OPTIONS FOR THE TEACHING OF FOREIGN LANGUAGES, LITERATURES, AND CULTURES

Warren C. Born and
Kathryn Buck, Compilers

American Council on the Teaching
of Foreign Languages, Inc.
2 Park Avenue; Suite 1814
New York, N.Y. 10016

The work presented or reported herein was
performed pursuant to a Contract from the
U.S. Office of Education, Department of
Health, Education, and Welfare, under the
authority of Title VI, Sec. 602, N.D.E.A.
However, the opinions expressed herein do
not necessarily reflect the position or
policy of the U.S. Office of Education, and
no official endorsement by the U.S. Office
of Education should be inferred.

1978

Table of Contents

1

Introduction

This report presents the results of a survey of innovative foreign language curricula in U.S. colleges and universities undertaken in 1974-75 by the Modern Language Association pursuant to a contract with the U.S. Office of Education. The survey results published here comprise three sections: (1) seventy-seven detailed curriculum reports; (2) a catalog giving questionnaire data for each of nearly 1,700 qualifying survey entries; and (3) an index of institutions represented.

Procedures and Results

In March 1974, the MLA submitted a proposal to the U.S. Office of Education requesting funding for a survey of innovative foreign language curricula that would attempt to ascertain the nature of curricular changes being undertaken in the wake of declining enrollments and the disappearance of many traditional reasons for foreign language study. Previous assessments of the role of foreign language study had been concerned with measuring trends in course registrations and college entrance and degree requirements, and in doing so had rightly assumed the content of the bulk of foreign language study to be constant and generally limited to the study of language and literature within the context of the so-called liberal arts curriculum. Since the late 1960's, however, new directions in curriculum have become increasingly apparent; new roles and service functions have been assumed by some foreign language departments in response to broader trends in higher education. The goal of the proposed survey was to assess the nature of such roles, as well as the extent to which they are being recognized and filled. The survey proposal outlined four general working categories for classifying the new curricula--career-related, community-related, interdisciplinary, and non-traditional--and included plans for collection and dissemination of information on range, breadth, time period, and disciplines covered, as well as prerequisites, contact hours, staffing, methods, and instructional materials.

Following the award of the contract to the MLA, a questionnaire soliciting the desired information (see pp. 8-9) was mailed to the heads of each of the 3,182 U.S. two-year and four-year college and university foreign language departments on the MLA's master list. A second and final mailing was undertaken several weeks later. Responses to the survey numbered 1,650, or 52% of the total mailing. The community and junior college response represented 38% of those surveyed; four-year college and university response represented 58%. Some 960 respondents indicated they offered no qualifying courses or programs; others were disqualified as being "traditional," that is, typical of the customary offerings of language and literature programs. But because the remaining 690 departments with qualifying entries often reported more than one course or program, these departments are represented by a total of nearly 1,700 entries.

The qualifying responses were reviewed, revisions in the definitions of the four basic categories were made, and subcategories were developed on the basis of similarity and frequency of types of entries. The survey proposal had originally called for the selection of a small number of outstanding entries for closer study and visitation. But it was the opinion of the research staff and of a special advisory committee of practicing professionals, upon review of approximately 10% of all entries in March 1975, that a narrow selection would be not only highly arbitrary but unrepresentative of the contents of the survey. It was decided to attempt to study a more representative number of entries in greater detail.

The entries selected by the staff and reviewed by the committee--amounting to some 10% of the total--were chosen either for representativeness or for uniqueness, and for their strength; it was felt that they presented the complete range of survey entries, in both breadth and quality, and that an attempt should be made to obtain more detailed information about as many of them as possible. Letters were sent to the respondents asking them to provide a prose description of not more than 2,000 words for each designated course. Included with the request was a set of eighteen items to be considered as guidelines, but the authors were given free rein to discuss aspects of the courses or programs which seemed most noteworthy to them. Eventually, more than eighty curriculum models were received for use in Part One of this report.

Some descriptions received had already been published elsewhere (or had publication commitments) and are not included here. Since readers may wish to consult these descriptions, those not reprinted are listed below.

160, 161 "Reading Swedish, Danish, and Norwegian," Jere Fleck, University of Maryland, College Park. Unterrichtspraxis, 6, i (1973), 63-70.

1025 "Other-Subject Lectures in a Foreign Language: A Model for Interdisciplinary Collaboration," Charlotte Brancaforte, University of Wisconsin, Madison. Unterrichtspraxis, 9, ii (1976), 36-45.

1151 "Foreign Languages 101: A Cultural Introduction to Languages," Howard H. Keller and John W. Ferguson, Murray State University. Foreign Language Annals, 9 (1976), 50-55.

1346 "VERBA: A Computer-Assisted Course in Terminology," Joseph R. Tebben, Ohio State University. Classical World, 68 (1975), 299-304.

1387 "The German Semester," Rudolf Hirschmann, University of Southern California. Unterrichtspraxis, 8, i (1975), 78-81.

1388 "Intensive German," David P. Benseler, Ohio State University. Foreign Language Annals, 11 (1978), in press.

1478A "Self-Paced Language Learning: Spanish, German, French," Francis J. Dannerbeck, T. Bruce Fryer, and Carl H. Johnson, University of South Carolina. ERIC: ED 102 864.

1546 "French-Canadian Live-In," Helen Kilzer, Mary College. Foreign Language Annals, 11 (1978), 93-96.

Survey Categories

Career-Related

The career-related category, in which knowledge of foreign language and culture is treated in combination with, and often as ancillary to, career-oriented majors in a variety of fields, is the largest of the five major divisions. To some extent its size is the result of the research staff's decision to include all career training in this category, even though many programs could as easily have been classified as community-related, and in fact some programs of this type appear in that category. This decision had the effect of swelling career figures in the areas of health, law enforcement, and the social service professions, as well as in the areas of business, commerce, and industry. The research subcategory of etymology, a fairly common offering among Classics departments, is directed primarily to students preparing for health-care careers but represents vastly different skills from those taught in programs and courses in the health care category.

The survey explicitly excluded traditional courses training teachers of language and literature; thus, the only category to deal with teacher training as such is training for bilingual classrooms. Again, this category represents primarily training in conjunction with a knowledge of Spanish language and cultures, although recent legislation and legal action on both the federal and the state level can be expected to broaden the potential need for training in both language and bilingual methodology to include other "immigrant" languages.

Community-Related

The number of community-related entries was, as indicated above, significantly reduced by the decision to include all career training in the career category. The community-related category represents courses including persons from outside the college and university community for other than career-education purposes. Very often, courses in this category attract full-time students as well, and certain kinds of courses offered as part of a general curriculum often attract community members. It should be noted that the survey mailing list did not include university extension programs. In a few cases, questionnaires were forwarded to such divisions, but the community figures cannot be said to reflect accurately the number of such courses actually available; rather, they reflect numbers and types of offerings under the sponsorship of traditional departments of language and literature established basically to serve the full-time student population. The category of off-campus programs is at best a hybrid; courses offered for specific business firms might well fall within the career-related category, whereas many courses offered in institutions such as prisons and hospitals could qualify in either the community or the career category.

The category of English for speakers of other languages clearly cannot claim to represent the total of such courses actually being offered. A few were submitted by "umbrella" departments, such as Modern Languages or Language Arts, which include English, but just as many entries indicated that the ESL courses are being taught by Romance and Spanish departments. Just as it did not include extension programs, our mailing list did not include departments of English or special language institutes which in many institutions are responsible for teaching such courses.

Interdisciplinary

The large number of interdisciplinary courses and programs, those which combine the study of two or more different kinds of subject matter, one of which as a rule is language or literature, made a division into interdepartmental and departmental offerings both desirable and useful because of obvious differences in course structure, staffing, and administration. In addition to those entries in which the interdepartmental teaching arrangement was explicitly indicated, area departments such as Latin American Studies or Scandinavian Studies were considered for purposes of classification to be interdepartmental in nature. In cases where only one department was officially involved in teaching a course but relied heavily on participation from other departments or from outside the institution, the course was also considered to be an interdepartmental offering.

Entries in culture and civilization have been divided into the subsections of national and supranational. For example, a course entitled "German Culture and Civilization" was classified under the supranational heading if course content was stated to include a study of more than one country in which German culture is manifest. The other subcategories generally involve a pairing of the study of literature and/or language with topics in the arts or social sciences, or with specific themes and concepts.

Non-Traditional

The non-traditional category is the most diverse. It reflects innovation in instructional approach, location, subject matter, and student population. Entries in this category were expected to overlap, as most do, with other categories; but the non-traditional classification provides subcategories which are more methodological than topical and thus reflect important aspects of curricular development not necessarily or immediately apparent in the other classifications. In most of the programs listed in the non-traditional category, basic language skills are being taught, but in non-traditional ways (individualized, programmed, mediated, intensive), in combination with travel abroad or field projects, or any combination of these.

Literature in translation courses were included in the report, although the number recorded by the survey is undoubtedly far smaller than the number of such courses actually being offered.

In classifying all entries, it was often necessary to determine whether subject matter or instructional approach appeared to be the more important innovation of a course or program. The determination was frequently arbitrary, and for this reason cross-references have been provided for all other categories appropriate and important to each entry.

Use of the Report

The report is presented in three parts. The seventy-seven curriculum reports comprise Part One; the catalog of nearly 1,700 qualifying entries with all available questionnaire data for each comprises Part Two. Items in Part Two are numbered consecutively and are arranged according to the outline of categories which serves as the Table of Contents for Part Two. Entries which are accompanied by a curriculum report in Part One are identified by a bullet ●. The curriculum models in Part One are presented in categorical--and essentially numerical--order; next to each title is the number of the entry or entries in Part Two to which it corresponds. Cross-references have also been provided under subheadings in Part One in instances where a manuscript is pertinent to that subcategory but has its primary place in another subcategory.

The questionnaire data for each entry are coded in accordance with the format of the questionnaire, which is reprinted on pp. 8-9. The data for each entry are presented as received from the respondents. Where available, we have indicated the person(s) to be contacted following the institutional address. In each instance in which a series of boxes was provided for the respondent's use, each box has been assigned a letter--a, b, c, etc. Thus, if a respondent indicated under item 3, staffing, that the course is staffed in cooperation with other departments, the data printed for that item appear as "3-b;" in item 13, materials used, if the respondent indicated that films, audiotapes, and newspapers were used, the item appears as "13-a,d,f." In subcategories where certain texts were extremely popular, the title of the text(s) in item 14 was replaced by a letter. To determine the title(s) of the text(s) consult the bibliography immediately preceding the entries for that language.

Entries are arranged in alphabetical order of institution within the sub-categories or, in some instances, within national or language subdivisions. An alphabetical index of institutions represented in the report and the numbers of their entries is provided as Part Three of this report. Although the research staff has attempted to summarize accurately the information submitted by respondents, the Modern Language Association is not responsible for the accuracy of the material supplied.

Commonly used abbreviations in Part Two include:

admin	administration	incl	including
adv	advanced	ind	independent
alt	alternate	info	information
Amer	American	Inst	institute
anthol	anthology	inter	intermediate
anthro	anthropology	interdept	interdepartmental
AV	audio-visual	interdisc	interdisciplinary
bicult	bicultural	intl	international
biling	bilingual	intro	introduction
bus	business	Ital	Italian
c	circa	Jan	January
C	college	Jap	Japanese
CC	community college	JC	junior college
cen	century	jr	junior
Chi	Chinese	Langs	languages
civ	civilization	ling	linguistics
Cl	Classics, classical	lit	literature, literary
comp	composition, comparative	math	mathematics
cont	continuing	med	medical, medicine
conv	conversation	Mex	Mexican
cult	culture, cultural	MFLs	modern foreign languages
dept	department	MLs	modern languages
Dist	district	Mod	modern
div	division	nat	natural
docs	documents	ng	not given
econ	economics	poli	political
ed	education	Port	Portuguese
elem	elementary	prep	preparation
Eng	English	prof	proficiency
equiv	equivalent	pubs	publications
FL	foreign language	q	quarter hours
for	foreign	qtr	quarter
Fr	French	Rom	Romance
Ger	German	Russ	Russian
govt	government	s	semester hours
grad	graduate, graduation	SC	state college
GRE	Graduate Record Examination	Scand	Scandinavian
hist	history, historical	sci	science, scientific
hrs	hours	sec	secondary
HS	high school	sem	semester
hums	humanities	Sl	Slavic

smr	summer	tech	technical, technology
soci	social, sociology	trans	translating, translation
Sp	Spanish	U	university
spkrs	speakers	vocab	vocabulary
spr	spring	wtr	winter
sr	senior	wk	week
SU	state university	yr	year

This publication is intended to familiarize users with a range of courses and programs and the institutions in which they are being offered, as well as acquaint them with all other information provided by the respondents. It is hoped the report will not only stimulate curriculum development and review, but also promote individual, direct communication among department personnel in various institutions. From the catalog, an instructor can assess what is being done in other colleges and universities and can then contact directly the individuals in those institutions who might be of help in developing and evaluating foreign language curricula.

We wish to thank the U.S. Office of Education and the Modern Language Association of America for providing the resources and assistance which made the survey possible. We acknowledge also the assistance of our colleagues in the colleges and universities who provided material, especially those who took the time to supply the detailed course descriptions. We apologize to them as well for any mistakes or omissions. Thanks are due, finally, to Richard I. Brod, Director of Foreign Language Programs, MLA, who designed the survey questionnaire and provided general guidance; to the Project Advisory Committee; to Kenneth Tigar, Page Tigar, and Marilyn Sequerra for assistance in the preparation of the catalog; and to Carla Hayes and members of the MLA office services staff.

K.B.
W.C.B.

SURVEY OF CAREER-RELATED, COMMUNITY-RELATED, NON-TRADITIONAL, AND INTERDISCIPLINARY COURSES AND DEGREE PROGRAMS IN FOREIGN LANGUAGES IN U.S. INSTITUTIONS OF HIGHER EDUCATION, FALL 1974

United States Office of Education Contract No. 0-74-3207

Dear Foreign Language Chairman:

The Modern Language Association (MLA), in conjunction with the Association of Departments of Foreign Languages (ADFL), is undertaking a detailed study of current curricular offerings in foreign languages, *other than* the traditional instruction in language and literature. The four categories of courses and programs covered by the survey are defined below, with examples. The categories are broadly inclusive; we ask you to supply information on any and all courses or programs that fit into any of the categories. Please include courses and programs offered in the 1973-74 academic year, in the current academic year, or which may be offered in 1975-76.

The data obtained by the survey will be compiled in the form of a catalogue of courses and programs, indexed according to course title, content, and language. Information from the survey will also be used as the starting point for a detailed study of eight college programs, and for a major conference of curricular specialists to be held in June 1975. Progress reports on the survey will appear during the spring of 1975 in the *ADFL Bulletin* and other MLA publications; the catalogue, detailed study, and conference report are scheduled to be published in the fall.

INSTRUCTIONS

Please fill in the information requested in the box at the bottom of this page. Then, for each course or program, fill in the specific information requested on the reverse side. Two copies of the form have been furnished; you may photocopy additional forms if you need to describe more courses or programs.

Please return the questionnaires in the enclosed prepaid envelope. If you have no courses or programs to report, please return one questionnaire with that indication so that you will not be contacted in the follow-up mailing.

Thank you for your participation in this national survey.

Types of courses about which information is desired:

1. **Career-related:** Courses and programs in which knowledge of foreign language and culture is treated as ancillary to career-oriented majors in a variety of fields, e.g., business, journalism, social sciences, natural sciences, medicine, law. (*Specifically excluded* are programs relating to the training of teachers of foreign language and literature on the school or college level.) Examples of courses to be included are translator training programs and curricula in international business.
   Examples: "Executive German;" "Spanish for Health Professionals."

2. **Community-related:** Courses and programs designed to meet specific local needs of a community or other constituency served by the college. "Community" may include adult (post-college-age) population, occupational groups, ethnic minorities, etc.
   Examples: "Spanish for Policemen" in which the students are full-time members of police departments; "French for Travel."

3. **Interdisciplinary:** Courses and programs which combine the study of two or more different kinds of subject matter. One of the disciplines involved must be language or literature. Include area studies programs only if they involve formal study of foreign language or literature. (*Specifically excluded* are programs in comparative literature and comparative linguistics, unless they involve work in other *disciplines*, e.g., philosophy, anthropology.)
   Examples: "Politics and the Novel in Latin America;" "Literature and Religion in Modern France;" "Medieval Studies."

4. **Non-traditional:** May involve innovations in the location of instruction (off-campus, e.g., factories, prisons), the approach (computer-assisted), the student population, credit arrangements, and the like. This category may overlap with any of the other three.
   Examples: "Spanish for Native Speakers;" "Total Immersion Course in Chinese;" "Non-Credit Self-Instructional Course in Arabic."

Institution: _____

Department: _____

Name of Chairman: _____

Total number of programs described in this response: _____

OMB No. 51-S74034
Approval Expires August 1975

1974-75 MLA CURRICULUM SURVEY
PROGRAM DESCRIPTION SHEET

Course (or Program) Title: _____

Institution: _____ Department: _____

Whom may we contact for further information? _____
_____

1. Number of registered students last time course was offered: _____

2. Contact Hours: _____ per week for _____ weeks

3. Staffing:
    ☐ Entirely within the department
    ☐ In cooperation with other departments
    ☐ In cooperation with persons outside the institution

4. In what year was the course first offered? _____

5. How many times has the course been offered, including the current semester? _____

6. How frequently is the course offered?
    ☐ Every semester or quarter
    ☐ One semester or quarter per year
    ☐ Other (please specify) _____

7. When is the course offered?
    ☐ Regular day session
    ☐ Evening session

8. Credit:
    ☐ _____ semester/quarter hours (circle appropriate unit)
    ☐ No credit given

9. Student population taking course:
    ☐ Full-time students
    ☐ Non-matriculated students
    ☐ Other (please specify) _____

10. Prerequisites: _____
    _____

11. Course Content: (If desired, enclose or attach descriptive material from the college catalog.)
    _____
    _____
    _____
    _____

12. Course Methods/Organization:
    ☐ Lecture   ☐ Taught in English
    ☐ Discussion   ☐ Taught in a foreign language
    ☐ Oral reports
    ☐ Group projects
    ☐ Laboratory

13. Materials Used:
    ☐ Films
    ☐ Slides
    ☐ Videotapes
    ☐ Audiotapes
    ☐ Periodicals
    ☐ Newspapers
    ☐ Other (please specify) _____

14. Texts Used: _____
    _____
    _____
    _____
    _____
    _____

Any additional material (course outline, syllabus, etc.) you wish to send would be welcome.

Please return to: FL Research Center, MLA, 62 Fifth Avenue, New York, N.Y. 10011

Part I: Selected Curriculum Reports

CAREER-RELATED

Translation and Interpretation

STUDIES IN TRANSLATION: FRENCH (12)

Edric Cane
Department of Languages and Linguistics, Occidental College

Studies in Translation was conceived as an essential element of the curriculum when a language-track option was added to the literature emphasis of the undergraduate French major. The aim of the language track was to create a major for students who were interested in language, but not necessarily in literature, and who intended to seek careers in non-teaching fields where language skills would be an asset. In other words, the creation of the language track was a means of attracting a broader spectrum of students and of preparing language majors for a broader choice of careers. Two features of the language-track option are the required equivalent of a minor in a field other than the student's chosen foreign language--such as economics or political science--and a course teaching more advanced language skills and practical use of the foreign language. Studies in Translation is among the latter.

As the only translation course given for French majors, its objectives are limited; its alumni are not professional translators! I wanted the course to focus on the skills of translation and interpretation, and allowed extra proficiency in the foreign language to be only a by-product to which no systematic effort or time would be devoted. Only students with advanced proficiency in French were accepted in the course, and at least three quarters of the work was done from French into English, which made it possible to devote only occasional attention to subtleties of French grammar. No systematic effort was made to enrich vocabulary or knowledge of French idioms.

The goals I set for Studies in Translation were born of practical experiences as a translator and interpreter. Perhaps the outstanding feature of these experiences was their variety and the impact of such variety on each translation task. Sensitivity, open-mindedness, flexibility, good judgment, and imagination are required in finding a satisfactory translation for individual words, phrases, and sentences, and these are the qualities which are at the heart of what a course in translation must attempt to convey. It is by constantly striving for such attitudes in the students that one will communicate what is most essential in the practice of translation. By their nature, these qualities are the antithesis of routine.

To translate is to transform an original in order to maximize its intended impact for an audience incapable of adequately understanding the original. This implies sacrificing some elements and taking great care to preserve others. Such choices are seldom obvious or simple, and the quality of a translation rests on the sophistication with which it is made. A simple paradigm may be the translation of films. If the face of the person who speaks is not visible, one may translate more or less as one would for a play. If the lips are visible, the synchronization of the sounds with the motion of the lips becomes an essential element of the original which cannot be sacrificed: labials and the general rhythm must be retained in the translation. If instead of dubbing one is preparing sub-titles, care must be taken to keep them unobtrusive, so that they do not destroy the immediacy of the original; a long sentence may be best translated by two words in order to preserve the essential quality of the original as much as possible. The same kind of analysis and

11

adjustment has to be made with every change in subject matter, genre, medium of expression, target audience, and the circumstances of the translation itself. This is why sensitivity, flexibility, open-mindedness, imagination, and good judgment are vital.

To foster these qualities, the course stressed variety in subject matter and style of the material to be translated--literary texts, songs, newspaper articles, letters to the editor, business letters, advertisements, and technical reports. It also stressed variety in the circumstances of the translation--written and oral, carefully prepared and impromptu. We also used material which a local firm needed to have translated, including both letters which the firm needed to understand and foreign material which it would ultimately publish.

The class met twice a week for two-hour sessions, each of which generally consisted of three groups of activities aimed at written translation, oral interpretation, and stylistic differences between French and English as they relate to translation. Before class, each student prepared a translation of the passages for the day, and we would then try to reach a common version judged best by consensus. Generally, I would not come with my own version of the texts, because English is not my native tongue and because a common quest is more valid if a 'best' version has not already been established. On occasion, we would refer to, learn from, and criticize published translations of the passages.

Different kinds of exercises were done in oral interpretation. These ranged from oral translation of written passages prepared with the help of a bilingual edition to simultaneous interpretation in the language lab. In the first of these we used a bilingual edition of French short stories. The students prepared rather long passages for the class in which they read in English from the French text, using whatever mix of translation skill and memory they desired. This was a good initiation to the mental process of speaking in English as fluently and naturally as possible while being cued in the foreign language.

Simultaneous interpretation was practiced for short periods during the second half of the course. The class met in a room adjoining the language laboratory, and no time was lost if we moved for even ten or fifteen minutes, the initial maximum students could stand this strenuous exercise. Recorded radio interviews and news broadcasts were generally used. It was not found pedagogically helpful to edit a few extra seconds of silence into the broadcasts, as I had initially attempted. No great fluency was achieved in the rather short time devoted to this demanding technique, but the students felt challenged by the experience and by their undeniable progress.

In addition to practical training in written and oral translation, time was devoted during each two-hour session to a systematic and theoretical study of some problems of translation. This was done with the help of Vinay and Darbelnet's Stylistique comparée du français et de l'anglais (Nouvelle édition, Didier, 1964) and an expensive accompanying Work Book I(Nouvelle édition, Didier-Beauchemin, 1965). The aim was to clarify some basic stylistic differences between French and English and to familiarize the student with means of dealing with the translation problems which these differences imply. For each session, the students read portions of the books and prepared exercises in the workbook. We discussed the books and corrected the exercises in class. The textbook was found too theoretical for a one-term introductory translation course; to benefit fully from it would have required much more time. For next year's offering we will use only the workbook, and I will present the most important notions relevant to the specific exercises.

The students were asked to evaluate the course at the end of the term, and their answers to the questionnaire were strikingly concurrent. They all enjoyed the course, its informal atmosphere, their own constant participation, and the manipulation of language; they judged it 'good' on a scale of 'excellent,' 'good,' 'adequate,' 'fair,' and 'poor,' in relation to other courses taken at the college. They, too, felt the text by Vinay and Darbelnet was too technical for their purposes. In answer to a question on the intellectual development fostered by the course, they stressed that the course was practically oriented and that the question therefore did not apply; I think they failed to perceive that the constant effort to broaden their conception of what alternatives were open to them and to acquire flexible approaches to changing circumstances and subject matter had as much to do with intellectual development as if the course had been devoted solely to mastering the complex theoretical analyses of the textbook.

I, too, enjoyed the course, and I think it achieved its goals reasonably well: it provided language majors with a basic initiation to the skills of translation and interpretation; it emphasized the mental attitudes necessary for various types of translations; it was sufficiently general to expose students to the various arts of translation and interpretation; and, not having been too dogmatic, it provided a good basis for more systematic study in a specialized institution.

STUDIES IN TRANSLATION: GERMAN (26)

Leland S. Babcock
Department of Languages and Linguistics, Occidental College

The catalog description for Studies in Translation reads: "The translator's art. Problems and techniques of translation from German to English." The course was first offered in fall 1974 as part of a new language-track major developed to meet the needs of an increasing number of students who wish to become translators and interpreters, or who are preparing for careers in business, industry, and service professions in which fluency in German is an asset. The goals of Studies in Translation, required in the curriculum of the new major, are accuracy and reasonable speed, and practice in translating a variety of essentially non-literary texts. The prerequisite for the course, which meets four times a week for eleven weeks, is the completion of the equivalent of six terms of German.

Five students, four of whom were seniors, enrolled in the course in fall 1974. Two of the students were majoring in German, one in music, one in political science, and one was undecided.

The course focused upon practical rather than theoretical aspects of the art of translation. Thus, the majority of class sessions was devoted entirely to the correction, discussion, and analysis of translation assignments. Only three hours were devoted entirely to lectures; in fifteen other sessions, short lectures were given at the beginning of class.

The three major lectures dealt with a survey of the history of the art of translation, an overview of the general and special techniques employed in translation, various theories of translation, and the role of the translator as technician and artist. For those who wished to pursue the subject matter of the lectures further, we placed three books on library reserve from our limited library resources in the field: G. Mounin, Die Uebersetzung: Geschichte, Theorie, Anwendung (Muenchen: Nymphenburger Verlagshandlung, 1967); W. Friedrich, Technik des Uebersetzens (Muenchen: Max Hueber Verlag, 1972); F. Güttinger, Zielsprache: Theorie und Technik des Uebersetzens (Zürich: Manesse Verlag, 1963).

The short lectures focused on an analysis of translation techniques, such as transposition, modulation, and equivalence, and on specific problems associated with translating from German into English. Among such problems were the proper method of handling subjunctive constructions, extended adjective constructions, passive constructions and their substitutes, and anticipatory da(r)- constructions. At the conclusion of each lecture, mimeographed materials were distributed which illustrated the various points of the lecture and provided a number of practice sentences. Some of the sentences were translated in class, and techniques and problems were discussed. The instructor assigned the balance of the sentences as part of the next day's homework assignment. The short lectures and accompanying activities fell entirely within the first half of the course.

The choice of materials to be translated from German into English was based upon variety of subject matter, variety of styles, difficulty of texts, and inherent interest of the subject matter of the texts. We did not assign the students a textbook for the course, but we did require them to subscribe to the weekly newspaper Die Zeit, from which we drew extensively for material. In addition, we provided a wide variety of texts in mimeographed form from various advanced readers and collections of essays or articles, and from journals such as Universitas.

From Die Zeit we chose, in consultation with the students in most cases, articles concerned with current political, social, economic, and environmental problems. Text materials in mimeographed form included, among others, excerpts from Freud's "Die 'Kulturelle' Sexualmoral und die moderne Nervösität," Mann's "Briefwechsel mit Bonn," Schopenhauer's "Ueber Schriftstellerei und Stil," "Gewalt des Fernsehens, Gewalt im Fernsehen - in der Sicht der Soziologie," and Storm's novelle "Hans und Heinz Kirch." The materials assigned gave ample opportunity for the student to experience a variety of styles and, because the subject matter was varied, exposed them to a large, practical vocabulary. In all cases, we sought materials which were both challenging and of inherent interest.

Daily assignments for translation were almost always short--not more than thirty-five lines for difficult passages, perhaps twice as many for less complex ones. This encouraged students to complete homework assignments carefully; lengthy assignments would have required more than two hours--a discouraging burden for such exacting work--or led to careless translations for the sake of completing the assignment. Moreover, short assignments enabled the class to cover all the material carefully within the 55-minute class. Toward the end of the course the students were able to complete longer assignments without feeling time pressure or sacrificing accuracy.

Students were instructed to prepare all translations in writing and to do so neatly, since their homework would occasionally be submitted. The instructor always directed them to prepare questions about translation problems they encountered. These questions were taken up at the beginning of the hour and often gave the instructor the opportunity to review methods and techniques of translation. At the conclusion of the question session, the text was dealt with sentence-by-sentence. Each student was directed to read one or two sentences; his rendition was then judged and, if necessary, corrected. Often two or three renditions were compared, which led to lively arguments at times. Although this procedure worked well, we found that the student reading the translation was often required to repeat it, since the other students were unable to retain what he had read. A solution is to have each student's homework mimeographed for distribution to other members of the class.

At unannounced intervals, the instructor called for the homework to be handed in, either after it had been corrected in class or at the start of the class session. In the latter case, he made detailed corrections which gave him an accurate indication of the progress of each student. When homework was called in at the beginning of the hour, the instructor distributed a short passage (usually taken from the same article as the homework) for sight translation. This procedure allowed the student to test mastery of translation techniques and of recognition vocabulary. Sight translation was used sparingly at the beginning of the course but with increasing frequency toward the end.

The monotony and loss of vitality which result from adherence to a rigid routine were avoided by using varying approaches from time to time. For instance, from the middle of the course onward quite long passages, often complete articles the equivalent of two newspaper columns, were occasionally assigned. The students were required to read the entire passage and to be prepared to summarize each paragraph in English. Each student was assigned a small segment of the article for written translation. In turn, each student was asked for his summary of a paragraph, after which the individual who had prepared a written translation of the paragraph was asked to judge the accuracy and completeness of the summary. We found this to be the most efficient method for checking rapid translation.

Occasional use of the following techniques was found to be useful, interesting, and challenging. (1) The instructor finds, or composes, a series of sentences, each of which contains a flaw. The flaw may consist of an inaccurate translation of a word or phrase, or a mishandling of a translation technique. The students are asked to find and correct the flaw. (2) The instructor distributes an excerpt from an already existing translation together with the German original. The students are asked to judge the quality of the translation. Is the translation accurate at all times? Does it flow naturally and capture the spirit of the original? If so, how? If not, why not? The first technique can be used at all stages of the course; the second should be employed only in the latter stages of the course.

Student questionnaires completed at the conclusion of the course were generally highly favorable. One or more of the five students indicated the following: (1) the course

14

exceeded their expectations; (2) they realized how careless their reading of German had been heretofore; (3) they were now aware of a great number of words, phrases, and idioms which they had unwisely taken for granted and had therefore mistranslated; (4) they were now much more confident readers of German; (5) they had greatly expanded their command of recognition vocabulary; (6) they now had a greater appreciation of both English and German. Two students indicated that the course occasionally became monotonous, and another remarked that one or two selections were too long or too difficult for the abilities of the class at the time they were introduced. I, as the instructor, must agree with these criticisms. In future offerings, closer attention will be paid to the sequence in which the materials are introduced, one or two selections which proved uninteresting, excessively complex, or replete with antiquated vocabulary or constructions will be eliminated, and auxiliary techniques such as those described in the preceding paragraph will be more fully utilized.

Studies in Translation is a necessary and very useful addition to our curriculum for the language major. It fits well into the Department of Languages and Linguistics' efforts to provide courses which more nearly meet the needs of the college population at large. The administration has been supportive of these efforts, but for current budgetary reasons requires us to implement the program without increases in staffing. In consequence, we have eliminated one section of advanced intermediate German and have consolidated two literary survey courses into one in order to inaugurate two advanced language courses.

We also feel that courses such as Studies in Translation can do much to lay to rest the current claims that language study is no longer relevant for the majority of students. The science departments at the college have always supported our traditional course in scientific German and, while it is too early to be certain of the impact of this course, additional departments have indicated that they welcome our efforts to provide their students with practical training in foreign languages.

TRANSLATOR TRAINING PROGRAM (27)

Edith Murdaugh
Department of German, Queens College, CUNY

The Translator Training Program began in fall 1972 as an honors course. Due to the interest it aroused, it became a regular department course series. The program is now structured as follows:

German 41 Introduction to the Principles and Problems of Translation: comparative grammars, points of contrast between English and German vocabularies, characteristics of prose styles and levels; written translations of selected materials of moderate difficulty and simultaneous translation from spoken German.

German 42 Translation of Materials from the Humanities and the Social Sciences: materials on the popular or general level as well as scientific and technically specialized materials.

German 43 Translation of Materials in Technology and the Physical Sciences: materials on the popular or general level as well as highly specialized articles in medicine, the biological and earth sciences, technology, etc.; problems of specialized technical vocabularies in the various sciences will be discussed.

German 44 Translation of Legal, Commercial, and Economic Materials: a rigorous course in translation of legal and commercial documents; materials describing the nature and structure of German stock companies, the European Common Market, and the German legislative and judicial systems.

Prerequisite for the program is two years of college German or the equivalent. (Exception is made for native speakers of German.) Translation is done almost exclusively

15

from German to English; mastery of formal English prose style is also required. At the end of the fourth semester, the student receives a letter certifying successful completion of the program. Whether the student may apply the translator courses toward completion of the major has not yet been decided; the decision will probably depend on enrollment.

There was some difficulty in obtaining textbooks on the art of translation, although once subject fields to be studied were determined, materials to be translated were readily available. The courses are taught, whenever possible, by native English speakers as part of their normal teaching load. The courses can be taught by most of the native English speakers in the department, although there is a core group to which the courses are regularly assigned. The first-semester course is currently being taught by a linguist, and we hope this will continue.

At present, enrollment is fairly modest and expected to remain so; the program is considered 'training' rather than part of the arts and humanities, and we are unwilling to encourage our good literature students to change to 'vocational' courses, however sophisticated the courses may be. For the same reason, the department is currently unwilling to give credit toward the B.A. in German for these courses.

The administration is pleased with the program, although it is too soon to tell whether it has contributed to a particular image of the department. The program has produced its first graduates, but it is too early to determine whether they can compete in the professional translation market. The content of the individual courses has changed from semester to semester but has stabilized this year with the completion of permanent course syllabi. As coordinator of the program, I believe that translator training is a valuable addition to a foreign language program as long as it contributes to—or at least does not detract from--the highest goal of the department, which is to stimulate the intellects of its students through exposure to foreign literatures and ideas.

THE TRANSLATORS AND INTERPRETERS PROGRAM (30)

Ulrike Lieder and Walter F. W. Lohnes
Department of German Studies, Stanford University

With a decreasing number of immigrant-translators, continuing efforts to establish standards of professionalism in the field of translation, and the growing significance of intercultural communication, the need for formalized translator training at the university level has become ever more apparent in recent years. In 1970 there were only two institutions of higher learning offering translator training programs in the United States, whereas at least seven major European universities had been maintaining highly successful translator and interpreter institutes since the end of World War II. The need for formalized translator training coincided with a trend toward diversification, offering alternatives to the traditional literature-oriented curricula, in university language departments. As developments in the past few years have shown, translator training courses seem to offer a recognized alternative.

The Translators and Interpreters (T and I) Programs in the Departments of German Studies and Slavic Languages and Literatures were introduced in September 1971. In the case of German Studies, the Translators Program was a local consequence of the overall restructuring of departmental programs. The T and I Program was established at the undergraduate level, one of the only two undergraduate certificate programs of its kind in the United States at the time. At the undergraduate level, the program leads to a Certificate in General Translation in conjunction with a bachelor's degree in any field. At the graduate level, a Certificate in Advanced Translation or in Interpretation may be earned in conjunction with a master's degree.

The German Translators Program is a three-year program, open to students of all majors, and should be started in the sophomore year. The first year of the program is basically a second-year language course, with emphasis on reading and listening comprehension. It is followed by a four-quarter series of courses called Translation of

16

Texts in the Social Sciences. Each of the first two quarters focuses on two or three areas in the social sciences, such as sociology, anthropology, law, economics, political science, etc. The last two quarters of the program are devoted to a translation workshop in which each student produces an independent, original translation in his field of study. This project is usually eighty to one hundred pages long; it may be a short book or a series of articles on a topic or on related topics, but it should represent a challenge as well as a contribution to the American study of the field.

The program was initially funded by special Stanford University funds for innovative courses; following an evaluation by the Dean's and Provost's Offices, it became part of the regular programs offered by the Department of German Studies. It is listed together with the other departmental offerings in the catalogue and is routinely announced to first- and second-year students of German, along with other programs and options offered by the department.

In 1972, a translators program in Chinese was initiated but had to be cancelled after two years. At that time, an interdepartmental committee on translation was established, and the three departments jointly sponsored lectures and panels on translation. This interdepartmental cooperation received a boost when three Stanford language departments were actively involved in organizing and leading the Fourth American Translators Association Summer Translation Workshop at Stanford on 23-27 June 1975. A member of a fourth language department (English), an active translator himself, joined the effort by delivering a lecture. We hope to strengthen and broaden this interdepartmental cooperation in the field of translation, particularly in view of plans for another ATA Summer Translation Workshop at Stanford in 1977.

Since its inception in 1971, the basic structure of the Translators Program has remained relatively unchanged, although individual courses were changed, expanded, and refined. The program has grown slowly but steadily, with an annual average of five students receiving their Certificates in General Translation since 1973.

While the program may lead to a career in translation, it is primarily designed as an ancillary program, providing students with an additional skill which might serve to open career opportunities in the field of international relations, international business, and the like. We have increasingly deemphasized the pre-professional aspect of the program as the market did not and does not seem to warrant the production of 'translators-only.' On the other hand, a chemist or an engineer with a foreign language background seems to have better chances of finding employment than one without. The experience of our certificate holders seems to bear us out--so far, none has made translation a career. Most chose to continue their education at the graduate level; two are presently studying at graduate schools of international relations, two are currently enrolled at the Stanford Law School, while others are attending German universities, planning to earn Ph.D.'s upon their return to the United States. Only one, a 1975 graduate and certificate-holder, plans to work as a free-lance translator. It will be most interesting to see how she fares, and we hope to receive some feedback for the program from her experience.

Good textbooks for translation courses are virtually unavailable. There are general treatises on principles of translation, intercultural communication, etc., but not much that lends itself easily to classroom use. What little there is is intended for Germans learning English as a foreign language and not always suitable. Most of the practice texts have to be collected from newspapers, periodicals, promotional literature, etc. This does offer the advantage that texts can be topical, up-to-date, and tailored to students' interests. We are also fortunate in having a number of translation agencies in the vicinity which are more than willing to provide texts for practice purposes.

All courses in the program can be handled by one full-time staff member, a Diplomdolmetscherin from the University of Mainz. In order to provide diverse views and prevent students from being 'stuck' with the same instructor for three years, the courses could be divided among two staff members as part of their regular teaching loads. It is, however, of great importance that all courses be taught by trained or experienced translators or interpreters. In this respect, the program is dependent on one or two individuals. To diversify instruction, we have 'borrowed' a translator and interpreter (with five working languages) from the European Community in Brussels for the 1975-76 academic year. Both instructors are teaching a half load in the T and I Program and half in other departmental programs. During the winter quarter, the regular instructor will be on leave to serve as an interpreter for the Olympic Winter Games in Innsbruck, Austria.

Credit earned in the program may not be applied toward a German Studies major because students from all majors are enrolled. Interest in literary translation in the department antedates the establishment of the T and I Program by many years. A number of dissertations were translations with major introductions and scholarly annotations; recently, two of our doctoral candidates translated, independent of their dissertations, two major works of literary criticism. The department strongly supports such undertakings as eminently worthwhile scholarly activities.

It seems to be an impossible undertaking to train American-born and -educated first-rate translators able to compete with the graduates of the European university institutes; there is too little foreign language training too late. By comparison, a German translator student setting out to earn a degree has had nine years of training in one foreign language and seven years in another, as well as numerous opportunities to practice language skills through inter-European youth exchange programs or trips abroad, and spends a minimum of four years studying translation almost exclusively (plus, for the chosen few, interpretation) and the culture and civilization of the respective lands.

An attempt to emulate such a vigorous training system at an American university appears to be an infeasible proposal at present. The compromise we practice in the T and I Programs, providing our future physicists, physicians, political scientists, lawyers, historians, and also Germanists with an ancillary, marketable skill, seems to be a happy one. The ultimate success of our approach remains to be seen, but the activities of our graduates so far seem to indicate that we are heading in the right direction.

Research   (See ms. 486)

Business/Commerce/Industry   (See also mss. 486, 890, 974)

BUSINESS FRENCH AND BUSINESS SPANISH (180, 240)

Paul Gaeng
Department of Romance Languages and Literatures, University of Cincinnati

(The author was a member of the Department of Romance Languages and Literatures at the University of Cincinnati when this report was written.)

While we had no direct evidence of potential student interest in a joint program with the College of Business Administration, we felt that we had to offer new options to our language majors. My counterpart in the German Department and I went to the dean of the College of Business Administration in the summer of 1972 and proposed setting up the joint program. The first recipients of the Certificate in Business Administration graduated in June 1975.

We have encountered no administrative problems concerning this program. I serve as the faculty advisor for both French and Spanish majors who wish to earn a Certificate in Business Administration. The two three-quarter courses given in the program, Business French and Business Spanish, are taught by two faculty members as part of their regular load. The courses are dependent on these two instructors; if they were not available, we would have to search for personnel with this particular competence.

Neither Business French nor Business Spanish is acceptable for major credit; these are elective credits. Both courses may be taken in lieu of the lower-level composition and conversation course which is a prerequisite to advanced composition and conversation; only the latter carries major credit. Business French and Business Spanish have achieved their objectives: the teaching of technical vocabulary in the fields of economics and international business, and the composition of acceptable business letters in the foreign language.

Students have expressed satisfaction with the two courses; colleagues in the department have accepted the courses and the concept of the joint program. The attitude of faculty members trained in literary traditions has become more flexible in view of the realities of the job market. Were it not for the flexibility of the undergraduate program, we might be faced with a crisis on the graduate level, because we, as other universities, depend on the undergraduate program to support the graduate program. The courses have elicited a great deal of interest on the campus, particularly on the part of central administration, which is very supportive of them. I would suspect that we did gain some departmental majors as a result of this option.

It is too early to say to what extent students have graduated into business careers. Students who have made inquiries in the local business community and in the eastern and western metropolitan areas have received some encouraging reactions and expressions of interest from business firms.

Business French. The following texts were used during the three-quarter course: Mauger and Charon, Le français commercial, Manuel I, and Brueziere and Charon, Le français commercial, Manuel II. In the first quarter, the history of French economy is reviewed in its cultural setting, slowly introducing the student to unfamiliar terminology, with reading and conversation using the new terminology.

In the second quarter the more technical aspect of the course begins, the writing of business letters. The Manuel is divided into twenty-four chapters, each of which deals with a different aspect of business. In each, there are samples of letters, which I supplemented with material from texts I had consulted in France. Students were required to write letters according to instructions given in French, a kind of directed letter composition. In the third quarter the work of the second was continued, but directions were given in English in an attempt to recreate actual situations students would encouter in the business world. Students were assigned letters to be written to customers and principals in France, as well as letters to be translated into English and into French.

Business Spanish. (My colleague, Edward Coughlin, supplied this description of his course.) The following texts were used in this three-quarter course: Ugarte, Gramática española de repaso; Jackson, Manual de correspondencia española; and Rosenthal and Rudman, Redacción de cartas comerciales simplificada. Material from Vivas, Fundamentos de correspondencia comercial, which the students did not have, was also used.

Initially, a review of Spanish grammar is undertaken since the course is primarily intended for third-year students of Spanish. The remainder of the course is dedicated to learning commercial terminology and the essentials of writing letters in Spanish. The Rosenthal and Rudman text is helpful with information about and examples of the various types of business letters, such as sales, mail orders, credit, collection of accounts, employment, complaints and adjustments, recommendations, acknowledging receipt, etc. The Jackson text contains examples of social letters in addition to business letters, and the class practices various types of letters one might write to a friend.

Recently during the final quarter, the class created a company in which the students served as heads of the various departments: management, manufacturing, advertising, national sales, international sales, accounting, credit, personnel, purchasing, shipping, and art and design. (With seventeen students in the class, we did not have a separate department for each student.) The company was a brewery situated in Mexico with various branches, including one in the United States. The students gave oral reports dealing with their departments detailing the activities during the previous year and, in some cases, including projections for the future. The class appeared to enjoy doing the reports, and I would consider including the same type of project each quarter.

THE INTERNATIONAL BUSINESS OPTION (181, 203, 241)

Helga Slessarev
Department of Germanic Languages and Literatures, University of Cincinnati

The International Business Option is one of the responses of the department to student criticism regarding the impracticality of their training for careers other than teaching. While we retain our faith in the value of a liberal arts education as the basis for personal growth regardless of the student's professional future, we did not want to be unresponsive to those students who want information about German life and institutions beyond the scope of literature. We therefore offer sufficient courses on the undergraduate and graduate levels for an M.A. in German Studies.

The International Business Option is, in a sense, a sub-program of the German Studies Option. Just as a student can select courses in political science and economics in preparing for foreign affairs study, courses in accounting, marketing, and management can be selected in preparing for a career in business. The goal is knowledge of language, German studies, and business administration on the level of a combined M.B.A. and B.A. in German Studies.

The program was instituted because of student interest and the interest of representatives of local business in employing young people with such training. It was not difficult to work out the details for students of both departments: students in business administration have to take certain courses in the language department and vice versa. Each student is advised by a member of each department. Materials for some of the required courses in the language department, such as composition and conversation courses on various levels, have been expanded to include business vocabulary. Some knowledge of business terminology is now also required for the traditional major. For students electing the International Business Option, we are establishing extra programs and increasing use of the language laboratory.

One course, The German-Speaking World Today (see IV.E.), is designed to train the student to apply his knowledge of American business management and marketing to that of Germany and has become particularly crucial for students in the Option.

EXECUTIVE GERMAN (212)

Kristine Trendota
Department of German, College of St. Catherine

In September 1972 our department initiated a major program in Executive German. The development of the program reflects, and in fact is a direct function of, the existence in close proximity to the college of a variety of public and private multinational corporations, e.g., Minnesota Mining and Manufacturing Company and Cargill, Inc., the nation's largest private trader and processor of agricultural products. The program has benefited from the established academic credibility of the college with the local business community and from the aspirations of today's students. The presence of the U.S. Department of Commerce in Minneapolis and the office of the Minnesota Department of Economic Development in St. Paul also contributed to the appropriate setting for such a program. At the time Executive German was proposed to the Curriculum Committee of the college, however, its initiator had only an intuitive sense of local potential and possibilities for providing service to the community.

On at least one occasion during the golden years of the 1960's, a foreign language department of my acquaintance indignantly rejected the request of a local company to translate some business correspondence. If this kind of behavior was typical in the past, it is unrealistic for a language department today to expect much community awareness of the need for foreign languages. The current interest in high school career days and in course offerings geared to broad appeal may help undo this isolationism, provided that

20

foreign language departments make an effort to cultivate off-campus relationships. Our communication-oriented discipline ought to be one of the most enthusiastic about interaction with the world of business, yet we have been slow to recognize this. In retrospect, the historic lack of cooperation between the foreign language profession and business is particularly regrettable in the case of German. West Germany's 'economic miracle,' together with its economic momentum within the European Economic Community, should have produced much earlier than now the establishment of business-oriented German studies.

Thanks to the lack of red tape at a school the size of St. Catherine's (ca. 1,500 students) and the encouraging support of the president of the college, Executive German was announced in the college catalog for 1972-74. It has already inspired wide interest among businesses, other local colleges, and secondary schools.

We have concluded that an open-minded and flexible relationship between the conventional teaching-oriented German major and the new executive-oriented program is in the best interest of the students, since it can provide opportunities for concurrent employment in education and in business. Sporadic work performed by teachers at the request of companies, such as document evaluation--not only a reliable translation into business English but also advice as to the most suitable course of action by a company-- can now be accomplished with a considerable degree of professionalism. In view of the job market and a growing sense of uncertainty in both education and international business, curricular planning with occupational goals should offer room for career mobility. We also hope that greater participation in business, and thus in the life of the community, will in turn create a greater need for foreign language teachers in the community. (Thanks to the program, a few executives have come to the college to study German.)

Given the diversified industrial situation in the state, there is career promise in Executive German, an autonomous program which can be combined with different majors. Not a redefinition of the foreign language and literature major, it is intended to serve as an undergraduate introduction to international commerce, with the prospect of futher education and training either under the sponsorship of hiring companies in their own programs or in graduate school.

In principle, each program participant is encouraged to cultivate an individualized path, whether in an established or an innovative direction. The range of student interests facilitates internships and job placement and reduces competition within the group itself. Mindful of the role of agriculture and of the food processing industry in Minnesota's economy, one double major combines Executive German with Foods and Nutrition, a traditionally popular field at St. Catherine's. According to a commodities broker who came as a guest speaker to the college, the alliance of a foreign language with biology initiated her career. In the April 1974 issue of Fortune (p. 28), the combination of linguistic skills and a professional specialty, e.g., law, accounting, or chemistry, was invaluable for employees, who earn as much as $40,000 a year, at All-Language Services, Inc., of New York City.

General departmental requirements for the new major consist of from six to ten courses, depending on language proficiency and high school background. Included within this framework is the typical three-part sequence of Executive German I and II and one semester of Individual or Experimental Study. Three courses are shared with the teaching-oriented major: Civilization, German Literature of the Twentieth Century, and German Drama Masterpieces. The two literature courses are included because of the college's fundamental commitment to liberal education. The drama course was selected for its connections with the vigorous theater life in the Twin Cities and on the assumption that business executives usually can enjoy opportunities to attend the theater when they travel. At least one departmental January interim is recommended; these focus on contemporary customs and values.

Possibilities for experiential learning under the auspices of a local business with faculty supervision are sought, and at least one summer abroad leading to a project completed for credit is recommended. In either case, a double accountability, namely to the school and to the working society, is sought. Mini-traineeships, in which a student participates upon invitation by a company in lieu of a January interim class, are increasingly popular. The on-location experience can precipitate dramatic increases in career consciousness and interest. All requests for experiential studies during the interim must be approved by the Curriculum Committee. Firms usually provide a methodic overview of operations with divisions acting as successive hosts, and the student keeps a daily journal of experiences. To the satisfaction of students and parents, the interims can lead to summer employment for the proven trainee.

In the catalog for 1974-76, Executive German I and II have the following course descriptions:

(I) Introduction to business German and West Germany's role in world trade. Interpretation and discussion of current business news in the German and American press. Informal lectures from resource persons. Visits to multinational companies in the Twin Cities area. Prerequisite: Completion of intermediate college level German or equivalent of 3-4 years of German in high school.

(II) Increased responsibility in the translation and evaluation of authentic current German business press. Each student works on an individualized market study project. Prerequisite: Executive German I or its equivalent with permission of the instructor.

The purpose of the third semester, featuring individual or experiential studies, is to give the student a specialization. The experiential component involves an off-campus locale and work evaluation by outside experts. To illustrate, one student worked part-time in the Credit Service Center of Montgomery Ward and compared American and German customer credit policies; another prepared her individual study on the advertising techniques of the Bleyle Company of West Germany, an exporter of clothing to the United States.

An outline of program objectives, prepared in consultation with business executives in the Twin Cities and on file with the Career Planning and Placement Office of the college, contains practical details. For Executive German, the description of working skills is:

(1) Solid undergraduate groundwork in basic grammar, vocabulary, and culture.
(2) Introduction to business terms, concepts, and practices as needed for translation, oral interpretation, document evaluation, and active company representation, e.g., at industrial fairs.
(3) Development of skills in the consultation of reference materials and current periodicals.
(4) Experiential learning (traineeship) with an international company at least during our January interim.

Essential to successful training in Executive German is exposure to commercial prose. In addition to an orientation to such material, the student must be willing to practice close textual analysis. The inclusion of authentic business communications as instructional materials proves to the students that casual treatment of vocabulary can result in financial loss.

At first it was a problem to find appropriate textbooks for the program. Still unavailable are bilingual textbooks published in the United States using American rather than British terminology and practice. Such texts are badly needed; when published, they could also assist those high school teachers who express interest in the introduction of business-oriented German programs. In addition, the market for bilingual textbooks could well include vocational schools, one of which in Minneapolis-Saint Paul offers commercial Spanish and is highly regarded by the business community. Imported textbooks were discovered through Inter Nationes in Bonn, a government-sponsored cultural agency. A shipment of reference books accompanied the requested textbooks.

Der Kaufman by Franz Bäumchen (Munich: Max Hueber Verlag, 1972) serves as a good introduction to business German. The opening scene is a dialogue in a grocer's shop, and a gradual progression with concurrent grammar review leads to a discussion of international trade. Thus, students with no background are gradually guided into it. The same author wrote <u>Deutsche Wirtschaftssprache für Ausländer</u> (Munich: Max Hueber Verlag, 1973) for use by more experienced readers. <u>Deutsche Handelskorrespondenz</u> by Rudolf Sachs (Munich: Max Hueber Verlag, 1969) involves not only the writing of business letters but also provides pertinent information on the conduct of international business. The German consulate in Chicago, whose support for Executive German included an introduction to the German-American Chamber of Commerce, provided <u>Tatsachen über Deutschland</u> (Bonn: Presse-und-Informationsamt der Bundesrepublik, 1972), copies of which students borrow from the department. Statistical projections and charts in this reference book provide another resource of vital importance. Dynamics of international business are also presented through reading assignments and bulletin board displays made from current, leading periodicals.

An up-to-date view of West Germany demands awareness of the European Economic Community. EEC authorities provided, usually without charge, various printed materials in German and English. Needless to say, developments in the EEC are reflected in the creation of a new and specific terminology and present a demanding challenge. Students' knowledge of the EEC is tested as part of the final comprehensive examinations in the two courses.

In order to prepare graduates for entry into the rapidly changing global market, considerable emphasis is on current information and intensive use of company literature. These donated materials come from German as well as American sources. An easy way to begin a departmental collection of items such as annual company reports--which in the case of some multinational corporations are written in several languages and are convenient information sources for technical terminology--was to fill out the postage-paid reply cards offered by <u>Fortune</u> in its May, June, and July issues. Materials soon began arriving without previous request.

Resource persons have been indispensable for the up-to-date interpretation of terms and texts and for access to information not necessarily available in print. (Business executives are in turn helped when they face linguistic problems or wish tapes.) The educational purpose of the inclusion of real letters has been agreeable to professional translators, who in turn also occasionally ask the department for cooperation. Students are stimulated by such spontaneous activity.

It is neither a valid nor realistic practice to teach assorted commercial terms or how to write a few letters without giving students some awareness of economic movements. Furthermore, superficiality and dullness will not spark the interest of students and prepare them for entry into the complex world of international trade relations. Our German students learn to appreciate the dynamics of commerce by reading, among other literary selections, the famous passage on the Grosse Zirkulation in the first chapter of Goethe's <u>Wilhelm Meisters Lehrjahre</u>.

In an effort to present as many up-to-date insights into career opportunities as possible, several speakers have been invited for informal briefing sessions. All guests proved generous distributors of materials concerning their occupational areas and have become permanent resource persons. In some cases they have given us potential placement contacts in financial services and banking. In order to make the most of the speakers' expertise, students are asked to submit questions in advance; this opportunity for input and personal contact guarantees good attendance. Recently a woman member of the Federal German Parliament with a background in retail business was welcomed with a record number of seventy-two questions.

The lecture of an insurance executive/marine specialist, aided by a company film, featured packaging and transportation, an acute and complex problem area not yet solved by the trend to containerization. Having impressed his listeners with the international tasks of today's traffic management specialist responsible for orderly deliveries, he left the following basic message: the multilingual era in business has arrived; fluency in foreign languages is necessary in telephone conversations with clients; families are often hired as units, and the linguistic and cultural background of an executive's spouse also counts as an employment essential.

St. Catherine's also provides for unsalaried 'courtesy appointments' as a way of opening lines of communication off-campus. The appointees are helpful reminders to the students of the need for survival--and success--in the business world. In the spring of 1974 two such courtesy appointments were made in the Executive German program. A native German manager employed by a German-Swiss manufacturer of industrial machinery with a plant in Minneapolis accepted the invitation, as did a woman who had been an international trade representative in a high-level position with the Minnesota Department of Economic Development and is currently an international planning manager in a private firm. Their contributions to Executive German included informal lectures, materials, special work assignments, invitations to off-campus events, contacts with various experts, and addresses of potential employers.

In fall 1973 the Minnesota Department of Economic Development entrusted the students with the preparation of the German version of Minnesota Profile, a 55-page compendium on the state for industrial and commercial purposes containing data pertinent to foreign investment. Since the beginning of Executive German, the interest of the business community has been an encouraging factor. As an integral part of the program, the students have enjoyed guest privileges at monthly seminars organized by the Minnesota World Trade Association, and they assist in the operation of the annual Minnesota World Trade Day. The faculty member in charge of Executive German received membership in the Association and in April 1975 was elected to a three-year term as the only professional educator on its board of directors.

Announcements of course offerings were printed in Minnesota Progress, the monthly digest of economic activity published by the Minnesota Department of Economic Development. The Minnesota World Trade Newsletter aided the Department of German in becoming better known for its translation services. As the latest cooperative development, business executives have come to the department for tapes of German readings dealing with their areas of professional interest. With the February 1975 issue of the Chamber's monthly German American Trade News, participants in the program changed from readers to being read about.

When Minnesota Profile was published, each member of St. Catherine's team received a personal letter from Governor Wendell R. Anderson commending the group's work in promoting the state's image abroad. A strong German heritage in Minnesota was linked with the desirability of commercial relations with Germany as being "most important to the state's economy." (That the presence of an ethnic group in a state can be a significant factor in the decision-making process on the part of potential investors was pointed out in the Wall Street Journal in an article on investors' concern with language barriers.) In Governor Anderson's description of the project as a "civic contribution," the Department of German finds an inspiring definition of its function as a service department beyond institutional boundaries.

PROYECTO DESARROLLO ECONOMICO (259A)

Toby Tamarkin
Foreign Language Department, Manchester Community College

Proyecto Desarrollo Económico is patterned after a program that has been offered successfully for four years at Manchester Community College in cooperation with the Ebony Businessmen's Association in Hartford, Connecticut. Members of the college staff met with representatives of the Spanish-speaking community and, particularly, the Puertorrican Businessmen's Association to outline the need for this type of program and to determine the best way for the college to help serve this need.

Because the twelve credits awarded the two-semester course are given through our Extension Division, the materials used in the course are those which are used in the regular business classes, and the staff involved are full-time teachers at the college, obtaining approval from the Curriculum Committee was not difficult.

The project is publicized in a variety of ways. An informative brochure was prepared in Spanish and mailed throughout the community. Advertisements were placed in local newspapers, and there were announcements on local radio and television news programs and on special talk shows in both Spanish and English. The Businessmen's Association has been helpful in recruiting students through personal visits and phone calls to members of the community; and the local Small Business Association asks that Spanish-speaking businessmen requesting loans enroll in the program if they have not had formal business training.

Three instructors work with representatives of the Businessmen's Association. A member of the Business Department at the college and a member of the Puertorrican Businessmen's Association serve as co-directors of the project. All lessons and worksheets dealing with accounting and the special financial records problems of the small businessman are prepared by the member of the Business Department. An instructor of marketing discusses basic problems facing small businesses regarding purchasing, merchandising, promotions, personnel, etc. A member of the Spanish Department with a background in accounting and business translates all materials to be used with the class into Spanish and presents the Spanish portion of classroom instruction. This trio and some part-time staff (secretarial help, audio-visual personnel, and additional translators) meet for a two-hour preparation period once a week. During this time they produce a bilingual televised tape for the lesson to be studied (bilingually) and review all materials to be presented to the class. Materials and information are given the students in both Spanish and English in order to help the businessman improve English skills and to familiarize him with specific business terminology in both languages.

The staff teaches as an overload and is paid from a grant. The course is dependent on individual instructors with expertise not only in the subject matter, but in dealing with groups in the community. Student motivation to continue in the program is a key problem, since all students work full-time and have family responsibilities. Attendance is kept as high as possible through a series of planned 'awards' which prevent students from drifting out of the course. For example, the same class is offered two nights a week so a student who must be absent is able to attend on another night; the television tape provides students who have missed a few lessons with the opportunity to catch up at their own convenience; coffee and doughnuts are provided when the class begins; regular notes of commendation are sent in the mail to all students informing them of their progress; and a graduation ceremony includes dinner, printed certificates, greetings from the college president, and television coverage.

Although the course has a slower pace than regular classes at the college, students must complete the same objectives that merit twelve credits in the regular college program. Students who complete this program are eligible to become part-time or full-time students in a business program at the college. They may also have earned credit-by-exam for their expertise in the Spanish language, so that it is possible to become a student in the regular program with a total of eighteen credits earned toward the sixty required for an associate's degree. About one-third of those who earn the twelve-credit certificate of completion enter the regular college program. Several have earned promotions in their jobs.

The project, as is true of any program designed to help serve the community, does promote a good image of the college to the public. All parties concerned--the community members, the students, the teachers, and the institution itself--benefit from and appreciate el Proyecto Desarrollo Económico.

PROGRAM IN INTERNATIONAL MANAGEMENT (301)

Woodrow W. Baldwin (Management)
Departments of Management and Foreign Languages, Simmons College

Our program in International Management was developed a few years ago to meet a need which we sensed for persons with a background in both management and language. The trend in the last few years for American companies to expand their markets to include branches in foreign countries has increased demand; the export-import business and the location of government bureaus in foreign countries have for many years provided opportunities for persons with the unique combination of language and management skills; the increased sophistication of international business and the opening of more opportunities for women in management have combined to make the field particularly attractive for women. Opportunities abound for persons wishing placement either in the United States or abroad. There had been considerable student interest; in fact, we had students for whom we worked out special programs before the formal program was established.

The only opposition we encountered on the part of the faculty was from the language faculty. They initially rejected our program proposal, but then took the initiative a year later to contact us to see if we were still interested. The program had to be approved by the Curriculum Committee and the faculty, but there was no opposition. The program is so new we have had no experience yet with administrative problems. Students are considered to be in the Department of Management even though they receive counseling from both departments. There are as yet no alumni of the program. The Program in International Management is not dependent on a single instructor or group of instructors and would be available regardless of the composition of the faculty. The only course that we are establishing especially to accommodate these students is a course in international marketing which will be offered for the first time during the 1975-76 academic year. It will be taught by a new faculty member whose primary interest is marketing.

The program is an interdepartmental major, and all courses carry the usual credit. Students wishing to pursue a concentration in International Management would take approximately half of their work in the Foreign Language Department and half in the Management Department. In the Management Department, they would be expected to take Finance Accounting, Dynamics of Management, Marketing, and International Marketing, and either Production Management, Personnel Management, or Organizational Behavior.

The student in International Management is expected to complete sixteen semester hours above the intermediate level in either French or Spanish. The foreign language component is intended to provide the ability to function successfully in the four basic skills of language. The student's program in language depends upon fluency and individual interests. Cultural background as well as practice in the foreign language are acquired through the study of certain courses in literature. The following are particularly recommended: (Spanish) Caribbean Spanish, Twentieth Century Readings, Composition and Advanced Conversation, Spoken Spanish, Spanish Field Work Seminar, General View of Spanish Cultural History, and Hispanic American Cultural History; (French) Readings in French Literature, Composition and Conversation, Spoken French, Advanced Composition and Conversation, and Stylistics. The specific language courses are selected through consultation with an advisor in the Department of Foreign Languages. In addition to these required courses, the following electives are recommended: International Economics, International Relations, and American Foreign Policy. The student must also satisfy the college senior seminar requirement in either the Department of Management or the Department of Foreign Languages.

Health Care

SPOKEN SPANISH FOR DOCTORS AND NURSES (362)

Judith Valles Davis
Department of Foreign Languages, San Bernardino Valley College

Spanish for Medical Professions is the result of a request to the Department of Foreign Languages. The Department of Public Employees of the City of San Bernardino informed the department of an urgent need for public health nurses to be able to communicate in Spanish with patients and their families. In order to meet the needs of nurses in the county, an arrangement was made whereby classes could be held at the Department of Public Employees during the lunch hour. The nurses were given a ninety-minute lunch break in order to attend class sessions and still eat lunch. The class met for three one-hour sessions per week.

When the course was submitted to the Curriculum Committee, it received unanimous approval and has been in the curriculum for nine years. Due to enrollments, the course has been self-supporting. In fall 1975, it became a transfer course because of the increasing demand for bilingual (English/Spanish) nurses. As of 1974-75, the nursing program of the State College of San Bernardino requires a course in Spanish for the medical professions.

As a result of scheduling problems, the noon program at the Department of Public Employees was discontinued and incorporated into regular offerings in the evening program at the college. Every semester the class has thirty-five to forty students. After one semester of specialized Spanish, students continue in standard courses offered in Spanish.

Ninety-eight percent of the students are already doctors, dentists, nurses, medical receptionists, X-ray technicians, lab technicians, and public health employees. This constitutes a heterogeneous group within the health care profession. The instructor has to gear the class to the needs of the particular students in order to achieve the goal of each class--to provide a vehicle of communication with a patient to obtain vital information regarding the health of the patient and his family. Classes vary from semester to semester; some have been composed entirely of hospital nurses, which allows course content to be fairly uniform. Even then one is dealing with the needs of different duties and assignments, such as intensive care, obstetrics, post-surgical, receiving, emergency, lab, supervision, and diet.

The course is geared toward medical terminology, phrases, sounds, and practice in understanding. The goal is to be able to obtain in Spanish all the information needed. Questions are memorized and are worded in such a way to require a "Sí," "No," or other very brief response. Published material of this nature is virtually nonexistent, and that which is available is generally cumbersome and inflexible. The students themselves provide the majority of course content and continuity. They know what it is they must be able to tell the patient, and they know what information they must be able to obtain from the patient. The success of the class depends on the instructor's resourcefulness in being able to provide a succinct phrase or two which will afford the essential communication, and on his knowledge of the type of Spanish spoken in the area.

The students have been, for the most part, extremely grateful. It is a reward to quote one of them who said: "It's like another world; it's like opening a door that has been there all your life, but you've kept it closed out of fear and ignorance. The happiest and most rewarding experience for me since I have taken this course was when I was able to tell a crying woman in the emergency room, 'No tenga miedo. Su hijo está bien. No es nada serio.' It was worth my lunch hours to see the happiness and relief expressed on her face, and to know that I did not have to prolong her anxiety trying to find an interpreter."

SPANISH FOR LAW ENFORCEMENT AND CORRECTIONAL PERSONNEL (394)

Harold L. Colvocoresses
Department of Foreign Languages, Manchester Community College

Spanish for Law Enforcement and Correctional Personnel has been taught without interruption for the past five years, and during that period classes have been consistently filled. I shall try to explain the circumstances which led to the creation of the course, the manner in which the course was constructed, and the results which have been obtained from it.

Spanish for Law Enforcement and Correctional Personnel is a two-semester course at the first-year-college level. It has no prerequisites. Classes meet three hours per week in both day and evening sections; students earn three hours of credit per semester or six hours for the academic year. The course emphasizes basic conversation as heard in the streets of North American cities with large Spanish-speaking populations. Reading and writing in Spanish are included in the course, as are the main points of basic grammar, but these receive less emphasis than conversation. The course has also been taught in several other Connecticut community colleges. To date, over 400 students have been enrolled in the course at Manchester.

The course serves the needs of law enforcement students and of cities and towns of central Connecticut. These communities have large Puerto Rican populations, with smaller groups of Cubans, Peruvians, Colombians, and other Spanish-speakers.

The advantages of training in conversational Spanish for police and correctional personnel became evident during the summers of 1969 and 1970. These were years in which the city of Hartford was torn by riots in which the Spanish-speaking population was often involved. The inability of police to communicate with Spanish-speakers reduced their effectiveness and contributed to misunderstanding and distrust on both sides.

I was convinced that some knowledge of basic Spanish and some insight into Hispanic cultures would make the police more effective and would promote cooperation and confidence. The director of our law enforcement degree program supported this view and offered to include such a course as a recommended elective for our associate degree in Law Enforcement. The Curriculum Committee concurred, and in June 1970 the writing started. By September of that year our Spanish Workbook and Laboratory Manual for Law Enforcement Officers, accompanied by twenty-four audiotapes in Puerto Rican and Cuban voices, was ready.

The preparation of the course involved investigation and planning in several areas. There were conferences with officers in the Community Relations Division of the Hartford Police Department, who described the most frequent problem situations involving Spanish-speakers as well as certain routines for police reporting and interrogation. Such situations and procedures were incorporated into the dialogues of our Workbook and Laboratory Manual. In San Juan, Puerto Rico, I visited the headquarters of the police force and obtained their Spanish training manuals. These included not only useful terminology, but such items as a list of Spanish instructions issued by police to parents who fear drug involvement of their children. These were also incorporated into the book.

The nature of the student body and the use students would be making of Spanish determined the scope and nature of the course. Most students would be police or correctional officers who could not spare more than three hours per week for the course. This ruled out an intensive course. Two semesters of study seemed necessary

28

to acquire the desired ability in basic conversational Spanish. These officers would be dealing chiefly with a Puerto Rican population, so Puerto Rican speech would be stressed, including street slang. There are twelve units for each semester of the course, including dialogues, audiotapes, and exercises, usually of the question-and-answer type combining verb drills and conversational situations.

The twenty-four taped dialogues involve a variety of city experiences and law enforcement topics and develop vocabulary suited to each. They include: meeting a newly-arrived Puerto Rican or Cuban; giving directions; helping a Spanish-speaker find a job; aiding the sick; reporting fires; traffic problems and regulations; automobiles and automotive parts; robbery, burglary, arrest, search, and interrogation; narcotics; crowd control at the scene of a fire or elsewhere; and others.

Such dialogues are coordinated with and reinforce the study of Spanish grammar, including the subjunctive mood. As a reference grammar we use the Department of Justice publication, A Practical Spanish Grammar for Border Patrol Officers. From it we delete such Mexican expressions as might prove unsuitable for use in the northeastern states.

Speakers were recruited from the Hartford Hispanic community to play the roles on our tapes. These included Puerto Rican police officers, a Puerto Rican journalist, a professor, and a Cuban family. The voices of men, women, and children were represented. All the speakers were urged to use slang, casually rather than carefully, on the premise that the students must be able to understand street speech. The tapes were made in our language laboratory and, while they are not professionally perfect, they have proved effective for our purpose.

The first year we taught the course was one of experimentation, of discovering the rate at which such a class could progress, what would interest the students, and how best to explain the material. In the process, certain administrative and methodological approaches proved their worth. For instance, when possible, it is best to offer both morning and evening sessions which progress at the same rate. Such an arrangement permits police and correctional personnel, who often work swing shifts, to attend either section and keep up with the class despite changing work schedules. In doing this, we have always had two full sections, and students' moving back and forth has not caused appreciable congestion in either class.

It is important to bear in mind the academic backgrounds and goals of the students. Students in these fields of work may be ill at ease with English grammar. A scholarly approach may terrify, embarrass, and 'turn them off.' Simple explanations of grammar and the relation of the language to daily life should be stressed.

This relation of the language to the daily life of its speakers can be very productive when time is taken to explain elements of Hispanic culture--such as the importance of small courtesies, the need to avenge an insult, economic conditions, homes and foods of Puerto Rico, life in the barrio of New York City, and the Puerto Rican markets and restaurants of Hartford. Such digressions bring rewards in enthusiasm and future learning.

When conversation is a prime objective, every student should participate in every session. Nevertheless, students easily become embarrassed. Allowing them to repeat in chorus for a few days permits them to hide mistakes in the din of voices. Soon they will be more at ease and good individual performance can be stressed.

Role playing is used extensively. As early as the third week, when a few phrases and some regular, present tense verbs have been acquired, each student is asked to create a short dialogue representing a practical work situation and to deliver it in class, choosing a partner if necessary. The students seem to enjoy the dialogues, dream up humorous or dramatic situations, and learn as they go. The process is repeated frequently throughout each semester.

When time for laboratory work is not available, it may be necessary to integrate taped dialogues with the class work. This is time consuming but has the advantage of allowing the instructor to supervise the laboratory operation, to correct pronunciation, and to explain new terms. We have been forced to use this method recently, and the results have been satisfactory.

Tests and final examinations seem most suitable when they emphasize those oral skills which the student hopes to apply in his work. Here old-style dictation and individual dialogues can be useful. A series of Spanish questions to which the students must supply correct answers will combine verbal skills and conversational flexibility.

The amount of work demanded of the students appears comparable to that of the average freshman language course. The career objective creates, however, a different emphasis on skills. Grammatical perfection is deemphasized in favor of the ability to communicate orally. In this course the student will learn less about the Alcázar of Seville or the Shrine of Guadalupe and more about Hispanic city life in the United States, government agencies, emergency situations, and crime. Superior students in the course have, nevertheless, continued successfully in a traditional second-year course.

In a course of this type the instructor should expect to be particularly active in the classroom and to offer more special help during office hours. Absenteeism, necessitated by emergencies in the students' jobs, may run higher than in a typical college class. A weakness in our program is the lack of adequate time for additional laboratory work and practice. Given the exigencies of the students' occupations, I can see no way to overcome this deficiency. If it were possible to extend class and laboratory time to five hours per week, the students' mastery of the language would probably be greatly enhanced.

Spanish for Law Enforcement and Correctional Personnel has unquestionably bolstered enrollment in the Foreign Language Department. During the past five years it has drawn hundreds of students to the study of Spanish who might not otherwise have thought of such a thing. In many cases it has stimulated an interest in the Spanish-speaking population among the students, an attitude which may contribute to both learning and improved community relations.

A review of student performance over the past five years sheds some light on the achievement of goals proposed for the course. We had hoped that, at the end of an academic year, students would have a fair understanding of spoken street Spanish, a limited ability to communicate with Spanish-speakers, and some insight into the customs and values of a Hispanic community. Each year some students, perhaps twenty percent, have surpassed these modest goals, showing high ability and interest in Spanish. The majority of the students, an estimated sixty percent, have enough facility to increase their effectiveness when dealing with Spanish-speakers. The results justify the effort, and teaching these groups has been a rewarding experience.

Performing Arts

ELEMENTS OF FOREIGN LANGUAGE (471)

Charles L. Nelson
Department of Foreign Languages, Eastern Kentucky University

This course presents the structure, pronunciation, and intonation patterns of French, German, Italian, Latin, and Spanish. The course meets once a week for a period of two-and-a-half hours. It is taught by professors each of whom is a specialist in one of the languages; each language is accorded four weeks of study. Since Latin is the base for all except German, the course begins with the study of Latin. Then Italian and Spanish are introduced, followed by German. French is the last language studied, because the pronunciation of French is considered to be the most complex for a student who has never studied a foreign language. Each professor grades work in his own language area, and the five areas are averaged for the final grade.

The course was originally designed for students of music, especially voice, at the request of the Department of Music. Students had indicated an interest in such a course, and one voice professor complained she spent more time teaching foreign language pronunciation and intonation than she did teaching voice. Students and professors from other departments began to express interest in the course, and it was opened to all students.

The Department of Communications provides most of the students for the course, since its majors in television and radio are among those who most need to acquire spoken fluency. Students in anthropology, art, business, drama and speech, law enforcement, political science, and the natural sciences also find the course helpful. Elements of Foreign Language cannot be credited toward a major, since it is a special course with limited objectives.

The course has achieved its goals. Contact hours and the amount of material covered are comparable to other classes. It is too soon to determine what effect the course will have on regular department offerings, but some students enrolled in the course have expressed interest in studying foreing languages upon the completion of Elements of Foreign Language. Evaluation of the course is undertaken by the Department of Foreign Languages and has resulted in an increase from one to three credit hours awarded. The instructors believe the course to be an excellent one, and student opinion has been very favorable.

Miscellaneous   (See also ms. 974)

TECHNICAL FRENCH (486)

Arthur J. Knodel
Department of French and Italian, University of Southern California

The idea for Technical French arose from requests of students in the field of international relations who felt the need for more specialized vocabulary training and exercise in the use of conventional forms of diplomacy and commerce. Students in other fields expressed a similar interest, and a course proposal was prepared early in 1974. No major problems were encountered in obtaining approval of the course by the University Curriculum Committee, as creation of the course was part of a general revision of the undergraduate French-major requirements.

Technical French consists of those French words and expressions that are connected with narrowly-defined but widely-referred-to areas. Thus, very general terms such as manger, aller, maison, se passer de, justice are not considered 'technical;' terms such as débiter un compte, azote, revendication, vesicule biliaire, and programmer un ordinateur are.

Although Technical French was designed chiefly to attract non-majors, the course may be counted toward the requirements for a French major. It is normally taken as a third-year, junior-level course. To date, Technical French has been offered only once. The course is taught as part of the instructor's normal teaching load and is not dependent upon an individual instructor.

Thirteen students enrolled in the course, six of whom were from the International

31

Relations, Journalism, Pre-Dental, and Public Administration Departments. The course was taught chiefly in English, with frequent presentations and discussions in French. All exercises were corrected in class, with student participation and answers to student questions. Spoken and written French were always corrected for grammatical errors and errors in usage, but collaterally rather than as the main issue.

Students were obliged to familiarize themselves with the specialized reference books in the various divisions of the university library, and they were encouraged to use the limited but useful departmental collection of standard and specialized dictionaries and manuals. Extensive use was made of Le Monde hebdomadaire and France-Amérique, as well as materials from the French Embassy and the French Cultural Services.

There are ten area units plus one personalized unit dealing with the area of specialization indicated by the student. The ten area units are: transportation and mail; commerce and finance; politics and diplomacy; telecommunications; journalism and publicity; performing arts and sports; life sciences and medicine; agriculture; physical sciences; and industry. Class preparations involve looking up technical terms and idioms in various dictionaries, manuals, specialized texts, and periodicals. Written assignments may be any or all of the following: 'detail' exercises; version (French to English); thème (English to French); dissertation (short compositions or letters in French).

It is too early to assess the effects of the course on the departmental image and more traditional offerings, but student commentary has been extremely favorable. I find the course challenging and satisfying despite certain gaps; for example, all students felt there should be a unit on basic legal terms. One of the major problems is to keep the course from being simply a vocabulary-building exercise, although that function is an extremely important one. There is no doubt that the course can be extremely profitable for the students, but the basic truth holds: the instructor of the course must be very well-informed, enthusiastic about the material, and constantly available to the students.

COMMUNITY-RELATED

Off-Campus Programs   (See also ms. 362)

EAGLE UNIVERSITY (693, 705)

C. P. Brown
Department of Foreign Languages, Western Kentucky University

Western Kentucky University is one of eleven consortium institutions which provide educational opportunities to military personnel, their dependents, and civilian employees at Fort Campbell, Kentucky. The concept is not one of a traditional campus university, but rather a gathering of the best courses and programs nearby institutions can offer in order to fulfill the needs of the Fort Campbell community. The typically random selection of courses provided in extension classes of these institutions was not considered adequate.

32

The academic programs are provided by members of the consortium, all of which are accredited by the Southern Association of Colleges and Schools. Credits earned are actually credits earned at these institutions respectively, but the management of the consortium rests with the military installation; the arrangement is known as Eagle University. Annual visits by representatives of the Southern Association are made to insure that standards are maintained.

Formal approval was obtained from military authorities and institutional governing boards. Approval was granted on a permanent or continuing basis. The administrative operation is funded by the Army, including special tuition assistance for qualified military personnel. A library of more than 60,000 items serves Eagle University. Outstanding classroom and laboratory facilities, including those of the post schools, are available. Eagle University began operation in fall 1972. Western Kentucky University has been a member of the consortium since its inception.

Each quarter, through preregistration, military families and civilian employees of the post indicate their needs and desires for specific classes. Some areas of instruction are provided consistently by one institution. Other, more general academic areas get support from several institutions. In these cases, the ability of an institution to provide instruction at the time specified is crucial to the decision about who will take responsibility for the course. Students attending classes at Eagle University may take continuing education classes, or they may work toward a bachelor's or a master's degree. In a typical quarter, one hundred classes are in session.

Eagle University terms and classes are closely coordinated and scheduled in conjunction with the military training activities at Fort Campbell. A unique weekly and bi-weekly arrangement of classes interlaces educational activities with military duty so that there is essentially no conflict. Quarter terms do not necessarily coincide with either quarters or semesters at the institutions providing instruction.

Departments which traditionally have offered extended campus classes under other arrangements have welcomed the opportunity to participate in this consortium arrangement. Departmental participation is vountary; a department can decline participation in a given semester or agree to participate depending on the availability of assignable teaching load.

Staff teach courses either as part of a normal load or as overload. (If an instructor is teaching a graduate course in a given semester, he may not teach a course as overload at any level.) The courses are not dependent on a single instructor or group of instructors. All courses offered are a part of normal offerings. Faculty participants enjoy teaching mature, highly motivated students, but teaching schedules and travel arrangements are primary problems, which means that skill courses, such as beginning language courses, which should be offered daily or almost daily, usually meet for several hours no more than one day per week.

The Department of Foreign Languages at Western Kentucky University has been assigned classes in French, German, Russian, and Spanish. These classes are about the same size as comparable classes on our campus. Typically, those who enroll in a language course have either just returned from a tour of duty in a country where that language is spoken or expect to be assigned to an area where knowledge of the language will be useful. They have concrete reasons for studying a particular language. A few are also interested in meeting academic requirements for a degree. The typical student is highly motivated.

Since many students enrolled in courses at Eagle University are taking these courses for college credit, the offering institution exercises the same kind of control as for courses offered on campus. However, teachers recognize the need to alter the syllabus of a course to meet the needs of these students. In a language course, the primary aim is use of the spoken language. (Only beginning courses have been offered to date.) Course materials are similar to those used on campus. Though no specialized military terms or vocabulary are introduced in the course, situations which a military family might encounter in an overseas assignment are the focus of the course.

Miscellaneous and General (See mss. 259A, 362, 394, 890, 985)

INTERDISCIPLINARY (INTERDEPARTMENTAL)

Culture and Civilization (See also 1023, 1566, 1678A)

THE FAR EASTERN STUDIES-CHINESE MAJOR (789)

G. J. Riccio
Department of Area-Language Studies, United States Naval Academy

The Far Eastern Studies-Chinese major was established during the 1970-71 academic year as one of five area studies majors administered and directed by the Area-Language Studies Department. The other area studies majors are: Latin American Studies-Spanish, European Studies-French, European Studies-German, and Soviet Studies-Russian. Each of these majors, like area studies majors generally, is interdisciplinary in character, combining study of an area-related language, indicated in the hyphenated names of the programs, with courses taken in other departments, specifically history, political science, and economics. The total number of credit hours necessary to fulfill requirements of these majors ranges from thirty-three to forty; the Far Eastern Studies-Chinese major requires forty, twenty-two credit hours in language and eighteen in other disciplines. At the more advanced levels of the language sequence, emphasis is placed on the target culture and military-related subjects in addition to further development of communicative skills.

The development of this program, and of the other area studies majors, was the outgrowth of a major revamping of the curriculum initiated in the late sixties. Principal among the changes resulting from this curriculum revision was the establishment of twenty-four academic majors or areas of concentration from which the students could select a preferred field of specialization. The language department, whose designation as the Area-Language Studies Department coincided with the establishment of the majors programs, was charged with the development of area studies majors; the administration believed this type of major, with its emphasis on imparting a reasonable degree of proficiency in one language along with knowledge in depth about a given country or region, had more relevance in an undergraduate program aimed at providing the educational background and training of a future naval officer than the more traditional literature- and linguistics-oriented major. Once the area studies concept was proposed, there was no doubt that one of them should deal with the important and critical Far East. There was no identifiable student interest prior to the establishment of the program, but it was expected that a reasonable minimum of students interested in a professional military career would choose the Far Eastern Studies-Chinese major, and this supposition has proved valid. The number of students in the program has been averaging about ten per class, sufficient for maintaining the program on a permanent basis.

When the program was still in the planning stage, there was opposition on the part of some faculty in the social sciences to allotting an excessive proportion of the major--in their view--to language study, i.e., to courses in Chinese. It was argued that given the scope of an area study program, which attempts to explore socio-religious, philosophical, historical, political, and economic developments in some depth, and given the limited number of credit hours in which to achieve this objective, the most effective use of the time would be made by deemphasizing language, devoting no more than one-third of the total credit hours to such study. Eventually this view was overruled by the administration (the academic dean and the superintendent in consultation with boards that oversee the Navy's educational programs), and the resulting decision provided the credit-hour distribution noted above.

Following resolution of this initial difference of opinion, departments have worked in harmony with each other and, indeed, the Chinese language instructor was called upon to teach a course in Chinese political and military systems in another department when a staffing problem arose there. Courses offered in the participating departments have been agreed upon through consultations among the respective chairmen, and a desire for effective coordination of all the component parts of the major has marked the deliberations. A measure of this coordination is found in changes already made in one or two courses offered by other departments in an effort to strengthen the elements that make up the major.

In the Chinese language courses, the Yale series (revised 1968) has constituted the basic text materials. Although these texts are adequate, there has been a growing awareness in the profession of a need to develop materials that more accurately reflect the social patterns in the People's Republic of China. Some of this can be attempted by adapting Chinese publications or by using materials for Chinese language instruction developed by the University of Peking. The latter reflect a very traditional approach to language learning methodology, and, consequently, though valuable for the image they project of China today, they must be and have been supplemented by instructor-prepared materials to make them more effective as a language learning instrument. It is hoped that by the 1976-77 academic year materials with the desired features will be available and will end the present reliance on the series.

Insofar as courses in the other disciplines are concerned—such as Modern History of China and Japan, Chinese Political and Military Systems, Political and Military Development of Southeast Asia, U.S. and Far Eastern Relations, as well as more generalized courses bearing indirectly on the area under study, such as courses on the theory and practice of communism and courses in international law—text materials are abundantly available. Our library holdings, which have been markedly expanded in the past ten years, are considered solid and more than adequate to support the program.

The language component of the course is dependent on a single instructor who has had to develop and teach, as his normal load, virtually all the courses since the major was established. It would not be possible to continue the program in its present format were this instructor not available. The course he has developed is, perhaps, somewhat more demanding than other language courses offered in the department, especially since the first year of the course is intensive, with five contact hours per week compared to three per week in the other languages. On the whole, the results have been quite satisfactory; a number of majors have succeeded in obtaining a rating on the armed services language proficiency scale which represents a creditable degree of competence in the language. The course is highly rated by other faculty members in the department, and student evaluations solicited at the end of each term generally reveal a high degree of motivation and sense of achievement. The language course itself may or may not have improved the department's image on the campus, although undoubtedly a course in a language still not generally offered in many undergraduate institutions carries with it the natural lure of the exotic; a number of students who take Chinese—the curriculum requires language study only for students majoring in the so-called non-technical fields—are not Far Eastern Studies majors.

The Far Eastern Studies-Chinese major is career-related in the sense that the nation   clearly needs increasing numbers of persons, including military personnel, who have in-depth knowledge of the Far East and its peoples. Our vital, albeit controversial, interests and responsibilities in that area of the world have grown considerably since World War II; present and future commitments argue strongly in favor of a Far Eastern area program at the Academy, the source of the bulk of our career naval officers. Since the program is still relatively new (the first Far Eastern Studies-Chinese majors were graduated in 1972), it is still too early to speak of the students who have 'graduated' into careers related to this field. (The Navy's normal personnel rotation patterns evidence no automatic or direct link between a student's academic area of specialization and his career pattern, except the reasonable expectation that his specialty will insure consideration for future assignments when such qualifications apply.) One of the first graduates in this major has already been advised that he is being considered for duty as the assistant naval attaché in Singapore, and it is hoped that future graduates will be similarly assigned during their naval careers.

The only change contemplated, other than changes in text materials mentioned earlier, is the possibility of offering students the option of either Chinese or Japanese language study in recognition of the significant role Japan continues to play in the Pacific and the strong military and political ties that bind our country to this major Asian power. While arguments may be sound for permitting this option, present enrollment prospects, given the reduced numbers of non-technical majors at the Academy, make it unrealistic; at present, it is better and more cost-effective to have one good and reasonably well-subscribed Far Eastern Studies major than two weak ones.

The Far Eastern Studies-Chinese program has a definite place in the curriculum at the Naval Academy. It is one of the more popular area studies majors, despite the special challenge the language component poses, and, unlike some of the other programs in which the enrollment has fluctuated considerably from one year to the next, it has consistently drawn a good percentage of the total number of area studies majors. Both this and the Soviet Studies-Russian area major have enjoyed consistent patterns of enrollment, and there is every expectation that they will continue to do so. The challenge of the unfamiliar and the fact that these areas are and will continue to be of critical importance to the military and to the nation undoubtedly account for sustained interest in this field of study.

THE USSR TODAY (815)

James D. Wilmeth (Foreign Languages and Linguistics)
Departments of Foreign Languages and Linguistics, Political Science, and History, University of Texas at Arlington

In developing the course The USSR Today, the viewpoint of the Soviet and East European Center, a division of the Department of Foreign Languages and Linguistics, was that, since the Soviet Union is our principal competitor in all forms of human endeavor, a survey course on the main characteristics of the USSR should be available to students. In our view, such a course should encourage them to learn about the Soviet Union (and to continue learning after graduation) in order that they as adults can make responsible decisions about relations between the two countries.

In fall 1971, the Soviet and East European Center proposed the course because it had, in addition to the altruistic, a selfish motive--to interest more students in the study of the Russian language. Conversely, in Russian language classes, there was abundant evidence that students wanted more information about the Soviet Union than is provided in language instruction. Faculty in the Political Science Department also felt there was evidence that such a course would be popular.

The course had to be approved by curriculum committees of the three departments which would be involved in the course (Foreign Languages and Linguistics, Political Science, and History) and then by the University Curriculum Committee. The Committees of the Departments of Foreign Languages and Linguistics and of Political Science readily approved the course, but opposition was encountered in the History Department because they did nott have a Soviet specialist. Consequently, the History Department did no participate in the course in fall 1972. During that year a Soviet specialist was hired, and the Department joined the program at the beginning of the following academic year.

Administrative problems have been minor. A teacher from the Soviet and East European Center is coordinator for the course as part of his normal workload. Part-time instructors from Political Science and History, as well as from Economics, lecture on an overtime basis. The course is dependent on a coordinator, and if one were not available, the course would not be offered. The coordinator could be from any of the three participating departments.

There is a wide selection of films and books available from Soviet and American sources. During the first year, American textbooks were used, but during the last two years we have used Soviet texts written in English.

HUMANITIES CORE PROGRAM (844)

Joseph Lowin (Language and Literature)
Departments of Language and Literature, and History, Touro College

The novelty of the Humanities Core Program lies not in its subject matter, which is traditional in the extreme, nor in its method of instruction, which is highly conservative in its emphasis on the active participation of the student in the educational process, but in the application of the interdisciplinary approach and team-teaching techniques to a bread-and-butter program and in the central position the core occupies in the academic structure of the college.

Touro College is a small, liberal arts college in New York City, founded in 1971 for the purpose of demonstrating "the relevance of the Jewish heritage to the general culture of Western civilization." One of the basic tenets of the educational philosophy of Touro is

> that there is educational significance in a rigorous curriculum which reviews the cultural and literary contributions of classical, medieval, and contemporary societies in a context of historical experiences as the prelude to the pursuit of a particular academic interest. (Touro College 1974-75 Catalog, page 21).

The basic means of implementing this ideal is the Humanities Core, a two-year, twenty-four credit program required of all students.

This program is described as offering "a multifaceted approach to the study of Western European traditions, ideas, and experiences. Readings in literature and philosophy are integrated into a program which surveys the development of Western European civilization from the Bronze Age to modern times"(Ibid., page 47). The first semester is devoted to Greek and Roman civilizations. The second deals with medieval civilization. In the third, the students study the period from the Renaissance to the eighteenth century, and in the fourth, modern European civilization. The sections are limited to fifteen students and are conducted as informal discussions. Lectures are used occasionally to provide continuity, but it is generally felt that if the material were sufficiently structured to be handled in the lecture format, it could be included in the reading assignments. Slides, tapes, and other teaching aids as well as museum trips occasionally supplement discussion, but, in general, we use no gimmicks.

The uniqueness of the program is in the integration. During the first year of the Core and of Touro's existence, three instructors were involved, one each from the Departments of History, Literature, and Philosophy. There was no attempt to coordinate the program and little communication among the instructional staff. The result was often confusion for the students and little opportunity to build upon and reinforce material presented in each section. The decision was made to coordinate the program, and a basic format was developed which has worked successfully for three years, with a fair amount of staff turnover. Each six-credit course is now taught by two instructors, one from the History Department and one from the Literature Department. Each instructor submits a reading list which is then reviewed and coordinated with that of his colleague so that the same authors, ideas, or movements are discussed in both segments--though from different perspectives--at approximately the same time during the semester.

This requires a certain degree of flexibility on the part of the staff. One work may be chosen in preference to another because it can also serve the needs of the other instructor. If, however, an instructor feels strongly that a particular work should be included or that more time should be allotted a specific period than his colleague can justify, this can be arranged. Although, in general, the organization is chronological, portions can be treated according to literary genres or themes, and their use can serve to facilitate the coordination. Each segment has its own integrity. There is practical coordination as well, so that instructors of later sections can build on this foundation. In discussing Racine's Phèdre, for example, comparisons can be made to Euripides' treatment of the myth. Most of the faculty who have been involved in the program are enthusiastic about the Core.

Certain devices have been used to foster integration of the material. One syllabus, covering both segments, is distributed to the students. In the first year of the program, joint exams are given. Although this can create minor problems of communication, the

37

benefits obtained by requiring students to review the material for both segments at the same time more than compensates for the inconvenience. As often as possible, reference is made in one segment to the readings or material covered in the other, and students are encouraged to relate the ideas and concepts introduced in one to the problems posed in the other. Finally, a single grade is given for the six-credit course. These features help to present the texts as documents to be analyzed from many different points of view as well as reinforcing individual presentations.

Although the instructors are chosen from particular disciplines, the aim is to make the presentation broader than this limitation might suggest. Our definition of civilization includes all of human experience. In addition to literature and history, the course regularly includes an introduction to philosophy, as well as such fields as art history, social and economic theory, comparative religion, etc. To a great extent, the scope of coverage depends on the particular instructors' interests. In the past, this has been supplemented by special lectures by other members of the faculty, but as the school has grown and the number of sections multiplied, these could not be offered on a sufficiently consistent basis. To compensate, we have proposed to offer a Humanities Forum, a series of evening lectures which all students in the Humanities Core program will be expected to attend. It will also be open to other students as a form of continuing education in humanities.

One program was offered this year to inaugurate the Humanities Forum. An instructor from the Department of Communications conducted a program in which students were shown portions of the Japanese film, The Seven Samurai, and were asked to think about the possibility of presenting the Humanities Core through the medium of film. The reaction of the students was that, while the visual experience contributed to their understanding of descriptive passages, such as the battle scenes in the Iliad, film, in general, was limited to externals and lacked the specificity and objectivity that could be achieved through the written word. Next year's series will include programs on archaeology, art history, numismatics, history of science, music, and film.

Within the basic framework of requirements, the Humanities Core also serves as an introduction to another requirement, the Senior Thesis. Core students are required to write themes and research papers, based on primary sources, which develop their writing skills as well as a critical approach to scholarship. As one of the required programs, the Core also serves as an introduction to many advanced courses in the humanities and the social sciences. Both of the departments most directly involved in offering the Core consider it basic to their program, although in establishing standards for their majors, they give recognition to the program in different ways. The English and Comparative Literature Department grants six credits toward a major to students who have completed the Humanities Core. The History Department presupposes that students have completed the Core and is therefore prepared to accept nine credits in related fields toward the thirty credits required to major in history.

In other departments not so directly involved in the program, the faculty can build on the common body of knowledge imparted in the Core. In psychology or religion, for example, the instructor can assume that students are familiar with Greek and Roman religion and mythology, Christianity, Islam, and non-religious deterministic schools of thought. In economic theory, students have been exposed to various schools of thought as well as general historical trends. If anything, there is sometimes a tendency to exaggerate the success of the Core on the part of faculty members teaching advanced electives, since they usually come in contact with the most motivated students in their field and have found them well-prepared for advanced work.

The reactions in other disciplines have not always been so favorable. Instructors in the sciences and in business administration have sometimes expressed resentment of the demands of a program which their students may be less prepared to handle. Sometimes their objections are couched in more general terms of rejection of a required program per se. With the passage of time, however, this opposition has become less vocal as the validity of the program is generally recognized. Opponents have sometimes found themselves on the defensive in having to justify purely vocational objectives. There have been repeated suggestions on the part of members of the Jewish Studies faculty to organize a Core of Jewish Studies, which is a tribute to our success.

Student reaction also varies according to interests and advancement in the program. Initially, there is some hostility to a required program, but this is usually overcome within a matter of weeks. At that point, the students begin to notice much that they had never before seen or understood. They begin to pick up references to classical antiquity and come with enthusiastic accounts of museum visits, etc. They begin to recognize similarities to problems and attitudes in their contemporary world. By the end of the first semester, a number of students have volunteered that they are happy that the course was required, since they would not otherwise have participated. Students who have completed the program can also attest to a very practical value in the Core after having taken the LSATs and Medical Boards.

The experience at Touro seems to show that innovative concepts and approaches can be successfully combined with the most traditional ideas and educational values. One might also add that the manifold functions of the Core within the academic framework of a small college have made it not only academically sound but financially expedient.

PORTUGUESE STUDIES (890)

Gilbert R. Cavaco
Modern Language Department, Providence College

The present program in Portuguese language, literature, and culture was introduced into the curriculum in September 1969. Portuguese had been taught earlier but was discontinued in the early 1950's. The impetus for reinstatement came from both the Modern Language Department, because of requests for the language due to the increased number of Portuguese-speaking immigrants in the area, and the Political Science Department, which was spearheading a degree program in Latin American Studies and needed a Portuguese component to complete it.

Portuguese was phased in, one course at a time. (As instructor, I also taught courses in Spanish until reaching a normal nine-hour teaching load in Portuguese.) By 1971, a full thirty-six hours of Portuguese had been accepted by the Committee on Studies and included in the catalogue. Portuguese was now offered as a minor in the Modern Language Department.

Early in 1973 the first proposal for the B.A. in Portuguese was submitted to the Committee on Studies, but it was not accepted as presented. In our opinion, this was due to three factors: (1) the major was proposed at a time when languages were not doing well; (2) a full major within the department would have been established with only one instructor; and (3) the instructor had not yet come up for tenure. What did result, however, was a concentration in Portuguese granted under the B.A. degree in Individualized or Interdisciplinary Studies, and the assurance that there was no apparent opposition to either the instructor or the proposal.

The original proposal was reworked and resubmitted in May 1974. The program now took on a new character. In the intervening year, the instructor had been in close contact with members of the Portuguese-speaking community as well as with employees of various local and state agencies who, as part of their normal duties, came in contact with Portuguese-speaking immigrants. Much of the discussion with each of these groups revolved around the same basic problem--communication. This gave the instructor the idea of developing a program of studies flexible enough to provide sufficient course work in Portuguese to allow for some degree of proficiency in the language in combination with course work in another area, such as social work, business, public administration, etc.

The requirements for the new B.A. in Portuguese Studies were set at twenty-four hours of Portuguese at any level in conjunction with a minor area of eighteen hours (or two minor areas of twelve hours each) which could be taken in any department or program. This left the student with thirty hours (or twenty-four) of free electives which could be used to tailor a program which would not only meet the career goals of the student, but would also conform to the realities of the job market. It was even possible, through careful selection of courses, to complete the requirements of as many as three different majors. Upon entering the junior year, the student could decide which degree he wished to receive--Portuguese Studies, Latin American Studies, or Political Science, to name a few of the many combinations already worked out.

Included with the new proposal were letters of support from the Modern Language Department as well as other departments and programs. There was also administrative support for the program. Each department or program was asked to submit a list of at least eighteen hours of course work in the respective field of specialization which, in conjunction with competence in Portuguese, would benefit not only the community but also students looking for jobs. A petition, circulated by students of Portuguese and signed by nearly two hundred student supporters of the program, was also included. The petition stated that, although the signers were not necessarily interested in pursuing such a course of study, they believed that students who were should be afforded the opportunity to do so. In the meantime, the instructor came up for tenure and was granted a deferred decision pending completion of his written and oral examinations for the Ph.D. This action was construed as a strong vote of confidence for the instructor and the program. Both the position and the program could have been cut very easily at this time. The proposal was unanimously accepted by the Committee on Studies and the Faculty Senate.

The B.A. in Portuguese Studies was officially instituted in September 1974 with two students, one a freshman and the other a junior who had been concentrating in Portuguese under a program of Individualized Studies. The latter was not only the first Portuguese major, but also the first Portuguese major to study abroad. She received a generous grant from the Instituto de Alta Cultura in Lisbon and completed her junior year at the University of Coimbra in July 1975.

By mutual consent of the instructor and the chairman of the Modern Language Department, and with the permission of the administration, the program was placed under the aegis of the Department of Modern Languages. This was done primarily to avoid creating a special program requiring a separate number designation, and to avoid having to appoint a director and establish a new budget. Similarly, the Director of the Providence-in-Europe program would handle the study abroad programs in Portugal and Brazil. No new courses had to be created, and one instructor could handle the Portuguese component until such time as increased enrollment warranted the hiring of another. No special funds were needed at this time, but it was acknowledged that some funding would be necessary as the program continued to develop.

The Providence Journal-Bulletin and a TV program (The Portuguese Around Us) helped advertise the program. Also, we published a brochure for distribution to those high schools from which we draw a large number of students. Our students and faculty have also been a prime source of publicity for the program in encouraging their friends and students to inquire about it.

In 1971 the language requirement was dropped. Needless to say, this caused us a great deal of consternation. Portuguese enrollments, however, have continued to increase--six in 1969, fourteen in 1970, twenty-one in 1971, twenty-three in 1972, forty-two in 1973, and fifty in 1974. The projected enrollment for 1975 is between sixty and seventy, eight to ten of whom will be Portuguese Studies majors; half of the total are incoming freshmen. During the summer, 1,070 freshmen will be registered, and it is very likely that some of these students will take Portuguese as an elective. Student interest continues to play an important role in strengthening and developing the program.

Enrollments are also increasing in the School of Continuing Education, and this summer, for the first time since Portuguese was introduced, two courses are being offered. We also have a consortium arrangement with some of the local institutions. One of these grants its students a degree in Portuguese for thirty hours of course work with us.

This past year we registered students in Portuguese from such majors as humanities, psychology, English, biology, social work, political science, education, modern languages, business management, philosophy, Latin American studies, and music. Our Portuguese majors for next year have declared the following combinations to date: Portuguese/business/economics; Portuguese/Latin American studies/accounting; Portuguese/Latin American studies/social work. In some cases it will not be possible to complete three majors. Students can also take advantage of courses available in the evening and summer programs.

The present program consists of elementary and intermediate Portuguese, advanced conversation and translation, Portuguese and Brazilian civilization, a survey of Portuguese and Brazilian literature, the Portuguese and Brazilian novel, and a tutorial. The elementary and intermediate Portuguese courses are offered annually and the four other courses are offered on a flexible cycle. Student interest and need determine which course is offered. Also, it is possible to take the literature and civilization courses on a tutorial basis.

All courses in Portuguese follow the same basic description as their counterparts in other languages, with the exception of advanced conversation and translation. The translation portion of the course allows the student to work with periodicals or journals related to individual career goals. Students are encouraged to use a good dictionary and to contact Portuguese-speaking members of the community engaged in that career for additional words and expressions. This serves to produce a list of useful terminology for the student and to introduce him to people in the community with whom he will be working. Use of the Portuguese Times in the conversation portion of the class allows the student to acquire everyday vocabulary and to keep in touch with events in the Portuguese-speaking community. Two other works are used as basic texts: Willis' An Essential Course in Modern Portuguese, an excellent traditional grammar; and Keates' A Manual of Spanish and Portuguese Prose Composition, which provides excellent practice in translating articles from periodicals, newspapers, journals, etc. from many fields of specialization. A key to the translations is also available.

It is impossible to evaluate our program at this time because our first Portuguese Studies major did not graduate until June 1976. We can say, however, that other faculty members in our department, as well as those in other departments and programs, are taking a second look at what we are doing, since Portuguese Studies is one of the fastest growing programs on campus. Providence College has granted some form of scholarship aid to seven of the projected Portuguese Studies majors for next year; five are incoming freshmen. The college has further strengthened its commitment to Portuguese by granting the author a letter of intent to tenure upon completion of his seventh year, and, although still not confirmed, it is very possible that another instructor will be hired for the fall, at least on a part-time basis. The Instituto de Alta Cultura and the Fundação Calouste Gulbenkian, both of Lisbon, Portugal, have been generous in providing grants for both instructor and students for summer or full-year study in Portugal. The library has also been generous in providing us with part of a grant it recently received. This unsolicited donation has enabled us to augment our meager holdings in Portuguese.

Our program in Portuguese Studies has developed as far as it can with only one instructor. With the addition of another well-qualified instructor and some funding, we would hope to: (1) introduce an intensive course in conversation; (2) program the translations with their specialized vocabulary into our computer system; (3) purchase some portable monitors for the computer; (4) build a library of Portuguese-language journals and periodicals in many different fields of specialization; (5) establish an M.A.T. in Portuguese Studies to provide training for secondary and bilingual school teachers who wish to introduce our program into their school; (6) establish a workshop to develop badly needed materials in Portuguese; (7) build our Portuguese holdings in the library and our audio-visual materials; (8) establish a Portuguese-speaking language house on campus which would provide a total-immersion experience; (9) establish a speakers' bureau made up of Portuguese-speaking professionals from the community; and (10) establish a scholarship fund for Portuguese Studies majors who need financial assistance. These are but a few of the areas we hope to explore. We feel there is no limit to the service this program could render the community and the nation.

SCANDINAVIAN LIFE AND CIVILIZATION (894)

Niels Ingwersen
Department of Scandinavian Studies, University of Wisconsin, Madison

Scandinavian Life and Civilization is a three-credit course, open to freshmen, which has been given every spring semester for the past fifteen years and which has gradually increased enrollment to its present 200 students. One faculty member acts as coordinator of the course by planning the sequence of lectures, films, and panels, overseeing the production of a publicity folder, introducing the various lecturers to the class, attempting (if possible) to link the lectures together, and--most importantly-- being present during each class hour. The coordinator, who changes from year to year, is the only faculty member who receives credit for the course; all other lecturers teach their hour or hours--very willingly--as overload. Arrangements with lecturers from other departments are made on an individual basis.

Between twenty and thirty lecturers participate in the course; of these, seven or eight are members of the Department of Scandinavian Studies, and their lectures--on such topics as the Viking age, Scandinavian mythology, Scandinavian languages, Scandinavian history, literature, and film--form the core of the course. In addition, specialists from other departments offer lectures--often using slides, films, tapes, etc.--on a wide variety of topics, such as social problems, music, urban planning, the press, and immigration. These lectures vary greatly from year to year, since the department attempts to involve new 'Scandinavianists' on campus (including graduate students', as well as visitors and guest lecturers from Scandinavia. Moreover, since several major lecturers may be absent during a given term, it is necessary to recruit new participants as replacements as well as to include new fields and perspectives.

This situation tends to give the course a loose structure, but it has the obvious virtue that no one lecturer is indispensable, and, consequently, the course can be given every year. By practice and trial and error a very general model for the course has been developed which could be adopted easily by any fairly large university with some Scandinavianists in residence.

Most students take the course as an elective, but students in Scandinavian Studies can apply the credits toward their major. Both students and staff regard the course as an introductory survey of Scandinavian culture, one that gives the interested undergraduate the opportunity to consider which aspect of Scandinavia he or she finds to be particularly fascinating and worthy of further pursuit.

The course is designed for freshmen and sophomores--no knowledge of a Scandina- vian language is required--but is elected by many advanced undergraduates. All lecturers must presume that the large majority of their audience has no background knowledge of Scandinavia. Since some twenty people speak during the semester, the niveau is bound to vary; nevertheless, although the course is quite elementary and many-splendored in nature, the student who takes it merely for its undeniable entertainment value will soon discover that she or he will do well to prepare meticulous notes for the rigorous examinations. The course is by no means easy, and, in some ways, it may be too challenging: the student is confronted with a wide array of fields, some of which he or she may find very difficult; the coherence of a history or literature course can be approached here only in a superficial manner; some lectures may be too advanced; and--most detrimental of all the problems--no basic textbook exists (some paperbacks and numerous mimeographed sheets help, but the student must basically rely on his or her notes). This badly needed textbook, which will do much to create coherence and to give background information, is in preparation, but it will be a year or two before it can first be used on a trial basis.

In spite of these obstacles, student evaluations indicate the course is popular with them. As a rule, they enjoy the wide array of topics and the many speakers and find the loose interdisciplinary character of the course both appealing and intellectually stimulating. A solid proportion takes other courses in the department during subsequent semesters.

One problem caused by the large enrollment is loss of contact with the students in the classroom. A large class easily intimidates the meek students, and the lecturers seem less inclined to encourage questions. Ideally, small discussion groups should be scheduled every week, but the present budget does not permit the hiring of teaching assistants for this purpose, and the department is hesitant to ask the various lecturers to add additional hours to their already heavy teaching loads. In order to remedy the situation, the department has included a number of panel discussions, often inviting students who have been to Scandinavia, and has encouraged students taking the class to submit written questions in advance. Recently, the students have also been involved in determining the content of the three examinations--one is given after each five-week period; students are asked to submit examination, questions for both the objective and the subjective portions of the examination and the final examination is composed from these suggestions.

The above description should indicate that the format of the course, if not necessarily the individual lectures, is quite traditional; the audience is also quite traditional, in the sense that it consists mainly of regular university students. Some part-time students belonging to older age groups have, however, shown a continuing interest in the course, and it is very common for 'visitors' to sit in on a number of lectures.

Whereas the course is quite traditional, it has inspired less traditional uses of the university's educational resources. Certain units of the course, e.g., Scandinavian film, the Viking age, Scandinavian arts and crafts, have been given in expanded form in cooperation with University Extension as experimental one-week workshop summer school sessions on Washington Island in northern Wisconsin. These workshops have attracted a large and varied audience. The course has obvious potential as a radio or television class, though such a transformation would involve a thorough revision of its present format. One change, which will go into effect in 1976, is the elimination of most of the literature lectures--they will constitute a separate course--in favor of an expansion of the offerings in the arts and the social sciences.

Some years ago, there were relatively few 'Life and Civilization' classes on campus, but during the last five years many departments have instituted such courses, a fact which seems to indicate that a definite need exists and deserves to be met. In general, faculty members find it exciting to offer a few fairly elementary lectures in their specialty and find, too, that cooperation with colleagues in other fields is highly stimulating.

With the rise of interdisciplinary studies in American education and with the healthy growth of Scandinavian studies nationwide, it is pertinent that graduate students be given training in planning and offering such Life and Civilization courses. Lately, the department has noticed that its job-seeking graduates (Ph.D.s and M.A.s) have been asked by their prospective employers whether or not they are capable of teaching and coordinating a general course in Scandinavian life and civilization.

THE EUROPEAN STUDIES PROGRAM (904)

Z. Philip Ambrose (Classics)
Center for Area and International Studies, University of Vermont

In 1969 the College of Arts and Sciences of the university repealed its requirement that all students take two years of English, one year of foreign language at the intermediate level or above, and a laboratory science course. It further repealed the requirement that majors in language and literature and in music take history and a second foreign language at the intermediate level. Although majors in the humanities and social sciences are still usually required to study some foreign language, the net result of the changes was a sharp reduction in staff in departments of English and of foreign languages, especially modern languages. This was viewed with alarm and discontent by most of the faculty in the humanities; we had long been proud of our liberal arts tradition, especially evident, for example, in the healthy position of classical languages.

Among the countermeasures to this apparent trend was the formation of the Committee on Comparative and General Literature. The Committee created a system of literature-in-translation courses. These team-taught courses, e.g., The Development of European Prose Fiction, were successful and popular, with enrollments from fifteen to thirty-five.   Staffing such courses, however, proved to be a problem because of the reduction in faculty caused by the drop in enrollment in foreign language courses. Clearly, teaching positions in foreign languages were not going to be authorized to staff courses in literature-in-translation, and something had to be done to increase the interest in foreign languages per se.

Members of the Committee on General and Comparative Literature began to work out a scheme which would cost no money, increase standards, sponsor a renewal of interest in foreign languages, and give a new raison d'être to existing study-abroad programs and a unifying purpose to the approximately 240 courses in the university catalogue which deal in some way with Europe.   This became the European Studies Program, an affiliate of the college's Center for Area and International Studies.

The Center already had good programs in Asian, Canadian, Latin American, and Russian/East European Studies, all requiring some study of foreign language.   These programs are staffed by faculty from traditional departments and directed by an executive committee which has a freer hand in curriculum matters than the departments. The new European Studies Program (Western, Northern, and Mediterranean) has faculty representing all the departments of humanities, fine arts, and social sciences.   Students may choose to emphasize any field in these divisions and may simultaneously fulfill a standard major in these areas.   Currently there are a dozen majors, representing concentrations in art, geography, German, Greek, ancient and medieval history, Romance languages, Latin, and political science. For a new and rigorous program, this response is gratifying.

There are four groups of requirements for the European Studies major:
(1) At least eighteen hours of advanced courses in one European area or topic determined through consultation with an advisor and with approval of the European Studies Subcommittee of the Area and International Studies Program (e.g., Medieval and Renaissance Studies);
(2) Fifteen hours of additional advanced courses related to Europe; the total of (1) and (2) shall include nine hours of advanced courses in European literature and fine arts and nine hours of advanced courses in social science relating to Europe;
(3) Six hours of a European foreign language related to the area or topic of (1) and at the 200 (senior and graduate) level.   Those who have concentrated in a foreign language in (1) shall offer six hours of a second language at the 100 (upper class) level or above in addition to the requirements of (2).   Variants in the language requirement may be made by the advisor, depending upon the area of interest (e.g., ancient/medieval history or archaeology, where an ancient and a modern language would be required);
(4) The general distribution requirements of the College or Arts and Sciences, normally through a broad selection of courses dealing with Europe.

The rigor of the program lies in four features: (1) all courses must be at the upper-class level or above; (2) all students must take at least six hours of a European language at the senior and graduate level; (3) those students who make a European language the core of their major must take a second foreign language at the upper-class level or above; (4) every student's program must have the approval of an advisor and the affiliated faculty.   These standards were considered carefully as an incentive for those language students who otherwise would not study a second foreign language or would not take courses in the history, geography, politics, or economic and social structure of the people(s) who use the language in which they were concentrating. The requirements also assure that the student of social sciences learns to handle sources and documents in the foreign language of the area of his interest and that students of English literature with an interest in comparative studies not rely upon translations exclusively. The rigor of the program is balanced by the flexibility which it affords the student who, wanting to keep open options for a field of graduate study, is wary of consigning himself too much to one department.

The fact that the program called for no additional funding made opposition negligible. It is hoped, however, that success of the program will result in more funding for foreign languages and advanced courses.   Already we can point to last year's highly successful Medieval and Renaissance Studies Program (a group of courses from several departments for students living in one dormitory) and a six-week summer seminar in Assisi as

44

innovations for which the program is in part responsible. A special goal is the reintroduction of Italian into our curriculum, as we believe it will be difficult for a strong interest in the European Renaissance to tolerate the absence of instruction in Italian mandated by loss of requirements and staff.

The program also provides a compelling motive for students to study abroad. One major spent last year in the university's German Program in Salzburg, another at the Intercollegiate Center for Classical Studies in Rome, and another is studying French and Spanish in Norway (sic). Next year one major will have a leave of absence to work in Germany while preparing an honors project in central European geography.

A program so young obviously must look forward to many changes before reaching maturity. Next year will be the first year with senior majors. Four of them have elected to write a senior honors thesis. They will meet together twice a month with their advisors to give progress reports on their work; we hope this will create a greater sense of collegiality among the majors and give them an opportunity to share approaches to Europe which, though differing in time, topic, and method, may be mutually helpful, informative, and enjoyable.

It is too early to tell whether we shall succeed in renewing foreign language study at the University of Vermont. It has been possible, however, to offer the university Modern Language Review Committee this model of the breadth which the study of foreign languages should entail. Our highest aim is to show that in a liberal arts college true philology is everybody's business: the ability to read accurately all the evidence--written and unwritten, material and artistic--leading to a better understanding of our world.

AREA STUDIES MAJORS (906)

Clarence A. Kraft
Departments of Foreign Languages, Political Science, and History, Willamette University

Faculty members from the Departments of Foreign Languages, Political Science, and History met several years ago to explore the possibility of joint majors and proposed new majors in French Area Studies, German Area Studies, and Hispanic Area Studies. Inasmuch as the proposal required no additional staff and no additional courses, the new major programs were approved. After the programs had functioned for a year, faculty members in English and Russian were invited to propose majors in British and in Soviet Area Studies respectively, following the basic format of the French, German, and Hispanic Studies programs. A broader major, International Studies, was also created.

Traditionally, the Foreign Language Department has offered literature-oriented majors in French, German, Russian, and Spanish. In the past, many of our language majors have completed a second major in political science. The new area studies majors allow students to combine areas of interest, especially advantageous for students who do not qualify for double majors. In practice, however, several of this year's graduates have completed triple majors--foreign language, political science, and area studies. For the good language students not interested in pursuing a literature major, the program provides an option in which core courses for an area studies program can be combined with additional electives in foreign language.

Student reception of the new options offered by the area studies majors has been good. This is evident from the number of combined majors declared in the last few years. Incoming freshmen and high school students visited by the admissions staff have shown particular interest in combining traditional subject areas. It is too early for testimonials or for career preparation evaluation. Some students who have declared a major in Hispanic Area Studies are hopeful of using this preparation, along with courses in education, in the field of bilingual and bicultural education, which is becoming an important field in certain parts of Oregon.

I feel the new area studies programs have a good chance of continued success and growth. An added benefit of the programs has been closer cooperation and understanding among several of our departments.

THE FRENCH FILM: SOCIAL CONTENT (907)

Richard Pini (Romance Languages)
Departments of Romance Languages and Dramatic Arts, Amherst College

The Dramatic Arts Department had given a course on the history of film, and there was strong feeling among students and faculty in our department that film was a major socio-aesthetic venture in contemporary France and should be in the departmental curriculum. It was suggested that we pool our resources in the creation of a course, which was first offered in spring 1971 and has been in the catalogue since then. The only difficulty encountered related to structure, since we decided to use a format of two courses with one common session per week and one separate session per discipline per week, with common materials for viewing but not necessarily for reading.

The French departments of the other institutions in the Valley (Hampshire, Mount Holyoke, Smith, and the University of Massachusetts) showed interest once we had initiated the course. A French film course was to rotate among the five institutions on a yearly basis, with each institution free to define the content of the course. In 1974-75 it was again our turn to offer the course; potential student interest was clear in 1971, and student participation then and at the other institutions in ensuing years warranted continuing the course. Credits earned may be applied toward the departmental major.

There has been no difficulty in obtaining films on a rental basis for use in the course. Funding came from the Dramatic Arts Department in 1971 and from the Dean of Faculty in 1974. There is greater difficulty in obtaining appropriate reading material. My part of the course was taught in French, partly because the only readings useful for the subject are in French (Pivasset, Annie Goldmann). In fact, there isn't much to read on the subject, and often we relied on Bazin, whose film criticism picks up many important strands. Some inevitable problems arose in choosing materials and in the necessary compromises in emphasis for the interdisciplinary approach, but the interplay of different points of view was worth whatever was lost in coherence. Healthy disagreement caused by differing approaches proved stimulating for the students. I liked the interdisciplinary structure and the colloquium nature of the teaching, though it was helpful to have independent sessions as well.

My interest is not in film as an adjunct to the teaching of literature or as a genre to be examined historically, but as an art form in its own right and as the depiction of social contexts. Certainly, seeing moving pictures representing various aspects of French society and talking about its fictional representation enhanced a sense of the foreign culture and its socioeconomic underpinnings. What was perhaps the most difficult to discern was how the ideology of the film maker, the relationship of his consciousness to social circumstances and structures around him, appeared in the modes of narration or in other presentational techniques. The difficulty in methodology and the problems in understanding the assumptions such a course makes seem greater here than elsewhere, although film is probably more easily accessible to students, at least initially, than many other materials. But film is at one and the same time too easy to 'get into' and too foreign to our usual critical approaches. The former necessitates a certain wrenching of our consciousness away from the obvious. The latter makes the critical language difficult to acquire because the presentational techniques, the rhetoric, are not familiar to us; very few of us have used them, whereas most students and professors have some sense of the problems of writing. These are difficulties facing anyone using film with undergraduates. Added to them are the problems of a sociological approach to any art form.

A major problem of such a course, and perhaps a major attraction as well, is that the professor is in a position of some instability at the crossroads of various areas of speculation--the aesthetics of film, the sociology of the industry, the sociology of the audience, the relationship of fiction to society, and the specificity of French films or French culture. He may not, to say the least, be familiar with all aspects of these subjects, so to some degree he is constantly learning and improvising. This can be exciting and intellectually stimulating. Yet, a course should afford the instructor as well as the student new insights into the material. Though the instructor should obviously not be irresponsibly juggling his and the students' ignorance, the process can be one of discovery for both parties.

The Social Sciences (See also mss. 907, 976, 985, 986, 1023, 1566)

THE B.A. IN LETTERS (973)

Alan F. Nagel
Program of Comparative Literature, University of Iowa

The undergraduate B.A. major in the School of Letters was designed in 1971 by a committee representing all departments of language and literature. While a few undergraduate general and comparative literature courses had been offered by faculty of English and comparative literature, and courses combining literature and film or literature from a social science perspective were being given from time to time, these offerings were sporadic and represented the periphery of courses of study in national languages and literatures.

The committee discussed several basic issues: the relative merits of a strict focus on literature; the extent of general humanistic emphasis; possible requirements of national and historical variey, of language study, and of philosophy, linguistics, and criticism. The resulting major offers two tracks, one involving reading entirely in translation, the other including at least two courses--six credit hours--of literary study in a foreign language beyond the proficiency required for the B.A. in liberal arts. Specific required courses were not established. General requirements of demonstrable historical, national, and linguistic distribution and a commitment to individual student-adviser relations replace any specific requirements in the design of the major.

Devising and instituting the new major has met little opposition, much general interest, and some active support. The Major in Letters is not intended to take students from the literature and language departments, but to provide an option for students with strong interests in literature and the humanities who often choose other fields rather than a strictly nationally-centered course of study. A few general changes in the departments have also worked to the benefit of the major. In 1971 there was only one intensive language course; such courses are now offered in five languages, particularly for undergraduates who have already satisfied the B.A. proficiency requirement. Several departments have begun to offer courses taught in English with reading in the foreign language, thus drawing students interested in reading but not in oral language performance. National departments are teaching a variety of courses in literature in translation, and some have added general courses of national culture and civilization which attract students both from within the department and from Letters. In turn the Letters courses allow a student to begin literary study in foreign areas before acquiring foreign language proficiency, with resulting increases in general literary sense and critical thinking among students interested in the national literature courses. These results have not been realized to the extent desired, and there is hope that new introductory courses in criticism, genres, and themes will help in these areas.

Several courses designed specifically for the Letters major have been given in the past three years. Following the model of the English Semester begun at Iowa in 1968, a Letters Semester on narrative was offered in 1973-74. This is a ten contact-hour, twelve credit-hour course team-taught by three faculty members, including a variety of texts, classical and modern, oral and written. The intensive experience of the course emphasizes discussion, writing of critical exercises, parodies, and creative imitations, as well as dramatic scenes prepared by students. Interdisciplinary courses on literature and psychology (1973-74), and on literature and society (1974-75) have been offered with some success. These courses are team-taught, and the Letters program has been fortunate to find faculty from English, comparative literature, psychiatry, and history able to participate in such courses as part of their regular teaching load. As a matter of principle, the team-teaching involves full-time participation of the faculty in the classroom. The Program of Comparative Literature, which oversees and administers the Letters major, has provided teaching assistantships to enable doctoral students completing their dissertations to teach in some of these courses.

As of 1974-75, a new course, Crosscurrents of Literature, is being offered as an introduction for students interested in general, international, and comparative literary study. The course focuses upon a basic theme or critical issue in literature, varying from semester to semester, in order to introduce basic concepts and tactics of reading, writing, and thinking critically in literature. Such a course, originally held by the committee to be unnecessary, is now considered essential for beginning students..

Any new program in a large university runs the risk of being lost in the shadows of conventional divisions. Publicity for the major has come in general through normal university channels of catalogue announcements and publicity brochures. In the case of specific courses, descriptive announcements are distributed to all related departments or units of the university. A general listing of all courses recommended for students in the major, according to announcements of the individual departments, is assembled before each semester and distributed to all departments of the School of Letters. Prose course descriptions seem particularly important in announcing a course having a very general title and content which varies from semester to semester, as well as in distinguishing courses of more general appeal from those designed for specialists. Since virtually all courses are cross-listed between Letters and one or more other departments or programs, the major is not so easily identified. The introductory "Crosscurrents" course and a series of visiting faculty who will teach short courses integrated with regular courses in 1975-76 are steps in the direction of making the major better known on the campus. Plans are being formulated for team-taught courses in future years.

Students enrolled in the major are as diverse a group as in any other general humanities major. There have been some surprises, particularly the lower interest than expected (about one third) in the translation track, and the happy development that about one third of the students completing the major in the first three years have added a second and sometimes a third language while completing the major. Students have gone on to graduate study in literature, professional schools, and employment in varied areas.

The problems of the major at this point stem from matters of organization. Since the major is not primarily career-oriented, there is a need to maintain a general humanistic emphasis without losing the coherence of a literary focus. Budgetary stringencies and the realities of departmental relations periodically threaten any such interdepartmental endeavors as the Letters major, which depends so heavily on cooperation among several departments. Attempts to develop interdisciplinary team-taught courses have been only partially successful, because of occasional difficulties in releasing faculty time from departments (especially outside the humanities) and the complexities of planning three or more semesters in advance, necessary for some ventures of this kind.

The concept of providing for individual departments or faculty members to initiate courses and receive credit for courses in the Letters major is a workable solution to a bugaboo of interdepartmental and interdisciplinary teaching. Fear that the Letters courses compete with departmental offerings has no basis. So long as the several departments remain committed to the Major, the cross-listing of courses provides a practical option for faculty to work on the peripheries of their primary areas without seeming to transfer allegiance from their professional department. The results of translation courses and intensive language teaching have been beneficial in bringing some students to pursue several courses in a department they might otherwise not have discovered.

The major in Letters at this point has achieved the initial goals of providing a flexible and open undergraduate course of study in literature for students whose interests are not limited to the traditional national divisions. Fewer innovative courses have been offered to date than some faculty envisioned, whether because of inertia, the limited autonomy of a non-departmental unit, or the difficulties in funding the major team-teaching efforts desired. The near future offers many opportunities, especially in the increasing common interests of the several literature departments and of faculty in other departments of the humanities and social sciences.

INTERNATIONAL AFFAIRS MAJOR (974)

Josef Roggenbauer (Foreign Languages and Classics)
Departments of Foreign Languages and Classics, Business and Economics, History, and Government, University of Maine at Orono

Opportunities for productive careers in international affairs are becoming more numerous as a result of increasing personal, commercial, and political contacts among individuals and nations. To help satisfy the need for trained personnel in government service, international organizations, and international business, the university offers an interdepartmental major in International Affairs in the Departments of Business and Economics, Foreign Languages and Classics, History, and Government.

A student choosing this major will follow a carefully planned program throughout four years of study, taking certain required courses in each of the four departments. At the end of the sophomore year, the student will choose a major in International Affairs in one of the departments. The program is administered by the Committee on International Affairs, which, in addition to providing direction to the program and guidance to students, helps place students in suitable positions following graduation.

During the first two years, the student fulfills basic requirements of the College of Arts and Sciences. Among such requirements are an introduction to economics, United States (and/or European) history, introductory or intermediate courses in a modern foreign language, and American government. Students should also consult their department advisor in International Affairs regarding recommended courses. To enter the junior year of the program, students must have a minimum grade point average of 2.0 or permission of the Committee on International Affairs.

The essential requirements of the respective programs in International Affairs are:

International Affairs in Economics

(1) At least twenty-four hours in economics in addition to the introductory course. Among such courses may be Comparative Economic Systems, Economic Development, International Trade and Commercial Policy, International Economic Theory and Policy, and Culture and Economic Development.

(2) At least nine hours each in (a) history and (b) political science from among the following courses or from among others with an international focus:

(a) History of European Civilization, Asian Civilization, European Diplomatic History, Problems of Latin America, American Diplomatic History, War, and Canadian External Relations;

(b) Current World Problems, Democratic Goverments of Europe, Communist Governments, International Relations, United States Foreign Policy, International Law, and International Organization.

(3) At least one year of a modern foreign language beyond the intermediate course.

(4) Additional electives relating to international affairs arranged in consultation with the major advisor, selected from a wide variety of courses in anthropology, economics, comparative literature, foreign languages, history, journalism, philosophy, political sciences, psychology, sociology, agricultural and resource economics, and civil engineering.

International Affairs in Foreign Languages

(1) Courses required for a major in foreign languages, i.e., a minimum of thirty hours in the subject field beyond the intermediate level.

(2) At least nine hours each in economics, history, and political science from among the courses listed above under International Affairs in Economics or from among others with an international focus.

(3) Additional electives relating to international affairs arranged in consultation with the major advisor.

International Affairs in History

(1) At least twenty-four hours in history in addition to the introductory courses. Among such courses may be those listed above under International Affairs in Economics.

(2) At least nine hours each in economics and political science from among the courses listed under International Affairs in Economics or from others with an international focus.

(3) At least one year of a modern foreign language beyond the intermediate course.

(4) Additional electives relating to international affairs arranged in consultation with the major advisor.

International Affairs in Political Science

(1) At least twenty-four hours in political science in addition to the introductory course. Among such courses may be those listed under International Affairs in Economics.

(2) At least nine hours each in economics and history from among the courses listed under International Affairs in Economics or from others with an international focus.

(3) At least one year of a modern foreign language beyond the intermediate course.

(4) Additional electives relating to international affairs arranged in consultation with the major advisor.

This interdepartmental program is now in its tenth year. Ninety-seven majors have been graduated during that period, fifty-nine of them choosing political science as their area of concentration. The chairman of the Committee on International Affairs was instrumental in promoting student interest and cooperation between departments. He, I, and the chairpersons of the Departments of Economics and History submitted a proposal to the Educational Policy Committee and to the Arts and Sciences faculty in 1964. The reception of the proposal was unanimously favorable, perhaps for the following reasons: four department chairpersons had pledged the full support of their staff; the program did not require special funding; all courses for the proposed program were already in existence and taught as normal staff load; it was expected--and proved correct--that students would appreciate being rewarded for seeking a wider intellectual horizon, and that they would also derive direct career benefits from this diploma.

Approximately one half of the B.A.'s in International Affairs continued with graduate studies in the field either at the University of Maine or at other graduate schools. (The University of Maine presently offers a master's degree in International Relations in the History and Government Departments, as well as a master's degree in associated fields in the Business and Economics Department and in the Foreign Languages and Classics Department.) Many students entered government service careers, some practice law, some are employed in international business organizations.

The International Affairs Program has been particularly advantageous for the Foreign Language Department, since hitherto most majors in economics, history, and political science considered language courses beyond the one year Arts and Science requirement non-essential, and since more foreign language majors--due to fewer opportunities in the job market, especially in teaching--now find it useful to pursue a broader field of studies.

Other interdepartmental programs have subsequently been introduced, following a similar pattern of combining existing courses regularly taught by the staff of the cooperating departments: a B.A. in French with a Franco-American Studies option and a

B.A. in Spanish with a Latin American Studies option. Each program is administered by a faculty committee representing the various departments.

In future summers, a seminar in international affairs will be offered by one of the participating departments. Each seminar will consider a different topic of general concern and will be open to graduate students as well as to undergraduates with consent of the instructor. A number of noted scholars and public officials will participate in the program. The Committee on International Affairs will assist students seeking opportunities as summer interns in appropriate government agencies, business concerns, and international organizations.

We feel these study options and internships add a broader view to a major and aid the liberal arts tradition as they help students bring usable knowledge into the world of work.

Themes and Concepts (See also mss. 1023, 1678A)

THE CITY AS CREATIVE CENTER: PARIS, BERLIN, NEW YORK (976)

Ulf Zimmermann (Modern Languages)
Departments of English, History, and Modern Languages, Carleton College

This two-term course was initially intended as an integrative exercise for seniors. It was not planned to relate necessarily to specific careers, though we hoped it would find some immediate application in relation to 'city-connected' things, and for some students it has. One, for example, is now writing pieces on the city for a Minneapolis newspaper. The need for the sequence was determined in terms of student interests and needs.

A three-year grant from the National Endowment for the Humanities was available for funding the course, which is taught by a team of three faculty members--a French historian, a Germanist, and a comparatist with a specialty in American studies. When arrangements with other departments were necessary, they were made by means of amicable reciprocation and cooperation. The course, with its historical and cultural perspectives, is substantially dependent on a group of instructors; moreover, its success as a team-taught course is very much dependent, I suspect, on the three particular staff members involved.

The course has probably been more rigorous for both students and faculty than many more traditional ones. Being interdisciplinary, the course covered slightly more material than traditional courses, attempting perhaps somewhat too much at times, but students seem to have been very satisfied judging by their final, integrative, independent efforts and by the number of people interested in participating in the future. Perhaps the main skill learned (if it hadn't been already, which is all too often the case) was the preparation and presentation of various kinds of performances (papers, lectures, demonstrations, etc.).

The course can be taken for credit toward a departmental major, including French literature and urban studies, by prior arrangement with a faculty representative of the department in question. This is possible because the students are already advanced, with good backgrounds in their own, usually related, majors, because each instructor represents his discipline as thoroughly as possible, and because members of other departments are willing to credit our efforts.

The course has improved interdepartmental morale and seems to have established a very gratifying image for itself. Several improvements are planned for the future. The next offering will be only one term, but more intensive and probably more faculty-directed, since there seemed to be a demand for the latter on the part of the students.

We have found that for our constituency it would be useful to open the course to juniors. Students with sufficient background, experience, and interest will take the course fall term, studying urban history, literature, and culture by means of lectures, discussions, papers, etc., buttressed by slides, films, and guest speakers and participants. Students can enroll in a tutorial the following term; the tutorial study will result in a public presentation before the college and community audience. (This year three of twelve students chose to do this.)

No difficulties have arisen in obtaining materials for the course. General themes planned for the next offering include the city in fiction, the physical and historical city, the city visualized, the city and the stage, and the culture of bohemia and other subspecies of city life.

Our main 'bibliographical Baedeker' to the city as creative center lists both 'main thoroughfares' and 'side streets and alleys.' Main thoroughfares are Balzac's Lost Illusions, Roger Shattuck's The Banquet Years, Bertolt Brecht's The Threepenny Opera, Alfred Döblin's Berlin, Alexanderplatz, Harold Clurman (ed.), American Plays of the 1930's, Malcolm Cowley's Exiles' Return, and Henry Roth's Call It Sleep. Side streets and alleys are poetry and prose of Charles Baudelaire, Honore de Balzac's A Harlot High and Low, Alfred Jarry's Ubu Roi, Emile Zola's L'Assomoir, Vicki Baum's Grand Hotel, Otto Friedrich's Before the Deluge, Wolf von Eckardt's and Sander Gilman's Bertolt Brecht's Berlin, John Dos Passos' USA, Theodore Dreiser's Sister Carrie, F. Scott Fitzgerald's The Great Gatsby, and Alfred Kazin's On Native Grounds.

A lengthier bibliography provides a checklist and a basis means of orientation for weaknesses in particular areas; we have more extensive and increasingly specialized lists available as students come to be more interested in particular topics.

PARIS: BIOGRAPHY OF A CITY (985)

John D. Erickson (French and Italian)
Departments of French and Italian, History of Art, and History, University of Kansas

Paris: Biography of a City, offered in spring semester 1974, was devised as an interdepartmental, interdisciplinary course under the auspices of the Interdisciplinary Program. It was felt that on the basis of previous courses in that program, a good deal of potential student interest had been generated. The course was designed by three principal organizers and instructors from the Departments of French and Italian, History of Art, and History. Guest lecturers on French film and music, and on Americans in Paris were scheduled.

Paris: Biography of a City was given in cooperation with, though not exclusively for, a university-wide program developed at the university in recent years, "Outreach," which has as its objective the development of community-related projects. Of 150 students, perhaps two dozen non-regular students attended. The course was offered once a week, from 7:00 to 9:30 p.m., to make it easily accessible to the community. The majority of students were juniors and seniors. Pre-M.A. graduates in the course were required to do extra work, usually a term paper.

In planning the syllabus, the instructors intended to offer subject matter that, while cutting broadly across disciplines, would limit itself to the three primary areas of literature, art history, and history in an attempt to examine a cross section of the political, social, and cultural life of a major European city. We chose to go into as much detail as possible by limiting the course to the period from the Franco-Prussian War to the present. The instructors all specialize in this period and felt it would reflect a coherent view of the development of contemporary French society and that the majority of students, unfamiliar with French culture and language, would more easily relate to modes of contemporary life based on principles and concepts of Western thought underlying their own society.

My colleagues in the Department of French and Italian and I generally believed that, despite the retention of essentially unmodified language requirements at the university, to continue to retain them we would have to make the curriculum as flexible as possible without 'watering down' the basic requirements on the undergraduate and graduate levels. The Paris course was part of an effort to stimulate student interest in foreign culture and the realization of the importance of pursuing such knowledge as an essential part of their regular academic training. The Paris course combines, along with its interdisciplinary aspects, French culture and literature-in-translation. While trying whenever possible to relate the course to the immediate environment of the students, we sought to point up differences between French habits and thought and our own, and to fit them into a cohesive pattern of life as perceived by the French, not by the American tourist.

We experienced no special difficulty in obtaining approval for the course. Most problems were of a technical nature--the need to have rooms and equipment when scheduled. No special funding was required since instructors were credited for teaching time. The greatest administrative difficulty existed in dividing up the numbers of students so that each contributing department would be allocated equivalent funds in budgeting. In offering this course again, we shall require a small amount of funding for production of slides (which will become the property of the individual departments). The course demanded effort to integrate the total presentation. It meant exchanging notes and lectures before class, consulting regularly on numerous details, attending every class as a lecturer or participant, and being present for open discussions following class.

Some problems arose in obtaining materials for the course, particularly in the area of French literature. I found it difficult at times to adhere to the Parisian format. Some works lent themselves well to it, such as Emile Zola's L'Assommoir, which provided an excellent commentary on the Parisian working class of the time. But if one limits oneself to the most significant literary works, it is not always easy to fit them naturally into a format illustrative of the life of Paris during a particular period. Among authors read were Baudelaire, Zola, Huysmans, decadent and symbolist poets, Jarry, Proust, Apollinaire, the surrealists, Sartre, and Ionesco. Students were disconcerted by the inordinate amount of literature, particularly since only two primary history texts and two art history texts were required. They felt literature dominated the course too heavily, and I must agree.

For my own part, I found it exceedingly unnerving to teach literature in the way the course demanded. My orientation is to the qualities of the literary text as a primary, aesthetic object, not to the literary text as a means to study extra-literary phenomena, such as society, culture, history, and psychological attitudes. I found myself torn between emphasizing the literary qualities of the text and treating the text as a document rather than a work of art. If I participate in such a course again, I will limit the number of readings as severely as possible and teach primarily not literary art, but cultural history. I can see no other alternative in such a course.

I do not want to leave the impression that this course was undemanding. The students probably worked harder than they would in a regular course, but their course evaluations indicated that the majority liked the course and some thought it invaluable. Several students have asked when we plan to offer it again.

The instructors feel the course achieved the proposed goals. It proved to be an attractive supportive course for a language and literature program. Students were not allowed to take it for credit toward a major in French because use of the original language was not required. Nonetheless, the Paris course was fully approved by the department. It has encouraged the study of foreign culture in translation and even inspired some students to enroll in one of the contributing departments.

We hope to offer the course in the near future as part of the "Outreach" program at a special, newly established, off-campus branch in Kansas City. In this event, the course would meet one evening a week and attract solely non-regular students who elect to take it for pleasure and to prepare for travel abroad. The course could be followed, were one ambitious, by a group tour conducted by the instructors, who could offer the course in residence during the spring semester and as study and travel abroad during early spring or summer. Allowing for state regulations for public institutions, the course could even utilize the advertising facilities of commercial travel organizations cooperating in the travel arrangements. In more modest form, however, Paris: Biography of a City already has proved exceedingly attractive as a course offering.

1913 (986)

J. Theodore Johnson, Jr. (French and Italian)
Departments of French and Italian, and History of Art, University of Kansas

A visiting professor in the History of Art Department, who had worked with the research team sponsored by the Centre National de Recherche Scientifique in Paris and had concentrated on the year 1913, sparked my interest and that of Jeanne Stump, History of Art, in teaching a course on that year. Professor Stump and I are specialists respectively in the art and literature of the late nineteenth century and the early twentieth century, particularly in France; we both are strongly inclined toward interdisciplinary courses and approaches, and we felt that it would be exciting to offer a course on the year 1913 in spring 1975.

The lectures, readings, and discussions focused upon the burst of artistic creativity in Europe and America early in the twentieth century, a creativity which reached its height in 1913 and was interrupted by World War I. The main emphasis was on visual arts and on literature in France, but reference was made to the broad spectrum of literary, philosophical, aesthetic, political, popular, and technical concerns of the era. The only prerequisite for the course was junior standing or above. Course credits were applicable toward the French major. Undergraduates and graduates were required to take two examinations plus the final examination; graduate students wrote a research paper on a topic relevant to their field of research, e.g., French literature, political science, art history.

Students were required to read Werner Haftmann's Painting in the Twentieth Century. Literary texts were in English translation, although students able to do so were encouraged to read the works in the original. These included: Guillaume Apollinaire, Selected Writings; André Gide, Lafcadio's Adventures; and Marcel Proust, Swann's Way. We showed several documentary films, such as Great War, Part I, Sinking of the Titanic, Recovery of the Mona Lisa, and two Griffith films, The Battle of Elderbush Gulch and Judith of Bethulia, as well as documentary films on early cinema. We had only a minimal film budget and regretted not being able to afford to rent more films. Recommended, but not required, were Wylie Sypher, Rococo to Cubism in Art and Literature; Virginia Cowles, 1913: The Defiant Swan Song; and the three volumes of essays L'Année 1913: Les Formes esthétiques de l'oeuvre d'art à la veille de la première guerre mundiale, edited by L. Brion-Guerry.

The organization of the course was kept fairly 'loose' in order to cover the material adequately, but not necessarily in sequentially-linked fifty-minute blocks. Concentration on one year predicated this non-linear approach. Some of the most exciting sessions were those toward the end of the semester when my colleague and I would both make brief presentations on specific problems along with a graduate student presenting his work, and we would all be struck by the way certain principles, concerns, and forms kept emerging. I had opened the course with several introductory lectures entitled "From Naturalism to the 'Reel' World." These lectures were designed to give students a background against which the artistic productions of 1913 would come to play. My colleague's major lectures included "Experiment in Color: Fauves and German Expressionists," "Developments in Cubism," "Orphism and Orphist Painting," "The Russians Come to Paris," "Architectural Program of the Théâtre des Champs-Elysées," "Futurist Painting," "Architecture and Sculpture in 1913: A Brief Survey," "Art Circles: Picasso-Stein in Paris in 1913," "Pittura metafisica," "England and the New Spirit," "The Armory Show," "The Blue Rider," and "Developments Toward Abstract Art."

I gave several lectures examining such topics as "Crosscurrents in French Literature: 1913;" "Concrete Poetry from Mallarmé to Cendrars;" several lectures each on Apollinaire, Proust, and Gide; and then several brief concluding lectures ranging from panoramic surveys of literature in other countries to brief asides on ragtime, Joplin, and Ives. Guest lecturers from the university presented lectures on Stravinsky's Rite of Spring (Music); "European Turmoil: 1913" (History); "The World of Physics: 1913" (Physics); "Aeronautics in 1913" (Chemistry); "Philosophy-Revolution-Lenin" (Philosophy); "Edwardian Literature: The Long Indian Summer" (English); Carl Sternheim's play 1913 (German); and a remarkable illustrated sound collage "1913: The American Scene" (Journalism and Radio).

We are eager to offer the course again when our teaching schedules allow, and we'll try to condense certain aspects and include representative works from several other literatures. We found that some of the visual arts students were not prepared to handle literature and exams; most of the literature students were able to handle the art and history. Colleagues in other departments were quite interested in the course. We found them to be quite cooperative, and we were unable to accommodate all those who wished to be guest lecturers. The course was cross-listed under three separate departments: French, History of Art, and Humanities. We had thirty-five students in the course, over half from History of Art, and the rest divided between French and Humanities.

Miscellaneous

HUMANITIES PROGRAM (1023)

Eva R. Frayne (Humanities-German)
Division of Communications, Parkland College

In the summer of 1969 interested faculty members from the Communications and Social Science Divisions formed a Humanities Committee for the purpose of designing an interdisciplinary, team-taught humanities sequence. Two years and many meetings later, we taught our first series of courses, entitled Man and the Divine, Man and Society, and Man and Man. The one-year sequence fulfills the humanities requirement for a large number of degree and certificate programs both at Parkland and at transfer institutions.

We advertised the first year with a flier designed by the art member of the team showing a pre-Columbian sculpture and stressing the multi-media, team-taught, interdisciplinary approach. We had approximately fifty students the first quarter, 100 the second, 150 the third. We limited the enrollment to 150 students (six sections), since courses in English literature, music appreciation, and art appreciation were beginning to show an alarming drop. During the next four years, enrollment fluctuated between 120-150 students, and courses in art and music appreciation as well as in literature have slowly risen again in enrollment.

Since the seven members of the team also teach courses in their specialites (English, foreign languages, history, philosophy, art, and music), the realignment of students was not catastrophic. On the contrary, we now have students taking art, music, and literature courses because they developed an interest in these fields in a humanities course.

Fortunately, the administrative structure presented no obstacles to interdisciplinary teaching. The college is divided into six divisions, of which two, Communications (English, foreign languages, music, art) and Social Science (philosophy, history) participate in the humanities sequence. The sequence is listed under the offerings of the Communications Division. Two instructors from the Social Science Division are regular members of the team and teach two to three courses each year as part of their regular load. The other instructors come from Communications (English and foreign languages).

Each course carries four credits and meets two hours on Fridays for a large-group lecture, film, or slide showing and one hour on Mondays and Wednesdays for discussion in groups of approximately twenty-five. Each instructor is responsible for a discussion section, assignments, tests, grades, etc. The Friday sessions alternate between presentations by the various discussion instructors and lectures by the art and music staff members, who do not teach discussion sections. In addition, we draw on interested members of the college, the University of Illinois, and the community who have special talents or experiences to offer. For example, we have had a pianist and a string quartet perform and discuss their music. The National Academy of the Dance presented a program of classical ballet, and graduate students and a professor of dance from the University of Illinois gave a modern dance recital. In view of increasing interest in Asia, we have had karate, yoga, and ikebana demonstrations as well as lectures by natives of India and Pakistan. We have had African music and dance performances and exhibitions of instruments. In general, we have found an enormous fund of good will and interest in the community and among the faculty.

The team, consisting originally of seven members, has lost the original art instructor and is losing one of the foreign language instructors this year. (We have also had three interns from the University of Illinois who have either assisted instructors or have taught sections of their own.) Even though we follow broad outlines, the loss or addition of a team member inevitably introduces changes. We are confident, however, of the continued life of the sequence, regardless of the change of personnel.

The underlying goals are to stimulate the imagination and expand the vision of students (and faculty). In the first course, we studied the Egyptians and the relations between man and gods as recorded by the ancient Greeks in their literature (one epic and one play), their art and architecture (slides of sculpture, vases, temples, and a trip to a local museum), and their philosophy (lecture and film on Socrates and Plato). Then we leaped across centuries to the Western European Middle Ages and looked at its art, architecture, literature, and philosophy. We studied the cathedral at Chartres (film and slides), some of the Canterbury Tales, and had a lecture on St. Augustine and Thomas Aquinas. Some medieval music as well as modern compositions, such as Orff's Carmina Burana and Britten's Ceremony of Carols, fit in well, and once we showed The Hunchback of Notre Dame. (Leaping centuries has its problems but is by no means unfeasible. If nothing else, it stimulates the students' curiosity about the intervening centuries.) Two years ago we introduced a unit on gods and men in pre-Columbian civilization in America--the Aztecs, Incas, and Mayans--and elicited good student interest.

Highlights of study in the second course are Renaissance painting in Italy and Northern Europe, a play by Shakespeare, Rousseau and Romanticism, and the music of Beethoven. Occasionally there is time to include units on the French Impressionists and on opera.

The third course has tended more and more toward Asian humanities, with a unit on India (film: Pather Panchali) and one on Japan (film: The Seven Samurai). Along with the reading of modern Asian short stories, we stress some Asian non-verbal ways of achieving peace of mind, body, and soul, such as Zen and yoga. Dance, eastern and western, classical and modern, has also found a niche in this particular course.

For materials we first experimented with handouts, progressed to an interdisciplinary humanities text, and now use a selection of paperbacks including: (1) Ernest Gombrich, The Story of Art; (2) The Odyssey, translated by Robert Fitzgerald; (3) The Canterbury Tales, translated by Lumiansky; (4) The Signet Shakespeare Series; and (5) Greek Tragedies, edited by Greene and Lattimore. We have not yet found a satisfactory paperback on Oriental cultures.

According to some students, the humanities sequence is the best thing they have encountered in college. They like the variety and the freedom to pursue various interests stimulated by the material. Some would have liked more structure and organization but still liked the course very much. The attitudes among the instructors range from a desire to help the students formulate an integrated world view to an effort to expose them to a multitude of cultural stimuli of the past and present, which cannot always be fit into a neat pattern. Eventually we hope to achieve a balance between integration and enrichment.

Since the college is changing from quarters to semesters in fall 1975, the content of the sequence has had to be redistributed and now appears as follows in the catalogue:

HUM 101: Cultural Values in the Western World
Exploration of Western culture as expressed in art, music, literature, history, and philosophy. (Team-taught with a multi-media approach.)

HUM 102: Cultural Values in the Non-Western World
Exploration of non-Western cultures (pre-Columbian, Oriental, African) as expressed in art, music, literature, history, and philosophy; their influence upon modern man. (Team-taught with a multi-media approach.)

INTERDISCIPLINARY (DEPARTMENTAL)

Culture and Civilization (See also mss. 1339, 1348, 1361, 1551)

TANDEM COURSES IN FRENCH CIVILIZATION (1045)

Newell R. Bush
Department of Foreign Languages, University of North Carolina, Charlotte

Inheriting responsibility in 1969 for the traditional course in French civilization required for majors in our department, I continued the established historical-cultural syllabus during the first year but found it less than satisfactory. Our language majors were not very enthusiastic about history, even French history; all of them were being subjected to some chronological study in the required literature survey courses, and, whenever possible, persuaded to take appropriate courses in the Department of History. Many of them were planning to be teachers, but only a few would have an opportunity to visit France before graduation. The rest would have met only one or two native-born French persons, usually faculty members, prior to becoming teachers of the French language and culture in high schools.

These and other factors emphasized the need for greater emphasis on modern France, particularly on the French people, in our program. All language teachers have experienced the intoxicating increase in classroom interest when yielding to the temptation to relate a travel anecdote. Usually we feel guilty about neglecting the lesson and seldom go on to other stories, despite their obvious success, under the suspicion that we are being taken in by students who have an eye on the clock. This phenomenon occurs with language majors as well, and their curiosity is even greater because of their personal stake in such information. Perhaps we should have recognized long ago the opportunity we had to take advantage of this kind of curiosity by introducing systematic study of cross-cultural contrasts along with literature and language.

I had been acquainted with the widely-read Village in the Vaucluse by Laurence Wylie, at that time already a bit out of date but representing the kind of information I felt students would welcome, along with other work by that author and others. Village was actually a sociology text and is so listed on the back cover of the paperback edition.

As such, it offered a new approach to studying a European civilization in the context of a modern language course. Unfortunately, it was written in English and therefore not exactly suited to our purpose; the school edition in French did not appear until later and was relatively short-lived.

The first time I offered the course, I used Deux Villages, a shortened, translated, paperback version of Wylie's book which contained most of the same illustrations. Student evaluation was quite favorable. A year later, the college-level text Le Français by Wylie appeared and has been used as our main text ever since. The class has also used the original Village in the Vaucluse in the Harper paperback (now out of print) and John Ardagh's The New French Revolution as supplementary texts.

The old syllabus was completely revised based on the topics in Les Français, all dealing with a sociological or anthropological study of the French people. I also scheduled a series of short films, rented from the French-American Cultural Services, most of them fifteen- to twenty-minute color documentaries on modern France. However, I was not prepared to abandon history entirely and assigned outside readings with periodic quizzes on La France et sa Civilisation by Jacques Hardré. Classes were oriented toward more discussion, a change which proved all the easier because of the lively interest in cross-cultural contrasts. It is not difficult to provoke discussion on such topics as French attitudes toward child-rearing and discipline, which are so strikingly different from our own. In this connection, the class was assigned an article on France from Childhood in Contemporary Cultures by Mead and Wolfenstein. French-born faculty members with children were invited to discuss this topic with the class. (Whenever available, exchange students were invited as well.) Students were equally interested in contrasts with the French educational system and, especially, the revolt of the university students in 1968 and subsequent attempts at educational reform.

The idea for a course in French civilization conducted in English for non-majors had long attracted me, even before I learned of Professor Wylie's similar course at Harvard. Even as an undergraduate, I had chafed at the absence of socio-cultural courses about specific foreign countries taught by natives or by faculty members who had lived extensively in such places. Courses 'in translation' offered by language departments, although excellent for someone wanting to study literature, simply do not fill the bill. Students who are unable or unwilling to study several languages to qualify for advanced civilization courses should be given an opportunity to study the same subject in English.

My main purpose in offering the course in English was to attract students to the language department who might otherwise never set foot in our building. I found many who were keenly interested in France, yet could not enroll in French language classes because of other requirements. It was soon made clear to them that the course would be no easy road to three hours of credit nor could it be applied toward the language requirement. In the first two classes, students were majors from a wide variety of departments. Some were Spanish or German majors; others came from the Departments of Geography, History, English, Nursing, Political Science, and Business.

My first action before taking formal steps toward college and faculty approval was to broach the idea to colleagues in the History Department who were already teaching general courses in western civilization for freshmen. The specialist in French history favored the course and helped select some of the texts and readings. Geography faculty had no objections, since they offered no courses on France alone. Political science faculty agreed for the same reason and promised to encourage students to enroll.

The course was approved and listed as a French course 'conducted in English' and primarily for non-majors. The number 209 was chosen to suggest similarity in content with the French language sister course, French 309, and to indicate its availability to freshmen and sophomores (no prerequisite). Both courses carry the same title and catalogue description, i.e., "a study of the French people, past and present, with emphasis on cross-cultural contrasts in attitudes and values." Semester schedules indicate which language is being used; since I alone teach the courses, they have not been offered simultaneously.

Enrollments have varied from ten to fifteen students. We have found that some publicity is necessary, if only to clarify the nature of the course to faculty advisors. Unless this is done, they will tend to be skeptical and discourage advisees from enrolling.   A slightly more detailed course description is usually circulated to appropriate departments before preregistration. Even a few signs were posted stressing the 'No French Required' aspect.   Another problem for students is whether the course can be applied to the general humanities requirement for graduation.   Our registrar at first refused to so classify what he rather condescendingly referred to as a 'civ' course. Unlike literature-in-translation, its classification is not self-evident and must be worked out with the administration.

At present, the course given in English may not be applied for credit toward a French major, although it is open to majors for elective credit.   One student decided to major in French after completing the course and was obliged to take the course in French because of our requirement that majors take all advanced work in the target language.   Thus, French 309 is required and is somewhat tailored for majors.

There have been problems in finding appropriate texts for both courses, especially in finding the right audio-visual materials.   For the course in French, aside from Les Français, the best of the possible replacements, Civilisation Française Contemporaine by Michel Paoletti, is either too difficult for our third-year students or not thorough enough, as is the case of Camille Bauer's La France Actuelle, an excellent text but oriented to intermediate-level language classes.   French embassy films, while attractive and quite up-to-date, are aimed at a travel and tourist audience.   Very few have the combination of sociological and human interest that is needed in the course.   One of the best examples, now old, is a film called Nous entrerons dans la carrière, which shows how different from their fathers and grandfathers French young people are today.   Some full-length feature films are excellent, but expensive to rent.

Appropriate bibliography for the course in English is no problem; the challenge is to select the right length and level of readings and resist the temptation to assign too much.   A basic source is In Search of France by Hoffman, et al., a Harvard symposium study combining all the social sciences.   Others include The Bureaucratic Phenomenon by Michel Crozier, a well-known French sociologist, Crane Brinton's Americans and the French, and paperback translations of well-known classics, e.g., The French by François Nourissier and The French: Portrait of a People by Sanche de Gramont.   Better prepared students might be assigned part or all of Tristes Tropiques by Claude Lévi-Strauss and The Words by Sartre, both available in paperback translations.

Inexpensive texts for such a course are not quite as easy to find.   John Ardagh's New French Revolution is superb, but the cultural contrasts are all with British society.   Our students also refer to this thorough study as "more than you need to know about France," Other small texts in English, such as France in the Modern World by Niles M. Hansen, are excellent and concise but lack the warm, human element characteristic of Wylie's books.   I have therefore been using dittoed sheets translated from Les Français (my own versions) pending completion of the up-dated English language edition. Students are also asked to read Village in the Vaucluse before going into Ardagh's more recent descriptions of France.   Chapters such as "Peyrane and the Outside World" fit very well with Wylie's "Le Comportement Politique."   The same films are used in both courses, since nearly all may be ordered with English commentary.

The best evidence of approval by my colleagues in German and Spanish was their decision to offer similar courses as part of their regular major programs. German has also started a course in English with a somewhat more impressive title. By moving in this direction, the department is in a better position to cooperate in a proposed interdisciplinary degree program and is attracting students, some of whom subsequently decide to resume language study as juniors or seniors. Graduating teachers have been nearly unanimous in their favorable evaluation of the course in French.   The most enthusiastic testimonials have come from students who have later gone to study in France. Several said this preparation had prevented them from turning anti-French in sheer exasperation.   Others found it especially helpful in attempting to teach cultural relativism and in helping students look at American culture from a different point of view.

I hope to improve the course by bringing in outside lecturers more frequently. Most will come from other departments, but members of the community with special qualifications, as well as all visiting French business executives, will be approached.   I would like to arrange a joint meeting of the class with members of the local Alliance française. When funds are available, it would be ideal to bring in a university exchange student as a part-time assistant to join the discussions as a member of the class. There will also be an effort to invite officials of multinational corporations doing business in France to discuss such problems as employment, sales techniques, and advertising.

I have enjoyed teaching the course and have found it necessary to get into some personal 'recycling.' This has enriched my teaching in the regular language and literature courses, indeed, it has added a new dimension to both.

OTHER CULTURES THROUGH HUMANISTIC STUDIES: FRENCH CULTURE, HISPANIC CULTURE (1054, 1141)

Raquel Kersten (Spanish) and Louise Witherell (French)
Division of Humanism and Cultural Change, University of Wisconsin-Green Bay

Trying to describe these courses on paper is like trying to catch a fast-swimming fish from the rear with one hand! Details of syllabus, texts, films, and student presentations change with each succeeding year and with changing events in French and in Hispanic cultures. Perhaps surveying the development of the courses will provide a sense of what it has been and what it will continue to be.

When our innovative branch of the University of Wisconsin came into being, it was decided that there would be a series of core courses required of all students, no matter what their field of specialization. These courses were grouped under the title Liberal Education Seminars. At first there was a four-year sequence, in which the junior year (Junior LES) was designated as dealing with an 'other-culture' experience. Today the LES sequence has been somewhat shortened; sophomore and junior LES years have been reduced to a three-unit sequence called Intermediate LES, some of which may include the concept of other-culture experience.

It was in response to the need for courses for the Junior LES that foreign language instructors began developing culture courses. Since they were to serve the entire student population, they attempted to survey all aspects of culture from all angles. Originally, we were to do the survey in one semester, after which the student would travel with the class group to the target country and conduct a research project related to a field of specialization. This plan assumed that the trip was financially possible for the student. As an alternative, we would give a second on-campus course in which the culture of the target country was examined in greater depth or from a different perspective than in the first semester. For example, in the first semester of the Spanish sequence (Latin America Today), writers, artists, and musicians are studied to learn how Latin Americans perceive their culture. In the second semester course (As Others See Us--The United States through the Eyes of Latin American Essayists, Novelists, Poets, Dramatists, and Artists), Latin American cultures are used as a basis for interpreting U.S. culture.

A student can get LES credit for the course, as well as Concentration and Option credit (foreign language). With the reorganization of the LES program and staffing, approval for this course was less readily available. It appeared that faculty would have to split contracts with LES as well as conduct the overseas trips; our foreign language is now too small to do this. It was decided to revise the other culture courses into Concentration/Option form only. Hence, the current title which relates to the Concentration in Humanism and Cultural Change: Other Cultures through Humanistic Studies. All students must have a concentration major in addition to LES. The courses also fulfill state certification recommendations for a civilization course for French or Spanish majors and minors.

Approval for this course is as permanent as anything is in an innovative institution. The staff teaches the course as part of the normal load. The course has no special funding, but a modest sum is available for film rental. Subscriptions to foreign periodicals and library books keep us up to date. No extra time was given to course development.

The following description of the French course provides an example of how we proceed. The instructor is in full charge of the first few weeks, giving the students time to be introduced to the problem of studying another culture and to choose one area of the syllabus to research and present to the class as one day's lecture. The first few weeks are devoted to French history and the relationship of twentieth-century France to earlier periods. The instructor lectures, recent documentary films from France are shown, and the students are assigned readings. The instructor provides an introduction to French history, at least up to the Revolution, on the theory that most undergraduates are ill-prepared to study the earlier centuries independently. There are suggested topics for each day with documentary films when appropriate, as well as basic background readings required of the entire class for each day.

More recent historical subjects appeal to some students, and they volunteer to do presentations relatively early in the semester. Other students choose topics such as urbanism, provincial life (Wylie's Village in the Vaucluse is required reading despite its limitations in time and space), agriculture, industry, the economy, the status of women, sports, popular amusements, film or other aspects of the arts, the French reputation for excellence, publishing, food, or education. The syllabus tries valiantly to cover all angles of culture in the broadest sense of a humanistic approach. Obviously, we intend to have something for everyone, and if a student's particular interest is not already represented, we find a way to include it. The instructor discusses any topics that may be neglected by a given group of students. We have had very good results and even some rare good times as a result of this freedom of choice.

Texts which fit our needs are difficult to find. For those receiving French credit, appropriate selections from Bouraoui's Créaculture I and II provide an introduction; unfortunately, no equivalent in English has been found. Cobban's A History of Modern France, Volume 3 (paperback) is required of all students, and the Paris Guide Michelin is used to emphasize how much of the past exists physically in the midst of the present.

There is no final exam; class participation throughout the semester plus the oral and documented written presentation of the research topic are adequate bases for a grade. If we have not had a French native as a student in the class, I invite one toward the end of the first semester to answer questions about French and American cultural similarities and differences. Fortunately, there are some culturally sensitive native French available in the community. I invite such a guest only at the end of the term; to do so earlier would be to risk uninformed questions on the part of the students. At the end of the semester, I also like to show the French film On l'appelle France; the students usually have a delighted sense of déjà vu!

The second semester, also open to all students, is perhaps less original in that it uses recognized twentieth-century works of literature exclusively as sources of information. But they are read for their reflections of some of the aspects of French culture which were studied in the first semester. (The second semester may be taken out of sequence, or by itself, but is of more value to the student if taken after the first semester.) For a study of how France looks at its own past we read Anouilh's The Lark and Proust's Swann's Way; for a study of France's concern with wars and internationalism, Malraux's Man's Fate and Camus' The Plague; for a study of urbanism and the provinces, Gide's Counterfeiters and Mauriac's Thérèse; for a study of ecology and pollution, Giono's early work; for a study of flight and space, Saint Exupéry's Night Flight. Within any work, of course, we look beyond the specific cultural strength of the work for many cultural details. Since the course is not restricted to those who know French, the works used are limited to those for which English versions are readily available. We have also occasionally included such works as Robbe-Grillet's Jealousy, Jarry's Ubu roi, Beckett's Molloy, Ionesco's Rhinoceros, and works by Feydeau, Simenon, Cocteau, and others. Nearly any work can be used if examined from a culturally sensitive perspective.

As the student's special contribution to the second semester, a cultural theme is chosen to follow through the semester's reading and to serve as the basis of a term paper. The topic might be family relationships, attitudes toward education and educational practices, or the status of women. Again, as in the first semester, there is no exam; grades depend on the quality of class participation and the term paper. Student reaction to this second semester has been positive, often marked by surprise at the discovery that ordinarily they would have read only for cross-cultural similarities and would have tended to skim over cultural differences as quaint or unimportant, or to misunderstand them.

Students in both French and Hispanic sections have evaluated the course sequences highly. The courses may have attracted some students to the study of French or Spanish, but since the courses are offered at the junior level, as they must be for Concentration/-Option credit, they are scheduled too late for general recruiting purposes. Testimonials from students are numerous and include many cards from former students traveling abroad and requests from recently-graduated teachers for some of the course materials.

We believe that the course, with its insistence on student participation in teaching a part of the course and its flexibility in terms of the student's choice of what will be taught, is both exciting and successful.

SEMINAR IN GERMAN CIVILIZATION (1058)

Frank L. Borchardt
Department of German, Duke University

This seminar grew out of the first offering of a lecture course in German civilization. The lecture course was conducted in English, open to the university community at large, and credit was given toward the German major on the condition that reading was in German. Student demand created the seminar in order to treat in greater depth various issues raised in the course. The logistics of creating the seminar posed few problems. Departmental offerings had long included general undergraduate seminars in German literature in English translation to correspond to similar lecture courses, and these provided an adequate rubric for the new seminar. Since one goal of the seminar was to reach students outside the department, the readings and discussion were to be in English; for that reason it could not be credited toward the major.

Limiting the participants to a reasonable number (10-15) presented the greatest difficulty. Need for the new seminar had not become evident until late in the lecture course on civilization. Public notice in the form of two posters had to announce time and place, since deadlines for normal channels had passed. This publicity attracted an undesirably large number. The first offering of the seminar bore this handicap, but for the second offering a year later we ruthlessly restricted the number.

The students suggested the first third of the twentieth century as the topic for the seminar. (The lecture course, as a general survey organized historically, had treated all periods superficially, but the modern suffered most by coming at the end of the semester.) The designation 'Expressionism' seemed to provide a handy foil for the diverse cultural activities of the period, and the seminar chose as its objective an explanation of that term. Topics for discussion followed the sequence: painting, sculpture, and graphics; architecture; theater and film; poetry; artists and politics.

Each student chose a book on each topic and presented a summary of the reading to the seminar, which met Monday evenings for two or three hours. The seminar exploited available cultural resources, such as the state museum, educational television, film series, public library films, and residential and commercial buildings. No specific materials or events were organized just the seminar.

Visual arts began the seminar due to their relatively easy accessibility. Books in English on the topic abound. The seminar first permitted relatively free discussion of the works on their own terms removed from historical context. Soon, however, students reported on nineteenth-century academic art in Germany, on fauvism, cubism, futurism abroad, and on their historical backgrounds. Discussion returned to the works in an attempt to find common features and thereby a definition of a style.

Progressing to the discussion of architecture, we moved beyond our specific period to the monumental public buildings of the 1930's and to modern architecture in general. The imaginary and actual architecture of the expressionists connected the discussion of art with the general discussion of modern architecture. Students also reported on turn-of-the-century architecture in Germany, France, and the United States to establish backgrounds for our study. Each time the seminar was offered, the discussion of architecture proved most interesting and unpredictable. It stimulated consideration of social planning, history, government, technology, and more. The students had, it seemed, never stopped to analyze their own routine experience of buildings or the effect of the various constellations of buildings among which they live and work. The German component easily retained its significance due to the pervasive influence of Bauhaus. The theatrical architecture of the expressionists brought the discussion back into focus and made the connection to expressionist drama.

In drama, as in the other topics, the primary works shared attention with historical backgrounds--both antecedent and contemporary. Film, as available, illustrated the dramatic word. The difference in taste between then and now and there and here presented good opportunity for discussion of principles of cultural history, a discussion which permitted passage beyond differences in taste to the origins of modern theatrical forms in the wide-ranging experimentation of the expressionist period. Familiarity with drama texts eased the entry into expressionist poetry, but discussion remained brief and served mainly to provide evidence for previous insights. The seminar recognized the special problems of language in relation to poetry and decided that translation was not an appropriate medium.

Finally the seminar turned to the intense involvement of the arts in the social criticism of the age, both as a topic per se and as a summary of the semester's work. Each student then attempted to synthesize the discussions in a term paper. The papers revealed high interest, good work, and occasional insight.

The results were, in each case, gratifying. During and after the seminar, various students reported activities, such as voluntary or semi-voluntary museum visits during which they recognized a Klee or Kokoschka from across the room. They told of newly-developed sensitivity to the organization of space in architecture and new awareness of the rudiments of the language of film--angle, editing, texture, etc. Although they found it difficult to articulate, I am convinced that the students acquired something approximating historical perspective: a sense of the relationship of style to specific time and place, and of the development of trends in style.

The seminar did not pretend to offer preprofessional training. It was a general humanities course in the broadest, least pragmatic sense. It was meant to provide a service to students in other literatures and the social sciences who were curious about German cultural history. The subject was preponderantly, but by no means exclusively, German: problems both broader and narrower than a strictly national phenomenon were investigated. The substance was, thus, as much comparative cultural history between times and places as it was German cultural history. This approach seems to have served both the interests of the students and the cause of German studies particularly well. It gave points of reference and tried to retain a sense of proportion. American students have heard of Frank Lloyd Wright, perhaps even of Louis Sullivan, and have seen examples of American monumental architecture, if only the local post office. To ignore them in a German cultural history in favor of Bauhaus and the fantasies of Speer is pedagogically unsound and intellectually irresponsible. The similarities that warrant simultaneous consideration carry at least as much weight as the differences that might justify separate study. The comparative approach also corrects the inclination to remove German cultural history from the mainstream of western civilization, to have culture spelled with a capital 'K,' and to dismiss the popular or vulgar as extrinsic or unworthy.

Even though the period under consideration was limited, the subject matter was extremely broad. The course was classified as a lower-level undergraduate seminar; the atmosphere was extremely informal, and digressions were not discouraged. Nonetheless, the students read no fewer than six book-length studies, organized the information for oral presentation on no fewer than six occasions, responded to the presentations of peers, and wrote papers of moderate length. The seminar, thus, represented a fair amount of work--not excessive but also not light. The informal atmosphere demanded constant attention and participation, so that in-class work clearly rose above the level of lecture courses.

The happy experience of the sequence of a lecture course on civilization and a seminar on a special topic is leading to further experimentation. Students in history and political science have approached the department inquiring about the possibility of a course on East and West Germany. Such a course is being introduced with readings in German for German majors, in English for others. It has a fully satisfactory preregistration. A follow-up seminar on the model of the Seminar in German Civilization is being contemplated. In each case, these courses bring students to the department who otherwise would not be there. The intangible effects seem to be excellent. Other departments have taken favorable notice of these activities. New language enrollments among present students (excluding incoming freshmen about whom we have no statistics) are increasing sharply.

THE BUCKNELL EXPERIENCE IN SOVIET RUSSIA: SOVIET SOCIETY, THE CULTURAL HISTORY TOUR OF RUSSIA, RUSSIAN CULTURE, AND READING PRAVDA (1085, 1257, 1258)

Robert Beard
Department of Modern Languages, Literatures, and Linguistics, Bucknell University

Bucknell offers a two-course sequence on Soviet society and Russian culture, with an optional January interim in Russia. The sequence is designed to equip students with a genuine understanding of the Soviet Union with a modest investment of time and effort. Taken together with elementary and intermediate language courses, this guarantees solid reading knowledge and basic speaking proficiency in Russian, first-hand experience of Soviet Russia and all the major cultural and historical centers, and general understanding of the Marxist-Leninist principles of Soviet society as well as the cultural traditions of Russia.

The academic courses were introduced in 1969, before the language requirement was dropped and such courses became prevalent in the United States. They were begun as a result of a student interest poll which demonstrated that the reading of belles lettres was a minor motivation in a student's choice to learn Russian. More frequently, interest in the politics or economics of the Soviet Union influenced the decision.

Since all our courses are departmental courses and departmental curricula are considered the prerogative of the department involved, no administrative approval was required beyond a pro forma nod from the dean (who did support the proposal). From 1965 to 1968 enrollment in third-year Russian courses varied from one to three. When nineteenth- and twentieth-century drama courses were introduced in 1968, they each attracted three students. In 1969 Soviet Society attracted nine, six of whom completed the course. Enrollments increased to eight in each course, but since 1973 they have been declining. Bucknell abolished the language requirement in 1971. Last year the enrollment fell below the five required to give the course, and it was cancelled. Nonetheless, student response to both courses remains positive, so Soviet Society was 'tested' this year as a second-year course in an attempt to reach a broader spectrum of students earlier. As of next year, both courses will be regular second-year offerings on an experimental basis. One of the successful aspects of last year is that five of the eleven students electing it have decided to take the third-year course in Russian drama.

Soviet Society

Soviet Society is designed to provide basic insights into the history, economy, geography, social organization, and politics of the Soviet Union while the student continues advanced language training. One of the aims of the course is to confront the student with the Marxist-Leninist interpretation of the Soviet Union as compared to the bourgeois interpretation. Toward this end, two basic texts are employed: Sovetskii soyuz, ed. N.N. Sofinskii et al., and an American text such as Alex Inkeles' Social Change in Soviet Russia. Sovetskii soyuz is an overview of Soviet society written for foreign students entering Soviet institutions of higher learning. It deals with every aspect of

Soviet society, including education and religion, in journalistic language; thus, it is an excellent vehicle for a social science survey of the Soviet Union.

The course is conducted in Russian, except on those occasions when visiting professors who do not speak Russian are present. Some classroom time is devoted to viewing and discussing filmstrips from the Soviet Union and Super 8mm films produced in Russia by Bucknell's Program in Russian. The use of visual media as a supplement to reading materials is particularly important in courses dealing with societies with which the student has had no direct contact. For this reason films, filmstrips, and slides are substantial parts of all Russian courses at Bucknell, but play an especially important role in Soviet Society, since it is considered a background course for the trip to the Soviet Union.

Since Sovetskii soyuz was not intended as a language learning text, adapting it to the course presented a special problem. Even in advanced courses, it is imperative that the texts be glossed in order to cover significant amounts of material during the semester. Unfortunately, there is a dearth of appropriately glossed reading materials in Russian. The Program in Russian had long since initiated efforts to devise an effective system of glossing (see R. Beard "Dynamic Glossing," SEEJ, 19:49-57) and apply that system to selected reading materials in its Russian drama courses. When Sovetskii soyuz was chosen as the basic text for Soviet Society, glossing the text by this method was undertaken.

The Cultural History Tour of Russia

The Cultural History Tour of Russia fits into the January interim program which Bucknell uses. The month is set aside for curricular experimentation and academic activities which are incompatible with the regular semester format. In fall 1969, the first Cultural History Tour of Russia was planned, designed to make a first-hand experience of the cultural landmarks covered in the spring semester course, Russian Culture, possible for majors and other students. In its four years of operation since 1970, 141 students, including fourteen of our nineteen graduated majors have taken advantage of its opportunities. (All other majors have participated in summer programs; some have participated in both.)

Although the Cultural History Tour of Russia is designed as a laboratory for both the Soviet Society and Russian Culture courses as well as an independent study tour of Russia for non-majors, Russian Culture was selected to be the basis of the tour, not only because its subject matter fell more within the purview of our instructional staff, but also because both art and music are palpable and sensuous, demanding direct contact. Seeing a collective farm and a match factory does not reveal so much about central planning as witnessing the Bolshoi perform Moussorgsky reveals Russian music. An understanding of the function of party congresses is accessible without direct contact in a way understanding the function of the two St. Sophias in the history of Russian art is not. The opera, ballet, and concert schedule of our tour varies with the concert season. Musical events, chosen to reflect subject matter of the second half of the Russian culture course, are also attended by the instructor, who gives a historical and interpretive commentary on pertinent performances.

The itinerary is: (Prague) Kiev-Moscow-Vladimir/Suzdal-Moscow-Novgorod-Leningrad-Pushkin/Pavlovsk-Leningrad (Warsaw-Prague). This represents an attempt to follow roughly the development of the history of Russian art. In the Soviet Union, the interpretations of native guides are augmented by lectures by the Bucknell instructor(s). Evenings and spare time on trains and busses are frequently spent in group discussions with the instructor(s) and occasionally with Soviet youth. There are no formal classes or written work, since the excitement of a month of group travel makes it advantageous to delineate clearly the experiential from the academic components of our program.

Russian Culture

Russian Culture is an upper-level language/culture course designed to provide basic insights into Russian music and art--folkd, ecclesiastical, and classical--while continuing with advanced language training. The course centers on major developments in Russian music and art of the nineteenth and twentieth centuries, emphasizing the origins of Russian national classical music in folk and church music and its influence on twentieth-century Soviet and Western music. Readings in music include biographies of composers, articles on major movements, plots and descriptions of the musical structure of ballets, operas, etc; the same emphasis has been applied to art. Considerable attention is devoted to interconnections between art and music on the one hand, and Russian literature and history on the other.

There was no suitable text for this course; the Program in Russian was compelled to produce (R. Beard, ed.) Istoriia russkoi kul'tury: Khrestomatiia po iskusstvu i muzyke. In an attempt to integrate the various components of the course and to integrate the course with the Cultural History Tour, the readings were selected with considerable care. For example, some biographies were adapted from filmstrips produced in the Soviet Union which are readily available through Russian language bookstores in this country. Other readings were taken from the programs of the Bolshoi Theater. These programs are particularly appropriate for third-year students, since they are written by experts for mass audiences in the Soviet Union; their style is colloquial, but they are academically sound. Moreover, those students who have participated in the January tour will have read several of these programs while enjoying the Bolshoi in Moscow, and the recurrence of program material in the reading text will vivify the reliving of the experience in the classroom.

We also try to take a few slides during the performance to show while studying individual operas and ballets in the course. We shoot at least a thousand feet of Super 8mm movie film along the itinerary of the tour for use in class to reinforce the academic study of Russian art by recreating the direct experience: students see themselves seeing the objet d'art.

Readings in Pravda

Readings in Pravda was a January interim project which was undertaken only once. The idea was a popular one, however, and it was implemented again as a semester seminar with five students and incorporated into a one-to-two-week component of Soviet Society. The intent now is to offer it at approximately two-year intervals as a seminar on contemporary topics for advanced students or as a regular course.

The original January course was intended as an exercise in 'reading between the lines.' News items in Pravda were selected, read, and in some instances translated and analyzed for the meanings of the political clichés. Particular emphasis was placed on revealing the underlying assumptions of these clichés. For example, when a former general in the Red Army argues in a letter printed in Pravda that Solzhenitsyn, having been raised "on our native bread," is treasonous because he slanders the Soviet Union, close examination reveals that an underlying assumption of the letter--and consequently of the editorial policy of Pravda is patriotic debt to one's country because it feeds you. Similarities and differences in the nature of assumptions made by the Soviet press and the American press were studied by comparing articles in Pravda with those dealing with the same events in The New York Times and in the local press.

As a senior seminar in 1974 a different approach to the material was initiated. During the first week of class, students in the seminar went through the previous seven years' issues of Pravda, selecting fifteen to twenty articles having to do with a topic they were studying in another course in a department other than the Modern Language Department. The remainder of the semester was spent reading and occasionally translating these articles and periodically reporting on them to the group. The objective of the course was twofold: (1) to integrate Pravda's view of the particular topic into the term paper the student was writing in the outside course; and (2) to develop from the material in Pravda a term project for the seminar. One student with a double major in Russian and International Relations did a computer-assisted content analysis of speeches by Brezhnev which seemed to indicate a drop in the Communist leader's hostility toward the United States. Another did a comparison between Soviet and American views on the success of Comecon.

Two years ago, two weeks of the Soviet Society course were set aside specifically for reading letters and critical articles in Pravda concerning the various institutions we had read about in Sovetskii soyuz. Students found it interesting to compare the text's laudatory treatment of the Soviet transportation system with letters of complaint and humorous articles in Pravda about difficulties Soviet citizens encounter travelling by train, to compare the textbook's description of business and collective farm managerial organization with letters to the editor on corruption in the managerial ranks, or to compare the textbook's description of vacation and rest benefits for the Soviet worker with a humorous article on how business trips can be turned into unofficial vacations. Of the three applications of readings in Pravda, this one generated the most enthusiasm, and we are now considering making a regular course of a composite of these approaches.

Additional information available in October 1975

The enrollment in Soviet Society is seven (of thirteen completing the preceding segment, Russian 102, last spring). This includes one freshman, but still it is above the fifty percent of returning students we normally expect to continue in Russian since five of the thirteen in 102 were graduating seniors. This gratifying increase in elementary Russian is at least partially the result of a mild advertising campaign discussing the new program and directed toward underclassmen. In comparison to eleven enrolled in 101 last year, we now have nineteen and one auditor.

Our translation courses have increased enrollments, partially due to new titles and partially due to a new faculty member. Our enrollment total of eighty-four is nine above the previous high and is very near the average teaching lead for two full-time faculty; in fact, we are exactly self-supporting this semester.

My analysis is that our recovery is attributable to good teaching, which in our case includes the use of Soviet sources--propaganda and all--translation courses in literature, and the use of textual material other than literature in the second year. My six third-year students have assured me they will not continue if their only course choice for next semester is Russian poetry. Reading Pravda will therefore be offered as an alternative. One student who dropped out this semester has promised to sign up next semester if that course is offered.

CHICANO LITERATURE (1102)

Walter A. Dobrian
Department of Spanish and Portuguese, University of Iowa

The course in Chicano Literature was first given in spring 1973 by the Department of Spanish and Portuguese. Need for the course was determined by student interest, especially from small groups of Chicanos and from a number of Anglos who wished to learn more about the Chicanos and their culture. Interest in such a course was also expressed by three faculty members in the Department of Spanish and Portuguese and by a graduate student in the English Department. Community members were alerted to the existence of the course and encouraged to attend it, with course credit being optional.

Problems encountered in obtaining approval for the course consisted mainly in tacit but obvious displeasure on the part of several senior faculty of the Department of Spanish and Portuguese. The chairman was reluctant to release time from other courses for the faculty to teach the course. Through collective insistence on the part of the small number of interested faculty, the opposition was overcome. Approval, once granted, was permanent. The course does not have special funding at present, although at the outset the TA participant from the English Department did receive some government funding for general work in the area of minority studies.

Administrative problems have been minimal. The course was cross-listed as an interdisciplinary subject in the schedule of courses. Cooperation among the cross-listed Departments of Spanish and Portuguese, English, American Civilization, and the School of Letters has been excellent. An unexpectedly large enrollment of fifty-five students the first time the course was offered required the addition of two extra teachers in order to keep class size small. Staffing was the responsibility of the Department of Spanish and Portuguese. After some initial reluctance, the chairman agreed to allow this course to be taught as a normal part of a teacher's load. Obtaining materials was initially difficult, due to their relative scarcity. Appropriate materials are now readily available.

The course was originally divided into three sections of eighteen or nineteen students each. One of the sections was team-taught by two instructors. The other two sections were taught by individual instructors. Since its inception, enrollment in the course has declined to one good-sized section of about twenty students. It continues to be taught on a regular basis, roughly every other semester plus summers, with a faculty member or Chicano TA serving as instructor. There is at present no problem in staffing the course and no absolute dependency on a single instructor.

Chicano Literature has been extremely well-received by students and compares favorably with traditional offerings in the department in all respects. The course is given in English, but students may choose to do some of the readings in Spanish. The course may be taken for credit toward a departmental major.

Colleagues in the department who are fairly familiar with the course rate it very highly. Older and more conservative members of the department tend to dismiss it as inferior or ignore it. As far as we can ascertain, the course is highly thought of in other departments, as well as in the administration. Student evaluations of the course are consistently very high. It has indeed improved departmental morale, especially among younger faculty and graduate students, and has improved the department's campus 'image.' It also appears to have attracted students to the department's regular offerings.

Chicano Literature has been very useful to students who have gone on to teach Spanish, as well as to those who have gone on to teach social studies and into bilingual education. Anglo students feel they have experienced an awakening to a culture about which they were largely ignorant or misinformed. Chicanos generally applaud the fact that the course is given, although some of the more militant among them would have it taught by militant Chicanos. Instructors generally leave the course each semester with a feeling of satisfaction for having accomplished something different, enlightening, and stimulating. The only changes contemplated are to keep abreast of all recent changes and developments in the field of Chicano studies and to obtain new materials as soon as they are available in order to incorporate them, if appropriate, into the course.

EUROPEAN CULTURE AND CIVILIZATION (1106)

Johannes M. Spronk
Department of Foreign Languages, Eastern Oregon State College

Combining our undergraduate courses in French, Spanish, and German culture and civilization into the course European Culture and Civilization was the partial realization of a suggested six-to-eight-hour interdisciplinary block, Our European Heritage. In the midst of curricular reorganization, it seemed reasonable to suggest this interdisciplinary course on European culture and civilization as a cooperative effort of the Departments of History, Sociology-Anthropology, Music, Art, and Foreign Languages. When it became apparent that we would not be able to implement the interdisciplinary suggestion under our curricular reorganization, the Department of Foreign Languages decided to combine its three language sections on culture and civilization into a two-term course, European Culture and Civilization.

The organization of the combined course was relatively simple. Each section retained its own number, and the students were allowed to sign up as if for either a French, Spanish, German, or English language section. In addition to the students normally enrolled in the Culture and Civilization courses, we expected to attract interested students who lacked foreign language competency. Each of the three foreign language instructors assumed responsibility for a specific number of general subject areas; inasmuch as this course was given in lieu of existing courses, it became part of their

68

normal load. Students received three hours of credit for each term under the section number. The instructors conferred on course content, objectives, and examinations, and papers were graded by all instructors. Since the course did not require a new course number and could be handled within the present framework of the department's offerings, approval was easily obtained.

Offering this type of course seemed justified. First, it avoided duplication in the discussion of similar developments in the three national cultures. Second, it avoided a certain cultural and linguistic chauvinism which has so often been the result of specialization in a specific language and its culture(s), and, finally, it made more efficient use of staff and classroom space. According to the college president, it was a step in the right direction.

A number of problems had to be considered. We had previously used French, Spanish, or German as our language of instruction, but in combining language groups we had to resort to English. We also had used text material designed for the study of a national culture and written in the language of that particular culture. We did not want to replace these texts with one in English. We therefore decided to retain the texts in the respective languages, but to add a number of general readings in English. The following texts were assigned: La France au Cours des Ages, Colette Dubois Brichant; Deutsche Kulturgeschichte, Hans W. Kelling; Panorama de la Civilización Española, Francisco Ugarte.

A number of works were made available in English and put on reserve. Among the works selected for the first term were: The Mediaeval Church by Baldwin; Caesar's Gallic Wars in translation; Moncrieff's translation of The Song of Roland; Huizinga's Waning of the Middle Ages; Lucki's History of the Renaissance; Artz' Humanism, 1300-1500; and The Pageant of Europe by Stearns. For the second term we assigned a number of plays in the original language as well as in translation. These works included Corneille's Cid, Racine's Phèdre, Lessing's Nathan der Weise, and Zorilla's Don Juan Tenorio. We also assigned a number of relevant articles from Horizon. Filmstrips and recordings were used to illustrate the development of architecture, art, and music.

We had originally intended to present the development of European culture and civilization during the first term, and to discuss contemporary aspects during the second, but it was too difficult to do justice to the many aspects of European civilization within the thirty hours of the first term. Hence, we covered origins until the Siglo de Oro during the first term.

In order to stress the relationship between language and culture, we first examined the origins and development of the Romance and Germanic languages. This made it possible for us to point to the influence of the Roman, Arabic, and Gemanic civilizations as evidenced within the modern languages. From this we moved to concepts of feudalism, Christianity, and courtly love, linking them to specific events and specific artistic and literary productions within each of the cultural areas. This made it possible to compare such works as La Chanson de Roland, El Cantar de Mío Cid, The Lay of Ludwig, and Waltharius. Contrasting the ideals of heroic literature with those of courtly love, the students examined customs and expressions which linked the latter to the twentieth century. In a discussion on medieval education, we were able to point to its lingering influence on contemporary education. The continuing presence of medieval art, architecture, and music was easily illustrated by filmstrips and recordings. An examination of the Renaissance and its role in shaping cultural and intellectual values and the contributions of Humanism, the Reformation, and the Counter Reformation to the intellectual, spiritual, and artistic aspects of the various cultures in Europe helped illustrate interrelationships among the various national cultures.

Because of increasing divergence among the national cultures, the second term proved more difficult to structure. We organized the course around certain great figures, movements, cultural developments, and concepts. The course covered: Absolutism, Baroque, Rationalism, Classicism, the Philosophers and the Enlightenment, Empiricism, the French Revolution, Romanticism, the Industrial Revolution, Realism, and Naturalism. We discussed the artistic and cultural significance of Don Juan Tenorio, the development of classical guitar, the vision of Versailles, and Goethe and Schiller. Students who were unable to read another language read the works in English. In order to help students organize the large amount of factual information, we used study questions which motivated supplementary reading and resulted in improved examination papers.

Fifteen students enrolled for the first term: ten of them enrolled in the second term. Most took the course as a requirement for their foreign language major in education; others took it as an elective. Students' lack of background was a problem which, coupled with the variation of texts, forced us to present much of the factual material in our lectures; some students resented this. It might have been better to have students research factual aspects and discuss their findings during the class period.

My colleagues and I considered the new approach quite successful, although not all students would agree. Students wrote thoughtful examination papers showing an understanding of national cultures within their European context, and their performance compared favorably with that of students in the separate courses. Certain students displayed the same linguistic and cultural chauvinism toward other cultures which I have observed in some foreign language teachers. Although I expected a certain amount of it, the extent surprised me. It is hoped that one function of the combined class will have been to make future language teachers aware of antagonisms created by cultural chauvinism.

Further curricular change, involving a reduction in load, made it necessary to reduce our offerings. We subsequently contacted the History Department and decided to enroll our students in a course sequence which would cover much of the same material as European Culture and Civilization. The language student will still be able to read much of the material in the language of concentration. We have also organized interdepartmental courses in cooperation with the Political Science Department. Students in a course on the political novel were able to do their work on the French novel. In another course, certain students used French materials for their work on a study of the French administrative system. The Business Department is also willing to cooperate in offering options in languages and business.

FRENCH-SPEAKING CULTURES AND LITERATURES OUTSIDE EUROPE (1109)

Monique J. Pourny
Department of Modern Languages, Anchorage Community College

The program consists of a six-course cycle: a survey course and five courses on French-speaking Black African, North African, Caribbean, Asiatic, and Canadian cultures and literatures. The cycle may be entered at any point. There is minimal duplication of content in the survey course and the other five sections.

This program is a result of my personal interest. In 1969-70, I tentatively included some cultural and literary material from these areas in first- and second-year classes; student interest was high. A program proposal was then sent to the administration; there was no great enthusiasm. Alaska, I was told, was not the place for such a program. However, I was allowed to offer the first two courses in 1970-71 on a trial basis. The enrollment was two to three times the usual for an upper-division class, even though there had been no other advertising but word of mouth and inclusion in the schedule. In 1971-72 the program was accepted as a special topic course. This is its present status. No special funding has been made available.

From the beginning, the main difficulty was to obtain materials. Textbooks were agonizingly slow in reaching us--when they did. We kept receiving out-of-stock and out-of-print notices. Photocopying my personal material also presented problems; our budget was so tight that either the students or I had to pay for any extensive reproduction. Student cooperation was marvelous; much photocopying was done off campus at no cost.

During the first two years, the courses were offered at the third-year level. They were 'heavy' courses in the amount of reading and class attendance required. Emphasis, however, was not on memorization, but on understanding and development of a sensitivity to other modes of thinking and feeling. At that time, all classes were taught in English with optional reading of the texts in the original. Approximately two thirds of the students were fluent in French. Many political science and anthropology majors participated; some subsequently began to learn French or decided on a refresher course in order to be able to read the original texts. Credit toward a French major was granted, provided the term paper was written in French.

Students were enthusiastic about the course; it provided a new dimension. Several felt very uncomfortable at first; occidentals were not what they appeared to be in these writings. However, the human quality of the literature quickly won them over. Two went on to graduate school with a specialization in this field. Two more joined the Peace Corps in Africa. Several teachers incorporated some of the material into their high school classes with very good response.

At this point, I was transferred from the Fairbanks to the Anchorage campus. Since no one else had the interest and background needed, the program was discontinued in Fairbanks. My initial contract did not make allowance for these courses; but this year I was given an overload contract to start teaching them again. Although we did not have much funding, I was allowed to purchase some slides, filmstrips, and movies.

Several changes have been made in the program. First, it is now individualized, with reading assignment options according to the student's field of specialization. Second, it is offered simultaneously in French and in English. Discussion of the texts takes place in class. Each group is given the questions on the assigned reading; one group proceeds in English and one in French. To obtain French credit, all readings and assignments must be done in French. English speakers receive Humanities credit. Third, because these are very demanding courses, they are now offered at the 400 level. Fourth, starting in fall 1975, various instructors served as guest speakers in such areas as history, anthropology, philosophy, art, and music. By 1977 all of the six courses in the cycle will have been offered.

FRANCOPHONE CIVILIZATION OUTSIDE FRANCE (1113)

Thomas Cassirer
Department of French and Italian, University of Massachusetts-Amherst

Francophone Civilization Outside France is a semester course introduced by the Department of French and Italian in fall 1973 and offered every semester since then as part of the departmental curriculum. To date it has been taught in English with no reading knowledge of French required. French majors can and do take the course but are not given major credit since class discussion, exams, and research reports are in English. In the future, we may also offer the course in French, making it more accessible to our majors.

The course has been planned and taught by four members of the department, each of whom has special competence in a particular area of francophonie--Canada, Belgium, Switzerland, and Africa and the Caribbean. It was conceived with the ambitious objective of offering a cross section of students--not just French majors but also students majoring in social and natural sciences--an introduction to the contemporary situation and the historical background of areas which receive little attention in other courses at the university or are taught in a very different cultural and historical context. Moreover, the course was conceived not only as a presentation of the Francophone areas of Canada, Belgium, Switzerland, Africa and the Caribbean, but was also intended as an introduction to such contemporary phenomena as the struggle for cultural identity; bilingualism and its social, cultural, and linguistic effects; cultural nationalism; the effect of cultural, as distinct from political, colonialism; and the interaction of European and Third World cultures.

71

The organization we devised is a hybrid between a survey-lecture course, a seminar, and a course in directed individual research. The first part is divided into four segments of approximately two weeks, during which each faculty member introduces his/her area through a series of lectures and the discussion of a few brief reading assignments. After four, six, and eight weeks we schedule a discussion session in which the four instructors and the students try to bring out parallels and contrasts between the various areas. At the end of each two-week segment there is also a take-home quiz that permits the student to summarize and discuss the substance of the lectures and the reading.

During this first part of the course, the students are expected to decide on an individual research project. This is done in stages: there is a first deadline by which each student must declare a geographical/cultural area of interest, plus an alternate to avoid the situation where one faculty member carries a disproportionate share of the projects. Once the area has been approved, the student is expected to arrange an interview with the faculty member most expert in that area in order to define a research topic by a second deadline. After the topic has been formulated, the student's principal work for the course consists of research and the preparation of a report and a bibliography.

After the series of lectures and discussion sessions, (normally during the last two or three weeks of the semester), each student gives an oral report on his/her project and distributes a bibliography on the topic. The written report is due the last day of class and is read and graded by two instructors, one of whom is the project director. There is also a final examination, composed of essay questions requiring the student to think about the course as a whole and to identify themes and problems common to the various francophone areas.

The most important and successful component of the course has been the research project. Here students are given wide latitude to define a topic and to plan work within the limits of the available resources. Our intention is to offer students the opportunity to explore a new interest, and consequently we judge their performance more on their ability to gather bibliography, to orient themselves, and to identify significant themes and problems than we do on their ability to write a finished presentation on a circumscribed topic. Some of the best papers have taken the form of a report on current research, in which the student communicated methods of research and the excitement of discovering a new field of knowledge rather than the mastery of a given body of knowledge. The emphasis on research rather than on the finished term paper has allowed students to treat a wide variety of topics: Language and Status of the Creole in Haiti; The Role of the Catholic Church in Education During the Quiet Revolution; French-Speaking Switzerland: The Land and Its Folkways (illustrated with slides); The Impact of African Traditional Art on Picasso and Cubism; The Language Problem and Education in Belgium; The Cultural Impact of the French Educational System on West Africa.

The lecture-survey part of the course has presented greater problems. The most obvious difficulty arises from the sheer mass of material. Most of the students come with little if any knowledge of the geographical/cultural areas of francophonie, and the task of the instructors is further complicated by the fact that students are expected to devote most of their reading time to their own project, so that the lectures must cover all the essential knowledge which the students are expected to absorb. To judge by the final examinations, the lectures seem to fulfill this purpose quite well, at least for the better students. Some of the students' written course evaluations, however, criticize the lectures for being 'too historical,' and we have become keenly aware of how difficult it is to strike a balance between historical background and contemporary civilization, especially in the case of francophonie--where the present is incomprehensible except in terms of the past. The remedy would seem to lie not so much in a complete revision of the lectures--they must of necessity explain the historical process by which things have become what they are now--but in the introduction of additional material on the contemporary situation.

Such material is not readily available, especially in English, and this is undoubtedly one of the main problems in the course. If we want to continue and develop this course, we shall have to put together our own reading material and visual aids for class use. This has not been due to any lack of support by the chairman, who in fact gave the initial impetus to the course, but to budgetary concerns and the fact that the course is team-taught. It seems impossible to count one course as part of the regular load of four faculty, and yet students and faculty agree that team teaching is essential for the success of such a civilization course. Student evaluations, in particular, have stressed the extent to which the range of the course and the lively atmosphere in the classroom are due to the interaction among four faculty with differing backgrounds and points of view.

The course is unquestionably a success in so far as it has made students aware of areas of the world that were unknown to them, and in so far as it has offered them the opportunity to explore some aspect of francophone civilization on their own. It has made it possible for students to relate this civilization to such diverse fields of interest as anthropology, psychology, history, education, religion, political science, and art. Our best students have consistently praised the course because it did not confine them to the absorption of a specific body of knowledge and because it taught them how to discover, define, and explore their personal interests. On the other hand, we need to do a great deal more in the way of systematizing, coordinating, collecting materials, and defining the subject in order to give better guidance to the average student. This will be a main objective of the reorganization of the course.

Four semesters' experience has also left us with questions which might be of interest to others attempting such a civilization course. How can we focus more consistently on the theme of francophonie in order to avoid the centrifugal effect of bringing in the non-francophone culture of each of the areas? Is it realistic to cover all four areas in one course or should we reorganize the material into two courses, one of which would deal with Belgium and Switzerland, the other with American and African francophonie? Should we restructure the topic into one course in English, oriented toward non-French majors and perhaps available as an alternate track to the required language courses, and a second one in French for majors and other advanced students? If so, how would these two differ in organization and material covered; should the one in French relate the subject matter more explicitly to the civilization of France? How can we more systematically identify our potential student audience, particularly those who normally have no contact with the French Department? Should we consult with area studies programs, with colleagues in anthropology, history, and geography? So far we have been so busy mastering the rudiments of what for all of us was a new type of course that we have not engaged in this form of academic public relations.

These questions are part of the inevitable growing pains we experience as we reach out into unfamiliar territory, both intellectually and pedagogically. This brief report on an ongoing experiment should not end on such a tentative note, however, for in the past four semesters we have established that it is possible to interest students with a minimal background in a field as new as francophonie, and that it is quite feasible for them to carry out original research projects even in such a wide-ranging introductory course. The research projects of our better students, in fact, have taught us a good deal about the potential of combining the study of French and francophone culture with an interest in a great variety of other academic specialities.

THE LITERATURE AND CULTURE OF THE SPANISH-SPEAKING IN THE U.S. (1122)

Gerard R. Clarke
Department of Foreign Languages, Allentown College of St. Francis de Sales

The goal of the course is to explore, through the novel, poetry, drama, and essay, aspects of bilingualism and biculturalism of Puerto Ricans, Cubans, Mexican-Americans, and Chicanos living in the United States. The need for such a course was expressed by participants in recent professional meetings and workshops, by many teachers who encouraged the development of such a course for its potential value to the local school districts, and by students.

Since this is an interdisciplinary course, members of other departments were consulted with regard to emphasis and bibliography. It is an 'Integrating Course' and is open to all students. (Each student must take five Integrating Courses. For this reason, lectures and most readings were in English.) The course is comparable to traditional offerings of the department in rigor and amount of material covered. The course can be taken for credit toward a departmental major in Spanish; in this case, readings must be in Spanish.

Student evaluation of the course has been highly favorable. Several students hope to teach in a bilingual environment and believe that the course is a necessary part of their training and has made them aware of the problems that exist within the Spanish ethnic groups in this country. The course has also attracted two new students to the department's regular offerings, and a few inquiries regarding the course have been received from outside the college community.

I found teaching the course to be very challenging; it required a great deal of reading and evaluation of materials. In addition, I required a rather extensive reading list, and we had many discussions regarding the similarities and differences in the cultural, linguistic, and personal values of both the Anglo and the Hispanic societies. Inexpensive texts are available in every area except the literature of Cubans in exile. While such material does exist, it is in Spanish, whereas Puerto Rican and Chicano literature can be found in both the original and in translation. An effort was also made to try to keep abreast of material published in current periodicals. While the course was very demanding for me, the students seemed to enjoy its immediacy and relevance.

THE HISPANIC WORLD TODAY (1130)

Antonia Inglesias Searles
Department of Foreign Languages and Literatures, Hope College

The department was undertaking a curriculum revision, and as a member of the curriculum committee I suggested that--in addition to the traditional courses on Spanish and Latin American civilizations being offered in Spanish--a course in English be added to present cultural, social, political, economic, and educational aspects of Spain and Latin America to a broader audience. I was sure that such a course would be successful, but I confess to being surprised and gratified by the campus-wide popularity of the course.

There had been evidence of student interest. Students in my elementary Spanish courses wanted to know more about Spain and Latin America than it was possible to teach in those courses, and students in the upper-level literature courses often had insufficient knowledge of the culture of the contemporary writers they were studying.

Established on a trial basis, the course has become a permanent feature of our curriculum and is offered every semester, usually with two sections of approximately thirty students each. For our college of 2,100 students, this is a large number for a course of this nature; it has become one of the most popular courses in our department.

I have selected two main textbooks, James Michener's Iberia and Jean Franco's The Modern Culture of Latin America: Society and the Artist. I selected Iberia because I could not find a more appropriate book, but it has turned out to be a good text for three reasons: (1) it is a popular book in the United States, a bestseller which most of the students have either read or heard about; (2) it is written by a man of their culture and is therefore an example of how a popular American writer views a foreign culture; (3) it is not nor does it pretend to be a scholarly book and tends toward generalized observations and points of view, giving in the process many wrong ideas about Spain which provide good points for discussion. Though it is true that I have wanted to replace Mr. Michener's book, it is also true that I have not been able to find a better one. Since I visit Spain frequently and am in constant touch through family and friends who live there, I am provided with many Spanish books, journals, newspapers, and other publications with which to supplement and correct the views in this text. Current periodicals--American and foreign--are also in constant use in the course.

In our study of Latin America we consider the last 150 years, beginning with "Modernismo," because, as Mrs. Franco states in her book, they were the first group of professional Latin American writers. Through this book the students acquire an insight into what Latin American is today, and into what the continent represents for the world from cultural, social, economic, and political points of view. I felt the students would profit from a knowledge of what Latin America has been since the modernists, and the success of the course and the students' reactions to this approach have borne out this judgment.

Part of the course is devoted to a study of Spanish-speaking minorities in the United States. All students, not only the minority students, show a great interest in this aspect of the course.

Every day, students present five-to-ten minute oral reports as points of departure for class discussion. I end the period by synthesizing class discussion and my own ideas. Every student is responsible for writing a research paper of fifteen to twenty pages, and I have been surprised at the excellent quality of a number of papers. Students have complete freedom in choosing a topic, but I ask them to submit the topics for approval at the beginning of the term to be sure they choose themes they can handle with the resources in the college library supplemented by my materials and those of professors from other departments, especially in political science. As of 1975 the range of themes will be limited, since the reading and evaluation of these papers, encompassing a wide range of topics, has demanded more time than is commensurate with the rest of my teaching load. In addition to the term paper and oral reports, students are responsible for two take-home exams, one on each major area of the course.

Perhaps the single significant difficulty encountered in offering the course is the need for more library and film materials. (I have a good private library and many other materials, but predominantly in Spanish.) We need, of course, money to supply the library with materials for the course, and we are limited in the amount we can spend for individual courses.

In 1973 a Luis Buñuel film, Viridiana, was shown as part of a foreign film festival at the college, and in 1974 a Buñuel Festival was held on campus, sponsored by our department and the Cultural Affairs Committee of the college. We showed The Exterminating Angel, Nazarin, and Tristana. During 1975 we hoped to have a "Cinema Novo Brasileiro" festival, with showings of three or four representative films of this movement, but lack of funds limited us to one film, O Padre e a Moca.

I think the course is regarded highly. It has been popular among students from all schools of the college, and the administration is pleased with the high enrollments. Many of the students in pre-professional programs, such as medicine, report that the knowledge acquired in the course has been useful to them in understanding minorities and in their entrance exams. Spanish majors and other foreign language majors taking the course report that it has been a great asset to them in their work or graduate studies.

YIDDISH LITERATURE: FROM SHTETL TO SUBURBIA (1147)

Sol Gittleman
Department of German and Russian, Tufts University

This course grew out of the interest of one instructor in the department. It is quite specifically a product of the 1970's, a manifestation of growing student interest in ethnicity. The greatest contribution that Black Studies programs have made to the traditional academic curriculum was in awakening departments to student interest in ethnic origins. Chinese, Chicano, and Puerto Rican studies have a natural place in literature and language, sociology, history, and political science departments.

Jewish students were among the first, in the post-Cambodia period, to rediscover ethnicity. This course was intended to respond to that interest. The course was based on the classical Yiddish literature of the nineteenth century, but required reading included the fields of history, anthropology, and religion, as well as the fiction of Bellow, Malamud, and Roth. (The English Department offered no objection, since they had been teaching Gide, Mann, Kafka, and Dostoyevsky for years!) Beginning as a special topics, general education course with an advanced number and no prerequisites, it had a first-term registration of eighty-four. By the third offering, registration was 193. (In view of such interest, the language laboratory has purchased tapes, and we are offering Yiddish language on a self-taught basis to a dozen students.)

There is no major in Judaic Studies, but this course counts toward the Plan of Study major in Jewish Studies, a program based in four departments. The Hillel Foundation on campus was eager to publicize the course, because--although it was given without any political or religious bias--it was sufficiently identified with Jewish awareness.

The off-campus impact has been nothing short of astonishing. Requests come in almost daily for lectures at synagogues, Jewish community centers, and study groups; the instructor cannot keep up with demands from tne general public. Parents of students in the course have written--perhaps as many as one hundred letters thus far--to the department and to the instructor, asking if they might participate in the classroom discussions.

The university administration cooperated, and the university librarian, faced with the realization that a new field of general education was opening, allocated an additional, unspecified amount for book purchases in the general area of Judaica. Initially, the course was taught by the instructor on an overload basis. Now it is a regular part of his load. The dean, realizing the importance of the course, allocated an increase in the instructional budget, so the regular German course which was part of the overload could be offered by a part-time instructor.

The department has become central to the development of the modest program in Judaica on the campus. This can happen in a small liberal arts curriculum that does not offer a major in such a field. We have formed a working committee with representatives of other departments, but our department remains the center of activity in the field. We have gained visibility and purpose on the campus with a substantial course, demanding academic respectability, open to all students regardless of educational background. A primary purpose of this general education course in Yiddish culture is to provide the students with a conceptual understanding of ethnicity, not merely glib consciousness-raising. Gentile students are encouraged to take the course, and they may write term papers on their particular ethnic heritage: Italian, Irish, Armenian, Chinese. As a result, the course is able to transcend its Jewish orientation and has become the center of a growing ethnic studies program of the campus.

A CULTURAL INTRODUCTION TO LANGUAGES: STUDENT PERSPECTIVES (1151)

Kathryn Buck

In October 1975, the survey research coordinator visited Murray State University pursuant to USOE contract stipulations that a number of programs of major interest be the subject of closer investigation. The purpose of the visit was to conduct interviews with students who had taken "A Cultural Introduction to Languages" (see FLA, 9 [1976], 50-55), since a major goal of the course, in addition to its immediate pedagogical goal of introducing students to basic concepts of language, linguistics, and culture, is to challenge attitudes and pre- and misconceptions regarding the nature and importance of language study and its relationship to other disciplines in an attempt to encourage more students to begin or continue formal language study.

Twenty-three of the forty-five students who had taken the course in the three times it had been offered were available for interviews. Follow-up questionnaires were mailed to all students; responses were received from twenty-seven. The responses which follow are from both the interviews and the questionnaires; the total of responding students is thirty-three of the forty-five (73%).

In the interviews and the questionnaires, the major areas of investigation were: (1) the effect of the course on student attitudes toward the value and importance of studying and knowing a foreign language; (2) the effect on the interest in and the likelihood of future language study; (3) the relationship of material in the course to the student's major and potential applicability of course material in that field; and (4) opinions on the usefulness of the course at different educational levels.

Students' reasons for taking the course included the understandable interest of a language major, general interest in languages and other cultures, the attraction of a teacher's reputation, the desire to study something different from the student's major field, and the need to fill a term's schedule.

As effects of the course on their attitudes toward the value and importance of studying and knowing a foreign language, more than a quarter of the students cited new or increased interest in understanding other cultures, and in four instances the conviction that it is a significant gesture to have at least some familiarity with the language of a country in which one is not a native in the hope of avoiding the 'ugly American' reproach. Others indicated that this introduction to language and culture had provided insights into the origins of prejudice and broadened their perspectives on other cultures and peoples, and that previously held opinions on other cultures had changed during the course of study. Questioned on possible changes in their perceptions of English, over half cited an increased awareness of their native language--of origin, structure, and idiom, and of its relative, limited position in the world--and a greater sensitivity to non-native English speakers.

Most students who already had studied language and who felt positively about it nonetheless experienced increased interest in further language study as a result of the course. Only eight students indicated that their interest in language study was not greater. (Five of these felt their interest was already high.) All those who had not previously studied a language indicated they were now more inclined to do so. Thirteen of the respondents indicated they are likely to begin language study in the future. Of the seven who indicated they were not likely to do so, five cited lack of time in their schedules. (The majority of students responding were already juniors or seniors at the time they took the course.) One student cited the serious consideration of a job opportunity in Quebec as a reason for the likelihood of future language study. For at least one, interest was related to the learning of sample dialogues in four major languages: "I enjoyed it. It was the first time I'd ever tried, and it gave me a thrill. We did it as a group, or I never would have done it. When everyone is speaking and not doing any better than you, you really enjoy it. It made it seem easier, made me feel that if I ever really wanted to take a class, I could do well in it."

All but ten of the respondents indicated they had encountered material in the course related to their major fields which they had not encountered in their major department's offerings. For example, a geography major explained that the major is basically concerned with physical geography, and that he had done no work on the interrelationships among culture, language, and geography--which he felt was closely related to what a geography major should include--prior to taking the course. Another geography major felt the possible applications of material presented in the course would be virtually endless. Another student in political science/geography felt the many potential applications were obvious. A home economics/social work major felt the course material would be applicable to her in future work situations. She cited greater ability to understand processes of word formation, which she felt would be of value to her under any circumstances, and stressed the importance to her of being aware of different cultures: "Home economics is not merely a study of 'the American way' but of home and family relationships around the world. If you're a person with more broad-minded views, then you're going to be a better professional and more objective in your relationships with other people. I feel that I've become more objective." A business management/marketing major explained: "I have a better understanding of communication. A background in languages will help in understanding the feelings of people I will meet." A business education major wrote: "If one is involved in international business or trade, the understanding of other cultures which is gained through this course can help." A student in journalism/radio-TV communications was certain of the applicability of language training in those fields and stressed the ability to communicate effectively as the key to understanding. Nursing and pre-medical students stressed the wide variety of people with whom they will come into contact and felt they would be more able to understand aspects of different cultures and the people who are products of them. One of them stated: "I think the course instilled more respect in me and that I am less ethnocentric now. If I had taken the course when I was a freshman, I might have put aside the time to study a foreign language; perhaps in graduate school I will."

Students of language also found the course offered them training which they had not otherwise encountered. A retired French teacher "learned something new in every session." A Spanish major felt the information on the origins of language helped her understand the historical influence of language on literature and music. An English/history major believed that exposure to different languages (in conjunction with a minor in Russian) will be helpful to her; she hopes to include some of the course material in her own teaching. She reported having done individual work with a Vietnamese student during her student teaching. She felt that her study of language, though not Vietnamese, helped her in working with the student, and that she was probably less apprehensive than a teacher who had never studied a language other than English might have been.

An elementary education major responded: "It is important to me to obtain as much general knowledge as I can in all fields that I feel a child might come in contact with in daily life, and language is a great part of that life. In my opinion, the course would be an excellent one for all elementary education majors." This view was corroborated by another, a language major doing practice teaching in Russian at the elementary level in the university school: "These children wanted to know what the people are like in Russia; that's what most of their questions were about. 'What are the people like?' 'Where's this city?' 'Where's that?' They want to know about the people and about the culture, even a. their age—grades 4-6. They want to learn the language, because they always ask 'How do you say...?' "

An observation made in a conversation between two of the students interviewed involved what could be one of the unique contributions of the course to the students' general education. The students both explained that, although they had taken courses in sociology and anthropology in which they were introduced to the concept of cultural relativism, neither acquired a feeling for its specific manifestations or consequences until taking A Cultural Introduction to Languages. Both attributed this to the fact that the foreign language teachers could offer first-hand experience and knowledge of different cultures and cross-cultural matters, and that such first-hand knowledge of different cultures is selcom encountered in other disciplines: "You learn that you shouldn't judge other cultures by your own. I've had sociology and anthropology, and we learned about cultural relativity in those courses. But you can learn the definition for it and never feel it. I was made to realize it more in A Cultural Introduction to Languages. I think it was because the instructors had traveled in these countries, and they knew what they were talking about."

All students indicated that they recommend the course to their friends. All but three indicated they would recommend the course for college freshmen in particular. Two who answered in the negative took offence at the narrowness of the question, stressing the course was for everyone. Asked why they would recommend it for freshmen, many students indicated that it would help them decide whether or not to study language while they still had time to do so. Others felt that it was a good general orientation to the subject area and it made a good introductory course, that the interdisciplinary aspect might help people decide what subjects they might like to pursue further, or that it was especially good for people who wouldn't have time to study a language. All but five students indicated they would have been interested in a similar course--with appropriate modifications--in high school.

The major and only general complaint made by a number of students in the interviews was the limited class time available in relation to the variety and amount of material to be considered. But none could suggest any way of deleting material in order to make a one semester, three-credit-hour offering more realistic. Instead, almost all suggested that the course be extended to a two-semester offering, because they also wanted more time and subject matter than one term provided. They were quite adamant in their willingness to commit six credit hours of study to such an expanded course.

The course definitely seems to have been a valuable offering for these students, in terms of both personal education and career applicability. The questionnaires and interviews indicate that most of them were not strangers to language study, and most, though not all, already had a positive attitude and certain insights about what that study could provide. Although such students have been providing healthy enrollments for the course every semester, their comments also indicate there is a larger audience to be considered, especially among those whose reaction to hearing a friend was taking the course was reported to be: "What are you doing taking this class? You're nuts; you're going to be into something that's too hard! You're not going to like it!" as well as among those who, upon hearing a friend return to the dorm reporting "Hey, I spoke German today" or "I spoke French today," became interested and "wanted to know all about it."

The Arts (See also ms. 1464)

FRENCH PLAY PRODUCTION (1158)

Michael Spingler
Department of Foreign Languages and Literature, Clark University

First given in fall 1972 and designed for students who have completed the equivalent of intermediate college French, French Play Production combines intensive work in spoken French with the practice of theater arts. Course goals are predicated upon the belief that students may significantly improve their language skills and, at the same time, intensify their knowledge of French drama through an exploration of the creative possibilities of play production. Since its inception, the course has been offered five times, and the university has also sponsored two summer Theater Workshops in France.

The course provides a direct experience of the theatrical synthesis within which the text, the actor, and the spectator operate. It concentrates on one playwright, studied in terms of all the problems peculiar to the staging of his plays. In addition to consideration of styles of acting and directing, considerable research is devoted to the dramaturgy, thematic concerns, social context, and aesthetic philosophy of the playwright's period. Playwrights studied to date have been Beckett, Ionesco, Genet, Molière, and Anouilh.

79

Since a different playwright is studied each semester, students may repeat the course for credit. Although the particular content of the course may vary from term to term the goals and methods remain fundamentally the same.

Previous experience in theater arts is not a prerequisite for the course, and, although many of the fundamentals of acting and staging are learned through class activities, the course does not pretend to train actors or directors. Instead, the rehearsal situation is considered to be an extension of the dialogue approach to language learning, one which diminishes the contrived nature of the dialogue by giving it a precisely defined goal. This goal is not primarily the staging of the play, but rather the use of performance activity as a means of deepening one's facility with the understanding of the text.

Thus, the course might best be called a seminar-workshop. Its method is one in which the theory, criticism, and practice of dramatic art are fused. A work is considered from four perspectives--those of the playwright, the director, the actor, and the spectator. This requires that drama be explored not only as a literary genre, but also as an art based upon both verbal and plastic expressions. Such study recognizes the necessity of research, criticism, and interpretation for the successful realization of the play upon the stage, and it also recognizes that the experience of performance can lead to the discovery of new significance in the text. The course, therefore, does not separate literary study and performance; it attempts to unite the two by approaching performance not as a final product but as an investigatory process which, when brought to a text, is the fundamental tool in analysis and exploration of the work.

Classes in play production are conducted entirely in French. The first week is devoted to certain fundamental principles essential to the course. This week only, students sight-read a text, and an initial evaluation of their strengths and weaknesses in spoken French is made so that each student is aware of particular problems of diction, articulation, and intonation upon which to work. The basics of stage movement and speech are introduced, and the student is acquainted with the nature and character of theatrical space. Scene presentation is the central activity of the class. It is essential that the scene to be presented in class for the next several weeks be assigned in the first week, since considerable outside preparation is expected before the initial presentation, and adequate lead-time must be allowed.

The scenes are to be presented with the seriousness and concentration essential to a stage performance; they are memorized. Scenes are never considered in isolation from the complete play. Just as the object of an explication de texte cannot be totally divorced from the entire work, so the scenes done in class are analyzed and criticized in terms of the whole play, or, where appropriate, in terms of the author's total work. For each presentation, one student is responsible for the basic mise en scène and serves as an 'eye' with which the other students may see themselves as they prepare. All students participating in a particular presentation are responsible for discussing their decisions and choices concerning the staging of the scene. Following each presentation, the class engages in discussion and critique of the scene in which the perspectives of metteur en scène, actor, and spectator are explored in an effort to arrive at a fresh perception of the text. Frank and constructive mutual criticism is one of the most important class activities, and the students continually test their insights and ideas before other members of the class. In addition, extensive critical readings have an important part in discussions and evaluations.

Each scene is modified and revised on the basis of discussions and critiques and is presented again. Certain scenes will be presented several times during the term, so that the class may observe the growth and evaluation of a dramatic conception of a text. As the course progresses, problems in dramatic aesthetics such as mode, tempo, image, and sequence of impressions are introduced in addition to more fundamental notions of character and plot as ways of analyzing the playwright's work. In addition to preparation of the scene, two papers of seven to ten pages are required, based on the student's experience and perception of the scene work done in class and reflecting developing skills in conceptualizing the written text in terms of a possible staged event.

During the term, a number of scenes become the object of more intensive work in preparation for a final class project, which may be a lecture demonstration, excerpts from a play, or a one-act play to be presented to the university and city community. Class activity has lead to a number of successful productions, including Beckett's En Attendant Godot and Ionesco's La Cantatrice Chauve and Jaques ou la Soumission. These public performances have helped attract students to the French program and have generated widespread university interest in the Department of Foreign Languages and Literatures.

Student response to the course has been enthusiastic. The average class enrollment has been around fifteen, with the smallest class numbering ten students and the largest nineteen; the latter is significant considering the small size of the university and the fact that the course is for third-year students and above. Some students have taken the course two or more times, and some have gone on to study theater arts and comparative drama. The administration has supported the course because it represents, through its combination of language, literature, and theater arts, the kind of interdisciplinary study which the university encourages.

FRENCH THEATER WORKSHOP (1159)

Andreé Kail
Department of French, University of Colorado

The workshop course began as a non-credit activity more than twenty years ago and became a credit course six years ago in recognition of student and faculty efforts and time. There was never a problem in obtaining approval for the course, in part because previous performances had been successful and well-received, and in part because the course description submitted for approval clearly indicated the literary and linguistic merits of the course. Furthermore, no special funding has been necessary or requested, since the small amount necessary had been provided by departmental funds (twenty-five or thirty dollars) and the French government for French cultural events. Assistance from the Theater Department has been available for props and costumes, lighting equipment and verification that these conform to fire codes, and make-up when no such expertise has been available among students enrolled in the workshop. Sometimes it has been difficult to arrange for a rehearsal and performance theater.

The course is dependent on the instructor's experience and interest in drama performance. Due to the necessity of a flexible schedule and, at times, daily effort on the part of the instructor, it is difficult to offer the course every year. An interested and qualified graduate student who could be spared other teaching assignments would be welcome as an instructor.

The course is open to majors as well as non-majors with at least two years of college French or who are otherwise qualified. Less qualified students are welcome for non-speaking cooperation. The course carries three credit hours.

After a play has been selected, preferably by the instructor with opinions from students, classes meet regularly during the first month of the semester to discuss the play's importance to the history of theater, the playwright's other works, and characters, style, settings, message, etc. There is an examination at the end of this period. (Classes are conducted in French, and the examination is written in French.)

The play is then read, in groups and individually, for pronunciation and diction, and students are assigned parts according to their linguistic ability and fitness for a part. They must study in the lab with tapes on which the play has been recorded by the instructor. If the play has been recorded professionally, the recording is made available to the students and also played to the class at the beginning of these sessions. When the students have mastered most of the pronunciation problems and are well acquainted with their parts, rehearsals on the stage begin. For two weeks prior to the performance, there are nightly rehearsals.

Students are expected to help with the props, costumes, and sets, which may involve some work on the weekend preceding the performance. Graduate students may be asked to contribute some time coaching actors during the last week.

Colleagues in the department have been pleased with the opportunities such a course offers. The play is made available for reading in French classes above the first year, and instructors usually devote one hour to discussing the play to facilitate understanding and encourage students to attend the performance.

Workshop participants have been very enthusiastic; they have improved their French tremendously and been encouraged to continue their language studies. The plays have brought praise to the Department of French and good relations with the Theater Department; majors from the latter have also participated in the course.

MUSIC IN GERMAN LITERATURE AND THOUGHT (1173)

Hartmut Kaiser (German)
Department of Foreign Languages and Literatures, Clark University

The desire on the part of the department to experiment with non-traditional approaches to the teaching of literature, encouragement by the administration for new courses of an original and substantive nature, and personal fascination with the relationship of literature and music led me to develop a course entitled Music in German Literature and Thought.

The course, first given in 1972 and in a modified version in 1975, has the following objectives: (1) to offer students an integral, full-semester, educational experience of general humanistic nature for which there are no specific prerequisites; (2) to point out the value of interrelating various areas of study; and (3) to acquaint them with German cultural history by shedding light on significant aspects of it.

Poetry was excluded from the reading list because it is particularly difficult to handle in translation. I further decided to restrict the reading to prose works written during the past 180 years, since prior to the Romantic period the influence of music on German literature was not highly significant, though by no means absent; for the Romanticists with their ideas of synthesizing the arts, music became an important force whose impact could be felt in numerous literary creations.

I structured the course by establishing the following general groups of works based on the function music plays in them: (1) works in which music has a symbolic function; (2) works in which an identified composition plays an important role; (3) works in which a musician is the hero; and (4) works in which musical forms are mirrored in the narrative structure.

The reading list presented a compromise between a chronological arrangement and the above categories. Problems were encountered in obtaining reading material, since not all selections are available in inexpensive editions, but with the cooperation of the library I compiled a reserve shelf which contained two or three copies of all those works either unavailable or too expensive to buy. Two modern short stories were translated specifically for the course and distributed in mimeographed form. Future repetitions of the course might stimulate more such translation projects which could eventually result in a collection justifying publication.

Precisely because we were concerned with the relationship between two arts, it was necessary to establish from the beginning that literature and music are two different media of artistic expression. Throughout the course a conscious attempt was made not to succumb to the temptation of terminological vagueness and meaningless associations. From our initial discussions about generic differences, three major areas of divergence emerged. First, words, in addition to their sound structure, connote something, i.e., they have a specific lexical meaning, while no such meaning can be associated with pure musical sound. Second, literature results from a succession of words; a succession of tones results in melody. Literature is, strictly speaking, limited to this horizontal dimension, but music is not. Two or more melodic lines are possible simultaneously (counterpoint), and there is no equivalent in literature for the vertical dimension of music (harmony). Third, prose literature is not normally created for the purpose of being performed, but most music is. Even dramatists and poets have almost no way of stipulating how their works ought to be executed. Composers of music, on the other hand, have an almost inexhaustible range of possibilities at their disposal with which to specify such aspects of performance as tempo, pitch, volume, timbre, mood, and style.

Most compositions referred to in the literary works were recorded on cassettes and placed on reserve in the library. Students were expected to listen to them and to familiarize themselves particularly with those sections which were pertinent to our discussions. In addition, they listened to music not specifically identified by composer and work, but clearly enough designated, e.g., "a very ancient Italian Mass" or "sacred oratorios." I sought advice from the Department of Music regarding the selection of appropriate and enjoyable compositions.

The topic of the course was music as a subject of literature, but its treatment varied widely. The class discovered that the subject of music can be used in many different narrative functions. Because of the nature of the topic, our discussions centered on the specific function of music in each work, e.g., symbolical, thematic, stylistic, or structural, and, as a result, several analytical methods were employed.

The extraordinary and ambivalent power of music, on the one hand inspiring and uplifting and on the other hand destructive, was a recurring theme. Because music is non-verbal, it was believed to be linked closely with the human psyche and emotions, and to intensify them. Interesting questions about the interrelationships between music and the German psyche were raised in view of the asocial attitudes, unrealistic views, and political backwardness which contributed to the catastrophic events of this century.

An area of great importance for our investigation was the way in which various writers tried to communicate a musical experience or describe a piece of music with words. It was here that the concept of 'verbal music' (cf. Steven Paul Scher, Verbal Music in German Literature) entered our discussion and that we began to observe some of the fundamental differences between language and music. Only one author, Thomas Mann in Doctor Faustus, used the technical vocabulary of musicologists to describe musical compositions.

For the most part, various types of imagery were employed to try to capture in words the mood and the essence of certain compositions. Some imagery derived from natural phenomena such as light, sound, and fragrance. Other imagery related to religious experience or was set in emotional, especially erotic, terms. In a few instances music was described pictorially as an elaborate tableau. It was noted in passing that the musical counterpart of such extended images is program music, which among other things attempts to tell a story in tones. Since music has frequently been the subject of philosophical inquiry in Germany, works by Schopenhauer and Nietzsche were included in the reading list and proved to be an indispensable aid to understanding the works of Hesse and Mann.

The final area of investigation dealt with works in which musical forms are reflected in the narrative structure. With varying degrees of success, writers have often attempted to imitate certain musical structures. This is clearly the topic which requires most expertise and circumspection. While parallels of form and structural devices do exist between the two arts, they usually remain approximations. The most easily discernible of such devices is the leitmotiv, which has been adapted by writers from Wagner's compositional technique. We also analyzed a rather convincing example of the structural principle of theme and variation, as well as attempts on the part of two different writers to employ the sonata allegro form as a narrative framework. Several literary items seemed suitable to explore to what extent approximations of (double or triple) counterpoint are possible in literature. The purpose of such questions was not so much to find an unqualified affirmative or negative answer, but rather to develop in the students a sense for the structural similarities and differences in the two arts.

The course seemed to have wide appeal. Students from almost all departments were represented, including German and music majors in addition to many who had not yet decided on a major. More than two-thirds of the students expressed the desire to take more courses of such an interdisciplinary nature. The reading list was considered excellent by most students, who also believed that their understanding of music, literature, and the German character had deepened. They registered surprise about the diversity with which different authors dealt with musical experiences.

I was gratified by results of the student evaluation of the course and do not contemplate major changes for the next offering. I would, however, seriously consider omitting some of the German titles in favor of suitable works from other literatures, such as A. Huxley's Point Counter Point, L. Tolstoy's Kreutzer Sonata, and H. de Balzac's Gambara. It is also possible that I will include poetry in the future.

LITERATURE AND MUSIC: TOWARD A DEFINITION OF CULTURE (1174)

W. V. Blomster (German)
Program in Innovative Education, University of Colorado

In 1949 Aspen, Colorado--at that time still somewhat of an isolated mountain ghost town--was chosen as the site of the American commemorization of the two-hundredth anniversary of Goethe's birth. The success of this program led its founders to envision Aspen as a center for continuing active engagement in the arts and humanities, inquiring into their nature, meaning, and relationship to modern life. The Aspen endeavors have continued and grown under the conviction that the major difficulty of our age is a matter of the spirit.

It seemed that the manifold activities in Aspen could offer a university program an enviable background for a more narrow academic program of an interdisciplinary nature. My wife, a European-trained pianist with a graduate degree in literature and with teaching experience in a humanities program, designed this program along modest lines, seeing great advantage in a course which the two of us could handle with no need for vast logistical support which would cause problems in a program far from the campus.

The program was organized totally outside the department of which I am a member in order that the established program would in no way suffer from the demands of the new offering. A sensitive dean in Arts and Sciences recognized the virtue of our suggestion and gave our proposal support and financing through the Program in Innovative Education organized at the university in 1973, the first year in which our program was offered. A special student fee of $25 is assessed to cover the overhead which we would not have on campus. Otherwise regular university tuition applies.

The program consists of two courses in which all students must enroll, involving nine hours of classroom work per week, required attendance at three regular concerts (numerous other performances are available), and informal discussion and critique. Six hours of academic credit are given. The literary portion of the program deals with works in which music is dominantly present--especially Nietzsche's Birth of Tragedy, Mann's Doctor Faustus, and Hesse's The Glass Bead Game. All reading is in English. The music portion of the program deals with matters of form, analysis, and music history from a humanistic perspective. What, for example, is the relationship between sonata form and the Enlightenment? How do concepts such as monism and dualism find expression in the fugue on the one hand and in the sonata on the other? Music is seen as a reflection of an age. The focus of the course adjusts as much as possible to the concert programs performed in Aspen. The 1974 program was a unique experience in that the Aspen Conference on Contemporary Music celebrated the Schoenberg Centennial with the performance of over a dozen works by that composer; this offered a superb perspective on the Schoenbergian aspects of Mann's Faustus.

We originally entitled the program Literature and Music: The Crosscurrents; we found, however, that we were trying too hard to point to identical features and phenomena in the two art forms, the validity of which we have come to doubt more and more. We have, therefore, renamed the program Literature and Music: Toward a Definition of Culture. This is an obvious borrowing from Steiner's In Bluebeard's Castle, where the phrase stands as a subtitle, harking back, in turn, to Eliot's Notes Towards the Definition of Culture. We now use Steiner's book as a basic text. We are moving more in the direction of something that might be called a sociology of culture, and in 1974 we required that the term paper which the students write have "Toward a Definition of Culture" as a subtitle; they were free to define the content. We found the resulting work stimulating and gratifying. Much of the value of the program seems to lie in removing students from the standard campus situation and working within a larger environment in which the classroom serves only to provide a perspective on that which plays beyond it: the concerts, lectures, ballet performances, and many other artistic and humanistic endeavors which center there.

The program is restricted to summers for obvious reasons; it is approved from summer to summer, but it is hoped that it will continue on a regular basis. Publicity is a problem since there are no special funds available to the program. We rely heavily upon information distributed on campus and in Aspen during the winter when the town is overrun by skiers. (A happy feature has been the response of Aspen itself to the program. The town, which has a community college program through Colorado Mountain College, has been pleased to have a full-fledged university program operating there. The Chamber of Commerce and the recently organized Aspen Foundation have also been very cooperative.) Releases go out through the University Information Service, and the campus newspaper has been helpful with publicity.

The course meets for a period of four weeks and five weekends; it is an extremely intense exercise during this time. Consequently, all major readings must be completed prior to arrival in Aspen. We feel that the course demands a great deal of the students-- perhaps not in terms of sheer bulk, but simply because all the work has to be done--and done thoroughly--if any benefit is to be derived from the course. We have been particularly impressed by the type and quality of students who have enrolled in the program. While they were undoubtedly of above-average intellectual ability, it is not this alone which distinguished them. It was rather a sincere concern for the human state, the relation to the realm of the spirit, and the impact that the product of the spirit might have upon life.

The only factor which has somewhat disappointed us is the small number of students enrolled in the program. We had assumed in the beginning that the program would be tremendously over-subscribed, but this has not been the case. We have had twenty-six students per summer, and 1975 will be about the same. This is a comfortable enrollment in the eyes of the administration; I feel forty would be an optimal maximum.

There is not a great deal which can be said about the relationship of the program to the German Department. My own teaching efforts for the past several years have centered upon teaching beyond the normal departmental program: literature in translation, interdisciplinary programs, etc. Numerous students from these courses sign up for the Aspen Program; others from the program enroll for my courses when they return to the campus, but on the whole I do not think students have been encouraged by the Aspen Program to learn German. The Department receives credit for the enrollment in the program and thus benefits indirectly from it.

The students in the program have been positive and enthusiastic in their reactions. There are few places in the world where one could offer such a program, and the impact which it has is great. We are pleased to see students from earlier summers making plans to spend vacations in Aspen in order to return to the setting of so much meaningful activity.

THE GERMAN OPERA (1181)

Paul A. Schons (German)
Department of Foreign Languages, College of St. Thomas

The German Opera was proposed for introduction into the curriculum at a time when popular demand for vocational training, practical education, and preprofessionalism had made a strong beginning. Other courses and sequences being introduced at that time were frequently justified on the basis of demonstrable application to career needs of students.

The course in German opera was introduced without documentation indicating application to career needs and without student requests for such a course. It was introduced on the basis that it would fit the concept of liberal arts, that there was a lack of this content in the current curriculum, and, most importantly, that the course content represented something worth knowing.

It was something of a surprise that the course was accepted without opposition, first by the Educational Policies Committee and then by the general faculty. (The music department had first given its blessing.) The course, conducted in German, was then listed with other offerings in German without any serious attempts at publicity other than an enthusiastic word here and there to a student who might be interested. It was also a pleasant surprise that the number of students who registered by the beginning of the fall semester was among the greatest we had had in any advanced language course for many years.

Students were not overwhelmingly those with majors in German or music, but with concentrations in such diverse fields as mathematics, economics, business, pre-medicine, etc. They were not lovers of opera; most, in fact, had never seen or heard an opera. They were not even lovers of serious music. They had arrived independently at the conclusion that this would be something 'worth knowing.' Soon after the beginning of the course, the students concluded that this was not only something worth knowing but also very interesting and enjoyable.

Word-of-mouth became excellent publicity for the course. There were soon inquiries and words of encouragement from a broad section of students and faculty. When the course was offered a second time--sooner, in fact, than an advanced course would normally be repeated in a small department--the enrollment was again as large. There have been requests to offer the course again soon, to give it in English, and to offer a continuation course.

Enrollments for the course have been among the largest in our department for many years. This is still not a vast number of students. The department itself, though growing, is relatively small and the opera course is selective in its prerequisites--four years of high school German or four semesters of college German; thus, the eligible population is rather restricted.

Nine to twelve operas are treated during the semester. It is important, when student background is limited, to begin with works which are light and immediately comprehensible, such as Die Fledermaus, and then to progress to more complex works carefully, based on the students' growth in comprehension. It is more desirable to proceed thematically than chronologically. The texts, lectures, recordings, discussions, and assigned papers are exclusively in the German language. Our students are undergraduates, however, and, since some of them may yet have difficulties in reading the volume of material required, they are invited to use translations of the texts parallel to their reading in the original. This procedure seems to be as effective in vocabulary building as the search for individual words in a dictionary and more effective in the development of structural comprehension. In the case of the opera, there is a decided advantage in this procedure in that students acquire an immediate understanding of the desirability of using texts in the original language. Since opera texts must be translated to fit the music as well as the ideas presented, students very soon see the marked differences, especially in poetic integrity and presentation of ideas. They see the significance of language in image development, humor, and dramatic impact. Even students taking The German Opera as their first advanced-level German course can readily perceive the significant changes and losses in the translation. Both times the course had been offered, students have soon begun to compete in pointing out to each other the striking discrepancies between the translations and the originals.

A two- to four-page paper in German on each opera is required. A survey of secondary literature is available, but, since the course is introductory at the undergraduate level, the papers are to be position papers rather than research papers. It seemed more important at this level and in this course that students spend their time with the operas themselves, rather than with secondary literature. It also seems important to general education that students be given a situation where they must think out an interpretation on their own before having a thought directed or conditioned by literature or lecture. (The papers on a given opera are due prior to lectures and discussion on that opera.) The subjects of the papers are assigned, although students are encouraged to alter the subject in conference with the instructor if they wish. The assigned subjects mix critical analysis, such as "The Use of the Number Three in Die Zauberflöte," with comparative subjects, such as "Fidelio and the Current American Concept of the Liberated Woman." The latter have tended to evoke papers of much greater length than required. Students have also shown a tendency to take greater pains with the quality of the German in the case of subjects they find more interesting.

The course is within the German sequence, and credit may be applied to the German major; thus, though the music of the operas is treated as integral to an understanding of the work, primary emphasis is on the literary texts. In this respect, the course is not a great divergence from a traditional literature course. Many of the texts of German operas, such as Woyzeck, Elektra, or Die Dreigroschenoper, are excellent literature in their own right. On the other hand, several operas, such as those of Mozart or Wagner, although not normally treated within a traditional survey of literature, are, as operas, very interesting and certainly fall within the legitimate investigative area of Germanistik.

In a course in opera, however, one must soon pass beyond the bounds of the traditional literature course, for the sounds of opera are of paramount significance in the appreciation and comprehension of the total artistic work. Thus, the instructor must possess characteristics beyond those required in a literature course, able to enjoy fully both the music and the literature and with sufficient experience in music to be able to point out and demonstrate, with the aid of indexed tapes and a cross-referenced text, how the music intensifies and formulates the dramatic characters, how the music supports the plot and idea development, and how the drama clarifies the musical mood. These matters could be accomplished by team-teaching, but it would seem that a far superior instructional model is presented to the students by one person able to encompass the whole.

It would seem further that an introductory course in a national opera falls quite properly within the foreign language sequence pertaining to that nation. An instructor in a foreign language can most reasonably be expected to be familiar not only with the music of the cultural area in question, but also with the language, literature, and history of the people within which a national opera grew. It is most likely that it will be the foreign language teacher who will be most anxious to integrate these matters.

The presence of a tape player or other means of reproduction is necessary in the classroom at all times. The musical dimension brings the drama to life and must be an integral part of the presentation and discussion. Although it is impossible because of time restrictions to play the complete operas in class, students have the complete operas available to them. We used a library tape center open from 8:30 a.m. to 10:30 p.m., and students used the center with very little urging on the part of the instructor. I think they were motivated to do so for two reasons: (1) opera is written to be heard and it is natural to listen to an opera; and (2) students readily realize that to speak of an opera intelligently, one must have heard it.

The fact that students spend a great deal of time outside of the classroom listening to and enjoying excellent German is very important. Expanded passive contact with the language results in more rapid than normal progress in the acquisition of both active and passive language skills. Listening to opera involves language learning in association with musical moods, rhythms, and tones; these associations have a positive effect on the retention of vocabulary and structure.

The enthusiasm which students have developed for German opera has remained strong after the conclusion of the course. Students still in college as well as those who have graduated have made a point of informing me of particularly good productions they have seen in the United States and in Europe. In general, students seem to feel we have shared a rather unique experience in our approach to the German opera, and a sense of a lasting bond has developed between teacher and students.

The presence of a popular course in opera within our department has had a positive effect on attitudes toward the department on the part of students and faculty. Several members of the faculty who have openly questioned the worth of literature in our standard curriculum have expressed interest and encouragement with respect to the opera course. Students who are studying languages other than German have requested that the course be given in English. Several students at the lower levels of German instruction have indicated that on the advice of friends they plan to continue with German at least far enough to take this course.

A foreign national opera seems less foreign than a foreign national literature and to have much stronger value associations. In the formation of a value association, the first necessary step is familiarity. In each of the nations which has produced a significant opera, that opera has had a much broader exposure to the general American population than has the literature. At least the names of the composers, the titles of the operas, and perhaps musical themes, if not the operas themselves, are present in the collective consciousness.

The German Opera, besides being of value in itself as part of the education offered in our liberal arts college, serves a secondary function in introducing students to the study of German literature. Having read an opera text by Büchner, Brecht, or Kleist, they become interested in knowing more about these and other writers and about the culture and the language within which they worked.

ORAL INTERPRETATION OF GERMAN POETRY, AND RADIO PLAY WORKSHOP: AN ENVIRONMENTAL APPROACH TO LANGUAGE LEARNING (1185, 1186)

Heinz Geppert (Foreign Languages, German)
Division of Humanism and Cultural Change, University of Wisconsin-Green Bay

A good environment for language learning can be created by involving students in projects that extend the classroom and require team effort in organization, memorization of lines, and performance. Students use a foreign language in a realistic and creative situation, and the language comes alive for them. This involvement with the language in a workshop environment can take many forms, from puppet plays to poetry recitals, in which students find continuing application for their efforts. While working together, they become better acquainted with each other and the instructor, and material learned in this way is retained more successfully because it has become more meaningful. Students often remember a poem, song, or memorized role for years. Above all, real communication takes place when students perform for an audience. Courses of this kind not only serve the department and the college or university, but performances reach the high schools and the ethnic community as well, and can help generate enthusiasm for and interest in foreign language study.

Oral Interpretation of German Poetry was offered as a result of a student poll taken by the Department of German Language and Literature at the University of Wisconsin in 1971 and has since been taught at this institution. The course is listed in the catalog as follows:

Oral Interpretation of German Poetry: Poetry is intended to be spoken and heard. Therefore, the purpose of this course will be to take advantage of the unique possibilities poetry presents both as a written and an oral means of expression. The course will first consider the subject in broad terms, with various examples from German poets to illustrate how poetry functions on a variety of levels. Students will be able to see how spoken language is alive, how its inner dynamics communicate on a level beyond the written work, and how creative use of language by the speaker can impart widely varying effects to the same poem. Next, individual students will select poems for interpretation and presentation, exploring in the process the widely varied forms of expression that poetry affords the listener and speaker. Among the many themes which can be selected by students are: the musical possibilities of language; dramatic elements in the poetic ballad; poetry as political and social commentary; poetry of protest; poetic imagery in poems of war; poetry of the absurd. The final class project will be a public, bilingual poetry reading entitled "An Hour With Brecht," Eine Stunde mit Brecht.

The course was also advertised on campus with posters designed by an art student.

The class, offered in the January interim, met five times weekly for two hours during four weeks and every evening of the last two weeks for rehearsal purposes. The basic text was Paths to German Poetry: An Introductory Anthology (Foltin and Heinen, eds.) in addition to a collection of poems chosen thematically and used in typewritten, photocopied form. (A valuable source for the teacher of oral interpretation is the Guide to Oral Interpretation by Louise M. Scrivner.)

Considering the small size of the institution and the decreased student body during the interim period, the enrollment of ten was rather surprising. The character of the class was determined by the students' varying backgrounds in the German language and by their own personal interests and experiences. Only three had previously been abroad, one had only one year of German, and only one, an English major, had experience in speech and drama.

The first class meetings were used to discuss and determine class content and goals. It was decided that the main objectives were a better understanding of poetry as a specific form of literary expression and the effective oral communication of such works. The students felt they needed means to understand an author's intellectual and emotional range, and wanted to learn how to interpret these in relation to their own experience.

As a speech art, oral interpretation is between public speaking and acting. The first week, therefore, was spent with the instructor leading students to various examples in the texts. Reciting a ballad by Meyer would imply a different approach than, for example, a poem by Enzensberger. In the first, retaining individual identity, the reader suggests a character or characters; in the latter the reader may assume a matter-of-fact tone or impart an element of anger. The instructor was able to observe that students did not have as many difficulties understanding poetry as an artistic form of expression--its symbols, meanings, and structure--as they had in speaking in front of the other class members. This hesitancy was not due simply to the fact that the material was 'foreign,' although it might have had some initial bearing, but rather to the demands poetry makes through its emotional content. It seems that the element most needed for this learning experience was trust in each other. To reach that goal, the class spent time together after class, getting to know each other better; the instructor was able to observe the individuals gradually becoming more comfortable with the material and with each other.

While students were selecting poems for oral recitation and discussion in class, including short biographies of the authors, preparations were made for the public reading. We decided upon a cross-section of Brecht's poetry arranged by groups of earlier and later poems and by related themes in a variety of short and longer poems, starting the program with "Vom armen B.B." ("On the Poor B.B.") and ending with "An die Nachgeborenen" ("To Posterity"). We decided upon a bilingual presentation in order to attract a larger audience. Different students were designated to read the German and the English versions, which led to interesting variations of interpretation. For the English versions, we used translations by Eric Bentley, Sidney Bremer, and Michael Hamburger.

The class was very enthusiastic about the project, although some students continued to battle misgivings about speaking in public. These were overcome, however, by using white face make-up with black accents in the form of question marks and other patterns, and costumes which would represent certain professions or attitudes (soldier, nun, cleaning woman, prostitute, etc.). The students felt less personally identified with the voices and characters of the poetry; it was not they who were speaking, rather they were demonstrating certain characters, very much in keeping with the Brechtian concept of alienation.

The reading was advertised with posters and short articles in school and city newspapers. The Art Department let us use one of their studios for the reading. It had small, adjustable spotlights on tracks and the disarray of easels and sketches everywhere created a special atmosphere. We made use of stools of different heights and platforms- even a stepladder turned into a prop for a very effective interpretation of "Gegen Verführung" ("Against Temptation"). The blackboard was covered with German news- papers with predominantly political headlines. The visual elements were not to interfere with the words themselves, but rather were designed to aid understanding of the material.

Other elements included in the presentation were theatrical elements of blocking, the delineation of movements, gestures, entrances, and exits. As each poem was read, more and more readers would join the person(s) already on stage. The same procedure was used for exits so that at the end of the reading only two students were left, facing each other, reciting the German and English versions of "To Posterity," which had a definite impact on the audience. (One would choose the strongest readers for such key poems.) Another technique was to use a chorus of speakers for parts of some works, such as "Apfelböck" or the Mahagonny poems. By this time most of the students had lost their initial shyness. They felt very comfortable within the group, especially since class criticism never left the realm of the positive and the class had been basically designed as a group activity, with the teacher trying to avoid the monologue/lecture approach in analytic interpretations.

The attendance at "An Hour with Brecht" was very good. The informal seating arrangement allowed between 100 and 120 persons in the studio. Among the audience were administrators who had taken German some years ago, members of the Drama Department, students of all disciplines, and many townspeople and high school students. We had arranged a Kaffee und Kuchen reception at which cast and audience could meet in one of the lounges. Another student provided guitar music, playing Bob Dylan songs which he felt were appropriate. There is perhaps no greater compliment to a teacher than students saying that they were able to participate in an interesting learning experience, that they have been more than just a number in a classroom, and that they have also learned to overcome some of the difficulties in speaking in front of an audience. (Most of the students participated in the following semester's play production workshop of Grass' Hochwasser.)

A similar oral approach to language learning was offered in connection with a workshop using a Hörspiel (radio play) as a text. Since most radio plays depend almost exclusively upon the creation of verbal images, texts are usually easier to understand than other forms of literary expression. The emphasis was again on reading aloud from the printed page with proper pronunciation and intonation. Discussion of the work followed each session. Although our main concern was the improvement of verbal skills, attention was paid to bringing a literary work of art alive. While performing the thoughts and feelings of the characters in the radio play verbally, many students were able to turn the printed page into a living work, providing enough initiative to design a "German Reader's Theater" production as the final project for the workshop.

The students involved in this workshop were enrolled in second- and third-year German classes, and participation was on a voluntary basis, although credit was given since it involved many weeks of rehearsal and memorization. (Even though it was to be read, the interaction of speakers/characters among each other made this necessary.) As a text we chose Ludwig Harig's Ein Blumenstück (Neues Hörspiel, Suhrkamp), which is ideal for a project such as this. First, the language is very simple-children's songs and games, nursery rhymes, passages from fairy tales and textbooks, diary quotations of a concentration camp commander--and most of the images are repeated throughout the hour-long play. The text also lends itself to the participation of a variable number of readers, since the author did not assign the lines to any given voice. After several readings, characters crystallize: a narrator describes the scene--the site of a former concentration camp in a bucolic German landscape--punctuated by numerous interruptions from a group of pupils playing nearby. Additional voices are those of a teacher, priest, prophet, camp commander, and Himmler.

After assigning roles, or voices, based on the natural qualities a student possesses which make the part appropriate, we began rehearsals. The first weeks were spent on the improvement of pronunciation, enunciation, and intonation. Meaning and intent were discussed, in German, in relationship to single roles as well as to the play as a whole. During this time, a certain concept of presentation formed. We decided to use an environmental-theater method. Students from the Drama Department designed the lights and worked on the set, which was to evoke remnants of a concentration camp. The actual reading or play area was in the middle of the room, fenced with barbed wire toward the audience on both sides. On opposing walls we erected platforms made of burnt wood from which the voices of authority would speak. The floor was covered with dry leaves, and stools were placed within the enclosed area for the students. The whole effect was that of an arena, and the question then was how to get the readers to their chairs most effectively. After the audience was seated with the aid of two strong searchlights, there was total darkness in the room, and sound effects created an atmosphere of machine-gun fire, barking dogs, and screaming people; as the stage lights went on, the students entered singing and giving flowers to members of the audience until they reached their places within the enclosed area.

We had again advertised the performance through posters and newspaper articles. Invitations to high schools and other colleges in the vicinity were sent, along with a description of the play in English and copies of the play in German so they could be read in advance in some of the classes. We charged no admission. Three performances were scheduled, and all were well attended, especially the matinee for high school students. A coffee hour following the play was again successful in facilitating a meeting of high school teachers, students, and the German-speaking citizens of the community.

Although acting experience is not required for these projects and they are mainly designed to encourage language skills, literary, theatrical, and cultural aspects of the works become apparent to the student and make it more than a language course per se. For German majors, graduate students, and future language teachers, experience with productions such as these can be an invaluable addition to their training. Practice in speaking a foreign language in front of a classroom and performing for an audience--the latter a 'real' rather than contrived situation--develop skills and confidence, and provide the future teacher with experience in a method of teaching language and literature using an oral approach.

By reading in a group with the teacher and other students as guides, a student can lose a sense of insecurity and uncertainty with regard to understanding a text. The oral group-project approach provides immediate feedback; the student is more confident because the activity includes and depends upon everyone.

The benefits to those beyond the class have already been discussed. Briefly, public performances, no matter how informal, serve the department, the college or unviersity, and the high schools and ethnic community as well, both in providing an opportunity for the community to experience the material being studied, and in maintaining and generating interest and enthusiasm for language study.

(The above report is based in part on Heinz Geppert, "Language Learning Through Involvement," in Second Language Teaching 75. Proceedings of the Twenty-Sixth Annual Meeting of the Pacific Northwest Council on Foreign Languages, ed. Hector Hammerly and Isabel Sawyer [The Conference, 1975], Pt. 2, pp. 107-14.)

SPANISH THEATER COURSE WITH INTERNSHIP OPTION; CINEMA COURSES (1191, 1198)

M. P. Holt
Department of Modern Languages, Staten Island Community College, CUNY

Recognizing the need to provide attractive elective courses in foreign languages and literatures in a college where language study is optional (except in certain health programs which require Spanish), the Department of Modern Languages has diversified its offerings of language courses designed for specific professional needs and of courses which have evolved from those dealing in a traditional manner with foreign literatures and cultures. In the latter area, the bilingual Spanish Theater Internship program has been the most successful in fulfilling its goals and, perhaps, in creating a model that can be adapted to situations in many other colleges and universities.

Spanish Drama in Translation existed in the curriculum as one of several offerings in European literature in translation, and the course was first scheduled for spring semester 1972. It was immediately apparent that more than half of the students enrolled were of Hispanic background and spoke or read Spanish with some fluency. This group was permitted to do any or all of the reading, papers, and tests in the original language, while the other students did their work entirely in English.

Although Spanish Drama in Translation was not offered the following year, I accepted four Spanish-speaking students for independent study with the idea of combining the study of individual plays with attendance at Spanish language theaters in New York City. One of the works studied was Sastre's Escuadra hacia la muerte, and the director of the Spanish theater group Nuestro Teatro permitted my students to observe and participate in backstage activities during the run of that company's production of the play. As a result of this experience, a revision of the course description of Spanish Drama, with provisions for an internship component and a bilingual approach, was submitted to the college curriculum committee. Although there was some question of appropriate credit (both for student and teacher) for a course that was divided between classroom instruction and off-campus activities, the change was approved.

Fall semester 1973 provided an opportunity for testing the concept, and what emerged was a further modification of the course necessitated by the realities of the schedules and life patterns of our students. Nuestro Teatro had scheduled a bilingual production of Buero-Vallejo's Concierto de San Ovidio, a major example of contemporary Spanish drama and an involved and difficult play which required considerable technical support in production. I had hoped to bring each of the fifteen students in the class into some aspect of the production--design, lighting, publicity, and acting. Several, because of family commitments, outside jobs, and other personal considerations, simply could not be in Manhattan for rehearsals or other evening activities for enough time to make their participation meaningful. Consequently, special projects were devised for these students to enable them to continue with the course.

This led to a decision to separate the internship element from the course, making it an option for additional credit. Each student would still be required to become involved in a theater project that would be different from the traditional term paper and could range from a design for the production of a play to a semester of attending productions of New York's Hispanic theaters and preparing critical oral and written reports on the experience.

When the course was offered again in spring 1975, the problems had been solved, and enrollment increased to twenty-five, of whom twenty-three completed the course successfully. Five students elected the internship for three additional credits, participating in production of Buero's El tragaluz. At the beginning of the semester, each student chose either to work in Spanish (for language and literature credit) or in English (for literature-in-translation credit). Most chose Spanish, and discussions sometimes jumped from one language to the other with little or no complaint from those whose Spanish was minimal or nonexistent.

The works to be studied depended on the availability of English translations, a continuing problem for all courses that attempt to offer Spanish literature in English. Titles ranged from the Golden Age comedies La vida es sueño and El burlador de Sevilla to twentieth-century plays by Lorca, Casona, Buero, and Sastre. One of the most successful was Buero's Las Meninas, which I was able to include because I had access to an unpublished translation.

At the beginning of the course, a few classes amounted to traditional lectures, but at all times the plays were treated as productions to be imagined visually and not as works embalmed on the printed page. All students attended performances of one or more of the plays they had read, and slides and films were used to illustrate scenes from several others.

Results became increasingly gratifying during the semester, as students with no previous experience in theater began to ask for titles of books that would tell them more about Lope de Rueda or the Velázquez they had encountered for the first time in Las Meninas, or to relate the plays of Lorca to their own cultural and social experiences in a number of Hispanic countries and to talk intelligently about virtues and flaws of performances they attended.

As an extension of theater internship activities, several Hispanic actors and students have participated in the production of videotapes for our department's series for hospital and professional workers. To my knowledge, only one student who took part in the internship has gone on to become professionally involved (in television), but all have come to consider theater a normal part of their experience. Obviously, most colleges and universities are not close enough to New York's Hispanic culture to relate the classroom experience to it directly; but closer cooperation with theater departments and utilization of production facilities may well provide the means for a similar learning experience in which dramatic literature is studied as living theater.

SPANISH PLAY PRODUCTION (1192)

Rodolfo Cardona
Department of Spanish and Portuguese, University of Texas at Austin

Our play production course has been offered for several years; the course was created in the belief that students who are expected to prepare a full-length play (or three one-act plays) for public performance work harder than they would for a traditional conversation course and therefore learn more than in such a course. To stage a play well, the student must acquire a fluency which is practically impossible to achieve in any other course, however much the latter may emphasize oral skills. In order to be understood, lines must be delivered naturally, with correct intonation for the context, and with perfect pronunciation. I have observed that students involved in producing and staging a play gain in one semester what others require two years to accomplish. A play production course is also the best and least expensive surrogate for study abroad.

There are, of course, limitations to this type of course. First, the course can never be required, even of majors, for not every student is willing or able to submit to the experience; students who register for the course have already at least a mild interest in acting. Second, there can be only limited enrollment. Last, instructor and students have to be willing to spend more than the three hours per week reflected in course credits. (We schedule the class with a laboratory in order to allow for extra rehearsal time.) The course is open to any student who has completed the language requirement or its equivalent. For this reason, exact course content is difficult to determine prior to the beginning of classes.

Recently I experimented with the use of hand puppets. This was advantageous in helping shy students overcome a reluctance to speak. Producing a puppet voice and speaking from behind a puppet stage greatly reduced self-consciousness. The experiment worked beautifully, and, even in one extreme case, I was able to obtain remarkable production of correctly spoken Spanish.

Actual play production began with a very simple work, an adaptation of Lope de Rueda's Las aceitunas. The results encouraged us to tackle a more challenging piece, Cervantes' Entremés del Viejo Celoso. We presented both plays with great success to an audience of faculty members, graduate students, undergraduate majors, and other students. For our final production, we combined puppet and stage plays. We opened with the Cervantes' work, followed by El delantal blanco, a one-act play by the Chilean Sergio Bodanović (and included in the textbook En un acto which we use for our conversation classes), and closed with a play for puppets and actors, García Lorca's Retablillo de Don Cristobal.

The play production course had other advantages. In addition to providing the possibility of improved language production to a group of English-speaking students, it offered a small group of Mexican-Americans who participated in the course the opportunity to improve diction and enlarge active vocabulary. The combination of 'anglos' and 'chicanos' afforded a wonderful opportunity for camaraderie and participation in a joint project, the presentation of the puppet plays to Mexican-American children in the Spanish-speaking section of the city.

I am hopeful that the course will continue this type of project in the future, since a community such as ours presents an unusual opportunity to combine learning with the dissemination of culture.

The Social Sciences (See also mss. 1085/1257/1258, 1102, 1348, 1359)

LATIN AMERICAN LITERATURE OF SOCIAL CONFLICT (1215)

John Means
Department of Spanish and Portuguese, Temple University

The course is part of the Spanish and Portuguese Department's Puerto Rican Studies degree program, and also a component of the college's undergraduate and graduate certificate programs in Inter-American Studies. Although the majority of students are Spanish majors, the political aspects of the course, being somewhat cross-disciplinary, are of interest to students specializing in Inter-American Studies or Puerto Rican Studies. The course is applicable to both departmental majors and certificate programs.

No problems were encountered in obtaining approval for the course, except that its initial title, Latin American Literature of Politics, was changed to the present title in deference to the Political Science Department.

The course covers the literature of Latin America, especially Brazil, which bears most directly on the region's socio-political process and the complexity and adversity of national problems during the nineteenth and twentieth centuries. Political literature, for the purpose of the course, does not signify political manifestos or analyses of the functions of governmental systems; it signifies those works of fiction, drama, poetry, and essay which have awakened collective examination of national character and conscience. The works are primarily the aesthetic outgrowth of the political ambience, especially such writing as accompanied and expressed early nineteenth-century struggles for independence and subsequent socio-political perspectives. Foremost among Brazilian writers who have sought to discover and document the changes brought about by revolutions in rural and urban life are novelists Jorge Amado, José Lins do Rêgo, Graciliano Ramos, and Joao Guimaraes Rosa, and playwright Alfredo Dias Gomes.

Material covered is approximately one-half to two-thirds Spanish-American, and one-third to one-half Brazilian in content. Our Hispanist who specializes in this area of Spanish-American literature teaches the Spanish-American segment, and a Brazilianist with a background in political science teaches the Brazilian material. The course is part of the normal teaching load for each. It is dependent on the availability of the two professors, and if both were unavailable it probably would not be offered.

Since the course is designed to appeal to non-language majors as well as to Spanish or Portuguese majors, and since reading materials include both Portuguese and Spanish

94

writings, all reading materials must be available in English translation. This imposes certain limitations, particularly in the Brazilian area. The only method of introducing students to those writings which are still untranslated is to assign special report topics to advanced language students who can study the materials and report to the class. However, eighty to ninety percent of all material for which students are held responsible is available to them in English as texts or as supplementary library assignments.

The course is as rigorous as the more orthodox course offerings in the department and covers quantitatively more material than the average Spanish course, since readings and lectures are in English.

The course has been well-received by students, though enrollments are not above departmental averages. To a minimal degree, usually as a result of the course's applicability to Inter-American Studies credit, the course has attracted students from the social sciences who would not otherwise be enrolled in a language department. We have received no substantial feedback from other departments or the administration.

LA VILLE DE PARIS AUX XVIIe ET XVIIIe SIECLES (1220)

Catherine Lafarge
Department of French, Bryn Mawr College

Changes in curriculum can take place either to respond to students' demands for a particular course or to allow a faculty member to share with students the results of a research project he or she has undertaken. In the case of La Ville de Paris aux XVIIe et XVIIIe Siècles, it was a combination of both. I first became interested in the theme of Paris in eighteenth-century French literature about ten years ago while studying a novelist who used Paris as the setting for his novel; over the years I have tried to see the problem in a larger context--beyond the eighteenth century and the novel--and study the impact the capital had on authors of as many various genres as possible, including letters, diaries, and journals.

I first offered a course on the theme of Paris in seventeenth- and eighteenth-century French literature. This knowledge of the literary representation of Paris, a representation necessarily distorted by the writers, led me to learn more about the geography, economics, sociology, and politics of the city. Simultaneous with my explorations of non-literary aspects of the problem was a burgeoning of student interest in the history of cities such that the college created a Growth and Structure of Cities major, and a need for the course for which I had been gathering materials became obvious.

Though the title might suggest that the course could be conveniently divided in half, it soon became obvious that such a division was not feasible. History and literary history rarely lend themselves to this arbitrary break into centuries. The seventeenth and eighteenth centuries are a case in point, as the two dates most relevant to the beginning and the end of this period are 1594 (Henri IV's arrival in Paris) and 1789 (the beginning of the French Revolution). Thus, more appropriately, the course could have been called Paris under Five Bourbon Kings (Henri IV and Louis XIII, XIV, XV, and XVI). The dominant role played by the kings of France in their capital's history hinted at by this alternative title will become more evident in the course content sketched in the following paragraphs.

Starting with a seventeenth-century concept of the city as a rather large group of houses usually surrounded by walls, it was shown how during these two centuries Paris had been transformed from a medieval city into a modern capital. Maps were used to illustrate this revolution and expansion. The role played by land developers and individuals in the growth or creation of certain districts was pointed out, e.g., Cardinal de Richelieu's impetus in the building of the Palais-Royal district. A certain familiarity with the topography of the capital during the period was acquired--how, for instance, the ancient division into three parts, "la Cité" (the island on which Notre Dame stands), "l'Université" (the left bank), and "la Ville" (the right bank), gave way to a larger and more varied Paris, in which narrow and unpleasant streets contrasted with new squares and numerous gardens surrounding palaces, private houses, and convents.

The next part of the course dealt with population. Arriving at a realistic estimate of Paris' population is no small challenge, as there is no census for the period studied, and all but a few records of birth and death burned in the City Hall fire of 1871. Attention was given to alternative methods which could be used to obtain a more or less accurate figure.

Henri IV's arrival in 1594 opened the way for an important chapter in the history of Paris, once again a royal city. The king living in the Louvre, his official residence, governed the kingdom and the capital. The Louvre itself, a symbol of what was to happen to Paris, progressively lost its medieval appearance and became a more spacious palace as it was considerably enlarged to house the king's entourage and government. Henri IV, interested in his people, wanted to make Paris a more livable city; with Henri IV a new trend began, and from then on the kings and their ministers were responsible for many of Paris' embellishments. These contributions were dealt with at some length.

Paris was then studied as a government center. The composition and working of the royal counsels held in the Louvre, the Parliament, and its many courts located in the Palais on the island of "la Cité," and the city government meeting in the Hôtel de Ville were analyzed. It was stressed that Henri IV's clever interventionist policy virtually put an end to the city's independence, and Louis XIV gave Paris a powerful master in creating the office of lieutenant general of police.

Paris was also the economic capital of the kingdom. Parisian financiers were called upon on numerous occasions to subsidize the kings' wars. John Law invented a system which eventually led to bankruptcy, but, while it lasted, it attracted many eager speculators and large sums of money to the city. The period under study saw the birth of many Parisian industries. In the seventeenth century, Sully and mercantilist Colbert were responsible for this new cause of growth in the capital. The point is developed that a century later the importance of these artisans was recognized by the philosophes, as witnessed in the long descriptions and many illustrations of the Encyclopédie.

An attempt was made to show more about everyday life by studying a cross section of working Parisians, all dwelling in a small district bordering the Seine. A limited sampling of inventories drawn after death was used for this purpose. Finally, three important aspects of life in the city were only too briefly mentioned: medical care in the hospitals, intellectual life in the university and the salons, and religious life in churches and convents.

If this outline appears to describe a rather ambitious program for a one-semester course, it should be said that each of the parts was treated with varying degrees of depth and breadth, depending on the availability of documents on these various aspects. I tried to cover those about which I personally had the greater knowledge.

I asked each student to give one oral report and write two papers, choosing any interdisciplinary topic which could be adequately documented. For the oral report I insisted that students use the college's large slide collection. A few topics by students were "The Development of the Marais District in the Seventeenth Century," "The Building of the Ile Saint-Louis," "The Problem of Supplying Water to the City," "The History of the Theater in Eighteenth-Century Paris," and "Le Nôtre's Embellishments of Paris."

The course was interdisciplinary and listed in three departments. As it was not a literature course, it could not be taken as credit toward the major in French literature; it could, however, be taken as credit toward both the French Studies and the Growth and Structure of Cities majors. The curriculum committee granted me permission to teach the course for an indefinite period of time and as often as other commitments would allow. The French Studies program would welcome similar courses in the medieval period or the nineteenth and twentieth centuries.

Faculty acceptance appears to have been widespread, as not only members of my department were interested in it but also faculty who teach in the Growth and Structure of Cities program and who come from varied departments (political science, history, history of art, sociology, economics, Greek, Latin, classical and Near Eastern archaeology, anthropology, and chemistry).

In my judgment, this course and courses like it are a great enrichment of the college curriculum from the point of view of students, who are offered an alternative to the more traditional courses, and from the point of view of faculty, who too often are restricted by traditional curricula. I believe that any course which allows the liberal arts student to view a broader context should be encouraged by all as a benefit to the entire college community.

A LA RECHERCHE DE LA FRANCE (1226)

Bruce Cronmiller
French Department, Lawrence University

We are a small university and know many of our students fairly well. From what they talk about and from questions they ask, we get a good idea of (1) what they want to know- -very important from the point of view of student motivation, (2) what they do not know- -even more important, and (3) what they need to know--most important of all.

For example, a student in anthropology asks about the position of women in French society. Is there a women's lib in France? A student in history asks for documentation of French claims of superiority over other nations. A student planning to study in France wants to know what the Sorbonne is. A student wants to know the meaning of the terms monde and milieu and to understand something of the relationship between these two concepts and social background. An American student wants to know what it is like to be a native French student, what the concours and the grandes and écoles are and what they stand for. Of course, almost any informed Frenchman can answer these questions; the answers seem elementary and obvious. However, as far as the American is concerned, these questions are utterly baffling; the answers lie outside the scope of his experience and culture.

What are the implications of questions such as the ones I have cited, questions that are asked again and again, year after year? What is the teacher of French to make of these questions? I think that from such questions we may draw the following conclusions. First, American students are only dimly aware of French society, and this awareness is encumbered more often than not by all sorts of misconceptions and misinformation. Second, we simply cannot take for granted that our students, whatever other courses they may be taking, are reading Le Monde in their spare time, not even the columns devoted to their special area or areas of interest. In fact, we cannot assume that they are keeping up in any way with current developments in French life. Third, there is a clear need for programs of study that teach students some of the fundamentals in these areas. Students need avenues of approach and knowledge of materials which will help them answer their own questions.

There are a few first-rate texts; they are teachable--interesting, specific, provocative, discussable; the information in them is reliable and up-to-date. As primary texts I use Wylie's texts and Ortali's Entre nous. These serve as the basis for discussion, in addition to a novel or two, and perhaps some of the Maigret series of Simenon. For background reading, I recommend Christin and Lefebvre's Comprendre la France and Michaud's Guide France with its admirable diagrams of the educational and political structures of France. I refer students also to the Guide Michelin (Vert) de Paris and to Adragh's The New French Revolution, which is not so new any more, but useful.

But there are still two main difficulties in finding suitable texts. One is in finding a wider variety of texts that keep pace with changes taking place in France. The second is that of finding a text that gives unity and coherence to the program. Such a text does not exist. It is clearly up to the teacher, and absolutely essential, to delineate the scope and limitations of the course.

I have taught the civilization courses here--as part of my normal load--since I arrived, partly because they interest me and partly because nobody else seems to want to teach them. I proposed them and have shaped and modified them over the years. This shaping and modification is based on some successes and quite a few failures. This is perhaps bound to be the case with all such experimental, exploratory work.

There were no problems encountered in obtaining permanent approval for the course. My colleagues have given me their full support, but I can't recall many instances where a colleague in another department has sent a student to take the course. Student reaction is favorable, and I have the administration's full cooperation and approval. I think the course has probably improved our image on campus, enhancing our reputation as an innovative, experimental department. In order to fulfill departmental requirements for graduation, students are required to take at least one civilization course, so this counts for credit toward the departmental major.

For me, this kind of course is not an alternative to a literature course. The two types of courses are complementary. A student of French who knows his Racine and Saint-Simon--it was a colleague of mine who pointed this out to me--knows his French political and social structures; but, I would add to that, a student who is acquainted with how the French deal with each other in daily encounters and with how they go about business in their national life is better equipped to appreciate Racine and Saint-Simon.

JUNGIAN PSYCHOLOGY AND GERMAN LITERATURE (1234)

Sterling Bennett
Department of Foreign Languages, California State College-Sonoma

In a small rural college and in the present cultural climate, courses taught in German, no matter how catchy the material and name, do not attract large crowds. Thus, we offer foreign literature courses in translation. This situation has forced us to broaden the area heretofore known as German literature and language.

Jungian Psychology and German Literature was publicized college-wide by a Foreign Language Department poster. In it each language area described the courses it would be offering in English. A more thorough description was sent to the Department of Psychology, both for the obvious reason and because their enrollment makes up a large part of the total college enrollment. A description was also sent to the Department of Interdisciplinary Studies. The course was cross-listed under Psychology, Foreign Language (German), and Foreign Literature in English.

Anticipating an unwieldy enrollment on the basis of preregistration, I asked a psychology student to assist in the course. Somewhat to my surprise, the Psychology Department donated a modest but worthwhile sum to this end. The student led discussion workshops, spent two class hours explaining Jungian terminology, assisted in reading final exams, and served as agent provocateur during discussions.

Course material was not hard to find. Students were asked to keep a dream journal and were required to read the following works in English:

Parzival (Wolfram von Eschenbach), Faust I and II (Goethe), The Golden Pot (E.T.A. Hoffmann), Cat and Mouse (Grass), Narcissus and Goldmund and Steppenwolf (Hesse), "The Penal Colony" and "A Country Doctor" (Kafka), as well as The Origins and History of Consciousness (Eric Neumann), The Hero with a Thousand Faces (Campbell), and Man and His Symbols and Memories, Dreams, Reflections (Jung). I further recommended A Primer of Jungian Psychology by Calvin Hall and Ann Faraday's The Dream Game, and read portions of Tieck's Der Runenberg, Mann's Death in Venice, and the "Snow" chapter from The Magic Mountain, translating as I went. Not surprisingly, the list turned out to be too long. Even the best students in the group of about thirty bogged down in Neumann and in Faust II. Toward the end of the semester I eliminated the works by Hesse. My assistant held two discussion-workshops on Neumann at her home.

For the many who had seemed to have learned otherwise, I made up a list of questions about the works being read, hoping to demonstrate that there are no right answers, but that many worthwhile questions are possible. When I thought the proper moment had arrived, I optimistically gave a fifty-minute midterm examination. They could write on either of two questions. Part of my optimism extended to my instructions at the beginning of the examination, in which I wrote, "In writing your answers, try to keep your sentences simple. Try to express only one idea in each sentence. Pretend you are writing for a ten-year-old and that it is important that he or she understands what you are saying."

After many hours of correcting, editing, and commenting, I passed the tests back. Most of the writing was confused, complex, and disorganized; the grades were low. It was evident to everyone that the reading list would need more attention. There was a storm of protest about the possibility, even the advisability, of writing clearly. The questions were complex, the time short. I held my ground and, in a course devoted to exploration of the unconscious and reflections of it in literature, found myself defending consciousness, clarity, and light in general. Even more confusing, I was defending simplicity. After a few days, the majority of the students admitted verbally and tacitly that their writing and thinking had not been as clear as it could have been. I for my part had learned that criticism of a young person's writing is often received as criticism of the individual. I began to see that many students assumed they were communicating and being understood.

In attending to the non-rational part of the course, not to be overwhelmed by the idea that it was all around us anyway, I asked that a dream journal be kept. The syllabus read, "As a written exercise, each student will write a fairy tale--a personal myth, his or her story of four to six pages. Although based on motifs and themes which appear in the dream journal, it is not to be a simple, direct transcription of dream content. The second portion of the written exercise will be three to four pages of written analysis, a consideration of the personal myth in the context of class reading and discussion." Later, I changed this part of the requirement, dealing with the problem through a question on the final examination which asked, "What have you learned about your personal symbolism through your story, through those of others, and through the readings and discussions in this course?" As a third part of the exercise, I told them I would like them to read their stories to the rest of the class.

As an example, I wrote a story based on my dream motifs and read it to the class. When the time came for them to do likewise, we had several experiences in common, for instance, that it is not easy to sit in a circle with twenty-five or thirty other people and emerge as a differentiated, secure, rational individual.

Apart from this, it turned out that writing the myth could be easy. The students were not to follow models; they were not be Manns or Hesses; they were to begin with their dream motifs, messages which were really about them, and then expand, literally writing whatever came to mind. Those who followed the directions unwittingly produced all the archetypes discussed throughout the course. Much personal darkness emerged, always safely in symbolic forms. When the darkness was confronted and accepted by the stories' protagonists, it was inevitably transformed into something friendly and life-giving.

From those who simply recorded dreams, we learned something else: the recorded dream is only marginally intelligible and meaningful, and even then rarely to anyone but the dreamer. The obscure story of the unconscious requires the conscious storyteller and through storytelling reveals something to everyone. Further, it was discovered that hearing a person's story seemed an ancient, almost religious experience, after which one could say, "I know your story; we are connected; in some way I have become a little responsible for you. We are part of the same world-family-history." The recounted dream did not produce that effect.

The final examination was praised for its form and content, whether rightly or wrongly. The writing was only somewhat better this time, although the creative writing had often been outstanding. I was tempted to conclude from this that students will learn to write better by writing 'creatively' about themselves and their worlds in their own way. The students liked the final because it was equally balanced between the objective and the subjective. Two questions were objective and weighed heavily in the grade. The first required an explanation of Jungian terms, the second an identification of texts. A third question asked about the differences between the recounted dream and the recounted story, and a fourth was subjective and offered the student an opportunity to reflect on what he or she had learned in taking the course.

In retrospect, the course was very challenging for me and I think for the students as well. The reading selections turned out to be well-chosen, especially Faust II, which, before my interest in Jung, had always seemed so impenetrable. The students liked hearing German read, and several asked about learning the language in our Individualized Instruction Program. The enrollment of thirty, higher than usual for an upper-division course in our area, helped us survive.

GERMAN EXPRESSIONISM: THE ROAD TO HITLER (1240)

Sol Gittleman
Department of German and Russian, Tufts University

This course and several similar ones in the department are the result of a conscious philosophical and educational decision on the part of the teaching staff: to move the German Department into the mainstream of general education on our campus. We had to consider some hard facts. First, the German major was becoming increasingly irrelevant in the world of the late sixties and early seventies. Language requirements were disappearing, liberal arts colleges were accepting larger and larger percentages of pre-medical students and professionally-oriented types who leaned heavily toward the social sciences. It was conceivable, unless something were done, that vast numbers of students would pass through the undergraduate curriculum and never set foot in a German class, because there was nothing there to attract them. We were threatened with extinction, and we responded by deciding that the importance of German life and letters could be given a more central role and greater visibility by creating a highly interdisciplinary course, involving the use of films, slides, and readings from fields such as history, psychology, science, and literature, while at the same time taking full advantage of the historical similarities between a unique pairing of historical moments: Weimar Germany and America of the sixties.

The course was first offered as a Special Topic in the German Department, a procedure which does not involve Curricula Committee approval. By the time the course had been offered a second time, enrollment had passed 100 students. (Of these, eighteen were engineers, and thirty-four were pre-medical majors; the rest represented majors in almost every department of the university.) The course was applicable as a distribution requirement in the humanities, but more than half the students indicated they took the course out of interest and not to fulfill any requirement. By the time the course went to the faculty Curricula Committee for approval and inclusion in the department listings, German Expressionism: The Road to Hitler had enrollments approaching 200 students. The faculty committee approved without dissent and encouraged other departments to create such general education courses.

The key to gaining the committee's approval was in maintaining academic respectability while providing the non-specialist point of view for the students. The course required two hourly exams and a term paper. The term paper could be written with the individual's major in mind: engineers enjoyed learning about Bauhaus; physicists discovered the humanistic aspects of Einstein and Planck; others wrote on topics such as

German silent films (everyone saw Caligari, Nosferatu, Metropolis, and M), painters of Der Blaue Reiter and Die Brücke (there were illustrated slide lectures), and the rise of National Socialism. Students were often writing on a subject for the first time, and this was taken into account by the instructor.

The basic required reading includes photocopied material from An Anthology of German Expressionist Drama (ed. Sokel) and from The Modern Theatre, Vol. I (ed. Eric Bentley). In addition, Kaiser's Gas I, Kafka's The Penal Colony and Other Stories, Nazi Culture (ed. George Mosse), Kracauer's From Caligari to Hitler, Grass' The Tin Drum, and Freud's Civilization and Its Discontents are read. A list of supplementary recommended reading is also provided.

The course has grown to an enrollment of 300 per offering. The Dean of Faculties has given the department an additional $1,000 for the purchase of a slide collection as well as several films, which have been turned over to the university library as part of a permanent film collection. Almost every department of the university now provides courses of a general educational nature, without any prerequisite, for a student audience which is primarily juniors and seniors. In our department, each faculty member is now responsible for one such course per year, which counts as part of the regular teaching load. We allow our majors to take these courses for credit, but insist that reading be in German. Departmental registrations in language courses have been significantly affected: we have had a fifteen percent increase in elementary and intermediate German classes, and more than half of these students became interested in German through one of these culture courses given in English.

Our campus image is exceptionally good. We have a vital educational role on campus, and the response to the Expressionism course, as well as to the several other similar courses in the department, has been gratifying. Expressionism: The Road to Hitler fully accomplished what it set out to do; it placed into focus the central role of Germany in the past seventy years of western civilization; it brought an understanding of this role to a large number of potential community leaders who otherwise might never have discovered its significance; and it took a department out of its isolation and provided it with an educational mandate.

LATIN AMERICAN LITERATURE IN A SOCIAL CONTEXT (1250)

Jean Franco
Department of Spanish and Portuguese, Stanford University

For the student not from that culture, Latin American literature presents some of the problems of ancient and medieval literature; that is, unless students are able to enter imaginatively into experiences that are alien to them they are likely to be able to produce only impoverished readings of texts. In the native culture, this accumulated experience includes unvoiced signs and tacit knowledge of appropriateness, conditions which affect the meanings attached to discourse. Not only is this experience missing in students brought up outside the culture, but they are also often unaware of the conditions in which literature is produced and, therefore, of historical evolution and interdependency.

Latin American Literature in a Social Context was designed to supply some of these dimensions which are missing from the student's experience. The course related literary problems to history, anthropology, and sociology and raised questions about the dynamics of the relationship between metropolitan and dependent cultures.

In winter 1973 I set up a pilot course for students who did not speak Spanish. In summer 1974, I planned a new course to be taught in Spanish, designed for advanced undergraduate and graduate students. I received help from the Faculty of Humanities and Sciences, who allotted a research assistant and money to finance the preparation of teaching materials, since the course would include a great deal of material not necessarily available in bookstores.

Because the Spanish Department is small, I anticipated fifteen to twenty students and planned the class as a seminar, meeting three hours a week for undergraduates with an extra hour for graduate students. The course was offered within the Department of Spanish and Portuguese and counted toward the major. Undergraduates and graduates were evaluated differently: undergraduates took midterm and final examinations; graduates wrote papers. Undergraduate students who wished to be evaluated by term paper rather than by examination were free to make the choice but were asked to do so before the fourth week of any quarter.

I conducted most of the seminars, but graduate students were encouraged to participate as instructors. For instance, an anthropology student in the class contributed slide material and gave a lecture on archaeological data in the first part of the course on indigenismo. In the second quarter, a graduate student gave lectures on aspects of cultural nationalism of Argentine Spanish from a sociolinguistic point of view; by the third quarter, graduate students contributed extensively, and six of them participated by conducting seminars or parts of seminars.

In the first quarter, we studied the relation of the indigenous peoples and Hispanic society. The course drew on a wide variety of texts including Indian oral literature, the works of the conquistadores, travel accounts, contemporary narrative, and poetry in order to isolate the problem of conflicting cultures with different and often opposing value systems. Topics such as the development of the Caliban and 'noble savage' stereotypes were discussed. We used film and slide material as well as printed texts.

In the second quarter, the topic was cultural nationalism. This part of the course concentrated on nineteenth- and twentieth-century essay, narrative, journalism, drama, and poetry. The course traced the Romantic origins of the notion of the Volksgeist, and the problems discussed included that of the supposed 'originality' of American experience, the idea of landscape as a determinant of national character, psychoanalysis and the national character, and the historical novel as a mode of exploring national reality.

The third quarter topic was literature and revolution from 1959 to 1973. The course dealt with the mood of disillusionment with the Mexican Revolution which gathered momentum in the 1960's, the Cuban Revolution and the development of its policy toward art, the guerrilla movement and the notion of praxis, the nature of revolution when applied to the literary text, reflectionist theories of literature, semiotic theories, and the notion of art as unalienated activity.

I found it useful to begin with traditional literary criticism familiar to students and to move on to the problem of relating ideology to different kinds of text. The use of a great variety of texts--not only novels and poems but also essays, speeches, oral literature, and travel accounts--made a more eclectic approach necessary, and material from semiotics and sociology of literature was also useful. While not entirely satisfied with the theoretical framework, I believe this can be improved when the courses are repeated.

The best testimonials to the program have been the interest of the Chicano students, who formed a good proportion of the undergraduates taking the course, the evidence of continued student interest (three applied for and obtained grants to study in Latin America during the summer), and the stimulus that was given to graduate students to expand their area of interest. Graduate students who took the course came from the following disciplines: Spanish and Portuguese, French, economics, anthropology, linguistics, and comparative literature; students of literature were encouraged to question and discuss the relationships between literature and history, linguistics, and social structures, while students from non-literary disciplines were encouraged to see literature as a mode of cognition offering valuable insights relevant to their own discipline.

I intend to offer the course again in 1976-77. The problems covered will relate specifically to connections between oral performance and writing. Because there is considerable graduate student interest in oral history, natural narrative, and oral performance, I would like to draw on the active participation of graduate students in linguistics, history, and anthropology in linking the study of the oral and the written with problems of popular and elite literature.

LANGUAGE, ETHNICITY, AND SOCIETY (1265)

Lawrence Biondi
Department of Modern Languages, Loyola University

Chicago is a cosmopolitan city in the truest sense of the word, made up of a large number of ethnic communities--ethnic in both the language used and the culture manifested by its members. Multi-ethnic communities are found throughout Chicago and some of the suburbs. Such ethnic neighborhoods have traditionally attracted immigrant families to establish residency in a particular geographical area where their language is spoken and their culture is understood, accepted, and appreciated.

Loyola University is a large metropolitan university. Many of its students are second- and third-generation children who reside in various ethnic neighborhoods. Since Loyola is situated in a multi-ethnic city and the United States is celebrating its bicentennial, the course Language, Ethnicity, and Society was created to offer students the opportunity to develop greater awareness and appreciation of the large numbers of ethnic communities in the Chicago area. One means of understanding the complex nature of an ethnic community is to grasp the intrarelationships of: (1) the language(s) used (English and/or a foreign language); (2) the ethnicity manifested in the particular neighborhood by the foreign language and culture; and (3) the society--how the members of a particular ethnic community function within a large American city in accepting or rejecting American values and beliefs.

There were no major obstacles in receiving permanent approval for this course from the Academic Council; the course's purposes, goals, and orientation were found justifiable. There is no special funding for the course.

To date the course has been offered only once, in fall 1974; twenty-three students enrolled. It differs from other courses offered in the Modern Languages Department in that there are two distinct major components: a theoretical component and a practical one. An understanding of the functions of language within a society in general and within various ethnic communities in particular was one major goal of the course. This goal was reached principally through selected readings, class lectures, and discussions. On the practical level, each student had to be involved in an ethnic community of his own choosing and do fieldwork in an ethnic community as the basis of an ethnography of the community under study. The ethnography had to deal with linguistic, cultural, and social aspects of the group's ethnicity. Toward the end of the course, each student presented a twenty-minute oral report on the community and prepared a written ethnography for submission to the instructor. There were two major examinations, a mid-term and a final.

The course was publicized principally through the university catalog. In addition, flyers were distributed throughout the university, especially to students in sociology, political science, English, urban ethnic studies, history, education, and psychology. The catalog has cross-listed the course in the Sociology, Urban Ethnic Studies, and Education Departments.

There have been no administrative problems arising from this newly-created course. I teach the course as part of my normal teaching load; since I am the only trained sociolinguist in the department, I doubt if the course would be continued if I were not available. The course can be taken for credit toward a departmental major in the departments under which it is cross-listed. Undergraduates made up the major portion of the enrollment, though the course is also open to graduate students for graduate credit.

The course has given the department a slightly better image in that this and several other sociolinguistic courses are giving students a better opportunity to broaden their language/linguistic backgrounds. Our department is becoming more known by other departments as a department 'on-the-move' and not afraid to make changes. Students were pleased with the course. The only frequent criticism was that too much detailed knowledge of the reading selections was expected. In general, I was very pleased with the course, the students' performance, and what they appeared to gain from the course.

Themes and Concepts

ITALIAN FOLKLORE (1277)

Juliana D'Amato
Department of Italian, Albertus Magnus College

The reappraisal of ethnic traditions and the high concentration of Italians in our area made me aware of the need for a course in Italian folklore. Response to allusions to folkloric content in beginning Italian and literature classes convinced me that students were fascinated by the material. I discussed various possible approaches to the subject with colleagues from many departments and decided to offer a course for the students of Italian in Italian. The faculty has been unanimously favorable and actively helpful in providing names of scholars in other colleges and universities who might be of help. The Sociology, Music, and Art Departments have been particularly helpful, and the Drama Department has offered its services.

A great deal of difficulty arose in obtaining books, all of which must come from Italy. As a consequence, the original syllabus had to be revised and parts had to be eliminated. This necessity had positive results because it forced me to proceed at a slower pace and gain in depth what was lost in breadth. As we proceeded, the material proved to be more than adequate. Basic required texts are Invito al folklore italiano (Roma: Studium, 1963), Il Folklore (Roma: Studium, 1969), and Guida allo studio delle tradizioni popolari (Torino: Boringhieri, 1971). A lengthy list of supplementary texts placed on library reserve is also provided.

There is no doubt Italian Folklore has achieved its educational goals. It has made students aware of the roots of Italian culture, increased appreciation of an ancient civilization, and developed a willingness to investigate the 'why' rather than be satisfied with the 'what' of unfamiliar facts. I believe the course guarantees optimum learning, because the student is totally involved in its development. The student is expected to make choices of preference in the material to be considered, touch every phase of life, and constantly appraise, evaluate, compare, decide, and judge. The material embraces not only the past but the present. The student arrives at the understanding that folklore and traditions are evolving constantly and are an active part of contemporary civilization.

The course carries credit toward a departmental major. Faculty, administration, and students have enthusiastically endorsed the course. Although one student found the course too demanding to complete, the rest were very happy and their enthusiasm attracted much attention. The enrollment in upper-division courses has doubled, and at present the class of 1977 has five declared majors. Many factors account for this, of course, and it would be impossible to say exactly what part the new course has played.

PHILOSOPHY IN FRENCH LITERATURE (1278)

Blair Hanson
Department of Modern Languages, Allegheny College

Philosophy in French Literature is an interdisciplinary course carrying three semester hours credit. It has been taught once a year during each of the past three academic years within the framework of a single department. It is one of several courses in foreign literatures given in English, which were proposed by the Department of Modern Languages and approved by faculty vote during the academic year 1971-72, following the dropping of the foreign language requirement for graduation. There was no predetermined evidence of need for these courses; they represented an attempt to utilize faculty time due to the loss of the foreign language requirement. Nor was there any evidence of potential student interest--on the contrary, only a hope that these courses could attract students to our area of the campus. The class each year has included students from almost every department in the college, and Philosophy in French Literature is accepted by the Philosophy Department toward a major in philosophy. It does not count toward a major in French, since it is given in English and most students do their reading from English translations.

Students enrolled in the course have repeatedly volunteered comments about its excellence. Several said it made them want to learn French, but time will tell whether they actually enroll in foreign language courses.

Philosophy in French Literature is an elementary or introductory level course open to anyone who is interested, with no prerequisites. It is intended to be a rigorous experience even though approached from a beginner's point of view. The lengthy reading list, examinations, papers (two short or one long), and class discussions require a great deal of work, especially when one realizes that they are concentrated into twenty-eight classes of seventy minutes each. The students, usually a mixture of freshmen and sophomores with a few juniors and seniors, do not seem to mind the work as long as the ideas are challenging.

The course appears to have been successful in drawing students by word of mouth. There has been no planned publicity other than announcement in the college catalogue. The instructor has reason to believe that it achieves its goals of bringing together areas of philosophy and French literature of which students are not usually aware and helping students realize the relationships that exist between philosophy and literature in general.

The reading list may change occasionally, but the format for the course will remain essentially the same. The course introduces the student to several French and non-French philosophers, investigates the relationship between them and the writings of some French littérateurs, and encourages critical reading. The instructor gives sixteen lectures on movements, philosophers, and writers, including: Humanism--Montaigne; Classicism--Descartes, Corneille, Jansenism, Pascal, Racine, and F. Mauriac; Enlighten-ment--Montesquieu, Leibnitz, Pope, Voltaire, Diderot, J-J. Rousseau; Existentialism--Gide, Bergson, Proust, Malraux, Saint-Exupéry, Sartre, and Camus, with a guest lecturer from the German staff giving a talk on Nietzsche prior to the one on Gide. For the ten class discussions, students read five of Montaigne's essays, Descartes' Discourse on Method, Corneille's Le Cid, selections from Pascal's Thoughts, Racine's Phaedra, F. Mauriac's Vipers' Tangle, one of Montesquieu's Persian Letters, Diderot's Jacques the Fatalist or Voltaire's Candide, one of J-J. Rousseau's discourses or extracts from one of his major books, Gide's The Immoralist, Proust's Swann's Way, Sartre's "The Wall," No Exit, and The Flies, and Camus' Caligula and The Misunderstanding. They also read one of five novels (Saint-Exupéry's Night Flight or Wind, Sand, and Stars, Malraux' Man's Fate, Sartre's Nausea, or Camus' The Plague) for an individual oral discussion with the professor. They write two short papers of five to seven pages each or one long paper and take a mid-term and a final examination. Optional readings are encouraged in Nietzsche, Bergson, and Sartre.

I warn the students about not always trying to see a cause and effect relationship between a philosophy and a work of literature and explain that similarities sometimes exist largely because of 'the times.' I tell them about the problems of reading an author in translation and the dangers of over-simplification in this rapid, overall view of such a tremendous field. I try to convey an idea of the extent to which philosophy can be literature, and to which literature can be used as a medium for expressing philosophy. And, of course, I point out the general French skepticism about philosophical 'systems' on the whole and the extent to which many French philosophers and men of literature carry on the long French tradition of being moralists.

MYTH IN PRACTICE AND THEORY (1282)

Mabel Lang
Department of Greek, Bryn Mawr College

Myth in Practice and Theory was developed an an alternate to Greek Literature in Translation in 1972, when there was much student interest in the content of Greek literature but less in the form. The development of the course came about as a consequence of a previous senior conference in which students and instructor explored the ramifications and cross-cultural connections of several Greek myths. Since at that time mythology was a subject of great interest and Greek mythology the most familiar and easiest route into the subject as a whole, the proposal for the course met with enthusiastic approval both among students and in the Committee on Curriculum. There was no special funding, nor was the course publicized in any fashion other than the regular announcement of new courses.

The original format of the course was as follows, with some variations and expansions in its second and third years: about 100-150 pages of reading a week, including both myths of various cultures on a particular theme and presentations of various theories of myth-- religious, philosophical, anthropological, psychological, sociological, structural; every third or fourth week an assigned short paper on a particular theme or interpretation; two class meetings a week devoted two-thirds to lecture and one-third to discussion; a third hour for which the class was divided into groups of seven to ten for either further exploration and interpretation of the assigned reading or critical discussion of the individual student papers.

There have been no administrative problems, but we have encountered some difficulty in finding paperback editions of appropriate myth collections and consequently have been overly dependent on reserved books. The instructor taught an overload because of the tripled third hour, but it is unlikely that the course would have the same unity and impact if divided between or among instructors, since each would necessarily have different approaches and emphases.

Students said the course was eye-opening and thought-provoking; it not only required hard work in reading, thinking, and writing, but proved to be more rigorous and more rewarding from the students' point of view than the more orthodox Greek Literature in Translation. Because its approach is neither literary nor linguistic, it is not credited toward a departmental major. It attracts students from a wide variety of disciplines, some of whom consider taking up the study of either the Greek language or its literature.

After the first and second offerings, students were asked if the course should be repeated and how they would like to see it changed. The response was largely affirmative and accompanied by suggestions either for widening or narrowing the scope--both of which were attempted in different ways.

CLASSICAL MYTHOLOGY (1323)

Mary R. Lefkowitz
Departments of Greek and Latin, Wellesley College

Classical Mythology was designed as an antidote to the more traditional mythology course we used to offer, in which emphasis was on routine memorization and restatement of the influential old stories. Now, students still read the myths, but not in a textbook like Gayley or Hamilton, where the editor has removed annoying contradictions; instead, all readings are in ancient sources, often presenting two or three authors' versions of the same myth. Students are asked to be sensitive to each author's emphasis and to try to account for changes in plot and detail. At the same time, the sequence of readings helps explore and describe the fundamental patterns underlying myths with different names and geography.

We begin slowly, considering first what various interpretative methodologies can tell us about the basic plot of familiar myths, using as texts Apollodorus' account of the houses of Laius and Atreus. We spend the next six weeks of a thirteen-week semester analyzing myths about creation, gods, and goddesses, using as sources principally Hesiod's Theogony, selected Homeric Hymns, Ovid's Metamorphoses, and Euripides' Bacchae.

Of particular interest to all students is the two- to three-week period we spend on the representation of the female experience in myth and the sociological background that produced it, perhaps because students are directly affected by the knowledge that ancient definitions of the significant events in a woman's life survive intact in much of our literature and in many of our customs. For many, this section of the course demonstrates more effectively than conventional observations the persistence of a traditional literary theme or artistic style and why it is important to know what happened in fifth-century Athens.

The rest of the semester concerns heroes (and one heroine); readings, now more extensive, include the Odyssey, Apollonius of Rhodes, the Aeneid, Apuleius' Golden Ass, and Lucian's Lucius and True History. Class time is devoted to discussion of the reading; students are asked to bring texts to class so that we can study certain passages in detail. There is no formal lecture or recitation: I will ask questions about what we have read and students volunteer answers; they are encouraged to ask at any point for background information and to suggest new lines of interpretation.

Three short papers ask the student to apply the problem-solving skills derived from the course reading to material not considered in class, to explain a new ritual, or to write or rewrite a myth that illustrates a particular experience to a particular audience, e.g., "You are a guide at the temple of Dionysus in Patras; explain to a group of Christian tourists why you are carrying your god in a chest down to the river;" or "You are a Christian priest in the third century A.D.; in order to keep your converts' allegiance in a troubled time, tell a story of a Christian saint who can do for man what Zeus or Apollo could do." Playing a role encourages the student to base 'speech' as much as possible on ancient sources and to use some imagination in the process. Supplementary readings in the histories of Greek religion, anthropology, and theories help students develop factual and theoretical background.

Working with more than one textbook creates some practical problems. Occasionally a required text does not arrive at the bookstore on time, and we have to use an inferior translation, rearrange readings at the last minute, or photocopy frantically. Sometimes the class proceeds more quickly or more slowly than the announced assignment. Students must ask or find out for themselves the background information that is not supplied in the translations or by the instructor. These last difficulties, however, appear to have pedagogical value: students realize that what they learn depends on themselves as much as on the instructor. But the greatest educational advantage of the approach is that it establishes immediately that there is no single correct interpretation. Confronting this reality is often painful. But, unless one understands the existence of multiplicity and learns to rank values, one cannot begin to think successfully in abstract terms or to do the kind of critical thinking of which our graduates should be capable. It might also be objected that limiting the course to readings in ancient texts restricts inquiry into modern applications. However, students in other disciplines are urged to discuss in class how our reading applies to what they've been doing in other courses or to what they have been reading outside the Classics.

Student response to this unconventional and demanding course has been enthusiastic. Most students find the course to have far more practical value than they had imagined. They come thinking that it will help them identify events and characters in pre-twentieth-century art and literature or in Freudian psychology. They leave realizing that the narrative patterns of the ancient myths still provide the basic syntax for the plots of contemporary novels and stories, and in many cases determine what we perceive to be the meaningful events and sequences in our own lives. Many continue to use information and techniques acquired in Classical Mythology in work in anthropology, psychology, and non-Classical literature. A few begin Greek or return to Latin because they like what they have been reading. Classics majors find the course helpful for cultural background and review.

Enrollment has risen from an average of thirty in the 1950's to an average of ninety in the last eight years, an encouragingly large number for an optional course in a college of 1,800 students. Since the enrollment helps balance smaller courses in Greek and Latin literature, we have not wanted to limit the class size. But the large numbers place special burdens on both students and instructor that cannot be alleviated with the present budget arrangements.

Grading assistance is available only for twenty or thirty students; the grader, to be fair and informed, must attend classes regularly, since there is no single textbook and emphasis changes from year to year. It is impossible to learn everyone's name and to give the kind of individual attention we ordinarily provide in classes of thirty or under. We urge students to work on papers in teams, so they can teach each other and reduce the number of papers we need to grade. Good students thrive even under these conditions and perhaps because of them; others, after some initial uncertainty, develop the skills and confidence to work on their own. But, ten to fifteen percent perform at minimal or unsatisfactory levels. The find the course 'confusing,' the paper assignments and grading 'unfair.' Undoubtedly some of these students are not reachable, and their attitudes have little or nothing to do with this class. Others we might have been able to encourage if we had time to work with them individually and to assign shorter, more frequent papers.

I have, and I try to convey that I have, the feeling that I am learning with and from my students. Each class can bring new insights to every text. I am delighted when one of us discovers in some contemporary work or ritual an affinity to what we have seen in ancient myth. Certainly it is gratifying to be able to help other people take pleasure in the literature which I have chosen to spend my life studying. But I think the excitement students and I seem to get from the course derives in part from the way they have been encouraged to approach the material--to learn by discovery and application, realizing that throughout their lives they can continue to use what they have learned in the course.

Miscellaneous (See also ms. 1348)

THE GERMAN-SPEAKING WORLD TODAY: MODERN TOPICS (1339)

Alan Galt
Department of Germanic Languages and Literatures, University of Cincinnati

The German-Speaking World Today extends over three quarters, with classes meeting three times weekly. It was designed as an essential element in two special programs of the German Department: the undergraduate major in German Area Studies and the International Business Option. (The former is an alternative to the traditional major in German language and literature, and the latter is an interdisciplinary program which permits students to graduate either with a degree in Business Administration and a certificate of competence in German, or vice versa.) In practice, the course has also appealed to German majors in the traditional program, as well as to a number of students from other disciplines. In the 1974-75 academic year, three such non-majors, all from the natural sciences, completed the course. (Two were second-generation German-Americans, and the third had traveled extensively with her German-speaking Hungarian fiancé, accompanying him on visits to his relatives in Austria.)

Because the class has not yet grown to full size--the maximum was nine participants in winter quarter 1975--it has been possible to develop a disciplined informality and spirit of cooperation and co-determination. Within a framework provided by the instructor, the students agree upon topics which are to be the subjects of mutual study and group discussion. In addition, the last two weeks of each quarter are left free for reports and discussion of topics of individual interest.

Under this system, long-range planning is not always possible, and occasionally the instructor is challenged by the need to discover and develop materials in a short time. In accordance with the interests of the students and the instructor's developing areas of competence, the following topics were treated in 1974-75: in the first quarter, a thorough survey of the physical, political, and 'tourist' geography of all four German-speaking countries; in the second quarter, legal systems and constitutional provisions, comparison of governmental structures, present-day domestic and foreign policy, political parties, and brief treatment of topics of individual interest, such as Swiss yodelling and West German medical insurance plans; in the third quarter, concentration on West Germany--major industries and industrial firms, professions and trades, the economy, educational reform, manner and style of life, social customs, folk traditions and festivals, the German's self-image and the foreigner's image of the German, and topics of individual interest.

These courses may be taken by anyone who has fulfilled the basic language requirement--a one-year five-hour course or a two-year three-hour course. Within the limitations of the students' modest proficiency in the language, we attempt to use German as much as possible. This has meant, in practice, that the instructor's lectures have been about ninety percent in German, and the student reports and group discussions about fifty percent.

The sequence is part of the regular curriculum of the German Department and is included in the normal course load of the instructor. It has always had the enthusiastic support and commitment of the departmental faculty; provision would be made for it even if the present instructor were not available. The only apparent threat is due to the generally low enrollment of all advanced German courses; to counter this trend, the department has instituted a vigorous program of advertising and recruitment in its basic language courses. Enrollment is strengthened by the fact that the course is not only accepted, but actively recommended for German majors. (Almost no courses are specifically required.)

The selection of texts and materials is not easy. Two reasons preclude the use of any single textbook: the instructor's desire to present aspects of all four German-speaking countries fairly, and the need to maintain the flexibility to accommodate student interests. Fortunately, the department began to develop a collection of books, brochures, and public documents several years ago. Most assigned reading has been selected from these sources, which are lent to the students. To cover the need for class reading assignments, photocopies are used; in lieu of purchasing textbooks, each student contributes $5 each quarter to the 'Copy Fund.' At the end of the quarter a refund or additional assessment adjusts the balance.

The instructor, trained in German literature and the methodology of language teaching, is working to develop new areas of competence and has learned much which will improve the next offering of the course, although no fundamental changes are foreseen. Students have been strongly positive in their opinions of the course, as expressed in casual remarks as well as formal surveys.

A SUMMARY OF CURRICULAR INNOVATIONS (1110, 1128, 1224, 1225)

Juana A. Hernández
Department of Modern and Classical Languages, Hood College

In fall 1973, the Department of Modern and Classical Languages revised its curriculum in an attempt to bridge the gap between humanistic and practical aspects of contemporary language study. The traditional humanistic objective of foreign language study as a way of acquiring a new perspective on oneself and one's own society was widened and enriched by the new curriculum.

In determining current needs, we requested suggestions from recently-graduated majors, met with junior and senior majors, and sought advice from retired members of the department as well as from members of other departments and colleagues at other institutions. We established two main goals: to offer the student body a useful learning tool and exposure to a foreign way of life and thought, and to offer advanced courses for those interested in specializing in the field of foreign languages.

We decided to strengthen course offerings related to the former by introducing additional civilization and cross-cultural courses (France Today and Latin America Today were already in the curriculum). This established a two-year sequence of civilization courses at an intermediate linguistic level. The new courses are:

(1) The French Press: reading and discussion of French periodicals and newspapers; articles in various fields of cultural, economic, political, and scientific interest. (3 credits)

(2) Women in France: roles and images of women in French society and literature. (3 credits)

(3) French Outside France: the concept of Francophony; readings from one or several areas of concentration, e.g., Canada, Haiti, the Caribbean, Asia Minor, Africa; and the concept of négritude. (3 credits)

(4) Women in the Hispanic World: the roles and images of women in Hispanic society and literature. (3 credits)

(5) Chicanos, Puerto Ricans, and Other Spanish-Speaking Americans: historical and cultural background; economic, social, and linguistic problems of Hispanic groups in the United States. (3 credits)

(6) The Hispanic Press: reading and discussion of Spanish periodicals and newspapers published in Spain, Latin America, and the United States; articles in various fields of historical, economic, political, and scientific interest. (3 credits)

These new cross-cultural courses can be taken for credit toward the major, since we recognize the need to prepare students in these areas. These innovations, as well as others geared to more advanced students, have resulted in an enrollment increase of sixty-five percent over spring 1974, greatly improving department morale and our campus image.

The cross-cultural courses were also an attempt to attract non-language majors to the department, offering them courses more relevant to their particular areas of interest (sociology, psychology, history, etc.). For language majors, the department now provides a well-balanced curriculum leading to a career in teaching, preparation for graduate studies and for entry into industry and commerce, and an introduction to translation and interpretation as a career.

NON-TRADITIONAL

Approach
(See also mss. 486, 693, 1158, 1159, 1185/1186, 1191, 1192)

COMMUNICATION WITH THE FRENCH (1348)

Laurence Wylie
Department of Romance Languages and Literatures, Harvard University

I proposed to offer a new course--Communication with the French--in the French Department for spring term 1975. This experimental course would be open to about fifteen students who had had the equivalent of one semester's study of French. The goal was to expand the concept of language teaching to the level of communication, combining the intellectual study of communication and culture with specific analysis and practice in role acting.

I began academic life as a French language teacher, the first step in what has turned out to be a lifelong preoccupation with the problem of understanding and communicating with the French people. To further this understanding, I have been involved in various disciplines, including anthropology, in which I recently taught the course Cultural Differences in Body Concept, Body Movement, and Nonverbal Communication. I wanted to apply the principles and knowledge I had acquired to the teaching of French, to return to my point of departure using knowledge and experience gained through these interdisciplinary forays.

Undoubtedly, the most depressed area in universities today is that of language study. The basic problem is, and always has been, a simplistic and therefore unrealistic concept of language teaching. Language learning has been assumed to consist of learning to exchange combinations of sounds and words and sentences. Other channels of communication have been either ignored or thought to be minor supporting factors, with no concern for what Sapir decades ago called "that elaborate and secret code that is written nowhere, known by none, and understood by all." In the last few years students of nonverbal communication (alas, I know no better expression for this concept) have 'proven' what everyone has always 'known:' verbal communication is only a part, often only a minor part, of the process of communication. Inevitably then, language courses focused uniquely on verbal channels were rejected by most college students as ineffective and irrelevant.

In Kinesics and Context, Birdwhistell writes:

There is good reason why Johnny has so much trouble learning to write. Writing must derive and abstract both spoken and body motion activity. If Johnny is taught that he is dealing only with lexically bound speech material, he has to deny reality to be literate. The multimodal universe of television may teach this, and he may very well revolt against the teacher who overbelieves in words. If our formulations are correct, the grammarian must turn to body motion for data to make sense out of a number of areas now hidden in the parts of speech (pp. 162-63).

In bringing to bear in the development of this course the knowledge and experience I have acquired in the fields of language, civilization, anthropology, visual studies, and nonverbal communication, the course work would involve three approaches: (1) analysis of communication, (2) study of communication in its cultural and social context, and (3) role-playing to reenact communication episodes. The focus of study would be on short series of French and of French/non-French interactions recorded in sound and film.

111

It is well-known that much essential and powerful communication is subliminal; it can be observed only by slowing it down, stopping it altogether, and examining it repeatedly, so that its nuances and progressions can be perceived. This cannot be done with standard movie projectors which normally turn at fixed speeds. In recent years, scholars working in the field of nonverbal communication discovered a way to adapt equipment to their purpose in fitting a certain obsolete model of a 16mm Bell and Howell projector with a hand crank and blower. The modifications enable one to study film at any speed and, thus, observe a social interaction repeatedly frame by frame, even stopping it for analysis of a single frame, if necessary, then playing the units over and over again a whole short sequence reveals its meaning. It is through such analysis that important discoveries have been made recently regarding the nature and relationship of different channels of communication.

It appears that there are four closely interlocked channels corresponding to four principal factors: sound, motion, space, and time. Thus, what one seeks to observe in a communicational episode is the nature and relationship of verbal expression, body movement, spatial position, and rhythm.

Little need be said here of the first channel, since it has traditionally been the center of interest in language study. However, certain aspects usually ignored must be emphasized, e.g., all oral utterances, not only 'meaningful' words, must be considered elements of communication; sound must be related to the absence of sound, for silence is in itself a crucial element of communication; voice quality and intonation must receive much more attention. Above all, verbal expression must be related closely and at every point to the other communicational channels.

The importance of body movement is scarcely a novel concept. It has, however, been curiously ignored in favor of more 'intellectual' factors. Except for a vague nod in the direction of formal gestures, that is, those conventional gestures that replace or emphasize verbal expressions (la barbe and le bras d'honneur, for example), the study of body movement has been restricted chiefly to the dance, the theater, and therapy. What we needed to concentrate on in this course is that unconscious movement which is the key to Sapir's secret code. Relatively little is known about this area, so research must go along with teaching. We must understand: (1) how respiration affects meaning; (2) cultural differences and implications of posture and muscle tension; (3) how different parts of the body are involved, and how together they form a message. Usually we confine our conscious attention to facial expression, but the whole body often tells us more. We must try to understand the mysteries of the power of gaze, and how it is utilized differently in different cultures. Hall and his students have demonstrated how much can be learned about cultures by the analysis of walking, i.e., la demarche. The point in space at which a motion is made may have important implications. A pointing finger implies quite different messages if it points at waist level, eye level, or above the head! Movement must be qualified as to direction, amplitude, speed, effort, and what Laban has called 'flow,' that is, its bound or free quality. (Probably the greatest danger in studying this channel is getting lost in details. Birdwhistell ventures that there are 20,000 possible facial expressions!)

The third channel involves the spatial relationships of bodies to each other and to surrounding objects, the study of what Edward Hall has called proxemics. This is an area in which cultural differences cause a great deal of misunderstanding, for each culture, indeed each subculture, has its tacit rules governing the appropriate distances at which individuals communicate in different circumstances. Generally speaking, the personal space 'possessed' by an individual is deeper in the United States than in France, and variations in the use of this space have meaning. The comparative study of French and American proxemics has not been undertaken. It is undoubtedly related to differences in the sense of body boundary. Fisher has shown that individuals differ considerably in their sense of vulnerability of the physical boundary of their self, and this sense has important repercussions on their behavior. Guiora relates this concept to an individual's ability to accept different communicational codes. From the generalizations based on this research, I infer that there are also important cultural differences between French and Americans in this regard. The sense of body boundary must be related to the role of touch in communicational interaction, for there are well-recognized cultural and situational differences in the unwritten rules governing touching. Through the analysis of all these aspects of body movement recorded on film, we can try to make the unwritten rules explicit.

112

The fourth channel of communication, the least known but the most important, is that of rhythm, undoubtedly the real key to Sapir's secret code. Recent research has shown that effective communication between two individuals depends on their success in establishing unconsciously a synchronous coordination between speech and body movement in the appropriate space. This synchrony is learned very early in life, perhaps in the womb. (William Condon has recently observed that at the age of twenty minutes a normal baby already moves synchronously with the rhythm of speech of people nearby!) These basic rhythms differ notably from culture to culture, and it is usually this difference that causes fundamental discomfort in intercultural communication. Fred Erickson's research has demonstrated the crucial differences in body movement rhythms among people of different subcultures, especially black and white, in the United States. I feel certain that the contrasting rhythms of French and English verbal expression represent a more basic difference in rhythm, but this area must be explored.

The first half of a two- or three-week period was devoted to the analysis of an interactional episode on a film clip. At the same time, the students were expected to become aware of the social and cultural context of the episode. This implied a kind of explication de texte based on anthropological concepts and methods used in my general education on French civilization.

The second half of the period devoted to an episode was quite different. It was the reenactment of the communicational situation. At this point, the course became a sort of acting course in which the students tried to utilize what they had observed and understood in order to play the roles of the individuals involved in the episode. I have always thought that language learning was really play-acting, but the exercise is more effective in this instance because of the deeper understanding the students will have acquired of the whole communication. The use of mechanical devices also helped us gain time and effectiveness. Here I turned to the use of videotape. The learning process was speeded enormously by instant playback, so that students could immediately see their mistakes. I found that mutual criticism of students by themselves was an effective means of progress, but with the visual evidence of videotape the learning process could be made even more effective.

Making and using films and using video equipment can be expensive, and I secured a grant from the Northeast Fund in order to purchase and rent equipment and make and process materials to be used in the class. Normal commercial and teaching films are no good for such a course, because they are concerned with art and beauty or because they focus on verbal expression and do not provide long sequences showing the whole body. One has to make and accumulate one's own materials.

The administration was very enthusiastic at the prospect of a course that might bring life to language teaching; departmental colleagues were bewildered but permissive; student response was excellent. With only word-of-mouth publicity, fifty students wished to enroll in the course; I could select only twelve. The course is accepted for credit toward a departmental major in either Romance Languages or Anthropology; other departments are indifferent. The course has gained a considerable reputation. The four teaching fellows in French who attended the course claim it has changed the ways they do and will teach. Student satisfaction was very high; the varied skills acquired were quite different from others they had learned.

Throughout the course, the class and I talked a great deal about goals and methods and achievement. We agreed that it was an exciting learning experience for us all, but that the problem was infinitely tougher than I had assumed. I was asking them (1) to become conscious of the tension and rhythm in their own communication in English-- phenomena they were not even aware of before, (2) to perceive and analyze parallel phenomena in French communication, and (3) to imitate this behavior until it became natural to them. All of this in one semester! (It takes a psychoanalyst months and years to help an individual become aware of unconscious behavior.) Nonetheless, I think I am right in believing that in order to 'speak French like a Frenchman' one must behave like a Frenchman in body tension, movement, and rhythm.

This raises another question in language teaching. How much can we expect of our students? Most of us have not achieved the perfection that was the goal of my course. At what point shall we declare ourselves satisfied with the achievements of our students?

Success depended a great deal upon body expression, which is related to role-playing, to acting ability. This ability varies enormously among people. There were four black girls in the class who understood the problem best, because to have succeeded in a white world (to have gained admission to Radcliffe), they had to be able to communicate effectively with whites. They were bilingual, or rather, bicorporal, in their communication. One day they put on a demonstration for us, first talking together as blacks as though we did not exist and then talking as part of our group.

A French woman also came to the course regularly. We learned a great deal by trying to teach her to speak English like an American. She was no more successful than the rest of us, but at least she is now aware of the problem. One of the French teaching fellows said after assuming French tension and rhythm for about five minutes: "I can't stand it any longer. I'm tired and I feel suffocated." For a term project, three of the students made a videotape demonstrating exercises to make one's body more French. The fundamental exercise has to do with holding the pelvis level. I doubt that many French teachers can be persuaded that this is a proper and necessary exercise in French classes!

In a word, what do we mean by 'teaching French?'

DECU AND TUCO: A TUTORIAL APPROACH TO COMPUTER ASSISTED INSTRUCTION (1356)

Charles W. Hoffman
Department of German, The Ohio State University

The Department of German has integrated Computer Assisted Instruction (CAI) into its two basic language courses, German 101 and 102. DECU (Deutscher Computer Unterricht), consisting of forty-two sections, is the CAI program for German 101; TUCO (Tutorial Computer), with twenty-four sections, is its counterpart for 102. The program was developed by Susan Severance, research assistant and coder, and me over a period of three years. It was tested in a single class and became fully operational in 1974. Since then it has been offered to every student in the two basic language courses on a voluntary basis and without charge. Between twenty-five and forty percent of all students enrolled in German 101 and 102 take advantage of the computer's assistance.

DECU and TUCO make use of the IBM Coursewriter III/version 3 computer language and of the university's IBM 370/model 158 computer. Students registered for the program do their CAI work at any of the sixty-five terminals in twenty-three locations on the campus; access to terminals is from 8 a.m. until 11 p.m. on weekdays and until noon on Saturdays.

The goal of the two programs is to provide individualized and highly controlled instruction in German grammar to supplement the first-year course. DECU and TUCO make use of the principles and practices of the tutorial method; they enhance and fortify a program of well-balanced language instruction. Neither is intended as an autonomous teaching device, divorced from the teacher and the classroom. Rather, they are meant to be additional educational tools which will not duplicate instruction that can be performed better and cheaper by teacher, textbook, or language laboratory. Students enrolled in a beginning German course can use DECU and TUCO as they would an individual tutor. This is possible because the computer is able to store large numbers of hints and quantities of information which relate to the difficulties and mistakes most likely experienced by a student learning German. Like any good tutor, the programs anticipate the student's problem and give the kind of advice which can help overcome particular learning difficulties. As the word 'tutorial' implies, there should be a close working relationship on a one-to-one basis between instructor and student. Such tutoring takes place in DECO and TUCO, where all feedback is geared to the student's individual response.

The CAI programs also eliminate unchecked errors that occur in classroom practice or homework assignments. To be made aware of mistakes and learn from them is a decisive factor in mastering a foreign language, but unfortunately the correction procedure in traditional instruction is often hit or miss. The student may, for a variety of reasons, never be sure of having the correct answers on a homework assignment, may not be listening when the instructor explains and corrects mistakes, and may not understand the explanation or take the time to ponder it--and teachers overlook mistakes made by their students. In DECU and TUCO mistakes cannot be overlooked; the student is guided by the computer toward the right answer, and at the same time grammatical patterns and correct structures are reinforced. A branching system permits acceleration or remedial work according to individual needs. CAI work can thus relieve the teacher of certain necessary but rote efforts, such as going over a grammar homework assignment. Classroom time is freed for other types of language instruction.

To monitor each student's progress, the instructor can receive a weekly synthesized account of the student's work (e.g., type of response, response time, areas of difficulty, etc.). This can help identify problems that need more attention in the classroom, though it should be admitted that our experience so far shows too few instructors making regular use of this opportunity. The student receives a printout at each CAI session and can analyze progress as often and for as long as desired. (This, by the way, is one of the advantages of the type-out computer system over the otherwise more convenient cathode ray tube.)

How did the German CAI program come about? The university has for some time been a leader in the general development of computer assisted instruction. At present there are sixty-five operational programs in sixteen different fields on the Columbus campus with eight more in various stages of development. Since DECU and TUCO were viewed from the start as only an adjunct to elementary language instruction, it would be an exaggeration to say that a pressing need gave them their impetus. Our elementary German program, based on a balanced four-skills approach and supplemented by good language laboratory facilities, could clearly stand on its own. But after examining the soundness of CAI and the possibilities it held for providing yet another tool for language learning, the German Department decided to take advantage of the opportunity the university's facilities and experience presented. The availability of computers and terminals, the assistance generously provided by the Computer Center staff, the encouragement of the College of Humanities, the competent help of a research assistant (a graduate student in German), and the willingness of a member of the staff to author the program were among the most important factors that brought DECU and TUCO into existence.

The two CAI programs in German were developed without outside funding. The Ohio State University, however--and especially the College of Humanities--furnished valuable support. Computer facilities were put at the disposal of the author, and he was able to visit several other universities to gain information about different CAI programs. For the first year and a half, no special remuneration for work on the project was available, but as it neared its completion, the College of Humanities appointed a full-time research assistant. Once it was understood that the German CAI program was to serve only as a voluntary adjunct to the existing instruction, there was general support for its development and introduction on the part of departmental faculty.

Communication about the use and goals of such a new device of educational technology is of course crucial if it is to be accepted by students and teachers. At various stages during the years of development and again when the program was completed, the German Department displayed, demonstrated, and explained DECU and TUCO, both locally on campus and nationally via presentations by the author at conventions. The department also keeps available a short information sheet describing the two programs ("DECU and TUCO: Computer Assisted Instruction in German Grammar"). This pamphlet, together with other pertinent material, is given to all instructors of German 101 and 102 prior to the beginning of a new quarter. Since many of them are graduate teaching associates, this material is also part of a special brochure prepared for all new GTAs ("A Guide for Teaching Associates"). Instructors are asked to inform their students at the first class meeting of the availability of DECU and TUCO, and those students interested in using the programs are invited to a special meeting at which the programs are further explained. If a student then decides to use CAI, registration with the Computer Center is arranged and work at the terminal can begin immediately.

The Department of German has conducted two small pilot studies to test the effectiveness of the CAI programs as a learning tool, to learn about the acceptance of DECU and TUCO by their users, and to 'debug' programming mistakes. Parallel sections of German 101 and 102 were set up, with the same instructor teaching both a CAI section and a non-CAI section. The class taught with the CAI adjunct met four times a week instead of the regular five sessions. For the purposes of comparing performance, identical tests were given to the students in both sections. At this point the results must still be considered inconclusive, for on one occasion the CAI users performed better than their non-CAI counterparts, while on another the situation was reversed. The German Department at the University of Cincinnati, which has used DECU, conducted a similar pilot study with a greater number of students (75), and in that study the CAI group performed considerably better than did students instructed solely in the classroom.

Although the pilot studies revealed interesting facts about the effectiveness in error reduction in certain segments of the two programs, they suffered from several handicaps which should be avoided in other such undertakings. First, the number of students participating was too small--fifteen or fewer in each section. Second, there was only random selection of students for the parallel sections. If results are to be meaningful, there should be an equal distribution of below-average, average, and above-average performers in each group. This would of course require pre-selection on the basis of high school records, the American College Test, the Scholastic Aptitude Test, or some similar criterion. Finally, the students who used CAI were not sufficiently supervised in their work with the program (time spent at the terminals, completion of program segments before the test, etc.). Lack of staff capacity, time, and money--as well as administrative obstacles beyond the control of the department--account for the shortcomings.

The debugging process was greatly helped by these pilot studies, however, and the positive acceptance of DECU and TUCO by its users was established beyond all doubt. The vast majority of students who had worked with both programs indicated strong approval of this method of individualized tutorial instruction. To the question "If you were now beginning German and had a choice between a section using CAI and one without it, which would you choose?" more than eighty percent of the students who had used CAI replied that they would again elect to study German with this additional help and would recommend it to others. Student comment was also collected concerning the DECU program on an attitude questionnaire at the University of Cincinnati. Some sample responses: "I enjoyed the give and take...;" "I was amazed at the computer's personality...;" "...it made me like German best of all my subjects...;" and "I was glad to see that the University of Cincinnati is using advanced techniques, especially in a language..."

Other German Departments having access to adequate computer facilities at their campuses have become interested in Ohio State's DECU and TUCO. The University of Cincinnati, South Dakota State University, and the University of Iowa have requested and received permission to use both programs for their beginning German courses.

The Department of German is pleased to have CAI instruction as an additional tool for its elementary language instruction. At the same time, we share the view of CAI authors and developers at other universities that this is a form of teaching which is still experimental and in what probably amounts to a primitive stage. No great claims should yet be made for CAI, and the advertisement of such programs is best kept low-key. We know that DECU and TUCO have confirmed the belief among students here that the German Department is greatly concerned with providing up-to-date and effective elementary language teaching. We know too that the students who have used the programs like them and find them helpful. But CAI has not improved the general student view of language learning, nor has it attracted masses of additional students into our sections of beginning German.

Perhaps the most valuable feature of CAI programs such as DECU and TUCO is their versatility. They can be used as a mechanism for review, perhaps even replacing one regular class session per week. (Such usage is bound to attract the attention of college administrations, since, while staff costs continually increase, the cost of computers and computer use is decreasing.) They can become an integral part of individualized instruction programs or a compulsory component of foreign language instruction, as is the case with the CAI program in the German Department at the University of Minnesota. They can function as highly controlled homework assignments or as testing devices. These are but a few of the possible uses.

The author of DECU and TUCO feels that the greatest potential, at least for these two

116

programs, lies in their use as a tool for remedial work. From the computer the student not only receives clues designed to lead to the correct answer of a particular grammatical point but is also given a better understanding of the problem itself. Then, too, work at the computer terminal requires the kind of attention and concentration which is an important factor in language learning. A number of our students who had not previously been using DECU or TUCO and who were failing or in danger of failing 101 and 102 were strongly urged to begin working with the computer and to review all segments of the CAI program already covered for their course. They were also asked to continue using CAI until the completion of the course. All but one of these students subsequently passed with grades of C or better.

A few thoughts which go beyond mere description are perhaps in order by way of conclusion. CAI programs like DECU and TUCO are not miracle devices, and it is both unjustified and unreasonable to hope for the salvation of language learning from them. As must be the case with any sophisticated new tool of educational technology, there are many mistakes still to be made and a great deal of learning yet to be done as we gain experience. There is a danger that technology may be allowed to dictate rather than simply assist the learning process. Nevertheless, we consider it established that CAI programs offer valuable self-instruction and an escape from rigid lock-step teaching. They make possible a controlled, individualized, and highly accurate means of learning German grammar which can be readily integrated with other aspects of language learning. We are convinced that both our educational goals and the needs of our students can be effectively served by the great potential of computer assisted instruction.

LANGUAGE AND SOCIETY (1359)

Winfred P. Lehmann
Department of Linguistics, University of Texas at Austin

With my project going well, buoyed in addition by Guggenheimisch euphoria, I decided in the middle of a year freed for research to plan a new course: Language and Society. Linguistics was beginning to creep out of its concentration on formulae supposedly "concerned primarily with an ideal speaker-listener, in a completely homogeneous speech-community" (Noam Chomsky, Aspects of the Theory of Syntax, Cambridge, Mass.: MIT Press, 1965, p. 3) and exalted under the label 'theory.' Sociolinguistics had made advances over predecessors of fifty years ago, attracting some attention in the process. Moreover, after almost twenty years of activity, the computer seemed capable of manipulating the patterns around which language was built. It seemed appropriate, then, to plan a course in which the mechanics of linguistics was taught by a computer, permitting the instructor to present the basic ideas of the field succinctly, even jovially, to the students.

In addition, the College of Education had requested an elementary course in sociolinguistics. Besides its capacity for teaching the "most intelligent and best prepared students ever to enter our universities," most in addition brought up on the new math, the computer might readily handle the hordes of aspiring teachers of English and of other languages who were finally to be taught something about language.

The course was constructed around three components designed to achieve these objectives. The computer component, as the most novel, will be described at greatest length. The lecture/discussions concerning the matters to be taught by the computer were constructed around topics such as Milne's "Why don't you spleak painly?" During the week dealing with syntactic rather than phonological analysis the Shakesperarian: "Find tongues in trees." The week for typological study was introduced under Woolcott Gibbs's "Backwards ran sentences till reeled the mind."

Social implications of language use were to be investigated largely by the students themselves in preparing a short term paper. A number of potential topics were handed out. Among those chosen most often were some which dealt with variety in language, such as "How the language used in telephone conversations differs from normal language," "Misleading advertising," and "How to say nothing and succeed in politics. (Substitute for politics: administration, advertising, journalism, the legal profession, literary criticism, science)."

Popular topics dealing with attitudes toward language were: "People who observe language taboos are dumb" and "Reasons for expanding your vocabulary and getting ahead in the world." The last, meant to provide leads for ironic treatment, was invariably taken seriously, a consequence that may not even be due to indoctrination by the Reader's Digest when one observes a Classics Department touting a course on improving word-power by scrutinizing the Greek and Roman elements in the English vocabulary.

A third set of topics dealt with mastery of more than one language, including "Why English is a funny language. (Substitute for English your native language if you first learned to speak Chinese, Turkish, Uzbek, Ibo, etc.)" and "None in the modern world can be considered educated unless hse has studied one or more foreign languages." (The pronoun in the last sentence, lifted from Buwing Yang Chao, How to Cook and Eat in Chinese, New York: John Day, 1945, p. xvi, never escaped remodeling, unless I typed the handouts. The impact of women's lib on language, like that of most social activities, resembles a bludgeon's rather than a rapier's.)

Support for entrance into an apparently ideal setting seemed readily forthcoming from a large grant awarded to the university for computer-based education—or so it seemed. The grantees, apparently swayed by the experience of a humanist with computers from the time that software seemed an outrageous neologism, and receptive to including a course outside the natural sciences in their string, provided a grant—though as usual less than that requested. Still, it was enough to persuade an experienced scholar, who had written a remarkable dissertation on teaching a non-Latin script by means of the computer, to abandon her leisure and undertake the difficult labor of preparing the proposed computer modules.

Since the course was new, it had to be approved by the department. What might seem like a routine or even welcome matter to anyone noting the growing interest of administrations in students was subjected to long delay and debate. The governance of the department had fallen into the hands of converts to the new linguistics, who believed that no one person could any longer be a general linguist; phonology, or even syntax, was a massive enough study to master. Anyone who vaunted himself on the possibility of giving a course in general linguistics, and in addition its implications for society, must have succumbed to dotage. After months of deliberation the course was finally authorized.

Thereupon, preparation of the modules was undertaken. In spite of the delays, time seemed adequate to produce an initial battery of six modules for teaching the elements of phonology, thereupon those necessary for syntax. The modules for conveying some of the findings of sociolinguistics might be completed in the fall, when the students were mastering the elements of phonology and syntax.

With much consultation, modules were produced, tested, and readied for the fall. In the meantime, the College of Education had retreated from its earlier decision; its masses of students were retained to fill the traditional education courses on the most advantageous number of windows in classrooms facing the north, or any other direction. Yet their change of mind turned out to be most welcome when the capabilities of the computer became clear. The terminals available were scarcely adequate for the thirty or so students who signed up for the course.

The space allotted for this report permits reference to only a few individuals of the relatively many intelligent and alert students who have taken the course. One, about thirty-five, had passed through a hippie phase and a successful business career, only to find his prime interest in a humanistic education. Like most of the other students, he was greatly taken by the first module, which was designed to teach what linguists mean when they define language as a system of communication. After completing the module, he admitted in wonderment that he had never expected a computer to be able to teach him anything.

In the first presentation of the course, the modules consisted essentially of short selections of texts with questions which the students were to answer. The staff providing technical assistance found that the presentation of phonology made inadequate use of the computer's possibilities, and in a further neologism characterized the modules as 'page-turning.' Other hazards arose. The prime purpose of the grant turned out not to be the development of computer-assisted courses, but rather to determine the reaction of users to computer-assisted instruction and to disseminate such instruction. In the middle of the semester, the executive program governing all programs was abandoned, and the modules were useless during a long period when the computer spent its energies testing a new one.

Though students accepted the arrangements with grace, the computerized portion of the course left a few things to be desired. On the other hand, many of the papers were remarkably good. One woman produced the best report I have seen on the use of tabooed words by female college students.

The experiences in the second semester the course was given were a near repeat of those in the first, except that this time the computer was judged inadequate and was replaced--an operation as lengthy and painful as the average divorce. But the remainder of the course went acceptably.

In the meantime, the computer modules were being redone. Now they were aimed at giving students practice in deriving sentences and constructing tree diagrams. Students used a CRT--a device like a TV tube, but with a typewriter keyboard and a light pen for writing on the CRT. A CRT is marvelous, for a student can study examples, draw diagrams, indicate answers, and get immediate responses--though at some cost. Moreover, such activities require complex programs and considerable computer memory which the project's computer lacked. So a third revision of the program was undertaken.

At this time, another requirement of the project came to be felt--the aim of transfer to other institutions. Since those most likely to adopt such programs are impecunious colleges, rather than universities with long experience in using computers, the slow, inexpensive, clattering teletype terminal seemed more adaptable than the splendid CRT. In this phase of the project, ten syntax modules were produced. The modules are programmed in Extended Basic and can be run on either a teletype or a CRT. (Anyone interested in details can obtain documentation from the Final Report of Project C-BE at the University of Texas at Austin or from Dr. Solveig M.V. Pflueger. The modules are available for use elsewhere.)

In the last semester, Project C-BE obtained a hookup with one of the lavishly supported computer projects; the linguistics students were able to use its modules for the instruction of phonology.

The course will be given a fifth time this fall, presumably with some advantages from previous experiences. Can its findings also assist others? One may. Despite the trials, the computer modules contributed to reducing the length of time used for the 'language' part of the course, leaving more for the 'society' part, for which the students have more interest. Computer-aided, or based, instruction will further improve and speed the teaching of the basics of linguistics. I am grateful, then, to the National Science Foundation, to the enterprising principal investigators who secured and furnished the funds for this part of the course, and to those who arranged the modules and the programs, notably Dr. Pflueger. But the grant has now expired. Future computer applications will be at the mercy of the university administration, which is badgered by legislators and newspaper pundits about the amounts spent on the rapacious computer, which outsiders view as the newest status symbol of universities.

The 'society' part of the course is not subject to such problems. In the last semester, visits were arranged to two schools for the deaf to provide perspective on possible contributions of linguistics to social problems. Seeing phonetic representations, rather than spelled forms, in actual use for ten-year-old children gives something of a fillip to the tedious process of mastering phonetic transcription. Any such community involvement is welcomed greatly by the serious students in the class. One of the very best students to have taken the course has done excellent work on speaking in tongues.

If instructors planned a similar course, or any course using computers, they would be strongly advised to have their hardware, software, and courseware in complete readiness before the semester began. Although courses brought in from elsewhere will seem to have shortcomings, instructors would be unwise to produce their own modules as the course proceeded. The student of today has been accustomed to a gadget's working since first peering into a TV screen at the age of ten days. Routine and dull material is far more acceptable than a non-operating computer. Whatever the IQ level of the contemporary student, it's much higher than the frustration level.

It would also be well to avoid experimentation with such a course unless tenure is well in hand. If there were any doubts about Kingman Brewster's view that the chief purpose of tenure is to protect one from one's colleagues, they can be dismissed. Young instructors should spend their time fattening a publication record, preferably on slightly outmoded, safe topics, such as transformational grammar or phenomonological literary theory. The perfect classroom visual aid--a solid surface on which figures can be drawn with a piece of chalk--has been in use since the stone age; much of the period persists in the persons of students and instructors.

A SURVEY OF RUSSIAN CULTURE AND CIVILIZATION (1361)

William D. Buffington
Department of Foreign Languages and Literatures, Purdue University

A Survey of Russian Culture and Civilization is the title of a course developed for television broadcast. The course was the product of cooperation among the Purdue Telecommunications Center, the Department of Foreign Languages and Literatures, and the Continuing Education Administration.

For the fall and spring semesters in 1973-74 and 1974-75, Purdue University made use of the facilities of the local television cable company to broadcast courses designed for the general public. This was one of the first courses to be broadcast. It consists of forty-five taped presentations, each thirty minutes long. Three lectures were broadcast a number of times during each week of the semester, which made it possible for the student to view the programs conveniently and to see the televised presentations more than once if desired.

The course was publicized through normal university channels, newsletters, the student newspaper, posters, the local newspaper, and was listed in the local TV program guide.

Because the course was intended to reach the community, it was presented in English. The instructor assumed that the viewer had no knowledge of Russian and very little awareness about Russia and Russians. He also assumed that the viewing audience would include those hostile to anything Russian.

The series traced the development of selected aspects of Russian culture and civilization and emphasized highlights of Russian participation in and contributions to the civilization of man. Particular attention was focused on the great monuments in Russian art, architecture, music, folklore, literature, and also on what might be called the Russian life style--its heritage and its present-day aspects in the Soviet Union. One of the general purposes of this course was to make these subjects less strange, exotic, or hostile.

The course represents a synthesis and modification of courses regularly taught to Russian majors and minors in the Department of Foreign Languages and Literatures. Thus, the course was created especially for television and for the broad spectrum of the viewing audience. The wide range of topics allowed the instructor to select those topics most appropriate for television and to make the fullest possible use of the potential of television. A conscious effort was made to avoid televising a lecturer at his desk. To illustrate the major concepts of the course, slides, recordings, filmstrips, posters, pictures, realia, and artists' drawings were used. All these were blended in a way which would be impractical, if not impossible, in the ordinary classroom setting. These resources had been assembled by the instructor in his own travels to the USSR and in his years of teaching Russian.

120

During the preparation and taping, the instructor received one-fourth released time in the spring semester and one-half time during the summer of 1973. He retains the option to revise any of the videotapes, although no revisions are contemplated at this time. There has been some discussion about re-taping the series for color broadcast.

Since it is not possible in a television course to have the usual kind of interaction between instructor and students, the author justified the use of television by exploiting what the medium can do with sight and sound to produce memorable effects, to make impressions on the imagination, to stimulate interest in learning more about the subject. Thus, visual images, pictures, drawings, realia, etc. were used to illustrate word or music; music and sound were used for backgrounds of visual images. Each half-hour segment became a unique combination of sight and sound, a montage of effects, all stored on videotape for rebroadcast. As a book stores the thoughts of the author for retrieval by the reader, each television tape has stored the efforts of the instructor for later viewing, thus multiplying those efforts by making them available to many people at many times. During the semesters when the course was televised, the instructor continued his normal teaching duties.

The student is supplied with a course outline and syllabus, which includes text references, an outline of each program, and suggested study questions. At the end of the course, the student may take the final examination for three hours of university credit. (As the course is taught in English and all readings are in English, departmental majors may not apply this course toward degree requirements.)

The course has been well-received in the community and has been positively evaluated by those colleagues who recognize both the advantages and limitations of television. As the development of such a course represented a pioneering effort at Purdue, the planning and creation of the presentations received necessary endorsements of the department, school, and administration without difficulty. No other faculty or departments were involved in the project. Although there were some reservations expressed after the broadcasts began about some of the programs belonging more properly in other academic areas, such as history, these reservations dwindled when the course was viewed in its entirety and course objectives were understood.

The greatest response has come from those who view the broadcasts but do not elect to take the course for credit. About thirty persons have gained credit for the television course, but its impact extends beyond that number. The broadcast of the series has contributed to the public image of the department and the university as agencies of concern for the education of the people.

SUMMER IMMERSION COURSE IN SPANISH (1410)

Norman Arbaiza
Department of Foreign Languages and Literatures, Rockland Community College

The idea for the course was in part generated over the last few years by the inquiries of high school seniors who had not studied a foreign language in high school on the assumption that the foreign language requirement in colleges is dead, found out later that this was not the case in their major field, and wondered what to do. These inquiries, combined with student complaints regarding the time required to attain minimal competency in a language and our knowledge of a successful summer program elsewhere, encouraged us to establish a summer immersion course in Spanish.

There were no special problems in designing the course, and no special funding was required. The course was offered in summer 1974 under the aegis of the Division of Continuing Education, which does an excellent job of getting publicity into every household in the county.

The enrollment represented a mixed group of students, including the expected high school graduates, as well as teachers, policemen, healthworkers, foreign language teachers seeking a second competence, a couple planning to retire to Costa Rica, and others.

The course met six class hours a day, five days a week, for forty-four days; in addition, there were two to three hours of home assignments daily. Twelve credit units were awarded for successful completion of the immersion course, representing a traditional four-semester curriculum. A team of one instructor and one paraprofessional taught the morning sessions, and a second team taught the afternoon sessions. The paraprofessionals were assigned principally to one-to-one small-group work. Since both instructors were men, it was important that both paraprofessionals be women, so that the students would be familiar with both male and female voices. It was also considered important that both have Spanish as their primary language, since when they were alone with students they would not make mistakes. It was thought best that one paraprofessional be Spanish and the other Latin American, that both be educated, and that neither speak with a strong regional accent. We also sought people who seemed to be interested in teaching, would empathize with the students, and who, in their first months in this country, had gone through the same process learning English that the students were undergoing learning Spanish. Two women of the twenty interviewed were selected, and the quality of their assistance was excellent.

During the equivalent of the first two semesters, mornings were devoted principally to sound production, listening comprehension, reduction of the sounds to writing, and extemporaneous oral and question-answer work; afternoons were devoted mainly to grammar, both inductive and deductive. During the third 'semester,' the mornings were largely spent reviewing grammar, and the afternoons reading about Spanish civilization and culture with accompanying lectures and discussions in Spanish. This continued in the afternoons of the fourth semester, while the mornings of the final semester were devoted to one-hour lectures or group conversation in Spanish on the material covered in the lectures. The main distinction between morning and afternoon techniques in the fourth semester was that in the morning we used no textbook, thus requiring practice in the comprehension of fairly complicated material presented orally without printed reference; students were encouraged to take notes they could confirm later by checking the textbook. By the same token, in the afternoon sessions, we concentrated on the textbook and the development of reading comprehension.

It seemed wisest to use the paraprofessionals primarily in one-to-one and small-group situations, since they were not experienced classroom teachers and could have been under severe strain if required to handle a class alone for an hour or more. They were, however, occasionally used with the whole class in order that not all dictations and question-answer sessions be directed exclusively by either male or female voices. Perhaps the chief value of the paraprofessional was in dealing with the individual problems of the students, which an instructor in an ordinary day-session class would presumably handle during office hours. Such individual problems involved pronunciation or a difficult point of grammar, which in an intensive course tend to be lost or ignored if there are no paraprofessionals. We also asked the students to use the usted form of address to the instructors and the tu form to the paraprofessionals, in order to train them equally in the use of the forms.

At the college, each elementary or intermediate semester in foreign language requires sixty hours of class time. Since the academic hour is fifty minutes long, a total of 12,000 clock minutes is available in four semesters. An equal amount of class time was obtained in forty-four days with the following schedule:

Period	Time	Clock minutes in class	Break between classes (minutes)
I	9:00 - 9:50	50	10
II	10:00 - 10:50	50	10
III	11:00 - 11:40	40	50 (lunch)
IV	12:30 - 1:15	45	10
V	1:25 - 2:10	45	5
VI	2:15 - 3:00	45	--
		275	

(275 minutes times 44 days equals 12,100 clock minutes.)

122

It is traditionally said that out-of-class work ought to be twice the number of hours per week as the course yields credits. Since each semester is a three-credit course, there is a presumption that each student is doing six hours per week of work outside of class, which would mean a total of ninety hours a semester, or a total of 360 hours over four regular semesters. In our immersion course, they may have fallen short of this, since they averaged about three hours of out-of-class work a day. The intensity of the work, in my opinion, easily made up the difference.

Neither instructor involved in the course in 1974 was available again in summer 1975, but at least one plans to be in 1976 and during that summer will be able to produce a detailed plan which could be followed by any other department instructor.

There is no question in the mind of either instructor that as much or more was accomplished in the summer as during four regular semesters. The same tests were used with equal or better results. Student satisfaction was high among the students who stayed with it; some could not tolerate the intensity and dropped out. At least three students took advanced Spanish courses, which they state they had had no intention of taking, subsequent to taking the immersion course. One French teacher has become certified in Spanish as well.

The next time the course is offered, in summer 1976, we plan to increase the time allotted the one-to-one and small-group sessions conducted by the paraprofessionals, especially during the first twenty-two days. Also we plan to have fewer field trips during the first half, since during the early weeks students become discouraged because they don't understand enough of the movie or other conversation; by the second half they do amazingly well.

INTENSIVE FOREIGN LANGUAGE STUDY (1414)

Norman A. Whitlock
Department of Foreign Languages and Linguistics, University of Texas at Arlington

Teachers have long complained of lacking the contact time necessary for foreign language classes. A survey here of beginning German classes indicated student interest in concentrated language study, and as a result an intensive course in German was initiated.

The intensive language class is made up of students who choose to complete fourteen semester hours--two years of foreign language study--in one semester of approximately 250 contact hours. The credits earned satisfy the foreign language requirement for a Bachelor of Arts degree and can be applied to a major or minor in the target language.

Success prompted the department to create additional intensive language courses in Spanish, Russian, French, and Portuguese. The intensive language courses do not require special funding or special educational materials; as a result, there were no financial problems to be overcome by the department or the administration. The student enrolls in four classes at one time--two beginning classes and two intermediate classes. Problems encountered with scheduling and room assignments were minimal. The students' acceptance of and satisfaction with the courses proved to be the best means of publicizing them; announcements of the courses were carried in the school paper and in local newspapers.

Intensive language courses are not dependent upon an individual instructor, but upon the number of instructors who are willing and able to teach courses of this type. The intensive course requires twenty or more class contact hours per week; therefore, the instructors are relieved of additional teaching assignments. Instructors have volunteered repeatedly to teach the intensive course; thus, it has not been necessary to assign the course to an instructor who would prefer to teach something else.

Positive evaluation of the intensive program has been seen in favorable comments from the students and faculty, an increase in the intensive program enrollment, requests for enrollment a semester in advance, the fact that many students continue studies in the target language after completing intensive study, the language majors and minors gained by the program, and the students' confidence to undertake a pleasure or study trip to Europe, Mexico, South America, or the Soviet Union. Students seem to favor this approach to foreign language learning, and it has created a new image and concept of language learning and teaching at the university.

We feel that the intensive course has achieved its educational goals. The student has the time and supervision necessary to master the skills for maximum language performance. The additional contact hours allow the teacher time to present in depth the material to be learned, time for aural/oral practice and evaluation, time for additional practice of difficult language patterns, and time for supplementary reading and written work.

The intensive language courses have the same behavioral objectives as the traditional language courses, and most of them use the same materials. By offering the traditional and the intensive language tracks simultaneously, we can compare and observe the success of the program. (See Ted E. Frank, "A Practical Approach to Intensive German and Its Results," Unterrichtspraxis, Spring 1973, p.5.) The instructor who teaches an intensive class often remarks on the class unity and involvement in learning the language--a unity and involvement rarely seen in the traditional classroom environment.

At present, the intensive language courses are offered on a rotation schedule: Spanish and German in the spring, Russian and French in the fall, and Portuguese in the summer. If enrollments in the intensive classes continue to increase, it is probable that the courses will be offered on a regular semester basis. Offerings in career-oriented intensive language courses in business, medical terminology, journalism, architecture, sciences, etc. are also being discussed, but as yet have not been developed.

MULTI-LEVEL FRENCH (1431)

Rosemary H. Thomas
Department of French, Forest Park Community College

The major benefits which we have enjoyed as a result of using the Multi-Level French program for the past six years have been:
-   making the teaching of elementary and intermediate courses more challenging, pleasant, personal, and interesting for instructors;
-   producing students who are willing and able to use the French they know with adequate fluency in real language situations by the end of their third semester;
-   allowing us to continue offering intermediate and advanced courses even though they usually attract too few students to be offered under the minimum-enrollment policies of the college;
-   allowing us to offer to all students the benefits of contact with a native French informant and free tutoring from an advanced student when they need help;
-   allowing us to adapt our expectations and teaching to the individual abilities and prior learning experiences of our students;
-   allowing us to achieve a slow but steady rate of growth commensurate with the growth of the college's total enrollment;
-   making the French program a source of pride for the college, a recipient of good will from a majority of colleagues in other departments, and a frequent focus of public relations attention.

These benefits, which also represent needs to which the development of Multi-Level French was a response, have been produced using original programmed materials in an open-classroom, multi-level format with individualized contracts and with teacher aides in the class. Both components of Multi-Level French, the materials and the class format, have been revised a number of times in response to the demands of real situations, and both continue to be revised, although revisions at this time tend to be relatively peripheral.

In performance on the Modern Language Aptitude Test, our students achieve a median thirty-five percentile and generally range from the fifth percentile or below through about the sixty-fifth percentile. If they have transferred from other colleges, it has generally been because they have failed courses there. Their past foreign language experience is usually spotty at best. Many have never studied a foreign language. They range in age from high school juniors to senior citizens and in motivation from minimal to fanatic. We needed to find some way of giving most of these people a successful foreign language experience that would satisfy their usual desire for short-term performance results and that would also insure their acceptability into transfer courses at universities. The potential drop-out rate for non-academic reasons often went as high as twenty percent of a section. We needed to find a way for students to drop out and return as their lives permitted, without losing credits they had already worked for or forgetting material they had already learned. Foreign languages were considered a low-priority item in the junior college structure by a number of administrators and were the target for a number of efforts toward elimination. We needed to find ways of demonstrating that we do render important services to a varied clientele to whom the college gives priority, and we needed to gain administrative esteem for what we do in our classes.

We began by writing the programmed materials. In its present, semi-final form, the program consists of approximately 1,100 multi-response frames (approximately thirty stimulus-response units per frame) on audiotape with accompanying worksheets. For the majority of the frames, each item is accompanied in the workbook by a line drawing depicting the situation to which the stimulus and response are related. Students must use the pictured situation to understand the stimulus and to infer the correct response. All frames consist of stimulus-response units which must be processed directly in French. Each frame takes an average of seven to ten minutes to complete. Responses, except in spelling and writing frames which are scattered throughout the materials, are both oral and motor (the motor part usually involves marking the picture in some way or keeping score of right and wrong responses). All items have confirmations, and scoring instructions are given for each frame. On the basis of points scored, the student is directed either to go on to the next frame, to redo the frame just completed, or to consult the instructor for help.

Frames are grouped into modules of approximately forty to fifty frames. One credit is earned for each module completed. In class and in assignment contracts, a module is scheduled to last three weeks. Students who have not come close to completing a module during the first three-week period for which it was scheduled may be directed to spend a second three-week period on the same module instead of going on.

A part of the program's success relates to the great amount of practice which it affords students in responding correctly to language stimuli in French. Part of it, however, also comes from what was included in the programmed materials. Before writing frames, we wrote a pedagogical grammar of French. We assumed that French structure can be divided into derivation rules and substitution rules. The derivation rules, both morphological and syntactic, comprise the total stock of different types of operations which are needed in basic, everyday French. The program teaches one example of each different type of rule thoroughly. Substitution rules are those morphological and syntactic operations which share the same mechanics as derivation rules, but whose semantic shape is different.

We have found consistently that once students have learned the total stock of derivation rules (this takes ten modules or credits), they are easily able to treat the other grammatical features they come across in reading and listening as lexical substitutions in the structures they already know how to manipulate. They often spontaneously and correctly deduce the difference between the basic form they have been taught and the analogous form with which they have now come into contact. They consistently process syntax and morphology for meaning, and they consistently produce sentences which are consistent with the logic of French structure. They do make many errors in writing and speaking, but these tend to be mostly errors in lexicon and in surface structure rather than in deep structure.

The programmed materials serve as the basis for the elementary and intermediate classes. At the beginning of each semester, each student receives an assignment contract, with specified frames to be done by specific dates and handed in for checking, and specified module exams and tests to be taken at precise times. The instructor also has a copy of each student's contract. The instructor checks off assignments on this copy, as they are handed in, and makes pertinent notations. In this way it is always possible to find quickly how an individual student is progressing, both quantitatively and qualitatively. A library of cassette and reel-to-reel copies of the frames is maintained, and students may borrow tapes in order to work on their own tape recorders wherever and whenever it is convenient. If they prefer, they may use tapes and recorders in the school learning laboratory.

Twenty students is the maximum enrollment for a section of Multi-Level French. Each section is taught by an instructional team composed of a faculty-level teacher aided by a native French informant and an advanced student who has already successfully completed most of the program. All three work with small groups of students during class time. Costs are minimal: The native assistant does not have outside preparation or grading to do and is paid $4-5 per hour worked; the student is paid the minimum wage for fifteen hours of work per week, about half of which is spent as an assistant in class and half of which is spent tutoring on an individual basis.

When they register for Multi-Level French, students choose only the number of credits they wish to complete. On the first day of class, the French staff places each student at a level in the program according to prior learning experiences. There are four elementary and intermediate levels, and each has five different class numbers (for one through five credits). If students were to choose a placement level at registration, they would be faced with twenty different classes to pick from, all called 'Elementary French' or 'Intermediate French.' Generally, we allow students to sign up for three, four, or five credits initially. The average number of credit hours per student for any given French section is around four (usually ranging from 3.85 to 4.15). Thus, we count a Multi-Level French section as a four instructor-credit teaching assignment.

There are three different Multi-Level French courses, with different numbers listed in a class schedule; each is for a different number of credits. All are scheduled at the same time in the same room. Total maximum enrollment for all three is twenty students. After students have been placed in an elementary or intermediate French section on the first day of class, we make up new class lists, using the different French courses and their different computer numbers. We then send these to the computer center with instructions to cancel the Multi-Level French sections and transfer the students listed to the new courses we are just submitting. We are, of course, grateful to our registrar for helping us work out this system. Students wishing to add credits during the semester, as a good number do, may do this through the normal 'drop and add' procedure, which the computer is equipped to handle.

Each section meets for three hours a week (90 minutes twice a week). The semester is divided into five 'module periods' of three weeks each. Students are divided into three to four groups according to their level in the programmed materials. Class agendas are planned so that each student group of four to six students has three twenty-five-minute activities with three different staff members during each class meeting.

About half the activities relate to the programmed materials. The other half are enrichment activities--films, slides, tapes, games, projects, conversations, articles, poems. Doing the enrichment activities, students practice using French in a real language situation and learn to use the derivation rules studied in the program.

At the end of each three-week module period, the instructor reviews each student's progress and holds a brief, individual interview. A class day is set aside each three weeks for interviews and module exams; students who have finished the modules they signed up for may add more; students who have fallen behind for whatever reason may be directed to start a module again; students who are not functioning well within the small group may be changed from one group to another; students who have finished their work for the semester may be given a final grade and processed out of the class. If a student signs up for three credits, keeps on schedule, and does not add more credits, he or she will have finished slightly after midterm. Most students who do this add more credits.

Meticulous record-keeping and class preparation, with workable and detailed agendas for the small-group activities, are absolutely essential. Improvisation is extremely difficult and not very effective in such a complex situation.

It would be difficult to implement a multi-level, open classroom in which groups moved around and engaged in different activities simultaneously without a relatively large class space; the noise level would be too distracting in a normal twenty-five or thirty student classroom. We use a large language laboratory room. We don't use the booths in class, but there is enough room around the periphery for small groups to meet, play tape recorders, and talk without unduly disturbing groups doing other things.

Initially, provisional approval was obtained for the program, but it has worked so well and solved so many problems that it is now considered the norm for our French courses. A number of different instructors and assistants have been involved. Usually we try to train a new instructor for a semester before he or she assumes responsibility for a multi-level section. Currently, we do this by having an experienced instructor share the responsibility for a section with a new instructor for a semester. (They share both the pay and the work.) We try to keep ahead of new staff needs so that we are not caught short without experienced staff for an unstaffed section.

By and large, we find that students transferring into our program from other colleges who have passed their French courses place at about the point where they would be if they had taken a similar amount of previous credit in our department. Likewise, students who transfer from our program to other colleges before finishing three semesters of French are generally able to succeed in the new French department. However, most students who will go on with French finish our program before taking courses elsewhere in French, even when this means continuing French at Forest Park while taking courses at other universities in the area.

The programmed materials need a final revision for professional workbook composition and tape recording. We are also still working to perfect ways of satisfying needs specific to students at different levels of achievement through types of activities and scheduling in the multi-level classroom. But we are generally pleased with the results of our program and with the benefits it has produced.

INDIVIDUALIZED INSTRUCTION IN FRENCH (1435)

Judith Baughin
Department of Foreign Languages, Raymond Walters College-University of Cincinnati

During the past several years, I have experienced problems all too common to foreign language teachers today--the decline of liberal education, changing standards that threaten the language department, emphasis on practical vocational courses, and increasingly varied backgrounds and achievement levels among college students, to name just a few. Faced with these pressures, I had for some time sought, with many colleagues, a new pedagogical outlook that, if not a panacea, would at least provide fresh insights and the flexibility essential to the rapidly changing language teaching field. It was under these circumstances that I became attracted to individualized instruction. After hearing such programs described and discussed, and attending a two-week workshop on individualized instruction, I decided to introduce individualized instruction in one of my elementary French courses in the 1973-74 academic year.

Raymond Walters College is a two-year junior college, one of sixteen divisions of the University of Cincinnati. It is not a 'branch,' but rather a fully autonomous college within the university, granting associate degrees in general and technical education. Unlike many similar two-year colleges affiliated with universities, departments in Raymond Walters College are fully independent, with no control of any kind by the baccalaureate and graduate departments in other divisions of the university. About one-third of our students are in two-year career-oriented or technical programs; another one-third are in transfer or pre-baccalaureate programs; the remaining one-third fall into expanding continuing education category, part-time students who will often move into full-time technical or baccalaureate programs. The college has an open enrollment policy; however, the location of the institution in the northeastern suburbs of Cincinnati and the variety of programs offered have brought us generally higher caliber students than ordinarily found in many other open-enrollment schools.

Most but not all students taking foreign language at Raymond Walters are in the baccalaureate transfer programs, especially in liberal arts, although our pre-medicine program supplies a number of students each year to our German classes. As has been true throughout higher education, our liberal arts enrollment has fallen noticeably. On the other hand, challenges to the foreign language prerequisite for the baccalaureate degree in the College of Arts and Sciences at the University of Cincinnati appear to have been defeated, and as a result the two-year pre-liberal arts program in our college retains a language requirement. In addition, our language classes are attracting more and more older, continuing education students whose different educational backgrounds make individualized instruction particulaly appropriate for them.

I encountered no administrative or departmental difficulty in initiating an individualized program. Under the highly developed system of faculty responsibility for governance that exists in our college, I had to submit my proposal both to my department and to a faculty curriculum committee. The latter must approve all new curriculum offerings, but, in this case, the committee interpreted individualized instruction not as a new course but simply as a change in the technique of instruction, which is of course inherently the prerogative of any teacher. Although the administration plays no direct role in curriculum questions within our college, their cooperation was necessary to establish some of the special procedures needed for grading and registration; they supported the needed modifications enthusiastically.

I teach two five-credit-hour elementary French classes, but I 'individualized' only one. Initially I did this to have a control class--with regularly scheduled work in a more or less conventional format--against which I could measure the success of the individualized approach. Even though after two years of experience I am more than ever convinced of the benefits of teaching under the individualized concept, I have decided to retain the control or conventional class, because I have found that some students prefer the more highly structured learning environment. Although individualized instruction provides the most efficacious means by which many students may learn a language, it is not for all students. A major problem is getting students into the class offering the most suitable technique for them. Some academic advisers--who schedule classes for students in our college--believe that the individualized method is only for students with low achievement records; others see it as only proper for those with the highest levels of performance. Two years of experience have taught me that the ability level of the student is not the determining factor: individualized instruction is for both slow- and fast-paced students. Many other considerations--personalities and backgrounds of students, degree of self-discipline, time available for study, etc.--should provide the criteria for placing a student in the individualized system.

Procedures have evolved over a two-year period. Individual paces are permitted, but students must initially register for five units of credit each quarter for three quarters. If the five units are not completed by the end of the quarter, an 'N' (no grade) is given and does not affect cumulative grade-point average. A student may, however, do more than five units, possibly completing fifteen units in two quarters. The only grades given for completed work in the course are 'A' or 'B,' since a student must achieve at the eighty per cent level in both oral and written tests before being allowed to continue into the next unit. Thus, individualized instruction guarantees proficiency; the variable is time, not level of performance. Unless scheduled for specific activities, such as a conversation group, the student is not required to attend class and may use the assigned class time in any way. I am available during each class contact hour, giving assistance to those who need it, working with students on a one-to-one basis, testing students both formally and informally, and conducting conversation groups on a predetermined schedule.

In both the control and individualized classes, I try to emphasize the four basic skills equally. In the beginning, I had some doubts about how well students could master audiolingual skills under an individualized approach, so I put particular emphasis on satisfactory achievement in these areas. We have a fully equipped language laboratory with a full-time attendant, and students can spend whatever time they need working with taped drills designed to fulfill the audiolingual objectives of each unit. Tapes are available to complement the textbook, and I have prepared taped drills geared to learning activity packets. The laboratory is open most evenings and on Saturdays, and students have used its facilities frequently during these hours. No special amount of time is required in the laboratory; it is strictly up to the student, who knows that a certain level of audiolingual proficiency must be demonstrated in each unit before proceeding to the next.

Every unit has two sets of learning activity packets with specific objectives. The first contains grammar explanations, exercises to supplement the grammar lectures, and pretests; the second deals with oral-aural objectives, such as conversation and dialogue, new vocabulary and idioms, and other structural elements. The student may take the oral and written unit tests when prepared and must reach at least an eighty percent proficiency level in both. Tests may be repeated as often as necessary, but in such cases the student takes an alternate form. Both the written and oral tests are taken in the language laboratory. Since there is a full-time attendant, the student may take tests when convenient. I keep a file on each student, with an analysis of test scores, weaknesses, and strengths.

In spite of some difficulties and necessary adjustments, I believe the two years of individualized instruction have been notably successful. Enrollment in my French classes has remained steady at a time when the number of students in the Liberal Arts Program--the source of most of our language students--has declined. Students who have either failed a foreign language in high school or who have never had a foreign language before frequently make significant progress in an individualized class, and I am certain that the same student would have dropped out of a regular class before having given language study an adequate chance. There may be many reasons for such failure in a conventional group--poor study habits, lack of experience in a foreign language, fear of language or of taking tests. An individualized class helps the student make the necessary adjustment to foreign language study, but, even more to the point, I believe that students in the individualized program have learned a great deal about themselves. They tend to become much more realistic about their own abilities and weaknesses.

I have had one full-time student tutor (one of my former students) assist during the past year. She has helped in class by drilling individual students on specific points, answering questions, and giving special help to the slower-paced students. Since there are many levels in this class, such assistance has proved especially valuable. I have also been pleased with the way in which all members of the class, regardless of the various levels, have demonstrated a willingness to help one another. Peer tutoring has been much more common in my individualized class than in the conventional one. Student evaluations have shown extremely positive reactions to the individualized approach. A sampling of student comments includes:

I have found that in working and being a full-time student I encountered some difficulty during the first few lessons of French grammar and consequently got behind in my lessons. If I had been taking French in a conventional class I would have been forced to drop out or take a lower grade with a lesser degree of learning. As a result of this individualized teaching method, I am now progressing at a satisfactory rate and feel that I can accelerate with a higher degree of proficiency.

The individualized French instruction has been a fantastic opportunity for me to learn a new language... Learning at my own rate has been an incentive, because it's helped erase old grammar hang-ups. It's helped convince me that it is not how fast one learns but how much. I do feel self-motivation plays an important part.

Setting up an individualized instruction program requires more than the customary amount of dedication on the part of the teacher. In the beginning, I was completely exhausted by the time necessary to prepare learning packets, alternate tests, and other materials. Much time must be made available to students who need help and encouragement. Extensive taping of oral drills is particularly time-consuming, but once the first materials were prepared, I was able to organize my time much more efficiently. Still, anyone using individualized instruction must realize that it places great demands on the instructor's time. This is especially true during the spring term, when achievement levels are more varied than earlier in the year.

As indicated earlier, I am not convinced that individualized instruction is for everyone. I have lost a few students, and I feel certain that some of them need the constant pressure of the control class. I have also concluded that a limited amount of regular class attendance should be mandatory even under the individualized method (at least two of five class periods each week). I have found that students in the individualized class who attend regularly usually do not fall behind as much as those who do not attend as often. It is the student who rarely comes to class who most frequently has difficulty completing work or who falls far behind and eventually loses interest altogether. I have also found it desirable to set a minimum amount of work that a student must complete in order to register for the next quarter, even when receiving an 'N' for the previous quarter. This is essential for both student and instructor, because a student who gets too far behind not only gets discouraged but finds it increasingly difficult to finish the work. Although the basic idea is to allow the student time to proceed independently, it is better for the student and the teacher if a minimum pace is maintained.

Individualized instruction undoubtedly offers an important new approach for the foreign language teacher in the present troubled environment of academe. Each teacher needs to establish a program according to the particular situation--the nature of the students and the demands of the community. But above all, as language teachers today, we must recognize that our students are our clientele and that we must meet their individual needs. Individualized instruction presents the greatest potential for language teachers to meet this obligation.

BEGINNING AND INTERMEDIATE INDIVIDUALIZED GERMAN (1440)

Philip H. Beard
Department of Foreign Languages and Literatures, California State College-Sonoma

Need for individualized instruction was determined on the basis of experience teaching first- and second-year German courses by the traditional approach with all the well-known frustrations, notably the discrepancy in learning rates among students and the attendant impossibility of teaching all students effectively.

Our goal in the individualized approach is to enable the student to communicate lucidly in spoken and written German as fast as possible given the individual's aptitude, motivation, and past training. Highly motivated, high-aptitude students can finish the course's five credit units of work in less than a full semester and move on to more advanced material, receiving credit at semester's end for as many units as they complete. Students who need more than the average amount of time to master a given unit will finish the semester with fewer than five credits, but this does not affect the grade for units completed.

To insure that progress in the course is firmly based on mastery of each segment of material, the minimum requirement for moving on to the next study unit is an 80% score on each chapter exam. This assures students of an 'A' or 'B' for each unit completed; no lower grades, incompletes, or no-grades are assigned. Generally, the satisfactory completion of two chapters of text will earn one unit of credit.

All students are required to attend one conversation session per week, to complete workbook sections corresponding to the text, and to use the language laboratory. In the lab, tapes accompanying the text are available, as well as audio flashcard readers for performing repetition exercises and improving pronunciation. Additional materials which the students are encouraged to use include the Guten Tag film series and printed and recorded cultural materials.

Development of the program was heartily encouraged; approval is permanent. Very little special funding was necessary; the main outlay was $750, provided from departmental funds, for three special tape machines.

Publicity has been primarily by means of departmental flyers sent to high schools and junior colleges throughout California, as well as to sister institutions in the state college system. Locally, publicity has been through the periodic distribution of informational leaflets and newspaper articles.

Administrative problems have been the prime area of difficulty encountered in setting up the courses. The main question has been how, without thoroughly disrupting the present system of awarding course credits, to institute a variable-unit system in which the student need not decide until quite late in the semester how many credit units he or she will finally earn. The accommodation arrived at with the registrar provided for standard enrollment procedures: each student initially enrolls for the traditional number of units the student is expected to complete, i.e., five for the first year and three for the second. About a month prior to the end of the semester, units can be added or dropped on the basis of the student's progress to date and of individual student-instructor agreements. This variability, it should be noted, is necessitated by the high quality standard built into the course.

No difficulties have arisen in obtaining materials. The text employed (Rogers and Watkins, German through Conversational Patterns) is easily adapted to the individualized approach.

The courses make up part of the instructors' normal load and could conceivably be taught by anyone capable of teaching by the standard method, but individual instructors have expressed doubt as to whether they would enjoy using the individualized method with the fragmentation of student-teacher contacts which it implies.

The courses seem to be reaching their educational goals. Student comment has been overwhelmingly positive, but the sampling is still too small to indicate reliably whether the method is responsible for any measurable increase in skill-learning effectiveness. The number of credit units earned and the amount of course material covered compare favorably with the traditionally-taught courses, and the students demonstrate on the whole a greater-than-average enthusiasm for speaking the language. To what extent this is due to intangibles, such as group affinity or the spread of individual aptitudes encountered in these specific classes, cannot yet be determined.

The only formal evaluation to date as been from students, who have been uniformly enthusiastic in their appraisal of the courses. They cite the reduced pressure, easy atmosphere, and guaranteed high performance level as those aspects of the individualized approach which they value most highly. Faculty and administration feedback, while less regular, has also been uniformly positive. A few other faculty members have voiced an interest in restructuring some of their courses accordingly.

Without question, these courses have contributed to the image of the department as being interested in innovative techniques and willing to invest extra time to meet student needs. No data have yet been compiled to determine whether other departmental offerings have benefited directly from the existence of these courses, but it seems at least likely.

The only change we are contemplating at present is requiring an attendance minimum in order to make the courses stronger relative to traditional 'high-pressure' courses. Our experience has been that attendance and achievement drop off markedly when students are subjected to the pressure of midterm exams and papers for other courses. The 'carrot' of being able to complete more units than would normally be possible has not proved as effective a motivator as we had hoped; therefore, we are considering introducing a little more 'stick.'

GOAL-DIRECTED LANGUAGE ACQUISITION PROGRAM: GERMAN (1443)

Guenter Pfister
Department of Germanic and Slavic Languages and Literatures, University of Maryland-College Park

The basis of a goal-directed program is the partnership between student and teacher. Both are equal partners working toward an established goal, e.g., ninety percent mastery of all tested material. Thus, it is of utmost importance that the goal is defined, the partnership is understood, and testing designs to measure relative success in reaching the established goals are at hand.

The course is designed to give students practice with all four language skills. Reading and dialogue material in the text portray the German people as products of their culture. Comparisons and contrasts are used to heighten the student's awareness of the impact of American culture and the individual's attitudes and values. Oral tests are given regularly in class to determine mastery of the speaking skill. The degree of mastery of the three remaining skills and a knowledge of German culture is measured by two written exams and one two-hour final. Scores of ninety percent correct on both of the one-hour exams constitute an 'A.' Sixty percent success on the final exam is necessary to pass the course.

Both teacher and student have responsibilities to fulfill in order to reach the goal. The student is expected to attend class regularly, participate orally, and complete assignments. The instructor is expected to attend staff meetings, review concepts to be covered in the week's work, and rate written assignments regularly so that a student can correct errors promptly. Assignments and oral and written tests are diagnostic in nature; they are an aid in determining areas in which the student and/or the instructional process is weak.

Enrollment in the beginning language course at the university necessitates several sections, usually taught by teaching assistants. To assure the quality of instruction as well as standardized evaluation procedures, a course director needs to establish clear administrative procedures and guidelines. Each year, teaching assistants new to the program are required to take a teaching methods course given by the program director. Weekly meetings of the entire staff provide the setting for discussing problems and planning. The director also serves as a resource person, visiting classrooms to observe the problems and strengths of individual teaching assistants and offering his expertise.

The individual teacher is responsible for diagnosing areas in which the student needs extra help. The responsibility to diagnose and correct weaknesses in the instructional process falls necessarily to the course director. Constructing tests and determining grading scales and numerical goals are duties of the director. Establishing goals puts the director squarely under the pressure of his colleagues; thus, ninety percent or better reflects a traditional and accepted goal area for an 'A' in the course, and sixty percent mastery as the minimum goal for a passing grade is also a well-established measurement in the university community. Instructional goals can be of a different nature, but any course director is well advised to examine the goals of department and institution before departing from the procedures accepted by his colleagues. In my experience with the program, seventy percent of the students mastered eighty percent or better of the material tested. Ten percent of the students failed to reach the sixty percent goal.

Success in the program is measured by written and oral tests; thus, the evaluation of test performances must be done as objectively as possible. Furthermore, since several instructors are teaching the course, objective criteria are important to minimize discrepancies among sections.

Oral tests are administered every two weeks. Numbers are written on the board which represent questions in German. Each student picks a number, and the instructor asks the question which that number represents. The student responds orally. From dialogues or class discussion, the student should be able to provide a complete sentence answer to all questions. This response is graded according to the following criteria:

Natural and meaningful response, free from error in vocabulary, grammar, and pronunciation; a complete sentence.   A

Meaningful response with minor errors in vocabulary, grammar, and pronunciation; a complete sentence. C

Response with major errors in vocabulary, grammar, and pronunciation; a complete sentence. D

Irrelevant or unintelligible response, response not attempted, or not a complete sentence. F

(Note: If a response is not a complete sentence, it should be appraised as 'F,' unless it represents a phrase from a dialogue or any other material based on the text which the student is trying to learn. The intermediate 'B' grade has been eliminated in the evaluation of oral performance in order to enable the instructor to make decisions as quickly, consistently, and objectively as possible on the basis of the more clearly defined and disparate criteria for the 'A' and 'C' grades. Experience has shown that this system also enables the student to understand more easily why a particular grade is assigned.)

Written exams consist of two multiple-choice sections of twenty-five items each--one dealing with grammatical concepts, the other with the recognition of cultural contrasts in the target language--questions to which the student provides complete-sentence answers, and a choice of theme topics requiring a nine- to eighteen-line response. Answers to questions are graded using the following system:

Complete rational sentence, correct in all respects, one spelling error allowed.
3 points

Complete rational sentence, one or two grammatical errors, two or three spelling errors.
2 points

Complete rational sentence, three grammatical errors, four spelling errors.
1 point

Either an incomplete sentence or an irrational or incoherent answer. 0 point

Themes are evaluated using five criteria:

Assignment

The student has written 9 complete sentences.	5 points
The student has completed 2/3 of the assignment.	3 points
The student has completed 1/3 of the assignment.	1 point
The student has completed less than 1/3.	0 point

Spelling

The student has spelled all vocabulary correctly.	5 points
The student has spelled 2/3 of the vocabulary correctly.	3 points
The student has spelled 1/3 of the vocabulary correctly.	1 point
The student has spelled less than 1/3 correctly.	0 point

Grammar Structures

All grammar structures are correct.	5 points
2/3 of the grammar structures are correct.	3 points
1/3 of the grammar structures are correct.	1 point
Less than 1/3 of the grammar structures are correct.	0 point

Continuity

All the sentences contribute to the topic.	5 points
2/3 of the sentences contribute to the topic.	3 points
1/3 of the sentences contribute to the topic.	1 point
Less than 1/3 of the sentences contribute to the topic.	0 point

Native Ability

The student's contribution is of native ability.	5 points
The student's contribution is close to native ability with small errors.	3 points
The student's contribution is faulty and includes direct translation from the mother tongue which leads to distortion.	1 point

The student's contribution is faulty and incoherent.   0 point

The grade is determined from the total of all points.

Such testing allows student and teacher to pinpoint weaknesses in either active or recognition parts of the test. Correlation between all scores of the individual sections reveals possible weaknesses.

This goal-directed program emphasizes partnership between student and teacher, relies on objective testing, and necessitates open communication between director and staff. The program is accepted by all members of the department. The director holds the position of associate professor and has the freedom to make decisions affecting changes in procedure without unnecessary delay.

PROGRAM I: RUSSIAN (1455)

Rodney L. Patterson
Department of Slavic Languages and Literatures, State University of New York at Albany

Program I (PI) is a system of self-paced, contract-graded instruction in the first two semesters of elementary Russian grammar (101, 102). It originated in 1972 at the University of California, Davis and was established at SUNY-Albany in fall 1974. PI is offered in a one-room learning center, Russian Room (RR), which is open for individualized tutoring and testing approximately thirty-five hours weekly. Not designed to replace the lock-step system of instruction, PI serves rather as an alternate system designed to serve a broader spectrum of students. Because experience indicates that PI students progress at a slower pace than lock-step students, prospective majors are encouraged to remain in the traditional classes. (PI carries full credit toward the departmental major.) PI is staffed by a director and four graduate assistants. Staff meetings are convened from time to time to discuss problems and explore means of improving the program.

PI has no organized classes or other regularly scheduled activities. However, PI students are strongly encouraged to attend lock-step sessions for grammar lectures, pattern drills, and conversational practice. In short, PI students may work entirely on their own, visiting RR only for testing, or they may arrange their own intensive Russian course by visiting RR often. Lock-step students may transfer to PI at any time, but PI students, unless they have kept pace with the regular classes, may not transfer to the lock-step sections.

Contracts specifying the grade desired for the course (A=92%; B=86%; C=78%; S/U=70%) are available for PI students, who are urged to choose the 'A' contract because it can be negotiated downward at any time (not to fall below 70%). Signing a contract permits a student to make five attempts to pass each unit of grammar (chapters in the Stilman and Harkins Introductory Russian Grammar) at contract level. A student failing to pass at contract level after five attempts (using alternate exams) must renegotiate the contract downward. Contracts are not obligatory in PI; students may choose to take only one exam per unit and have their final grade determined by averaging their unit scores.

Beginning with unit 4, five exams and their correction keys were written for each chapter of the grammar and filed in RR. A standardized method of correcting the exams was devised so that any two staff members, correcting the same exam, would arrive at the same grade.

RR is conveniently located near the department. It is equipped with desks, a couch, end tables, file cabinets, a blackboard, lamps, posters, coffee urn, etc. Funding was provided for the purchase of a videotape recorder and an automatic Singer Caramate slide projector with synchronized audiotape; these machines and the Beseler Cue/See super-8 mm movie unit with synchronized audiotape will be used by future PI students for self-instruction in phonetics, the alphabet, and grammar.

A student believing to have mastered a given unit of grammar at contract level arranges to be tested in RR. All tests (no one of which the student takes twice) are taken in the presence of a PI instructor, who corrects the test immediately, pointing out to the student the types of mistakes made and means of eliminating them. Each student is encouraged to use the language laboratory and to visit RR as often as possible for practice in conversation, pattern drills, and translation exercises. Students are not allowed to take more than one test per unit on a given day, though they may take tests on different units. Completed tests may be studied by students in RR, but may not be removed; they are retained in the student's folder. All pertinent data concerning the tests are filed in RR and in the director's master file.

The PI staff assumes responsibility for keeping complete records of the students' grades until the regular time for their submission to the registrar. A student enrolling late in the semester (PI has open enrollment) and not finishing the required course work is given an incomplete, which may later be removed at leisure. Immediately upon completing the work, the student may enroll in the second semester of PI. As in lock-step 101, PI-101 students must complete fourteen units of the grammar (at contract level, if they have contracts); PI-102 students must complete the remaining thirteen units of the text.

Sixty-two students enrolled in Russian 101 in fall 1974. Acquainted with the option to leave their lock-step sections to study in PI, they were nevertheless strongly urged to remain in 101 at least through the introductory lectures on phonetics and the alphabet. A large number did so. By mid-semester, twenty-six students were studying in PI, while thirty-six remained in lock-step sections. Of the twenty-six PI students, all but two had chosen 'A' contracts. Midterm progress of the students enrolling in PI at the beginning of the semester represented a range of one to ten units, a median of four units, and a mean of four and a quarter units. At semester's end, twenty-eight students were in lock-step sections and twenty-five were in PI. Of the twenty-five PI students, five had managed to complete the required fourteen units on or before the end of the semester (one had completed Unit 15); the remaining twenty received incompletes. Of the students receiving incompletes, four had yet to pass their first exam, three had finished Unit 4, two had finished Unit 5, one had finished Unit 6, two had finished Unit 7, three had finished Unit 8, one had finished Unit 9, one had finished Unit 10, and three had finished Unit 13. The average student finished seven-and-a-half units. The average progress of students who had entered PI at the beginning of the semester was slightly higher (eight and three-tenths units). An average of 1.53 attempts was made by each student to pass each unit of grammar. Three students found it necessary to renegotiate their contracts downward. Two students dropped PI-101, and seven withdrew from lock-step 101.

Usually offered only in the fall, Russian 101 was offered for the first time during a spring semester as PI-101; four students enrolled. At the beginning of the spring term, fifty-nine students were studying elementary Russian, either in the lock-step system or in PI. At the end of the spring term, the students fell into the following categories: one new PI-101 student withdrew and three finished fewer than fourteen units; two PI-101 (fall term) students completed 101 requirements and continued in PI-102, four completed 101 requirements and did not continue in PI-102, and seventeen had yet to finish 101 requirements; one PI-102 student finished Unit 18, four finished Unit 19, two finished Unit 22, and eleven finished Unit 27 and received their contract grades; five PI-102 students had yet to finish Unit 14; one withdrew; six lock-step 102 students finished the course (Unit 27), and two lock-step students withdrew.

Of the eleven PI-102 students who successfully completed their course work at contract level, nine took the MLA Cooperative Foreign Language Test (1965, form LA). Their scores were as follows:

Listening	Reading	Total
39	44	83
44	47	91
41	47	88
36	36	72
23	40	63
39	43	82
41	46	87

42	48	90
43	50	93

On the listening part of the exam, the mid-percentile ranking ranged from 44 to 98, with a 96 percentile median and a 91 percentile mean; on the reading part, the range was 65 to 100, with a median of 89 and a mean of 89.

Five of the six lock-step 102 students were tested:

Listening	Reading	Total
35	41	76
30	43	73
35	40	75
45	46	91
39	46	85

On the listening part of the exam, the mid-percentile ranking ranged from 78 to 100, with a 91 percentile median and an 87 percentile mean; on the reading part, the range was 91 to 98, with a median of 95 and a mean of 95.

Although collecting such data from standardized testing is indispensable in any attempt to judge the effectiveness of PI, one must treat the scores cautiously. Certain factors warrant special consideration, e.g., of the eleven students finishing PI-102, many faithfully attended the lock-step sessions and several enrolled in PI in mid-term in order to avoid the lock-step final exam (PI does not have a final exam). Furthermore, the sampling is obviously not yet large enough to warrant generalizations.

The need to explore means of revitalizing and improving undergraduate instruction in Russian is evident in MLA statistics, which reveal little growth in Russian enrollments at the college level since 1970. My own experience also indicates that most lock-step systems of elementary Russian instruction serve certain students poorly, e.g., gifted linguists who tend to be bored in language classes geared to C+/B- students, poor linguists who can still do well given more time to study, and students who have little time to study anything but their majors and who are unwilling to jeopardize their GPA--hence their admittance into graduate programs--by studying a 'difficult' foreign language.

No problems were encountered in obtaining provisional approval for PI at SUNYA. The administration has been most supportive of it. The Slavic faculty does not oppose PI, but neither has it been supportive, with the exception of the chairperson and one colleague. The attitude of most members of the department is probably best described as skeptical, but withholding judgment until sufficient data can be analyzed. Thanks to the patience and cooperation of the registrar and the support of the dean of humanities and the chairperson of the department, administrative problems have been minor.

PI depends primarily on the director's willingness to see to its continuation; it would probably be discontinued were he not available. Both the director and one colleague who served for a time in RR contributed their free time to PI, although a portion of the director's assigned duties included some PI activities.

In addition to constructive criticism which was considered in planning modifications in PI, participating students had praise for the program's flexibility, which allowed them to study when they wanted and at their own rates. They expressed appreciation for the thirty-five hour weekly schedule of RR and for the comfortable atmosphere of the learning center. Several students, who dislike lock-step lectures and recitation in general, expressed reservations about continuing second-year Russian because it does not have the PI option. Most students appreciated not having to prepare for exams on a predetermined schedule that too often led to 'cramming' instead of learning. Most students felt that the immediate correction of exams, with simultaneous tutoring, was invaluable.

I believe that PI is promising in spite of certain limitations, e.g., that PI students' progress through the required material is slower, generally, than that of lock-step students. The fact that most students choose challenging 'A' contracts should not be overlooked. Furthermore, experience indicates that students generally come to RR prepared to pass the tests, which are long as well as challenging, at contract level. During the spring term, for instance, the average PI-102 student required only 1.48 attempts to pass each unit at contract level. The relative lack of subjective elements in the correction of exams substantially alters the image of the instructor, who now tends to be viewed by the students more as a friendly consultant and diagnostician than as a judge whose stern decisions are mysteriously conditioned by the concept of the curve.

PI's open enrollment attracts more students, often those who have withdrawn from another course, yet wish to maintain a full load. Because of PI's flexibility, the department can now offer both 101 and 102--at least in the PI version--each semester, and currently in the summer. PI tends to minimize the number of withdrawals. The fact that most students eventually transferred to PI indicates that in their view the program better served their needs than the lock-step system.   However, their perception of their needs was not necessarily wise (I refer to the fact that some excellent lock-step students transferred to PI mainly to avoid a final examination).

RR is useful as a cultural center for the department as a whole, for faculty meetings, and as a center for testing new audio-visual software. PI allows a greater number of graduate students to do practice teaching under the supervision of an experienced teacher. It is also conducive to experimentation in cross-student instruction under the supervision of the PI instructors.

During the first year of PI at SUNYA it was impossible to do more than create five variations of translation tests for each of the twenty-three units. However, since the exams already created may now serve for a second year, oral and aural exams can be added, thus raising the program's standards. (Students whose career needs do not include a knowledge of spoken Russian should not be forced to take the new exams.)

In order to motivate students who are unable to pace themselves properly, a minimal goal (e.g., one-third that of the lock-step sections) will probably be imposed on PI students. Such imposed discipline was recommended by PI students during the first year. Also, a student who has passed a certain point in the grammar (e.g., the eighth chapter in PI-101) will not be allowed to drop the course.

Greater efforts will be made to acquaint graduate assistants with effective teaching techniques, and new graduate assistants will be required to review and demonstrate their mastery of the first-year grammar before beginning service in the program. Greater faculty participation will be sought. A separate track of PI, utilizing a different grammar, may eventually be introduced for students desiring to learn scientific Russian.

INDIVIDUALIZED FIRST-YEAR SPANISH PROGRAM (1458)

Charles W. Stansfield
Department of Spanish and Portuguese, University of Colorado

The Department of Spanish and Portuguese began to experiment with individualized instruction in spring 1972 in an effort to solve the recurring problems of expanded class size and the high cost of language teaching. We adopted a set of programmed materials which allows students to work at their own speed and requires a greater degree of individual commitment.

One of the first problems encountered was the direction of self-pacing. While some students exceeded normal advancement, a larger number fell hopelessly behind. We therefore established a policy of allowing students to fall only one week behind before assigning an 'F' for the uncompleted unit. We have found that setting such completion dates forces everyone to do the unit before that date and keeps them from falling so far behind that it becomes impossible to catch up or participate with the rest of the class in conversational practice. Students may still move as far ahead as they wish, even to the point of not having to attend class at all.

As some ten percent of the students advanced so far that class attendance was no longer helpful, it became necessary to substitute alternate kinds of learning activities. Consequently, we now make increased use of resources such as foreign films and the foreign language house.

Another necessary change concerned repetition of examinations. A student was allowed to repeat any exam as often as he wished and receive the highest grade achieved. However, some students made a habit of taking the test at least once for practice, thereby placing an unreasonable burden on the TA's who grade the tests. Now, students are allowed to repeat tests only once, and both grades are averaged together; this forces students to prepare seriously for each examination.

First-year Spanish is composed of two five-semester-hour courses numbered 101 and 102 or 105. Spanish 105 is parallel to 102 but is limited to people who did their first level of work in high school or at another university. Students attend five fifty-minute classes per week. The program uses three different teaching strategies in the following manner.

Tuesday and Thursday sessions, involving large groups of students (200-250) with a single teacher, present aspects of the course which do not require teacher-student interaction. On Tuesday, a multi-section lecture on Spanish grammar and culture is presented using transparencies, an overhead projector, and a wireless microphone. Questions from the audience are permitted and occasional pattern drills are conducted to apply concepts previously described. Thursday is reserved for testing, and students may take written tests on any of the twelve programmed units comprising each course. Tests are prepared by the lecturer and are delivered to the appropriate TA for grading each Thursday afternoon. They are returned to the students during Friday's class, at which time they may decide whether they want to take the test again one week later, provided the completion date for that unit has not yet arrived. Tests are returned to the TA at the end of the period. Since the course is self-paced, the lecturer must bring tests for several different units each Thursday.

The Monday, Wednesday, and Friday classes are taught to small groups of twenty or fewer students by a teaching assistant, referred to as a 'drill session leader.' Although programmed grammar units are done independently, a situational dialogue accompanies each, and these are handled in the drill sessions, with four classes devoted to each dialogue. During these classes no lecturing is done, and grammar is not presented either deductively or through pattern practice. On the first day, the drill session leader introduces the dialogue and corrects student pronunciation. On the second day, he reviews the dialogue to insure that students have memorized it, conducts question-answer practice on the dialogue content, and gives students dialogue expansion material composed of synonyms, antonyms, and other substitution vocabulary. The third day is devoted to personalization of the dialogue: students practice speaking in an unstructured conversational situation similar to that portrayed in the dialogue. On the fourth day of a unit, the drill session leader gives an oral test to each student in the class. The test comprises fifty percent of the unit grade and generally involves reciting the dialogue, answering questions on it, and personalization employing dialogue expansion vocabulary.

Students may retake these oral tests during their TA's office hours. A student passing both the oral and written test for a unit before the first day of dialogue presentation is excused from attending class for that unit. Once the class begins to officially study the unit, students must wait until the fourth drill session to take the oral test. This prevents the TA from being deluged with requests for early tests following introduction of the material.

Drill session leaders are required to keep six office hours per week. While this is twice that required by other departments, it is necessary for the individualized program. Students are encouraged throughout the course to come in for practice, ask questions, take oral tests ahead of time, and retake tests.

Independent study is employed to teach grammar through the programmed booklets the student works through on his own. It also includes the language laboratory, which is open six days and five nights per week, thus giving students ample opportunity to practice with the tapes.

Once students become accustomed to learning independently, many like to expand the technique to include unstructured application of their skills. This is particularly true of those students who advance ahead of the group and no longer attend class. Therefore, the department publishes a bi-weekly newsletter of events in the community involving Spanish language or culture. Here, students are informed about the Spanish-language radio station in Denver, movies playing at Denver's three Spanish cinemas, special events such as campus lectures on the Hispanic world, foreign films, a local Spanish mass, and cultural programs of the foreign language house and the local United Mexican-American Students organization. In addition, students are encouraged to have lunch at the weekly language table in the student union and to have supper at the language house whenever possible.

In response to a request from the department, the university's Bureau of Audio-Visual Instruction presents Spanish- and English-language films on Latin America from noon to 1:00 p.m. each Tuesday on closed-circuit television. Receivers for viewing are available at fifty-one campus locations; a description of films to be shown is also printed in the newsletter.

Students in second-semester courses, particularly those who completed the first level in high school, have frequently forgotten much material. The departmental office maintains a supply of first-level programmed texts which can be used by students wishing to review.

The primary instructional resource is the series of twelve small programmed textbooks called Basic Spanish published by Individual Learning Systems of San Rafael, California. Each text is composed of two units treating a different morphological or syntactic problem of the language. For instance, unit eleven in book six covers irregular forms of the preterite and imperfect tenses, while unit twelve covers some of the more idiomatic uses of tener, ser, estar, hacer, and gustar.

Each unit is itself divided into two parts. Part A gives a narrative description of the language, similar to that which might be found in any traditional grammar text. Each statement is followed by sentences illustrating the grammatical point in question. After completing this section, the student takes a mastery test located at the end of each unit. If all responses are correct, the student may go on to the next unit. If not, part B, a programmed treatment of the same concept, is studied. After completing the section the student again takes the mastery test, usually obtaining a perfect score. Failing to obtain a perfect score, the student can consult the TA or lecturer for assistance.

In addition to the twelve programmed volumes, the series includes a Student Guide which contains a picture of each of the twenty-four situations, pronunciation exercises, and worksheets which are to be completed in the language laboratory. The drill session leader has an Instructor's Guide containing suggested expansions of each dialogue. Also available are three sets of color posters illustrating the dialogues.

In a program of this type, provision must be made for the orientation and in-service training of all teachers. Therefore, the department grants released time for the following people to supervise and participate in program management. A faculty coordinator designs the instructional system and approves or disapproves changes, including activities for the training of all incoming TA's, is responsible for materials, books, and tapes being available and in sufficient stock, observes all TA's at least once during the fall semester, meets frequently with all TA's to discuss problems and answer questions, teaches a graduate-level course in college foreign language teaching which all incoming TA's must take, conducts a three-day pre-service workshop in the fall, and has overall responsibility for the program. The faculty coordinator generally spends twelve to fifteen hours per week on the program, including time spent on the course in college foreign language teaching.

An assistant coordinator assists the faculty coordinator and is classified as a teaching assistant. This person is always an experienced teacher who can win the respect of the other TA's. The assistant coordinator may assist the faculty coordinator in all functions and is prepared to take charge if necessary. Additional regular duties include publishing the newsletter of coming events and community resources, conducting the weekly Spanish-language table with one drill session leader, and assisting in the distribution and proctoring of Thursday examinations. The assistant coordinator observes each TA at least three times per semester, meets weekly with the faculty coordinator and lecturers, and is also called upon occasionally to construct visual aids for other TA's.

Lecturers are responsible for teaching and testing grammar during the Tuesday and Thursday large-group sessions. They also meet weekly with the faculty coordinator and assistant. In addition, they prepare suggested dialogue expansions for distribution to drill session leaders, and they discuss the coming unit with them at the weekly coordination meeting. They also distribute copies of the laboratory tape script, so that drill session leaders will know which concepts and vocabulary are being emphasized there. While lecturers teach only two classes per week, they are credited and paid for three hours teaching and classified as teaching associates.

A multi-faceted organizational plan will not guarantee a successful program. The plan itself may be faulty, thus causing a deterioration rather than an improvement in instruction. Since evaluation of any program is essential in determining its success, the department has been interested in any feedback that might shed light on how we are doing. In this respect, the following facts have increased our confidence that we are on are on the right track:

(1) During the 1972-73 academic year, seven TA's who had also worked with Lado's Contemporary Spanish the previous year taught in the Basic Spanish program. Each reported that student achievement in the four skills seemed noticeably higher in the individualized program. Especially impressive was student achievement in the skills of speaking and writing.

(2) During the ten-week summer term, the department has traditionally offered two five-week intensive courses covering levels 101 and 102. The following table illustrates the change in enrollment patterns which occurred after instituting individualization in spring 1972.

Summer Spanish Enrollments by Course and Year

	1970	1971	1972	1973	1974
101	33	28	66	67	71
102	30	30	50	48	68
Total	63	58	116	115	139

Registration for the second five-week session during the summer of 1973 produced seventy-one requests for Spanish 102. Financial difficulties within the college made it impossible to offer a third drill session so that twenty-three requests were turned down, and the department acceded to placing the forty-eight students who had preregistered for the course into two sections. The magnitude of this increase can be appreciated by considering that the total university enrollment dropped by ten percent during summer 1972 and remained at that level during summer 1973.

(3) During fall semester 1972, a student course evaluation was administered to all sections of 101 and 102. (Spanish 105 did not exist at the time.) The mean rating of respondents in each of twenty-five categories was determined by computer analysis, and this rating was compared with the mean of each category for the entire university. Respondents in 101 ranked the course and their instructors above the university mean in each of the twenty-five categories, while 102 students ranked the course and their instructors above the university mean on eighteen of the categories. When one considers that these are courses for non-majors, the results are even more gratifying.

Until fall 1971, the Department of Spanish and Portuguese used teaching associates in first-year classes composed of thirty or more students, the same organization presently used by the other foreign language departments. But the teaching associate, having full responsibility for a class, earns 22.7% more per hour than a teaching assistant. Since the assistant teaches six hours per week and the associate only five, the difference in pay amounts to only 2.7% more in favor of the associate. In terms of actual pay received, the difference is only $80.00 per year. With the teaching assistant teaching 25% more students for 2.7% less, the result is a gross saving of 27.7%. When the salaries of the lecturers and the assistant coordinator are subtracted, actual savings still amount to 15.2%. Thus, the program has reduced our cost per student credit hour from $10.28 to $8.92.

Since each fall some ten percent of the students complete Spanish 101 before Thanksgiving, arrangements were made in 1973 for them to continue into 102 before Christmas. Those who complete at least one-fourth of 102 during this period are allowed to enroll in a special spring section covering both second- and third-semester Spanish. In January 1974, this select group consisted of twenty-five students, eighteen of whom completed all third semester work and received credit for both courses. The remaining seven received credit for 102 after voluntarily returning to a regular section of this class. While no standardized test was given, the students in the special course appeared to do generally better than students enrolled in regular third-semester sections, and all of those who were not graduating seniors stated their intent to continue the study of Spanish, taking either a minor or major in the language.

SPANISH CIVILIZATION AS REFLECTED IN THE ARTS (1464)

Marta de la Portilla
Department of Foreign Languages, Manhattanville College

A Spanish proverb states, "Necessity sharpens the intellect;" in English the same thought is expressed as "Necessity is the mother of invention." This is perhaps the most concise explanation of the origin of Spanish Civilization as Reflected in the Arts.

For some time I had been trying to individualize portions of our Spanish instruction and to create a survey of the artistic and cultural manifestations of Hispanic civilizations and their proper interrelationship. Due to a sudden shortage of teaching personnel, it became necessary to make the fullest possible use of our audio-visual facilities, and I designed a series of presentations for individualized use involving an audio cassette, slides, and supplementary readings.

The program presents study materials in the four basic skills; the student listens to the tapes, takes notes and answers questions in writing, reads supplementary selections, and discusses the work in weekly meetings with the instructor. The cassette, recorded in Spanish, is a guide to the visual material. Each unit also includes test questions for the student to use in evaluating comprehension of the material and usually ends with musical selections preceded by brief introductions. Supplementary readings in literature or from another discipline are also accompanied by questions.

At the beginning of the course, each student is interviewed and, in accordance with previous preparation and interest, a program is prepared, and the student is given an outline indicating the work to be done each week. Sixteen units is the minimum the student is allowed to complete.

The materials are available to students daily from 8 a.m. until 9 p.m. in the Audio-Visual Department. There they use a rear-screen projector which also coordinates the cassette and Carousel slide tray. At any moment, the student can interrupt the presentation to repeat a sequence. Students come for a weekly consultation during office hours and submit unit evaluation forms. During the first year, we did not have this weekly discussion procedure, but the results indicate it is warranted. At the end of the semester, students take an examination; the final grade is a combination of performance on this examination and on the weekly evaluations.

The course has been offered for the past three years and carries three credit hours at either the 300 or 500 level. A varied group of students has shown interest in the course. Spanish majors take it as an elective; students from other departments with sufficient knowledge of Spanish take it as independent study; high school teachers easily fit it into their own teaching schedules and find it suited to their needs and interests.

This type of course offers advantages in that it presents no schedule conflicts, provides for individualized instruction, and demands systematic study from students. Disadvantages are the expense of purchasing the visual aids, the initial demands of preparation, the inability of some students to work independently, and the lack of daily contact between teacher and student--which means that difficulties cannot always be resolved and commentary made at the most appropriate time. Nevertheless, the course has had positive results, and series on Spanish literature and on Spanish America are now being prepared.

Off-Campus

(See also mss. 30, 212, 1054/1141, 1085/1257/1258, 1174, 1191, 1265)

LES ACTUALITES FRANCAISES (1551)

Michelle Buchanan
Department of French and Italian, University of Southern California

Les Actualités Françaises was created when the department decided to offer a summer session in France. As director-administrator of the program, I chose to structure it along strictly linguistic and cultural lines. Literature courses, especially in shortened sessions, shortchange students who, away from their home campus, seldom find the necessary scholarly resources to help them in their research projects. Undergraduate students, non-majors and majors alike, choosing to go to France or anywhere else for summer study, do so primarily to spend some time abroad and to establish contact with the people. At that level, there is little interest in scholarly research and little desire to spend hours in classrooms doing the same things one has to do on the home campus.

It was therefore decided to offer language and conversation courses for beginners under native instructors, advanced composition for experienced students, and Les Actualités Françaises for all students with reading knowledge of French at or above third-semester level. With the support of my colleagues and evidence of interest from potential program participants, the course proposal was submitted to our university curriculum committee which approved it as part of our regular program.

By its very nature, Les Actualités Françaises, conducted in English, must reflect the changing concerns of France each time it is offered. It must have built into it the necessary flexibility to present evolving social, political, and economic situations confronting the French people. Its basic structure may remain fairly constant while allowing shifting emphasis from one area to another.

As students unfamiliar with French history and culture would not be able to grasp or analyze much of the information they encounter, the instructor's first responsibility is to offer the foundation necessary to their understanding of contemporary France. As an introduction, a rapid overview recalls the basic attributes of French regions, their differences, and their role in the development of major urban areas in the long-range plan for decentralization.

During the session, the following topics are covered: (1) social structure and the role of religion as a sociological phenomenon; (2) political life, governmental institutions, their role and relative importance; (3) French youth, with its major problem areas of education and employment; (4) agriculture, heavy industry, transportation, and the growth of the tertiaire service industries; (5) France as a world contributor to basic research and its technological applications; (6) the communications media of newspapers, radio, television, cinema; (7) France and its relations with other European countries, the Third World, and the United States.

Soon after classes start, areas of major interest in present-day France are identified, and students, singly or in pairs, decide which one they will study in depth for detailed and

142

up-to-the-moment class presentation. To do so, they are to choose a daily newspaper and/or a weekly periodical of national distribution in which they will follow coverage of their particular topic. Newspapers and weeklies are selected with a clear understanding of their general political leanings: socialist, UDR, conservative, communist, or broad readership. Each lecture by the instructor is followed by a student discussion of current events reflecting and reinforcing their growing awareness of France's actuality.

Some topics of major interest in summer 1974 were the reorganization of the Office of Radio and Television, the prison system (prison rioting being a major headline), women's growing role in society and government (the appointment of several women to Giscard d'Estaing's cabinet), birth control and abortion, and Common Market problems.

Although reading newspapers and periodicals is a major way to perceive the country's mood and concerns, involvement with the French themselves is essential to add the human dimension necessary to fix the reality of those concerns. With this in mind, the written assignment for Les Actualités Françaises is the preparation of a 'cultural' (for want of a better word) journal, in English. Such an assignment transcends the limits of a summer session. In their journals, the students are to write, in analytical reporting fashion, of their encounters with native French people, of discussions, and of reactions to different cultural patterns. The project forces the students to think about their French experience as it happens, and, after the journals are returned to them, they have an invaluable record of their summer in France.

The course requires constant intensive involvement on the part of students and instructor in order to be a successfully enriching experience. The cultural journals are a gold mine of perceptive comments. For many students, it is the beginning of a better understanding of another people and another country. The department plans to continue its summer session in France, and at present no changes are contemplated in the structure of the program offerings.

Les Actualités Françaises offered on the home campus would present few problems, except of course for the preparation of the cultural journal. With a good 'French connection' in a bookstore, preferably in Paris, dailies and weeklies could be airmailed with very few days' delay. The unavailability of French radio and television material is of minor importance, as the continued government control of the media makes them merely another official tool of news dissemination. With materials available in our International Relations Library, or any other good library, students would be able to research and develop topics of major interest and, thus, achieve the original purpose of the course.

MEXICO: A MODERN REVOLUTION (1566)

Douglas K. Benson (Modern Languages) and Robert Stockton (Sociology)
Departments of Modern Languages and Sociology, Hastings College

Over a period of five years many students had asked the language department to organize a tour to Mexico, and it was as a result of this interest that the travel course was planned. But we realized that a course for language majors only would not be academically feasible; a language-oriented guided tour could not begin to study the phenomenon that is Mexico. Thus, we scheduled activities for Spanish-speaking students, but the course was conducted in English or with the Spanish-speaking students acting as interpreters.

The purpose of the course is to study social and cultural change as they relate to revolution, and to concentrate on events in Mexico from 1910 to the present as a specific model of ongoing revolution. An important consideration in this study was the examination of cultural and artistic expression as a corollary of social change and the development of national pride and self-awareness.

Octavio Paz' The Labyrinth of Solitude was selected as a required text for upper-division students. It is one of the most lucid treatments of the Mexican character and history and one of the better examples of artistic essay in modern Mexico. The basic text for the course was Cumberland's Mexico: The Struggle for Modernity. In addition, all students read Oscar Lewis's Five Families, Mariano Azuela's The Underdogs (Los de abajo), and Carlos Fuentes' Where the Air Is Clear (La región más trasparente). The two novels were chosen because they exemplify a high level of artistic achievement as well as a variety of attitudes toward the revolution and its aftermath.

During the first week, classes were held on campus and were designed to acquaint students with the backgrounds of modern Mexico, including pre-Columbian achievements and their influence on the present. The forces leading to Díaz' overthrow and the subsequent struggle for power were examined in light of the original ideals of the early revolutionaries. Then we compared the achievements of Cárdenas and his successors to those ideals. The first week was also devoted to instilling a sense of cultural relativity in the students before we left on the journey.

In addition, upper-level students gave reports on their areas of specialty: art students spoke on Posada, Rivera, Orozco, Siquieros; Spanish students on the directions of modern Mexican prose, drama, culture; social science students on the economic, political, and educational trends of the twentieth century. Thus, a level of expertise was brought to different dimensions of the problems that could not all be expected of the professors themselves. Filmstrips, music, movies, and other audio-visual materials gave the students a visual preparation for what to expect.

This approach proved its soundness during the travel portion of the course. As we moved through the Bajío region, we encountered many different types of imitative church and colonial architecture in European medieval and baroque styles, Mexican Indian baroque, and all possible combinations. Art students aided the professors in pointing out differences among these early examples and later contrasted them with modern and truly Mexican architecture and sculpture. The same was done with painting, music, anthropology, land use patterns, etc.

Knowledge was gained by a 'composite' approach; students were exposed to different aspects of modern Mexico and its heritage and encouraged to consider them in light of revolutionary goals and trends. Synthesis was sought on an individual basis, and progress was detailed in journals of the trip kept by each student. The interaction and mutual discovery on the part of the students was most impressive. Professors tried to keep students from applying too closely the criteria they had learned to everything they saw, but they refrained from turning the trip into a guided tour, and generally made comments only on elements that might create confusion or on those which are common to many developing nations and their aspirations and cultural expression.

The rationale for a multifaceted approach to Mexico and its revolution is obvious-- all parts of Mexican society were affected; indeed, Mexico did not come into being until the 1930's as a direct outgrowth of the collective pride which came from the success of the revolution. Mexico cannot be understood in terms of only language, society, economics, or politics, but rather as a synthesis of these elements and their interrelationship. Thus, an interdepartmental approach was the only logical one.

The only problems encountered in getting official approval were mechanical ones, such as point of departure, accommodations, and the like. The language department is strongly supported by the administration and by at least half of the faculty. The course was given full approval and was publicized through regular channels--posters, newspaper articles and ads, memos to faculty. On a small campus such as ours, there is a good deal of faculty interaction; nevertheless, groundwork for breaking down artificial interdepartmental barriers had to be done by the language department. A direct approach has been quite effective. When we have an idea for a particular emphasis in a course, or if we wish to develop a double major, we approach the instructor or department involved. We have been turned down infrequently since our record of success has been high. Indeed, these classes attract more students into each department then either department can possibly hope to attract individually.

The Mexico course was not used as a model for future Mexico courses, although such courses are now in the planning stage, but rather for future interdepartmental courses such as Hispanic Music, Developing a Life-Concept Through Philosophy and Literature, Literature and the Film, etc. These can generally be worked into regular terms, and in

144

the past none of the courses has resulted in an overload for the instructor. The month-long January interim is especially useful, and the Mexico course functioned very well under this plan. Since the course was developed as a model for specific repetition in the future, we attempted to avoid dependency on individual faculty.

Interdepartmental courses are somewhat less than satisfactory for language skill development, but our language classes have always had a high culture content and work especially well in this context. Indeed, the Mexico course and its prospective successors could not possibly be duplicated by another department in depth of cultural knowledge or academic rigor. For this reason, and because the language department is willing to impart its knowledge and experience to others as well as to request assistance from other departments, the Department of Modern Languages has an improved image. For example, several departments now suggest and encourage language and cultural study as useful adjuncts to their fields, including business, sociology, music, English, journalism, and pre-med.

The administration has become more aware of the advantages of our programs and supports them fully. Students are able to relate their fields to the study of language, culture, and literature, and their interest is growing; we have many repeat students. Many students have mentioned that because of the scope of this approach they were later better able to relate many of the things they learned to fields unrelated to language study.

We feel highly motivated to develop other courses in which several departments are involved, in which students are asked to contribute their individual expertise, and in which each instructor's duties involve relating to other disciplines. The interdepartmental approach allows students to perceive the basic differences in approach between, for example, a humanist and a social scientist, and to realize the value of each. The synthesis of disciplines shows the student ways in which other complex topics can be studied.

This type of course has had no detrimental effect on language skill courses. The latter continue to be taught on a regular basis, and the special courses are taught as the opportunity presents itself. There is one other bonus: an increasing number of students taking elementary and intermediate language courses--and who are not doing so to satisfy any requirement of the college. A significant number of these had their initial contact with language department members in interdepartmental courses.

In-Translation   (See mss. 1045, 1054/1141, 1551, 1566)

Miscellaneous

VALUES OF FOREIGN CULTURES (1678A)

Gwyndola P. Fish
Department of Modern Foreign Languages, Mars Hill College

Several years ago, the foreign language requirement came under fire, and members of the department, realizing the days of the requirement were numbered, began to look for

145

additional ways of justifying their existence. An inquiry was made into the value of foreign language study in an attempt to isolate aspects which could be independent of the language-learning process. An initial program of foreign culture courses taught in English was created. It had both strengths and weaknesses, and, although some students were encouraged by the courses to continue foreign language study, the number was small.

In 1972 the college began working toward adoption of a 'competency-based' curriculum. The concept involved in such a curriculum was that a student would graduate on the basis of acquired competencies, i.e., because of what the student had learned to do, rather than on the basis of having taken a specified number of courses. Under the competency system in general education, students meet competency requirements in six areas: communication skills, personal development, values, aesthetics, science, and synoptics. The major represents a seventh competency area.

The Values Competence Statement stipulates that a graduate of the college understand the major values of the native and of one foreign culture and be able to assess the significance of those values. In theory, students are able to study, travel, and develop competence on their own in any way they see fit, simply requesting that a values assessment team evaluate their competence. But few choose such independent study because most have a very limited cultural exposure. Therefore, courses in American and foreign cultures have been designed in order to help the student develop competence in this area.

With the adoption of the Values Competence, values as reflected in the foreign culture became the specific focus of the courses. Many faculty members had reservations about the propriety and feasibility of such an arrangement. How can one teach values? Where does indoctrination begin? Would 'ethics' perhaps be a better word? As a result of the department's early efforts to analyze what the foreign culture course could offer the student, we were able to establish some criteria for meeting the requirements of the competence. They are:

(1) knowledge of and ability to compare the contemporary political structure of a major foreign culture and of the native culture;
(2) knowledge of and ability to compare major art forms and artists of a major foreign culture and the native culture;
(3) knowledge of and ability to compare the religious heritage of a major foreign culture and the native culture;
(4) knowledge of the economic system and conditions of a major foreign culture;
(5) knowledge of the social structure of a major foreign culture;
(6) knowledge of the major historical events as they relate to the foreign culture in its entirety.

The student is expected to compare and assess relationships continuously between the major values of the native and the foreign culture.

Foreign culture courses with the values orientation will be taught for the third time in fall 1975. It is too soon to draw conclusions about the general success of the program, but we have been able to observe that: (1) students have more interest in and tolerance of other people; (2) the student body as a whole demonstrates greater global awareness; (3) there has been some increase in the number of students who want to study a foreign language.

The classes have been lively and have included various types of activities--debates, discussions, oral reports, eating, games, dancing, singing, viewing films and slides, and hearing visiting lecturers. It is difficult to find materials appropriate for the courses, and faculty members must rely heavily on their own experience. Classes meet one hour a day, four days a week. Because so much of what happens in the course happens in the classroom, attendance is considered vital, and students are permitted only a limited number of absences.

Sample course outlines are available. The courses are taught in the areas of Greek and Roman, French, Spanish, German, and Oriental cultures.

146

Part II: Catalog of Survey Entries

CAREER-RELATED

Translation and Interpretation

CHINESE

1. CHINESE-ENGLISH TRANSLATION
Federal City C; FLs; Washington, DC 20001.
1-4; 2-3x10; 3-a; 4-73/74; 5-1; 6-sufficient demand; 7-a; 8-3q; 9-a; 10-inter prof; 11-intensive practice trans Chinese into Eng; 12-a,b,c,d,t; 13-e,f; 14-ng.

2. ENGLISH-CHINESE TRANSLATION
Federal City C; FLs; Washington, DC 20001.
1-3; 2-3x10; 3-a; 4-73/74; 5-1; 6-sufficient demand; 7-a; 8-3q; 9-a; 10-inter prof; 11-intensive practice trans English to Chinese; 12-a,b,c,f,g; 13-e,f; 14-ng.

FRENCH

3. FRENCH TRANSLATION
Adelphi U; Langs; Garden City, NY 11530.
Josette Smetana
1-10; 2-3x16; 3-a; 4-70; 5-5; 6-b; 7-a; 8-3s; 9-a; 10-adv prof; 11-study of comparative structures & idioms to overcome lang barrier with spoken word as interpreter, written word for the translator; poli, lit, hist, soci texts studied; 12-b,c,d,f; 13-e,f; 14-Dider, Chemin de la Traduction, Domaine anglais; Whitmarsh & Jukes, New Advanced French Course.

4. FRENCH TRANSLATION
Allegheny C; MLs; Meadville, PA 16335.
Blair Hanson
1-7; 2-3½x9½; 3-a; 4-72/73; 5-3; 6-b; 7-a; 8-3 1/3; 9-a; 10-adv prof; 11-Designed to give students insight into problems, techniques of trans & acquaint them with the tools & practical aspects of trans work. Texts to be translated will be taken from lit, natural & social sciences, business; 12-c,f; 13-e,f; letters, poems; 14-ng.

5. TRANSLATOR-INTERPRETER PRO-GRAM
U of California; Fr & Ital; Santa Barbara, CA 93106.
Donald R. Westman
1-new; 2-8x30; 3-a; 4-fall 75; 5-0; 6-a; 7-a; 8-8q; 9-grad students; 10-B.A. or consent; 11-1-yr certificate program of 6 courses: 1,2) Intro to Trans, Fr-Eng, Eng-Fr; 3,4) Intro to Interpretation, Fr-Eng, Eng-Fr; 5)

Adv Trans, Fr-Eng; 6) Conference Interpreting; 12-a,e,f,g; 13-d,e,f; 14-Masselin, Le francais scientifique et technique (2 vols); Brueziere, Le francais commercial (2 vols); Rozan, Le prise de notes en interpretation consecutive.

6. COMMERCIAL FRENCH TRANSLATION
Colby-Sawyer C-New Hampshire; MLs; New London, NH 03257.
David Siesicki
1-2; 2-3x14; 3-a; 4-74/75; 5-1; 6-demand; 7-a; 8-1 course unit (3.3s); 9-a; 10-adv prof; 11-trans, structural & stylistic analysis of commercial lang, ling & stylistic differences between Canadian & European Fr; 12-b,c,d,e,f,g; 13-e,f, commercial correspondence, reports, articles; 14-ng.

7. ENGLISH-FRENCH TRANSLATION
Federal City C; Fr; Washington, DC 20001.
1-6; 2-3x10; 3-a; 4-73/74; 5-1; 6-demand; 7-a; 8-1 course unit (3.3s); 9-a; 10-adv prof; 11-Eng to French trans; 12-b,c,d,f,g; 13-e,f; 14-ng.

8. FRENCH-ENGLISH TRANSLATION
Federal City C; Fr; Washington, DC 20001.
1-7; 2-3x10; 3-a; 4-73/74; 5-1; 6-c; 7-a; 8-3q; 9-a; 10-inter prof; 11-Fr to Eng trans; 12-b,c,d,f,g; 13-e,f; 14-none.

9. INTERPRETER'S STUDIES
U of Massachusetts; Fr & Ital; Amherst, MA 01002.
Daniel Martin
1-est 20-30; 2-(2 courses of) 3x13; 3-b; 4-spr 75; 5-0; 6-a; 7-a; 8-3s; 9-a; 10-good comprehension of Dutch, Fr, Ger, Ital, Port, Russ, or Sp and a basic reading knowledge of Fr; 11-2 courses, one each in consecutive & simultaneous trans; 12-e,f; 13-d,e; 14-Rozan, La prise de notes en interpretation consecutive; Herbert, Manuel de l'interprete; Seleskovitch, L'Interprete.

10. INTRODUCTION TO CONSECUTIVE AND SIMULTANEOUS INTERPRETING
Montclair SC; Fr; Upper Montclair, NJ 07043.
Robert Glick
1-ng; 2-3x16; 3-a; 4-72; 5-3; 6-b; 7-a; 8-3s; 9-a; 10-adv prof; 11-the field of cross-cult communications (emphasis on Fr-speaking

world) & practice in techniques of simultaneous & consecutive interpreting, Fr-Eng,
Eng-Fr; 12-b,c,f,g; 13-d,e,f; 14-from a' variety of fields: legal, commercial, lit.

11. TRANSLATION I & II (CONCENTRATION
IN TRANSLATION & INTERPRETATION)
Montclair SC; Fr; Upper Montclair, NJ
07043.
Robert Glick
1-ng; 2-3x16; 3-a; 4-71; 5-5; 6-a; 7-a; 8-3s;
9-a; 10-adv prof; 11-2 sem sequence in
techniques of trans, Eng-Fr, Fr-Eng, vocab,
comparative sentence structure, analysis,
expression of ideas & images; 12-a,b,c,f,g;
13-d,e,f; 14-from a variety of fields: legal,
commercial, lit.

12. STUDIES IN TRANSLATION: FRENCH
Occidental C; Langs & Ling; Los Angeles,
CA 90041.
Edric Cane
1-9; 2-4x10; 3-a; 4-74; 5-1; 6-every other
yr; 7-a; 8-4s; 9-a; 10-adv prof, permission;
11-emphasis on practice: written trans,
oral interpretation, simultaneous trans; variety in materials & purpose of trans; 12-
b,d,e,g; 13-d,f; 14-Darbelnet, Stylistique
comparee du francais et de l'anglais, & especially accompanying workbook.

13. FRENCH TRANSLATION
Queens C; FLs; Charlotte, NC 28207. E.
Cobb
1-ng; 2-3 wks; 3-a; 4-to be offered Jan 76;
5-0; 6-every 3 yrs; 7-a; 8-2; 9-a; 10-elem
prof; 11-3 hrs per day of trans in science or
hums; 12-b,c,g; 13-e,f, native spkrs; 14-ng.

14. TECHNIQUES OF TRANSLATION:
FRENCH
Stephens C; FLs; Columbia, MO 65201.
Albert J. Delmez
1-12; 2-3x7; 3-a; 4-70; 5-4; 6-b; 7-a; 8-1½q;
9-a; 10-adv comp skills; 11-ng; 12-b,c,f,g;
13-e,f; 14-materials from magazines, periodicals, some literary prose.

15. TRANSLATION
Trinity C; French; Washington, DC 20017.
Eda Levitine
1-10; 2-3xsem; 3-a; 4-73/74; 5-1; 6-every
2nd yr; 7-a; 8-3s; 9-a; 10-inter to adv prof;
11-trans, written & oral, Fr-Eng & Eng-Fr
using articles selected from various sources
& dealing with materials pertinent to various majors; 12-b,c,d,e,g; 13-a,b,e,f; 14-
see 11.

16. FRENCH TRANSLATION
U of Tulsa; Letters; Tulsa, OK 74104.
Anthony A. Francis
1-9; 2-3x15; 3-a; 4-73; 5-2; 6-every 2nd yr;
7-a; 8-3q; 9-a; 10-inter prof; 11-sci & lit
trans Fr-Eng, individualized instruction according to students' fields of study; 12-
a,b,c,f; 13-e,f; 14-Stack, Reading French in
the Arts & Sciences; Bonnerot, Les chemins
de la traduction.

See also 201, 475, 476.

GERMAN

17. GERMAN TRANSLATION
Allegheny C; MLs; Meadville, PA 16355.
Dieter Lotze
1-8; 2-3½x9½; 3-a; 4-72/73; 5-3; 6-b; 7-a; 8-
3 1/3s; 9-a; 10-inter prof; 11-designed to
give insight into problems & techniques of
trans & to acquaint them with tools & practical aspects of trans; texts to be trans will
be taken from lit, sci, business, other fields;
12-a,c,written, f; 13-ng; 14-professor's
materials.

18. TRANSLATOR-INTERPRETER   PRO-
GRAM
U of California; Ger & Sl; Santa Barbara,
CA 93106.
John T. Waterman
1-new; 2-20x36; 3-a; 4-74/75; 5-0; 6-a; 7-a;
8-16q; 9-a; 10-B.A. any field plus 1 yr of
study in Ger-speaking country, satisfactory
score on Adv Ger Test of GRE; 11-Post B.A.
yr of study leading to certification; 12-
a,d,e,f,g; 13-a,b,c,d,e,f; 14-ng.

19. ENGLISH-GERMAN TRANSLATION
Federal City C; FLs; Washington, DC
20001.
1-3; 2-3x10; 3-a; 4-73/74; 5-1; 6-b; 7-a; 8-
3q; 9-a; 10-inter prof; 11-Eng to Ger trans;
12-b,c,d,e,f,g; 13-e,f; 14-ng.

20. GERMAN-ENGLISH TRANSLATION
Federal City C; FLs; Washington, DC
20001.
1-3; 2-3x10; 3-a; 4-73/74; 5-1; 6-b; 7-a; 8-
3q; 9-a; 10-inter prof; 11-Ger to Eng trans;
12-b,c,d,e,f,g; 13-e,f; 14-ng.

21. TECHNIQUES OF INTERPRETATION OF
GERMAN
Federal City C; FLs; Washington, DC
20001.
This course extended over period of 2 qtrs;
further info ng.

22. SPECIAL   TOPICS: TRANSLATING
GERMAN
Kent SU; Ger & Sl Langs & Lits; Kent, OH
44242.
Herman K. Doswald
1-ng; 2-4x10; 3-a; 4-74; 5-1; 6-every 2nd yr;
7-a; 8-4q; 9-a; 10-adv prof; 11-intro to
trans of German commercial, tech, sci, and
lit texts into Eng; 12-a,b,c,f; 13-e, materials from lit anthologies, histories; 14-
Savory, The Art of Translation.

23. SPECIAL TOPICS: ADVANCED TRANS-
LATING OF GERMAN
Kent SU; Ger & Sl Langs & Lits; Kent, OH
44242.
Herman K. Doswald
1-ng; 2-4x10; 3-a; 4-74; 5-ng; 6-every 2nd
yr; 7-a; 8-4q; 9-a; 10-intro course in trans;
11-trans adv Ger commercial, tech, sci, lit
texts into Eng; 12-a,b,c,f; 13-e, selections
from lit; 14-Handbuch der Kultur.

24. TRANSLATION I & II
Montclair SC; Ger; Upper Montclair, NJ
07043.

148

1-13; 2-3x16; 3-a; 4-73/74; 5-2; 6-b; 7-a; 8-3s; 9-a; 10-inter prof; 11-Trans I emphasizes Ger into Eng; Trans II emphasizes Eng into Ger; material taken from legal texts, poli statements, newspaper articles, sci pubs; 12-b,g; 13-e,f, govt pubs; 14-Kottmann, Kaufmaennischer Schriftverkehr; James, Writing and Communicating in Business; Gewehr & von Schmidt, Reading German in the Social Sciences.

25. SPRACHFERTIGKEIT
Occidental C; Langs & Ling; Los Angeles, CA 90041.
Erich Frey
1-10; 2-4x10; 3-a; 4-74; 5-2; 6-b; 7-a; 8-4s; 9-ng; 10-inter prof; 11-practice in trans & interpreting of non-lit contemporary Anglo-American materials from newspapers, magazines, books into Ger; 12-b,e,g; 13-c,e,f; 14-none.

26. STUDIES IN TRANSLATION: GERMAN
Occidental C; Langs & Ling; Los Angeles, CA 90041.
Leland S. Babcock
1-5; 2-4x10; 3-a; 4-74; 5-1; 6-every other yr; 7-a; 8-4s; 9-a; 10-6 sems college Ger; 11-trans from newspapers, journals, stories; work on various trans problems & techniques; 12-a,b,c,f,g; 13-e,f; 14-none.

27. GERMAN FOR TRANSLATORS
Queens C; Ger & Scand; Flushing, NY 11367.
Rolf Kieser
1-12; 2-3x15; 3-a; 4-73; 5-3; 6-a; 7-a; 8-3s; 9-a; 10-Ger 1-4; B plus average; permission; 11-4 course sequence; texts taken from nat & soci scis, govt, commerce, lit & contemporary affairs; 2 additional courses in Ger lit or Ger civ; 12-a,f,g; 13-e,f, Ger books on tech & law; 14-ng.

28. TECHNICAL TRANSLATOR'S CERTIFICATE GERMAN PROGRAM
Rose-Hulman Inst of Technology; Hums; 5500 Wabash Ave, Terre Haute, IN 47803.
Peter F. H. Priest
1-30; 2-3-5x120 (4 yrs); 3-a; 4-73/74; 5-ng; 6-continuously; 7-a; 8-48q; 9-a; 10-demonstrated for lang prof; high verbal & math SAT scores; 11-elem & inter skills, sci lit; 12-a,b,d,e; 13-e,f, patents, tech reports, trade catalogs; 14-ng.

29. TRANSLATION TECHNIQUES
Southern Illinois U; FLs & Lits; Carbondale, IL 62901.
Howard French, German Section
2-yr sequence, 14s, initiated 74, offered continuously in sequence; current enrollment is 4; courses offered during regular day session; student population comprised of full-time students; first year grammar study & written Ger emphasized, contrastive study of styles through trans and readings of representative texts; second yr trans & readings of original Ger texts in soci sci, natural sci, & hums, examination of reference works, individual trans in stu-

dents' fields of specialization emphasized. Courses taught in Eng by lecture, discussion, oral reports; periodicals & newspapers are utilized. Texts first year: Bergethon, Grammar for Reading German; Spann & Goedsche, Deutsche Denker und Forscher; Lehmann, Rehder, & Beyer, Spectrum.

30. TRANSLATORS AND INTERPRETERS PROGRAM
Stanford U; Ger Studies; Stanford, CA 94305.
Ulrike Lieder
1-20-30; 2-ng; 3-a; 4-71; 5-ng; 6-continuously; 7-a; 8-ng; 9-a; 10-completion of first-yr college Ger; 11-program leads to Certificate in General Translation at A.B. level, and in Advanced Trans or Interpretation at M.A. level; can be combined with degree programs in any subject matter area, incl Ger; student eligible for Certificate in General Trans end of 9-course sequence designed to strengthen lang competence & knowledge of contemporary Ger, introduce problems of trans, mainly Ger to Eng, incl trans workshop; adv trans courses available beyond 9-course core, as well as intro to simultaneous & consecutive interpretation, conference terminology & precis-writing; lit trans workshop offered if interest warrants; students may spend 1-3 quarters abroad; 12-14-ng.

31. THEORY AND PRACTICE OF TRANSLATION
U of Texas; Ger Langs; Austin, TX 78712.
A. Leslie Willson
1-new; 2-3x14; 3-a; 4-75; 5-0; 6-b; 7-a; 8-3s; 9-a; 10-jr, inter prof; 11-study of methods with practical exercises in trans of texts, sci & tech as well as lit; 12-a,c,d,f; 13-e,f, lit texts; 14-ng.

32. GERMAN FOR TRANSLATION
Villanova U; MLs; Villanova, PA 19085.
Gudrun McGee
1-new; 2-8x4; 3-a; 4-75; 5-1; 6-b; 7-b, smr; 8-b; 9-srs & grad students from Villanova & vicinity; 10-ng; 11-grammar, extensive practice in trans from textbook & specialized material of interest to individual student; 12-ng; 13-e; 14-Jannach, German for Reading Knowledge.

33. GERMAN SCIENTIFIC TRANSLATION
U of West Florida; Eng & FLs; Pensacola, FL 32504.
Stanton Millet
1-15; 2-5x10; 3-a; 4-72; 5-2; 6-every 2nd yr; 7-a; 8-5x2q; 9-a; 10-ng; 11-basic elements of grammar, key words & expressions, trans; 12-a,b,c,d,f; 13-e,f; 14-Hieble, Die Welt von Heute und Morgen; Hirschhorn, Scientific and Technical German Reader; Van de Luyster, Naturforschung von Heute.

See also 209.

ITALIAN

See 218.

PORTUGUESE

34. TRANSLATION: PORTUGUESE-ENGLISH, ENGLISH-PORTUGUESE
Georgetown U; Port & Interpretation & Trans; Washington, DC 20007.
Maria I. Abreu, Margareta Bowan (Port)
1-8; 2-3x28; 3-b,c; 4-50; 5-ng; 6-a; 7-b; 8-3s; 9-a,c; 10-examination; 11-adv level trans of texts chosen mostly from newspapers & magazines dealing with current topics in variety of fields; each three-hour course is a unit in itself; 12-b,c,g; 13-e,f; 14-ng.

RUSSIAN

35. SPECIAL TOPICS: TRANSLATING RUSSIAN
Kent SU; Ger & Sl Langs & Lits; Kent, OH 44242.
Herman K. Doswald
1-ng; 2-4x10; 3-a; 4-74; 5-1; 6-every 2nd yr; 7-a; 8-4q; 9-ng; 10-adv prof; 11-continuation of tech and sci trans, Russian into Eng, begun in the course "Scientific Russian;" 12-a,b,c,f; 13-e,f; 14-Meader, Scientific Russian.

36. TRANSLATION WORKSHOP
Middlebury C; Russian Summer School; Middlebury, VT 05753.
Helena Moroz, School of Translators & Interpreters, Laurentian U, Sudbury, Ontario.
1-24; 2-5x6; 3-a; 4-74; 5-1; 6-a; 7-a; 8-2½s; 9-a; 10-examination, inter prof; 11-training in written trans Russian-Eng, using variety of texts, including the daily press & tech lit; 12-a,b,g, individual consultation; 13-ng; 14-Magner, Russian Scientific & Technical Readings.

37. TRANSLATING RUSSIAN
U of New Mexico; Mod & Cl Langs; Albuquerque, NM 87131.
Byron Lindsey
1-new; 2-3x17; 3-a; 4-75; 5-1; 6-b; 7-a; 8-3s; 9-a; 10-inter prof; 11-analysis of grammar, reading-trans of non-lit & lit texts, some training in oral comprehension; 12-b,c,e,g; 13-d,e; 14-Phillips, Concise Russian Review Grammar; Gottlieb, Improve Your Russian Comprehension; others.

38. TECHNICAL TRANSLATOR'S CERTIFICATE PROGRAM
Rose-Hulman Inst of Technology; Hums; 5500 Wabash Ave, Terre Haute, IN 47803.
Peter F. H. Priest
1-20; 2-3-5x120 (4 yrs); 3-a; 4-73/74; 5-ng; 6-continuously; 7-a; 8-48q; 9-a; 10-demonstrated for lang prof in high school; high verbal & math SAT scores; 11-elem & inter skills, sci lit; 12-a,b,d,e; 13-e,f, patents, tech reports, trade catalogs; 14-ng.

39. RUSSIAN TRANSLATION TECHNIQUES
Southern Illinois U; FLs & Lits; Carbondale, IL 62901.
Joseph Kupcek, Russian Section
1-9; 2-3x16; 3-a; 4-74; 5-1; 6-a; 7-a; 8-3s; 9-a; 10-elem prof; 11-intro to trans of hums, soci sci & sci material, accompanied by grammar; techniques, procedures, methodology, art of trans; course also designed for students majoring in other than For Lang & Lit; 12-a,b,c,d,e,f; 13-e,f; 14-Dewey & Mercereau, Reading & Translating Contemporary Russian.

See also 211.

SPANISH

40. TRANSLATION TECHNIQUES AND PROBLEMS OF TRANSLATION
Adelphi U; Langs; Garden City, NY 11530.
Nicholas Carbo
1-24; 2-3x16; 3-a; 4-73; 5-3; 6-b; 7-a; 8-3s; 9-a; 10-intro trans course; 11-2 course sequence, continuation & expansion of trans study designed to develop & refine skills; review of specialized lang & idiomatic expression; development of specific skills for use in various fields; 12-a,d,f,g; 13-e,f; 14-Manrique, Arte de traducir el ingles; Mounin, Los problemas teoreticas de la traduccion; Stockwell, The Grammatical Structures of English and Spanish.

41. ORAL INTERPRETATION AND TRANSLATION FROM ENGLISH TO SPANISH
Federal City C; FLs; Washington, DC 20001.
1-7; 2-3x10; 3-a; 4-73/74; 5-2; 6-b; 7-b; 8-3q; 9-a, part-time; 10-adv prof; 11-development of prof in trans (idiomatic) thought patterns from Eng to Sp; 12-c,d,e,f,g; 13-d,e,f; 14-ng.

42. ORAL INTERPRETATION AND TRANSLATION FROM SPANISH TO ENGLISH
Federal City C; FLs; Washington, DC 20001.
1-7; 2-3x10; 3-a; 4-73/74; 5-2; 6-b; 7-b; 8-3q; 9-a, part-time; 10-adv prof; 11-development of prof in trans (idiomatic) thought patterns from Sp to Eng; 12-c.d,e,f,g; 13-d,e,f; 14-ng.

43. PRACTICUM IN TRANSLATION
U of Maryland; Sp & Port; College Park, MD 20742.
Henry Mendeloff
1-ng; 2-3x15; 3-c; 4-75/76; 5-0; 6-every 2nd yr; 7-b; 8-3s; 9-a,c (special students); 10-inter prof; 11-trans of tech, sci & lit materials from Sp to Eng; 12-a,d (& individual projects), f,g; 13-e,f, other materials from appropriate sources; 14-none.

44. TECHNIQUES OF TRANSLATION
Meramec CC; MFLs; Kirkwood, MO 63122.
Jennie Davis
1-7; 2-3x15; 3-a; 4-75; 5-1; 6-every 2nd yr; 7-a; 8-3s; 9-a; 10-inter prof; 11-study of variant meanings, practice in selection of equivalents, trans of business letters, newspaper articles, sci articles, lit selections, recipes; 12-a,b,d,f; 13-e,f; 14-Sp-Eng dictionary.

45. TECHNICAL TRANSLATION, CONSECUTIVE AND SIMULTANEOUS INTERPRETING

150

Northern Arizona U; MLs; Flagstaff, AZ 86001.
Orazio Giusti
1-new; 2-12xsem; 3-a; 4-75; 5-1; 6-a; 7-a; 8-12s; 9-a; 10-major & verbal prof; 11-ng; 12-a,b,d,e,f,g; 13-d,e,f; 14-tech pubs.

46. THE ART OF TRANSLATION
Skidmore C; MLs & Lits; Saratoga Springs, NY 12866.
Sonja Karsen
1-ng; 2-3x12; 3-a; 4-72; 5-2; 6-every 2nd yr; 7-a; 8-3s; 9-a; 10-inter prof; 11-trans of lit, hist, poli, soci, & tech texts from Sp to Eng; 12-b,c,d,f; 13-e,f; 14-Arrowsmith, The Craft and Context of Translation; Brower, On Translation; Karsen, Versos y Prosas de Jaime Torres Bodet.

47. PROBLEMS OF TRANSLATION
U of South Dakota; MFLs; Vermillion, SD 57069.
Enrique Ollivier
1-new; 2-2x16; 3-a; 4-new ; 5-0; 6-every 2nd yr; 7-a; 8-2; 9-ng; 10-inter prof; 11-trans of 3 books & articles from magazines & newspapers; 12-b,d,f,g; 13-c,d,e; 14-Ollivier-Pelletier, Mexico, Pais Encantador; Usigli, Corona de Sombras; Casona, La Dama del Alba. Additional material is used for trans from Eng to Sp.

48. TECHNIQUES OF TRANSLATION: SPANISH
Stephens C; FLs; Columbia, MO 65201.
Albert Delmez
1-10; 2-3x7; 3-a; 4-70; 5-4; 6-b; 7-a; 8-1½q; 9-a; 10-adv comp skills; 11-ng; 12-b,d,f,g; 13-e,f; 14-materials from magazines, periodicals, lit anthols.

49. READING AND TRANSLATION IN SPANISH FOR GRADUATE STUDENTS
Tarrant County JC; MFL; Fort Worth, TX 76119.
E. Guzman
Further info ng.

50. SPANISH TRANSLATION
U of Texas; MLs; El Paso, TX 79968.
Diana Natalicio
1-38; 2-3x15; 3-a; 4-74; 5-1; 6-b; 7-b; 8-3s; 9-a,c (part-time); 10-adv prof; 11-techniques of Eng to Sp & Sp to Eng trans, incl instantaneous oral, lit, bus & other forms of trans; 12-a,b,e,f,g; 13-d,e, documents; 14-Microcosm: College and the World, and Encuentro: Ensayos de la Actualidad.

51. SPANISH FOR TRANSLATORS
Washington U; Rom Langs; St. Louis, MO 63130.
Joseph Schraibman
1-12; 2-3x15; 3-a; 4-74; 5-1; 6-ng; 7-a; 8-3s; 9-a; 10-adv prof; 11-ng; 12-b,d,g; 13-e,f; 14-individual texts selected with students.

52. TRANSLATING & INTERPRETING: ENGLISH-SPANISH, SPANISH-ENGLISH
Wilson C; Sp; Chambersburg, PA 17201.
Jose Diaz
1-7; 2-15x4; 3-a; 4-74; 5-1; 6-every 2nd yr; 7-Jan term; 8-3; 9-a; 10-inter prof; 11-ex-

perience trans & interpreting, simultaneous trans, simulated court cases, legal techniques, lit trans; 12-b,d,e,f,g; 13-d,e,f,court cases; 14-none.
See also 256, 506.

MULTI-LANGUAGE

53. TRANSLATOR TRAINING PROGRAM
Baruch C, CUNY; Rom Langs; 17 Lexington Ave, New York, NY 10010.
Violet Horvath
1-12; 2-(8 courses of) 3x15; 3-a; 4-74; 5-1; 6-b; 7-a; 8-3s; 9-a; 10-inter prof; 11-Fr or Sp. Trans: Theory & practice, the first of 8 courses leading to a certificate from the American Translators' Association; 12-a,c,f; 13-e,f; 14-Penguin French Reader; The Gimmick, vol 2.

54. THE MUSIC OF MEANING
Carnegie-Mellon U; MLs; Pittsburgh, PA 15213.
J. Rosenberg
A writing workshop, emphasizing trans from Fr & Ger, although students who wish to work in other langs accepted. Trans studied as method of cognition, as a craft, as a branch of fine arts. Bilingualism neither necessary nor desirable; reasonable reading knowledge of 2nd language is a prerequisite. Admission by consent, 3 contact hrs per wk; sem course, 9 units.

55. TRANSLATION THEORY: LITERARY, SCIENTIFIC/TECHNICAL
Carnegie-Mellon U; MLs & Lits; Pittsburgh, PA 15213.
Juris Silenieks
1-ng; 2-1-2x14; 3-a,c; 4-ng; 5-2; 6-a; 7-a; 8-varies; 9-a; 10-2 yrs of college or equiv; 11-workshops in Ger, Russ, Fr & Sp; 12-d,f; 13-e,f; 14-ng.

56. SEMINAR IN TRANSLATION
Immaculata C; MF & Cl Langs; Immaculata, PA 19345.
Sr. Maria Lucy
Further info ng.

57. MAJOR IN TRANSLATION AND INTERPRETATION
Kearney SC; FLs; Kearney, NB 68847.
Ari Sosa
1-40; 2-(8 courses of) 3x15; 3-a; 4-72; 5-3; 6-a; 7-a; 8-3s/course; 9-a; 10-inter prof; 11-grammar, civ, conversation, trans, phonetics, hist, interpretation, Fr, Ger, or Sp; 12-b,e,g; 13-e,f, docs to be translated; 14-ng.

58. TRANSLATION: THEORY AND PRACTICE
U of Maine; FLs; Orono, ME 04473.
Josef Roggenbauer
1-74; 2-3x15; 3-a; 4-70; 5-5; 6-b; 7-a; 8-3s; 9-a; 10-reading fluency in a for lang; 11-intro to theories & problems of trans for the student interested in professional trans from a for lang into Eng; 12-a,b,d,f,g; 13-e,f; 14-Savory, The Art of Translation.

59. TRANSLATOR PROGRAMS

151

Marygrove C; FLs; Detroit, MI 48221.
E. DuBruck
1-18; 2-(3 courses each of) 3x15; 3-a; 4-73;
5-4; 6-Workshops I & II in terms 1 & 2
respectively; Workshop III via independent
study; 7-a; 8-3s/course; 9-a, part-time; 10-
inter prof; 11-3 workshops per lang: Fr,
Ger, or Sp: 1) trans of modern fiction into
Eng; 2) trans of modern fiction into for
lang; 3) trans from 1st to 2nd for lang, or
independent trans project in field of
specialization, practice in oral interpretation; 12-a,b,d,e,f; 13-a,d,e,f; 14-Hendry,
Your Career in Translating and Interpreting; Ludtke, History of Romance
Vocabulary; Gassler, From Sentence to
Word: Comparative Translation; and
others.

60. CERTIFICATE IN TRANSLATION AND
INTERPRETATION
Monterey Inst of Foreign Studies; Trans &
Interpretation; Monterey, CA 93940.
Etilvia Arjona
1-50; 2-ng; 3-b; 4-67; 5-continuously since
67; 6-a; 7-a; 8-ng; 9-a; 10-MFL B.A. or B.A.
with accompanying strong knowledge of
MFL; 11-joint M.A./Certificate Program;
overseas study not required but highly
recommended; in addition to traditional
courses, area studies are also required; 12-
a,b,e,f,g; 13-b,d,e,f, stencils, dittoes; 14-
ng.

61. TRANSLATION AND INTERPRETATION
CURRICULUM: CERTIFICATE PRO-
GRAMS
Monterey Inst of Foreign Studies; Trans &
Interpretation; Monterey, CA 93940.
Etilvia Arjona
1-59; 2-2 to 3 yr curriculum, credits vary
according to course; 3-a, b for M.A. studies;
4-68; 5-continuous; 6-a, incl smr; 7-a; 8-
varies; 9-a, part-time students; 10-B.A. in
lang or equiv; translators need Eng plus
major lang, interpreters need Eng plus 2
major langs; 11-practica, courses &
seminars, comprehensive exams, fieldwork
for interpreters, thesis and defense for
translators; 12-a,b,c,d,e,f,g; 13-d,e,f,g,

overhead projections; 14-prepared by staff.

62. TRANSLATION WORKSHOP
C of Mt St Vincent; MFLs; Bronx, NY
10471.
Kathleen Knowles
1-15; 2-3x15; 3-a; 4-spr 75; 5-1; 6-b; 7-a; 8-
3s; 9-a; 10-sr lang majors; 11-ng; 12-a,e,f;
13-a,e,f; 14-excerpts from newspapers &
magazines, lit, bus correspondence, soci &
nat sciences.

63. CERTIFICATE IN TRANSLATION
SUNY; Comp Lit; Binghamton, NY 13901.
Marilyn Gaddis Rose
A 3-course curriculum, either lit or non-lit
emphasis, for grad students in the Schools
of Arts & Sci, General Studies, Management, & Advanced Tech. Fluency in the
source lang, effective expression in the
target lang, knowledge of the subject(s) to
be trans is required. The Trans Workshop is
the core course of the curriculum. It
presents lit & methodology of trans; staffed
by a team of published translators representing the major lang areas. Curriculum
instituted Sept 74.

64. PROFESSIONAL TRANSLATING PRO-
GRAM
Notre Dame C; FLs; Cleveland, OH 44121.
Mary Cesarie
1-30; 2-(4 courses of) 3x64 wks (2 yrs); 3-
b,c; 4-73; 5-first sequence complete; 6-a;
7-b; 8-3s each; 9-a, most have B.A.; 10-adv
prof in the for lang & in written Eng; 11-Fr,
Ger, Latin, or Sp intro to professional trans,
workshop in general trans, workshop in bus
correspondence, seminar in selected topics
(based on student's major); 12-a,b,c,e,f; 13-
a,b,d,e,f, guest speakers; 14-Finlay, Translating; and others.

65. TRANSLATION
U of Southern Mississippi; FLs; Hattiesburg, MS 39401.
Roger Johnson Jr.
1-45; 2-4x11; 3-a; 4-72; 5-2; 6-b; 7-b; 8-3s;
9-a; 10-inter prof & interest in tech trans;
11-theory & practice; 12-a,b,d; 13-b,e,f,
other docs; 14-none.

Education: Training for Bilingual Classrooms

66. CHINESE/JAPANESE-ENGLISH BILIN-
GUAL PROGRAM
Seton Hall U; Asian Studies; South Orange,
NJ 07079.
John B. Tsu
1-30; 2-25x36; 3-b; 4-74; 5-2; 6-each yr for
2 sems; 7-a; 8-18s; 9-a; 10-B.A. in Chin or
Jap or related studies; 11-emphasis on

biling ed for teachers of Chin/Jap-Eng
biling ed, 2 sem course; 12-a,b,d,f,g; 13-
a,b,c,d; 14-ng.

FRENCH

67. CODOFIL FRENCH FOR IN-SERVICE EL-
EMENTARY TEACHERS
Nicholls SU; FLs; Thibodaux, LA 70301.
Gary G. McCann, Joseph Saltzman
1-48; 2-3x15; 3-c; 4-73; 5-5; 6-a; 7-b; 8-3s;

9-in-service elem teachers; 10-elem teaching license; 11-complete program spans 2 yrs with evening classes during fall & wtr sems & 4-wk smr program each smr. Upon completion, teacher receives certificate as "Second Lang Specialist (Fr)." Stresses lang skills, professional prep (applied ling), and cult and civ (incl a study of children's lit in Fr); 12-b,c,d,g; 13-a,b,c,d; 14-A la Fran-caise; plus primary texts.

See also 89, 546.

SPANISH

68.   SPANISH FOR ELEMENTARY EDUCA-
        TION
        Annhurst C; Sp; RR #2, Woodstock, CT 06281.
        Rosa M. Garcia
        1-4; 2-3x4; 3-a; 4-75; 5-1; 6-inter-session wtr; 7-a; 8-1s; 9-a; 10-ng; 11-for students who know no Sp; basic words, phrases and info needed when working with children and parents; 12-a,c, taught in both langs; 13-b; 14-ng.

69.   SPANISH FOR THE CLASSROOM
        TEACHER
        U of Arizona; Rom Langs; Tucson, AZ 85721.
        Charles Olstad
        1-new course; 2-4x14; 3-a,c; 4-spr 75; 5-0; 6-b; 7-a,b; 8-4s; 9-a, classroom teachers; 10-working practical knowledge of Sp; 11-vocab usage as required by the elem & sec school teacher of other subjects in Sp; 12-a,b,d,g; 13-sample for textbooks; 14-ng.

70.   SPANISH FOR COLLEGE PERSONNEL
        Barry C; FL; Miami, FL 33161.
        Ellen Leeder
        1-16; 2-2x16; 3-a; 4-73; 5-2; 6-a; 7-a; 8-1s or 0, depending on written work; 9-a, part-time & college staff; 10-none; 11-mostly oral work; 12-b,c,g; 13-a,b,d; 14-ng.

71.   CONVERSATIONAL SPANISH FOR PUB-
        LIC SCHOOL TEACHERS
        Boise SU; FL; Boise, ID 83725.
        J. Rodriguez, Counseling
        1-17; 2-4x18; 3-b,c; 4-fall 74; 5-2; 6-a; 7-b; 8-4s; 9-b, teachers already on job in Nampa Schools; 11-basic conv Sp; 12-ng; 13-ng; 14-ng.

72.   SPANISH CLASSROOM VOCABULARY
        California SU; FL & Lits; Fullerton, CA 92634.
        J. Kiraithe
        1-first time spr 75; 2-2x15; 3-a; 4-75; 5-first time; 6-b; 7-b; 8-2; 9-a, students with BA working for teaching credits; 10-upper-div standing; 11-specific vocab needed to teach in biling schools; 12-a,b,c,d,g; 13-textbooks for elem grades in Sp; 14-ng.

73.   SPANISH FOR BILINGUAL EDUCATION
        California SU; FLs & Lits; Northridge, CA 91324.
        Maja Reid
        1-25; 2-3x15; 3-a; 4-fall 74; 5-2; 6-a; 7-b; 8-3s; 9-a; 10-adequate competency; 11-to

prepare students wishing to teach within biling format; 12-b,d,g; 13-e,f; 14-ng.

74.   INTRO TO BILINGUAL ED
        Calvin C; Fr & Sp; Grand Rapids, MI 49506.
        Edna Greenway
        1-14; 2-15x3; 3-c; 4 first time, Jan 75 interim; 5-none; 6-to be determined; 7-a; 8-3½s; 9-a; 10-2 sems of a for lang; 11-prepares ed students for biling instruction in primary and sec schools; 12-a,b,d,f,; 13-a,c,e; 14-ng.

75.   PRACTICAL ORAL SPANISH
        Clarendon C; FL; Clarendon, TX 79226.
        Dixie Howard
        1-20; 2-ng; 3-a; 4-spr 75; 5-1; 6-a; 7-b; 8-3s; 9-b; 10-ng; 11-oral use of lang with minimum of grammar and writing; participants are people who teach Sp-speaking children, professionals, storekeepers, people who employ Sp speakers; 12-e,f,g; 13-a,d,e; 14-ng.

76.   FOUNDATIONS AND CURRICULUM
        U of Connecticut; Rom & Cl Langs; Stamford, CT 06903.
        Juan Leach, U CT, Storrs, CT 06268
        1-6; 2-3x15; 3-b; 4-fall 74; 5-1; 6-uncertain; 7-b; 8-3s; 9-b; 10-ng; 11-a grad program for teachers; courses include: "Teaching ESL," "Cult Divergence," "Teaching Multi-Cult Population," "Biling Education," "A Practicum," "Special Investigations," "Methodology for Biling, Bicult Classes," "Seminar in Caribbean Culture"; first course offered Sept 74; 12-a,b,c,f; 13-ng; 14-ng.

77.   METHODOLOGY FOR THE BILINGUAL
        CLASSROOM
        Emmanuel C; Boston, MA 02115.
        Margaret Pauline Young
        1-10; 2-4x15; 3-a (team taught); 4-72/73; 5-twice; 6-b; 7-a,b; 8-4s; 9-a, students from Simmons C; 10-adv prof; 11-methods of teaching basic skills to Sp-speaking children in biling program on elem level; open to qualified jrs & srs; 12-a,b,c,d,e,g; 13-b, all types of realia used in an elem classroom; 14-basic texts for reading, writing, math (New) used with Sp-speaking children in their own country.

78.   ELEMENTARY EDUCATION-BILINGUAL
        EMPHASIS
        Emporia Kansas SC; FLs; Emporia, KS 66801.
        David E. Travis
        New interdepart major program. Includes courses in soci, anthro, race and ethnic relations and "Seminars in Understanding" (e.g. Child of Poverty). Further info not available.

79.   WORKSHOP: BILINGUAL COMMUNICA-
        TION
        Hardin-Simmons U; Abilene, TX 79601.
        Don R. Whitmore
        1-new course; 2-3x16; 3-a; 4-75; 5-0; 6-b, on demand during smr; 7-a,b; 8-3s; 9-a, part-time grads, school teachers; 10-equiv-alent to inter Sp; 11-vocab and usage of Sp

153

as spoken by Mex-Amer in elem school classrooms. Terms for teaching subject areas such as math, sci, soci studies. Approaches to lang skills for non-speakers of Eng; 12-a,b,d,f,g; 13-a,d,e,f; 14-to be selected.

80. M.A. IN BILINGUALISM
Hofstra U; Sp; Hempstead, NY 11550.
Isabel Cid Sirgado
Interdisc program with course work in the following areas: lit; ling; hist; cross-cult studies; pedagogical orientation. Students participate fully in both cults, to achieve a biling and bicult understanding of Hispanic and American ways of life.

81. WORKSHOP OR INSTITUTE IN CONVER-SATIONAL SPANISH FOR EDUCATORS
Houston Baptist U; Lang; Houston, TX 77036.
Marion R. Webb
1-25; 2-1-3/4x25; 3-c; 4-74/75; 5-4; 6-a; 7-b; 8-3s; 9-teachers & principals, Houston Ind School Dist; 10-none; 11-conv, directed toward elem school teaching level. Dealing with Sp-speaking students in classroom and school context, and parents. For more adv students, content teaching in Sp; 12-d,g; 13-a,b,c,d; 14-Webb & Tabery, Communicating in Spanish for Educators.

82. SPANISH REQUIREMENT FOR STUDENTS MAJORING IN EDUCATION
City C, CUNY; Rom Lang; New York, NY 10031.
Raquel Chang-Rodriquez
1-ng; 2-5 (elem) and 3 (inter) x 14; 3-a; 4-69; 5-18; 6-a; 7-a; 8-4 & 3s; 9-a; 10-none for beginning; 2 yrs of H.S. Sp for inter; 11-sequence designed to give students oral competency in Sp and to familiarize them with the ethnic character of the Sp-speaking community; field work in the community; 12-a,b,d,g; 13-e,f; 14-primary texts.

83. SPANISH FOR EARLY CHILDHOOD
Kingsborough CC; FLs; Manhattan Beach, Brooklyn, NY 11235.
Julio Hernandez-Miyares
1-3; 2-2x15; 3-a; 4-74; 5-3; 6-a; 7-a; 8-2s; 9-a; 10-none; 11-ng; 12-b,e,g; 13-c,d, textbook, workbook; 14-ng.

84. SPANISH FOR EDUCATIONAL ASSISTANTS
Kingsborough CC; FLs; Manhattan Beach, Brooklyn, NY 11235.
Julio Hernandez-Miyares
1-ng; 2-3x15; 3-a; 4-71; 5-8; 6-a; 7-para-professionals; 8-3s; 9-a,paraprofessionals; 10-3 levels; 11-ng; 12-b,e,g (with Eng explanations); 13-c,d,g,textbook & workbook; 14-Hernandez-Miyares & Elio Alka Spanish for Educational Assistants.

85. BILINGUAL EDUCATIONAL ASSISTANCE PROGRAM
La Guardia CC; Lang; Long Island City, NY 11101.

Flora Mancuso
1-100; 2-12x10; 3-b; 4-74; 5-1; 6-a; 7-a,b; 8-full credit; 9-a, working paraprofessionals; 10-ng; 11-problems of Sp-speaking children in NY public schools; 12-a,b,d,f,g; 13-a,b,c; 14-primary texts.

86. INTENSIVE SPANISH WORKSHOP
Lone Mountain C; Sp; San Francisco, CA 94118.
M.P. Valdes
1-6; 2-8x6; 3-c; 4-smr 74; 5-2; 6-smr; 7-a; 8-4s; 9-teachers, soci service workers; 10-none for 1st; inter prof for 2nd; 11-specially designed for teachers and future teachers of biling projects, soci workers, psychologists or counselors working or preparing to work with Sp-speaking minorities; lang skills and cult (cult stressed in 2nd course); 12-a,b,c,d,e,g; 13-a,b,c,d,e,f; 14-primary texts.

87 HISTORY AND THEORY OF HISPANIC BILINGUALISM
U of Massachusetts; Sp & Port; Amherst, MA 01002.
William G. Milan
1-30; 2-3x14; 3-a; 4-spr 74; 5-2; 6-b; 7-b; 8-3s; 9-a,b, part-time; 10-course in Hispanic ling; 11-study of biling: soci, psych, ling; biling as socioling phenomenon; results of biling: Pidgins, Creoles, substrata, adstrata, superstrata, diglossia, formation of lang; contact of langs; lang planning & legislation; 12-a,b,f; 13-ng; 14-Fishman et al, Bilingualism in the Barrio; Fishman, Sociology of Language; Alatis, Bilingualism and Language Contact.

88. SPANISH FOR TEACHERS
Monterey Inst of Foreign Studies; Langs & Civs; Monterey, CA 93940.
Burt H. Seidenberg, Ovid C. Fuente
Special smr 75 workshop; intensive study; further info ng.

89. BILINGUAL EDUCATION
New York U; FLs & Biling Ed; New York, NY 10003.
Annette S. Baslaw
Courses offered to train professionals in teaching of school subjects with a biling approach (Lang Arts, Sci, Soci Studies, Math) in either Sp or Fr. Also courses in theory, practice of biling ed, workshops in both Sp and Fr biling ed, and a course in cross-cult analysis. Other courses include: The Vernacular Lang of Puerto Rico and Hispanic Dialectology; The People and Cult of Puerto Rico; The People and Cult of Haiti; The Educational Relevance of Afro-Spanish Lit; The Educational Relevance of the Lit of Haiti. Int Understanding through Films. M.A., Ph.D., Ed.D. programs.

90. BEGINNING SPANISH FOR ELEMENTARY TEACHERS
Odessa C; FLs; Odessa, TX 79760.
Matt Rees
1-30; 2-3x16; 3-a; 4-fall 73; 5-1; 6-on demand; 7-b; 8-3s; 9-teachers, to qualify

154

under the new state biling ed program; 10-none; 11-limited basic structure, with content for classroom and parental contact situations. Special attention to the border Sp and Chicano Sp; 12-a,b,d,f,g; 13-Eng situational convs, put into Sp on request; 14-Espanol a lo Vivo.

91. SPANISH AS A SECOND LANGUAGE: FOR EMPLOYEES IN EDUCATIONAL INSTITUTIONS AND PUBLIC SERVICE AGENCIES
Pasadena City C; FLs; Pasadena, CA 91106.
Marina Cobb
1-54; 2-2x9; 3-c; 4-fall 73; 5-3; 6-a; 7-a,b; 8-1q (not applicable to B.A. except in certain programs); 9-teachers, teacher-aides, police officers; 10-none; 11-con practice in elem Sp stressing specialized vocab and basic expressions; 12-d,f,g; 13-d; 14-ng.

92. MIGRANT TEACHER EDUCATION INSTITUTE
Salisbury SC; ML, Eng Ed; Salisbury, MD 21801.
John K. Knowles, ML Dept.
1-30; 2-4x15; 3-b,c; 4-Jan 75; 5-1; 6-state-related program given each spr; 7-4 hrs Sat; 9-inservice teachers; 10-none; 11-Sp lang, Hispanic cult, ESL methods and materials of pre-school ed; 12-a,b,d,e,f,g; 13-a,b,c,d; 14-ng.

93. BILINGUAL EDUCATION
Southwestern U; FLs; Georgetown, TX 78626.
Regine Reynolds, Francisco Betancourt
1-new course; 2-4 yr program; 3-b; 4-74; 5-ng; 6-a; 7-a,b; 8-ng; 9-a, area school teachers; 10-basic knowledge of Sp; 11-complies with requirements of the Texas Ed Agency for certification in Biling Ed; 12-a,c,d,f,g; 13-ng; 14-ng.

94. INTENSIVE SPANISH COURSE FOR ENGLISH MONOLINGUAL TEACHERS IN BILINGUAL SCHOOLS

Tarrant County JC; MFLs; Fort Worth, TX 76119.
Ernesto Guzman
1-ng; 2-30x3; 3-c; 4-smr 74; 5-1; 6-smrs; 7-a; 8-b (credit for biling teacher certification); 9-non-Sp- speaking biling teachers in FWISD; 10-none; 11-fundamental skills of Sp lang, emphasis: hearing, understanding, speaking, to improve skills of teachers in biling school & to provide understanding of Mex-Amer cult; 12-a,e,g; 13-multimedia; 14-Barker, Espanol para el Bilingual; Materials for Monolinguals, ILS.

95. INTRODUCTION TO SPANISH IN THE ELEMENTARY SCHOOL
Tennessee Technological U; FLs; Cookeville, TN 38501.
Juanita Shettlesworth
1-10; 2-3x10; 3-a; 4-73; 5-2; 6-b; 7-a; 8-3q; 9-a; 10-none; 11-intro, emphasizing pronunciation, to aid elem school teachers in use of ed TV and other materials; 12-a,b,c,g; 13-b,c,d,e; 14-none.

See also 313, 314, 321, 325, 348, 419, 421, 431, 437, 440, 442, 506, 514, 660.

MULTI-LANGUAGE

See 965.

GENERAL

96. PREPARATION FOR THE BILINGUAL/BICULTURAL CREDENTIAL
U of San Diego; Ed; Alcala Park, CA 92110.
Patricia Lowry
First offered in 73. Further info ng.

97. TEACHING ENGLISH TO SPEAKERS OF OTHER LANGUAGES
U of Southern Mississippi; Eng & FLs; Hattiesburg, MS 39401.
Bonnie Brennager, Eng Dept.
1-ng; 2-ng; 3-b; 4-73; 5-ng; 6-ng; 7-ng; 8-ng; 9-a; 10-ng; 11-curriculum includes courses leading to regular certification for sec school teachers in Eng and FLs. Courses in Latin required; 12-a,b,c,d,e,f,g; 13ng; 14-variety.

Research

READING

French

98. SCIENTIFIC FRENCH
Federal City C; French; Washington, DC 20001.
1-new; 2-3x10; 3-a; 4-new; 5-0; 6-ng; 7-ng; 8-3q; 9-a,c; 10-inter Fr; 11-reading modern texts, primarily nat & soci scis; 12-a,b,c,d,f,g; 13-e,f; 14-ng.

99. INTRODUCTION TO TECHNICAL, SCIENTIFIC, AND COMMERCIAL FRENCH
Hood C; Lang; Frederick, MD 21701.
1-11; 2-3x1 sem; 3-a; 4-spr 75; 5-1; 6-a; 7-a; 8-3s; 9-a; 10-adv prof; 11-texts for discussion & vocab development, correspondence, written work; 12-a,b,c,g; 13-e; 14-various.

99a. SCIENTIFIC FRENCH
Howard U; Rom Langs; Washington, DC

20059.
Jacques Antoine
1-8; 2-3x18; 3-a; 4-ng; 5-ng; 6-b; 7-a; 8-3s;
9-a; 10-inter prof; 11-trans course for
students desiring Fr for advanced study in
sci; 12-a,c,g; 13-ng; 14-ng.

100. FRENCH READINGS IN THE GENERAL
SCIENCES
U of Illinois; Fr; Urbana, IL 61801.
1-11; 2-4x16; 3-a; 4-71; 5-1; 6-depends on
enrollment; 7-a; 8-4s; 9-ng; 10-inter prof;
11-reading background in general sci works;
12-a,b,f,g; 13-ng; 14-Reading Proficiency
in French: Physical Sciences; Reading
Proficiency in French: Biological Sciences.

101. FRENCH SCIENTIFIC VOCABULARY
FOR PHYSICS AND CHEMISTRY
Lenoir Rhyne C; ML; Hickory, NC 28601.
Bohdan B. Kuropas
1-new; 2-3x12; 3-a; 4-ng; 5-0; 6-b; 7-a; 8-
3s; 9-ng; 10-inter Fr; 11-exposure to basic
sci terminology; 12-b,d,f; 13-a,e,f; 14-
Degand, Notions de physique; Degand,
Notions de chimie; articles from sci jour-
nals.

102. READING FRENCH FOR RESEARCH
U of Minnesota; Fr; Minneapolis, MN 55455.
Tom O'Donnell
1-new; 2-5x10; 3-a; 4-spr 75; 5-0; 6-b; 7-a;
8-5q; 9-a; 10-none; 11-acquisition of
reading prof in one qtr; 12-a,f; 13-e,f; 14-
Stack, Reading French in the Arts &
Sciences.

103. SCIENTIFIC FRENCH
Nasson C; Hums; Springvale, ME 04083.
Gilles E. Auger
1-7; 2-4x16; 3-a; 4-72/73; 5-3; 6-a; 7-a; 8-
4s; 9-a; 10-elem prof; 11-film trans from Fr
to Eng followed by film viewing; 12-
b,c,d,f,g; 13-a; 14-Siebert, Skills and Techniques in Reading French.

104. BASIC FRENCH FOR GRADUATE STU-
DENTS: RAPID READING
U of New Mexico; Mod & Cl Langs;
Albuquerque, NM 87131.
Vivien Bull
1-31; 2-3x2 sem; 3-a; 4-70; 5-2; 6-a,
annually or biennially; 7-b; 8-3s undergrad,
0 grad; 9-a; 10-ng; 11-fundamentals of
grammar, readings in sci and hums; 12-
a,b,e,f; 13-ng; 14-Stack, Reading French in
the Arts & Sciences.

105. FRENCH READINGS IN THE SCIENCES
U of New Mexico; Mod & Cl Langs;
Albuquerque, NM 87131.
Claude-Marie Senninger
1-new; 2-3x1 sem; 3-a,b; 4-76; 5-0; 6-b; 7-a;
8-3s; 9-a; 10-inter prof; 11-contemporary
sci material from books and journals; 12-
a,b,c,f; 13-ng; 14-ng.

106. FRENCH READINGS IN THE SOCIAL
SCIENCES
U of New Mexico; Mod & Cl Langs;

Albuquerque, NM 87131.
Claude-Marie Senninger
1-new; 2-3x1 sem; 3-a,b; 4-75; 5-0; 6-b; 7-a;
8-3s; 9-a; 10-inter prof; 11-contemporary
soci sci readings from journals, books,
newspapers; 12-a,b,c,f; 13-ng; 14-ng.

107. FRENCH FOR RESEARCH
SUCNY; For Studies Center; Oswego, NY
13126.
Patrick Sullivan
1-20; 2-3x30; 3-a; 4-70; 5-3; 6-alt yrs; 7-a;
8-6s, no partial credit; 9-a; 10-none; 11-
grammar essentials and readings in expository prose, development of skills in trans
and comprehension, readings to match
students' fields of interest; 12-a,b,c,d,f; 13-
e,f; 14-basic grammar and readings chosen
by instructor.

108. MILITARY AND SCIENTIFIC READINGS
IN FRENCH
U.S. Military Academy; FLs; West Point,
NY 10996.
Sumner Willard
1-9; 2-2½x16; 3-a; 4-67; 5-6; 6-b; 7-a; 8-
2½s; 9-a; 10-basic or accelerated course;
11-study of arms & services of France using
selected and edited passages from military
pubs, industrial standards also considered;
12-a,b,c,g; 13-a,b,c,e,f; 14-Military Readings in French.

See also 201, 486, 1429.

German

109. TECHNICAL GERMAN
Baldwin-Wallace C; FLs & Lits; Berea, OH
44017.
John R. Sinnema
1-6; 2-3x11; 3-a; 4-c30; 5-c30; 6-b; 7-a; 8-
3q; 9-a; 10-inter prof; 11-techniques in
trans expository Ger; 12-b,f; 13-e; 14-Van
de Luyster, German Readings in Science;
locally-prepared guides to trans techniques.

110. BEGINNING GERMAN FOR SCIENCE
MAJORS
Ball SU; FLs; Muncie, IN 47306.
Robert S. Sears
1-15; 2-4x11; 3-a; 4-71/72; 5-4; 6-3q
sequence each yr; 7-a; 8-12q for yr; 9-a; 10-
none; 11-basic grammar needed for reading
texts required for sci majors, readings to
build competence in reading comprehension
and trans of expository materials; 12-a,b,f;
13-ng; 14-Jannach, German for Reading
Knowledge; Jannach, Humanities and
Social Sciences; Van de Luyster, German
Readings in Science.

111. SCIENTIFIC GERMAN
Bennington C; Lang & Lit; Bennington, VT
05201.
Reinhard Mayer
1-1; 2-2x14; 3-a; 4-73; 5-2; 6-on demand; 7-
a; 8-ng; 9-a; 10-adv prof; 11-essays from
journals presenting material on subjects
being studied in the sci div; 12-b,c,f,g; 13-e;
14-Lehmann et al, Spectrum.

112. SPECIAL READINGS IN SCIENTIFIC GERMAN
Berry C; FLs; Mount Berry, GA 30149.
August J. de Berdt
1-3; 2-2x10; 3-a; 4-72; 5-3; 6-on demand; 7-a; 8-2/5q; 9-a; 10-adv prof; 11-readings from journals in cooperation with courses offered in chemistry; 12-b,c,e,g; 13-d,e; 14-articles from journals.

113. SCIENTIFIC GERMAN
Boston U; MLs; Boston, MA 02215.
Susan Cate
1-10; 2-4x17; 3-a; 4-71/72; 5-5; 6-a; 7-a; 8-ng; 9-a; 10-elem prof; 11-review of grammar, development of vocab for students concentrating in the scis; 12-b,c,f,g; 13-ng; 14-DeVries, German-English Science Dictionary; A Course in Scientific German.

114. SCIENTIFIC GERMAN
Central Connecticut SC; ML; New Britain, CT 06050.
Edward Force, Lothar Kahn
1-10; 2-3x16; 3-a; 4-71; 5-3; 6-on demand; 7-a; 8-3s; 9-a; 10-elem prof; 11-reading, vocab building, and trans; 12-a,b,f,g; 13-ng; 14-Dyck & Schwarz, Mensch und Welt; Hirschhorn, Scientific and Technical German Reader.

115. INTERMEDIATE GERMAN FOR SCIENTISTS AND BUSINESS MAJORS
U of Cincinnati; Ger; Cincinnati, OH 45221.
Helga Slessarev
1-80; 2-3x10 for 3q; 3-a; 4-60 (scientists), 73 (bus); 5-every yr; 6-b; 7-a; 8-3q per qtr; 9-a; 10-elem prof; 11-grammar review, general and specific sci and bus material; 12-b,c,d,f,g; 13-a,b,e; 14-Hieble, Die Welt von Heute und Morgen; Sparks & Vail, German in Review; Langenscheidt, Dictionary.

116. ELEMENTARY READING COURSE IN SCIENTIFIC GERMAN
Columbia U; Ger; New York, NY 10027.
Inge D. Halpert
1-13; 2-2x14; 3-a; 4-50; 5-c50; 6-a; 7-a,b,; 8-0; 9-a,b; 10-jr, sr, grad; 11-rapid survey of grammar, extensive reading program; for those with one yr to study the lang; 12-g; 13-e,f; 14-Van de Luyster & Curts, German Grammar for Science Students; Dyck & Schwarz, Mensch und Welt.

117. GERMAN FOR READING REQUIREMENT
DePaul U; MLs; Chicago, IL 60614.
W.V. Hoffman
1-new; 2-6x5; 3-a; 4-smr 75; 5-ng; 6-b; 7-b; 8-4; 9-ng; 10-none; 11-ng; 12-ng; 13-ng; 14-ng.

118. SCIENTIFIC GERMAN
Fairfield U; MLs; Fairfield, CT 06430.
Victor Leeber
1-20; 2-3x14; 3-a; 4-60; 5-regularly; 6-a; 7-a; 8-3s; 9-a; 10-elem prof; 11-ng; 12-b,f,g; 13-ng; 14-Phelps, The German Scientific Heritage; Rechtschaffen, German for Research; Van de Luyster, German Readings in Science.

119. SCIENTIFIC GERMAN
Federal City C; FL; Washington, DC 20001.
1-4; 2-3x10; 3-a; 4-73/74; 5-1; 6-b; 7-a; 8-3q; 9-a; 10-inter prof; 11-grammar review stressing syntax of expository prose, extensive reading of sci texts; 12-a,b,c,d,f,g; 13-e; 14-ng.

120. ADVANCED SCIENTIFIC GERMAN
Federal City C; FL; Washington, DC 20001.
1-3; 2-3x10; 3-a; 4-73/74; 5-1; 6-b; 7-a; 8-3q; 9-a; 10-Sci Ger; 11-reading and discussion of sophisticated sci texts in books and journals published in Ger-speaking countries; term project involves class report and written abstract of research topic in field of concentration; 12-a,b,c,f,g; 13-e; 14-ng.

121. SCIENTIFIC GERMAN
U of Hartford; FL & Lits; West Hartford, CT 06117.
J. Danielson
1-ng; 2-3x15; 3-a; 4-long ago; 5-c10; 6-b; 7-b; 8-3s; 9-a,b; 10-elem prof; 11-readings in the scis; 12-b,c,d,f; 13-e,f; 14-varies.

122. INTRODUCTION TO TECHNICAL, SCIENTIFIC, AND COMMERCIAL GERMAN
Hood C; Lang; Frederick, MD 21701.
1-8; 2-3x1 sem; 3-a; 4-spr 75; 5-1; 6-a; 7-a; 8-3s; 9-a; 10-adv prof; 11-texts for discussion and vocab development, correspondence, written work; 12-a,b,c,g; 13-e; 14-varied.

123. SCIENTIFIC GERMAN
U of Houston; Ger; Houston, TX 77004.
Harold Lenz
1-10/15; 2-3x15 for 2 sems; 3-a; 4-ng; 5-ng; 6-every yr; 7-a; 8-3s; 9-a, part-time grad students; 10-none; 11-streamlined presentation of grammar for reading purposes, reading and trans of prose; 12-a,d,f; 13-e,f; 14-Morgan & Strothmann, Shorter German Reading Grammar; Rechtschaffen & Homberger, German for Research.

124. GERMAN CONVERSATION AND READINGS IN SCIENCE AND MATHEMATICS
Indiana SU; FL; Evansville, IN 47712.
Lomberto Diaz
1-10; 2-4xsem; 3-b; 4-73; 5-2; 6-b; 7-a; 8-4s; 9-a; 10-inter prof; 11-ng; 12-ng; 13-ng; 14-Haynes, Deutsch in drei Laendern; materials chosen by instructor.

125. GERMAN CONVERSATION AND READINGS IN THE SOCIAL SCIENCES
Indiana SU; FL; Evansville, IN 47712.
Lomberto Diaz
1-9; 2-4xsem; 3-b; 4-73; 5-2; 6-b; 7-a; 8-4s; 9-a; 10-inter prof; 11-grammar review and conv, intense reading from soci sci, individual projects; 12-ng; 13-ng; 14-Hieble, Die Welt von Heute und Morgen; materials chosen by instructor.

126. SCIENTIFIC GERMAN
Indiana U; MFLs; Fort Wayne, IN 46805.
Virginia R. Craig

1-13; 2-4x15; 3-a; 4-69; 5-6; 6-b; 7-a; 8-4s for non-major; 9-a; 10-elem prof; 11-intensive treatment of structures and idioms encountered in expository writings, trans of sci materials from various disciplines; 12-b,c,d,g; 13-e; 14-Phelps, The German Scientific Heritage; Jannach, German for Reading Knowledge; DeVries, Scientific German Dictionary; material from various books.

127.　READING AND EXERCISES IN THE GERMAN OF THE SOCIAL SCIENCE PROFESSIONS
U of Kansas; Ger Lang & Lit; Lawrence, KS 66045.
Helga Vigliano
1-10; 2-3x15; 3-a; 4-71/72; 5-3; 6-b; 7-a; 8-3s; 9-a,b; 10-inter prof; 11-readings from current Ger newspapers & periodicals introducing journalistic style, terminology in fields of cult affairs, bus, politics; written exercises; 12-b,d,e,g; 13-e,f,g; 14-ng.

128.　SCIENTIFIC GERMAN
U of Missouri; FLs & Lits; St. Louis, MO 63121.
1-13; 2-3x15; 3-a; 4-67; 5-17; 6-a; 7-a; 8-3s; 9-a; 10-elem prof; 11-reading selected texts in nat and soci scis; 12-a,b,c,f,g; 13-e; 14-Nock, German Science Reader; Gewehr & Von Schmidt, Reading German in the Natural Sciences.

129.　BASIC GERMAN FOR GRADUATE STUDENTS: READING
U of New Mexico; Mod & Cl Langs; Albuquerque, NM 87131.
Rosemary Welsh
1-8; 2-3x2 sem; 3-a; 4-ng; 5-2; 6-on demand; 7-a,b; 8-3s undergrad, 0 grad; 9-a; 10-ng; 11-fundamentals of grammar, readings in scis and hums; 12-a,b,c,f; 13-ng; 14-Morgan & Strothmann, Shorter German Reading Grammar.

130.　GERMAN FOR SCIENTISTS
SUCNY; FLs; Geneseo, NY 14454.
Gifford P. Orwen
1-6/8; 2-3x15; 3-a; 4-71; 5-4; 6-b; 7-a; 8-3s; 9-a; 10-inter prof; 11-ng; 12-b,f,g; 13-f; 14-ng.

131.　GERMAN FOR RESEARCH
SUCNY; For Studies Center; Oswego, NY 13126.
Ralph Beckmeier
1-40; 2-3x16; 3-a; 4-71/72; 5-ng; 6-a; 7-a; 8-3s; 9-a; 10-none; 11-presentation of grammar and reading expository prose first sem; trans, development of comprehension, readings in specialized fields second sem; two sems, no partial credit; 12-f; 13-ng; 14-Law, How to Read German; various texts and supplemental reading material.

132.　READING GERMAN (first semester)
Pennsylvania SU; Ger; University Park, PA 16802.
Keith O. Anderson
1-25; 2-4½x10; 3-a; 4-71/72; 5-7; 6-b; 7-a; 8-3s; 9-a; 10-science major; 11-survey of grammar, reading tech prose; for students with one year to study the lang; 12-a,f; 13-ng; 14-Lehmann et al, German Language and Culture (plus exercise manual); Wishard & Diller, Spiel und Sprache.

133.　READING GERMAN (second semester)
Pennsylvania SU; Ger; University Park, PA 16802.
Keith O. Anderson
1-49; 2-4½x10; 3-a; 4-71/72; 5-6; 6-b; 7-a; 8-3s; 9-a; 10-sci major; 11-survey of grammar, readings in the student's field; 12-a,f; 13-ng; 14-Lehmann et al, German Language and Culture (plus exercise manual); Wishard & Diller, Spiel und Sprache.

134.　READING SCIENTIFIC GERMAN
Pfeiffer C; Lang & Lit; Misenheimer, NC 28109.
Nancy D. McLaurin
1-c6; 2-2x14; 3-a; 4-73/74; 5-1; 6-on demand; 7-a; 8-2s; 9-a; 10-inter prof; 11-ng; 12-ng; 13-ng; 14-ng.

135.　SCIENTIFIC GERMAN
Philadelphia C of Textiles & Science; Hums & Soci Scis; Philadelphia, PA 19144.
Lee L. Snyder
Two courses offered to chemistry majors to prepare them to read simple sci Ger.

136.　ADVANCED READING IN SPECIAL SUBJECTS
Reed C; Ger; Portland, OR 97202.
Ottomar Rudolf
1-6; 2-3x13/26; 3-a; 4-c60; 5-every yr; 6-a; 7-a; 8-1s; 9-a; 10-inter prof; 11-articles and books in students' field; 12-d, tutorial; 13-ng; 14-pubs in students' major field, selected by student or dept.

137.　SCIENTIFIC GERMAN
St. Bonaventure U; MLs; St. Bonaventure, NY 14778.
Bohdan S. Tomkiw
1-25; 2-3x14; 3-a; 4-60; 5-26; 6-a; 7-a; 8-3s; 9-a; 10-one or two yrs; 11-systematic review of grammar, reading, and trans of sci and tech works; 12-a,b,c,f,g; 13-b,e,f; 14-Radimersky, German Science Reader; DeVries, A Contemporary German Science.

138.　SCIENTIFIC GERMAN
Trinity U; FLs; San Antonio, TX 78284.
Registrar
1-15; 2-3x15; 3-a; 4-spr 71; 5-4; 6-b; 7-a; 8-3s; 9-a; 10-inter prof; 11-reading and trans of tech Ger in selected fields; 12-b,c,g; 13-f; 14-Hieble, Die Welt von Heute und Morgen.

139.　MILITARY AND SCIENTIFIC READINGS IN GERMAN
U.S. Military Academy; FLs; West Point, NY 10996.
Sumner Willard
1-30; 2-2½x16; 3-a; 4-66; 5-7; 6-b; 7-a; 8-2½s; 9-a; 10-inter prof; 11-tactics, space flight, atomic research, medicine, econ,

soci; 12-a,b,ɑ,g; 13-a,b,c,d,e,f; 14-Van de Luyster, German Readings in Science; Gierschik, Militaerische Lesebogen.

140. SCIENTIFIC GERMAN
Washington C; ML; Chestertown, MD 21620.
Erika Salloch
1-6; 2-3x28; 3-a; 4-70; 5-yearly; 6-a; 7-a; 8-ng; 9-a; 10-elem prof; 11-ng; 12-d,f; 13-e,f; 14-Lehmann et al, Spectrum.

141. SCIENTIFIC GERMAN
U of Wisconsin; FL; Platteville, WI 53818.
John G.W. Robertson
1-20; 2-2x16; 3-a,b,c; 4-68; 5-8; 6-b; 7-a; 8-2s; 9-a; 10-inter prof; 11-reading, trans, comp, discussion, explanation; visitors utilized; 12-a,b,c,d,g; 13-ng; 14-Van de Luyster, Naturforschung von Heute; Itter, German Workbook for Science Students.

See also 209, 689, 1352, 1381, 1382.

Italian

See 218.

Russian

142. ESSENTIALS OF SCIENTIFIC RUSSIAN
Case Western Reserve U; Sl & East European; Cleveland, OH 44106.
Thomas J. Watts
1-10/12; 2-3 per wk; 3-a; 4-ng; 5-ng; 6-alt yrs; 7-a; 8-3s; 9-a,b; 10-none; 11-basic grammar first sem, tech and sci texts second sem; 12-a,b,f,g; 13-e; 14-Warne, A Russian Scientific Reader; Waring, Russian Science Grammar; Magner, Russian Scientific and Technical Readings.

143. RUSSIAN FOR SCIENTISTS AND SOCIAL SCIENTISTS
U of Colorado; Sl; Boulder, CO 80302.
D.L. Plank
1-14; 2-3x16 for 2 sem; 3-a; 4-71/72; 5-4; 6-b in 2-sem sequence; 7-a; 8-3s per sem; 9-a; 10-none; 11-readings in the student's field; 12-b,f; 13-ng; 14-Plank, Russian for Scientists and Social Scientists.

144. SCIENTIFIC RUSSIAN
Emmanuel C; Russ; Boston, MA 02115.
Luba M. Dyky, Pranas A. Sveikauskas
1-9; 2-3x13; 3-a; 4-71; 5-2; 6-alt yrs; 7-a; 8-4s; 9-a; 10-inter prof; 11-reading and trans of sci material; frequent quizzes and sight trans; 12-b,f,g; 13-f; 14-Cooper, Russian Science Reader; Znamensky, Scientific Russian; booklets on sci topics pub in Moscow.

145. RUSSIAN IN SCIENCE, BUSINESS, INDUSTRY
Lehigh U; FLs; Bethlehem, PA 18015.
Anna P. Herz
1-new; 2-3x14; 3-a; 4-74/75; 5-1; 6-a; 7-a; 8-3s; 9-ng; 10-elem prof; 11-reading, limited conv, limited bus correspondence; 12-b,d,f,g; 13-a,e,f; 14-ng.

146. SCIENTIFIC, TECHNICAL AND BUSINESS

RUSSIAN
Macalester C; Russ; St. Paul, MN 55105.
Alexander Guss
1-ng; 2-ng; 3-a; 4-74; 5-1; 6-ng; 7-a,b; 8-ng; 9-a,b; 10-none; 11-intro to basic grammar, development of vocab, extensive reading of sci texts, training in the use of specialized dictionaries, 2 sem course; 12-ng; 13-ng; 14-ng.

147. SPECIAL RUSSIAN READING COURSE
U of Michigan; Sl; Ann Arbor, MI 48104.
Benjamin A. Stolz
1-20; 2-4x15; 3-a; 4-ng; 5-30; 6-a; 7-a; 8-4s; 9-a; 10-none; 11-reading for research in sci, math, soci sci, and hums; trans skill for Ph.D research; 12-b,f; 13-e,f; 14-Dewey & Mersereau, Reading and Translating Contemporary Russian; other materials as needed.

148. BASIC RUSSIAN FOR GRADUATE STUDENTS: RAPID READING
U of New Mexico; Mod & Cl Langs; Albuquerque, NM 87131.
Byron Lindsey
1-new; 2-3x2 sem; 3-a; 4-ng; 5-0; 6-on demand; 7-a; 8-3s undergrad, 0 grad; 9-a; 10-ng; 11-fundamentals of grammar, readings in sci and hums; 12-ng, 13-ng; 14-ng.

149. RUSSIAN FOR READING
SUCNY; For Studies Center; Oswego, NY 13126.
Edward Nordby
1-6; 2-3x30; 3-a; 4-71; 5-1; 6- 75/76; 7-a; 8-3s; 9-a; 10-none; 11-basic grammar first sem; adv grammar & reading for passive knowledge second sem; 12-a,f; 13-ng; 14-reading texts taken from the Large Soviet Encyclopedia; Dewey & Mersereau, Reading and Translating Contemporary Russian.

150. RUSSIAN
Pennsylvania SU; Sl; University Park, PA 16802.
Lorraine T. Kapitanoff
1-8; 2-4x10; 3-a; 4-63; 5-22; 6-fall & wtr qtrs; 7-a (wtr), b (fall); 8-3q; 9-a; 10-none; 11-for grad students, in majority of cases to fulfill degree requirements; intensive grammar instruction; 12-a,d; 13-d,e,f; 14-Kapitanoff, Russian 5.

151. RUSSIAN
Pennsylvania SU; Sl; University Park, PA 16802.
Lorraine T. Kapitanoff
1-18; 2-4x10; 3-a; 4-69; 5-12; 6-2 qtrs; 7-a (wtr), b (fall); 8-3q; 9-a; 10-none; 11-intensive grammar and trans course for students enrolled in tech disciplines; 12-a,d,f; 13-d,e,f; 14-Kapitanoff, Russian 5.

152. RUSSIAN FOR READING KNOWLEDGE
Rutgers U; Sl; New Brunswick, NJ 08903.
William W. Derbyshire
1-10; 2-3x15; 3-a; 4-72; 5-1; 6-alt yrs; 7-a; 8-3s; 9-a,b; 10-none; 11-alphabet, grammar, use of dictionary, identification of roots, reading of basic texts, readings in the

hums, soci sci, and sci; 12-a,f; 13-ng; 14-Dewey & Mersereau, Reading and Translating Contemporary Russian.

153. MILITARY & SCIENTIFIC READINGS IN RUSSIAN
U.S. Military Academy; FLs; West Point, NY 10996.
Sumner Willard
1-13; 2-2½x16; 3-a; 4-66; 5-9; 6-b; 7-a; 8-2½s; 9-a; 10-adv prof; 11-readings in military, tech, sci and journalistic materials; speeches on a military or sci topic; research paper; 12-a,b,c,g; 13-a,b,c,d,e; 14-Cooper, Russian Science Reader; Basic Military Terminology Exercises; Ross, Russian Military and Scientific Readings.

154. RUSSIAN SCIENTIFIC TRANSLATION
U of West Florida; Eng & FL; Pensacola, FL 32504.
Stanton Millet
1-7; 2-5x10; 3-a; 4-71; 5-6; 6-alt yrs; 7-a; 8-5q; 9-a; 10-none; 11-trans for sci majors; 12-a,b,f,g; 13-e; 14-Turkevich, Russian for the Scientist; Emery, Scientific Russian Guide.

155. SCIENTIFIC RUSSIAN
Western Michigan U; Mod & Cl Langs; Kalamazoo, MI 49001.
Roger L. Cole
1-5; 2-4x15½; 3-a; 4-fall 72; 5-3; 6-ng; 7-ng; 8-4s, no credit for grad students, faculty, staff; 9-ng; 10-none; 11-basic grammar and trans of sci and tech material; intended for undergrad majors in physical or soci sci desiring reading knowledge only; 12-f; 13-ng; 14-ng.

156. READINGS IN SCHOLARLY RUSSIAN
U of Wisconsin; Sl; Madison, WI 53706.
James Bailey
1-20; 2-4x16; 3-a; 4-73; 5-2; 6-b; 7-a; 8-4s; 9-a; 10-elem prof; 11-reading and trans of selected texts in the scis, soci sci, & lit; 12-a,b,f; 13-e,f; 14-all materials are reproduced.

See also 35, 1456.

Spanish

157. INTRODUCTION TO TECHNICAL, SCIENTIFIC, AND COMMERCIAL SPANISH
Hood C; MLs; Frederick, MD 21701.
Juana Amelia Hernandez
1-11; 2-3x1 sem; 3-a; 4-spr 75; 5-1; 6-a; 7-a; 8-3s; 9-a; 10-adv prof; 11-texts for discussion & vocab development, correspondence, written work; 12-a,b,c,g; 13-e; 14-various.

158. BASIC SPANISH FOR GRADUATE STUDENTS: RAPID READING
U of New Mexico; Mod & Cl Langs; Albuquerque, NM 87131.
S.R. Ulibarri
1-17; 2-3x2 sems; 3-a; 4-70; 5-2; 6-on demand; 7-a; 8-3s undergrad, 0 grad; 9-a; 10-ng; 11-fundamentals of grammar, readings in sci and hums; 12-a,b,c,f; 13-ng; 14-Landeira & Van Scoy, Mosaico Hispanico; Schmitt, Spanish Grammar.

159. READINGS IN CULTURE & SCIENCE
U of Texas; Sp & Port; Austin, TX 78712.
Phyllis Harmon
1-18; 2-3x14; 3-a; 4-68/69; 5-13; 6-a; 7-a; 8-3s; 9-a; 10-inter prof; 11-readings in various sci areas, emphasis on trans with some activities devoted to the spoken lang and acquisition of an active vocab; 12-a,g; 13-ng; 14-De Mello, Espanol contemporaneo; various texts in soci and natural sciences.

See also 256, 503, 507, 1678.

Multi-language

160. READING SWEDISH, DANISH AND NORWEGIAN
U of Maryland; Ger & Sl Langs & Lits; College Park, MD 20742.
Jere Fleck
1-22; 2-3x15; 3-a; 4-72/73; 5-5; 6-each fall (and each spr in evening); 7-a,b; 8-3s; 9-a, part-time, faculty; 10-none; 11-student is taught to 'decode' all three langs with use of a grammatical survey & dictionary; active skills are avoided entirely; 12-f, trans from texts; 13-ng; 14-ng.

161. READING SWEDISH, DANISH AND NORWEGIAN
U of Maryland; Ger & Sl Langs & Lits; College Park, MD 20742.
Jere Fleck
1-7; 2-3x15; 3-a; 4-73; 5-5; 6-each spr; 7-a,b; 8-3s; 9-a, part-time, faculty; 10-preceding elem course; 11-2nd sem of a 2-sem sequence course; students read a Scand play or novel; 12-f; 13-texts; 14-primary texts.

See also 1421, 1667.

ETYMOLOGY

162. GREEK AND LATIN ELEMENTS IN SCIENTIFIC TERMINOLOGY
Ball SU; FL; Muncie, IN 47306.
Jerry Kasparek
1-10; 2-1½x5; 3-a; 4-smr 74; 5-1; 6-b; 7-smr; 8-4; 9-a; 10-none; 11-prefixes, suffixes, roots; 12-a,f; 13-ng; 14-Ayers, Bioscientific Terminology.

163. ANALYSIS OF SCIENTIFIC TERMINOLOGY
Baylor U; Cl; Waco, TX 76703.
Roy F. Butler
1-25; 2-3x18; 3-a; 4-48; 5-20; 6-b; 7-a; 8-3s; 9-a; 10-jr; 11-sci vocab of Eng, based on Greek and Latin prefixes, stems, and suffixes; 12-a,f; 13-ng; 14-Butler, Handbook of Medical Terminology.

164. CLASSICAL BACKGROUND OF SCIENTIFIC TERMINOLOGY
Concordia C; Cl; Moorhead, MN 56560.
Stanley Iverson
1-32; 2-2x15; 3-a; 4-73; 5-2; 6-b; 7-a; 8-2s; 9-a; 10-none; 11-study of tech & sci terms from Greek & Latin; roots, prefixes,

suffixes, word formation, analysis; 12-a,b,f; 13-ng; 14-Nybokken, Greek and Latin in Scientific Terminology.

165. CADUCEUS AND LIBRA: LINGUISTICS OF CONTEMPORARY MEDICINE AND LAW
Goucher C; Cl; Towson, MD 21204.
Chester F. Natunewicz
1-20; 2-3x14; 3-a; 4-72; 5-4; 6-every two yrs, smr; 7-a; 8-4s; 9-a; 10-none; 11-Greek and Latin roots as applied to modern med and legal terminology; lang of med diagnosis and therapy; analysis of legal expressions and principles as canonically expressed in Latin formulae; 12-a,f; 13-ng; 14-instructor-developed materials.

166. ENGLISH ETYMOLOGY
Hampden-Sydney C; Cl; Hampden-Sydney, VA 23943.
Graves H. Thompson
1-36; 2-3x14; 3-a; 4-72; 5-4; 6-b; 7-a; 8-3s; 9-a; 10-none; 11-study of words derived from the cl langs; intended to broaden vocab; 12-a,b,f; 13-ng; 14-Burris & Cassou, Latin and Greek in Current Use; Ayers, English Words from Latin and Greek Elements; dictionary.

167. MEDICAL TERMINOLOGY
U of Illinois; Cl; Chicago, IL 60680.
A.P. MacGregor
1-70; 2-2x10; 3-a; 4-68; 5-10; 6-3 qtrs per 2-yr cycle; 7-a; 8-2q; 9-a, paraprofessionals in training; 10-biology major or minor; 11-analysis of Greek and Latin elements in med and zoological vocab with intensive drill of prefixes, suffixes, and roots; 12-a,b,f; 13-blackboard; 14-jeHarned, Medical Terminology Made Easy; Taber's Cyclopedic Medical Dictionary.

168. GREEK AND LATIN IN ENGLISH
U of Kansas; Cl; Lawrence, KS 66045.
Karl Rosen
1-15; 2-3x15; 3-a; 4-over 10 yrs ago; 5-unknown; 6-b; 7-b; 8-3s; 9-a; 10-none; 11-study of words drawn from Greek & Latin, attention to the needs of students of sci and others interested in the sources of Eng vocab; 12-a,b,f; 13-ng; 14-Ayers, English Words from Greek and Latin Elements.

169. THE GREEK AND LATIN ORIGIN OF ENGLISH
U of Maryland; Ancient Studies; Baltimore, MD 21228.
Walter K. Sherwin, Jay M. Freyman
1-40; 2-8x4; 3-a; 4-66/67; 5-6; 6-b; 7-wtr session; 8-2s; 9-a, part-time; 10-none; 11-lectures on hist of alphabet and etymologies; 12-a,f, recitation; 13-ng; 14-Brunner & Berkowitz, The Elements of Scientific and Specialized Terminology.

170. MEDICAL TERMINOLOGY FROM GREEK AND LATIN
Maysville CC; Eng; Maysville, KY 41056.
Natalie Jarzekowski
1-13; 2-3x16; 3-a; 4-74; 5-1; 6-a; 7-a; 8-3s;

9-a,b; 10-none; 11-roots, prefixes, suffixes; primarily for pre-med, pre-dent, pre-nursing, pre-vet; others admitted for help in vocab and writing; 12-b,f; 13-programmed material; 14-Smith & Davis, Medical Terminology.

171. MEDICAL VOCABULARY
Middle Tennessee SU; FLs; Murfreesboro, TN 37130.
T. Coy Porter
1-new; 2-3x15; 3-a; 4-fall 75; 5-0; 6-b; 7-a; 8-3s; 9-a; 10-none; 11-prefixes, suffixes, root words for med vocab; 12-a,b,d,f; 13-ng; 14-Brunner & Berkowitz, Elements of Scientific and Specialized Terminology; Gosser, A Word-Part Book for Medical Terminology; Dorland, A Medical Dictionary.

172. CLASSICAL BASIS OF VERBAL COMMUNICATION
Montgomery County CC; For Studies; Blue Bell, PA 19422.
Charlotte Anderson
1-new; 2-3x16; 3-b; 4-spr 75; 5-1; 6-a; 7-a; 8-3s; 9-a; 10-none; 11-Greek and Latin roots of Eng; word and sentence structure, vocab; words and phrases used in med and legal professions and in the scis and hums; Latin bases of Rom langs; intro to Greek and Latin alphabets; 12-f; 13-ng; 14-Wheelock, Latin; Burris & Cassou, Latin and Greek in Current Use.

173. SCIENTIFIC GREEK AND LATIN
U of Nebraska; FLs; Omaha, NE 68101.
Woodrow L. Most
1-30; 2-2x15; 3-c; 4-72; 5-3; 5-a; 7-a; 8-2s; 9-a,c; 10-none; 11-Latin and Greek derivatives; intended for students in med, dentistry, pharmacy, physical therapy, med technology; 12-a,b,f; 13-ng; 14-McCulloch, A Medical Greek and Latin Workbook; Dorland, Illustrated Medical Dictionary.

174. SCIENTIFIC AND SPECIALIZED TERMINOLOGY
C of Notre Dame; Cl; Baltimore, MD 21210.
Therese Marie Dougherty
1-12; 2-2x4; 3-a; 4-75; 5-1; 6-on demand; 7-a; 8-4s; 9-a; 10-none; 11-programmed study of sci terminology derived from Greek and Latin; includes study of ling principles of word building, Greek and Latin phrases in current use; 12-a,b,f; 13-ng; 14-Ayers, English Words from Greek and Latin Elements; Brunner & Berkowitz, The Elements of Scientific and Specialized Terminology; Asimov, Words from the Myths.

175. LATIN AND GREEK ELEMENTS OF SCIENTIFIC TERMINOLOGY
Seton Hall U; Cl; South Orange, NJ 07079.
Robert Antczak
1-52; 2-3x15; 3-a; 4-75; 5-1; 6-b; 7-a; 8-3s; 9-a; 10-none; 11-study of Latin & Greek vocab used in the physical scis; 12-a,b,f; 13-

ng; 14-Berkowitz, Latin and Greek Elements of Scientific Terminology.

176. ETYMOLOGY OF ENGLISH WORDS
U of Vermont; Cl; Burlington, VT 05401.
Z. Philip Ambrose
1-110; 2-3x14½; 3-a; 4-55; 5-c80; 6-a smr; 7-a,b, community; 8-3s; 9-a,b; 10-no knowledge of Greek or Latin; 11-words of tech and sci usage; 12-a,b,f; 13-ng; 14-Ambrose et al, English Etymology Volumes I & II.

See also 1346.

Business/Commerce/Industry

CZECH

177. CZECH FOR FARM AND RANCH WORKERS
Hill JC; Communications; Hillsboro, TX 76645.
Eugene Maroul
1-47; 2-2x18; 3-c; 4-74; 5-2; 6-a; 7-b; 8-2s; 9-a,b, evening school; 10-none; 11-basic Czech with emphasis on agricultural work situations; 12-a,b,e,f,g; 13-a,b,c,d,e,f; 14-Skrivanek, Modern Conversational Czech.

FRENCH

178. BUSINESS FRENCH
Central Connecticut SC; ML; New Britain, CT 06050.
Yvonne L. LaBrecque
1-10; 2-3x15; 3-a; 4-73; 5-4; 6-a; 7-a; 8-3s; 9-a; 10-inter prof; 11-development of skills geared to situations encountered in bus offices, foreign firms, travel agencies, etc; emphasis on composing bus letters, trans into Eng, interpreting; 12-b,c,d,g, dictations; 13-d,e,f; 14-Harvard & Rose, Bilingual Guide to Business and Professional Correspondence; Buckley, How to Write Better Business Letters; Chaffurin, Le Parfait Secretaire.

179. PROTOCOL OF COMMUNICATION IN FRENCH
Chaminade C; FL; Honolulu, HI 96816.
Eleanor Frierson
1-new; 2-3x15; 3-part-time lecturer; 4-75/76; 5-0; 6-b; 7-a; 8-3s; 9-a; 10-inter prof; 11-customary usage, vocab, and procedures in bus and govt correspondence and diplomatic negotiations; 12-b,c,e,g; 13-a,b,d,e,f, transparencies, charts; 14-ng.

180. BUSINESS FRENCH
U of Cincinnati; Rom Langs; Cincinnati, OH 45221.
Paul A. Gaeng
1-15; 2-3x30; 3-a; 4-74/75; 5-1; 6-a; 7-a,b; 8-3q; 9-a, cont ed; 10-inter Fr; 11-comp, conv, bus correspondence, written & oral trans from & into Fr; 12-b,c,g; 13-f; 14-Mauger, Charon, Brueziere, Le francais commercial I, II.

181. INTERNATIONAL BUSINESS OPTION: FRENCH
U of Cincinnati; Rom Langs; Cincinnati, OH 45221.
Paul A. Gaeng
A cont program for Fr majors with required courses in Bus Admin, leading towards Certificate in Intl Bus. Combines the B.B.A. degree requirements with approximately 27 hrs of lang. Further info ng.

182. COMMERCIAL FRENCH
Colby-Sawyer C; ML; New London, NH 03257.
Stanley E. Wenmark
1-5; 2-15x4; 3-a; 4-Jan 73; 5-2; 6-interim; 7-a; 8-1 unit; 9-a; 10-typing, inter prof; 11-review of office procedures in Fr; 12-a,b,d,e,f,g; 13-e,f, reports, correspondence; 14-ng.

183. FRENCH FOR HOTEL MANAGEMENT
CC of Denver; Fr; Denver, CO 80204.
Elizabeth Brigham
1-25; 2-3x12; 3-b; 4-75; 5-1; 6-b; 7-a; 8-3q; 9-a; 10-none; 11-geared for future chefs and maitre d's who will be working and studying in France; 12-a,f; 13-d; 14-How to Read and Write French.

184. BUSINESS FRENCH
Emporia SU; FL; Emporia, KS 66801.
David E. Travis
1-new; 2-3x15; 3-b; 4-fall 75; 5-0; 6-b; 7-a; 8-3s; 9-a; 10-inter prof; 11-bus forms, contracts, procedures; 12-a,b; 13-f, current bus forms; 14-ng.

185. BUSINESS FRENCH
Federal City C; FLs; Washington, DC 20001.
1-new; 2-3x10; 3-ng; 4-ng; 5-0; 6-ng; 7-ng; 8-3q; 9-a, part-time students; 10-inter prof; 11-techniques of bus correspondence; vocab of intl econ, bus law, accounting, banking; 12-a,d,f, g; 13-ng; 14-ng.

186. CONVERSATIONAL FRENCH
Greenville Technical Education Center; ML; Greenville, SC 29606.
1-18; 2-4x11; 3-a; 4-73; 5-6; 6-a; 7-b; 8-b; 9-b; 10-none; 11-for those who need Fr for bus or travel; two new Michelin plants in community; 12-a,b,e,f,g; 13-a,b,d,e; 14-Brown, French.

187. COMMERCIAL FRENCH

162

Indiana U of Pennsylvania; Rom & Cl Langs; Indiana, PA 15701.
Ludo op de Beeck
1-15; 2-3x14; 3-a; 4-spr 74; 5-1; 6-b; 7-a; 8-3s; 9-a; 10-inter prof; 11-practice in letter writing, use of tech terms, survey of bus practices and methods, problems of trans 12-a,d,g; 13-e,f, bus materials; 14-Francais Commercial, I-II.

188. TRANSLATING AND INTERPRETING FRENCH (two courses)
Lake Erie C; MLs; Painesville, OH 44077.
Ernest Pick
1-12; 2-4x10; 3-a,b; 4-74; 5-1; 6-b; 7-a; 8-3 per course; 9-a; 10-inter prof; 11- recommended for students majoring in intl bus; lit, sci, bus, govt trans and interpreting; 12-c,d,f; 13-e,f, transparencies; 14-various.

189. COMMERCIAL AND BUSINESS FRENCH
U of Maryland; Fr & Ital; College Park, MD 20742.
William MacBain
1-new; 2-3x15; 3-c; 4-spr 75; 5-1; 6-undecided; 7-b; 8-3s; 9-a; 10-inter prof; 11-acquire a mastery of econ vocab; readings, vocab; trans, summaries; 12-a,b,g; 13-e,f; 14-Maitrise de la langue francaise:..en commerce international; de Renty, Lexique de l'anglais des affaires.

190. BUSINESS FRENCH
U of Massachusetts; Fr & Ital; Amherst, MA 01002.
Micheline Dufau
1-18; 2-3x15; 3-a; 4-Sep 73; 5-3; 6-b; 7-a; 8-3s; 9-a; 10-inter prof; 11-familiarize students with vocab and terminology of Fr bus and financial lang; correspondence models studied, letters written, trans, essays; 12-b,g; 13-f; 14-Larousse, Le Francais Commercial, Vols. 1 & 2; Marabont, Dictionary- Le Francais Commercial.

191. COMMERCIAL FRENCH
Monterey Inst of Foreign Studies; Langs & Civs; Monterey, CA 93940.
Burt H. Seidenberg, Danielle Chavy Cooper
Special smr 75 workshop; intensive study; further info ng.

192. BUSINESS FRENCH
C of New Rochelle; Fr; New Rochelle, NY 10801.
Marie-Helene Messager
1-ng; 2-3x13; 3-a; 4-74/75; 5-1; 6-b; 7-a; 8-3s; 9-a,b; 10-inter prof; 11-commerce and Fr commercial lang; 12-a,c,f,g; 13-f; 14-Mauger, Le Francais Commercial, Manuel 1.

193. INTENSIVE FRENCH
SUNY Maritime C; Fort Schuyler, Bronx, NY 10465.
D. Todd, R. Wagoner
5 hrs per sem (elem or inter levels) for all students majoring in Marine Transportation; further info ng.

194. BUSINESS FRENCH
Northwest Missouri U; FLs; Maryville, MO 64468.
Elaine Mauzey
1-5; 2-3x18; 3-a; 4-73/74; 5-2; 6-b; 7-a; 8-3s; 9-a; 10-elem prof; 11-gives general knowledge of Fr as it pertains to bus, govt, econ; emphasis on written communications for bus and industry; 12-a,b,g; 13-d,e,f; 14-ng.

195. FRENCH FOR BUSINESS AND TRAVELERS AND MARINE CORPS
Notre Dame C; Fr; Manchester, NH 03104.
Frances Lessard
1-9; 2-2x14; 3-a; 4-73/74; 5-6; 6-a; 7-b; 8-4s or 0; 9-a,c; 10-none; 11-individualized or collective instruction; emphasis on conv; current vocab for bus, travelers; 12-c,e,g; 13-a,b,c,d,f, games, records; 14-Cadoux, Vous et moi (varies).

196. FRENCH FOR BUSINESS AND TRAVEL
Pasadena City C; FL; Pasadena, CA 91106.
Marina Cobb
1-new; 2-2x18; 3-ng; 4-fall 75; 5-0; 6-two-sem course; 7-b; 8-2s per sem; 9-b, community residents; 10-1st sem, none; 11-practical conv Fr for bus, travel, contemporary cult; 12-a,g; 13-a,b,c,d; 14-Living Language books and cassettes, instructor-prepared materials.

197. COMMERCIAL FRENCH
Skidmore C; MLs & Lits; Saratoga Springs, NY 12866.
Madeleine Ortoleva
1-new; 2-3x12; 3-a; 4-spr 75; 5-1; 6-every second or third yr; 7-a; 8-3s; 9-ng; 10-none; 11-primarily for students majoring in Fr and bus; emphasis placed on comp of letters as applied to commerce, industry, banking; 12-b,c,d,f,g; 13-e,f; 14-de Renty, Lexique de l'anglais des affaires; Maston & Charon, Manuel de francais commercial.

198. EXECUTIVE FRENCH
Temple U; Fr; Philadelphia, PA 19122.
Raymond J. Cormier
1-new; 2-3x14; 3-a; 4-75; 5-0; 6-b; 7-a,b; 8-4s; 9-b; 10-inter prof; 11-condensed cult-oriented grammar for review, speaking and reading, vocab and idiom study focused on bus terminology; 12-a,b,g; 13-e,f; 14-France: A Cultural Review Grammar; Review of Standard French.

199. FRENCH FOR BUSINESS MAJORS
Virginia Commonwealth U; FLs; Richmond, VA 23284.
William J. Beck
1-5; 2-3x15; 3-a; 4-74/75; 5-1; 6-a; 7-a; 8-3s; 9-a; 10-none; 11-2 sem course; 12-f; 13-ng; 14-ng.

200. BUSINESS FRENCH
U of Wisconsin; FL; Eau Claire, WI 54701.
Barbara Rolland
1-new as workshop; offered previously as independent study 72/73 with c3 students per sem; 2-ng; 3-a; 4-smr 75; 5-0; 6-ng; 7-smr; 8-3s; 9-new; 10-inter prof; 11-basic vocab, bus forms and cult material neces-

sary for offices of Fr firms or Amer firms doing bus with France; 12-a,b,d,e,g; 13-e,f, one wk simulated office practice; 14-Clas, Horquelin: Le Francais, Langue des affaires; Lange, Le Secretaire Ideal.

201. COMMERCIAL AND TECHNICAL FRENCH
U of Wisconsin; FL; Platteville, WI 53818.
John G.W. Robertson
1-15-20; 2-2x16; 3-a,b,c; 4-68; 5-7; 6-b; 7-a; 8-2s; 9-a; 10-inter prof; 11-reading, trans, composition, discussion, explanation of tech, commercial, sci texts, docs, contracts, correspondence; 12-a,b,c,d,g; 13-a,b,c,d,e,f, guest speakers; 14-Larousse, Le Francais Commerciale, I & II; Larousse, Le Parfait Secretaire; Jackson, Technical and Scientific French.

See also 99, 474, 475, 476, 478, 480, 486, 544, 546.

GERMAN

202. PRACTICE IN WRITTEN EXPRESSION AND BUSINESS GERMAN
Adelphi U; Langs & Intl Studies; Garden City, NY 11530.
Eva Friedman
1-10; 2-3x16; 3-a; 4-70; 5-3; 6-alt ys; 7-a; 8-3s; 9-a, various professionals; Specimens of German Script; 10-inter prof; 11-essays and narration, composition exercises incl commercial and private correspondence; 12-b,c,d,g; 13-e,f, commercial letters; 14-Kelling &Folsom, Wie man's sagt und schreibt; Lederer & Neuse, Kleines Aufsatzbuch.

203. INTERNATIONAL BUSINESS OPTION (GERMAN)
U of Cincinnati; Ger Langs and Lits; Cincinnati, OH 45221.
(See ms. #181)
Helga Slessarev
1-ng; 2-ng; 3-b; 4-73/74; 5-continuously; 6-a; 7-a; 8-credit giver; 9-a; 10-none; 11-continuing program for Ger majors with required courses in Bus Admin leading towards a certificate in Intl Bus; 12-a,b,f,g; 13-ng; 14-various.

204. SECRETARIAL SKILLS IN FOREIGN LANGUAGE: GERMAN
Clackamas CC; FL; Oregon City, OR 97045.
Magdalena M. Ladd
1-1; 2-3x11; 3-a,b; 4-73/74; 5-2; 6-b; 7-a; 8-3q; 9-a; 10-inter prof; 11-basic bus letter vocab, differences in letter styles and cult items, field trips, resource materials and centers; 12-a,b,c,g; 13-f, texts, films; 14-Sachs, Deutsche Handelskorrespondenz; Horten, Commercial Correspondence in Four Languages.

205. BUSINESS GERMAN
Emporia Kansas SC; FL; Emporia, KS 66801.
David E. Travis
1-new; 2-3x15; 3-b; 4-fall 75; 5-0; 6-b; 7-a; 8-3s; 9-a; 10-inter prof; 11-business forms, contracts, procedures; 12-a,b; 13-f, current business forms; 14-ng.

206. BUSINESS GERMAN
Federal City C; FL; Washington, DC 20001.
1-new; 2-ng; 3-ng; 4-ng; 5-0; 6-ng; 7-ng; 8-3q; 9-ng; 10-inter prof; 11-techniques of bus correspondence; vocab of int econs, bus law, accounting, banking; 12-a d,f,g; 13-ng; 14-ng.

207. CONVERSATIONAL GERMAN
Greenville Technical Education Center; ML; Greenville, SC 29606.
Margaret Rice
1-20; 2-4x11; 3-a; 4-ng; 5-6; 6-a; 7-b; 8-1; 9-b; 10-none; 11-for those who need Ger for bus or travel; many textile-related Ger firms in community; 12-a,b,e,f,g; 13-a,b,d; 14-Kessler, Deutsch fur Auslaender.

208. BUSINESS GERMAN
U of Illinois; Ger; Chicago, IL 60680.
Ernest S. Willner
1-new; 2-4x10; 3-a; 4-Jan 75; 5-1; 6-b; 7-a; 8-4q; 9-a; 10-adv prof; 11-tech vocab, oral, written communication for bus and industry; 12-a,b,c,f; 13-e,f; 14-Sachs, Deutsche Handelskorrespondenz; Korbinian, Der Praktikant; Baeumchen, Der Kaufmann.

209. TRANSLATING AND INTERPRETING GERMAN (two courses)
Lake Erie C; ML; Painesville, OH 44077.
Ernest Pick
1-ng; 2-4x10; 3-a,b; 4-74; 5-1; 6-b; 7-a; 8-3 course; 9-a; 10-inter prof; 11-recommended for students majoring in intl bus; lit, sci, bus, govt trans and interpreting; 12-c,d,f; 13-e,f, transparencies; 14-various.

210. BUSINESS GERMAN
U of Maine; FLs; Orono, ME 04473.
Josef Roggenbauer
1-new; 2-3x15; 3-a; 4-spr 75; 5-1; 6-b; 7-b; 8-3s; 9-a; 10-inter prof; 11-introduce students to terminology used in bus correspondence, invoicing, accounting, shipping; general discussions on the econ geography, industries, and commerce of Ger-speaking Europe; 12-a,b,d,f,g; 13-b,e,f; 14-Kershaw & Russon, German for Business Studies; Kirst & Manekeller, Moderne Geschaeftskorrespondenz.

211. BUSINESS GERMAN
Northwest Missouri SU; FLs; Maryville, MO 64468.
Elaine Mauzey
1-5; 2-3x18; 3-a; 4-73/74; 5-2; 6-b; 7-a; 8-3s; 9-a; 10-elem prof; 11-give general knowledge of Ger as it pertains to bus, govt, econs; special emphasis placed on written communications for bus and industry; 12-a,b,g; 13-d,e,f; 14-ng.

212. EXECUTIVE GERMAN
C of St Catherine; Ger; St. Paul, MN 55105.
Kristina Trendota
1-9; 2-4x15; 3-c; 4-fall 72; 5-6; 7-a; 8-24s (program consists of 6 sem courses); 9-a,b, bus persons; 10-4 sem Ger; 11-solid groundwork in grammar, intro to bus terms, concepts, and practices as needed for trans,

oral interpretation, doc evaluation, active company representation; development of skills in consulting reference materials & periodicals; experiential learning with intl company at least during Jan interterm (Full report published in the ADFL Bulletin, Nov, 1974.); 12-a,b,c,d,f,g; 13-a,e,f; 14-Baeumchen, Der Kaufmann; Baeumchen, Deutsche Wirtschaftssprache fuer Auslaender; Sachs, Deutsche Handelskorrespondenz; West German govt, Tatsachen ueber Deutschland.

213. COMMERCIAL GERMAN
Skidmore C; MLs & Lits; Saratoga Springs, NY 12866.
Sonja Karsen
1-new; 2-3x12; 3-a; 4-spr 75; 5-1; 6-every 2nd or 3rd yr; 7-a; 8-3s; 9-ng; 10-none; 11-primarily for students majoring in Ger and bus; emphasis placed on composition of letters as applied to commerce, industry, banking; 12-b,c,d,f,g; 13-e,f; 14-ng.

214. INTENSIVE GERMAN
U of South Carolina; Ger; Columbia, SC 29208.
Gerda Jordan
1-22; 2-35x10; 3-a; 4-smr 74; 5-1; 6-smrs; 7-a; 8-ng; 9-a; 10-none; 11-for students working for Master of Intl Bus Studies degree; 12-a,b,c,d,e,g; 13-a,b,c,d,e,f; 14-Feld et al, Anfang und Fortschritt; Bonnell & Sedwick, Conversation in German; Lederer & Neuse, Kleines Aufsatzbuch; Baeumchen, Der Kaufmann; Kirby, Auslese.

215. MAINTENANCE GERMAN
U of South Carolina; Ger; Columbia, SC 29208.
Gerda Jordan
1-17; 2-1½x 16; 3-ng; 4-fall 74; 5-1; 6-b; 7-a; 8-ng; 9-a; 10-Intensive Ger; 11-for students working for Master of Intl Bus Studies; intended to keep active the skills acquired during the previous smr; 12-a,b,c,g; 13-a,b,e,f; 14-Kelling, Deutsche Kulturgeschichte.

216. GERMAN FOR INTERNATIONAL TRADE AND COMMERCE
U of Texas; FLs and Ling; Arlington, TX 76010.
T.E. Frank
1-15; 2-3x15; 3-a; 4-72; 5-1; 6-alt yrs; 7-a; 8-3s; 9-a,b; 10-inter prof; 11-reading and writing correspondence; reading and writing tech reports; general study of contemporary bus trends; 12-a,b,d,e,f,g; 13-d,e,f; 14-Heintz-Schuppmann, Briefe schreiben, leicht gemacht; Renner & Sachs, Wirtschaftssprache; Langenscheidt, 100 Briefe Deutsch fuer Export und Import.

217. GERMAN FOR BUSINESS MAJORS
Virginia Commonwealth U; FLs; Richmond, VA 23284.
William J. Beck
1-8; 2-3x15; 3-a; 4-74/75; 5-1; 6-a; 7-a; 8-3s; 9-a; 10-none; 11-ng; 12-f; 13-ng; 14-ng.

See also 115, 122, 729, 730, 1339.

ITALIAN

218. TRANSLATING AND INTERPRETING ITALIAN
Lake Erie C; ML; Painesville, OH 44077.
Ernest Pick
1-ng; 2-4x10; 3-a,b; 4-74; 5-1; 6-b; 7-a; 8-3 course; 9-a; 10-inter prof; 11-recommended for students majoring in intl bus; lit, sci, bus, govt trans and interpreting; 12-c,d,f; 13-e,f, transparencies; 14-various.

JAPANESE

219. JAPANESE FOR TRAVEL INDUSTRY MANAGEMENT MAJORS
Brigham Young U; Communications & Lang Arts; Laie, HI 96762.
Jay Fox
1-25; 2-5x15; 3-b; 4-73; 5-4; 6-a; 7-a; 8-4s; 9-a,b; 10-none; 11-3-sem program; emphasis on basic conv in the travel industry; 12-a,b; 13-d; 14-Japanese for TIM Majors.

220. PROTOCOL OF COMMUNICATION IN JAPANESE
Chaminade C; FL; Honolulu, HI 96816.
Eleanor Frierson
1-new; 2-3x15; 3-part-time lecturer; 4-75/76; 5-0; 6-b; 7-a; 8-3s; 9-a; 10-inter prof; 11-customary usage, vocab, procedures in bus, govt correspondence and diplomatic negotiations; 12-b,e,g; 13-a,b,d,e,f, transparencies, charts; 14-ng.

RUSSIAN

221. RUSSIAN FOR BUSINESS
Douglass C-Rutgers U; Russ; New Brunswick, NJ 08903.
Luba H. Kowalski
Advanced comp & stylistics course dealing with fundamental bus vocab. Topics covered: Soviet retailing & supermarkets; containerization & packaging; Soviet economy; pollution & environmental problems; transportation & freight insurance; bus correspondence; simultaneous trans; typing. Text: Kohl, Business Russian.

222. BUSINESS RUSSIAN
George Washington U; Sl; Washington, DC 20006.
George Olkhovsky
1-new; 2-2½x13; 3-a; 4-spr 75; 5-0; 6-alt yrs; 7-a; 8-3s; 9-a,b, part-time students; 10-inter prof; 11-study of bus vocab, concepts of bus in Soviet context; 12-b,f; 13-e,f; 14-Kohls, Business Russian.

223. BUSINESS RUSSIAN
Georgetown U; Russ; Washington, DC 20007.
Robert Lager
1-new; 2-3x13; 3-a; 4-spr 75; 5-0; 6-a; 7-a; 8-3s; 9-a; 10-adv prof; 11-detailed analysis of the special usage of bus and journalistic Russ; special emphasis on vocab & various types of bus letters and forms; 12-a,b,d,g; 13-e,f; 14-Dorff, Business Russian.

224. BUSINESS RUSSIAN
U of Illinois; Sl Langs & Lits; Urbana, IL 61801.
Kurt A. Klein
1-19; 2-3 per wk; 3-a; 4-70; 5-1; 6-b; 7-a; 8-3s; 9-a; 10-inter prof; 11-based on text; 12-a,b,g; 13-f; 14-Kohls, Business Russian.

225. THE ART OF NEGOTIATING WITH THE RUSSIANS
Ohio SU; Cont Ed, Center for Sl & East European Studies; Columbus, OH 43210.
David A. Ricks, Finance
Special seminar given 2 hrs per wk 8 wks, 3 credits or no credit. General framework of dealing with Russ negotiators; specific problem areas. Authorities from US govt, Russ consulate, and 2 multi-national corporations will visit the seminar.

226. BUSINESS RUSSIAN
Southern Illinois U; FLs and Lits; Carbondale, IL 62901.
Joseph Kupcek
1-5; 2-3x16; 3-a; 4-74; 5-1; 6-b; 7-a; 8-3s; 9-a; 10-inter prof; 11-study of style of commercial lang, its application to the development of skills in bus correspondence; 12-a,b,c,d,f,g; 13-e,f; 14-Kohls, Business Russian.

See also 145, 146, 836.

SPANISH

227. CONVERSATIONAL SPANISH FOR AGRI-BUSINESS
Amarillo C; Cont Ed; Amarillo, TX 79178.
Clair Mayes
1-new; 2-3x15; 3-c; 4-ng; 5-0; 6-a, special groups; 7-b; 8-b; 9-b; 10-none; 11-mechanics, sound system, basic grammatical structures, special terminology, oral drills; 12-a,b,d,f; 13-records; 14-See It and Say It in Spanish.

228. CONVERSATIONAL SPANISH FOR RE-TAIL TRADE
Amarillo C; Cont Ed; Amarillo, TX 79178.
Clair Mayes
1-18; 2-3x15; 3-c; 4-74; 5-1; 6-a, for special groups; 7-b, 8-b; 9-b; 10-none; 11-mechanics, sound system, basic grammatical structures, special terminology, oral drills; 12-a,b,d,f; 13-records; 14-See It and Say It in Spanish.

229. BUSINESS SPANISH
Ball State U; FL; Muncie, IN 47306.
James Brown
1-21; 2-1½x5; 3-a; 4-74; 5-1; 6-alt yrs; 7-a; 8-4q; 9-a; 10-adv prof; 11-use of bus forms, bus letters, terms, commercial correspondence; 12-a,g; 13-sample letters; 14-Pittman Academy, La correspondencia moderna.

230. SPANISH FOR BUSINESS ENTERPRISES
Benedictine C; Spanish; Atchison, KS 66002.
John Lange
1-4; 2-18x3; 3-a; 4-74; 5-2; 6-b; 7-a; 8-3s; 9-a; 10-elem prof; 11-readings of bus texts, letters, journals; analysis of dual lang letters; letter writing; vocab, idiom building; 12-b,c,g; 13-e,f; 14-Commercial Spanish; Spanish Business Correspondence.

231. SPANISH FOR INTERNATIONAL TRADE AND DIPLOMACY
Bennett C; Communications; Greensboro, NC 27420.
Hortensia Sanchez-Boudy
1-6; 2-3x18; 3-a; 4-72; 5-1; 6-b; 7-a; 8-3s; 9-a; 10-consent of instructor; 11-mastery of bus and commercial terms used in intl trade & commerce; 12-a,b,c,f,g; 13-a,d,e,f; 14-ng.

232. INTERNATIONAL SPANISH CORRE-SPONDENCE
Bethany C; FLs; Bethany, WV 26032.
Santiago Garcia, Marjorie Carty
1-new; 2-4x15; 3-a; 4-spr 75; 5-0; 6-not determined; 7-a; 8-4s; 9-a; 10-inter prof, typing; 11-development of skills in bus & diplomatic letter-writing; familiarization with tech terms; methods of trans; comprehensive preparation for biling positions; 12-e,f,g; 13-ng; 14-Turk & Brady, Spanish Letter Writing; dictionary of commercial terms from Spain; locally-developed workbook.

233. COMMERCIAL SPANISH
Bethany Nazarene C; ML; Bethany, OK 73008.
Dolores Wood
1-new; 2-3x15; 3-a; 4-spr 75; 5-1; 6-alt yrs; 7-a; 8-3s; 9-a; 10-inter prof; 11-preparation of biling secretaries, accountants, office administrators, correspondence, special forms, terminology, lang typewriters, contrastive methods, sources, resources; 12-a,b,c,d,f,g; 13-ng; 14-ng.

234. ELEMENTARY SPANISH FOR BUSINESS STUDENTS
Boise SU; FL; Boise, ID 83725.
L. Valverde
1-11; 2-4x18 for two sems; 3-a; 4-fall 74; 5-1; 6-alt yrs; 7-a; 8-4s; 9-a; 10-none; 11-intro to basic lang skills useful for students in world of bus; bus terminology, pertinent readings, rudimentary writing, letter writing, reading of managerial, commercial transactions, short reports, resumes, memoranda; 12-ng; 13-ng; 14-ng.

235. SPANISH FOR BUSINESS CORRESPON-DENCE
Bowling Green SU; Rom Langs; Bowling Green, OH 43403.
Richard Hebein
1-new course; 2-3x10; 3-a; 4-ng; 5-0; 6-on demand; 7-a; 8-3q; 9-a; 10-inter prof; 11-commercial purposes with emphasis on bus letter writing; 12-a,b,g; 13-ng; 14-ng.

236. BUSINESS SPANISH
California SU; FLs & Lits; Hayward, CA 94542.
Vincenzo Traversa
1-13; 2-4x10; 3-a; 4-spr 74; 5-1; 6-b; 7-a; 8-

4q; 9-a, persons working in city offices; 10-2nd yr Sp; 11-Sp terminology used in bus & trade; 12-a,b,g; 13-material prepared by instructor; 14-de Meza, Business Letters Handbook.

237. ADVANCED SPANISH CONVERSATION-COMMERCE
U of California; Sp & Port; Santa Barbara, CA 93106.
R.E. Wilson
1-9; 2-2x10; 3-a,c; 4-spr 74; 5-1; 6-b; 7-a; 8-2q; 9-a; 10-inter prof; 11-conv sessions featuring the specialized vocab of commercial transactions and correspondence; role-playing; 12-b,c,d,g, visits to offices and factories; 13-e,f; 14-instructor-prepared materials.

238. SPANISH FOR BUSINESS
Centenary C of Louisiana; FLs, Bus; Shreveport, LA 71104.
Arnold Penuel
1-75/76; 2-1 to 3; 3-b; 4-75/76; 5-0; 6-a; 7-a; 8-1 to 3; 9-a; 10-varies with course; 11-program includes several different courses; bus courses, applied & adv applied Sp which include readings in appropriate journals; adv students required to work in field & take sem at Instituto Tecnologio, Monterrey, Mexico; 12-a,b,c,g; 13-a,b,d,e,f; 14-ng.

239. BUSINESS SPANISH
Central Connecticut SC; MLs; New Britain, CT 06050.
Orlando Gomez-Gil, Fred Lougee
1-40; 2-3x15; 3-a; 4-74; 5-3; 6-a; 7-a; 8-3s; 9-a; 10-inter prof; 11-study of the most important commercial activities: corporation, credit, insurance, stock markets, real estate, commercial correspondence, travel agencies, for trade, bus office; 12-a,b,c,f,g; 13-e,f; 14-Gomez-Gil, Tratado Practico de Espanol Comercial; Martin, Correspondencia Comercial.

240. BUSINESS SPANISH
U of Cincinnati; Rom Langs; Cincinnati, OH 45211.
Paul A. Gaeng
(See ms. #180)
1-22; 2-3x30; 3-a; 4-74/75; 5-1; 6-a; 7-a,b; 8-3q; 9-a, cont ed; 10-inter Sp; 11-comp, conv, bus correspondence, written & oral trans from & into Sp; 12-b,c,g; 13-f; 14-Rosenthal & Rudman, Redaccion de cartas comerciales simplificada.

241. INTERNATIONAL BUSINESS OPTION: SPANISH
U of Cincinnati; Rom Langs; Cincinnati, OH 45221.
(See ms. #181)
Paul A. Gaeng
Cont program for Sp majors with required courses in Bus Admin leading to Certificate in Intl Bus; combines B.B.A. degree requirements with approx 27 hrs of lang courses; further info ng.

242. SECRETARIAL SKILLS IN FOREIGN LANGUAGE: SPANISH
Clackamas CC; FL; Oregon City, OR 97045.

Magdalena M. Ladd
1-2; 2-3x11; 3-a,b; 4-73/74; 5-2; 6-b; 7-a; 8-3q; 9-a; 10-inter prof; 11-basic bus letter vocab, differences in letter styles & cult items, field trips, resource materials & centers; 12-a,b,c,g; 13-f; 14-Steel de Meza, Business Letter Handbook; Horten, Commercial Correspondence in Four Languages.

243. COMMERCIAL AND BUSINESS SPANISH
Colby C; ML; New London, NH 03257.
Stanley E. Wenmark
1-1; 2-varies; 3-a; 4-73; 5-2; 6-on demand; 7-a; 8-1 unit; 9-a; 10-adv prof, secretarial skills; 11-vocab, structures common to commercial, bus operations; trans; 12-a,b,c,e,f,g; 13-d,e,f; bus, industrial, govt reports & correspondence; 14-Steel de Meza, Business Letter Handbook.

244. COMMERCIAL SPANISH
Colby C; ML; New London, NH 03257
Stanley E. Wenmark
1-2; 2-15x4; 3-a; 4-72/73; 5-3; 6-b; 7-a; 8-1 unit; 9-a; 10-inter prof, typing ability; 11-general office procedures; 12-a,h,e,f,g; 13-d,e,f, bus materials; 14-Gregg, Tecnicas mecanograficas modernas; Steel de Meza, Business Letter Handbook.

245. SPANISH AND BUSINESS
U of Detroit; Langs & Ling; Detroit, MI 48221.
Marjorie Reas
1-new; 2-3 & 4x15; 3-b; 4-fall 75; 5-0; 6-a; 7-a; 8-3s; 9-ng; 10-elem prof; 11-bus terminology, practice in intensive conv; civ & cult; 12-a,b,d,g; 13-e,f, bus forms, office equipment; 14-ng.

246. BUSINESS SPANISH
Emporia Kansas SC; FL; Emporia, KS 66801.
David E. Travis
1-new; 2-3x15; 3-b; 4-fall 75; 5-0; 6-b; 7-a; 8-3s; 9-a; 10-inter prof; 11-bus forms, contracts, procedures; 12-a,b; 13-f, current bus forms; 14-ng.

247. BUSINESS SPANISH
Federal City C; FL; Washington, DC 20001.
1-6; 2-3x10; 3-a; 4-74/75; 5-1; 6-on demand; 7-b; 8-3q; 9-a, part-time students; 10-inter prof; 11-practical course in bus Sp; 12-a,d,f,g; 13-ng; 14-ng.

248. FUNCTIONAL SPANISH
Florida Atlantic U; Langs & Ling; Boca Raton, FL 33432.
Juan Estarellas
1-6; 2-4x11; 3-a; 4-74; 5-1; 6-not known; 7-b; 8-4q; 9-a,b; 10-none; 11-functional grammar, vocab for businesspersons, traveler; 12-a,e,f; 13-d; 14-Estarellas, Functional Spanish.

249. SPANISH FOR THE BUSINESS EXECUTIVE
Hofstra U; Sp; Hempstead, NY 11550.
Isabel Cid Sirgado
1-new; 2-ng; 3-ng; 4-spr 75; 5-0; 6-ng; 7-b; 8-b; 9-working members of community; 10-

ng; 11-ng; 12-ng; 13-ng; 14-ng.

250. BUSINESS CORRESPONDENCE IN SPANISH
Imperial Valley C; FL; Imperial, CA 92251.
Alicia Ortega
1-ng; 2-3x18; 3-a; 4-ng; 5-ng; 6-a; 7-a; 8-3s; 9-a; 10-none; 11-letter form, style, bus vocab, spelling, punctuation; emphasis on differences, similarities in Eng & Sp bus correspondence; 12-a,d,f,g; 13-ng; 14-Steel de Meza, Business Letter Handbook, Spanish/ English.

251. SPANISH FOR BUSINESS
Indiana SU; FL; Evansville, IN 47712.
Lomberto Diaz
1-new; 2-3 per wk; 3-b; 4-ng; 5-0; 6-b; 7-b; 8-3; 9-a, cont ed; 10-elem prof; 11-study of correspondence, docs related to bus in Spain and Latin Amer; 12-d,g; 13-e,f; 14-ng.

252. COMMERCIAL SPANISH
Indiana U of Pennsylvania; Rom & Cl Langs; Indiana, PA 15701.
Ludo op de Beeck
1-15; 2-3x14; 3-a; 4-spr 74; 5-1; 6-b; 7-a; 8-3s; 9-a; 10-inter prof; 11-practice letter writing, technical terms, survey of bus practices, methods, problems of trans; 12-a,d,g; 13-e,f, bus materials; 14-Villen & Pilar de Ron, Der spanische Korrespondent.

253. SPANISH BUSINESS
Ithaca C; FLs; Ithaca, NY 14850.
Douglas H. Armstrong
Will be offered fall 75; other info ng.

254. SPANISH SHORTHAND
Kansas City CJC; Hums & Bus; Kansas City KS 66112.
Cecilia Rodriguez
1-2; 2-2x17; 3-a; 4-spr 74; 5-1; 6-upon request; 7-a; 8-3s; 9-a; 10-elem prof, some knowledge of shorthand; 11-shorthand theory and principles; 12-b,c,g; 13-d; 14-Taquigrafia Gregg: primer curso.

255. COMMERCIAL SPANISH
Kean C; FL; Union, NJ 07083.
Charles Wendell
1-25; 2-3x14; 3-a; 4-69; 5-3; 6-b; 7-a,b; 8-3s; 9-a; 10-ng; 11-ng; 12-ng; 13-ng; 14-ng.

256. TRANSLATING AND INTERPRETING SPANISH
Lake Erie C; ML; Painesville, OH 44077.
Ernest Pick
1-ng; 2-4x10; 3-a,b; 4-74; 5-1; 6-b; 7-a; 8-3 course; 9-a; 10-inter prof; 11-recommended for students majoring in intl bus; lit, sci, bus, trans, interpreting; 2 sem course; 12-c,d,f; 13-e,f, transparencies; 14-various.

257. SPANISH BUSINESS
Lone Mountain C; Sp; San Francisco, CA 94118.
M.P. Valdes
1-5; 2-4x15; 3-a; 4-74; 5-1; 6-on demand; 7-a; 8-2s; 9-a, part-time students; 10-inter

prof; 11-written skills in bus correspondence; principles of bus writing, specific types of bus communications; 12-b,c,g; 13-e,f; 14-Cobo, Tratado de Correspondencia Comercial y Oficial.

258. BUSINESS SPANISH
Louisiana Tech U; FLs; Ruston, LA 71270.
Richard Ezell
1-12; 2-20x4; 3-c; 4-restructured in 74; 5-1; 6-smr; 7-a; 8-3; 9-a; 10-adv standing; 11-bus forms plus internship in Mex bus without pay; 12-b,c,d,e,g; 13-d,e,f, worksheets; 14-ng.

259. BUSINESS SPANISH
U of Maine; FLs; Orono, ME 04473.
Josef Roggenbauer
1-new; 2-3x15; 3-a; 4-spr 75; 5-1; 6-b; 7-b; 8-3s; 9-a; 10-inter prof; 11-intro study terminology, techniques commercial transactions--bus letters, forms, abbreviations; econ geography of Latin Amer, Spain, industries, commerce; 12-a,b,d,f,g; 13-b,e,f; 14-Garcia Martin, Correspondencia Comercial.

259A. PROYECTO DESARROLLO ECONOMICO
Manchester CC; FL; Manchester, CT 06040.
Toby Tamarkin, FL; Alan Gates, Bus 1-35; 2-6x30; 3-b; 4-73/74; 5-1; 6-every other yr depending on grant funding; 7-b; 8-12s; 9-members of Puerto Rican community through the P.R. Businessmen's Assoc; 10-none; 11-series of exercises in accounting, econ, marketing, sales; for more efficient handling of the mechanics of small businesses; 12-a,b,f,g individualized help, guest speakers; 13-c, materials prepared by the bus dept, trans into Sp; 14-ng.

260. COMMERCIAL SPANISH
Mankato SC; FL; Mankato, MN 56001.
Paul Waldorf
1-15; 2-4x11; 3-a; 4-ng; 5-3; 6-one qtr in alt yrs; 7-a,b; 8-4q; 9-a; 10-inter prof; 11-study of the lang of the bus world, stressing letter writing, similar techniques; 12-a,b,c,g; 13-d,e,f; 14-ng.

261. CONVERSATIONAL SPANISH
McHenry County C; Sp; Crystal Lake, IL 60014.
Rosemary Kurtz, Erwin Cornelius
1-25; 2-2x16; 3-a; 4-ng; 5-4; 6-b; 7-b; 8-1s; 9-b; 10-none; 11-practice in basic conv Sp necessary for daily contacts with those employed in ornamental horticulture; 12-a,e,f,g; 13-d; 14-MLA, Modern Spanish.

262. BILINGUAL SECRETARIAL COURSE (SPANISH)
Montgomery County CC; For Studies; Blue Bell, PA 19422.
Charlotte Anderson
1-new; 2-ng; 3-b; 4-Sept 75; 5-0; 6-2-yr program with courses every sem; 7-n g; 8-ng; 9-ng; 10-none; 11-follows Executive Secretarial program substituting Sp courses for electives and special projects in Office Procedure courses; 12-ng; 13-ng; 14-ng.

168

263. INTENSIVE SPANISH
SUNY Maritime C; Fort Schuyler, Bronx, NY 10465.
D. Todd, R. Wagoner
5 hrs per sem (elem or inter levels) for all students majoring in Marine Transportation; further info ng.

264. BUSINESS SPANISH
U of North Carolina; MLs; Wilmington, NC 28401.
A. Gonzalez-del-Valle
1-31; 2-3x16; 3-a; 4-fall 73; 5-4; 6-a; smr; 7-a; 8-3s; 9-a; 10-elem prof; 11-familiarization with terminology necessary for fields of econ, bus, accounting, nat scis; bus correspondence; currency systems; 12-b,c,g; 13-f; 14- Guias telefonicas de los Estados Unidos y paises de Hispano-America; Gonzalez-del-Valle & Gonzalez-del-Valle, Manual of Business Spanish; Rojas, Redaccion Comercial Estructurada; Vasquez, Diccionario de Correspondencia Comercial--Ingles-Espanol.

265. BUSINESS SPANISH
Northwest Missouri SU; FLs; Maryville, MO 64468.
Elaine Mauzey
1-5; 2-3x18; 3-a; 4-73/74; 5-2; 6-b; 7-a; 8-3s; 9-a; 10-elem prof; 11-gives general knowledge of Sp as it pertains to bus, govt, econ; emphasis on written communications for bus, industry; 12-a,b,g; 13-d,e,f; 14-ng.

266. ORAL & WRITTEN SPANISH FOR BUSINESS STUDENTS
Pace U; FLs; New York, NY 10038.
Anthony T. Sallustio
1-6; 2-3x30; 3-a; 4-fall 74; 5-1; 6-as needed; 7-b; 8-3s; 9-a; 10-elem prof; 11-practice in reading, writing bus communications; study of commercial documents, specialized vocab; conv practice; geared to bus admin students; 12-a,b,c,d,g; 13-e,f; 14-Larralde, Correspondencia Comercial.

267. SPANISH FOR BUSINESS AND TRAVEL
Pasadena City C; FL; Pasadena, CA 91106.
Marina Cobb
1-49; 2-2x18; 3-a; 4-fall 74; 5-1; 6-two-sem course; 7-b; 8-2s; 9-b, community; 10-1st sem, none; 11-practical conv for bus, travel, personal enrichment; contemporary cult of areas where lang is spoken; 12-a,g; 13-a,b,c,d; 14-Living Language books and cassettes; instructor-prepared materials.

268. SPANISH FOR BUSINESSMEN AND TRAVELERS
Regis C; MLs; Denver, CO 80221.
Sr. Joanne Donavan
1-6; 2-2x15; 3-a; 4-Jan 75; 5-1; 6-b; 7-b; 8-2s,b; 9-b; businessmen, police officers; 10-none; 11-basic grammar, everyday vocab; 12-g; 13-d,e,f; 14-Kany, Spoken Spanish; Nassi, Workbook in Spanish.

269. INTERNATIONAL FINANCE MAJOR
Rosary C; Bus & Econ, ML; River Forest, IL 60305.

Doris Rauenhorst
32 sem hrs of econ; 24 sem hrs adv lang work. Designed to produce a unique person who is skilled in both the knowledge and art of intl finance as well as the lang, hist, cult of one or more of the modern trading nations. Initiated in 72. Recommended that work be taken at the Rosary C program in Fribourg, Switzerland (U of Fribourg).

270. BUSINESS AND PROFESSIONAL SPANISH
St. Louis U; MLs; St. Louis, MO 63103.
Teresa de Johnson
1-14; 2-3x18; 3-a; 4-fall 74; 5-1; 6-a; 7-a,b; 8-3s; 9-a,b; 10-inter prof; 11-ng; 12-b,d,e,g; 13-a,b,c,d,e,f, psychodramatic settings; 14-Schmitt, Spanish Grammar; de Colon, Manual de Espanol Comercial; Frias, Diccionario Comercial.

271. COMMERCIAL SPANISH
Skidmore C; MLs & Lits; Saratoga Springs, NY 12866.
Ruth Chismall
1-new; 2-3x12; 3-a; 4-spr 75; 5-1; 6-every 2nd or 3rd yr; 7-a; 8-3s; 9-ng; 10-none; 11-primarily for students majoring in Sp & bus; emphasis placed on composition of letters as applied to commerce, industry, banking; 12-b,c,d,f,g; 13-e,f; 14-Predmore, Topical Spanish Review Grammar; Ramon, Correspondencia mercantil; Rosenthal & Rudman, Redaccion de cartas comerciales simplificadas.

272. BUSINESS CORRESPONDENCE IN SPANISH
U of South Dakota; MFL; Vermillion, SD 57069.
Gary Mikelson
1-new; 2-2x16; 3-a; 4-ng; 5-0; 6-alt yrs; 7-a; 8-2s; 9-a; 10-inter prof; 11-proper form for letters, bus primarily; tech vocab; bus activities in Sp-speaking countries; 12-ng; 13-ng; 14-Jackson, Manual de correspondencia espanola; Juncal, Manual Practico de Correspondencia Comercial; Steel de Meza, Business Letter Handbook, Spanish-English.

273. PRACTICAL CONVERSATIONAL SPANISH
South Plains C; Communications & Philo; Levelland, TX 79336.
Frank Gonzales
1-27; 2-3x16; 3-a; 4-68; 5-10; 6-a; 7-b; 8-3s; 9-b, bus people, farmers, ranchers; 10-none; 11-conv Sp with vocab used in bus, farming, ranching; 12-f,g; 13-b,d; 14-Gonzales, Practical Conversational Spanish.

274. BILINGUAL EXECUTIVE SECRETARIAL STUDIES
U of Southern Mississippi; FLs; Hattiesburg, MS 39601.
Roger Johnson Jr.
This major prepares students for interesting positions with intl companies. The program is administered by the Dept of Bus Ed and includes considerable practical instruction in Sp. Students normally

complete a portion of their studies in one of the Latin Amer centers recommended by the FL Dept.

275. BUSINESS SPANISH
Stephen F. Austin SU; MLs; Nacogodoches, TX 75961.
Elizabeth Davis
1-19; 2-3x14; 3-a; 4-74/75; 5-1; 6-b; 7-a; 8-3s; 9-a; 10-inter prof; 11-oral, written Sp; special attention to accurate & idiomatic expressions currently in use in the bus & tech fields; 12-a,b,c,d,f,g; 13-a,e,f, guest lecturers; 14-de Meza, Business Letter Handbook, Spanish-English; de Colon, Espanol Comercial, Manual de lecturas y ejercicios.

276. SPANISH CONVERSATION FOR RETAILING AND FASHION
Stephens C; FL; Columbia, MO 65201.
Albert J. Delmez
Offered spr 75; other info ng.

277. FARM AND RANCH SPANISH
Tarleton SU; Eng & Langs; Stephenville, TX 76402.
Russell Peterson
1-new; 2-3x18; 3-c; 4-spr 75; 5-0; 6-to be determined; 7-a; 8-3s; 9-ng; 10-none; 11-ng; 12-a; 13-ng; 14-ng.

278. BUSINESS CORRESPONDENCE IN SPANISH
Tarrant County JC; FLs; Hurst, TX 76053.
Jane Harper, Doris Key
1-5; 2-self-paced; 3-a; 4-spr 74; 5-2; 6-a; 7-a,b; 8-1s; 9-a, part-time students; 10-elem prof; 11-vocab of commercial terms used in bus letters; trans, composition, punctuation of letters; typing of letters; 12-e,g; 13-Sp bus letters; 14-Teijo, Moderna Correspondencia Comercial; Cacho, Practicas de Secretaria; Cacho, Mecanografia, Ejercicios para el segundo curso; Zalce, Ejercicios de Practica Comercial; Turk & Brady, Spanish Letter Writing.

279. CONVERSATIONAL SPANISH FOR BANKING AND FINANCIAL INSTITUTIONS
Tarrant County JC; MFL; Fort Worth, TX 76119.
Ernesto Guzman
Further info ng.

280. CONVERSATION SPANISH FOR COMMERCIAL AND RETAIL SELLING
Tarrant County JC; MFL; Fort Worth, TX 76119.
Ernesto Guzman
Further info ng.

281. CONVERSATIONAL SPANISH FOR HOTEL AND MOTEL PERSONNEL
Tarrant County JC; MFL; Fort Worth TX 76119.
Ernesto Guzman
Further info ng.

282. CONVERSATIONAL SPANISH FOR RESTAURANT PERSONNEL

Tarrant County JC; MFL; Fort Worth, TX 76119.
Ernesto Guzman
Further info ng.

283. BUSINESS SPANISH
Tennessee Technological U; FLs; Cookeville, TN 38501.
Gerd F. Mueller
1-6; 2-3x10; 3-a; 4-74; 5-1; 6-b; 7-a; 8-3q; 9-a; 10-none; 11-intro to development of reading skills with emphasis on bus correspondence, order forms, trade regulations; 12-a,b,g; 13-e, pamphlets; 14-Larralde, Correspondencia comercial.

284. SPANISH ORAL EXPRESSION, READING, AND COMPOSITION FOR BUSINESS MAJORS
U of Texas; Sp & Port; Austin, TX 78712.
Phyllis Harmon
1-new; 2-3x14; 3-a; 4-fall 75; 5-0; 6-to be determined; 7-a; 8-3s; 9-a,b, members of local bus community; 10-inter prof; 11-ng; 12-a,g; 13-ng; 14-ng.

285. BUSINESS SPANISH
U of Texas; ML; El Paso, TX 79968.
Diana Natalicio
Will be offered fall 75; other info ng.

286. CONVERSATIONAL SPANISH
U of Texas; MLs; El Paso, TX 79968.
Diana S. Natalicio
1-ng; 2-8x8; 3-a; 4-73; 5-3; 6-a; 7-b; 8-b; 9-b; 10-none; 11-basic conv Sp for those who need to live and conduct bus in the biling El Paso-Juarez area; 12-e,f,g; 13-a,b,d,e; 14-locally developed materials.

287. SPANISH BUSINESS CORRESPONDENCE
Thiel C; Langs; Greenville, PA 16125.
Dr. De Llanos
1-12; 2-3x14; 3-a; 4-spr 75; 5-1; 6-b; 7-a; 8-3s; 9-a; 10-instructor's permission; 11-examination of bus correspondence with regard to style and terminology; 12-a,b,g; 13-e,f; 14-Anorga Larralde, Manual de Correspondencia Comercial.

288. SPANISH FOR BUSINESS MAJORS
Virginia Commonwealth U; FLs; Richmond, VA 23284.
William J. Beck
1-6; 2-3x15; 3-a; 4-74/75; 5-1; 6-a; 7-a; 8-3s; 9-a; 10-none; 11-ng; 12-f; 13-ng; 14-ng.

289. CONVERSATIONAL SPANISH
Western Texas C; Communications & Letters; Snyder, TX 79549.
Edward Barkowsky, Wendell Jones
1-40; 2-3x16; 3-a,c (extension); 4-71; 5-4; 6-a; 7-a,b; 8-3s; 9-a,b; 10-none; 11-idiomatic expressions & conv stressed; for bus & professional people, farmers, ranchers, etc.; special section for law enforcement majors; 12-a,b; 13-a,d,e; 14-LaGrone, Entender y Hablar; Spanish for Law Enforcement Officers, Texts I & II, with workbooks.

290. BUSINESS SPANISH

170

U of Wisconsin; FLs; Eau Claire, WI 54701.
Angelo Armendariz
1-new; 2-15x3; 3-a; 4-May 75; 5-0; 6-interim course; 7-a; 8-3s; 9-a; 10-inter prof; 11-letter writing, general & commercial; completing forms; econ & industry of Spain & Sp Amer; 12-a,b,g; 13-d,e,f; 14-Ripolles, Tratado de correspondencia.

See also 70, 75, 157, 314, 321, 342, 343, 348, 418, 426, 445, 489, 490, 496-498, 502, 504, 506, 634, 660, 665, 694, 695, 700, 756, 772, 870, 883, 884, 1466, 1480, 1504.

MULTI-LANGUAGE

291. AMERICAN GRADUATE SCHOOL OF INTERNATIONAL MANAGEMENT
Glendale, AZ 85306.
Jorge Valdiveseo
Conducts an MA program in Intl Mgt; average enrollment 750 students per sem; FL mandatory; langs offered: Sp, Fr, Ger, Jap, Port, Chi; 15 hrs of FL are required; beginning lang course: 5 wkly contact hrs in conv, 2 in grammar; following level: 3 wkly hrs of conv, 1 hr of grammar; class size 8-10 students; school offers the following FL courses: Bus Correspondence; Bus Law; Soci, Poli & Econ Problems of Today; cult survey courses; various materials & texts.

292. BI-LINGUAL SECRETARIAL WORKSHOP
Berkshire CC; MLs; Pittsfield, MA 01201.
Martin Jonas
1-new; 2-3x15; 3-b; 4-Jan 75; 5-0; 6-as needed; 7-a; 8-3s; 9-a; 10-concurrent enrollment in 4th sem lang, shorthand, typing; 11-letter forms & procedures, dictation & typing in the FL, trans of letters; 12-b,e,f,g; 13-ng; 14-depends on lang, e.g., Le Parfait Secretaire.

293. FOREIGN LANGUAGE - INTERNATIONAL BUSINESS SCHOOL
Daniel Webster JC; Nashua, NH 03060.
John Furey
1-10; 2-ng; 3-taught by Rosetta Stone School of Langs; 4-74; 5-1; 6-a; 7-a; 8-3s; 9-a; 10-two yrs of H.S. Fr, Ger, or Sp; 11-designed to meet needs of bus, industry, banking, govt; oral practice, written work, conv sessions; 12-situational reinforcement; 13-a,e,f; 14-Inst of Mod Langs, Situational Reinforcement series.

294. CERTIFICATE PROGRAM IN BUSINESS ADMINISTRATION
Franklin Pierce C; MLs; Rindge, NH 03461.
Anthony M. Tremblay
New 4-yr program leading to certificate in Bus Admin & B.A. in Fr, Ger, or Sp.

295. TOUR ESCORT TRAINING
U of Maine; FLs; Orono, ME 04473.
Josef Roggenbauer
1-33; 2-3x15; 3-b,c; 4-fall 74; 5-1; 6-b; 7-b; 8-b; 9-b; 10-none; 11-team taught; familiarize students with regional geography, hist, govt, econ, procedures &

practices of tourism; 12-a,b,d,f; 13-a,b; 14-ng.

296. INTERNATIONAL ECONOMICS
Monterey Inst of Foreign Studies; Intl Econ & Intl Management; Monterey, CA 93940.
Robert S. Lande
Program leading to B.A. & M.A.; further info ng.

297. INTERNATIONAL MANAGEMENT
Monterey Inst of Foreign Studies; Intl Management; Monterey, CA 93940.
Donald G. Halper
1-15; 2-3x15; 3-a; 4-70/71; 5-4; 6-a; 7-a; 8-3s; 9-a; 10-ng; 11-M.A. program requires prof in at least 1 lang besides the native lang; 12-14-ng.

298. INTERNATIONAL STUDIES
Monterey Inst of Foreign Studies; Intl Studies; Monterey, CA 93940.
Stephen Garrett
1-20; 2-ng; 3-b,c; 4-74; 5-ng; 6-ng; 7-ng; 8-ng; 9-a,b; 10-no rigid prerequisites for admission, although in some instances make-up work at MIFS is required if student is deficient in soci scis; 11-multidisc, cross cult approach; acquisition of high degree of prof in FL; a,b,c,f; 13-ng; 14-ng.

299. TRAINING FOR SERVICE ABROAD
Monterey Inst of Foreign Studies; TSA; Monterey, CA 93940.
1-4; 2-30x6; 3-b,c; 4-67; 5-89; 6-upon demand; 7-a; 8-b; if credit is desired, must be requested & subject to written/oral test; 9-varies; 10-none; 11-course designed to train reps of Amer bus in lang & cult of destination country, incl private individuals traveling & studying abroad; 12-b,c,d,e,f,g; 13-a,b,d,e,f; 14-ng.

300. INTERNATIONAL CAREER TRAINING
School for Intl Training; Brattleboro, VT 05301.
Charles F. MacCormack
Grad program offering Master of Intl Admin; management, cross-cult awareness, understanding soci change, research methods, community development, area studies & lang; internship abroad.

301. INTERNATIONAL MANAGEMENT
Simmons C; FL, Mgt; Boston, MA 02115.
W. W. Baldwin, Dept. of Management
Interdepart concentration initiated 74/75; concentrator in Int Management expected to complete 16 sem hrs in either Fr or Sp above inter level (including lit courses for cult background).

302. LANGUAGE FOR AIRLINE PERSONNEL AND TRAVELERS
Staten Island CC; MLs; Staten Island, NY 10301.
M.P. Holt
1-12; 2-2x15; 3-a; 4-72/73; 5-4; 6-a; 7-b; 8-2s; 9-a,b; community members; 10-none; 11-basic expressions in Fr, Ger, Ital, Sp for intl travel; three langs included each time course is taught; 12-e,f,g; 13-c,d; 14-Bator, International Airline Phrase Book.

303. COMBINED MAJOR IN BUSINESS & FOR-
EIGN LANGUAGE
Susquehanna U; MLs, Business; Selinsgrove,
PA 17870.
Peter B. Waldeck
Program in planning stages. Slightly
reduced combination of bus & lang majors;
new lang course to develop skills above
inter level in context of bus terminology; jr
yr abroad incl internship in for bus &
academic study. Will include Fr, Ger, Sp.

304. BUSINESS--FOREIGN STUDIES
U of Tennessee; School of Bus; Martin, TN
38237.
William Baker
Proposed, not yet approved; further info ng.

305. BUSINESS ADMINISTRATION MAJOR
WITH FOREIGN LANGUAGE SPECIALI-
ZATION
Wartburg C; FLs; Waverly, IA 50677.
Albert R. Riep
1-4; 2-ng; 3-b; 4-74/75; 5-1; 6-a; 7-a; 8-ng;
9-a; 10-elem prof; 11-jr yr abroad is
required (Fr students-U of Montpellier;
Ger-U of Bonn, U of Vienna; Sp-U of
Navarra); program intended to make lang
skills of student effectively useful. For
lang courses in program not specifically
bus oriented, but student must take bus
courses in for university; 12-ng; 13-ng; 14-
ng.

See also 974.

Health Care

CLASSICS

See 165, 167, 171.

FRENCH

306. FRENCH CONVERSATION FOR OCCU-
PATIONAL THERAPY
Catonsville CC: FLs; Baltimore, MD 21228.
Marcelle J. Von Mayer, Enrique Corzo
1-12; 2-1 1/4x10; 3-a; 4-73/74; 5-2; 6-on
demand; 7-a,b; 8-0; 9-b; 10-none; 11-conv;
12-a,b,g; 13-a,b,d,transparencies; 14-in-
structor-prepared materials.

See also 474.

NAVAHO

307. BASIC MEDICAL NAVAJO
U of New Mexico; FLs; Gallup, NM 87301.
Alan Wilson
1-16; 2-2½x16; 3-a; 4-72; 5-2; 6-a; 7-a; 8-3s;
9-doctors, nurses, pharmacists, paramed
personnel; 10-none; 11-basic anatomy,
med, psychiatry, seasons, weather, occupations, etc; 12-b,c,d,e,f,g; 13-d, flash cards;
14-Wilson, Basic Medical Navajo; Wilson,
Breakthrough Navajo.

PORTUGUESE

308. PORTUGUESE FOR MEDICAL PERSON-
NEL
Rhode Island JC; FLs; Warwick, RI 02886.
William Pilkanis
1-20; 2-3x15; 3-c; 4-Jan 75; 5-1; 6-b; 7-b; 8-
3s; 9-b; 10-none; 11-completely oral emphasis with recreation of day-to-day hospital experience from nurse and patient
viewpoints; 12-g; 13-b,e; 14-none.

SPANISH

Texts used (#14):
a. Armengol & Aguilar, English-Spanish Guide
for Medical Personnel
b. Benitez, Practical Spanish for the Health
Professions

c. Bomse & Alfaro, Practical Spanish for
Medical and Hospital Personnel
d. ---, Practical Spanish for School Personnel,
Firemen, Policemen and Community Agencies
e. Conzemius & Conzemius, Spanish for Health
Professionals
f. Seymann, Basic Spanish for Health Personnel
g. Wolfe, Curso Básico de Español

309. CONVERSATIONAL SPANISH FOR
HEALTH CARE PERSONNEL
Amarillo C; Cont Ed; Amarillo, TX 79178.
Clair Mayes
1-new; 2-3x15; 3-c; 4-ng; 5-0; 6-a, special
groups; 7-b; 8-0; 9-b; 10-none; 11-mechan-
ics, sound system, basic grammatical structures, special terminology, oral drills; 12-
a,b,d,f; 13-records; 14-See It and Say It in
Spanish.

310. SPANISH FOR MEDICAL PERSONNEL
Angelo SU; ML; San Angelo, TX 76901.
O.W. Tetzlaff
1-new; 2-3x15; 3-a; 4-75/76; 5-0; 6-b; 7-a;
8-3s; 9-a; 10-none; 11-ng; 12-b,f,g; 13-ng;
14-c.

311. SPANISH FOR NURSES AND RELATED
PERSONNEL
Anna Maria C; MLs; Paxton, MA 01612.
N. Ramirez
1-18; 2-3x15; 3-a; 4-75; 5-1; 6-b; 7-b; 8-3s;
9-a, part-time; 10-in nursing or related
area; 11-patient needs, nursing care, hospital and community relations, etc; 12-
a,b,c,f,g; 13-b,e,f; 14-instructor-prepared
materials.

312. SPANISH FOR HEALTH CARE PERSON-
NEL
U of Arizona; Rom Langs; Tucson, AZ
85721.
Charles Olstad
1-35; 2-4x14; 3-a; 4-73/74; 5-3; 6-on
demand; 7-b; 8-4s; 9-a; 10-ng; 11-working
knowledge of grammar; vocab; speaking &

listening practice; 12-b,d,f,g; 13-ng; 14-locally-prepared materials.

313. SPANISH FOR HEALTH PROFESSIONALS, SOCIAL WORKERS AND EDUCATORS
Augustana C; Rom Langs; Sioux Falls, SD 57105.
Robert L. Bledsoe
1-10; 2-20x5; 3-a; 4-Jan 75 interim; 5-1; 6-alt yrs; 7-a; 8-l unit; 9-a; 10-elem prof; 11-combining professional knowledge with lang skill; 12-a,b,d,g; 13-e, booklets, pamphlets; 14-e.

314. SPANISH FOR THE PROFESSIONS
Austin C; ML; Sherman, TX 75090.
Juliette C. McClendon
1-new; 2-4x14; 3-a; 4-75; 5-ng; 6-b; 7-a; 8-4s; 9-a; 10-elem prof; 11-topics alt by sem and include health scis, law and bus, and ed; specific vocab and dialogues to suit topic; may be repeated for credit with different topic; 12-b,c,d,e,g; 13 a,b,c,d,e,f; 14-various texts by Antonio Carbajo.

315. SPANISH FOR NURSES
Barry C; FLs; Miami, FL 33161.
Ellen Leeder
1-18; 2-2x16; 3-a; 4-73; 5-1; 6-ng; 7-a; 8-0 or 1 hr depending on written work; 9-a, part time, staff; 10-none; 11-mostly oral work; 12-b,c,g; 13-a,b,d; 14-Angel & Dixon, Metodo Directo de Conversacion en Espanol; Angel & Dixon, Tests and Drills in Spanish Grammar.

316. SPANISH FOR HEALTH PROFESSIONS
Bergen CC; FLs; Paramus, NJ 07652.
Additional info not available.

317. SPANISH FOR NURSES
Bronx CC; ML; Bronx, NY 10453.
C. R. Monticone
1-75/80; 2-4x15; 3-a; 4-75; 5-1; 6-a; 7-a,b; 8-4s; 9-a,b; 10-none; 11-grammar; orientation toward med and hospital situations; 12-a,f; 13-c,d; 14-ng.

318. MEDICAL SPANISH
Brookdale CC; FLs; Lincroft, NJ 07738.
Albert C. Eyde
1-5; 2-3x17; 3-a; 4-73; 5-2; 6-on demand; 7-a; 8-3s; 9-a,b; 10-none; 11-terminology for med professions; 12-b,g; 13-d, posters; 14-locally developed.

319. SPANISH FOR THE HEALTH SCIENCES
U of California; Sp & Port; Los Angeles, CA 90024.
Jose M. Cruz-Salvadores
1-25; 2-5x10; 3-a; 4-wtr 75; 5-1; 6-hopefully a; 7-a; 8-4q; 9-students in health scis; 10-student of health scis or permission; 11-foundation course stressing audiolingual skills, problems of Chicano dialect and Los Angeles area; 12-ng; 13-ng; 14-Barcia, Lengua y cultura.

20 ADVANCED SPANISH CONVERSATION--HEALTH AND SOCIAL SERVICES
U of California; Sp & Port; Santa Barbara, CA 93106.
R. E. Wilson
1-15; 2-2x10; 3-a; 4-spr 74; 5-2; 6-b; 7-a; 8-2q; 9-a; 10-inter prof; 11-vocab for health and soci services; presentation of situations related to those fields; 12-b,c,d,g, role playing; 13-c,e,f; 14-pamphlets written in Sp.

321. SPANISH FOR HEALTH PROFESSIONS
California SU; FLs; Fresno, CA 93710.
Jose A. Elgorriaga
1-25; 2-3x18; 3-a; 4-70; 5-8; 6-a; 7-a; 8-3s; 9-a; 10-none; 11-preparation of professionals and paraprofessionals to work in health, ed, soci work, bus; 12-g, situational approach; 13-d; 14-b.

322. SPANISH FOR HEALTH PROFESSIONALS
California SU; FLs and Lits; Los Angeles, CA 90032.
E. D. Carter
1-25; 2-4x10; 3-a; 4-74; 5-1; 6-b; 7-a; 8-4q (0 for Spanish majors); 9-a; 10-none; 11-elem conv Sp focusing on vocab of med, law enforcement, or soci scis; basic grammar presented inductively; may be repeated for credit; 12-a,b,d,f,g; 13-d; 14-f.

323. SPANISH FOR THE HEALTH PROFESSIONS
California SC; FLs; Rohnert Park, CA 94928.
Rosa Vargas-Arandia
1-9; 2-3x15; 3-a; 4-fall 74; 5-1; 6-b or alt yrs; 7-a; 8-3s; 9-a; 10-none; 11-basic grammar with practice in pronunciation, speaking, understanding, and writing; vocab and ling patterns focus on needs of med personnel; 12-a,e,f,g; 13-b,d, dialogue illustrations; 14-Gaona & Tibbets, Basic Spanish (a programmed grammar).

324. SPANISH FOR HEALTH PROFESSIONS
California SC; FLs; San Bernardino, CA 92407.
W. C. Oliver
1-22; 2-4x10; 3-a; 4-fall 73; 5-7; 6-a; 7-b; 8-5q; 9-a, extension; 10-none; 11-basic conv with emphasis on vocab, expressions, and cult attitudes related to health; 12-b,f,g; 13-ng; 14-instructor-prepared text.

325. SPANISH FOR DENTISTS AND PROFESSORS
Catonsville CC; FLs; Baltimore, MD 21228.
Enrique Corzo, Marcelle J. Von Mayer
1-15; 2-1¼x10; 3-a; 4-72; 5-1; 6-on demand; 7-a,b; 8-0; 9-b; 10-none; 11-conv; 12-a,b,g; 13-a,b,d, transparencies; 14-instructor-prepared materials.

326. PRACTICAL SPANISH FOR THE HEALTH PROFESSIONS
Citrus C; FL; Azusa, CA 91702.
Nelly Rampoldi, Leopoldina Ahren
1-73; 2-2x20; 3-a; 4-74; 5-1; 6-a; 7-b; 8-2s; 9-a, professionals; 10-none; 11-ng; 12-a,b,c,d,e,g; 13-a,b,d; 14-b.

327. BASIC SPANISH FOR HEALTH PERSONNEL
County C of Morris; Hums; Dover, NJ 07801.
Carlo Prisco

1-10; 2-3x15; 3-a; 4-spr 73; 5-4; 6-a; 7-a; 8-3s; 9-a; 10-none; 11-oral communication; vocab directed at nurse-patient relationships; 12-a,b,c,e,g; 13-ng; 14-c.

328. SPANISH FOR HEALTH, MEDICAL AND SOCIAL WORKERS
Curry C; Lang & Lit; Milton, MA 02186.
Frances M. Kohak
Further info ng.

329. CONVERSATIONAL SPANISH FOR MEDICAL PERSONNEL
East Stroudsburg SC; FLs; East Stroudsburg, PA 18301.
Aurora Gonzalez
1-new; 2-3x15; 3-a; 4-75/76; 5-0; 6-alt yrs; 7-b; 8-3s; 9-a, nurses; 10-none; 11-basic conv skills; dialogues based on typical hospital situations; 12-b,d,g; 13-d, charts, realia; 14-ng.

330. SPANISH FOR NURSING PERSONNEL
Felician C; MLs; Lodi, NJ 07644.
Mary Noel
1-11; 2-3x15; 3-a; 4-spr 75; 5-1; 6-given experimentally; 7-a; 8-3s; 9-a; 10-none; 11-vocab, grammar, idioms of the various health fields; emphasis on communicating with patients; 12-e,g; 13-b,e,f, charts, transparencies; 14-f.

331. SPANISH CONVERSATION FOR MEDICAL EMPLOYEES
Foothill C; Lang Arts; Los Altos Hills, CA 94022.
Nayan McNeill, Ralph Lee
1-30; 2-3x11; 3-c; 4-72; 5-5; 6-a; 7-b; 8-2q; 9-hospital employees; 10-ng; 11-listening, speaking, med vocab; 12-b,e,f,g; 13-d; 14-ng.

332. VOCATIONAL SPANISH
Grossmont C; FL; El Cajon, CA 92020.
G. M. Washington
1-40; 2-4x6; 3-a; 4-72; 5-5; 6-a; 7-a,b; 8-3s; 9-a; 10-none; 11-fundamentals of Sp related to nursing & paramed specialties; 12-a,d,e,g; 13-ng; 14-Turk & Espinosa, Foundation Course in Spanish; locally-prepared handouts.

333. BASIC SPANISH FOR PRACTITIONERS IN THE HEALTH SERVICES
Holy Names C; FL; Oakland, CA 94619.
Sr. Miriam Daniel Fahey
1-18; 2-2½x10; 3-a; 4-71; 5-2; 6-alt yrs; 7-b; 8-2q; 9-b; 10-none; 11-vocab required to deal with everyday needs of patients; med terminology; basic structures and pronunciation; 12-d,g; 13-ng; 14-Sallese & Fernandez, Pan y mantequilla; Glosario Espanol-ingles para las Auxiliares de Salud.

334. CONVERSATIONAL SPANISH FOR HEALTH RELATED PROFESSIONS
Holyoke CC; Hums; Holyoke, MA 01040.
Gerhard M. Wilke
1-new; 2-2x15; 3-a; 4-75; 5-1; 6-b; 7-a; 8-2s; 9-a, professionals; 10-none; 11-stress on communication and understanding health-related terminology; 12-b,e,f,g; 13-d; 14-materials supplied by instructor.

335. SPANISH CONVERSATION--MEDICAL
Houston Baptist U; Langs; Houston, TX 77036.
Marion R. Webb
1-17; 2-3½x11; 3-a; 4-72/73; 5-5; 6-1 or 2 qtrs per yr; 7-a,b; 8-3q; 9-a; 10-none; 11-conv Sp in med areas to help health personnel communicate with patients; 12-c,g, small conv groups; 13-b,d, transparencies; 14-Tabery et al, Communicating in Spanish for Medical Personnel.

336. CONVERSATIONAL SPANISH FOR MEDICAL PERSONNEL
Illinois Wesleyan U; FLs; Bloomington, IL 61701.
Wilbur Nachtigall
1-18; 2-3x14; 3-a; 4-69/70; 5-6; 6-a; 7-a; 8-1 course unit; 9-a; 10-none; 11-dialogues, drills, exercises to increase oral skill; med vocab; 12-b,c; 13-d,e,f; 14-locally-prepared materials.

337. PRACTICAL SPANISH FOR MEDICAL PERSONNEL II
Imperial Valley C; Hums; Imperial, CA 92251.
James R. Stone
Second of 2 courses offering basic Sp oriented toward health personnel; course features extensive oral drills and role playing in med situations. Reference books include English-Spanish Glossary for Health Aides and Practical Spanish for Public Safety Personnel.

338. SPANISH FOR HEALTH PROFESSIONALS
U of Iowa; Sp & Port; Iowa City, IA 52242.
Oscar Fernandez
1-5; 2-5x16; 3-a; 4-72/73; 5-5; 6-a, smrs; 7-a; 8-4s; 9-a, nurses, hospital personnel; 10-none; 11-teaching hospital personnel to communicate with patients in their lang; 12-a,b,d,g; 13-a,b,c,d,e,f, songs, games, skits, diagrams; 14-e.

339. SPANISH FOR NURSES AND ALLIED HEALTH SCIENCE STUDENTS
Kingsborough CC; FLs; Brooklyn, NY 11235.
Julio Hernandez-Miyares
1-25; 2-2x15; 3-b; 4-73; 5-5; 6-a; 7-a; 8-2s; 9-a; 10-none; 11-designed for beginners who will have to communicate with patients & hospital personnel whose native lang is Sp; stress placed on conv aspects, emphasizing practical & meaningful hospital-related vocab; experience of total immersion created by use of many AV aids; 12-a,b,e,f,g; 13-c,d; 14-Hernandez-Miyares et al, Spanish for Nurses and Allied Health Science Students.

340. CONVERSATIONAL SPANISH FOR NURSES
Lehman C; Rom Langs; Bronx, NY 10468.
1-ng; 2-ng; 3-a; 4-73; 5-ng; 6-b; 7-a; 8-ng; 9-a; 10-ng; 11-ng; 12-b,g; 13-ng; 14-ng.

341. SPANISH FOR THE HEALTH PROFES-
      SIONS
      U of Lowell; Sp; Lowell, MA 01854.
      John Mendicoa
      1-65; 2-3x16; 3-a; 4-73/74; 5-ng; 6-a; 7-a,b;
      8-3s for nursing students, 0 in-service; 9-a,
      health professionals; 10-none, elem prof for
      adv section; 11-ng; 12-ng; 13-ng; 14-ng.

342. CAREER SPANISH
      Manchester CC; FL; Manchester, CT
      06040.
      Toby Tamarkin
      1-40; 2-3x15; 3-a; 4-73; 5-5; 6-a; 7-a,b; 8-
      3s; 9-a,b,c; 10-elem prof; 11-two-sem
      sequence, practical approach for career
      application in med, soci services, and bus;
      cult capsules; 12-f,g; 13-c,d, transparen-
      cies, realia; 14-instructor developed.

343. SPANISH FOR CAREERS
      Manhattanville C; Sp; Purchase, NY 10577.
      Marta de la Portilla
      1-12; 2-2xsem; 3-b,c; 4-spr 75; 5-1; 6-b; 7-
      a; 8-3s; 9-a, community; 10-adv prof; 11-
      vocab required in hospitals, bus, pub;
      special training in phonetics and letter
      writing; 12-b,c,g; 13-d,e,f; 14-Business
      Letter Handbook; c.

344. BASIC SPANISH FOR HEALTH PERSON-
      NEL
      Marian C; Sp; Fond du Lac, WI 54935.
      Maralyn Homiak
      1-5; 2-2¼x15; 3-a; 4-spr 75; 5-1; 6-a; 7-a; 8-
      3s; 9-a; 10-elem prof; 11-skills to meet
      immediate needs of persons involved in
      health fields; 12-b,c,d,c,g; 13-a,b,c,d,e,f,
      practice with Sp-speaking patients; 14-f.

345. BASIC SPANISH CONVERSATION FOR
      NURSES
      Molloy C; Sp; Rockville Center, NY 11570.
      Libe Aranguren
      1-18; 2-3x15; 3-a; 4-72; 5-15; 6-a, smr,
      intersession; 7-a,b; 8-3s; 9-a, part-time
      students; 10-none; 11-aural-oral practice in
      use of everyday lang; systematic develop-
      ment of conv idiom and vocab with em-
      phasis on that used in nursing; 12-c,d,e,g;
      13-ng; 14-instructor-prepared materials; a.

346. SPANISH FOR HEALTH PROFESSIONS
      Montclair SC; Sp & Ital; Upper Montclair,
      NJ 07043.
      Norman Fulton
      1-ng; 2-3x15; 3-b,c; 4-ng; 5-ng; 6-a; 7-a,b;
      8-3s; 9-a,b; 10-ng; 11-ng; 12-a,b,c,d,f,g; 13-
      d,e,f; 14-ng.

347. SPANISH FOR COMMUNITY RELATIONS
      PERSONNEL
      Montgomery County CC; For Studies; Blue
      Bell, PA 19422.
      Charlotte Anderson
      1-new; 2-ng; 3-a; 4-fall 75; 5-0; 6-a; 7-b; 8-
      ng; 9-ng; 10-none; 11-ng; 12-ng; 13-ng; 14-
      c,d.

348. CONVERSATIONAL SPANISH I
      Mountain View C; Community Services;
      Dallas, TX 75211.
      Joe Altick, Joyce Overholt
      1-52; 2-3x10; 3-c; 4-72; 5-7; 6-a; 7-b; 8-0;
      9-mainly businessmen; 10-none; 11-com-
      municative needs of doctors, nurses,
      teachers, ind foremen, travelers; mainly
      conv; 12-b,e,f,g; 13-e,f; 14-Madrigal, Open
      Door to Spanish.

349. SPANISH FOR MEDICAL PERSONNEL
      SUCNY; FLs; Brockport, NY 14420.
      Francisco Zayas
      1-18; 2-3x17; 3-a; 4-74/75; 5-2; 6-a; 7-b; 8-
      3s; 9-b, physicians, nurses, soci workers;
      10-elem prof; 11-med terminology; 12-g,
      small-group instruction; 13-charts; 14-c;
      Overjero & Fraile, Atlas del cuerpo
      humano.

350. SPANISH FOR MEDICAL STUDENTS
      SUNY; Sp, Ital, & Port; Buffalo, NY 14214.
      Jorge Guitart
      1-10; 2-5x15; 3-a; 4-72/73; 5-2; 6-a; 7-a; 8-
      4s; 9-a; 10-none; 11-lang training geared to
      med students; 12-a,b,e,g; 13-ng; 14-g.

351. SPANISH FOR MEDICAL & HOSPITAL
      PERSONNEL
      Orange Coast C; Lit & Langs; Costa Mesa,
      CA 92626.
      Mary L. McChesney
      1-new; 2-3x18; 3-c; 4-74/75; 5-1; 6-a; 7-b;
      8-3s; 9-b, hospital personnel; 10-none; 11-
      basic conv; emphasis on med vocab and
      hospital situations; 12-a,b,f; 13-d; 14-
      instructor-prepared materials.

352. SPANISH FOR MEDICAL PERSONNEL
      Pace U; FLs; New York, NY 10038.
      A. Sallustio, J. Dumbra
      1-14; 2-3x15; 3-a; 4-fall 74; 5-1; 6-
      unknown; 7-a; 8-3s; 9-a; 10-none; 11-basic
      vocab and conv patterns based on med
      situations; 12-b,g; 13-ng; 14-materials
      from public health office, physicians'
      guides, instructor-prepared materials.

353. SPANISH FOR MEDICAL PERSONNEL
      Pace U; FLs; Pleasantville, NY 10570.
      George Pappas
      1-25; 2-3x15; 3-a; 4-71; 5-6; 6-varies; 7-a,b;
      8-3s; 9-a,b; 10-none; 11-med vocab and
      idioms; 12-a,c,e,f,g; 13-a,b,c,d,e,f; 14-
      varies.

354. SPANISH FOR MEDICAL PERSONNEL
      Pacific Union C; ML; Angwin, CA 94508.
      James Scott
      1-22; 2-2x10; 3-c; 4-75; 5-1; 6-a; 7-b; 8-3q;
      9-a, professionals; 10-none; 11-crash
      course designed to aid hospital personnel in
      meeting patients' needs; med terminology
      not covered extensively, rather, students
      learn to communicate on a variety of
      subjects; 12-b,c,d,f,g; 13-realia; 14-
      Escandon, Spanish for Medical Personnel.

355. SPANISH AS A SECOND LANGUAGE:
      FOR PEOPLE IN MEDICAL PROFESSIONS
      Pasadena City C; FLs; Pasadena, CA 91106.
      Marina Cobb
      1-68; 2-2x9; 3-a; 4-spr 74; 5-2; 6-a; 7-a,b; 8-
      none for B.A.; 1 for A.A.; 9-a, doctors,

technicians, nurses, receptionists; 10-none; 11-sequence of two 9-wk courses; conv practice stressing specialized vocab and basic expressions; 12-g; 13-anatomy charts, equipment; 14-instructor developed.

356. SPANISH FOR HEALTH PERSONNEL
Phoenix C; FL; Phoenix, AZ 85013.
Martin H. Durrant
1-60; 2-3x16; 3-c; 4-68; 5-14; 6-a; 7-b; 8-3s; 9-nurses and doctors; 10-none; 11-basic conv Sp with emphasis on med terminology; 12-g; 13-ng; 14-f.

357. SURVIVAL SPANISH FOR NURSING AND MEDICAL PERSONNEL
U of Portland; English & MLs; Portland, OR 97203.
Manuel Jato Macias
1-19; 2-3x15; 3-a; 4-fall 74; 5-1; 6-a; 7-b; 8-3s; 9-a; 10-none; 11-basic structures, med terminology, role-playing; 12-b,d,e,f,g; 13-pamphlets; 14-Howell & Perez-Sabido, Spanish-English Handbook for the Nursing and Medical Profession.

358. SPANISH FOR MEDICAL PERSONNEL
Rhode Island JC; FLs; Warwick, RI 02886.
Olga Ingelse, William Pilkanis
1-ng; 2-3x15; 3-a; 4-fall 74; 5-2; 6-b; 7-a,b; 8-3s; 9-a,b; 10-none; 11-completely oral emphasis with recreation of day-to-day hospital experience from nurse and patient viewpoints; 12-b,g; 13-b; 14-Carreno & Larson, Spanish for Hospital Personnel; a.

359. SPANISH FOR MEDICAL AND PARA-MEDICAL WORKERS
Sacramento City C; Sacramento, CA 95822.
Maria Rekowski
1-18; 2-3x18; 3-a; 4-73; 5-5; 6-a; 7-b; 8-2s; 9-a, professionals; 10-in paramedical occupation; 11-teaches current and future workers in health occupations the vocab and structures needed in clinical situations; 12-a,e,f,g; 13-d; 14-instructor-prepared materials.

360. SPANISH FOR HEALTH CARE
St. Xavier C; FL; Chicago, IL 60655.
Safia F. Haddad
1-6; 2-9x4½ (Jan interim); 3-c; 4-73; 5-2; 6-b; 7-ng; 8-3s; 9-a; 10-elem prof; 11-designed to help nurses develop or increase ability to communicate with Sp-speaking patients; 12-a,d,e,f,g; 13-ng; 14-instructor-prepared materials.

361. SPANISH FOR NURSES AND MEDICAL PERSONNEL
Salve Regina C; Sp; Newport, RI 02840.
Heriberto Vazquez
1-39; 2-4x15; 3-a; 4-70; 5-8; 6-a; 7-a; 8-4s; 9-a; 10-none; 11-deals with daily requirements of the work and develops the ability to communicate with Sp-speaking patients; 12-c,g; 13-ng; 14-instructor-prepared pamphlets.

362. SPOKEN SPANISH FOR DOCTORS AND NURSES

363. SPANISH FOR NURSES
C of San Mateo; FL; San Mateo, CA 94402.
Rosa Sausjord
1-30; 2-ng; 3-c; 4-ng; 5-ng; 6-b; 7-b; 8-0; 9-b; 10-ng; 11-ng; 12-a,b,c,g; 13-a,b,d,e; 14-ng.

364. SPANISH FOR HEALTH PERSONNEL
Santa Monica C; FL; Santa Monica, CA 90405.
L.B. Faber
1-30; 2-2x18; 3-c; 4-74; 5-1; 6-a; 7-b; 8-2s; 9-full-time health professionals; 10-none; 11-basic Sp with emphasis on vocab necessary to the profession; 12-a,b,f,g; 13-charts, diagrams; 14-f.

365. SPANISH FOR HEALTH OCCUPATIONS
Santa Rosa JC; FLs; Santa Rosa, CA 95401.
Ruth Parle Craig
1-15; 2-3x17; 3-c; 4-fall 74; 5-1; 6-a; 7-b; 8-3s; 9-a,b, health professionals; 10-none; 11-2-sem sequence; listening comprehension and speaking; vocab centered on health occupations; 12-a,b, drill; 13-ng; 14-b.

366. ELEMENTARY SPANISH (SPECIAL SECTION FOR NURSING MAJORS)
Skidmore C; MLs & Lits; Saratoga Springs, NY 12866.
Regina Casalls
1-ng; 2-5x12; 3-a; 4-fall 74; 5-1; 6-b; 7-a; 8-3s; 9-a; 10-nursing major; 11-basic grammar, composition, conv, readings; 12-a,b,d,e,g; 13-b,d; 14-c, g.

367. CONVERSATIONAL SPANISH
South Plains C; Communications & Philosophy; Levelland, TX 79336.
Frank Gonzales
1-ng; 2-3x16; 3-b; 4-spr 75; 5-1; 6-b; 7-a; 8-3s; 9-a; 10-none; 11-designed for radiology tech and nursing students; basic med expressions; 12-class participation; 13-d; 14-b.

368. SPANISH FOR MEDICAL PERSONNEL
Southern Connecticut SC; FLs; New Haven, CT 06515.
Sandra Briggs
1-25; 2-3x15; 3-a; 4-spr 75; 5-1; 6-b; 7-a; 8-3s (does not count towards Sp major); 9-a; 10-elem prof; 11-basic med vocab and practice in conv; intro to Hispanic cult; 12-b,c,f, recitation; 13-a,b, records, radio broadcasts; 14-c; 201 Spanish Verbs.

369. SPANISH FOR NURSES
Southern Oregon C; FLs; Ashland, OR 97520.
Tomas Oquiza
Course is being developed now in response to community need.

370. PRACTICAL SPANISH FOR HOSPITAL PERSONNEL AND COMMUNITY

San Bernardino Valley C; FL; San Bernardino, CA 92403.
Contact: Judith Valles Davis
1-35; 2-3x17; 3-a; 4-67; 5-c15; 6-a; 7-b; 8-3s; 9-a,b,c; 10-none; 11-ng; 12-g; 13-a,b; 14-instructor-developed materials.

WORKERS
Staten Island CC; ML; Staten Island, NY 10301.
Marguerite Bomse
1-15; 2-2x15; 3-a; 4-71/72; 5-7; 6-a; 7-a,b; 8-2s; 9-a,b; 10-none; 11-basic communication for · physicians, nurses, and others dealing with.Sp-speaking clients; emphasis on tech and med terminology; 12-g; 13-a,c; 14-c;d.

371. CONVERSATIONAL SPANISH FOR THE MEDICAL PROFESSION
Tarrant County JC; MFL; Fort Worth, TX 76119.
Ernesto Guzman
Comprehensive course with conv & vocab for doctors, dentists, nurses, hospital personnel, receptionists, & others in related med fields who need to communicate in Sp. Course inaugurated fall 69; further info ng.

372. SPANISH ORAL EXPRESSION, READING, & COMPOSITION FOR HEALTH PROFESSIONS
U of Texas; Sp & Port; Austin, TX 78712.
Phyllis Harmon
1-new; 2-3x14; 3-a; 4-spr 75; 5-1; 6-to be determined; 7-a,b; 8-3s; 9-a,b, health professionals; 10-inter prof; 11-emphasis varies according to the interests of the students; limited study of grammar; 12-a,b,f,g; 13-e; 14-brochures produced by various institutions.

373. SPANISH FOR THE HEALTH PROFESSIONS

U of Texas; ML; El Paso, TX 79968.
Diana Natalicio
Will be offered fall 75; further info not available.

374. ELEMENTARY SPANISH HEALTH SCIENCE
Texas Woman's U; FLs; Denton, TX 70204.
Maurine Faulkner
1-19; 2-3xsem; 3-b; 4-spr 74; 5-3; 6-a; 7-a; 8-3s; 9-a; 10-none; 11-audiolingual practice needed by students in the health scis; 12-g; 13-d; 14-a.

375. SPANISH FOR CAREERS
Triton C; FL; River Grove, IL 60171.
Rita Flaherty
Will offer course for health careers fall 75; further info ng.

376. CONVERSATIONAL SPANISH IN THE MEDICAL FIELDS
Wagner C; FL; Staten Island, NY 10301.
M. S. Tirado
1-5; 2-3x15; 3-a; 4-74; 5-ng; 6-b; 7-a; 8-3s; 9-a, cont ed (without credit); 10-inter prof; 11-designed to develop ability to speak at a functional level through learning a limited amount of lively material so that through additional practice on the outside health professionals can master the patterns of the lang; 12-b,f; 13-b,e; 14-c.

See also 382, 418-422, 425, 426, 433, 434, 439, 440, 442-445, 489, 490, 497, 502, 504, 704, 764, 772, 1590.

Law Enforcement

CLASSICS
See 165.

SPANISH

377. SPANISH FOR LAW ENFORCEMENT OFFICERS
U of Albuquerque; Langs, Soci; Albuquerque, NM 87140.
Jorge N. Alarcon
1-16; 2-3x16; 3-b; 4-72; 5-3; 6-b; 7-a,b, according to need; 8-3s; 9-a, part-time; 10-none; 11-grammar, vocab & expressions related to law enforcement. Standard Sp & local dialects; 12-e,f,g, drills; 13-d,f, dialogues; 14Practical Grammar for Border Patrol Officers.

378. SPANISH FOR LAW PERSONNEL
U of Arizona; Rom Langs; Tucson, AZ 85721.
Charles Olstad
1-35; 2-2x14; 3-a; 4-73/74; 5-2; 6-on demand; 7-b; 8-2s; 9-police officers & trainees; 10-ng; 11-ng; 12-b,d,f,g; 13-

specially prepared ad hoc materials; 14-ng.

379. LAW ENFORCEMENT
Brookdale CC; FLs; Lindcroft, NJ 07738.
Albert C. Eyde
1-20; 2-3x17; 3-a; 4-72; 5-2; 6-on demand; 7-a; 8-3s; 9-a,b; 10-none; 11-law enforcement terminology; 12-b,g; 13-d, posters; 14-locally developed.

380. EMERGENCY SPANISH FOR POLICE AND FIREMEN
Bunker Hill CC; Communications; Charleston, ME 02109.
Harriet Hutchinson, Roger A. Richards
1-c25; 2-3x15; 3-a; 4-spr 75; 5-1; 6-periodically; 7-a,b; 8-3s; 9-a,b; 10-none; 11-conv course emphasizing terms & expressions for emergency situations; 12-b; 13-a,b,c,d,e,f; 14-to be selected

381. SPANISH FOR LAW ENFORCEMENT OFFICERS
California SU; FL; Fresno, CA 93710.
Jose Elgorriaga

1-30; 2-3x10; 3-c; 4-74; 5-2; 6-a; 7-b; 8-2s; 9-b; 10-none; 11-ng; 12-g, situational approach; 13-ng; 14-instructor prepared text (Gomez-Vidal).

382. SPANISH FOR PUBLIC SAFETY PERSON-NEL
C of the Canyons; FLs; Valencia, CA 91355.
D. Hellrigel
1-new; 2-3x10; 3-a; 4-spr 75; 5-1; 6-b; 7-b; 8-3q; 9-mostly part-time; 10--limited to students majoring in or currently employed in the fields of police science, fire science, nursing or emergency med services; 11-emphasis on communication; vocab suitable to specialized areas, extensive use of AV materials; 12-a,b,e,f; 13-d; 14-Moreno & Hayden, Practical Spanish for Public Safety Personnel.

384. SPANISH FOR CRIMINAL JUSTICE & SPANISH FOR HUMAN SERVICES
Corning CC; Hums; Corning, NY 14830.
Robert E. McEnroe
1-c15; 2-5x15; 3-a; 4-spr 75; 5-1; 6-a; 7-a; 8-4s; 9-a; 10-students in Police Science programs; 11-relevant conv Sp; 12-e,f,g; 13-d; 14-Garcia, Spanish for Law Enforcement Officers.

385. BASIC SPANISH FOR LAW ENFORCE-MENT OFFICERS I & II
County C of Morris; ML; Dover, NJ 07801.
Carlo Prisco
1-new; 2-3x15; 3-a; 4-75/76; 5-0; 6-b; 7-a,b; 8-3s; 9-a, working policemen; 10-none; 11-2-course sequence; basic conv for policemen & community workers. Vocab related to work situations; 12-a,b,e,f, situational dialogues; 13-d,f; 14-Garcia, Spanish for Law Enforcement Officers, Text and Workbook.

386. SPANISH FOR LAW ENFORCEMENT PERSONNEL
Curry C; Lang & Lit; Milton, MA 02186.
Frances M. Kohak
Further info not available.

387. SPANISH FOR LAW ENFORCEMENT
Cuyahoga CC; FLs; Cleveland, OH 44115.
Lenore V. Buford
1-12; 2-5x10; 3-a; 4-73; 5-2; 6-a; 7-a; 8-4q; 9-a, part-time; 10-none; 11-special section of Sp sequence with specialized vocab; 12-a,b,c,e,g; 13-d; 14-selecting new text; present one provided by U.S. Labor Dept very lacking.

388. SPANISH FOR LAW ENFORCEMENT OFFICERS
East Texas SU; Lit & Langs; Commerce, TX 75428.
Fred Tarpley
1-c75; 2-4x18; 3-a; 4-spr 75; 5-1; 6-a; 7-a,b; 8-4s; 9-a; 10-none; 11-freshman Sp conv specialized for law enforcement situations; 12-a,b,e,f; 13-a,d,e,f; 14-not yet selected.

389. SPANISH FOR LAW ENFORCEMENT (SPA 300)

Eastern Kentucky U; FLs; Richmond, KY 40475.
William M. Clarkson
1-new; 2-3x16; 3-a; 4-fall 75; 5-0; 6-a; 7-b; 8-3s; 9-a; 10-enrollment in College of Law Enforcement; 11-ng; 12-a,d,e,f,g; 13-a,b,d; 14-text being developed.

390. PRACTICAL SPANISH FOR PUBLIC SER-VICE PERSONNEL (POLICE)
El Centro C; Communications; Dallas, TX 75202.
Robert C. Bennett, George Ramsey
1-24; 2-3x15; 3-b; 4-74; 5-1; 6-a; 7-a,b; 8-3s; 9-a, police officers; 10-none; 11-basic Sp phrases and communication abilities for situations involving police action; 12-a,b,c,d,f; 13-a,d, student- written projects; 14-Moreno & Hayden, Practical Spanish for Public Service Personnel; Settgast & Anderson, Basic Spanish.

391. SPANISH FOR LAW ENFORCEMENT
Grand Valley SC; FL; Allendale, MI 49401.
P. E. Robert
1-ng; 2-5x10; 3-a; 4-73/74; 5-1; 6-on demand; 7-a,b; 8-5q; 9-a, police officers; 10-none; 11-basic expressions to enable immediate functioning in lang; 12-a,e,g; 13-a,b,c,d,e,f; 14-Dover texts, etc., instructor-prepared materials.

392. CONVERSATIONAL SPANISH FOR POLICEMEN
Holyoke CC; Hum; Holyoke, MA 01040.
Gerhard M. Wilke
1-26; 2-2x15; 3-a; 4-70; 5-8; 6-a; 7-a,b; 8-2s; 9-a, full-time policemen; 10-none; 11-communication and insight into cult; 12-e,f,g; 13-d; 14-none; materials supplied by instructor.

393. SPANISH FOR POLICEMEN
Kean C; FLs; Union, NJ 07083.
Charles Wendell
1-9; 2-3x15; 3-a; 4-73; 5-1; 6-b; 7-b; 8-3s; 9-a; 10-policemen in Criminal Justice Program; 11-ng; 12-ng; 13-ng; 14-ng.

394. SPANISH FOR POLICE OFFICERS
Manchester CC; FL; Manchester, CT 06040.
Harry Colvocoresses
1-60; 2-3x15 (two-sem sequence); 3-a; 4-71; 5-c8; 6-a; 7-a,b; 8-3s; 9-law officers studying part-time; 10-none; 11-normal 1st yr course, but using police vocab and situational dialogues (Puerto Rican and Cuban); 12-a,b,d,e,f,g; 13-d; 14-specially prepared workbook; Border Patrol Grammar Presentation.

395. PRACTICAL SPANISH FOR POLICEMEN
Montclair SC; Sp & Ital; Upper Montclair, NJ 07043.
Norman Fulton
1-ng; 2-3x15; 3-b,c; 4-ng; 5-ng; 6-a; 7-a,b; 8-3s; 9-a,b, part-time; 10-ng; 11-ng; 12-a,b,c,d,f,g; 13-d,e,f; 14-ng.

396. SPANISH FOR LAW ENFORCEMENT OFFICERS

Mt. Aloysius JC; MLs; Cresson, PA 16630.
Mariella Crowe, James Salony
1-6; 2-15x5; 5-3; 4-smr 74; 5-1; 6-b, double smr session; 7-varies; 8-12s; 9-a (criminology), part time; 10-none; 11-Sequence of 3 courses; Sp for policemen & community workers; conv patterns on routine matters of family, job, traffic, emergency situations with grammar support; 12-a,c,d,e,g, dialogues; 13-d, illustrated workbook, filmstrips, puzzles; 14-Spanish for Law Enforcement Officers-- Text 1 & 2, Workbook 1 & 2.

397. SPANISH FOR POLICE SCIENCE
Nassau CC; FL; Garden City, NY 11530.
Ignacio Vazquez
1-50-60; 2-4x15; 3-a; 4-74; 5-2; 6-a; 7-a,b; 8-4s; 9-a; 10-enrolled in Police Sci curriculum; 11-fundamentals of grammar and pronunciation; reading, writing, dictation, comprehension, and simple conv patterns; expressions for law enforcement officers; 12-a,b,c,e,f,g; 13-a,b,c,d; 14-Turk & Espinosa, Foundation Course in Spanish; Bomse & Alfaro, Practical Spanish for School Personnel, Policemen, and Community Agencies.

398. SPANISH FOR LAW ENFORCEMENT OFFICERS
U of Nebraska; FLs; Omaha, NE 68101.
Woodrow L. Most
1-20; 2-3x15; 3-a; 4-75; 5-1; 6-unknown; 7-b; 8-3s; 9-a; 10-none; 11-designed to give law enforcement students and current officers a practical working knowledge of Sp; job-related situations; 12-b,d,e,g, drill; 13-a,b,d; 14-Spanish for Law Enforcement Officers.

399. SPANISH FOR POLICE OFFICERS
Notre Dame C; FLs; Cleveland, OH 44121.
Sr. Mary St. Louis
1-20; 2-3x16; 3-c; 4-71; 5-3; 6-a; 7-b; 8-3s; 9-members of the LEEP Program—law enforcement; 10-hs grad; 11-regular elem and inter Sp; 12-b,e,g; 13-a,d; 14-Spanish for Beginners.

400. SPANISH FOR LAW ENFORCEMENT OFFICERS
Odessa C; FLs; Odessa, TX 79760.
Matt Rees
1-40; 2-3x16; 3-a; 4-74; 5-1; 6-on demand; 7-b; 8-3s; 9-policemen upgrading their qualifications; 10-none; 11-basic lang structure, vocab and conv; job-related; heavy Chicano content; 12-a,b,d,f,g; 13-specific requests from students; 14-used Spanish for Law Enforcement Officers & next time will use Border Patrol Spanish text.

401. SPANISH FOR LAW ENFORCEMENT PERSONNEL I & II
Pace U; FL; Pleasantville, NY 10570.
Prof. Tompakov
1-25; 2-3x15; 3-a; 4-73; 5-4; 6-a; 7-a,b; 8-6s; 9-a,b; 10-none; 11-stepping stone towards the speaking & understanding of Sp cult background to build awareness of attitude of community; little grammar; 12-a,b,c,d,e,f,g; 13-a,b,c,d, situational dialogues; 14-varies.

402. SPANISH FOR LAW ENFORCEMENT OFFICERS
Salve Regina C; Sp; Newport, RI 02840.
Heriberto Vasquez
1-c25; 2-4x15; 3-a; 4-ng; 5-ng; 6-ng; 7-b; 8-3s; 9-a, cont ed & law enforcement; 10-none; 11-daily requirements of police work; develops the ability to communicate with people who speak only Sp concerning their constitutional rights; 12-c,g; 13-pamphlets; 14-none.

403. SPOKEN SPANISH (PUBLIC EMPLOYEES)
San Bernardino Valley C; FL; San Bernardino, CA 92403.
Judith Davis
1-40; 2-ng; 3-c; 4-67; 5-13; 6-a; 7-ng; 8-3s; 9-a, policemen & soci workers, court clerks & probation officers; 10-ng; 11-memorization of dialogues appropriate to needs of students; 12-f,g; 13-ng; 14-instructor-prepared materials.

404. SPANISH FOR PEACE OFFICERS
San Jose SU; FLs; San Jose, CA 95192.
Roland Hamilton
1-new; 2-15x3; 3-a; 4-smr 75; 5-ng; 6-unknown; 7-ng; 8-3s; 9-b; 10-none; 11-ng; 12-a,d,e,f; 13-material developed for course; 14-ng.

405. SPANISH FOR LAW ENFORCEMENT OFFICERS & COMMUNITY WORKERS
Savannah SC; MLs; Savannah, GA 31404.
C. D. Koch
1-new; 2-4x20; 3-a; 4-75; 5-0; 6-a; 7-a; 8-3q; 9-a; 10-none; 11-comprehension and speaking ability; expressions in typical situations with Latin-Amers in U.S. cities; reading & writing; 12-b,e,g; 13-b,d; 14-Spanish for Law Enforcement Officers; workbook.

406. CONVERSATIONAL SPANISH
South Plains C; Communication & Philosophy; Levelland, TX 79336.
Frank Gonzales
1-32; 2-3x16; 3-b; 4-spr 74; 5-2; 6-a; 7-b; 8-3s; 9-a,b (law enforcement majors, inservice personnel); 10-none; 11-basic expressions used by officers, office personnel or those in judicial capacities; 12-audio, tutorial & class participation; 13-d, talking paper machines; 14-Conversational Spanish for Law Enforcement Personnel.

407. SPANISH FOR LAW ENFORCEMENT
Southern Oregon C; FLs; Ashland, OR 97520.
Thomas Oquiza
Course is being developed now in response to community need.

408. CONVERSATIONAL SPANISH FOR POLICE OFFICERS
Tarrant County JC; MFL; Fort Worth, TX

76119.
Ernesto Guzman
Further info ng.

409. SPANISH FOR CAREERS
Triton C; FLs; River Grove, IL 60171.
Rita Flaherty
1-15; 2-3x16; 3-a; 4-74/75; 5-1; 6-a; 7-b; 8-3s; 9-a; 10-none; 11-for fire & police personnel; 12-a,b,e,f,g; 13-d; 14-instructor-prepared text.

410. SPANISH FOR LAW ENFORCEMENT
Wayland Baptist C; Sp; Plainview, TX 79072.
Cecil Golden
1-25; 2-5x15; 3-a; 4-73/74; 5-2; 6-b; 7-a,b; 8-4s; 9-a; 10-none; 11-ng; 12-b,c,e,f,g; 13-d; 14--Basic Conversational Spanish.

411. CONVERSATIONAL SPANISH FOR LAW ENFORCEMENT OFFICERS
Weber SC; FLs; Ogden, UT 84403.
Oren E. Moffett
1-20; 2-5x10; 3-c; 4-73; 5-3; 6-a; 7-a,b; 8-5q; 9-a, part-time; 10-none; 11-intensive oral expression, listening, reading for law enforcement functions, phonetics, vocab, & short police-related dialogues, regional dialects, including profanity (for recognition only), cultural awareness; 12-b,g, audiolingual; 13-a,c,d,g, transparencies guest lectures, magnetic slapsticks; 14-Moffett, Conversational Spanish for Law Enforcement Personnel.

412. SPANISH FOR LAW ENFORCEMENT

OFFICERS I & II
Westchester CC; MLs; Valhalla, NY 10595.
Jacqueline Rosay
1-40; 2-3x16; 3-a; 4-72; 5-3; 6-b; 7-b; 8-3s each course; 9-part-time; 10-limited to those enrolled in fire sci & criminology program; 11-ng; 12-g; 13-a,b,d,e,f, transparencies, charts, drawings; 14-AMSCO Co., First Year Spanish; teacher-devised materials.

413. CONVERSATIONAL SPANISH
Western Texas C; Communications; Snyder, TX 79549.
Edward Barkowsky, Wendell Jones
1-40; 2-3x16; 3-a (but 2 sections taught by extension in nearby cities by local instructors); 4-71; 5-4; 6-a; 7-a,b; 8-3s; 9-a,b; 10-none; 11-skills in spoken Sp; idiomatic expressions & conv for law enforcement majors; 12-a,b; 13-a,d,e; 14-LaGrone, Entender Y Hablar; Spanish for Law Enforcement Officers, I & II, w/workbooks.

414. SPANISH FOR LAW ENFORCEMENT
Westfield SC; FLs; Westfield, MA 01085.
Raymond Ourand
1-60; 2-3x16; 3-a; 4-fall 73; 5-4; 6-a; 7-a; 8-3s; 9-a; 10-none; 11- basic conv Sp; vocab geared to law enforcement; 12-b,e,g; 13-d,g, guest lectures by police officers from community; 14-A Practical Spanish Grammar for Border Patrol Officers; Voces del Barrio; Puerto Rican Americans.

See also 91, 268, 289, 314, 322, 347, 370, 419, 420, 423, 425, 426, 428, 430, 437, 443, 444, 445, 450, 498, 757, 764, 772.

Social Services

FRENCH

See 546.

SPANISH

415. CONVERSATIONAL SPANISH FOR SOCIAL WORKERS
Amarillo C; Cont Ed; Amarillo, TX 79178.
Clair Mayes
1-16; 2-3x15; 3-c; 4-74; 5-ng; 6-a; 7-b; 8-ng; 9-b, soci work students; 10-none; 11-pronunciation, basic grammar, special terminology; 12-a,b,d,f; 13-records; 14-See It and Say It in Spanish.

416. SPANISH FOR CIVIL SERVICE PERSONNEL
Bergen CC; FLs; Paramus, NJ 07652.
Further info ng.

417. CHICANO LITERATURE BACKGROUND FOR SOCIOLOGY STUDENTS
Bethany Nazarene C; ML; Bethany, OK 73008.

Dolores Wood
1-new; 2-3x15; 3-a; 4-spr 75; 5-1; 6-alt yrs; 7-a; 8-3s; 9-a; 10-none; 11-attitudes and adjustments, value system, and historical factors pertaining to the Chicano as portrayed in Chicano lit; 12-a,b,c,d,f,g; 13-ng; 14-ng.

418. SPANISH FOR SOCIAL WORKERS, MEDICAL PERSONNEL AND BUSINESSMEN
Bloomfield C; Lang; Bloomfield, NJ 07003.
Clarence Fuller
1-10; 2-1½x12; 3-a; 4-72; 5-3; 6-b; 7-a; 8-½ unit; 9-a; 10-inter prof; 11-special vocab and idiomatic structures needed by those people communicating with Sp-speaking in their daily work; 12-a,b,g; 13-e,f; 14-no special text.

419. PRACTICAL SPANISH FOR PUBLIC SERVICE EMPLOYEES
Boise SU; Boise, ID 83725.
Carlin Otto

1-15; 2-4x18; 3-c; 4-Jan 75; 5-1; 6-b; /-b; 8-4s; 9-a,b; 10-elem prof; 11-for policemen, firemen, nurses, teachers, other public service employees who communicate on a functional level & to understand cult; 12-ng; 13-ng; 14-ng.

420. LEGAL SPANISH
California SU; FLs & Lits; Hayward, CA 94542.
Vincenzo Traversa
1-11; 2-4x10; 3-a; 4-fall 74; 5-1; 6-h; 7-a; 8-4q; 9-a, city employees; 10-inter prof; 11-vocab used in legal profession and in soci services; tech lang used in legal docs, and the same lang expressed in terms the layman can understand (for use with Sp-speakers in the U.S.); 12-a,b,g; 13-instructor-prepared materials; 14-Steel de Meza, Business Letters Handbook; Rabb: Dicionario de terminos legales; Last, Everyday Law Made Simple.

421. SPANISH FOR PROFESSIONALS
California SU; FLs & Lits; Northridge, CA 91324.
Maja Reid
1-ng; 2-3x15; 3-a; 4-fall 74; 5-2; 6-a; 7-b; 8-3s; 9-ng; 10-instructor permission; 11-practical conv Sp for professions such as teaching, soci work, public health; 12-b,d,g; 13-ng; 14-Da Silva, Beginning Spanish - A Concept Approach.

422. SPANISH FOR PUBLIC SERVANTS
California SU; Sp; Sacramento, CA 95819.
Jorge A. Santana
1-32; 2-3x14; 3-a; 4-ng; 5-7; 6-a; 7-b; 8-3s; 9-a,b; 10-elem prof (not for Sp majors); 11-vocab and structures for effective communication for interviews, home visits, etc; local dialect differences; 12-a,c,d,e,f,g; 13-c,d; 14-Benitez, Practical Spanish for the Health Professions.

423. ADVANCED SPANISH CONVERSATION (PROFESSIONAL EMPHASIS - LEGAL AND WELFARE TERMS)
U of California; Sp & Port; Santa Barbara, CA 93106.
R. E. Wilson
1-ng; 2-2x10; 3-a; 4-spr 74; 5-2; 6-b; 7-a; 8-2q; 9-a; 10-inter prof; 11-vocab useful for U.S. legal professions & welfare system; discussion related to those fields; 12-b,c,d,g, role playing; 13-e, pamphlets; 14-no text.

424. SPANISH FOR HUMAN SERVICES
Corning CC; Hums; Corning, NY 14830.
Robert E. McEnroe
1-new; 2-5x15; 3-a; 4-spr 75; 5-1; 6-a; 7-a; 8-4s; 9-a; 10-students in Human Services program; 11-relevant conv Sp; 12-e,f,g; 13-ng; 14-Garcia, Spanish for Law Enforcement Officers.

425. BILINGUAL PUBLIC SERVICE
Curry C; Sp; Milton, MA 02186.
Robert Forbes
1-ng; 2-ng; 3-b; 4-fall 74; 5-ng; 6-a; 7-a,b;

8-30s total; 9-a,b; 10-elem prof; 11-intensive spoken Sp: "Spanish for Law Enforcement Personnel" or "Spanish for Health, Medical, and Social Workers"; "History and Culture of Latin America" and psychology and soci courses; 12-a,b,c,e,f,g; 13-d,e,f; 14-ng.

426. PUBLIC SERVICE SPANISH
Cypress JC; Sp; Cypress, CA 90630.
Richard McIntosh
1-ng; 2-4xsem; 3-ng; 4-ng; 5-ng; 6-ng; 7-ng; 8-3s; 9-ng; 10-none; 11-for med, soci welfare, law enforcement, bus. Oral fluency for communication w/Sp-speaking public. Functional vocab for emergency situations; 12-e, drill; 13-situational dialogues; 14-Moreno & Hayden, Practical Spanish for Public Safety Personnel.

427. SPANISH FOR SOCIAL WORKERS
U of Delaware; Langs & Lits; Newark, DE 19711.
Ivo Dominguez
1-25; 2-2x7; 3-a; 4-73; 5-2; 6-a; 7-b; 8-0; 9-b; 10-none; 11-drill on phrases useful for soci workers; 12-b,e,g; 13-b; 14-instructor-prepared materials.

428. CONVERSATIONAL SPANISH FOR SOCIAL SERVICES
East Stroudsburg SC; FL; East Stroudsburg, PA 18301.
Dolores Smith
1-ng; 2-ng; 3-a; 4-ng; 5-ng; 6-b; 7-ng; 8-3s; 9-a; 10-elem prof; 11-practical conv for law enforcement and soci work. Situations in real life will be simulated in classroom dialogues; 12-b,d,e,g; 13-b,d; 14-Luna & Meneses, A Spanish Manual for Law Enforcement Agencies.

429. SPANISH FOR COMMUNITY WORKERS I, II
CC of the Finger Lakes; Lang Arts; Canandaigua, NY 14424.
R. S. Foster
1-22; 2-3x15; 3-c; 4-73/74; 5-3; 6-a; 7-b; 8-3s; 9-a,b; 10-none; 11-conv patterns & basic grammar; 12-a,b,c,d,e,g; 13-a,b,f; 14-Leslie, Spanish for Conversation, several others with specialized vocabs.

430. FUNCTIONAL SPANISH
Franklin & Marshall C; Sp; Lancaster, PA 17604.
R. V. Martinez
1-30; 2-3x15; 3-a; 4-74; 5-2; 6-on demand; 7-b; 8-3s; 9-policemen, soci workers; 10-none; 11-elem lang and cult; 12-d,e,f; 13-ng; 14-specially designed materials.

431. EVERYDAY SPANISH
Georgian Court C; Mod & Cl Langs; Lakewood, NJ 08701.
Mary Catharine Sullivan
1-20; 2-3x15; 3-a; 4-smr 73; 5-4; 6-a; 7-a,b; 8-3s; 9-a,b, community; 10-course has 2 divs, for students with no background & for those with some; 11-strictly oral for conv Sp; for present & future teachers, soci ma-

jors, soci workers, & community personnel; 12-b,c,d,f; 13-a,b,d; 14-Madrigal, Open Door to Spanish; Berlitz.

431A. APPLIED SPANISH FOR THE SOCIAL SERVICES
Howard U; Rom Langs; Washington, DC 20059.
Moraima de Semprun Donahue
1-118; 2-3x20 plus lab work; 3-a; 4-73; 5-8; 6-a; 7-a,b; 8-4s, b; 9-a,b, doctors, nurses, police officers, etc.; 10-none; 11-4-sem sequence available; 12-a,b,c,d,e,g; 13-d,e,f; 14-Applied Spanish for the Social Services (textbook and tape manual).

432. SPANISH-SOCIOLOGY MAJOR
Immaculata C; Mod Langs; Immaculata, PA 19345.
Sister M. Appolonio
Initiated in 1972, this major is designed to give future soci workers a knowledge of spoken and basic written Sp and Hispanic cult. Srs do field research or field work. Presently 8 students enrolled.

433. SPANISH FOR THE PROFESSIONAL
Loma Linda U; MLs; Riverside, CA 92505.
Leon Gambetta
1-37; 2-3x11; 3-b; 4-72/73; 5-6; 6-a; 7-b; 8-4q; 9-a,b, hospital personnel; 10-ng; 11-expressions needed for patient & health services/soci services; 12-g; 13-ng; 14-instructor-prepared text.

434. COMMUNITY SPANISH (FIREMEN AND NURSES)
Mesa C; Cont Ed; Grand Junction, CO 81501.
Leecy Wise, David Pilkenton
1-18; 2-3xq; 3-a; 4-74; 5-1; 6-unknown; 7-b; 8-3q; 9-b; 10-none; 11-basic greetings, intros & vocab; work-related dialogues; parts of body & emergency expressions; buildings and parts of houses; 12-a,b,d,f,g; 13-d, games; 14-instructor-prepared.

435. ELEMENTARY SPANISH
Millersville SC; FL; Millersville, PA 17551.
Beatrice M. Killough
1-18; 2-3x15; 3-a; 4-fall 74; 5-1; 6-undecided; 7-a; 8-3s; 9-PA Welfare Dept interviewers; 10-none; 11-regular Sp course with vocab adapted to needs of Welfare Dept workers; special dialogues; 12-g; 13-d; 14-MLA, Modern Spanish.

436. BASIC SPANISH CONVERSATION FOR SOCIAL WORKERS
Molloy C; Sp; Rockville Centre, NY 11570.
Libe Aranguren
1-9; 2-3x15; 3-a; 4-72; 5-3; 6-on demand; 7-a; 8-3s; 9-a, part-time; 10-none; 11-Aural-oral practice of everyday lang, emphasis on soci service careers; 12-c,d,e,g; 13-handouts; 14-no formal text.

437. PRACTICAL SPANISH FOR FIRE, LAW ENFORCEMENT, SCHOOL AND GOVERNMENT PERSONNEL
Monroe County CC; Hums; Monroe, MI 48161.

Paul E. Ross
1-5; 2-1½x10; 3-a; 4-74; 5-1; 6-ng; 7-Sat; 8-1s; 9-a,b; 10-none; 11-highly specialized tech approach; 12-a,b,g; 13-ng; 14-Bomse and Alfaro, Practical Spanish for School Personnel, Firemen, Policemen and Community Agencies.

438. SPANISH FOR COMMUNITY RELATIONS PERSONNEL
Montgomery County CC; For Studies; Blue Bell, PA 19422.
Charlotte Anderson
1-new; 2-ng; 3-a; 4-75; 5-ng; 6-a; 7-b; 8-ng; 9-ng; 10-none; 11-ng; 12-ng; 13-ng; 14-Bomse & Alfaro Practical Spanish for Medical and Hospital Personnel; and Practical Spanish for School Personnel, Firemen, Policemen and Community Agencies.

439. SPANISH FOR HEALTH PERSONNEL & SOCIAL WORKERS
Mt. Mercy C; Sp; Cedar Rapids, IA 52402.
Sr. Gloria Rivera
1-20; 2-3x13; 3-c; 4-75; 5-1; 6-alt yrs; 7-b; 8-3½s; 9-a, part-time; 10-elem prof; 11-cult of Mex Amer & Latin Amer; practical dialogues for nursing & soci work situations; 12-b,f,g; 13-b,e,f; 14-Duran, Introduction to Chicano Studies; Practical Spanish for Medical & Hospital Personnel; Practical Spanish for Community Agencies.

440. SPANISH FOR SOCIAL WORKERS, MEDICAL PERSONNEL AND TEACHERS
New York U; FLs; New York, NY 10003.
Annette S. Baslaw, Salvatore Corteselli
1-41; 2-3x15; 3-c; 4-69; 5-5; 6-a; 7-b; 8-3s; 9-a,b, part-time; 10-none; 11-2-sem sequence incl special vocab and idiomatic structures needed by those who communicate orally with Puerto Rican, Cuban and other Sp Amer clients in their daily work; 12-b,f,g; 13-ng; 14-ng.

441. SPANISH FOR FIREMEN
North Shore CC; MLs; Beverly, MA 01915.
Enrique Rueda-Puerto
1-19; 2-3x15; 3-a; 4-spr 75; 5-1; 6-a; 7-b; 8-3s; 9-a; 10-none; 11-ALM approach; basic Sp practical vocab for community professionals; 12-a,b,e,g; 13-d; 14-none; instructor-prepared manual.

442. SPANISH FOR SOCIAL AGENTS
Occidental C; Langs & Ling; Los Angeles, CA 90041.
Prof. Nieto
1-30; 2-5x10; 3-a; 4-spr 74; 5-1; 6-alt yrs; 7-a; 8-1q; 9-a; 10-elem prof; 11-designed for those in ed, med, & community service; discussion of cult aspects of Hispanic life; 12-a,b,d,e,g; 13-a,d; 14-Paz, The Labyrinth of Solitude; Anaja, Bless Me Ultima; Ralfo, Pedro Paramo; Spanish Review Grammar.

443. ELEMENTARY SPANISH I (CAREER SPANISH SECTION)
Orange County CC; Eng & FLs; Middletown, NY 10940.
Moses Stivers

1-c25; 2-3x15; 3-c; 4-spr 75; 5-1; 6-b; 7-a,b; 8-3s; 9-a; 10-none; 11-oral situations to be handled by nurses, policemen, & soci workers; 12-b,e,g; 13-a,c,d; 14-ng.

444. SPANISH FOR SOCIAL SERVICES
Pennsylvania SU; Sp, Ital & Port; University Park, PA 16802.
Martin S. Stabb
1-c20; 2-4½x10; 3-b; 4-spr 75; 5-1; 6-b; 7-a; 8-3s; 9-a; 10-inter prof; 11-practical Sp for soci workers, med personnel, law enforcement officers; emphasis on Puerto Rican vocab, idiom, and pronunciation; 12-b,e,g; 13-ng; 14-undecided.

445. SPANISH FOR COMMUNITY SERVICE I & II
Rockland CC; FL & Lits; Suffern, NY 10901.
Norman D. Arbaiza
1-48; 2-4x15; 3-a; 4-fall 74; 5-1; 6-a; 7-a,b; 8-3s; 9-a,b; 10-none for I; 11-for soci workers, nurses, law enforcement personnel, civil service employees, merchants; 12-a,b,e,f, situational dialogues & drills; 13-special lexical lists; 14-Spanish for Law Enforcement Officers; workbook, Practical Spanish for Medical & Hospital Personnel.

446. SPANISH FOR COMMUNITY WORKERS
Russell Sage C; MLs; Troy, NY 12180.
Adrienne Rogers, Marta Perez-Lopez, Helen Triantafilou
1-12; 2-3x13; 3-a; 4-fall 74; 5-2; 6-a; 7-a,b; 8-3s; 9-a; 10-elem prof; 11-for community-oriented professionals who work with Sp speakers, Sp cult; 12-b,e,g; 13-pictures, diagrams; 14-Bomse & Alfaro, Practical Spanish for Medical and Hospital Personnel.

447. SPANISH FOR THE SERVICE PROFESSIONS
Rutgers U; Sp & Port; New Brunswick, NJ 08903.
Jose Vazquez-Amaral
1-8; 2-3x16; 3-a; 4-spr 72; 5-3; 6-a; 7-a; 8-3s; 9-jrs, srs, grad students; 10-none; 11-cult & ling materials pertinent to specific job situations; basics of spoken Sp; oral practice through drills & model interviews; 12-b,f,g; 13-b,e,f; 14-none.

448. SPANISH FOR SOCIAL WORKERS
Salve Regina C; Sp; Newport, RI 02840.
H. Vazquez
1-new; 2-3x15; 3-a; 4-ng; 5-ng; 6-ng; 7-b; 8-3s; 9-a; 10-none; 11-to develop ability to communicate with people needing soci assistance and speak only Sp; 12-c,f,g; 13-pamphlets; 14-none.

449. SPANISH FOR FIREMEN
C of San Mateo; FLs, Fire Science; San Mateo, CA 94402.
Robert Dawson, Fire Science Coordinator
1-23; 2-6x3; 3-a; 4-74; 5-1; 6-on demand; 7-b; 8-1s; 9-part-time, usually in Fire Sci program; 11-pronunciation and basic grammar, fire & emergency service vocab; 12-a,f,g; recitation; 13-none; 14-teacher-prepared materials.

450. SPANISH FOR PUBLIC SAFETY PERSONNEL
Santa Ana C; FL; Santa Ana, CA 92706.
Lyle Johnson
1-35; 2-2x18; 3-a; 4-ng; 5-ng; 6-a; 7-b; 8-2s; 9-a, part-time on & off campus; 10-none; 11-designed for public safety personnel, firemen, & police, oral and written comprehension of basic words & phrases; 12-a,b,c,d,e,f; 13-a,b,d,e,f; 14-ng.

451. APPLIED SPANISH FOR HUMAN SERVICE WORKERS
Southern Illinois U; FL & Lits; Carbondale, IL 62901.
Mildred Wilkinson
1-12; 2-3x15; 3-a; 4-spr 75; 5-1; 6-a; 7-a; 8-3s; 9-a; 10-elem prof; 11-lang skills for future professionals in human services working with Sp speakers; 12-b,c,d,e,f,g; 13-a,b,d,f; 14-Sallese & Fernandez, Pan y Mantequilla; Bomse & Alfaro, Practical Spanish for School Personnel, Firemen, Policemen & Community Agencies; Bomse & Alfaro, Practical Spanish for Medical & Hospital Personnel.

452. SPANISH FOR SOCIAL WORKERS
Valparaiso U; FLs; Valparaiso, IN 46383.
Judy Peters
1-15; 2 3x14; 3-c; 4-71; 5-3; 6-on demand; 7-a; 8-3s; 9-a; 10-inter prof; 11-Sp lang situations encountered by soci workers; 12-a,b,c,d,g; 13-e,f; 14-Clark, Health in the Mexican-American Culture.

453. SPANISH FOR COMMUNITY SERVICE PERSONNEL
Villanova U; MLs; Villanova, PA 19085.
Harriet Goldberg
1-new; 2-3x13; 3-a; 4-75/76; 5-0; 6-b; 7-a; 8-3s; 9-a; 10-inter prof; 11-grammar review; specialized vocab; extensive conv practice; 12-ng; 13-ng; 14-Bomse & Alfaro, Practical Spanish for Medical and Hospital Personnel and Practical Spanish for School Personnel, Firemen, Policemen and Community Agencies; A. Bryson Gerrard, Beyond the Dictionary in Spanish.

454. OCCUPATIONAL SPANISH I & II
Westchester CC; MLs; Valhalla, NY 10595.
Jacqueline Rosay
1-20; 2-4x16; 3-b; 4-71/72; 5-3; 6-b; 7-a; 8-3s; 9-a; 10-elem prof; 11-for Food Service Administration & Human Services; 12-g; 13-a,b,d, transparencies, charts, drawings; 14-Turk & Espinosa, Foundation Course in Spanish.

455. CONVERSATIONAL SPANISH
Western Texas C; Communications; Snyder, TX 79549.
Edward Barkowsky, Wendell Jones
1-40; 2-3x16; 3-c; 4-71; 5-4; 6-a; 7-a,b; 8-3s; 9-a,b; 10-none; 11-skills in spoken Sp; idiomatic expressions & conv stressed. For bus & professional people, firemen, ranchers, etc; 12-a,b; 13-a,d,e; 14-La Grone, Entender Y Hablar; Spanish for Law Enforce-

183

ment Officers Text I & II, w/ workbooks.

456. SPANISH FOR SOCIAL SERVICES
Westfield SC; FLs; Westfield, MA 01085.
Raymond Ourand
1-60; 2-3x16; 3-a; 4-fall 74; 5-2; 6-a; 7-a; 8-3s; 9-a; 10-none; 11-basic conv; vocab geared to soci services; 12-b,e,g; 13-d; 14-

A Practical Spanish Grammar for Border Patrol Officers; Voces del Barrio; Puerto Rican Americans.

See also 86, 313, 320,321,322, 328, 342, 347, 349, 370, 380, 382, 385, 403, 405, 409, 412, 489, 497, 503, 660, 764, 870, 1252, 1417.

Performing Arts

FRENCH

457. FRENCH FOR MUSIC MAJORS
Houston Baptist U; Langs; Houston, TX 77036.
Phyllis B. Nimmons
1-new; 2-210 min x 12 wks; 3-a; further info ng.

458. FRENCH/MUSIC
U of Massachusetts; Fr, Music; Amherst, MA 01002.
Ursula F. Chen, Dept of Fr & Ital
1-8; 2-3x14; 3-a; 4-72/3; 5-3; 6-b; 7-a; 8-6s; 9-a; 10-none; 11-for vocal students where proper pronunciation of Eng,Ger, Fr, & Ital is essential. Dif. between spoken & sung Eng emphasized to free students of regional pronunciation; 13-songs and arias written in Eng, Fr, Ger & Ital; 14-Ursula Chen, Sing in English, French, German, & Italian.

459. FRENCH FOR MUSIC MAJORS
U of Missouri; MFLs; St. Louis, MO 63121.
Ingeborg M. Goessl
1-8; 2-3x15; 3-a; 4-wtr 74; 5-1; 6-variable; 7-a; 8-3s; 9-a; 10-none; 11-for music majors: pronunciation, diction reading; 12-a,b,f; 13-a,b,d, records; 14-Applebaum, Invitation to French Poetry; Opera: Faust; selected poems.

460. FRENCH FOR SINGERS AND BROADCASTERS
U of South Dakota; MFLs; Vermillion, SD 57069.
Alexander Hartman
1-new; 2-2x8; 3-a; 4-ng; 5-0; 6-every other yr; 7-a; 8-1s; 9-ng; 10-none; 11-ng; 12-b,f, & individual projects; 13-libretti; 14-ng.

461. FRENCH FOR SINGING
Tennessee Technological U; FLs; Cookeville, TN 38501.
Claire Saint-Leon
1-30; 2-2x10; 3-a; 4-73/74; 5-2; 6-b; 7-a; 8-2q; 9-a; 10-none other than major in music; 11-pronunciation, particularly in vocal lit, intro to basic conv; 12-a,b,c,g; 13-d; 14-ng.

See also 546.

GERMAN

462. GERMAN FOR MUSIC MAJORS
U of Missouri; MFLs; St. Louis, MO 63121.
Ingeborg M. Goessl
1-9; 2-3x15; 3-a; 4-fall 73; 5-1; 6-variable; 7-a; 8-3s; 9-a; 10-none; 11-primarily for music majors--pronunciation, diction, reading; 12-a,b,f; 13-d; 14-Waengler, Instruction in German Pronunciation; Bauer, Deutsche Volkslieder.

463. GERMAN FOR SINGERS & BROADCASTERS
U of South Dakota; MFLs; Vermillion, SD 57069.
Alexander Hartman
1-new; 2-2x8; 3-a; 4-ng; 5-0; 6-every other yr; 8-1s; 9-ng; 10-none; 11-ng; 12-b,f, individual projects; 13-libretti; 14-ng.

464. GERMAN FOR SINGING
Tennessee Technological U; FLs; Cookeville, TN 38501.
Frederick Heina
1-19; 2-2x10; 3-a; 4-73/74; 5-1; 6-b; 7-a; 8-2q; 9-a; 10-none, other than music major; 11-pronunciation, particularly in vocal lit, intro to basic conv; 12-a,b,c,g; 13-d; 14-ng.

ITALIAN

465. ITALIAN FOR MUSIC STUDENTS
Adelphi U; Langs; Garden City, NY 11530.
Romano Giachetti
1-20; 2-3x14; 3-a; 4-72; 5-1; 6-every 2-3 years; 7-a; 8-3s; 9-a; 10-none; 11-esp for music majors, extensive practice in pronunciation, reading, trans; material drawn from music hist, librettos, other related sources; 12-f,g; 13-e,f,g; 14-ng.

466. ITALIAN FOR STUDENTS OF VOICE
U of Arizona; Rom Langs; Tucson, AZ 85721.
Charles Olstad
1-new; 2-4x14; 3-a; 4-74/75; 5-ng; 6-ng; 7-a; 8-4s; 9-a; 10-ng; 11-pronunciation, phrasing, comprehension & interpretation of musical texts; basic grammar; 12-a,b,e,f,g; 13d,g, opera libretti; 14-Speroni-Bolino, Basic Italian.

467. FOREIGN LANGUAGE DICTION FOR VOICE MAJORS (ITALIAN)
Federal City C; FLs; Washington, DC 20001.
Marie M. Racine
1-12; 2-2x10; 3-b; 4-72/73; 5-3; 6-b; 7-a,b; 8-2q; 9-a; 10-none; 11-for voice majors to acquire the pronunciation of Ital for singing; 12-a,d,e,f; 13-d; 14-singers manual in Ital, Ger, Fr.

468. ITALIAN FOR MUSIC MAJORS
U of Missouri; MFLs & Lits; St. Louis, MO 63121.
Ingeborg M. Goessl
1-8; 2-3x15; 3-a; 4-wtr 73; 5-1; 6-variable; 7-a; 8-3s; 9-a; 10-none; 11-primarily for music majors; emphasis on pronunciation, diction, reading; 12-a,b,f; 13-d; 14-Colorni, Singers Italian: A Manual of Diction & Phonetics; Rebay, Invitation to Italian Poetry (record & manual); Cagno & D'Arlon Rapid Italian for Students and Tourists.

469. ITALIAN FOR SINGING
Tennessee Technological U; FLs; Cookeville, TN 38501.
David Viera
1-18; 2-2x10; 3-a; 4-73/74; 5-1; 6-b; 7-a; 8-2q; 9-a; 10-none, other than major in music; 11-pronunciation, particularly in vocal lit,

intro to basic conv; 12-a,b,c,g; 13-d; 14-ng.

MULTI-LANGUAGE

470. PHONETICS FOR VOICE STUDENTS
Boise SU; FL; Boise, ID 83725.
George A. Jocums
1-12; 2-4x4; 3-a; 4-Sep 74; 5-1; 6-b; 7-a; 8-4; 9-a; 10-none; 11-phonetics of Ital, Fr & Ger for voice majors; 12-ng; 13-ng; 14-ng.

471. ELEMENTS OF FOREIGN LANGUAGE
Eastern Kentucky U; FL; Richmond, KY 40475.
Charles L. Nelson
1-10; 2-3x16; 3-a; 4-fall 74; 5-2; 6-a; 7-b; 8-1s; 9-a; 10-none; 11-structure, pronunciation, intonation patterns of Fr, Ger, Latin, Ital, Sp; course specifically designed for students of music, radio, television, broadcasting, drama & speech; 12-f; 13-a,d; 14-none.

472. FRENCH 131, GERMAN 131, ITALIAN 131
Grand Valley SC; FL; Allendale, MI 49401.
P. E. Robert.
1-15; 2-5x10; 3-a; 4-73/74; 5-3; 6-c, 2q out of 3; 7-a; 8-5q; 9-a; 10-none; 11-for music students, emphasis on pronunciation, intonation, music vocab & development of reading skills limited to the repertoire; 12-e,f,g; 13-b,d; 14-compilation of materials by instructor with musical background.

Miscellaneous

CHINESE

473. CHINESE MILITARY READINGS
U.S. Military Academy; FLs; West Point, NY 10996.
Sumner Willard
1-3; 2-2½x16; 3-a; 4-70; 5-4; 6-b; 7-a; 8-2½s; 9-a; 10-inter prof; 11-Chinese military terminology through stories & dialogues; interrogation exercises, oral reports, group discussion; 12-a,b,c,d,g; 13-a,b,c,d,e,f; 14-Juan Chang, Chinese Military Reading; Illustrated Military Situation (Chinese) DLI, Monterey.

CLASSICS
See 1104.

FRENCH

474. FRENCH FOR THE CAREER ORIENTED PERSON
Anna Maria C; MLs; Paxton, MA 01612.
Mary Ann Quinn
1-new; 2-3x15; 3-a; 4-74; 5-0; 6-a; 7-a; 8-3s; 9-a, part-time or special; 10-elem prof; 11-to perfect speaking abilities for careers; specialized vocab to aid bicentennial foreign visitors in such situations as hotels,

restaurants, hospitals; 12-c,d,e,g; 13-a,b,d,f; 14-ng.

475. CAREER FRENCH
Bowling Green SU; Rom Langs; Bowling Green, OH 43403.
Richard Hebein
1-22; 2-4x10; 3-a; 4-73/74; 5-1; 6-on demand; 7-a; 8-3q; 9-a,c, majors & minors; 10-inter prof; 11-skills in trans; careers in tech, bus & research; 12-a,b,g; 13-ng; 14-Larousse, Le Francaise Commercial I & II.

476. FRENCH TRACK II
California SU; Fr & Ital; Sacramento, CA 95819.
Lo Verso Rosabianca
1-20; 2-9x14; 3-a; 4-fall 74; 5-1; 6-a; 7-a; 8-ng; 9-ng; 10-phonetics, adv grammar, comp & conv, ling, Fr civ; 11-program which includes bus Fr, 2 sems of trans, interpreting; 12-a,b,c,d,e,g; 13-a,b,c,d,e,f; 14-ng.

477. FRENCH FOR CAREER DEVELOPMENT
Carlow C; ML; Pittsburgh, PA 15213.
Marie Immaculee Dana
1-5; 2-4; 3-a; 4-74; 5-2; 6-b; 7-a; 8-2q; 9-a; 10-elem prof; 11-program consists of 4 courses each given once per yr in sequence; 12-b,c,g; 13-b,e,f; 14-ng.

478. PRACTICAL FRENCH
DePaul U; MLs; Chicago, IL 60614.
W. V. Hoffman
1-new; 2-6x5; 3-a; 4-smr 75; 5-ng; 6-b; 7b; 84; 9ng; 10none; 11for law, bus, travel; 12-b,d,f; 13-d,e; 14-no text.

479. FRENCH FOR ARCHITECTS
U of Illinois; Fr; Urbana, IL 61801.
1-7; 2-8x16; 3-a; 4-spr 71; 5-4; 6-depends upon enrollment; 7-a; 8-5s; 9-a; 10-none; 11-intensive Fr for students of architecture going to France; 12-a,b,f,g; 13-ng; 14-ng.

480. ACCELERATED FRENCH
Jacksonville SU; FLs; Jacksonville, AL 36265.
France A. C. Peterson
1-new; 2-3x28; 3-a; 4-75; 5-ng; 6-ng; 7-a; 8-6; 9-a; 10-none; 11-for those in bus, engineering, sci; 12-g; 13-a,b,f; 14-Mauger & Brueziere, Le Francais Accelere.

481. AGRICULTURAL FRENCH
U of Minnesota; Fr, Intl Agriculture; Minneapolis, MN 55455.
John Blackmore
1-10; 2-10x6; 3-b; 4-73; 5-1; 6-special smr project; 7-a; 8-b; 9-professional staff in broad field of agriculture; 10-permission of Office of Intl Agriculture; 11-basic Fr, materials relating to broad field of agriculture; 12-a,b,e,g; 13-b,c,d, visual aids; 14-Lenard, Parole et Pensee; EMC Corporation, Suivez la Piste; supplementary drill materials developed for Peace Corps language training program in agriculture (unpub).

482. FRENCH FOR MOROCCO
U of Minnesota; Fr, Intl Agriculture; Minneapolis, MN 55455.
John Blackmore
1-10; 2-5x10-20; 3-b; 4-72; 5-6-8; 6-one or two qtrs per year as prospective Peace Corps volunteers are recruited; 7-a; 8-5q; 9-a; 10-participation in intern program for prospective Peace Corps volunteers in broad field of agriculture; Fr as spoken in Morocco; 12-a,b,e,g; 13-b,c,d, posters, visual aids; 14-Lenard, Parole et Pensee; drills by Peace Corps.

483. CAREER-RELATED FRENCH
SUCNY; FLs & Lit; Plattsburgh, NY 12901.
Craig L. Sample
Will be offered 75/76; other info not available.

484. PRACTICAL FRENCH - FRENCH FOR CAREERS
St. Joseph's C; Fr; North Windham, ME 04062.
Anna McNaughton
1-13; 2-3x15; 3-a; 4-74/75; 5-1; 6-2-sem, alt yrs; 7-a; 8-3s; 9-a; 10-inter prof; 11-conv based on collection of magazine articles from Pour Parler; transcription of Fr material from tapes without use of script; letters; dramatized life situations; 12-b,c,d,e,g; 13-a,b,d,e,f; 14-Duche, Pour Parler; Cadoux, L'Envolee; Mollica et al, French Canadian Readings.

485. ADVANCED FRENCH FOR THE SOCIAL SCIENCES & HUMANITIES
St. Olaf C; Rom Langs; Northfield, MN 55057.
Loring D. Knecht
1-11; 2-3x14; 3-a; 4-72/73; 5-3; 6-b; 7-a; 8-1 course unit; 9-a; 10-inter prof; 11-read, discuss non-lit topics on adv level; 12-b,c,g, written reports; 13-e,f; 14-none, all from periodicals.

486. TECHNICAL FRENCH
U of Southern California; Fr & Ital; Los Angeles, CA 90007.
Arthur J. Knodel
1-12; 2-3x15; 3-a; 4-fall 74; 5-1; 6-every 3 sem; 7-a; 8-4s; 9-a; 10-inter prof; 11-basic terminology in politics, diplomacy & law; finance & econ; telecommunications; journalism, publicity, entertainment (incl. sports), physical scis; life scis; industry; individualized instruction & projects to develop mastery of tech Fr within each student's field; 12-a,b,f,g; 13-e,f, tech manuals, dictionary; 14-specialized text, mimeo handouts.

487. FRENCH FOR COMMUNICATION MAJORS
U of Texas; Fr & Ital; Austin, TX 78712.
Jean-Pierre Cauvin
1-16; 2-3x15; 3-a; 4-73; 5-4; 6-a; 7-a; 8-3s; 9-a; 10-elem prof; 11-to develop reading skills, advertising articles from Fr newspapers, scenario of a film, & a book about cinema; reading, trans, writing compositions; 12-a,f; 13-a,e; 14-Duras, Hiroshima mon amour; Morin, Les Stars.

See also 460, 471, 1427.

GERMAN

See 1025, 1439, 1444.

PORTUGUESE

488. MILITARY READING IN PORTUGUESE
U.S. Military Academy; FLs; West Point, NY 10996.
Sumner Willard
1-8; 2-2½x16; 3-a; 4-71; 5-4; 6-b; 7-a; 8-2½s; 9-a; 10-inter prof; 11-instruction in organizing, training, & operations of Brazilian army forces; expansion of military vocab; 12-a,b,c,d,g; 13-a,b,c,d,e,f; 14-USMA, As forces armada do Brasil.

See also 890.

SPANISH

489. SPANISH FOR PROFESSIONAL USE
Adelphi U; Langs & Intl Studies; Garden City, NY 11530.
James Stais
1-30; 2-2x16; 3-a; 4-69; 5-12; 6-a; 7-b; 83s; 9a, nurses, soci workers, bus people; 10-none; 11-oral prof; specifically oriented to needs of professionals with Sp-speaking clients; 12-c,d,g; 13-d,e; 14-f.

490. SPANISH FOR THE CAREER-ORIENTED PERSON
Anna Maria C; MLs; Paxton, MA 01612.
Mary Ann Quinn
1-new; 2-3x15; 3-a; 4-74; 5-0; 6-a; 7-a; 8-3s; 9-a; part-time or special; 10-elem prof; 11-to perfect speaking abilities for careers; specialized vocab to aid bicentennial foreign visitors in such situations as hotels, restaurants, hospitals; 12-c,d,e,g; 13-a,b,d,f; 14-ng.

491. SPANISH FOR THE PROFESSIONS
Austin C; ML; Sherman TX 75090.
Juliette C. McClendon
1-new course; 2-4x14; 3-a; 4-75; 5-ng; 6-b; 7-a; 8-4s; 9-a; 10-basic Sp; 11-designed to prepare professional person to deal with Sp-speaking clientele in Southwest; specific vocab and situation dialogs plus some reading of periodicals; 12-b,c,d,e,g; 13-a,b,c,d,e; 14-series by Antonio Carbajo for various fields.

492. CONTEMPORARY URBAN SPANISH
Baldwin-Wallace C; FLs & Lits; Berea, OH 44017.
Marguerite A. Klooz, John R. Sinnema
1-14; 2-5x11; 3-a; 4-73; 5-2; 6-b; 7-a; 8-5q; 9-a; 10-elem prof; 11 introduces the values, mores, lang, soci issues of Sp-speaking people of U.S.; 12-b,c,e,g; 13-a,b,c,d,e,f, visits to Sp-Amer groups; 14-Richard, Hispanoamerica moderna; Bomse & Alfaro, Practical Spanish for Social, Medical, & Educational Personnel.

493. BORDER SPANISH
Brigham Young U; Sp & Port; Provo, UT 84602.
J Halvor Clegg
1-25; 2-3x15; 3-a; 4-wtr 74; 5-1; 6-b; 7-a; 8-2; 9-a; 10-working knowledge of Sp; 11-ng; 12-a,b,g; 13-e; 14-ng.

494. SPANISH CONVERSATION PROFESSIONAL EMPHASIS - FOREIGN SERVICE
U of California; Sp & Port; Santa Barbara, CA 93106.
R. E. Wilson
1-16; 2-2x10; 3-a; 4-Jan 74; 5-2; 6-bq; 7-a; 8-2q; 9-a; 10-inter prof; 11-specialized vocab for situations likely to be encountered in U.S. Foreign Service abroad; discussion of responsibilities, & of political, econ, soci, & cult conditions of countries; 14-no text, current Sp newspapers, magazines, & govt publications read & discussed.

495. SPANISH FOR PROFESSIONALS
California SU; FLs & Lits; Fullerton, CA 92634.
J. Kiraithe, M. Diaz
1-new; 2-3x15; 3-a; 4-spr 75; 5-0; 6-on demand; 7-b; 8-3s; 9-ng; 10-none; 11-vocab oriented toward the specific group; 12-b,g; 13-ng; 14-ng.

496. CULTURAL ASPECTS OF SPANISH & ENGLISH
California SU; Sp & Port; Long Beach, CA 90840.
Beverly J. DeLong-Tonelli
1-new; 2-2x15; 3-a; 4-spr 75; 5-none; 6-b; 7-a; 8-2s; 9-a; 10-inter prof; 11-cult bases of colloquial speech (idioms, refrains, proverbs, common comparisons, and formulaic expressions, correspondence, telephone, classroom interview behavior) in the two langs; 12-a,b,c,f; 13-materials compiled by instructor; 14-Sapir, Culture, Language and Personality; Harvard & Ariza, Bilingual Guide to Business and Professional Correspondence; Gooch, Diminutive, Augmentation Prejorative Suffixes in Modern Spanish.

497. SPANISH FOR CAREER DEVELOPMENT
Carlow C; ML; Pittsburgh, PA 15213.
Marie I. Dana
1-5; 2-4x8; 3-a; 4-74; 5-2; 6-b; 7-a; 8-2s; 9-a; 10-elem prof; 11-program which includes following courses: Sp for Health Professions; Sp for Soci Scis; Sp for Art and Lit; Sp for Bus; 12-b,c,g; 13-b,e,f; 14-Espana en el Siglo.

498. PRACTICAL SPANISH
DePaul U; MLs; Chicago, IL 60614.
W. V. Hoffman
1-new; 2-6x5; 3-a; 4-smr 75; 5-ng; 6-b; 7-b; 8-4; 9-ng; 10-none; 11-for law, bus, travel; 12-b,c,d,f; 13-d,c; 14-no text.

499. SPANISH FOR TV AND RADIO BROADCASTS
Federal City C; FLs; Washington, DC 20001.
1-new course; 2-ng; 3-a; 4-ng; 5-0; 6-ng; 7-ng; 8-3q; 9-ng; 10-inter prof; 11-diction, pronunciation, intonation for students majoring in communication; 12-a,c,f,g; 13-d,e,f; 14-ng.

500. URBAN STUDIES WITH AN EMPHASIS IN SPANISH
Jackson SC; MFLs; Jackson, MS 39217.
Sarah Banks
1-ng; 2-ng; 3-b; 4-75/76; 5-0; 6-a; 7-a; 8-up to 16 q hrs; 9-a,b; 10-ng; 11-prepares urban affairs majors to deal w/Sp speaking living in urban areas; 12-a,b,c,d,e,f,g; 13-a,b,c,d,e,f; 14-ng.

501. SPANISH FOR RECREATION LEADERSHIP
Kingsborough CC; FL; Brooklyn, NY 11235.
Julio Hernandez-Miyores
1-20; 2-3x15; 3-a; 4-74; 5-2; 6-a; 7-a; 8-3s; 9-a; 10-none; 11-ng; 12-b,e,g; 13-c,d, textbook, workbook; 14-text & workbook being developed by Julio Hernandez-Miyores & Elio Alba.

502. SPANISH FOR CAREERS
Manhattanville C; Sp; Purchase, NY 10577.
Marta de la Portilla
1-12; 2-2 hrs each wk of sem; 3-b,c; 4-spr 75; 6-b; 7-a; 8-3s; 9-a, outside students; 10-adv prof; 11-specific vocab for professional use, phonetics, composition of appropriate letters; 12-b,c,g; 13-d,e,f; 14-Business Letter Handbook; Spanish for Hospital Personnel.

503. M.A. IN HISPANIC BILINGUAL-BICUL-
TURAL STUDIES
U of Massachusetts; Sp & Port; Amherst,
MA 01002.
Juan C. Zamora
1-11; 2-ng; 3-a or b; 4-73; 5-ng; 6-ng; 7-ng;
8-ng; 9-a,b; 10-B.A. or B.S. in related area,
fluency in Sp & Eng; 11-professional objectives of the students vary: teaching, research, soci studies, soci work, administration; program has structured core & specified electives; student may take electives
in many other fields. One third of the total
credits toward the MA fall within this last
category.

504. CONVERSATIONAL SPANISH FOR PRO-
FESSIONAL PEOPLE
Modesto JC; Lit & Lang Arts; Modesto, CA
95350.
Lowell A. Draper
1-35; 2-3x18; 3-a; 4-ng; 5-ng; 6-ng; 7-b; 8-b;
9-part-time students; 10-none; 11-designed
to teach spoken lang with emphasis on
special vocab needs of bus & professional
occupations; 12-a,b,d,e,g; 13-d, dialogues,
questionnaires; 14-Garcia, Hablemos en
Espanol; English-Spanish Glossary for
Health Aides.

505. INTRODUCTION TO SPANISH AND
SPANISH-AMERICAN LITERATURE AND
CIVILIZATION
Mount Vernon C; Sp; Washington, DC
20007.
Maria F. Carroll
A course in Eng designed to prepare profes-
sionals and paraprofessionals culturally to
work with Sp-speaking people. Course
approved, not yet scheduled.

506. PRACTICAL SPANISH FOR SPECIFIC
CAREER USE
Mount Vernon C; Sp; Washington, DC
20007.
Maria F. Carroll
1-new; 2-6x6; 3-a; 4-75/76; 5-0; 6-b; 7-a; 8-
3q; 9-a,b; 10-inter prof; 11-preparation of
professionals, paraprofessionals in fields of
public affairs, govt, childhood, bus administration, visual arts; 12-b,c,e,g; 13-ng; 14-
ng.

507. PROFESSIONAL SPANISH
U of New Mexico; Mod & Cl Langs;
Albuquerque, NM 87131.
Leon Marquez
1-7; 2-3x2 sems; 3-a; 4-74; 5-2; 6-on demand; 7-a; 8-3s; 9-a, faculty, staff; 10-ng;
11-intensive course for overseas field re-
searchers, emphasis on specialized professional vocab; 12-a,b,c,g; 13-ng; 14-Leavitt
& Stoudemire, Concise Spanish Grammar.

508. CAREER-RELATED SPANISH
SUCNY; FLs & Lit; Plattsburgh, NY 12901.
Craig L. Sample
Will be offered 75/76; other info ng.

509. INTENSIVE EXPERIENCE IN BEGINNING
SPANISH AND CULTURE

Rosary Hill C; MFL; Buffalo, NY 14226.
L. Aranibar Merrill
1-10; 2-3x10; 3-a; 4-Jan 72; 5-4; 6-on demand; 7-b; 8-b; 9-b, those needing Sp in
their professions; 10-none; 11-vocab
pertaining to different professions; 12-
b,f,g; 13-native speakers; 14-mimeo-
graphed materials.

510. ADVANCED SPANISH FOR THE SOCIAL
SCIENCES & HUMANITIES
St. Olaf C; Rom Langs; Northfield, MN
55057.
Frank Odd
1-2; 2-3x14; 3-a; 4-72/73; 5-3; 6-b; 7-a; 8-
3.5s; 9-a; 10-inter prof; 11-develop the
ability to read, write & discuss non-lit
topics in Sp on adv level of ling difficulty;
text drawn from press & pertinent journals
& books; 12-b,c,g; 13-e,f; 14-none.

511. CARIBBEAN SPANISH
Simmons C; FLs & Lits; Boston, MA 02115.
Mary Jane Treacy
1-12; 2-4x13; 3-a; 4-73; 5-5; 6-a; 7-a; 8-4s;
9-a; 10-elem prof; 11-vocab, grammar,
reading of popular Puerto Rican & Cuban
magazines, newspapers, short stories; study
of Caribbean speech patterns & vocab, for
those planning to work w/Sp speakers;
emphasis on cult differences; 12-a,b,c,g;
13-d,e,f; 14-various.

512. ORAL EXPRESSION, READING, & COM-
POSITION
U of Texas; Sp & Port; Austin, TX 78712.
Phyllis Harmon
1-24; 1-3x14; 3-a; 4-fall 72; 5-5; 6-a; 7-a; 8-
3s; 9-a; 10-inter prof; permission of in-
structor; 11-ng; 12-a,b,c,f,g; 13-a,b,d,e,f,
posters, special guest lecturers; 14-Iriarte,
Tres Telecomedias de Espana; Duran &
Duran Vivir Hoy.

513. MILITARY READINGS IN SPANISH
U.S. Military Academy; FLs; West Point,
NY 10996.
Sumner Willard
1-28; 2-2½x16; 3-a; 4-69; 5-54; 6-b; 7-a; 8-
2½s; 9-a; 10-inter prof; 11-discussion &
reading of guerilla warfare; classic survey
of military history & roles of Sp Amer
armies, practical drills; 12-a,b,c,d,g; 13-
a,b,c,d,e,f; 14-Guevara, Abra revoluciona-
ria; USMA, Lecturas militares; USMA,
Military Situations.

See also 649, 660, 763.

MULTI-LANGUAGE

514. INTERDISCIPLINARY PROGRAMS
Providence C; MLs; Providence, RI 02918.
Program permits students to coordinate &
integrate their program of study in MLs
with courses offered by related disciplines.
Preparation for a career in biling ed is also
available. Further info ng.

See also 974.

188

Tourism

CHINESE

515. MANDARIN FOR TRAVELERS
Rockland CC; FLs & Lits; Suffern, NY 10901.
Norman D. Arbaiza
Non-credit course; meets once or twice a wk for 10 wks; on demand, may be offered to fit the needs of a particular interest group; further info ng.

516. CHINESE FOR TRAVELERS
Santa Rosa JC; FLs; Santa Rosa, CA 95401.
Ruth Parle Craig
1-50 plus; 2-3x17, 2 sems; 3-a,c; 4-73; 5-2; 6-yr course offered every yr; 7-b; 8-3s per sem; 9-a,b, adults from community; 10-first sem none; second sem elem prof; 11-emphasis on travel lang and cult experiences; audiolingual approach with some reading and writing; 12-c,e,f,g; 13-a,b,d,e,f, foods; 14-de Francis; instructor-prepared materials.

DANISH

517. CONVERSATIONAL DANISH FOR TRAVELERS
CC of Baltimore; Eng & FLs; Baltimore, MD 21215.
Edward I. Meyers
1-15; 2-2x6; 3-a; 4-73; 5-1; 6-sufficient enrollment (10); 7-b; 8-1q; 9-b; 10-none; 11-ng; 12-a,b,f; 13-d,e; 14-Berlitz, Danish for Travel.

FRENCH

Texts used (#14):
a. Amado, En France Comme Si Vous y Etiez
b. Berlitz, French for Travelers
c. ---, Interpret Francais
d. Cohen, Say It in French
e. Kany & Dondo, Spoken French for Students and Travelers

518. CONVERSATIONAL FRENCH
Amarillo C; Cont Ed; Amarillo, TX 79178.
Charles Gaither
1-25; 2-2x10; 3-c; 4-70; 5-10; 6-a, special groups; 7-b; 8-0; 9-b; 10-none; 11-basic conv lang; 12-a,b,d,f; 13-ng; 14-Look and Learn French.

519. CONVERSATIONAL FRENCH
Augusta C; MLs; Augusta, GA 39094.
Thomas Riley, Cont Ed
1-12; 2-1½x10; 3-a; 4-70; 5-ng; 6-a; 7-a; 8-0; 9-b; 10-none; 11-basic vocab for travelers; 12-b,d,e,g; 13-d; 14-instructor-prepared text, Je me debrouille.

520. FRENCH FOR THE TOURIST
Austin C; Cont Ed; Sherman, TX 75090.
Ted Vestal
1-10; 2-1½x12; 3-a; 4-74; 5-1; 6-a; 7-b; 8-0; 9-community adults; 10-none; 11-conv approach, essential phrases for travel and communication; 12-a,b,e,f,g; 13-a,b,d; 14-none.

521. CONVERSATIONAL FRENCH FOR TRAVELLERS
CC of Baltimore; Eng & FLs; Baltimore, MD 21215.
Edward I. Meyers
1-20; 2-2x6; 3-a; 4-73; 5-2; 6-sufficient enrollment (10); 7-b; 8-1q; 9-b; 10-none; 11-ng; 12-a,b,f; 13-d,e; 14-b.

522. FRENCH FOR TRAVELLERS
Barry C; FLs; Miami, FL 33161.
Carroll Naves
1-10; 2-2x16; 3-a; 4-74; 5-2; 6-irregularly; 7-a; 8-0 or 1, depending on written work; 9-a, part time, staff; 10-none; 11-mostly oral work; 12-b,c,g; 13-a,b,d; 14-e.

523. FRENCH FOR TOURISTS
Bergen CC; FLs; Paramus, NJ 07652.
Further info not available.

524. FRENCH FOR TRAVEL
Bloomsburg SC; FLs; Bloomsburg, PA 17815.
A. Foureman
1-new; 2-4x5; 3-a; 4-spr 75; 5-1; 6-ng; 7-b; 8-b; 9-a,b, community; 10-none; 11-ng; 12-c,d,e,f,g; 13-a,b,c,d; 14-Quenelle, La France dans votre poche; Garnier, French-English Conversation; la France, Informations touristiques; Michand, Guide France.

525. FRENCH FOR TRAVELERS
Cabrillo C; Fr; Aptos, CA 95003.
Bette Silverblatt
1-25; 2-3x15; 3-c; 4-70; 5-4; 6-varies; 7-b; 8-0; 9-b; 10-none; 11-conv; 12-b,g; 13-ng; 14-a.

526. FRENCH LANGUAGE WORKSHOP FOR TRAVELERS
California SU; FLs and Lits; Northridge, CA 91324.
Maja Reid
1-c100; 2-8x2; 3-a; 4-71; 5-5; 6-a; 7-2 consecutive Sats; 8-1s; 9-ng; 10-none; 11-lang needs of persons traveling abroad; 12-b,g; 13-b,d; 14-instructor's own materials.

527. FRENCH FOR TRAVELERS
Catonsville CC; FLs; Catonsville, MD 21228.

Marcelle J. Von Mayer, Enrique Corzo
1-15/20; 2-2x15; 3-a; 4-71; 5-c9; 6-a; 7-b
mostly; 8-b; 9-b, sr citizens, businessmen;
10-none; 11-conv Fr; 12-a,b,c,d,g; 13-
a,b,c,d,e, transparencies, filmstrips; 14-in-
structor-prepared materials.

528. FRENCH FOR TRAVELERS
Centenary C of Louisiana; FLs; Shreveport,
LA 71104.
R. Johnson Watts
1-new; 2-3x6; 3-c; 4-75/76; 5-0; 6-ng; 7-b;
8-0; 9-b; 10-none; 11-basic patterns and
vocab; 12-e,f,g; 13-a,b,d,e,f; 14-materials
being developed.

529. MINI-FRENCH WORKSHOP
Central SU; FLs; Edmond, OK 73034.
Mildred H. Lyon
1-c12; 2-20x3; 3-a; 4-74; 5-1; 6-smr; 7-a; 8-
3s; 9-a, teachers, special interest students;
10-none; 11-basic vocab, basic grammar
constructions, skits, dialogues, cult units,
lab exercises; 12-a,b,c,d,e,g; 13-a,b,c,d,e,f,
realia; 14-provided by dept.

530. FRENCH FOR TRAVELERS
Clarke C; Fr; Dubuque, IA 52001.
Raymond K. Binder
1-6; 2-2x6; 3-a; 4-spr 74; 5-1; 6-probably
not again; 7-b; 8-1s; 9-b; 10-none; 11-words
and phrases useful to travelers; emphasis
oral, some writing; 12-b,f; 13-b; 14-a.

531. FRENCH FOR TRAVELERS
Curry C; Lang & Lit; Milton, MA 02186.
Frances M. Kohak
Further info not available.

532. FRENCH FOR TRAVELERS
East Central Oklahoma SU; FLs; Ada, OK
74820.
Nancy Shew
1-11; 2-2x9; 3-a; 4-74; 5-1; 6-yearly; 7-b; 8-
0; 9-adults in community; 10-none; 11-ng;
12-d,f; 13-a,b,d, maps, records; 14-various;
Living French (with record); guides to
France; b; c.

533. FRENCH FOR TRAVELERS
Foothill C; Lang Arts; Los Altos Hills, CA
94022.
Nayan McNeill
1-43; 2-3x11; 3-a; 4-74; 5-3; 6-a evenings, b
days; 7-a,b; 8-2q; 9-a, community; 10-none;
11-conv, reading, listening; 12-a,b,d,e,f,g;
13-d,f; 14-a; Resnick, Essential French
Grammar.

534. CONVERSATIONAL FRENCH
Harrisburg Area CC; Urban Devel Inst;
Harrisburg, PA 17110.
Hazel J. Brown
1-19; 2-3x6; 3-b; 4-74; 5-2; 6-a; 7-b; 8-0; 9-
b; 10-none; 11-for the traveler; emphasis on
expressing basic thoughts with correct pronunciation; reading a phrase book; 12-a,b,f;
13-a,b,e,f; 14-Berlitz, Self Teacher in
French.

535. FRENCH FOR FUN
Kent SU; Rom Langs & Cl; Kent, OH 44242.
Mark R. Rubin

1-10; 2-2x10; 3-a; 4-spr 73; 5-3; 6-a; 7-b; 8-
0; 9-general public; 10-none; 11-basic
vocab and grammar; 12-b,f,g, drill; 13-
a,b,e,f, games, mimeo materials; 14-none.

536. FRENCH FOR TRAVEL
Loyola U; ML Div; Chicago, IL 60626.
Andrew McKenna
Offered fall 74; other info not available.

537. FRENCH FOR TRAVELERS
Mansfield SC; FLs; Mansfield, PA 16933.
Brigitte Callay
1-17; 2-1/2/3x15; 3-a; 4-74; 5-2; 6-a; 7-a; 8-
variable 1/2/3s; 9-a,b; 10-inter prof; 11-ng;
12-b,c,d,g; 13-a,b,d,e,f; 14-ng.

538. FRENCH FOR TRAVELERS
Marymount C; FLs; Salina, KS 67401.
Francis Ellen Riordan
1-9; 2-2x10; 3-a; 4-74; 5-1; 6-irregularly; 7-
b; 8-0; 9-a,b; 10-none; 11-situations, conv
phrases; 12-e,g; 13-d,e, records; 14-a.

539. FRENCH FOR TRAVEL
Memphis SU; FLs; Memphis, TN 38152.
Frank Brantley
1-10; 2-2 or 3x11; 3-c; 4-68; 5-8; 6-b; 7-b; 8-
0; 9-b; 10-none; 11-practical course to assist travelers; 12-a,e; 13-d,e,f; 14-varies.

540. FRENCH FOR TRAVELERS
Molloy C; Fr; Rockville Center, NY 11570.
Pickman Gertz
1-25; 2-3x14; 3-a; 4-spr 74; 5-1; 6-b; 7-a; 8-
3s; 9-a,b,c; 10-none; 11-material needed
for travel in France; intro to cult; 12-f,g;
13-b, records, songs; 14-a.

541. PRACTICAL FRENCH CONVERSATION
U of Nebraska; FLs; Omaha, NE 68101.
Woodrow L. Most
1-20; 2-2x15; 3-part-time instructors; 4-71;
5-each sem; 6-a; 7-b; 8-2s, students are
encouraged to use Cr/NCr option; 9-a,
faculty, townspeople; 10-none; 11-pronun-
ciation and oral practice in everyday situations; no formal grammar; most take the
course in preparation for travel abroad; 12-
b,g, repetition, question-answer; 13-d; 14-
Madrigal, See It and Say It in French; b.

542. FRENCH FOR TRAVELERS
Neosho County CC; Sp & Fr; Chanute, KS
66720.
Dean of Instruction
1-6; 2-1x9; 3-a; 4-smr 74; 5-3; 6-a; 7-a,b; 8-
1s; 9-adults; 10-none; 11-pronunciation and
use of phrase book; 12-a,b,f,g; 13-d, song
manual; 14-Gossett, Phrase Book/Diction-
ary.

543. CONVERSATIONAL FRENCH
SUCNY; FLs & Lit; Plattsburgh, NY 12901.
Intended to develop shopping, bus, and rest-
aurant-directed skills; further info not
available.

544. FRENCH FOR BUSINESS & TRAVELERS
Notre Dame C; Fr; Manchester, NH 03104.
Frances Lessard
1-9; 2-2x14; 3-a; 4-73/74; 5-6a; 7-b; 8-4s,b;
9-a, Marine Corps personnel; 10-none; 11-
emphasis on conv, study of current vocab;

190

12-c,e,g; 13-a,b,c,d,f; 14-Cadoux, <u>Vous et Moi</u>.

545. FRENCH FOR TRAVELERS
Raymond Walters C; FL; Cincinnati, OH 45236.
Judith A. Baughin, Dorothy Wartenberg
1-15; 2-2x6; 3-b; 4-74; 5-1; 6-b; 7-b; 8-0; 9-b; 10-none; 11-basic phrases and sentences; questions and answers; info about the Fr and their customs; 12-b,d,e,g; 13-b,d,e,f; 14-b; locally-developed materials.

546. FRENCH FOR PRACTICAL COMMUNI-CATION
Salisbury SC; ML; Salisbury, MD 21801.
John R. Knowles
1-27; 2-3x15; 3-a; 4-73; 5-1; 6-b; 7-b; 8-3s; 9-anyone; 10-none; 11-situational lang for the traveler, businessman, elem educator, music major, soci worker; 12-a,b,d,e,f,g; 13-a,b,d, records; 14-<u>Practical French for Communication</u>; b; d.

547. FRENCH FOR THE BON VIVANT TRAVELER
Sam Houston SU; FLs; Huntsville, TX 77340.
Mary Gutermuth
1-new; 2-3x12; 3-a; 4-75; 5-1; 6-unknown; 7-b; 8-0; 9-b; 10-none; 11-basic conv skills developed through actual use in simulated situations; 12-d,g; 13-a,b; 14-none.

548. TRAVEL COURSE IN FRENCH
San Bernardino Valley C; FL; San Bernardino, CA 92403.
Judith Davis
1-ng; 2-3x17; 3-c; 4-70; 5-10; 6-a; 7-b; 8-3s; 9-a, community; 10-none; 11-general info, key phrases; 12-f,g; 13-a,b; 14-<u>Passport to French.</u>

549. SURVIVAL FRENCH
C of San Mateo; FL; San Mateo, CA 94402.
Rosa Sausjord
Six-wk course for travelers; further info not available.

550. FRENCH FOR TRAVELERS
Santa Ana C; FLs; Santa Ana, CA 92706.
Neil Benner, Bertha Detlof, Lyle Johnson
135; 22x18; 3a; 473/74; 54; 6a; 7-b; 8-2s; 9-a,b, part-time; 10-none; 11-conv approach; basic vocab and terminology; sound system; everyday expressions, useful phrases and expressions in travel situations; 12-a,b,c,e,f; 13-a,b,d,e,f, speakers; 14-<u>Living French</u>; various other materials.

551. FRENCH FOR TRAVELERS
Santa Rosa JC; FLs; Santa Rosa, CA 95401.
Ruth Parle Craig
1-50 plus; 2-3x17 2 sems; 3-a,c; 4-65; 5-10; 6-yr course offered every yr; 7-a,b; 8-3s per sem; 9-a,b, community; 10-first sem none; second sem elem prof; 11-travel lang and cult , audiolingual approach with some reading and writing; 12-c,e,f,g; 13-a,b,d,e,f, food; 14-Lovy, <u>Silhouettes de France</u>; e.

552. FRENCH FOR AMERICAN TRAVELERS

Schoolcraft C; Community Services; Livonia, MI 48151.
Ron Griffith
1-30; 2-2x8; 3-b; 4-71; 5-4; 6-a; 7-b; 8-0; 9-b; 10-none; 11-differences in cult, working knowledge of the most important basic experiences in the lang; 12-a,b,c,g; 13-a,b; 14-b.

553. FRENCH FOR TRAVELERS
Slippery Rock SC; MLs; Slippery Rock, PA 16057.
Charles Tichy
1-ng; 2-5x8; 3-a; 4-smr 74; 5-1; 6-every other smr; 7-b; 8-0; 9-community; 10-none; 11-usage and pronunciation of the phrases most needed; 12-a,f,g; 13-a,b,e; 14-b.

554. FRENCH FOR FAMILIES
U of Southern Mississippi; FLs; Hattiesburg, MS 39401.
Elizabeth Anglin
1-8; 2-2x6; 3-a; 4-72; 5-2; 6-b; 7-b; 8-0; 9-community; 10-none; 11-oral lang; 12-b,d,f; 13-a,c, posters; 14-none.

555. FRENCH FOR TRAVELERS
U of Southwestern Louisiana; FL; Lafayette, LA 70501.
Richard E. Chandler
1-12; 2-3x16; 3-a; 4-fall 74; 5-1; 6-on request; 7-b; 8-0; 9-thru univ college for C.E. units; 10-none; 11-practical conv approach; 12-a,b; 13-ng; 14-Brown, <u>French</u>; instructor-made materials.

556. FRENCH FOR TOURISTS
Spalding C; Hums; Louisville, KY 40203.
M. Janice Murphy
1-12; 2-1x10; 3-c; 4-73/74; 5-4; 6-a; 7-b; 8-0; 9-b; 10-none; 11-spoken lang and vocab; hist and cult noted; 12-b,f,g; 13-a,b; 14-none.

557. FRENCH FOR TOURISTS
Virginia Commonwealth U; FLs; Richmond, VA 23284.
William J. Beck
1-13; 2-2x10; 3-a, adjunct faculty; 4-71; 5-4; 6-a; 7-b; 8-0; 9-adults; 10-none; 11-ng; 12-a,g; 13-a,b; 14-b.

558. CONVERSATIONAL FRENCH
Walla Walla C; ML; College Place, WA 99324.
George L. Caviness
1-12; 2-2x10; 3-a; 4-73/74; 5-1; 6-b; 7-b; 8-2q; 9-b; 10-none; 11-intended for tourists or those interested only in the spoken lang; 12-e,g; 13-d; 14-mimeoed materials.

559. FRENCH CONVERSATION
Westchester CC; MLs; Valhalla, NY 10595.
Jacqueline Rosay
1-ng; 2-2x8; 3-a; 4-73; 5-4; 6-a; 7-Sats; 8-0; 9-b; community; 10-none; 11-special section for those with background in the lang; 12-g; 13-a,b,d,e; 14-materials prepared by instructors.

560. CONVERSATIONAL FRENCH FOR TRAVELERS

Westfield SC; FLs; Westfield, MA 01085.
Raymond Ourand
1-6; 2-3 for two sems; 3-a; 4-73/74; 5-2; 6-student response; 7-b (smr); 8-6s for two sems; 9-b, part-time; 10-none; 11-basic conv patterns, especially those needed by a tourist; 12-b,e,g; 13-a,b; 14-Mondelli, Conversational French One.

561. SPOKEN FRENCH FOR TOURISTS
William Paterson C; FLs; Wayne, NJ 07470.
Catherine A. Barry
1-7; 2-9x4; 3-a; 4-73; 5-1; 6-b; 7-b; 8-3s; 9-a,b; 10-none; 11-intro to France, its people, and tourist attractions; pronunciation; conv; 12-a,b,c,f,g; 13-a,b,d; 14-Larousse, Le Francais accelere.

562. FRENCH FOR TRAVELERS
U of Wisconsin; FLs, Extension Services; Eau Claire, WI 54701.
Edith O'Connor
1-ng; 2-2x10; 3-a; 4-73/74; 5-2; 6-b; 7-b; 8-0; 9-a, townspeople; 10-none; 11-lang instruction, civ; review, application, practice; 12-f; 13-a,b,d,e,f, native informants; 14-Madrigal, Open Door to French.

See also 186, 195, 196, 478, 717, 776, 777, 778, 779.

GERMAN

Texts used (#14):
a. Berlitz, German for Travelers
b. Schneider, Guten Tag: A German Language Course for Television

563. CONVERSATIONAL GERMAN
Amarillo C; Cont Ed; Amarillo, TX 79178.
Charles Gaither
1-16; 2-2x10; 3-c; 4-71; 5-7; 6-a; 7-b; 8-0; 9-b; 10-none; 11-basic conv lang; 12-a,b,f; 13-ng; 14-none.

564. CONVERSATIONAL GERMAN
Augusta C; MLs; Augusta, GA 39094.
Thomas Riley, Cont Ed
1-8; 2-1½x10; 3-b; 4-72; 5-3; 6-b; 7-b; 8-0; 9-b; 10-none; 11-basic conv for travelers; 12-b,d,e,g; 13-d; 14-material prepared by instructor.

565. GERMAN FOR THE TOURIST
Austin C; Cont Ed; Sherman, TX 75090.
Ted Vestal
1-10; 2-1½x12; 3-a; 4-74; 5-1; 6-a; 7-b; 8-0; 9-community; 10-none; 11-conv approach to learning essential phrases for travel; 12-a,b,e,f,g; 13-a,b,d; 14-none.

566. BASIC CONVERSATIONAL GERMAN FOR TRAVELERS
Ball SU; FLs; Muncie, IN 47306.
Robert S. Sears
1-25; 2-2x11; 3-a; 4-72/73; 5-4; 6-2qs a yr; 7-b; 8-2q; 9-a,b; 10-none; 11-beginning spoken Ger for travelers or those seeking employment in Germany; intro to pronunciation, basic vocab and expressions, elem structures; 12-a,b,e,g; 13-a; 14-Braun, Deutsch als Femdsprache, I.

567. GERMAN FOR TOURISTS

Bergen CC; FLs; Paramus, NJ 07652.
Further info not available.

568. GERMAN FOR TRAVELERS
Bethany C; FL; Bethany, WV 26032.
Leonora B. Cayard
1-13; 2-4x7½; 3-a; 4-72; 5-1; 6-infrequently; 7-a; 8-2s; 9-a,b; 10-none; 11-intensive conv intended for students planning to travel; 12-e,f,g, drill; 13-a,b; 14-a.

569. GERMAN LANGUAGE WORKSHOP FOR TRAVELERS
California SU; FLs and Lits; Northridge, CA 91324.
Maja Reid
1-c100; 2-8x2; 3-a; 4-71; 5-5; 6-a; 7-2 consecutive Sats; 8-1s; 9-ng; 10-none; 11-lang needs of persons traveling abroad; 12-b,g; 13-b,d; 14-instructor's materials.

570. GERMAN FOR TRAVELERS
Catonsville CC; FLs; Catonsville, MD 21228.
Marcelle J. Von Mayer, Enrique Corzo
1-15/20; 2-2x15; 3-a; 4-71; 5-c9; 6-a; 7-b mostly; 8-b; 9-b, sr citizens, businessmen; 10-none; 11-conv Ger; 12-a,b,c,d,g; 13-a,b,c,d,e, transparencies, filmstrips; 14-instructor-prepared materials.

571. GERMAN FOR TRAVELERS
Centenary C of Louisiana; FLs; Shreveport, LA 71104.
R. Johnson Watts
1-new; 2-3x6; 3-c; 4-75/76; 5-0; 6-ng; 7-b; 8-0; 9-b; 10-none; 11-basic patterns and vocab; 12-e,f,g; 13-a,b,d,e,f; 14-materials being developed.

572. GERMAN FOR TRAVELERS
Eastern Montana C; Langs; Billings, MT 59101.
Maurice M. Heidinger
1-5; 2-2x10; 3-a; 4-74; 5-1; 6-sufficient demand; 7-b; 8-2q; 9-a, part-time adults; 10-none; 11-survival course in learning to cope in Ger with basic life situations; 12-a,b,f,g; 13-a; 14-Bertin, Passport to German.

573. GERMAN FOR TRAVELERS
Foothill C; Lang Arts; Los Altos Hills, CA 94022.
Nayan McNeill
1-ng; 2-3x11; 3-a; 4-74; 5-3; 6-a evenings, b days; 7-a,b; 8-2q; 9-a, community; 10-none; 11-conv, reading, listening; 12-a,b,d,e,f,g; 13-d,f; 14-a; b.

574. GERMAN FOR TRAVEL
Indiana U; Ger; Bloomington, IN 47401.
Sidney M. Johnson
1-9; 2-4x6; 3-c; 4-73; 5-3; 6-b; 7-b; 8-0; 9-b; 10-none; 11-spoken lang and contemporary cult; 12-a,b,f,g; 13-a; 14-b, worksheets based on films.

575. BASIC GERMAN FOR TOURISTS
Madison C; FLs; Harrisonburg, VA 22801.
John G. Stewart
1-20; 2-2x7; 3-a; 4-spr 73; 5-1; 6-on de-

mand; 7-b; 8-0; 9-a,b; 10-none; 11-contemporary spoken Ger in everyday situations; conv, sentence patterns, simple readings, cult of the Ger-speaking countries; 12-e,g; 13-a,b; 14-b.

576. GERMAN FOR TRAVEL
Memphis SU; FLs; Memphis, TN 38152.
Frank Brantley
1-c10; 2-2 or 3x11; 3-c; 4-68; 5-8; 6-b; 7-b; 8-0; 9-b; 10-none; 11-practical course to assist travellers abroad; 12-a,e; 13-d,e,f; 14-varies.

577. PRACTICAL GERMAN CONVERSATION
U of Nebraska; FLs; Omaha, NE 68101.
Woodrow L. Most
1-20; 2-2x15; 3-c; 4-71; 5-each sem; 6-a; 7-b; 8-2s; students encouraged to use Cr/NCr option; 9-a, faculty, townspeople; 10-none; 11-pronunciation and oral practice, no formal grammar; most take course in preparation for travel abroad; 12-b,g, repetition and question-answer; 13-d; 14-Madrigal & Halpert, See It and Say It in German.

578. GERMAN FOR TRAVELERS
SUNY; Credit-Free Program; Buffalo, NY 14214.
Phyllis D. Sigel
1-9; 2-3x15; 3-ng; 4-72; 5-2; 6-sufficient registration; 7-b; 8-0; 9-community; 10-none; 11-enable the traveler to communicate in situations likely to be encountered abroad; 12-ng; 13-ng; 14-a; Shaw, Focus on German for Beginners.

579. CONVERSATIONAL GERMAN
North Hennepin CC; FL; Brooklyn Park, MN 55445.
Barbara K. Mantini
1-ng; 2-2x8; 3-ng; 4-75; 5-2; 6-ng; 7-b; 8-0; 9-ng; 10-none; 11-practical vocab for everyday situations encountered while traveling; cult and geography; 12-e; 13-b,d, maps, records; 14-ng.

580. TRAVEL COURSE IN GERMAN
San Bernardino Valley C; FL; San Bernardino, CA 92403.
Judith Davis
1-ng; 2-3x17; 3-c; 4-70; 5-10; 6-a; 7-b; 8-3s; 9-a, community; 10-none; 11-general info, key phrases; 12-f,g; 13-a,b; 14-Passport to German.

581. SURVIVAL GERMAN
C of San Mateo; FL; San Mateo, CA 94402.
Rosa Sausjord
Six-wk course for travelers; further info not available.

582. GERMAN FOR TRAVELERS
Santa Rosa JC; FLs; Santa Rosa, CA 95401.
Ruth Parle Craig
1-50 plus; 2-3x17, 2 sems; 3-a,c; 4-66; 5-9; 6-yr course offered every yr; 7-a,b; 8-3s per sem; 9-a,b, community; 10-first sem none; second sem elem prof; 11-travel lang and cult experiences; audiolingual approach with some reading and writing; 12-c,e,f,g; 13-a,b,d,e,f, foods; 14-teacher-prepared material.

583. GERMAN FOR AMERICAN TRAVELERS
Schoolcraft C; Community Services; Livonia, MI 48151.
Ron Griffith
1-30; 2-2x8; 3-b; 4-71; 5-4; 6-a; 7-b; 8-0; 9-b; 10-none; 11-differences in cult; working knowledge of the most important vocab and phrases; 12-a,b,c,g; 13-a,b; 14-a.

584. GERMAN FOR TRAVELERS
Slippery Rock SC; MLs; Slippery Rock, PA 16057.
Charles Tichy
1-ng; 2-5x8; 3-a; 4-smr 74; 5-1; 6-alt smrs; 7-b; 8-0; 9-community; 10-none; 11-usage and pronunciation of the phrases most needed; 12-a,f,g; 13-a,b,e; 14-a.

585. GERMAN FOR TOURISTS
Spalding C; Hums; Louisville, KY 40203.
M. Janice Murphy
1-9; 2-1x10; 3-a; 4-73/74; 5-2; 6-a; 7-b; 8-0; 9-b; 10-none; 11-spoken lang and vocab for travel; hist and cult highlights; 12-b,f,g; 13-a,b; 14-none.

586. ADVANCED CONVERSATIONAL GERMAN FOR TRAVELERS
Tarrant County JC; MFL; Fort Worth, TX 76119.
Ernesto A. Guzman
1-ng; 2-4x6; 3-a; 4-74; 5-ng; 6-ng; 7-b; 8-ng; 9-ng; 10-some previous knowledge; 11-practical conv Ger, active vocab buildup through topics and situations; 12-a; 13-d; 14-Embarrassing Moments in German and How to Avoid Them; Kary, Spoken German for Students and Travelers.

587. GERMAN FOR TOURISTS
Virginia Commonwealth U; FLs; Richmond, VA 23284.
William J. Beck
1-8; 2-2x10; 3-adjunct faculty; 4-71; 5-4; 6-a; 7-b; 8-0; 9-adults; 10-none; 11-ng; 12-a,g; 13-a,b; 14-a.

588. CONVERSATIONAL GERMAN
Walla Walla C; MLs; College Place, WA 99324.
George L. Caviness
1-12; 2-2x10; 3-a; 4-73/74; 5-1; 6-b; 7-b; 8-2q; 9-b; 10-none; 11-intended for tourists or those interested only in the spoken lang; 12-e,g; 13-d; 14-mimeoed materials.

589. GERMAN CONVERSATION
Westchester CC; MLs; Valhalla, NY 10595.
Jacqueline Rosay
1-ng; 2-2x8; 3-a; 4-73; 5-4; 6-a; 7-Sats; 8-0; 9-b, community; 10-none; 11-special section for those with some background in the lang; 12-g; 13-a,b,d,e; 14-materials prepared by instructors.

590. CONVERSATIONAL GERMAN FOR TRAVELERS
Westfield SC; FLs; Westfield, MA 01085.
Raymond Ourand
1-10; 2-3 for two sems; 3-a; 4-73/74; 5-1; 6-student response; 7-b (smr); 8-6s for two sems; 9-b, part-time; 10-none 11-basic conv patterns; 12-b,e,g; 13-a,b; 14-Vail &

Sparks, Modern German.

591. GERMAN FOR TRAVELERS
U of Wisconsin; MLs; River Falls, WI 54022.
Erwin F. Ritter
1-10; 2-3x6/8; 3-a; 4-72/73; 5-2; 6-b; 7-b; 8-0; 9-a, community; 10-none; 11-ng; 12-a,d,e,f; 13-a,d; 14-Schulz et al, Deutsche Sprachlehre fuer Amerikaner; a; b.

See also 207, 726, 729, 734, 776, 777, 778.

GREEK

592. GREEK FOR TRAVELERS
Foothill C; Lang Arts; Los Altos Hills, CA 94022.
Nayan McNeill
1-new; 2-3x11; 3-a; 4-ng; 5-0; 6-a evenings, b days; 7-a,b; 8-2q; 9-a, community; 10-none; 11-conv, reading, listening; 12-a,b,d,e,f,g; 13-d,f; 14-ng.

593. TRAVEL COURSE IN GREEK
San Bernardino Valley C; FL; San Bernardino, CA 92403.
Judith Davis
1-ng; 2-3x17; 3-c; 4-70; 5-10; 6-a; 7-b; 8-3s; 9-a, community; 10-none; 11-general info, key phrases; 12-f,g; 13-a,b; 14-ng.

594. GREEK FOR TOURISTS
Virginia Commonwealth U; FLs; Richmond, VA 23284.
William J. Beck
1-5; 2-2x10; 3-a, adjunct faculty; 4-71; 5-4; 6-a; 7-b; 8-0; 9-adults; 10-none; 11-guided by text; 12-a,g; 13-a,b; 14-Berlitz tourist lang book.

HEBREW

595. HEBREW FOR TRAVELERS
Rockland CC; FLs & Lits; Suffern, NY 10901.
Norman D. Arbaiza
Non-credit course; meets once or twice a wk for 10 wks; may also be offered to fit the needs of a special-interest group; further info ng.

596. HEBREW FOR TOURISTS
Virginia Commonwealth U; FLs; Richmond, VA 23284.
William J. Beck
1-0; 2-2x10; 3-a, adjunct faculty; 4-71; 5-4; 6-a; 7-b; 8-0; 9-adults; 10-none; 11-guided by text; 12-a,g; 13-a,b; 14-Berlitz tourist lang book.

ITALIAN

Texts used (#14):
a. Berlitz, Italian for English Travelers

597. ITALIAN FOR TOURISTS
Bergen CC; FLs; Paramus, NJ 07652.
Further info not available.

598. ITALIAN FOR TRAVEL
Bloomsburg SC; FLs; Bloomsburg, PA 17815.
A. Foureman
1-new; 2-4x5; 3-a; 4-spr 75; 5-1; 6-ng; 7-b; 8-b; 9-a,b, community; 10-none; 11-ng; 12-c,d,e,f,g; 13-a,b,c,d; 14-ng.

599. ITALIAN LANGUAGE WORKSHOP FOR TRAVELERS
California SU; FLs and Lits; Northridge, CA 91324.
Maja Reid
1-c100; 2-8x2; 3-a; 4-71; 5-5; 6-a; 7-2 consecutive Sats; 8-1s; 9-ng; 10-none; 11-lang needs of persons traveling abroad; 12-b,g; 13-b,d; 14-instructor's materials.

600. ITALIAN FOR TRAVELERS
Catonsville CC; FLs; Catonsville, MD 21228.
Marcelle J. Von Mayer, Enrique Corzo
1-15/20; 2-2x15; 3-a; 4-71; 5-c9; 6-a; 7-b mostly; 8-b; 9-b, sr citizens, businessmen; 10-none; 11-conv Ital; 12-a,b,c,d,g; 13-a,b,c,d,e, transparencies, filmstrips; 14-instructor-prepared materials.

601. ITALIAN WITHOUT TEARS
Kent SU; Rom Langs & Cl; Kent, OH 44242.
Mark R. Rubin
1-6; 2-2x10; 3-a; 4-fall 73; 5-1; 6-on demand; 7-b; 8-0; 9-public; 10-none; 11-expressions, cult info, drill in basic vocab and grammar; 12-b,f,g, drill; 13-mimeoed materials; 14-none.

602. ITALIAN FOR TRAVELERS
Macomb County CC; Hums; Warren, MI 48093.
Irving Panush
1-30; 2-2x16; 3-a; 4-ng; 5-ng; 6-a; 7-b; 8-2s; 9-ng; 10-none; 11-structural treatment to acquaint student with functional vocab and useful expressions; 12-f,g; 13-c,d; 14-Cavagna, Lo Dica in Italiano.

603. ITALIAN FOR TOURISTS
Madison C; FLs; Harrisonburg, VA 22801.
James N. Conis
1-11; 2-1¼x10; 3-a; 4-fall 74; 5-1; 6-sufficient demand; 7-a; 8-0; 9-a,b; 10-none; 11-pronunciation, basic sentences and dialogues, grammatical orientation; 12-b,c,e,f; 13-d, records; 14-Bosco Lolli, Incontro con l'italiano; Living Italian; mimeo and ditto materials.

604. ITALIAN FOR TRAVEL
Memphis SU; FLs; Memphis, TN 38152.
Frank Brantley
1-c10; 2-2 or 3x11; 3-c; 4-68; 5-8; 6-b; 7-b; 8-0; 9-b; 10-none; 11-practical course to assist travellers abroad; 12-a,e; 13-d,e,f; 14-varies.

605. ITALIAN FOR TRAVELERS
Rockland CC; FLs & Lits; Suffern, NY 10901.
Norman D. Arbaiza
Non-credit course; meets once or twice a wk for 10 wks; on demand, may be offered to fit the needs of a special-interest group; further info ng.

606. TRAVEL COURSE IN ITALIAN
San Bernardino Valley C; FL; San Bernardino, CA 92403.

194

Judith Davis
1-ng; 2-3x17; 3-c; 4-70; 5-10; 6-a; 7-b; 8-3s;
9-a, community; 10-none; 11-general info,
key phrases; 12-f,g; 13-a,b; 14-Passport to
Italian.

607. ITALIAN FOR AMERICAN TRAVELERS
Schoolcraft C; Community Services;
Livonia, MI 48151.
Ron Griffith
1-30; 2-2x8; 3-b; 4-71; 5-4; 6-a; 7-b; 8-0; 9-
b; 10-none; 11-differences in cult; basic;
12-a,b,c,g; 13-a,b; 14-a.

608. ITALIAN FOR TRAVELERS
Slippery Rock SC; MLs; Slippery Rock, PA
16057.
Charles Tichy
1-ng; 2-5x8; 3-a; 4-smr 74; 5-1; 6-every
other smr; 7-b; 8-0; 9-community; 10-none;
11-usage and pronunciation of the phrases
most needed; 12-a,f,g; 13-a,b,e; 14-a.

609. ITALIAN FOR TOURISTS
Virginia Commonwealth U; FLs; Richmond,
VA 23284.
William J. Beck
1-12; 2-2x10; 3-adjunct faculty; 4-71; 5-4;
6-a; 7-b; 8-0; 9-adults; 10-none; 11-guided
by text; 12-a,g; 13-a,b; 14-a.

610. ITALIAN CONVERSATION
Westchester CC; MLs; Valhalla, NY 10595.
Jacqueline Rosay
1-ng; 2-2x8; 3-a; 4-73; 5-4; 6-a; 7-Sats; 8-0;
9-b, community; 10-none; 11-special section for those with some background in the
lang; 12-g; 13-a,b,d,e; 14-materials prepared by instructors.

See also 737, 739, 776.

JAPANESE

611. JAPANESE FOR TRAVELERS
Catonsville CC; FLs; Catonsville, MD
21228.
Marcelle J. Von Mayer, Enrique Corzo
1-15/20; 2-2x15; 3-a; 4-71; 5-c9; 6-a; 7-b
mostly; 8-b; 9-b, sr citizens, businessmen;
10-none; 11-conv Jap; 12-a,b,c,d,g; 13-
a,b,c,d,e, transparencies, filmstrips; 14-in-
structor-prepared materials.

611A. CONVERSATIONAL JAPANESE
Chaminade C; FL; Honolulu, HI 96816.
Eleanor Frierson
1-spr 75; 2-8x10; 3-c; 4-75; 5-1; 6-h; 7-b; 8-
4s for those taking it for credit; 9-a,b, part-
time evening; 10-none for elem level; 11-2-
level program emphasizing idiomatic
material for policemen, tourists & tourist
industry personnel; 12-c,e,g; 13-b,d, transparencies, charts; 14-Young & Nakaj, Learn
Japanese.

612. SHORT COURSE IN JAPANESE FOR
VISITORS
U of Colorado; Oriental Langs & Lits;
Boulder, CO 80302.
Robert Bruns, Bureau of Ed Media

1-new; 2-ng; 3-ng; 4-ng; 5-ng; 6-ng; 7-b; 8-
2s; 9-ng; 10-ng; 11-ng; 12-f; 13-a,b; 14-to
be determined.

613. JAPANESE FOR TRAVELERS
Foothill C; Lang Arts; Los Altos Hills, CA
94022.
Nayan McNeill
1-18; 2-5x11; 3-a; 4-74; 5-3; 6-a evenings, b
days; 7-a,b; 8-3q; 9-a, community; 10-none;
11-conv, reading, listening; 12-a,b,d,e,f,g;
13-d,f; 14-ng.

614. JAPANESE FOR TRAVELERS
Santa Rosa JC; FLs; Santa Rosa, CA 95401.
Ruth Parle Craig
1-50 plus; 2-3x17, 2 sems; 3-a,c; 4-73; 5-2;
6-yr course offered every yr; 7-b; 8-3s per
sem; 9-a,b, adults; 10-first sem none;
second sem elem prof; 11-emphasis on
travel lang and cult experiences;
audiolingual approach with some reading
and writing, oral reports; 12-c,e,f,g; 13-
a,b,d,e,f, foods; 14-teacher-prepared
material.

See also 219, 745, 776.

NORWEGIAN

615. CONVERSATIONAL NORWEGIAN
Indiana U; MFLs; Fort Wayne, IN 46805.
A. Dennis Mead
1-22; 2-2x12; 3-a; 4-73; 5-2; 6-b; 7-b; 8-0;
9-a,b; 10-none; 11-basis for those wanting
to travel; 12-a,b,f,g; 13-a,b; 14-Elementary
Norwegian Grammar, Syntax and Conversation.

616. CONVERSATIONAL NORWEGIAN
North Hennepin CC; FL; Brooklyn Park, MN
55445
Barbara K. Mantini
1-new; 2-2x8; 3-ng; 4-75; 5-1; 6-ng; 7-b; 8-
0; 9-ng; 10-none; 11-conv skills and understanding; basic vocab and structures; 12-e;
13-d; 14-ng.

PORTUGUESE

617. CONVERSATIONAL BRAZILIAN PORTU-
GUESE
U of North Carolina; Univ Extension;
Greensboro, NC 27412.
Stephen C. Mohler, Rom Langs
1-14; 2-3x14; 3-b; 4-72; 5-2; 6-alt yrs; 7-b;
8-0; 9-b; 10-none; 11-emphasis on speaking;
12-b,e,g; 13-d,e; 14-Modern Portuguese.

618. PORTUGUESE FOR TOURISTS
Virginia Commonwealth U; FLs; Richmond,
VA 23284.
William J. Beck
1-4; 2-2x10; 3-c; 4-71; 5-4; 6-a; 7-b; 8-0; 9-
adults; 10-none; 11-guided by text; 12-a,g;
13-a,b; 14-Berlitz tourist lang book.

RUSSIAN

Texts used (#14):
a. Berlitz, Russian for Travelers

195

619. RUSSIAN FOR TRAVELERS
Catonsville CC; FLs; Catonsville, MD 21228.
Marcelle J. Von Mayer, Enrique Corzo
1-15/20; 2-2x15; 3-a; 4-71; 5-c9; 6-a; 7-b mostly; 8-b; 9-b, sr citizens, businessmen; 10-none; 11-conv Russ; 12-a,b,c,d,g; 13-a,b,c,d,e, transparencies, filmstrips; 14-instructor-prepared materials.

620. PRACTICAL RUSSIAN CONVERSATION
U of Nebraska; FLs; Omaha, NE 68101.
Woodrow L. Most
1-20; 2-2x15; 3-c; 4-74; 5-2; 6-a; 7-b; 8-2s; 9-a, faculty, townspeople; 10-none; 11-pronunciation and oral practice, no formal grammar; most take course in preparation for travel abroad; 12-b,g, question-answer, repetition; 13-d; 14-Khavronina, Russian as We Speak It.

621. RUSSIAN FOR TRAVELERS
Santa Rosa CC; FLs; Santa Rosa, CA 95401.
Ruth Parle Craig
1-50 plus; 2-3x17, 2 sems; 3-a,c; 4-66; 5-9; 6-yr course offered every yr; 7-b; 8-3s per sem; 9-a,b, community; 10-first sem none, second sem elem prof; 11-emphasis on travel lang and cult experiences; audiolingual approach with some reading and writing; 12-c,e,f,g; 13-a,b,d,e,f, foods; 14-teacher-prepared material.

622. RUSSIAN FOR AMERICAN TRAVELERS
Schoolcraft C; Community Services; Livonia, MI 48151.
Ron Griffith
1-30; 2-2x8; 3-b; 4-71; 5-4; 6-a; 7-b; 8-0; 9-b; 10-none; 11-differences in cult; basic vocab and phrases; 12-a,b,c,g; 13-a,b; 14-a.

623. RUSSIAN FOR TRAVELERS
Slippery Rock SC; MLs; Slippery Rock, PA 16057.
Charles Tichy
1-ng; 2-5x8; 3-a; 4-smr 74; 5-1; 6-every other smr; 7-b; 8-b; 9-community; 10-none; 11-usage and pronunciation of the phrases needed; 12-a,f,g; 13-a,b,e; 14-a.

624. RUSSIAN FOR TOURISTS
Virginia Commonwealth U; FLs; Richmond, VA 23284.
William J. Beck
1-5; 2-2x10; 3-c; 4-71; 5-4; 6-a; 7-b; 8-0; 9-adults; 10-none; 11-guided by text; 12-a,g; 13-a,b; 14-a.

See also 750, 776.

SPANISH

Texts used (#14):
a. Berlitz, Latin-American Spanish for Travelers
b. ---, Spanish for Travelers
c. Kany, Spoken Spanish for Students and Travelers
d. La Grone, Basic Conversational Spanish
e. Madrigal, See It and Say It in Spanish
f. ---, Open Door to Spanish
g. Richards et al., Spanish Through Pictures

625. CONVERSATIONAL SPANISH
Amarillo C; Cont Ed; Amarillo, TX 79178.
Charles Gaither
1-29; 2-2x10; 3-c; 4-69; 5-9; 6-a; 7-b; 8-0; 9-b; 10-none; 11-basic conv lang; 12-a,b,f; 13-ng; 14-e.

626. SPANISH FOR THE TOURIST
Austin C; Cont Ed; Sherman, TX 75090.
Ted Vestal
1-10; 2-1½x12; 3-a; 4-71; 5-6; 6-a; 7-b; 8-0; 9-community; 10-none; 11-conv approach to phrases for travel; 12-a,b,e,f,g; 13-a,b,d; 14-none.

627. BASIC CONVERSATIONAL SPANISH FOR TRAVELERS
Ball SU; FL; Muncie, IN 47306.
James Brown
1-45; 2-2x10; 3-a; 4-74; 5-1; 6-b; 7-b; 8-2q; 9-a,b; 10-none; 11-useful travel terms, basic cult concepts, elem grammar concepts; 12-a,f,g; 13-ng; 14-Berlitz, Spanish for Travelers.

628. SPANISH FOR TOURISTS
Bergen CC; FLs; Paramus, NJ 07652.
Further info ng.

629. CONVERSATIONAL SPANISH
Bismarck JC; MLs; Bismarck, ND 58501.
Barbara L. Egan
1-25; 2-2x12; 3-a; 4-74; 5-1; 6-b; 7-b; 8-0; 9-b; 10-none; 11-basics of grammar and vocab, travel vocab, conv practice; 12-a,f; 13-b; 14-d.

630. SPANISH FOR TRAVEL
Bloomsburg SC; FLs; Bloomsburg, PA 17815.
A. Foureman
1-new; 2-4x5; 3-a; 4-spr 75; 5-1; 6-ng; 7-b; 8-b; 9-a,b, community; 10-none; 11-ng; 12-c,d,e,f,g; 13-a,b,c,d; 14-ng.

631. SPANISH FOR TRAVELERS
California SU; FLs and Lits; Northridge, CA 91324.
Maja Reid
1-c100; 2-8x2; 3-a; 4-71; 5-5; 6-a; 7-2 consecutive Sats; 8-1s; 9-ng; 10-none; 11-lang needs of persons traveling abroad; 12-b,g; 13-b,d; 14-instructor's materials.

632. SPANISH FOR TRAVELERS
Catonsville CC; FLs; Catonsville, MD 21228.
Marcelle J. Von Mayer, Enrique Corzo
1-15/20; 2-2x15; 3-a; 4-71; 5-c9; 6-a; 7-b mostly; 8-b; 9-b, sr citizens, businessmen; 10-none; 11-conv Sp; 12-a,b,c,d,g; 13-a,b,c,d,e, transparencies, filmstrips; 14-instructor-prepared materials.

633. SPANISH FOR TRAVELERS
Centenary C of Louisiana; FLs; Shreveport, LA 71104.
R. Johnson Watts
1-new; 2-3x6; 3-c; 4-75/76; 5-0; 6-ng; 7-b; 8-0; 9-b; 10-none; 11-basic patterns and vocab; 12-e,f,g; 13-a,b,d,e,f; 14-materials being developed.

634. SPANISH MINI WORKSHOP

196

Central SU; FLs; Edmond, OK 73034.
Mildred H. Lyon
1-c12; 2-20x3; 3-a; 4-74; 5-1; 6-smr; 7-a; 8-3s; 9-a, teachers, special interest students; 10-none; 11-basic vocab, basic grammar constructions, skits, dialogues, cult units, lab exercises; 12-a,b,c,d,e,g; 13-a,b,c,d,e,f, realia; 14-materials provided by dept.

635. SPANISH FOR TRAVEL AND TRADE
U of Dallas; Sp; Irving, TX 75060.
Hazel Cazorla
1-ng; 2-ng; 3-c; 4-fall 75; 5-0; 6-ng; 7-ng; 8-b; 9-b; 10-ng; 11-basic conv Sp with some cult emphasis; vocab for interested tourist & businessman; bus letter writing; 12-b,c,d,g; 13-b,f; 14-ng.

636. CONVERSATIONAL SPANISH FOR THE TRAVELER
Delta C; Sp; University Center, MI 48710.
Robert Mee
1-35; 2-2x8; 3-a; 4-73; 5-6; 6-a; 7-b; 8-0; 9-residents of school dist; 10-none; 11- useful phrases; lang and pronunciation generalized for use in Europe or North/South Amer; 12-b,c,d,e,f; 13-b,d,e,f, maps, realia; 14-Ariza, Zarabanda.

637. SPANISH FOR TRAVEL
East Tennessee SU; Langs; Johnson City, TN 37601.
Cari Holland, Cont Ed
1-12; 2-2x10; 3-a; 4-67; 5-4; 6-2q a yr; 7-b; 8-0; 9-adults; 10-none; 11-words and idioms occurring most frequently in everyday situations; minimum grammar; 12-a,b,f,g; 13-ng; 14-d.

638. SPANISH FOR TRAVELERS
Foothill C; Lang Arts; Los Altos Hills, CA 94022.
Nayan McNeill
1-ng; 2-3x11; 3-a; 4-74; 5-3; 6-a evenings, b days; 7-a,b; 8-2q; 9-a, community; 10-none; 11-conversation, reading, listening; 12-a,b,d,e,f,g; 13-d,f; 14-e.

639. CONVERSATIONAL SPANISH
Fort Scott CJC; Sp; Fort Scott, KS 66701.
Johnny Bennett
1-12; 2-3x18; 3-a; 4-68; 5-7; 6-a; 7-b; 8-3s; 9-community; 10-none; 11-basic conv skills helpful to a tourist; 12-b,g; 13-a,b,c,d,e,f, overheads, realia, drawings; 14-none.

640. SPANISH FOR TRAVEL
Gadsden SJC; FLs; Gadsden, AL 35901.
Clarence Kirkley
1-26; 2-3x12; 3-c; 4-74/75; 5-1; 6-b; 7-b; 8-0; 9-a,b, sr citizens; 10-none; 11-pronunciation, oral dialogues, verbs, cult material; 12-e,f; 13-b,d; 14-A-LM Spanish.

641. CONVERSATIONAL SPANISH
Harrisburg Area CC; Urban Devel Inst; Harrisburg, PA 17110.
Hazel J. Brown
1-26; 2-3x6; 3-b; 4-73; 5-4; 6-a; 7-b; 8-0; 9-b; 10-none; 11-basic vocab and conv use of the lang; based on situations a traveler might encounter; 12-a,b,f; 13-a,b,e,f; 14-

Berlitz, Self Teacher in Spanish.

642. INFORMAL CONVERSATIONAL SPANISH
Henderson CC; Fr & Sp; Henderson, KY 42420.
Arch S. Lacefield
1-ng; 2-2x8; 3-a; 4-74; 5-1; 6-b; 7-b; 8-0; 9-b; 10-none; 11-useful idiomatic expressions, verb forms, conv expressions; no emphasis on reading or writing; primarily for travel; 12-b,f; 13-c; 14-c.

643. SPANISH IN STYLE
Kent SU; Rom Langs & Cl; Kent, OH 44242.
Mark R. Rubin
1-9; 2-2x10; 3-a; 4-wtr 73; 5-4; 6-a; 7-b; 8-0; 9-general public; 10-none; 11-asking directions, dealing with waiters and porters, greetings, understanding customs; useful vocab and basic grammar; 12-b,f,g, drills; 13-b,d, flashcards; 14-Pan y mantequilla; Look and Learn Spanish.

644. CONVERSATIONAL SPANISH
Lake-Sumter CC; Hums; Leesburg, FL 32748.
La Vera Garish
1-30; 2-3x16; 3-c; 4-70/71; 5-5; 6-b; 7-b; 8-3s; 9-adults; 10-none; 11-vocab development and speaking situations in everyday life; 12-a,b,d,f; 13-a,d; 14-Modern Spanish.

645. SURVIVAL SPANISH
Leeward CC; Lang Arts; Pearl City, HI 96782.
Carol Beresiwsky, Pat Harpstrite
1-8; 2-2x16; 3-a; 4-74; 5-2; 6-a; 7-a,b; 8-2s; 9-a,b; 10-none; 11-pronunciation exercises, useful phrases and dialogues, recreations of common situations encountered by travelers; 12-a,b,f; 13-a,b,c,f; 14-a, g.

646. SPANISH FOR TRAVELERS
Macomb County CC; Hums; Warren, MI 48093.
Irving Panush
1-30; 2-2x16; 3-a; 4-ng; 5-ng; 6-a; 7-b; 8-2s; 9-ng; 10-none; 11-structural treatment for functional vocab and expressions; 12-f,g; 13-c,d; 14-materials supplied by the dept.

647. SPANISH FOR TRAVELERS
Marymount C; FLs; Salina, KS 67401.
Francis Ellen Riordan
1-9; 2-2x10; 3-a; 4-74; 5-1; 6-irregularly; 7-b; 8-0; 9-a,b; 10-none; 11-situations, conv phrases; 12-e,g; 13-d,e, records; 14-See It and Say It in Spanish.

648. SPANISH FOR TRAVEL
Memphis SU; FLs; Memphis, TN 38152.
Frank Brantley
1-c10; 2-2 or 3x11; 3-c; 4-68; 5-8; 6-b; 7-b; 8-0; 9-b; 10-none; 11-practical course to assist travellers abroad; 12-a,e; 13-d,e,f; 14-varies.

649. PRACTICAL SPANISH
Mercer County C; FL; Trenton, NJ 08608.
Alfred Kolb
1-23; 2-3x15; 3-a; 4-70; 5-5; 6-b; 7-a; 8-3s; 9-a,b; 10-none; 11-conv on practical topics; grammar deemphasized; training for work

situations or travel; 12-a,b,c,d,e,f,g; 13-d,f, transparencies; 14-Richman, <u>Practical Conversational Spanish.</u>

650. SPANISH FOR TRAVELERS
Molloy C; Sp; Rockville Center, NY 11570.
Libe Aranguren
1-new; 2-3x15; 3-a; 4-75; 5-0; 6-ng; 7-a; 8-3s; 9-ng; 10-none; 11-conv idioms to help the traveler abroad; customs and cult differences; 12-b,c,d,g; 13-a,b,f, maps, ads, menus, realia; 14-ng.

651. PRACTICAL SPANISH CONVERSATION
U of Nebraska; FLs; Omaha, NE 68101.
Woodrow L. Most
1-20; 2-2x15; 3-c; 4-71; 5-each sem; 6-a; 7-b; 8-2s, students encouraged to use Cr/NCr option; 9-a, faculty townspeople; 10-none; 11-pronunciation and oral practice involving everyday situations; 12-b,g, repetition, question-answer; 13-d; 14-a; b; <u>Essential Spanish Grammar.</u>

652. SPANISH FOR TRAVELERS
Neosho County CJC; Sp & Fr; Chanute, KS 66720.
Dean of Instruction
1-6; 2-1x9; 3-a; 4-smr 74; 5-3; 6-a; 7-a,b; 8-1s; 9-adults; 10-none; 11-pronunciation and use of phrase book; 12-a,b,f,g; 13-d, song manual; 14-Gossett, <u>Phrase Book/Dictionary.</u>

653. SPANISH FOR TRAVELERS
U of North Carolina; FLs; Charlotte, NC 28213.
Ralph McLeod
1-15; 2-5x17; 3-a; 4-fall 74; 5-1; 6-ng; 7-b; 8-4s; 9-a,b; 10-ng; 11-useful vocab and structures; 12-f; 13-ng; 14-c.

654. SPANISH FOR TOURISTS
U of North Carolina; MLs; Wilmington, NC 28401.
Jackson Sparks, Carlos A. Perez
1-c25; 2-3x15; 3-a; 4-spr 74; 5-2; 6-b, smr; 7-a,b; 8-3s; 9-a,b; 10-none; 11-emphasis on useful vocab and phrases; oral practice; grammar deemphasized; 12-b,g; 13-a,b; 14-Gorden, <u>Living in Latin America</u>; dictionary; b.

655. SPANISH FOR FUN & TRAVEL
North Hennepin CC; FL; Brooklyn Park, MN 55445.
Barbara K. Mantini
1-12; 2-2x8; 3-a; 4-72; 5-4; 6-depending on demand; 7-b; 8-0; 9-community residents, sr citizens; 10-none; 11-conv skills; 12-a,b,d,e,f; 13-a,b,d,e,f, realia; 14-e.

656. SPANISH FOR TRAVELERS
Park C; ML; Parkville, MO 64152.
Arturo Sanchez
1-8; 2-3x8; 3-a; 4-74; 5-1; 6-irregularly; 7-b; 8-0; 9-b; 10-none; 11-intro to the lang; phrases and dialogues for a trip to Mexico; 12-b,c,g; 13-records, visuals; 14-<u>Speaking Spanish the Mexican Way</u> (records and booklet).

657. SPANISH FOR TRAVELERS
Rockland CC; FLs & Lits; Suffern, NY 10901.
Norman D. Arbaiza
Non-credit course; meets once or twice a wk for 10 wks; on demand, may be offered to fit the needs of a particular interest group; further info ng.

658. SPANISH FOR TRAVEL
Roosevelt U; Lang; Chicago, IL 60605.
Alice Zimring
1-14; 2-7x1 day; 3-a; 4-74; 5-1; 6-ng; 7-special one-day Sat course; 8-0; 9-b; 10-none; 11-basic vocab and structures; 12-c,g; 13-b, posters, signs; 14-faculty-prepared ditto material.

659. CONVERSATIONAL SPANISH FOR THE TRAVELER
C of St. Catherine; Sp; St. Paul, MN 55105.
C. A. Kleczynski
1-26; 2-20x4; 3-a; 4-Jan 74; 5-1; 6-interim offering, given once; 7-a; 8-4s; 9-a,b; 10-prior experience in learning for lang; 11-basic vocab & structures used for everyday conv; 12-b,d,g; 13-d, props for dramas acted out; 14-<u>Vamos a Ver</u>; <u>Hablemos en Espanol.</u>

660. SPANISH FOR PRACTICAL COMMUNICATION
Salisbury SC; ML; Salisbury, MD 21801.
John K. Knowles
1-28; 2-3x15; 3-a; 4-73/74; 5-1; 6-alt yrs; 7-b; 8-3s; 9-a,b; 10-none; 11-situational lang for the traveler, bus person, elem educator, soci worker; 12-b,d,e,g; 13-a,b,c,d,f; 14-Hall, <u>The Silent Language</u>; Angel & Dixson, <u>Metodo directo de conversacion en espanol.</u>

661. TRAVEL COURSE IN SPANISH
San Bernardino Valley C; FL; San Bernardino, CA 92403.
Judith Davis
1-ng; 2-3x17; 3-c; 4-70; 5-10; 6-a; 7-b; 8-3s; 9-a, community; 10-none; 11-general info, key phrases; 12-f,g; 13-a,b; 14-<u>Passport to Spanish.</u>

662. SPANISH FOR TRAVELERS
Santa Rosa JC; FLs; Santa Rosa, CA 95401.
Ruth Parle Craig
1-50 plus; 2-3x17; 2 sems; 3-a,c; 4-66; 5-9; 6-a first sem, b second sem; 7-a,b; 8-3s per sem; 9-a,b, community; 10-first sem none; second sem elem prof; 11-travel lang and cult experiences; audiolingual approach with some reading and writing, oral reports; 12-c,e,f,g; 13-a,b,d,e,f, foods; 14-b, c, f.

663. SPANISH FOR AMERICAN TRAVELERS
Schoolcraft C; Community Services; Livonia, MI 48151.
Ron Griffith
1-30; 2-2x8; 3-b; 4-71; 5-4; 6-a; 7-b; 8-0; 9-b; 10-none; 11-differences in cult; basic vocab and phrases; 12-a,b,c,g; 13-a,b; 14-b.

664. SPANISH FOR TRAVELERS
Slippery Rock SC; MLs; Slippery Rock, PA 16057.
Charles Tichy
1-ng; 2-5x8; 3-a; 4-smr 74; 5-1; 6-every

other smr; 7-b; 8-0; 9-community; 10-none; 11-usage and pronunciation of the phrases most needed; 12-a,f,g; 13-a,b,e; 14-b.

665. SPANISH FOR TRAVEL AND BUSINESS
Southern Connecticut SC; FL; New Haven, CT 06515.·
S. Mendez-Penate
1-new; 2-3x15; 3-a; 4-new; 5-0; 6-possibly smrs; 7-b, smr; 8-3s; 9-a, community; 10-none; 11-intensive drill in specialized vocab, verb tenses, and situations common to travel and bus; orientation to values, attitudes and living patterns; 12-a,b,f, recitation; 13-e,f; 13-Carbajo, Spanish for Banks and Savings & Loan Institutions, Spanish for Retail Selling, Spanish for Restaurants, Spanish for Hotels & Motels, Spanish for Airlines and Travel Agents, Bilingual Guide to Business and Professional Correspondence.

666. SPANISH FOR TOURISTS
U of Southern Mississippi; FLs; Hattiesburg, MS 39401.
Elizabeth Anglin
1-10; 2-2x6; 3-a; 4-72; 5-3; 6-b; 7-b; 8-0; 9-community; 10-none; 11-oral lang; 12-b,d,f; 13-a,c, posters; 14-none.

667. SPANISH FOR TRAVELLERS
U of Southwestern Louisiana; FL; Lafayette, LA 70501.
Richard E. Chandler
1-14; 2-3x4; 3-a; 4-smr 74; 5-3; 6-on request; 7-b; 8-0; 9-thru univ college for C.E. units; 10-none; 11-practical conv approach with emphasis upon situations a traveler is likely to find; 12-a,b; 13-ng; 14-instructor-made materials; Curso Basico.

668. SPANISH FOR TOURISTS
Spalding C; Hums; Louisville, KY 40203.
M. Janice Murphy
1-21; 2-1x10; 3-a; 4-73/74; 5-4; 6-a; 7-b; 8-0; 9-b; 10-none; 11-spoken lang and vocab for travel; hist and cult distinctions noted; 12-b,f,g; 13-a,b; 14-none.

669. BASIC CONVERSATIONAL SPANISH
Three Rivers CC; FL; Poplar Bluff, MO 63901.
Javier Alcaraz
1-14; 2-1½x15; 3-a; 4-73; 5-ng; 6-b; 7-b; 8-1; 9-cont ed students; 10-none; 11-basic materials for those traveling in a Sp-speaking country; real-life situations; 12-ng; 13-a,b,d; 14-instructor's hand-outs; b.

670. SPANISH FOR TOURISTS
Virginia Commonwealth U; FLs; Richmond, VA 23284.
William J. Beck
1-13; 2-2x10; 3-c; 4-71; 5-4; 6-a; 7-b; 8-0; 9-adults; 10-none; 11-guided by text; 12-a,g; 13-a,b; 14-b.

671. SPANISH CONVERSATION
Westchester CC; MLs; Valhalla, NY 10595.
Jacqueline Rosay
1-ng; 2-2x8; 3-a; 4-73; 5-4; 6-a; 7-Sats; 8-0;
9-b, community; 10-none; 11-special section for those with some background in the lang; 12-g; 13-a,b,d,e; 14-materials prepared by instructors.

672. SPOKEN SPANISH FOR TOURISTS
William Paterson C; FLs; Wayne, NJ 07470.
Catherine Barry
1-28; 2-3x17; 3-a; 4-72; 5-2; 6-b; 7-b; 8-3s; 9-a,b; 10-none; 11-intro to Spain, its people, and its attractions; pronunciation; conv; 12-a,b,c,f,g; 13-a,b,d; 14-c.

673. SPANISH FOR TRAVELERS
U of Wisconsin; FLs; Eau Claire, WI 54701.
Roma Hoff
1-10; 2-2x10; 3-a; 4-72; 5-4; 6-a; 7-b; 8-0; 9-b; 10-none; 11-cult, pronunciation, grammar, situational conv; 12-b,f; 13-b,e,f; 14-f.

674. SPANISH FOR TRAVELERS
U of Wisconsin; MLs; River Falls, WI 54022.
Erwin F. Ritter
1-10; 2-3x6/8; 3-a; 4-72/73; 5-2; 6-b; 7-b; 8-0; 9-a, community; 10-none; 11-ng; 12-a,d,c,f; 13-d; 14-b.

675. SPANISH FOR TRAVELERS
Yankton C; FL; Yankton, SD 57078.
Ambrose Schenk
1-6; 2-10x4; 3-a; 4-May term 74; 5-1; 6-ng; 7-ng; 8-3s, option to take at no credit; 9-a, community; 10-none; 11-vocab and idioms common in daily speech, pattern drills, basic conv, cult facets; 12-b,c,d,e,g; 13-a,b; 14-instructor-prepared convs.

676. PREPARATION FOR TRAVEL IN MEXICO
Yavapai C; FL; Prescott, AZ 86301.
Banisa de Laub
1-25; 2-2x15; 3-c; 4-73; 5-3; 6-a; 7-b; 8-2s; 9-a,b; 10-none; 11-ng; 12-a,b,c,d,e,f,g; 13-a,b,e,f; 14-McHenry, A Brief History of Mexico.

See also 248, 267, 268, 348, 498, 776, 777, 778, 779.

SWEDISH

677. SWEDISH FOR TRAVELERS
U of Washington; Scand; Seattle, WA 98195.
Birgitta Steene
1-12; 2-3x8; 3-a; 4-74; 5-3; 6-irregularly; 7-b; 8-0; 9-a,b, anyone; 10-none; 11-aural/oral methods; practice in speaking and info about cult and customs; 12-a,b,f,g; 13-a,b,f; 14-Lar er Svenska; Ovningsbok.

See also 776.

UKRANIAN

678. UKRANIAN FOR TRAVELERS
Rockland CC; FLs & Lits; Suffern, NY 10901.
Norman D. Arbaiza
Non-credit course; meets once or twice a wk for 10 wks; on demand, may be offered to fit the needs of a particular interest group; further info ng.

199

MULTI-LANGUAGE IN ONE COURSE

679. THE INTERNATIONAL TRAVELER: A
PRACTICAL INTRODUCTION TO THE
LANGUAGE AND CUSTOMS OF SE-
LECTED FOREIGN COUNTRIES
Boise SU; FL; Boise, ID 83725.
G. Jocums
1-25/30; 2-3x18; 3-a; 4-Jan 75; 5-1; 6-b; 7-
Sat am; 8-0; 9-b, community; 10-none; 11-
intro to hist, geography, cuisine, soci customs, and lang of selected for countries;
each country studied for 3 wks, one may
enroll for up to 6 segments; 12-a,f; 13-
a,b,e,f; 14-mainly touring materials.

680. TRAVEL LANGUAGE
U of Evansville; FLs; Evansville, IN 47701.
Janet Walker, Cont Ed
1-10; 2-2x9; 3-a; 4-spr 74; 5-1; 6-b; 7-a; 8-0;
9-b; 10-none; 11-useful phrases, simple
verbs, numbers, time, etc.; 3 wks each of
Fr, Ger, Sp; 12-a,f,g; 13-ng; 14-mimeoed
word lists.

681. LANGUAGES FOR FOREIGN TRAVEL
Guilford C; FL; Greensboro, NC 27410.
Rosalie Payne
1-17; 2-4x16; 3-a; 4-73/74; 5-2; 6-irregu-
larly; 7-a; 8-4s; 9-a,b, community; 10-none;
11-team taught; includes Fr, Ger, Ital,
Russ, Sp; pronunciation, basic vocab and
phrases; 12-e,g; 13-d, charts, realia; 14-
instructor-prepared material.

682. SPANISH-FRENCH-GERMAN FOR FUN
AND TRAVEL
Henry Ford CC; FL; Dearborn, MI 48128.

Wanda Chrobak
1-25; 2-2x15; 3-a; 4-Sep 74; 5-1; 6-b; 7-a; 8-
2s; 9-a, sr citizens; 10-none; 11-guided by
text; 12-f,g; 13-b,e,f; 14-Pei, Getting
Along in French; Pei, Getting Along in
German; Pei, Getting Along in Spanish.

683. TRAVEL TECHNIQUES FOR TOURISTS
TO EUROPE
Modesto JC: Lit & Lang Arts; Modesto, CA
95350.
Lowell A. Draper
1-27; 2-3x17; 3-c; 4-74/75; 5-1; 6-a; 7-b; 8-
0; 9-adult cont ed; 10-none; 11-principles of
how to travel; info about tourist centers;
food and hotel accommodations; money and
exchange rates; transportation; geography;
useful phrases in Ger, Ital, Sp and Fr; 12-
a,f; 13-b,e,f; 14-Berlitz, French, German,
Spanish, Italian, for Travelers; Rand, How
to Get to Europe and Have a Wonderful
Time; Rand, Enjoy Europe by Car; Rand,
Enjoy Europe by Train.

See also 302.

MULTI-LANGUAGE

684. LANGUAGE FOR TRAVELERS
Northern Arizona U; MLs; Flagstaff, AZ
86001.
Orazio Giusti
1-new; 2-3xsem; 3-a; 4-fall 75; 5-0; 6-a, one
lang each sem (Fr, Ger, Ital, Sp); 7-b; 8-3s;
9-a,b, community; 10-none; 11-basic
phrases for travel needs; 12-a,e,g; 13-d; 14-
ng.

Off-Campus Programs

ENGLISH AS A SECOND LANGUAGE

685. DIGITAL PROJECT
Inter American U; Eng & Ling; San German,
PR 00753.
Robert L. Muckley
1-60; 2-3x48; 3-a; 4-Sep 74; 5-1; 6-once a yr
throughout the yr; 7-a; 8-b; 9-employees of
local industry (Digital); 10-students chosen
by company; 11-geared to developing competence in oral and written Eng; 12-b,f; 13-
c,d,f; 14-locally produced material.

686. ENGLISH FOR SPANISH PRISONERS
Western Connecticut SC; FLs; Danbury, CT
06810.
John Dever
1-27; 2-4x15; 3-c; 4-73; 5-3; 6-b; 7-b, federal correctional inst, Danbury; 8-b; 9-in-
mates; 10-native Sp speaker; 11-functional
Eng, very basic course; 12-a,b,d,f,g; 13-e,f;
14-instructor-prepared materials.

FRENCH

687. ELEMENTARY FRENCH
Boise SU; FLs; Boise, ID 83725.
G. Jocums
1-10; 2-4x1 sem; 3-a; 4-smr 74; 5-1; 6-on
demand; 7-off campus; 8-4s; 9-prisoners at
state prison; 10-none; 11-elem Fr; 12-a,g;
13-d; 14-ng.

688. FRENCH
SUCNY; FLs; Plattsburgh, NY 12901.
Craig L. Sample
Offered at the Plattsburgh Air Force Base.

See also 723.

GERMAN

689. SCIENTIFIC GERMAN
U of North Carolina; Ger; Greensboro, NC
27412.
Anne Baecker

200

1-10; 2-3x8; 3-a; 4-74; 5-1; 6-uncertain; 7-b; 8-b; 9-personnel at research center in Greensboro; 10-elem prof; 11-grammar review, sci readings; 12-a,f; 13-ng; 14-Lederer, Basic German; Rechtschaffen & Homberger, German for Research.

690. CONVERSATIONAL BEGINNING GERMAN
St. Mary C; ML; Leavenworth, KS 66048.
Emilie Gordon
1-15; 2-3x10; 3-a; 4-spr 73; 5-1; 6-upon demand of Fort Leavenworth; 7-b; 8-b; 9-Fort Leavenworth personnel; 10-none; 11-condensed course of Ger grammar geared to conv; 12-a,b,e,g; 13-d; 14-Pfister, Deutsch durch Deutsch; laboratory manual.

691. ELEMENTARY GERMAN
Southern Illinois U; FLs & Lits; Carbondale, IL 62901.
Eugene F. Timpe
1-15; 2-2½x16; 3-a; 4-wtr 74; 5-2; 6-a; 7-b; 8-4s; 9-inmates at Menard State Penitentiary; 10-none; 11-development of basic skills; 12-a,b,f; 13-a,b,e; 14-Jannach, German for Reading Knowledge; lab workbook.

692. INTERMEDIATE GERMAN
Southern Illinois U; FLs & Lits; Carbondale, IL 62901.
Eugene F. Timpe
1-15; 2-2½x16; 3-a; 4-wtr 74; 5-2; 6-a; 7-b; 8-4s; 9-inmates at Menard State Penitentiary; 10-elem prof; 11-practice in spoken and written Ger, review of grammatical structure, reading of modern Ger authors, emphasis on cross-cult understanding; 12-a,b; 13-a,b,e; 14-Der Weg zum Lesen; Koepke, Die Deutschen Und die Oesterreicher; Ruder & McCormick, Lebendige Literatur.

693. EAGLE UNIVERSITY: GERMAN
Western Kentucky U; FLs; Bowling Green, KY 42101.
C. P. Brown
1-14; 2-4x10; 3-a,c; 4-72; 5-1; 6-on demand; 7-a,b; 8-3s; 9-military personnel; 10-none; 11-beginning course modified to meet need of military personnel who often are expecting an assignment to the area where the lang is spoken; 12-a,e,f,g; 13-a,b; 14-Guten Tag films.

SPANISH

694. CONVERSATIONAL SPANISH
Greenville Tech Ed Center; ML; Greenville, SC 29606.
Margaret K. Rice
1-16; 2-4 x open; 3-a; 4-74; 5-1; 6-course to continue until objectives are met; 7-late afternoon at plant; 8-b; 9-executives with company with holdings in Puerto Rico; 10-none; 11-course is designed to bring a group of businessmen to fluency in Sp as quickly as possible; 12-a,b,e,f,g; 13-d, cassettes for home practice; 14-Lamadrid et al, Communicating in Spanish.

695. SPANISH FOR SUPERVISORS IN A TEXTILE PLANT
Greenville Tech Ed Center; ML; Greenville, SC 29606.
Margaret K. Rice
1-50; 2-4x11; 3-c; 4-74; 5-1; 6-as needed; 7-a (in the plant); 8-b; 9-supervisors who need to communicate with South Amers in the plant; 10-none; 11-basic conv plus specific terms relating to textile machinery and production; 12-a,e,f,g; 13-d, cassettes were supplied for home study; 14-ng.

696. CONVERSATIONAL SPANISH
Henderson County JC; Lang Arts; Athens, TX 75751.
Ernest Holland
1-105; 2-3x16; 3-c; 4-74; 5-3; 6-based on need; 7-a; 8-3s; 9-prisoners; 10-none; 11-audiolingual approach; 12-f,g; 13-e,f; 14-Arjona et al, Lengua Espanola, Primer Libro.

697. INTRODUCTORY SPANISH
Mercer CC; FL; Trenton, NJ 08608.
Alfred Kolb
1-30; 2-3x15; 3-c; 4-71; 5-3; 6-b; 7-a; 8-3s; 9-a, prison inmates; 10-none; 11-standard 1st yr college Sp, taught both on campus & in prisons; 12-a,b,e,f; 13-a,d; 14-Leslie, Spanish for Conversation.

698. CHICANO AMERICAN LITERATURE
U of Nebraska; FLs; Omaha, NE 68101.
Woodrow L. Most
1-15; 2-3x15; 3-a; 4-75; 5-1; 6-uncertain; 7-b; 8-3s; 9-a, taught off-campus in Chicano Awareness Center for Chicano Amers; 10-permission; 11-specifically requested by the Chicano group in Omaha, and directed specifically to them; 12-a,b,c,g; 13-ng; 14-Romano, ed, El Espejo, The Mirror: Selected Chicano Literature; Valdez & Steiner, eds, Aztlan: An Anthology of Mexican American Literature.

699. SPANISH
SUCNY; FLs; Plattsburgh, NY 12901.
Craig L. Sample
Sp and other lang courses are offered to inmates of Dannemora Prison on an irregular basis.

700. SPANISH CONVERSATION AND STRUCTURE
Queens C; Cont Ed; Charlotte, NC 28207.
Gordon Freeman, Marjorie T. Kirby
1-30; 2-2x8; 3-a; 4-spr 74; 5-2; 6-on demand; 7-b; 8-b; 9-b; 10-membership in the particular engineering firm involved; 11-travel expressions, structure of the lang in order to deal with reading, writing, and conv; 12-a,b,c,e,f,g; 13-d; 14-Turk & Espinosa, Foundation Course in Spanish; mimeoed material.

701. SPANISH I
St. Mary C (Kansas State Penitentiary, Lansing, KS); ML; Leavenworth, KS 66048.
Virginia Monserrate
1-14; 2-5x14; 3-a; 4-72; 5-2; 6-a; 7-b; 8-5s; 9-b; 10-none; 11-practice in pronouncing,

speaking, understanding, reading, and writing; 12-g; 13-ng; 14-Wolfe, Curso Basico de Espanol.

702. SPANISH
U of Tampa; MLs; MacDill Air Force Base Center; Tampa, FL 33606.
Eustasio Fernandez, Capt. Schroeder
1-15; 2-3x14; 3-c; 4-64; 5-10; 6-a; 7-b; 8-3s; 9-evening students from the Air Force Base; airmen and their dependents; 10-ng; 11-ng; 12-a,b,g; 13-ng; 14-U.S. Air Force Academy textbooks.

703. CHICANO LITERATURE
Tarrant County JC; Eng, MFL; Fort Worth, TX 76119.
E. A. Guzman
1-18/20; 2-3x18; 3-b,c; 4-72/73; 5-3; 6-b, initial offering went two sems; 7-a, prison personnel now come on campus; 8-3s; 9-a,b; 10-college freshman Eng, elem Sp; 11-Chicano lit in all genres beginning with pre-Columbian poets of Mexico and proceeding to contemporary Chicano writers of U.S.; 12-a,f; 13-a,e,f; 14-Shular & Ybarra-Frausto, Literatura Chicana, Texto y Contexto; Simmen, The Chicano; Bario, The Plum Plum Pickers.

704. CONVERSATIONAL SPANISH FOR HOSPITAL PERSONNEL
Tarrant County JC; MFL; Fort Worth, TX 76119.
Ernesto A. Guzman
1-50; 2-2x24; 3-a,c; 4-73/74; 5-3; 6-b, on demand; 7-a; 8-0; 9-nurses & MDs from county hospital; 10-none; 11-practical conv

Sp for individuals who have little or no previous experience & knowledge of the lang; conceptual approach stressed, with vocab buildup through a variety of topics & situations related to hospital experience; 12-b,e,g; 13-a,b,c,d,e,f; 14-Carbajo, Spanish for Doctors and Nurses.

705. EAGLE UNIVERSITY: SPANISH
Western Kentucky U; FLs; Bowling Green, KY 42101.
C. P. Brown
(See ms. #693) 1-20; 2-4x10; 3-a,c; 4-72; 5-1; 6-on demand; 7-a,b; 8-3s; 9-military personnel; 10-none; 11-beginning course modified to meet need of military personnel who are expecting an assignment to the area where the lang is spoken; 12-a,e,f,g; 13-a,b; 14-Segreda & Harris, Listening, Speaking, Reading, Writing.

706. SPANISH
Western Oklahoma SC; Spanish; Altus, OK 73521.
Richard Maffry
1-10; course taught for 5 sem hours credit via talk-back TV to State Reformatory in Granite, Okla.; further info ng.

See also 431, 450.

MULTI-LANGUAGE

707. ELEMENTARY LANGUAGE
Hagerstown JC; Lang; Hagerstown, MD 21740.
Helen Kreykenbohm
Beginning lang offered evenings at Fort Ritchie military base.

English for Speakers of Other Languages

708. ENGLISH FOR KOREAN SAINTS
Brigham Young U; Communication & Lang Arts; Laie, HI 96762.
Jay Fox
1-22; 2-3x12; 3-c; 4-75; 5-1; 6-as requested; 7-b; 8-0; 9-businessmen and others; 10-member of the Church; 11-listening comprehension, reading, grammar, Church-related material; 12-b,f; 13-d; 14-English for Korean Saints.

709. TEACHING ENGLISH TO SPANISH SPEAKERS
Curry C; Lang & Lit; Milton, MA 02186.
Frances Kohak
Additional info not available.

710. PUERTA DE OPORTUNIDAD
Kalamazoo C; Rom Langs; Kalamazoo, MI 49001.
Betty Rita Gomez Lance
1-26; 2-5x10; 3-a, sr Sp majors; 4-72; 5-3; 6-c; 7-b; 8-0; 9-adults; 10-native lang Sp or

Port; 11-situational approach, functional lang, skits; 12-f,g; 13-a,b,c,d,e,f, flash cards; 14-varied.

711. ENGLISH FOR SPEAKERS OF OTHER LANGUAGES
Rockland CC; FLs & Lits; Suffern, NY 10901.
Norman D. Arbaiza
1-36; 2-25x8; 3-a; 4-fall 74; 5-1; 6-b; 7-a; 8-0; 9-prospective students; 10-equivalent of HS diploma; 11-immersion program; listening, speaking, reading, writing, pronunciation, spelling, sentence structure, dictionary use; required for students entering the college with deficient Eng skills; 12-a,b,c,f; 13-a,b,d, drawings; 14-American English series.

712. ENGLISH AS A SECOND LANGUAGE
Tarrant County JC; MFL; Fort Worth, TX 76119.
Ernesto Guzman

1-12; 2-3x15; 3-b,c; 4-69; 5-6; 6-a, as needed; 7-a,b; 8-3s for A.A. or certificate; 0 credit for transfer purposes; 9-a, community members; 10-none; 11-course structured on six levels; students placed at own level; material individualized, self-paced, packaged oral comprehension; 12-e,f; 13-a,d, packaged; 14-English 900 series.

713.	ENGLISH FOR SPANISH SPEAKERS
Tarrant County JC; FL; Hurst, TX 76053.

Jane Harper, Doris Key
1-new; 2-2x17; 3-a; 4-spr 75; 5-1; 6-a; 7-b; 8-0; 9-b, adults; 10-none; 11-functional Eng, emphasis on oral-aural ability, some writing; no formal grammar, repetition and situational reinforcement; 12-b,e,f; 13-realia; 14-Hall & Flamm, Orientation in American English (text and workbook).

See also 685, 686, 776, 1671, 1674, 1676, 1677, 1680.

Miscellaneous and General

CHINESE

714.	BASIC CONVERSATIONAL CHINESE
Tarrant County JC; Cont Ed; Fort Worth, TX 76119.
Ernesto Guzman
1-20; 2-3x6; 3-c; 4-74; 5-ng; 6-a; 7-b; 8-b; 9-b; 10-elem prof; 11-conv & cult; 12-a,b,e,g; 13-multi-media; 14-Modern Chinese, A Basic Course.

CZECH

715.	CZECH ETHNIC HERITAGE STUDIES
Kirkwood CC; FLs; Cedar Rapids, IA 52406.
Florence Masters
1-new; 2-1+x12; 3-b,c; 4-fall 75; 5-0; 6-a; 7-a,b; 8-8q; 9-adults; 10-ng; 11-purpose of program (& grant) is to develop an individualized interdisc learning system for general ethnic heritage studies, utilizing Czech lang & cult; 12-b,c,d,e,f,g; 13-b,c,d; 14-will develop own ABC book, fairy tales in trans, lang videotape film.

See also 177.

FRENCH

716.	FRENCH CIVILIZATION FOR SENIOR CITIZENS
Catonsville CC; FLs; Baltimore, MD 21228.
Marcelle J. Von Mayer, Enrique Corzo
1-30; 2-1⅜x10; 3-a; 4-74; 5-5; 6-on demand; 7-a; 8-0; 9-b, sr citizens; 10-none; 11-conv & lecture with slides; 12-a,b,f; 13-a,b,d, transparencies; 14-instructor-prepared materials.

717.	BEGINNING CONVERSATION
Everett CC; Fr; Everett, WA 98201.
Phyllis Harris
1-24; 2-2x10; 3-c; 4-74; 5-3; 6-a; 7-b; 8-2q; 9-a,b; 10-none; 11-beginning conv to facilitate travel, social & occupational contact; minimal grammar; 12-b,g; 13-a,b,c,d,e,f; 14-none.

718.	COMMUNICATING IN FRENCH
Lake Forest C; FLs; Lake Forest, IL 60045.
Jean-Luc Garneau
1-new; 2-3x7; 3-a; 4-wtr 74/75; 5-1; 6-on

trial basis to determine community interest; 7-b; 8-2s; 9-not known at this time; 10-none; 11-cult approach to France, its people, institutions, life; basic conv through AV aids; 12-b,c,f,g; 13-b,e, basic French readers; 14-Harris & Leveque, Basic Conversational French.

719.	FRENCH:	CONVERSATION	AND COMPOSITION
C of Notre Dame; MLs & Cont Ed; Baltimore, MD 21210.
Regina Soria, Frederick Van der Wens
1-20; 2-3x14; 3-a; 4-74; 5-1; 6-a; 7-b; 8-3s; 9-adults from surrounding communities; 11-basic patterns of speech, active use of spoken lang; 12-c,e,g; 13-d; 14-ng.

720.	CONVERSATIONAL FRENCH (Levels I and II)
Parkland	C;	Communications	Div; Champaign, IL 61820.
Kenneth Strickler
1-18; 2-2x11; 3-a; 4-ng; 5-ng; 6-wtr & spr qtrs, occasionally smr; 7-b; 8-2q general studies, not applicable toward degree; 9-b; 10-none for Level I; for Level II, elem prof; 11-conv with attention to cult; 12-b,c,d,e,g;	13-a,b,c,d,e,f;	14-internally generated handouts; dictionary and/or phrasebook.

721.	CONTINUING STUDIES: FRENCH
Rice U; Fr; Houston, TX 77001.
M. Raaphorst, Lynda Driokoll
1-20; 2-3x12; 3-c; 4-74/75; 5-2; 6-a; 7-b; 8-b; 9-adults; 10-none; 11-emphasis on conv; 12-e,g; 13-ng; 14-Parole et Pensee.

722.	ADVANCED	CONVERSATIONAL FRENCH
Tarrant County JC; Cont Ed; Fort Worth, TX 76119.
Ernesto Guzman
1-25; 2-4x6; 3-ng; 4-74; 5-ng; 6-a; 7-b; 8-b; 9-b; 10-elem prof; 11-practical conv Fr; 12-b,e,g; 13-multimedia; 14-Madrigal, Open Door to French.

723.	BASIC CONVERSATIONAL FRENCH

Tarrant County JC: Cont Ed; Fort Worth, TX 76119.
Ernesto Guzman
1-25; 2-2x6; 3-c; 4-73; 5-20; 6-a; 7-b, also off-campus on demand; 8-b; 9-b; 10-none for basic course; knowledge of lang required for adv course; 11-conv & cult; 12-a,b,e,g; 13-multimedia; 14-Madrigal, Open Door to French.

724. BASIC CONVERSATIONAL FRENCH FOR TEENAGERS
Tarrant County JC; Cont Ed; Fort Worth, TX 76119.
Ernesto Guzman
1-ng; 2-2x6; 3-c; 4-74; 5-ng; 6-ng; 7-Sat; 8-b; 9-teenagers; 10-none; 11-conv & cult of Fr young people; 12-ng; 13-multi-media, popular Fr music; 14-Madrigal, Open Door to French.

725. PREPARATORY PROGRAM IN FRENCH
Tarrant County JC; FLs; Hurst, TX 76053.
Jane Harper
1-ng; 2-2x12; 3-a; 4-proposed for 75; 5-none; 6-a; 7-after school hours of public schools; 8-b; 9-children ages 5-11; 10-none; 11-basic conv patterns, games, songs; 12-a,b,d,e,g; 13-a,b,c,d; 14-ng.

See also 985.

GERMAN

726. BEGINNING CONVERSATION
Everett CC; German; Everett, WA 98201.
Phyllis Harris
1-26; 2-2x10; 3-c; 4-69; 5-3; 6-a; 7-b; 8-2q; 9-a,b; 10-none; 11-beginning conv to facilitate travel, occupational or soci contact; minimum grammar; Ger cult; 12-b,g; 13-a,b,c,d,e,f; 14-Lederer, Basic German: An Introduction; Goedsche, Patterns of German Conversation; Hagboldt, Fabeln, Book Two.

727. CONVERSATIONAL GERMAN
Harrisburg Area CC; Urban Dev Inst; Harrisburg, PA 17110.
Hazel J. Brown
1-15; 2-3x6; 3-b; 4-74; 5-1; 6-a; 7-b; 8-b; 9-b; 10-none; 11-basic conv; 12-a,b,f; 13-a,b,e,f; 14-none.

728. BEGINNING GERMAN
Heidelberg C; Ger; Tiffin, OH 44883.
Frank D. Horvay, Albert Fink
1-1; 2-1 hr every two wks; 3-a; 4-74/75; 5-1; 6-a; 7-b; 8-3 or 4s; 9-special students; students with regular jobs; 10-college eligibility; 11-ng; 12-b,f,g; 13-d (cassettes); 14-using improvised material while awaiting non-traditional "boxes" with tapes, texts, workbooks from Germany.

729. PRACTICAL GERMAN
Jacksonville SU; FL; Jacksonville, AL 36265.
George Teague
1-new; 2-3x14; 3-a; 4-ng; 5-none; 6-2-sem sequence probably offered every other yr; 7-a; 8-3s; 9-a,b, open to anyone; 10-none; 11-practical Ger designed to give student, traveler, bus person basic knowledge of Ger, concentration on manipulation of high frequency expressions for practical application; 12-b,c,g; 13-a,b,e,f; 14-Schulz-Griesbach, Deutsche Sprachlehre fur Auslaender.

730. PRACTICAL CONVERSATIONAL GERMAN
Moorhead SC; Langs; Moorhead, MN 56560.
G. Theodore Schaum
1-11; 2-3x12; 3-a; 4-spr 72; 5-1; 6-has been taught only once due to shortage of staff; 7-b; 8-3; 9-a,b; 10-none; 11-intensive lang course designed to give participant working knowledge for pleasure, bus, & cult purposes, emphasis on speaking & oral comprehension in idiomatic Ger; 12-b,e,g; 13-b,e,f; 14-Berlitz, German for Travelers.

731. GERMAN FOR FUN
Mt. Hood CC; Lang & Speech; Gresham, OR 97030.
Ray H. Nelson
1-15; 2-3x11; 3-c; 4-66; 5-approx 20; 6-a; 7-b; 8-3q cont ed, non-transferable; 9-adults; 10-none; 11-conv, intro to Ger cult; applied ling approach; 12-a,d,e; 13-a,d,e, records, Ger games; 14-Lederer, Look and Learn German.

732. CONVERSATIONAL GERMAN
Parkland C; Communications Div, Champaign, IL 61820.
Kenneth Strickler
1-18; 2-2x11; 3-a; 4-ng; 5-ng; 6-wtr & spr qtrs, occasionally smr; 7-b; 8-2q general studies, not applicable to a degree; 9-b; 10-none for Level I; for Level II, elem prof; 11-conv with attention to cult; 12-b,c,d,e,g; 13-a,b,c,d,e,f; 14-internally-generated handouts, dictionary and/or phrasebook.

733. GERMAN SCHOOL FOR CHILDREN OF GERMAN-SPEAKING PARENTS
Queens C; Cont Ed, German; Charlotte, NC 28207.
Agnes Hostettler
1-15-14-10 (three groups); 2-2x8; 3-c; 4-74; 5-1; 6-a; 7-special aft class; 8-b; 9-children 4-16 yrs; 10-have Ger parents & speak Ger at home; 11-learning words, sentences, idiomatic expressions, reading & writing; no Eng used; 12-b,c,d,g; 13-g, mostly our own flash cards & pictures; 14-Deutsch fuer Dich; Deutsch 2000.

734. BLITZ GERMAN FOR BEGINNERS
C of St. Catherine; Ger; St. Paul, MN 55105.
Kristina Trendota
1-15; 2-15x3; 3-a; 4-74; 5-2; 6-special smr school offering for women with concurrent, free of charge enrichment program for children of those registered; 7-smr school; 8-2q; 9-a,b, sr citizens, housewives, tourists; 10-none; 11-intensive lang-in-cult course, multimedia approach, comprehensive final on lang & civ; 12-b,c,e,f,g; 13-a,d,e,f, posters, realia; 14-Schapers, Deutsch 2000.

735. CONVERSATIONAL GERMAN
Williamsport Area CC; Communications; Williamsport, PA 17701.
Frederick Sharar
1-8; 2-2x8; 3-3; 4-fall 74; 5-2; 6-a; 7-b; 8-b; 9-b; 10-none; 11-conv; 12-e,g; 13-d; 14-none.

See also 1025, 1357.

HEBREW

736. HEBREW
Grossmont C; FLs; El Cajon, CA 92020.
G. M. Washington
Requested by community leaders, 40 enrolled in eve div, spr 75; further info ng.

ITALIAN

737. ADVANCED ITALIAN CONVERSATION
California SU; FLs & Lits; Northridge, CA 91324.
Maja Reid
1-20; 2-3x15; 3-a; 4-75; 5-ng; 6-a; 7-b; 8-3s; 9-teachers, travelers; 10-some knowledge of the language; 11-reading, discussion; 12-c,g; 13-b,e,f; 14-Guardeschi: Il Mondo Piccolo di Don Camillo.

738. PANORAMA OF ITALIAN CULTURE
California SU; FLs & Lits; Northridge, CA 91324.
Maja Reid
1-35; 2-8x2; 3-a; 4-72; 5-3; 6-b; 7-Sats; 8-1s; 9-b, teachers; 10-none; 11-survey of Ital hist, lit, art, sci; 12-a,f; 13-b,e,f; 14-none.

739. BEGINNING CONVERSATION
Everett CC; Ital; Everett, WA 98201.
Phyllis Harris
1-20; 2-2x10; 3-c; 4-74/75; 5-3; 6-a; 7-b; 8-2q; 9-a,b; 10-none; 11-elem conv course to facilitate travel, soci & occupational contact; minimum grammar; info about people & customs of Italy; 12-b,g; 13-a,b,c,d,e,f; 14-none.

740. CONVERSATIONAL ITALIAN
Lock Haven SC; FL; Lock Haven, PA 17745.
P. Podol
1-25; 2-ng; 3-a; 4-74; 5-1; 6-annually; 7-b; 8-b; 9-b, community residents; 10-none; 11-emphasis on conv, some grammar, first 8 wks only present tense is used; 12-a,b,g; 13-d, xerox copies of dialogues, vocab, music; 14-none required, principal recommended text for which tapes are available: Speroni & Gabino, Basic Italian Revised.

741. ITALIAN FOR COMMUNICATION
C of Notre Dame; MLs & Cont Ed; Baltimore, MD 21210.
Regina Soria
1-25; 2-3x14; 3-a,c; 4-73; 5-4; 6-a; 7-b; 8-3s; 9-adults from surrounding communities; 10-none; 11-elements of grammar, conv material; 12-a,c,e,g; 13-d,e; 14-Battaglia, Nuova Grammatica per Straniers.

742. TWENTIETH CENTURY ITALIAN WRITERS
C of Notre Dame; Cont Ed; Baltimore MD 21210.
Regina Soria
1-ng; 2-3x15; 3-a; 4-spr 75; 5-1; 6-ng; 7-b; 8-ng; 9-ng; 10-elem prof; 11-reading lit, conv, writing; 12-b,e; 13-ng; 14-primary texts.

743. ITALIAN THROUGH CONTINUING EDUCATION
Southeastern Louisiana U; FLs; Hammond, LA 70401.
James F. Fournet
1-63; 2-3x16; 3-c; 4-spr 74; 5-2; 6-a; 7-b; 8-3s; 9-a, adults, auditors; 10-H.S. grad; 11-taught off-campus; practical conv course, little emphasis on grammar; 12-a,b,e,f; 13-a,b,d,e,f; 14-Lo dica in Italiano.

744. FUNDAMENTALS OF ITALIAN
Temple U; Ital; Philadelphia, PA 19122.
Raymond J. Cormier
1-15; 2-3x14; 3-a; 4-75; 5-none; 6-new course to be offered again only if there is sufficient interest; 7-a,b; 8-4s; 9-b; 10-none; 11-condensed grammar for review; stress on rapid acquisition of basic listening, speaking, reading, writing skills of contemporary Ital; 12-a,b,e,g; 13-b,c,e,f; 14-Orwen, Introduction to Italian.

See also 804, 1142.

JAPANESE

745. BEGINNING CONVERSATION
Everett CC; Jap; Everett, WA 98201.
Phyllis Harris
1-25; 2-2x10; 3-c; 4-72/73; 5-3; 6-a; 7-b; 8-2q; 9-a,b; 10-none; 11-informal elem conv approach for purposes of travel, occupation or socializing; minimum grammar; info about Japan (people, customs); 12-b,g; 13-a,b,c,d,e,f; 14-Martin, Easy Japanese.

NAVAHO

746. NAVAHO LANGUAGE
Navajo CC; Navaho Studies; Tsaile, AZ 86503.
Ruth Roessel, Jerold Judd
1-125; 2-3 to 9x16; 3-a; 4-69; 5-ng; 6-a; 7-a,b; 8-3s; 9-a,b, community, eve; 10-none (but program is sequenced I, II, III); 11-creative writing, conv; 12-a,b,e,g; 13-a,b, & Navajo typewriter material; 14-Morgan & Young, Navajo Language; Gosen, Navajo Made Easier; own text which will soon be published.

POLISH

747. INTRODUCTION TO POLISH CONVERSATION
East Stroudsburg, SC; FLs; East Stroudsburg, PA 18301.
Bernard S. Hawrylo
1-14; 2-3x8; 3-a; 4-74; 5-1; 6-b; 7-a; 8-2s; 9-a; 10-none; 11-trial mini-course in Polish conv; presented with teacher-prepared visual aids depicting every-day situations; some visuals also covering dialogues in Mowimy po Polsku, Bisko, Karolak, Wasilewska, Krynski; 12-f,g; 13-teacher-prepared visuals; 14-Mowimy po Polsku.

PORTUGUESE

748. ELEMENTARY INTENSIVE PORTUGUESE
California SU; Sp & Port; Long Beach, CA
90840.
John H. Schmitt
1-new; 2-10x15; 3-a; 4-spr 75; 5-1; 6-b; 7-b;
8-5s; 9-a,b, cont ed; 10-none; 11-equivalent
of 1 yr. of college Port in 15 weeks; 12-
a,b,e,f,g; 13-a,d,e,f; 14-ng.

749. PORTUGUESE TUTORIAL PROGRAM
U of Massachusetts; Sp & Port; Amherst,
MA 01002.
Antonio Andrade Jr.
1-12; 2-5x15; 3-c; 4-spr 74; 5-3; 6-a; 7-a; 8-
3s; 9-a; 10-1 course; 11-students serve in
schools with children who speak Port at
home; aim is to help children gain academic
skills & to learn as much as possible about
the Port Amer communities of the region in
the process; 12-b; students placed according to their fluency; 13-ng; 14-students
keep field notebook; research paper required.

RUSSIAN

750. BEGINNING CONVERSATION
Everett CC; Russ; Everett, WA 98201.
Phyllis Harris
1-18; 2-2x10; 3-c; 4-73/74; 5-3; 6-a; 7-b; 8-
2q; 9-a,b; 10-none; 11-emphasis on elem
conv for use in travel, limited soci &
occupational contact; minimum grammar;
12-b,g; 13-a,b,c,d,e,f; 14-no text.

SERBIAN

751. SERBIAN FOR THE SERBIAN
COMMUNITY
U of Illinois; Sl Langs &Lits; Chicago IL
60680.
Nicholas Moravcevich
1-15; 2-4x10; 3-a; 4-74; 5-2; 6-a; 7-b; 8-4q;
9-a,b; 10-none; 11-elem Serbo-Croatian;
12-a,b,c,e,f,g; 13-a,b,e,f; 14-Magner,
Introduction to the Croatian and Serbian
Language; Magner, The Student's
Dictionary of Serbo-Croatian.

SPANISH

752. CONVERSATIONAL SPANISH
Adams SC; FL; Alamosa, CO 81101.
Luis Trujillo
1-20; 2-3x10; 3-a; 4-60; 5-16; 6-alt qtrs or
on demand; 7-b; 8-3q; 9-community,
faculty, some students; 10-ng; 11-emphasis
on conv; 12-a,b,e,f; 13-d; 14-ng.

753. ELEMENTARY CONVERSATIONAL
SPANISH FOR NON-NATIVE SPEAKERS
Bee County C; Sp; Beeville, TX 78102.
Norman G. Damerau
1-36; 2-2½x15; 3-a; 4-68; 5-13; 6-a; 7-b; 8-
3s; 9-a, local citizens; 10-none; 11-conv
with particular emphasis on Sp spoken in
South Texas; 12-a,b,d,f,g; 13-a,b; 14-EMC,
Asi Son los Mexicanos; La Madrid, Bull,
Briscoe, Communicating in Spanish.

754. CONTINUING EDUCATION SPANISH

Bowling Green SU; Cont Ed; Bowling Green,
OH 43403.
1-10; 2-3x10; 3-b; 4-74; 5-3; 6-on demand;
7-b; 8-b; 9-b; 10-none; 11-tailored to the
group; 12-a,b,c,g; 13-ng; 14-ng.

755. FOREIGN LANGUAGE CLASSES FOR
CHILDREN
California SU; FLs & Lits; Northridge, CA
91234.
Maja Reid
1-fall & spr 200, smr 100; 2-1-2x12; 3-a; 4-
70; 5-6; 6-a, smr session; 7-a; 8-b; 9-
children 5-12; 10-consent of instructor; 11-
children grouped by age & experience in
small conv oriented classes taught by
native speaker; langs in program: Fr, Ger,
Sp, Chi, Hebrew; 13-a,b,d; 14-Sp: Me
gusta el espanol other languages use
instructors' own material.

756. SPANISH FOR FARM AND RANCH
WORKERS
Hill JC; Communications; Hillsboro, TX
76645.
David McCord
1-12; 2-2x18; 3-a; 4-75; 5-1; 6-uncertain; 7-
b; 8-2s; 9-a,b, eve school; 10-none; 11-conv
with emphasis on agricultural work
situations; 12-a,b,e,f,g; 13-a,b,c,d,e,f; 14-
Farm and Ranch Spanish; Spanish for the
Housewife; Espanol.

757. ADVANCED CONVERSATIONAL
SPANISH
Holyoke CC; Hums; Holyoke, MA 01040.
Gerhard M. Wilke
1-20; 2-2x15; 3-a; 4-73; 5-3; 6-b; 7-a,b; 8-
2s; 9-a, policemen and other interested
groups; 10-elem prof; 11-attention is given
to speaking & understanding the
contemporary colloquial idiom of the
native speaker; 12-b,e,f,g; 13-d; 14-
Conversations in Spanish: Points of
Departure.

758. SPANISH AS A FOREIGN LANGUAGE
Humacao Regional C; Sp; Humacao, PR
00661.
Jose Pomales
1-18; 2-3x18; 3-a; 4-74; 5-3; 6-a; 7-b; 8-b;
9-b; 10-none; 11-conv Sp; 12-e; oral-aural
approach; 13-d; lessons prepared by
teacher; 14-Espanol a lo Vivo (only as a
resource to be used by teacher).

759. CONVERSATIONAL SPANISH
Indiana U; MFLs; Fort Wayne, IN 46805.
Virginia R. Craig
1-22; 2-2x12; 3-b; 4-68; 5-13; 6-a; 7-b; 8-b;
9-b; 10-none; 11-designed for those
interested in learning to speak Sp; 12-
a,b,f,g; 13-a,b, records & visual aids; 14-
See It and Say It in Spanish; Spanish Made
Simple.

760. CONVERSATIONAL SPANISH
Jefferson SJC; Lang Arts; Birmingham, AL
35315.
Carl Vickery
1-7; 2-2x10; 3-b; 4-fall 72; 5-3; 6-on demand; 7-b; 8-b; 9-b: 10-none; 11-for conv

206

only; 12-a,b; 13-d; 14-<u>Conversational Spanish</u>.

761. COMMUNICATING IN SPANISH
Lake Forest C; FLs; Lake Forest, IL 60045.
Francisco Sosa
1-ng; 2-3x7; 3-a; 4-wtr 74/75; 5-1; 6-trial basis to determine community interest; 7-b; 8-2s; 9-ng; 10-none; 11-a cult approach to Sp-speaking countries, their peoples, institutions and lives; basic conv through AV aids; 12-a,b,f,g; 13-b,d, mimeoed material on grammar & folk stories; 14-ng.

763. MOLLOY SPANISH INSTITUTE
Molloy C; Sp; Rockville Centre, NY 11570.
Rose Teresa Amor
1-40; 2-4x13; 3-c; 4-69; 5-13; 6-a; 7-b; 8-3s; 9-majority are professional people with a need to learn Sp; 10-none; 11-intensive course in conv Sp designed to give student fluency in the lang; small groups, no larger than 8; 12-b,g; 13-units from Foreign Service Institute; 14-same as 13.

764. SPANISH CONVERSATION FOR COMMUNITY
C of Mount St. Vincent; MFL; Bronx, NY 10471.
Manuel Gonzalez
1-10; 2 2½x15; 3 a; 4-74; 5-2; 6-b; 7-b; 8-3s; 9-b; 10-none; 11-vocab & exercises relating to med, soci and correctional fields; 12-a,e; 13-a,e,f; 14-none.

765. SPANISH FOR ELEMENTARY STUDENTS
Northeastern JC; Hums Div; Sterling, CO 80751.
Joseph Mills
1-ng; 2-ng; 3-a & Div of Community Service; 4-ng; 5-ng; 6-ng; 7-Sat morning; 8-b; 9-elem school children; 10-ng; 11-ng; 12-b,g; 13-a,b,d; 14-ng.

766. CONVERSATION SPANISH (Levels I and II)
Parkland C; Communications Div; Champaign, IL 61820.
Kenneth Strickler
1-18; 2-2x11; 3-a; 4-69; 5-ng; 6-wtr & spr qtrs, occasionally smr; 7-b; 8-2q general studies, not applicable toward a degree; 9-b; 10-none for Level I; for Level II, elem prof; 11-conv with attention to cult; 12-b,c,d,e,g; 13-a,b,c,d,e,f; 14-internally-generated handouts, dictionary and/or phrasebook.

767. INTENSIVE SPANISH LANGUAGE PROGRAM FOR ADULTS
Rosary C; Sp; River Forest, IL 60305.
Sr. Philip Mary Reilly
1-23; 2-30x4½; 3-c; 4-smr 74; 5-1; 6-each smr; 7-a; 8-4s; 9-b; 10-none; 11-the course, with students grouped according to ability, is designed to give facility in the use of Sp as a tool to adults whose working/living situations require communication in Sp; the four lang skills are covered, but emphasis is given to listening comprehension, speech; cult presentations also; 12-a,b,c,d,e,f,g; 13-a,b,d,e,f, overhead projector materials; 14-primary text.

768. SPANISH CONVERSATION AND MEXICAN TOUR
Stetson U; FL; Deland, FL 32720.
Edwart Settgast
1-16; 2-2x6; 3-a; 4-fall 74; 5-1; 6-a; 7-b; 8-b; 9-adults from community; 10-none; 11-beginning Sp & 12-day study tour of Mexico; 12-d,e,f; 13-b,d, filmstrips; 14-<u>Asi son los Mexicanos</u>.

769. CONVERSATIONAL SPANISH
Tarrant County JC; MFLs; Fort Worth, TX 76119.
Ernesto Guzman
1-25; 2-18; 3-ng; 4-smr 74; 5-ng; 6-ng; 7-smr, 3 mornings per wk; 8-ng; 9-children 8-10 yrs old; 10-ng; 11-basic conv, songs, games; 12-ng; 13-ng; 14-mimeo material.

770. CONVERSATIONAL SPANISH FOR HOMEMAKERS
Tarrant County JC; MFLs; Fort Worth, TX 76119.
Ernesto Guzman
Further info ng.

771. SPANISH OF THE SOUTHWEST
Texas Lutheran C; Sp; Seguin, TX 78155.
Carmen Tafolla
1-new; 2-3x14; 3-a; 4-spr 75; 5-1; 6-b; 7-b; 8-3s; 9-a,b, community people; 10-elem prof; 11-conv Sp; emphasis on Sp of the Southwest; 12-b,c,d,g; 13-b,d,e,f; 14-ng.

772. CONVERSATIONAL SPANISH
Western Oklahoma SC; Sp; Altus, OK 73521.
Richard Maffry
Three-hour evening class to assist adults in talking to Mex Amers in the area; attended by doctors, lawyers, realtors, employers, and Mex Amers wishing to learn to write and read Sp.

773. ELEMENTARY SPANISH
Wharton County JC; FL; Wharton, TX 77488.
Julio C. Guerra
1-18; 2-2x6; 3-b; 4-ng, but given for many yrs; 5-ng; 6-a; 7-b; 8-b; 9-b; 10-none; 11-grammar, vocab; 12-a,b,e; 13-a,b,c,d, handouts; 14-none.

774. HISPANIC LANGUAGE AND LIFE
William Carey C; FLs; Hattiesburg, MS 39401.
Thomas W. Lott
1-10; 2-2x16; 3-a; 4-spr 74; 5-1; 6-b; 7-a (one day per wk in middle of day when children are in school); 8-b; 9-primarily housewives; 10-none; 11-intro to vocab & structure of lang; primary emphasis on all aspects of Hispanic cult: religion, philosophy, psychology; 12-a,b,f; 13-a,b,d, records, food, realia; 14-Alexander, <u>Today's Latin America</u>.

775. CONVERSATIONAL SPANISH
U of Wisconsin; FLs; La Crosse, WI 54601.
Ruth A. Nixon
1-14; 2-ng; 3-a; 4-74; 5-ng; 6-ng; 7-b; 8-b; 9-b, community adults; 10-none; 11-all

Xeroxed and dittoed material for basic stiuational conv; 12-g; 13-ng; 14-none.

See also 249, 259A, 286, 1460, 1494.

MULTI-LANGUAGE

776. CONVERSATIONAL COURSES
Bellevue CC; FL; Bellevue, WA 98007.
Edward Matkovick
1-200 (150 presently); 2-3x11; 3-a; 4-68; 5-5; 6-a; 7-b; 8-b; 9-adults from community; 10-none for beginning level; elem or inter prof for more adv courses; 11-practical conv useful for everyday communication; structure is self-learned by using workbooks and lab, variety of langs offered (Fr, Ger, Ital, Jap, Sp, Swedish, Russ, Eng for foreign born) cont ed program; 12-b,c,e,f,g; 13-a,b,d,f, transparencies; 14-ng.

777. ADVANCED FRENCH, SPANISH, GERMAN CONVERSATION
Catonsville CC; FLs; Catonsville, MD 21228.
Enrique Corzo
1-15; 2-2x15; 3-a; 4-75; 5-1 (Sp), 2 (Fr); 6-a; 7-a; 8-b; 9-a,b, sr citizens; 10-elem prof; 11-conv structure; 12-b,c,d,g; 13-a,b,d,e, transparences; 14-none, other than the instructor's sheet.

778. CONVERSATIONAL FRENCH, SPANISH AND GERMAN
Christopher Newport C; MFLs & Lits; Newport News, VA 23606.
L. Barron Wood
1-30; 2-3x10; 3-a; 4-spr 71; 5-3; 6-b; 7-b; 8-b; 9-b; 10-none; 11-cont ed program in Fr, Sp, & Ger, separate classes; direct method with emphasis on basic everyday speech patterns in each lang; 12-f,g; 13-a,b,d, various other AV materials; 14-basic texts by American Express & the Inst of Modern Langs, Inc.

779. LANGUAGE INSIGHT PROGRAM
Forest Park CC; Fr; St. Louis, MO 63110.
Rosemary H. Thomas
1-50; 2-8x16; 3-b; 4-73; 5-4; 6-a; 7-a,b; 8-12s; 9-adults returning to school; 10-none; 11-Eng composition, oral communication, readings in contemporary prose, basic Fr or Sp; 12-a,b,c,d,f,g; 13-a,b,c,d,e,f; 14-Escholtz, Clark, Rosa, Language Awareness; Morton & Thomas, Basic Programmed French Course; American Express Co., Hablamos Espanol; Bantam Dual Ed., French Stories or Spanish Stories.

780. CONVERSATIONAL FRENCH & SPANISH
Monroe County CC; Hums; Monroe, MI 48161.
Paul E. Ross
1-19; 2-2x10; 3-a; 4-71; 5-4; 6-a; 7-b; 8-b; 9-community adults; 10-none; 11-ng; 12-a,b,g; 13-ng; 14-Kany & Dondo, Spoken Spanish for the Student and Traveler; Spoken French for the Student and Traveler.

781. CONVERSATIONAL LANGUAGE
Tarrant County JC; MFL; Fort Worth, TX 76119.
Ernesto Guzman
1-ng; 2-2x6-12; 3-c; 4-67; 5-2 or 3 times every yr; 6-a; 7-b; 8-b; 9-b; 10-none for elem level;11-program offered in all langs & levels; given on campus regularly, off-campus to community groups on demand; 12-a,b,d,g; 13-multimedia; 14-ng.

MISCELLANEOUS

782. RENAISSANCE ROOTS OF MODERN CULTURE
Lone Mountain C; Fr; San Francisco, CA 94118.
Antoinette Knapton
1-50; 2-1 hr per day for 4 days (2 wkends); 3-b; 4-74; 5-1; 6-special intersession program for 74; 7-on 2 wkends; 8-2s; 9-b; 10-none; 11-lit, art, music, sci, hist, evolution of the sonnet form; 12-a,f; 13-d, short bibliography supplied; readings of sonnets in original lang: Fr, Eng, Ital; 14-none.

783. DRIVER'S LICENSE STUDY FOR THE SPANISH SPEAKING
Morgan CC; Evening C; Fort Morgan, CO 80701.
Clarence Sanders
1-20-25; 2-2x10; 3-a; 4-75; 5-1; 6-b; 7-b; 8-b; 9-b; 10-ng; 11-we are presently in the process of translating all of the Colorado drivers' tests & study material to Sp for this class; 12-a,b,g; 13-b; 14-instructor's own material.

784. SOLZHENITSYN: ARTIST AND THINKER
U of North Carolina; Cont Ed; Greensboro, NC 27412.
J. T. Baer
1-7; 2-2x10; 3-a; 4-fall 74; 5-1; 6-b; 7-b; 8-b; 9-community adults; 10-none; 11-survey of writings of Solzhenitsyn in trans; 12-a,b,c,f; 13-ng; 14-primary texts.

785. CONTEMPORARY WRITERS
Trinity C; ML; Burlington, VT 05401.
Nancy Audette
1-22; 2-3x13; 3-b; 4-73; 5-1; 6-when feasible; 7-b; 8-3s; 9-a, adult ed; 10-ng; 11-contemporary Fr, Sp, and Amer novelists; 12-a,b,c,d,f; 13-ng; 14-ng.

786. OLD ORDER AMISH RELIGION AND LIFE
C of Wooster; Ger; Wooster, OH 44691.
Fred Cropp, W. I. Schreiber
1-58; 2-3x10; 3-c; 4-70; 5-5; 6-b; 7-a; 8-one unit (of three); 9-a, townspeople; 10-none; 11-lang & culture; 12-a,b,f, bus trips to Mennonite churches and into the Amishland, writing papers; 13-a,b,f, guest speakers; 14-Schreiber, Our Amish Neighbors.

See also 1305.

208

INTERDISCIPLINARY (INTERDEPARTMENTAL)

Culture and Civilization

NATIONAL

Canada

787. CANADIAN STUDIES PROGRAM
U of Maine; FL; Orono, ME 04473.
Joseph Roggenbauer, A. Stewart (Library)
1-ng; 2-ng; 3-b,c; 4-74; 5-ng; 6-a; 7-a,b; 8-ng; 9-a; 10-ng; 11-12 hrs of "Canadian core" courses plus 18 hrs related work in at least 3 of 5 participating depts; 12-a,b,c,d,f,g; 13-a,b,c,d,e,f; 14-ng.

See also 904.

China

788. CHINESE CIVILIZATION
Oberlin C; East Asian Studies; Oberlin, OH 44074.
Dale Johnson
1-50; 2-3x13; 3-b; 4-72/73; 5-2; 6-b; 7-a; 8-3; 9-a; 10-none; 11-3 lectures wkly, one optional discussion; taught by 5 specialists in hist, art, intellectual development, lit & lang; 12-a,b,f; 13-a,b; 14-various.

789. FAR EASTERN STUDIES - CHINESE
US Naval Academy; Area Lang Studies; Annapolis, MD 21042.
Guy J. Riccio
1-28; 2-varies; 3-b; 4-70; 5-each yr; 6-a; 7-a; 8-36; 9-a; 10-none; 11-Chi basic, inter & adv level courses aimed at developing prof & awareness of salient characteristics of Chi culture and civ; 6 supporting courses offered by Depts of Hist, Poli Sci, & Econ; 12-a,b,c,f,g; 13-a,b,e,f; 14-various.

Czechoslovakia

See 715.

France

790. THE CIVILIZATION OF FRANCE
Bryn Mawr C; French; Bryn Mawr, PA 19010.
Alain Silvera
1-7; 2-3x13; 3-b; 4-71/72; 5-2; 6-every other yr; 7-a; 8-8s (full yr course); 9-a; 10-good command of Fr; 11-studies development of modern Fr life & cult in its hist context & explores values & attitudes of Fr society as manifested in lit, arts, politics, ed & religion; 12-a,b,c,d,g; 13-a,b,e,f; 14-various.

791. CONFERENCE FOR SENIORS
Bryn Mawr C; Fr; Bryn Mawr, PA 19010.
Michel Guggenheim
1-5; 2-2x26; 3-b; 4-73/74; 5-2; 6-a; 7-a; 8-16; 9-a; 10-for majors in Fr & majors in hist;

11-in the 1st sem, sr majors will study selected aspects of the hist, soci, & inst features of Fr civ, giving oral reports; 2nd sem they will work on a research project; 12-a,b,c,d,g; 13-a,e,f; 14-ng.

792. FRENCH STUDIES
Bryn Mawr C; Fr & Hist; Bryn Mawr, PA 19010.
Michel Guggenheim, Fr; Arthur Dudden, Hist
The major concentrates on a sequence of Fr & hist courses planned according to lit themes, genres, & topics studied in their hist setting, possibility of modifying pattern of concentration to include courses in such allied fields as poli sci, soci, philosophy, hist of art, or music, to be taken either at Bryn Mawr or Haverford; jr yr in France integral part of program.

793. FRENCH STUDIES
Emory U; Fr Studies; Atlanta, GA 30822.
Grant E. Kaiser
1-7; 2-1½x11; 3-b; 4-72/73; 5-2; 6-b; 7-a; 8-5q; 9-a; 10-combined with Fr, Hist, or Art Hist Major; 11-cult, hist, art, lang; Fr studies majors urged to take jr yr in France; 12-a,b,c,f; 13-library; 14-ng.

794. FRENCH SOCIETY AND CULTURE
U of Michigan; Rom Langs; Ann Arbor, MI 48104.
John Bowditch, Hist
1-35; 2-3x14; 3-b; 4-71; 5-4; 6-b; 7-a; 8-3s; 9-a; 10-permission of instructor; 11-interdisc study of soci & cult; 12-a,b,f; 13-a,b,c,d,e,f; 14-Fox, History in a Geographic Perspective; Ardagh, The New French Revolution; E. Morin, Plodemet; Wylie, Village in the Vaucluse; plus others.

795. FRENCH CIVILIZATION AND CULTURE
Northwest Mississippi JC; MFL; Senatobia, MS 38688.
Emily Mae Ballew
1-new; 2-3x32; 3-b; 4-75/76; 5-0; 6-every yr for 32 wks; 7-a; 8-3s; 9-ng; 10-elem prof; 11-civ & cult of Fr-speaking nations; to include hist, poli sci, art, music, archaeology, architecture plus lit pertaining to each segment; readings in Fr; 12-a,b,c,e,f,g; 13-a,b,d,e,f, filmstrips, pictures, articles; 14-various.

796. FRANCE TODAY
Saginaw Valley C; MLs; University Center, MI 48710.
Lynn Kerkstroeter
1-15; 2-4x15; 3-b; 4-75; 5-1; 6-will depend upon success of course; 7-a; 8-4s; 9-a; 10-none; 11-study of hist, lit, arts, soci institu-

tions of France, 1890-1970; 12-a,b,c,f; 13-b; 14-Nourissier, The French; Tannenbaum, Modern France.

797. FRENCH CULTURE THROUGH THE AGES
Stephens C; FLs; Columbia, MO 65201.
Albert J. Delmez
1-12; 2-6x7; 3-b; 4-62; 5-13; 6-a; 7-a; 8-3q; 9-a; 10-two courses in Fr civ taught in Fr; 11-deals with 20th cen thought, societal problems, politics, econ, art, architecture, lit, women's movement; 12-a,b,c,d,f; 13-a,b,e,f; 14-no formal text, various material.

798. FRANCE IN THE 12th & 13th CENTURIES
C of Wooster; Fr; Wooster, OH 44691.
D. Wilkin
1-7; 2-5x10; 3-b; 4-74; 5-1; 6-alt yrs; 7-a; 8-one course credit; 9-a; 10-none; 11-lit, architecture, soci, poli structures, music from 1080-1300; 12-a,b,c,f; 13-b,d; 14-various.

See also 921.

German

799. POLITICAL AND CULTURAL MOVEMENTS IN GERMANY BETWEEN THE TWO WORLD WARS
Amherst C; Ger; Amherst, MA 01002.
Donald O. White
1-13; 2-3x14; 3-b; 4-72; 5-2; 6-no longer to be offered; 7-a; 8-3s; 9-a; 10-ng; 11-interdisc study of interaction of art & hist in Germany, 1918-39; 12-b,c,f; 13-a,b; 14-various.

800. GERMAN STUDIES
Heidelberg C; Ger; Tiffin, OH 44883.
Frank D. Horvay
1-20; 2-ng; 3-b,c; 4-71; 5-4; 6-a; 7-a; 8-24s; 9-a; 10-inter Ger, Adv Ger Grammar; 11-12 Sem hrs in Civ, Lang & Lit; 12 sem hrs in German Hist, Econ, Poli Sci; may be taken at Heidelberg C or during Jr Yr in Germany; 12-a,b,c,f,g; 13-a,b,d,e; 14-ng.

801. GERMAN CIVILIZATION
Illinois SU; FLs; Normal, IL 61761.
Bodo Fritzen
1-23; 2-5x18; 3-b; 4-74; 5-2; 6-b; 7-a; 8-ng; 9-a; 10-none; 11-interdis study in hist, poli sci, lang; optional study abroad program; 12-a,b,c,f; 13-a,b,c,d,e; 14-ng.

802. MAJOR IN GERMAN LANGUAGE & CULTURE
Southern Missionary C; MLs; Collegedale, TN 37315.
Robert R. Morrison
1-new; 2-ng; 3-b; 4-74/75; 5-1; 6-a; 7-a; 8-30; 9-ng; 10-varies; 11-4-yr program built upon preexisting courses; includes courses in Ger, Sci, Eng, Hums, Religion, Math, Fine Arts; team-taught; 12-a,b,c,e,f,g; 13-a,b,d,e,f; 14-ng.

803. EUROPEAN STUDIES: GERMAN
US Naval Academy; Area-Lang Studies; Annapolis, MD 21042.

G.J. Riccio
1-21; 2-ng; 3-b; 4-70; 5-each yr; 6-a; 7-a; 8-36s; 9-a; 10-elem Ger; 11-European Studies Program with concentration in Ger; inter & adv lang courses, a civ course of 2 sems; 6 courses related to the area, offered by the Hist, Poli Sci & Econ Depts; 12-a,b,c,f,g; 13-a,b,e,f; 14-Tenbrock, Geschichte Deutschlands.
See also 949, 950, 951.

Greece

See 978.

Italy

804. LANGUAGE & CULTURE OF ITALY
Central Connecticut SC; ML; New Britain, CT 06050.
Gaetano Iannace
1-28 for credit, 25 auditors; 2-3x16; 3-b; 4-75; 5-1; 6-b; 7-b; 8-3s; 9-a,b, open to public free of charge; 10-none; 11-interdis lectures covering nature of lang, hist, art, theater, philosophy, sci & lit conducted in Eng; 12-a,b,c,d,f; 13-b; 14-Italian Literature in Translation.

Mexico

805. MEXICAN FOLKLORE
Monterey Inst of Foreign Studies; Langs & Civs; Monterey, CA 93940.
Ovid C. Fuente
General survey of Mexican myths, legends, popular lit, music, dances, costumes & arts & crafts; no prerequisite; taught in Sp; 2 credits; smr 74; further info ng.

806. INTRODUCTION TO MEXICO
Trinity U; Latin Amer Studies; San Antonio, TX 78284.
Richard D. Woods
1-12; 2-3x14; 3-a; 4-ng; 5-ng; 6-b; 7-a; 8-3s; 9-a; 10-none; 11-covering Pre-Columbian, Colonial, & Independence periods to present, multiple approaches from hist, soci scis, religion, fine arts, lit; 12-a,b,c,d,g; 13-a,b,d,e,f; 14-Quirk, Mexico; Wolf, Sons of the Shaking Earth; Paz, Anthology of Mexican Poetry; Gamio, The Life Story of the Mexican Immigrant; Millon, Zapata-The Ideology of a Peasant Revolutionary; Fuentes, The Death of Artemio Cruz; Lewis, Five Families.

See also 897, 1566.

Puerto Rico

807. PUERTO RICO
U of Vermont; Area Studies; Burlington, VT 05401.
Timothy Murad
1-13; 2-3x14; 3-b; 4-fall 73; 5-1; 6-only given once, future offerings contemplated; 7-a; 8-3s; 9-a; 10-only Sp lang ability; 11-hist, politics, lit; 12-a,b,c,f,g; 13-e,f; 14-ng.

Russia

808. RUSSIAN STUDIES
Bryn Mawr C; Russ; Bryn Mawr, PA 19010.

Ruth Pearce
1-ng; 2-ng; 3-b; 4-ng; 5-ng; 6-a; 7-a; 8-ng; 9-a; 10-variable; 11-gives student the opportunity to combine study of the Russ lang with study in depth in one of the following areas of concentration: Russ Hist, Russ Econ, Russ Phil. Residence abroad and in the Russ House is advisable; 12-a,b,f; 13-ng; 14-ng.

809. SOVIET STUDIES
Cazenovia JC; Lang & Lit, Hist & Soci Sci; Cazenovia, NY 13035.
N.E. Bently
1-8; 2-6x6; 3-b; 4-65; 5-9; 6-one module; 7-a; 8-3q; 9-a; 10-permission of the instructors; 11-revolution, civil war, NEP, Stalin, WW II, Krushchev, related lit, music, drama, films.

810. RUSSIAN STUDIES
Douglass C; Rutgers U; Russ; New Brunswick, NJ 08903.
Ludmilla B. Turkevish
Interdis major; courses in Russ lang & lit, econ, geography, hist, poli sci, soci.

811. RUSSIAN AREA STUDY
Macalester C; Interdept; St. Paul, MN 55105.
A.A. Guss
1-new; 2-ng; 3-b,c; 4-75; 5-0; 6-a; 7-a; 8-ng; 9-new course; 10-2 yrs Russ; 11-hist, lit, religion; study of poli, soci, econ insts of Soviet Union; 12-f; 13-a,e; 14-ng.

812. RUSSIAN STUDIES
Muhlenberg C; FLs; Allentown, PA 18104.
Arnds Ziedonis
Interdis program. Further info ng.

813. THE SOVIET UNION: YESTERDAY, TODAY & TOMORROW
Purdue U; FLs & Lits, Hist, Poli Sci; West Lafayette, IN 47907.
Herbert Eagle
1-80+; 2-3x15; 3-b; 4-spr74; 5-1; 6-b; 7-b, the course will be offered in day session in future; 8-3s; 9-a; 10-none; 11-interdis, geography, econ, politics, sci, ed, lit, art; 12-a,b,f; 13-a,b,e, political posters; 14-various.

814. BACKGROUND AND MAIN CURRENTS OF RUSSIAN CULTURE
U of Tennessee; Ger & Sl; Knoxville, TN 37916.
Martin D. Rice
1-97; 2-3x20; 3-b; 4-72/73; 5-3; 6-1 two-qtr sequence each yr; 7-a; 8-4q; 9-a; 10-none; 11-program in Russ lit & intellectual, religious, poli & soci hist; 12-a,b,c,d,f; 13-a,b,d,e; 14-various.

815. THE USSR TODAY
U of Texas; FL & Ling; Arlington, TX 76019.
James D. Wilmeth
1-97; 2-3x15; 3-b,c; 4-72/73; 5-5; 6-was a, but now b, because this spr a sequel course will be offered for the first time; 7-a; 8-3s; 9-a; 10-2 yrs of Russ for Russ credit; 11-

examines metamorphosis of the Communist Party; provides insight into the mind of the typical Soviet citizen; 12-a,f; 13-a,b,c,d, guest lecturers; 14-USSR 73; A Short History of the Soviet Union, both are written and published in the Soviet Union. Map of Russia, CIA. An oral or trans requirement is mandatory for those receiving credit in Russ lang.

816. SOVIET STUDIES-RUSSIAN
US Naval Academy; Area-Lang Studies; Annapolis, MD 21042.
G.J. Riccio
1-25; 2-varies; 3-b; 4-70; 5-each yr; 6-a; 7-a; 9-36; 10-none; 11-Russ-elem, inter and adv and a 2-sem civ course; 6 courses related to the area offered by Hist, Poli Sci & Econ Depts; 12-a,b,c,f,g; 13-a,b,e,f; 14-Vasys, Krypton, Iswolsky, Russian Area Reader; Johnson, Kaspin, Kostruba, Eyewitness (both for civ course).

817. RUSSIAN CIVILIZATION & CULTURE
U of Virginia; Sl; Charlottesville, VA 22903.
Jan L. Perkowski
1-60; 2-3x14; 3-b; 4-74; 5-2; 6-b; 7-a; 8-3s; 9-a; 10-none; 11-lit, hist, art, music, taught jointly by Sl & Hist Depts with other guest lecturers; 12-a,b,c,d,f; 13-a,b,c,d; 14-varies.

818. RUSSIAN WITH AREA STUDIES
Williams C; Russ; Williamstown, MA 01267.
Nicholas Fersen
1-4; 2-ng; 3-b; 4-67; 5-every yr; 6-a; 7-a; 8-ng; 9-a; 10-4 sems Russ; 11-a major program with courses in Russ lit (a few in trans), econ, hist, poli sci; 12-a,b,c,d,f,g; 13-ng; 14-ng.

819. RUSSIA IN THE 19TH CENTURY
C of Wooster; Interdept; Wooster, OH 44691.
Daniel F. Calhoun
1-40; 2-4x20; 3-b; 4-74/75; 5-1; 6-every other yr; 7-a; 8-10q; 9-a; 10-none; 11-2-course module exploring cult and political developments of 19th cen Russ; hist course in the fall and General Lit in the spr; a cohesive unit placing primary emphasis on hist & lit; 12-a,b,c,f; 13-a,b,e; 14-Mirsky, A History of Russian Literature: From Its Beginnings to 1900; primary texts.

Slovenia

820. SLOVENIAN LANGUAGE AND CULTURE
Southern Colorado SC; FL; Pueblo, CO 81005.
Monique Amerman
1-25; 2-3x11; 3-b,c; 4-fall 74; 5-1; 6-3 consecutive qtrs; 7-a,c; 8-3q; 9-a,b; 10-none; 11-2 hrs per wk spent in conv, rest of time instruction in major cult aspects of Slovenian; 12-a,e,f,g; 13-b,d; 14-special material for Slovenian.

Spain

821. SPANISH CIVILIZATION AND CULTURE
Stephens C; FLs; Columbia, MO 65201.

211

Albert J. Delmez
3-credit fall sem course providing general background in understanding the Spaniard and his heritage through hist, art, architecture, lit & philo. Taught in Eng. No prerequisites.

SUPRANATIONAL

African

See 898, 905.

Asian

822. ASIAN STUDIES PROGRAM
U of Alaska; Ling & FLs; Fairbanks, AK 99701.
Bruce R. Gordon
Includes Asian hist, art, philosophy, geography, & Jap & offers only a minor. Provides instruction through an interdis approach (at least 3 depts) and enables students to consolidate various course offerings into a cohesive program relevant to several major fields of specialization.

823. ASIAN STUDIES
Monterey Inst of Foreign Studies; Intl Studies; Monterey, CA 93940.
Claude Buss, Dennis Cohen
Program leading to M.A.; includes comparative & intl politics, intl econ, lit, consecutive interpretation, Eng & for lang trans.

824. EAST ASIAN STUDIES
Muhlenberg C; FLs; Allentown, PA 18104.
Stuart Lee
Interdisc program. Further info ng.

825. INTERDEPARTMENTAL MAJOR IN ASIAN CIVILIZATION
Randolph-Macon Women's C; Asian Studies; Ashland, VA 23005.
David F. Anthony
1-32; 2-flexible 6-24; 3-b; 4-65/66; 5-8 yrs; 6-a; 7-a; 8-6 to 24; 9-a and occasionally part-time businessmen taking Jap; 10-Asian civ course; 11-study of Asian cult & civ in order to develop an understanding of Asian value-systems, soci organization, govt, and aesthetics and thereby reduce the "cult distance" between Amers and Asians; 12-a,b,c,f; 13-a,e,f; 14-various.

826. EAST ASIAN AREA STUDIES
Washington U; Committee on Asian Studies; St. Louis, MO 63130.
Eugene Soviak
1-42; 2-ng; 3-b; 4-62; 5-ng; 6-a; 7-a; 8-ng; 9-a; 10-matriculation; 11-14 units (2 yrs) lang plus area courses; 12-a,b,c,f,g; 13-a,b,d,e,f; 14-varies.

See also 897, 904, 905.

Classical

827. ANCIENT CIVILIZATION
U of California; Cl, Hist; Irvine, CA 92664.
Richard Frank
1-ng; 2-3x10; 3-b; 4-75; 5-0; 6-a; 7-a; 8-4q; 9-a; 10-none; 11-cult & hist material dealing with the golden ages of Greece & Rome; 12-a,b; 13-ng; 14-various.

828. INTERDISCIPLINARY MAJOR IN CLASSICAL CIVILIZATION
Connecticut C; Cl; New London, CT 06320.
Mary Louise Lord
1-6; 2-4 yrs; 3-b; 4-73; 5-ng; 6-a; 7-a; 8-ng; 9-a; 10-ng; 11-Greek or Latin required; elective courses (at least 4 from these) in art hist, govt, hist, philosophy, religion; 12-a,b,c,f; 13-b, records; 14-ng.

829. PROGRAM IN CLASSICAL HUMANITIES
Kent SU; Rom Langs & Cl; Kent, OH 44242.
Betty J. Parks, Mark Rubin
Alternative to traditional major in ancient langs & lit; focuses attention on the whole of classical civ, emphasizing areas in humanistic studies relevant to all men in every age.

830. CLASSICAL CIVILIZATION MAJOR
U of Kentucky; Cl; Lexington, KY 40506.
Louis J. Swift
Major requirements: 18 credits within the Dept of Cl above the freshman level; 6 of these must be in lang courses; 14 credits above freshman level outside Dept of Cl; 8 credits in addition either from cl or in other depts within field of concentration (Hebrew and Islamic civ courses and Hebrew Lang accepted as part of major).

831. CLASSICAL STUDIES MAJOR
Salem C; Cl; Winston-Salem, NC 27108.
F.M. Lazarus
1-15; 2-3x13; 3-b; 4-spr 74; 5-3 (most courses); 6-a; 7-a; 8-3s per course; 9-a; 10-none; 11-Depts of Art, Cl Langs & Lit, Eng, Hist, & Religion & Philosophy; major requires prof in one cl lang; emphasizes broad approach to humanistic values; 12-a,b,f,g; 13-ng; 14-varies.

832. CLASSICAL CIVILIZATION CONCENTRATION
Syracuse U; Cl; Syracuse, NY 13210.
Louis Roberts
1-35; 2-3x17; 3-b; 4-72; 5-4; 6-a; 7-a; 8-3s; 9-a; 10-none; 11-offered with cooperation of Depts of Eng, Fine Arts, Hist, Philosophy, Poli Sci & Religion; no Greek or Latin required; while acquiring a general knowledge of cl civ, the student may concentrate on one or more aspects of it; 12-a,b,f; 13-a,b,d; 14-ng.

See also 998.

East European

833. RUSSIAN AREA STUDIES
U of Alaska; Interdept; Fairbanks, AK 99701.
Joseph J. Brenckle Jr.
This undergrad major is offered in an effort to develop the student's awareness of Alaska's Russ heritage. Courses designed to provide understanding of the cult, civ, poli insts, hist and philosophical foundations of Russia and the Soviet Union.

834. SOVIET STUDIES

Monterey Inst of Foreign Studies; Intl Studies; Monterey, CA 93940.
Leon Shoob
Program leading to M.A.; includes comparative & intl poli, intl econs, lit, consecutive interpretation, Eng & for lang trans; hist, thesis.

835. RUSSIAN & EAST EUROPEAN INTERDISCIPLINARY PROGRAM
SUNY; Sl Langs; Albany, NY 14222.
Alex M. Shane
1-new; 2-ng; 3-b; 4-75/76; 5-0; 6-unknown; 7-a; 8-60-70; 9-a, special students; 10-none; 11-proposed jointly by Depts of Hist & Sl Langs; program would lead to a BA in Russ & East European Studies with a concentration in lang or hist. With either concentration, the student would acquire broad, relevant experience and the necessary lang skills for the field. There would be opportunity for overseas study; 12-a,b,c,d,f,g; 13-a,b,d,e,f, records; 14-varies.

836. M.A. IN SLAVIC STUDIES
SUNY; Russ; Binghamton, NY 13901.
F.F. Seeley (Russian); B.H. Horwitz (Bus Management)
Main objective of the program (to begin 75-76) is to produce broadly-educated citizens versed in the cults of the Soviet Union and Eastern Europe and equipped to interpret those cults to their fellow citizens and/or act as intermediaries, at all levels, in the poli, econ, legal, ed and other relations which can be expected to develop between the US & the USSR & Eastern Europe.

See also 904, 906.

European

837. MODERN EUROPEAN STUDIES
Connecticut C; Ger; New London, CT 06320.
J.L. Gellinek
Interdisc program first offered in 74/75. Requires minimum of 1 lit course in 1 European lang; study of another European lang; courses in intellectual hist, hist of poli insts of Europe, electives in soci scis, arts & lits, with concentration in 1 area.

838. COMPARATIVE CULTURES
Midland Lutheran C; FL; Fremont, NE 68025.
Martin Trautrimas
1-27; 3-4x14; 3-b,c; 4-73; 5-2; 6-b; 7-a; 8-4s; 9-a; 10-none; 11-highlights of major European cults which contributed to & enriched Western heritage; 12-a,b,d,f; 13-a,b,c,d,e,f; 14-Comparative Culture & Government, booklets for Greece, Italy, France, Spain, Germany, Scandinavia, England.

839. CONTINENTAL EUROPEAN STUDIES
Millikin U; FLs; Decatur, IL 62522.
William N. Ferris
Further info ng.

840. WEST EUROPEAN STUDIES

Monterey Inst of Foreign Studies; Intl Studies; Monterey, CA 93940.
Juergen Bruhn
Program leading to M.A.; includes comparative & intl politics, intl econ, lit, consecutive interpretation, Eng & for lang trans, hist, thesis.

841. EUROPEAN STUDIES
U of San Diego; Interdisc Studies; Alcala Park, CA 92110.
Carl Guilbert
Program initiated 1972. Further info ng.

842. EUROPEAN STUDIES
Seattle Pacific C; Hums; Seattle, WA 98119.
Michael Macdonald
A new program to be offered 75/76. Students who wish to concentrate in European Studies may design a program which includes 30 credits in one for lang & 30 credits from courses offered in the School of Hums & the School of Soci and Behavioral Scis. A total of 23 upper-div credits is required. At least one qtr of study abroad or approved alternative is required.

843. FOCUS ON THE PAST: AN INTRODUCTION TO EUROPEAN CIVILIZATION

Sweet Briar C; All Hums Depts; Sweet Briar, VA 24595.
Robert Gilpin
1-50; 2-4x13; 3-b; 4-73/74; 5-3; 6-a, sr colloquia alt sem; 7-a; 8-3s; 9-none for freshman; completion of other program requirements for colloquia; 11-hist, lit, philosophy, econ, music, art; 12-a,b,f; 13-a,d; 14-various.

844. HUMANITIES SURVEY CORE
Touro C; Div of Hums; New York, NY 10036.
Joseph Lowin, R. Berlow
1-100; 2-6x12; 3-b; 4-71; 5-ng; 6-a; 7-a; 8-6q; 9-a; 10-required for graduation; 11-2-yr sequence offering the student a multi-faceted approach to the study of Western European traditions, ideas, experiences. Sequence consists of 4 courses: Greek & Roman Civ; Medieval Civ; Renaissance to 18th Cent; Modern European Hist; 12-a,b,c,f; 13-a; 14-readings in lit & philosophy.

845. CULTURAL AREA STUDIES-20TH CENTURY WESTERN EUROPE
C of Wooster; Fr; Wooster, OH 44691.
D. Wilkin (Fr) or D. Gedalecia (Hist)
A major program initiated 73/74: 4th level competence in one Western European lang; 6 courses in core area (e.g., hist, Fr, econ); 6 courses in related disciplines; sr thesis.

See also 898, 904, 1000, 1008.

French

846. EUROPEAN FRENCH STUDIES
Colby C-New Hampshire; MLs; New

213

London, NH 03257.
David Siesicki
A contract major to start fall 75. Goals: to develop skills & knowledge necessary to demonstrate understanding in depth of European Fr cult & civ; to attain direct experience living in a European Fr cult; to demonstrate the utility of this skill, knowledge & experience through a work/study project devoted to cult relations between the US & France.

847.   NORTH AMERICAN FRENCH STUDIES
Colby C–New Hampshire; MLs; New London, NH 03257.
David Siesicki
A contract major to start fall 75. Goals: to develop skills & knowledge necessary to an understanding in depth of Fr cult & civ in North Amer; to attain direct experience living in the North Amer Fr cult; to demonstrate the utility of this skill, knowledge, experience by a work/study commitment to the North Amer Fr community.

848.   FRANCO-AMERICAN STUDIES PROGRAM
U of Maine; FL, Anthropology, Econ, Hist, Soci; Orono, ME 04473.
Josef Roggenbauer
1-ng; 2-ng; 3-b,c; 4-71; 5-every sem; 6-a, also smr; 7-a,b; 8-ng; 9-a; 10-ng; 11-24 hrs of Fr lang plus 18 hrs of related work in at least 3 of 5 participating depts; 12-a,b,c,d,f,g; 13-a,b,c,d,e,f; 14-ng.

849.   FRANCO-AMERICAN STUDIES I AND II
U of Maine; FLs & Cls; Portland, ME 04103.
Monique Crochet
1-8; 2-2½x14; 3-b; 4-fall 74; 5-1; 6-b; probably but not certain, since this is experimental; 7-a; 8-3s; 9-a; 10-none; 11-multi-disc course focusing on the Franco-Amers of New England, their antecedents and contemporaries in Canada. Includes studies in hist, soci, poli sci, & lit; 12-a,b,f; 13-a,b; 14-Thompson, ed., Quebec Society and Politics; Wade, The French-Canadian Outlook; Greeley, Why Can't They Be Like Us?; Ringuet, Thirty Acres; Ducharme, The Delusion Family.

850.   EUROPEAN STUDIES: FRENCH
US Naval Academy; Area-Lang Studies; Annapolis, MD 21402.
G.J. Riccio
1-14; 2-ng; 3-b; 4-70; 5-each yr; 6-a; 7-a; 8-36s; 9-a; 10-elem Fr; 11-European Studies program with concentration in Fr; inter & adv lang courses, a civ course of 2 sems; 6 courses related to the area, offered by the Hist, Poli Sci, & Econ Depts; 12-a,b,c,f,g; 13-a,b,e,f; 14-Hardie, La France et sa civilisation.

See also 903, 905, 906, 1546.

German

851.   CONTEMPORARY GERMAN CULTURE
U of Pittsburgh; Ger; Pittsburgh, PA 15260.

John Neubauer
1-9; 2-3x14; 3-b,c; 4-73/74; 5-1; 6-b; 7-a,b; 8-3s; 9-ng; 10-none; 11-lectures, films, discussion on contemporary Austria, East & West Germany, Switzerland; lectures by invited specialist; 12-a,b,f; 13-a,b; 14-Dahrendorf, Society and Democracy in Germany; Grosser, Germany in our Time; Leonhardt, This Germany; Grass, Local Anaesthetic.

852.   POLITICS AND CULTURE OF MODERN GERMANY
U of Texas; Ger Langs; Austin, TX 78712.
Walter Wetzels
1-80 in various topical sections; 2-3x14; 3-b; 4-55; 5-40-50 times; 6-a, occasionally in smr; 7-a; 8-3s; 9-a; 10-jr standing; 11-varies, has included East Germany, Austria, Germanies, Switzerland today, art & architecture of Germany in 15th cen; 12-a,b,f; 13-a,d,e,f; 14-various.

853.   GERMAN AREA STUDIES
U of Washington; Gers; Seattle, WA 98195.
G. C. Buck
1-ng; 2-variable; 3-b; 4-74/75; 5-1; 6-a; 7-a; 8-variable; 9-a; 10-2 yrs lang study; 11-a major designed for students who wish to acquire a solid humanistic background oriented toward Germanics but who do not wish to concentrate on developing skills of lit analysis and/or active prof in all aspects of Ger grammar & stylistics. Students may choose to concentrate on one of 5 "core groups" - art & lit of the modern period; art & lit of the older period; hist of ideas; hist & sociology; ling; 12-a,b,c,d,f,g; 13-ng; 14-ng.

See also 906, 1018, 1387.

Hispanic

854.   MEXICAN-AMERICAN STUDIES
Adams SC; Soci; Alamosa, CO 81101.
Wilma Gomez Stump
1-25; 2-3x11; 3-b; 4-73; 5-2; 6-a; 7-a; 8-9q; 9-a; 10-ng; 11-Mex-Amer cult taught by concerned depts; 12-b,c,d,f; 13-a,d; 14-ng.

855.   LATIN AMERICAN STUDIES INTER-DISCIPLINARY COLLOQUIUM
Austin C; Area Studies; Sherman, TX 75090.
Juliette C. McClendon
1-1; 2-3x14; 3-b; 4-70; 5-5; 6-a,b, on demand; 7-a; 8-4s; 9-a; 10-open to Latin Amer Studies concentrators; to other students by permission; 11-an interchange of ideas presenting an integrated view of contemporary Latin Amer issues involving students, faculty of various disciplines represented in the Latin Amer Studies program; 12-a,b,c,f; 13-a,e,f; 14-ng.

856.   LATIN AMERICAN STUDIES
Baylor U; Interdept; Waco, TX 76703.
William Cooper;
Further info ng.

857.   LATIN AMERICAN AREA STUDIES
Beloit C; MLs & Lits; Beloit, WI 53511.
Donald A. Murray

New major not yet in operation. The courses will be taught by several depts other than MLs: hist, geography, econ, anthropology; both lang & lit courses are required. Courses will be open to all qualified persons of the non-academic community, though the major is designed for our own undergrad students.

858. LATIN AMERICAN STUDIES
Brandeis U; various; Waltham, MA 02154.
Donald Hindley
1-14 ng.

859. HISPANIC CULTURE AND CIVILIZATION
Bryn Mawr C; Sp; Bryn Mawr, Pa 19010.
Willard F. King
1-11; 2-3x13; 3-b; 4-74/75; 5-1; 6-a; 7-a; 8-4s; 9-a; 10-good reading & listening comprehension of Sp; 11-brief survey of the poli, soci & cult hist of Spain & Sp Amer concentrating on the emergence of specifically Hispanic values & modes of life, as identified by Spaniards & Span Amers & by sympathetic or antagonistic non-Spaniards; 12-a,b,c,d,f,g; 13-b,e,f, records, film-strips; 14-(a selection) Ortiz, Clases privilegiadas en la Espana de los Austrias; Tannenbaum, Ten Keys to Latin America; Castro, Structure of Spanish History; Jackson, Making of Medieval Spain; Gibson, ed., The Black Legend; Garcilaos, Comentarios.

860. HISPANIC STUDIES SENIOR CONFERENCE
Bryn Mawr C; Sp; Bryn Mawr, PA 19010.
Willard F. King
1-5; 2-2x14; 3-b; 4-71/72; 5-3; 6-b; 7-a; 8-4s; 9-a; 10-completion of previous requirements for Hispanic Studies Program, prof in Sp; 11-varies; 12-b,c,d,f; 13-e,f,g, books; 14-various.

861. HISPANIC CULTURE AND CIVILIZATION
Central Virginia CC; Hums; Lynchburg, VA 24504.
Edward A. Peniche
1-14; 2-3x30; 3-b; 4-72; 5-2; 6-a; 7-a; 8-9q; 9-ng; 10-1 Sp course; 11-study of Latin Amer life, civ & lit; interdisc approach; taught by members of Hist, Govt, Art & Eng Depts; 12-a,b,d,f,g; 13-a,b,c,e,f; 14-Iberoamerica: Sintesis de su Civilizacion.

862. SPANISH-AMERICAN AREA STUDIES
Clemson U; Lang; Clemson, SC 29631.
G. J. Fernandez, J. Arbena
1-5; 2-ng; 3-b; 4-fall 72; 5-every sem; 6-a; 7-a; 8-15s; 9-a; 10-2 yrs Sp; 11-a minor concentration requiring courses in hist, poli sci, Sp, agriculture, econ, geography; 12-a,b,c,f,g; 13-all; 14-ng.

863. IBERO-AMERICAN STUDIES
Eastern Kentucky U; FL; Richmond, KY 40475.
Kathleen K. Hill
1-ng; 2-ng; 3-b; 4-74; 5-ng; 6-a; 7-a,b; 8-ng; 9-a; 10-ng; 11-interdisc major in cooperation with Depts of Anthropology, Poli Sci,

Hist, Geography; 12-ng; 13-ng; 14-ng.

864. LATIN AMERICAN STUDIES SEMINAR
Emory U; Rom Langs; Atlanta, GA 30322.
Joaquin Roy
1-new; 2-4x8-10; 3-b; 4-to be offered; 6-a; 7-a; 8-5q; 9-a; 10-minimum requirement for LAS major; 11-topic will change every time; 12-b,d,f,g, (whether course will be taught in Eng or Sp will depend); 13-b,f; 14-ng.

865. LATIN AMERICAN STUDIES PROGRAM
U of Georgia; Rom Langs (and several others); Athens, GA 30601.
Manuel D. Ramirez
1-ng; 2-5x10; 3-b; 4-fall 74; 5-1; 6-a; 7-a; 8-5q; 9-a; 10-none for most of the courses; 11-courses in lit, civ, art, intl relations, poli sci, population theory and problems; 12-a,b,c,f,g; 13-b,e,f; 14-various.

866. LATIN AMERICAN CIVILIZATION
Grinnell C; Sp, Hist; Grinnell, IA 50112.
Dennis Parle
1-20; 2-3x14; 3-a; 4-74/75; 5-1; 6-2 sem course: civ I every 1st sem, civ II every 2nd sem; 7-a; 8-4s; 9-a; 10-none; 11-study of Latin Amer cult & hist, in 2nd sem emphasis on its developing nationalism; 12-a,b,c,f; 13-a,c, guest lecturers; 14-various.

867. LATIN AMERICAN STUDIES PROGRAM
Kent SU; Latin Amer Studies; Kent, OH 44242.
Doris J. Turner
Open to candidates for B.A. degree, curriculum structured to enable student to cross dept lines to pursue, with the mastery of Port and/or Sp, a major in Latin Amer Studies; students required to use elective hours in any of the recognized disciplines that support the program: Anthropology, Econ, Geography, Hist, Marketing, Poli Sci, Sociology or Sp; credit program in Mexico, wtr qtr.

868. LATIN AMERICAN AREA STUDIES
Lock Haven, SC; FL; Lock Haven, PA 17745.
E. J. Carney
An interdisc program initiated Jan 75; prerequisite is inter Sp; program involves Sp or Port lang & lit, Latin Amer cult, hist, geography, anthropology, art, music.

869. LATIN-AMERICAN STUDIES PROGRAM
U of Maine; FL, Hist, Anthropology, Poli Sci; Orono, ME 04473.
Josef Roggenbauer
1-ng; 2-ng; 3-b; 4-spr 74; 5-ng; 6-a; 7-a; 8-ng; 9-a; 10-ng; 11-24 hrs of Sp or Port lang combined with 18 hrs of related work in 4 participating depts; 12-a,b,c,d,f,g; 13-a,b,c,d,e; 14-ng.

870. AREA OF CONCENTRATION IN LATIN AMERICAN STUDIES
U of Missouri; Rom Langs; Columbia, MO 65201.
Program designed to provide a broad background in lang & soci sci for students

215

anticipating careers in govt service, teaching, or bus in the Latin Amer field; sufficient concentration in one discipline is also incorporated into the Area to provide a good foundation for adv grad study in any one of several fields--lang & lit, econ, hist, poli sci.

871. LATIN AMERICAN STUDIES
U of Missouri; FLs; Kansas City, MO 64110.
Jon Beeker
1-3; 2-ng; 3-b; 4-74; 5-ng; 6-a; 7-a; 8-ng; 9-a; 10-jr status; 11-interdisc program involving FL & Depts of Biology, Hist, Econ, Poli Sci, Geosciences, Soci; 12-all; 13-ng; 14-ng.

872. LATIN AMERICAN STUDIES
Monterey Inst of Foreign Studies; Intl Studies; Monterey, CA 93940.
Brian Johnson
Program leading to M.A.; includes comparative & intl politics, intl econs, lit, consecutive interpretation, Eng & for lang trans.

873. SPANISH AMERICAN CIVILIZATION
Monterey Inst of Foreign Studies; Langs & Civs; Monterey, CA 93940.
Ovid C. Fuente
Survey of hist, institutions, arts, soci & econ problems of Latin Amer; no prerequisites; taught in Sp; 2 credits; transfer class, Wisconsin SC; further info ng.

874. SPANISH CIVILIZATION AND CULTURE
Northwest Mississippi JC; MFL; Senatobia, MS 38688.
Emily Mae Ballew
1-new; 2-3x16; 3-b; 4-75/76; 5-every yr for full yr; 7-a; 8-3s; 9-ng; 10-elem Sp; 11-civ & cult of Sp speaking countries; to include hist, poli sci, art, music, archaeology, architecture; lit, pertaining to each segment; readings in Sp; 12-a,b,c,e,f,g; 13-a,b,d,e,f, filmstrips, pictures, articles; 14-various.

875. SURVEY OF LATIN AMERICA
Ohio U; Intl Studies; Athens, OH 45701.
Manuel Serna
1-62; 2-4x10; 3-b; 4-72; 5-4; 6-b; 7-b; 8-4q; 9-a; 10-none; 11-hist, geography, lit, music, art, sociology, govt; 12-a,b,f, book reports; 13-b; 14-Human Condition in Latin America; 100 Years of Solitude; Sons of the Shaking Earth.

876. LATIN AMERICAN STUDIES
Providence C; Latin Amer Studies; Providence, RI 02918.
Gilbert R. Cavaco
New 30-hr BA and 24-hr certificate program; students concentrate in one of the areas represented by the following disciplines: MLs, hist, anthro, econ, poli sci, or within other disciplines such as bus admin, the scis, etc.

877. LATIN AMERICAN STUDIES
Randolph-Macon Woman's C; Sp, Politics; Lynchburg, VA 24054.
Charlotte Stern, Ernie Duff

1-ng; 2-2x13; 3-b; 4-72/73; 5-2; 6-a; 7-a; 8-6s; 9-a; 10-reading knowledge of Sp & understanding of spoken Sp; 11-Sp lang & Latin Amer lit; 12-a,b,c,g; 13-a,e,f; 14-ng.

878. LATIN AMERICAN STUDIES
Rhode Island C; MLs; Providence, RI 02908.
Dix S. Coons
The program has a cognate requirement of 4 courses in Sp or Port, plus prof in either Sp or Port; further info ng.

879. HISPANIC HISTORY AND CULTURE
Roanoke C; FLs; Salem, VA 24153.
Mamie S. Patterson
1-60; 2-15x3; 3-b; 4-73; 5-2; 6-interterm-Jan; 7-a; 8-ng; 9-a; 10-none; 11-interdisc study of Hispanic civ, its hist & cult development & its influence in modern world; 12-a,b,f; 13-a,b,c,d,e,f, art books; 14-Atkinson, A History of Spain & Portugal; Pendle, A History of Latin America; Franco, The Modern Culture of Latin America.

880. HISPANIC STUDIES MAJOR
St. Olaf C; Interdept; Northfield, MN 55057.
An interdisc program (Sp, hist, econ, poli sci, soci) projected to begin fall 75; designed to enhance the student's understanding of Spain and Sp Amer; the program is grounded in a thorough knowledge of the lang. In addition to the rigorous lang requirement, 8 area-related courses are required.

881. HISPANIC-LATIN AMERICAN STUDIES
U of San Diego; Interdisc Studies; Alcala Park, CA 92110.
Carl Guilbert
Program initiated in 72 for full-time students; further info ng.

882. INTERCULTURAL STUDY: LATIN AMERICA
Simon's Rock Early C; Soci Studies, Sp; Great Barrington, MA 01230.
E. Misch, Rene Biher, John Dwyer
1-10; 2-ng; 3-b,c; 4-73/74; 5-2; 6-a; 7-a; 8-4-6s; 9-a; 10-ng; 11-hist & lit of Latin Amer; 12-a,b,c,g; 13-a,b,d,e,f; 14-various.

883. LATIN AMERICAN STUDIES PROGRAM
U of Southern Mississippi; Latin Amer Studies; Hattiesburg, MS 39601.
There are 2 majors within the program, Latin Amer Trade & Finance, & Latin Amer Studies. The curricula are interdept, intended to provide the specific knowledge and skills necessary for persons entering the world of intl bus in this hemisphere.

884. LATIN AMERICAN STUDIES
Stephen F. Austin SU; MLs; Nacogdoches, TX 75961.
Vivian M. Gruber
Program initiated 71. Required: prof in Sp; a minor from General Bus, Econ, Geography, Hist, Poli Sci, Soci or Sp; 6 sem hrs from specified courses in art, soci, psychology, philosophy, & electives within these areas.

885. LATIN AMERICAN CIVILIZATION AND CULTURE
Stephens C; FLs; Columbia, MO 65201.
Albert J. Delmez
3-credit spr sem course begun in 1970 emphasizing pre-Columbian, colonial & modern civs & cults & emergence of nations; taught in Eng; no prerequisites.

886. LATIN AMERICAN STUDIES: SPANISH
US Naval Academy; Area-Lang Studies; Annapolis, MD 21042.
G. J. Riccio
1-25; 2-varies; 3-b; 4-70; 5-each yr; 6-a; 7-a; 8-36s; 9-a; 10-elem Sp; 11-Sp: inter, adv lang courses plus civ courses on Spain & Latin Amer; 6 courses related to Latin Amer offered by the Hist, Poli Sci and Econ Depts; 12-a,b,c,f,g; 13-a,b,e,f; 14-Hilton, La America Latina de ayer y de hoy; Mallo y Castellano, Espana: Sintesia de la civilizacion.

See also 898, 903, 904, 905, 906, 958, 1015, 1024.

Middle & Near East

887. JUDAIC STUDIES
U of Missouri; FLs; Kansas City, MO 64110.
Joseph Schultz
1-5; 2-ng; 3-h; 4-71; 5-ng; 6-a; 7-a; 8-ng; 9-a; 10-jr status; 11-interdisc program involving FL & Hist Depts; 12-all; 13-ng; 14-ng.

888. NEAR EASTERN STUDIES
Monterey Inst of Foreign Studies; Intl Studies; Monterey, CA 93940.
Stephen A. Garrett
Program leading to M.A.; includes comparative & intl poli, intl econ, lit, consecutive interpretation, Eng & for lang trans.

889. ARABIC LANGUAGE AND CULTURE
Southern Colorado SC; FL; Pueblo, CO 81005.
Monique Amerman
1-12; 2-3x11; 3-b,c; 4-fall 74; 5-1; 6-3 consecutive qtrs; 7-a; 8-3q; 9-a,b; 10-none; 11-conv, 2 hrs per wk; cult aspects of Arabic; 12-a,e,f,g; 13-b,d, Arabic By Radio from the UAR Broadcasting Corp; 14-ng.

See also 905.

Portuguese

890. PORTUGUESE STUDIES
Providence C; MLs; Providence, RI 02918.
Gilbert R. Cavaco
1-50; 2-6-12x30; 3-b; 4-74/75; 5-1; 6-entire program offered every yr; 7-a (for BA degree) and b (no degree awarded); 8-24s; 9-a, eve; 10-none; 11-all courses in lang are taught comparatively with usage within the community; vocab in the conv segment is based on practical situations within the community; adv trans course focuses on topics which could prepare student for work within the community; 12-all; 13-a,b,d,f; 14-Leroy, Portugues para principiantes; Willis, An Essential Course in Modern Portuguese; Keates, Advanced Spanish and Portuguese Composition.

Scandinavian

891. SCANDINAVIAN SEMINAR
Mankato SC; FL; Mankato, MN 56001.
Wallace G. Esgate
1-26; 2-3x11-12; 3-b,c; 4-73; 5-2 (totaling 4qs); 6-fall & wtr qtrs, each yr; 7-b; 8-3q; 9-a; 10-none; 11-fall qtr-geography, mythology, hist, art, lit, architecture, religion, music & typical Scand celebration; wtr qtr-geography, religion, lit, art, emigration out of Scand, soci, art, music; 12-a,f; 13-a,b,d, maps, visuals; 14-various.

892. SCANDINAVIAN CULTURE & CIVILIZATION
U of Texas; Ger Langs; Austin, TX 78712.
John Weinstock
1-93; 2-3x14; 3-b; 4-73/74; 5-4; 6-a; 7-a; 8-3s; 9-a; 10-none; 11-geography, cult, art, hist, lit, mores, politics; 12-a,f; 13-a,e,f; 14-Hancock, The Politics of Post-Industrial Change; Higley & Field, Elites in Developed Societies: Sage, Njal's Sage; Strindberg, Six Plays; Ibsen, Four Great Plays.

893. SCANDINAVIAN EMIGRATION: HISTORY & LITERATURE
U of Washington; Scand; Seattle, WA 98195.
B. Steene
1-new; 2-3x10 or 5-week smr session; 3-b (hist); 4-new course; 5-0; 6-b; 7-a; 8-3q (2.5 in smr); 9-a; 10-grad; 11-grad seminar in Scand hist & lit; studied are forces behind Scand behind Scand emigration to U.S., structure of Scand communities in U.S. & lit by & about Scand emigrants; 12-a,f; 13-b; 14-various plus portions of Swedish & Norwegian Ph.D. dissertations.

894. SCANDINAVIAN LIFE AND CIVILIZATION
U of Wisconsin; Scand; Madison, WI 53706.
Niels Ingwersen
1-200; 2-3x15; 3-b; 4-60; 5-15; 6-b; 7-a; 8-3s; 9-a; 10-none, designed especially for freshmen; 11-life in Scand, emphasis on soci & cult conditions against geographical & hist background; 12-a,f; 13-a,b; 14-primary texts.

Uralic and Altaic

895. URALIC AND ALTAIC STUDIES
Indiana U; Uralic & Altaic; Bloomington, IN 47401.
Denis Sinor
Interdisc & cross-cult approach; 30-40 courses offered each sem; major langs offered are Hungarian, Finnish, Estonian, Turkish, Mongolian, Tibetan, and minor langs are taught from a ling point of view; undergrad & grad programs in Uralic, Altaic, Inner Asian, and Hungarian studies.

General and Miscellaneous

896. INTERNATIONAL STUDIES MAJOR
Allegheny C; MLs; Meadville, PA 16335.
Blair Hanson

217

First offered c20 yrs ago with Hist, Poli Sci & Econ Depts; has had 2 or 3 sr majors each yr; the major consists of at least 2 courses beyond the 2nd yr college level plus 6-8 courses each in hist & poli sci, with a basic knowledge of econ.

897. INTERDISCIPLINARY, INTERCULTURAL STUDY OF MEXICO, SOUTH ASIA, USA
Davidson C; Honors Center; Davidson, NC 28036.
Earl MacCormac
1-new; 2-3-5x30 for 3 yrs; 3-b,c; 4-to be offered 75-78 if it goes into operation; 5-0; 6-only once; 7-a; 8-5q each term; 9-a; 10-admission to the Honors Center; 11-intensive lang (Sp and eventually Hindi), team-taught seminars on comparative cult, political econ, lings; 12-a,b,c,e,f,g; 13-all; 14-ng.

898. INTERDISCIPLINARY PROGRAMS
U of Florida; Rom Langs & Lits; Gainesville, FL 32611.
J. W. Conner
The College of Arts & Sciences has undergrad interdisc programs (certificate) in Latin Amer Studies, Western European Studies, African Studies; one component in each is an interdisc seminar--topic varies.

899. INTERCULTURAL COMMUNICATIONS
Montana SU; Center for Intercult Programs; Bozeman, MT 59715.
Richard Landis
1-40; 2-2x10; 3-b; 4-73; 5-4; 6-a; 7-a; 8-3q; 9-a; 10-none; 11-oral communication centering on cult similarities & differences in perception; aimed at meeting needs of for students, Amer Indian students, non-Indian Amers; 12-a,b,c,d,f; 13-a; 14-Harms, Intercultural Communication; Deloria, Custer Died for Your Sins.

900. INTERNATIONAL STUDIES
Monterey Inst of Foreign Studies; Intl Studies; Monterey, CA 93940.
Stephen A. Garrett
Program leading to B.A. & M.A.; includes comparative & intl politics, intl econ, lit, consecutive interpretation, Eng & for lang trans.

901. INTERNATIONAL STUDIES
Newberry C; Interdepartmental; Newberry, SC 29108.
John Romeiser
Program begun in 71; though new major, college offers no new courses but does require lang study.

902. INTERDISCIPLINARY THIRD WORLD CULTURES PROGRAM
Northland C; MLs, Poli Sci; Ashland, WI 54806.

Daniel G. Small.
Looking into possibility of starting such a program, most likely in 76/77, but not yet even in planning stage.

903. INTERDISCIPLINARY MAJOR
Vanderbilt U; Interdept; Nashville, TN 37235.
Forrest Miller
Available to all qualified undergrads, who must submit a major program to a committee. Must include work in at least 3 disciplines for 48 hrs credit, such as Fr, Sp, Hist; a study of the 17th cen in lit, fine arts, hist, poli sci; each program is individual.

904. AREA AND INTERNATIONAL STUDIES
U of Vermont; Area Studies; Burlington, VT 05401.
J. P. Felt
Program initiated 73/74; requirements for concentration include the general distribution requirements in the College of Arts & Sciences, the for lang of the selected area, usually through the inter level; several options of courses in the soci scis & hums (incl fine arts); & specialized area courses, reading & research, college honors, & area seminars; the program focuses on Asia (East Asia, South & Southeast Asia, Western Asia); Canada; Europe (Western, Northern, Mediterranean); Latin America; Russia/Eastern Europe.

905. INTERNATIONAL STUDIES WITH LANGUAGE CONCENTRATION
Warren Wilson C; Interdept; Swannanoa, NC 28778.
William Mosher
1-10; 2-6-9x16; 3-b,c; 4-72; 5-6; 6-a; 7-a; 8-3s per course; 9-a; 10-none; 11-in this program the student may have a comparative track--Far East, Mid-East, India, Africa, France, Spain; an Area Studies track and must have a specific discipline such as econ, intl relations, lang; 12-a,b,c,d,f (and e,g for lang courses); 13-a,b,e,f, records, live demonstrations of dancing, foreign dinners; 14-varies.

906. PROGRAM IN INTERNATIONAL STUDIES
Willamette U; FL; Salem, OR 97301
C. A. Kraft
Program in Intl Studies with specialization in British, Fr, Ger, Hispanic & Soviet area studies; provides student with background in intl poli & econ while increasing his knowledge of the lang, lit, hist, art, philosophy & geography of the area of his specialization.

See also 300, 963, 1023, 1659, 1678A.

907. THE FRENCH FILM: SOCIAL CONTENT
Amherst C; Fr; Amherst, MA 01002.
R'. Pini
1-12; 2-3x14; 3-b; 4-71; 5-2; 6-every four
yrs a Fr film course is supposed to rotate
among the colleges of the valley; 7-a (b for
viewing); 8-one-course cr; 9-a; 10-reading
& speaking knowledge of Fr; 11-given with
Fine Arts; Fr films in terms of their
relevance to chosen aspects of Fr society
and relationship to the visual arts; 12-
a,b,c,e,f; 13-a; 14-Blaujoun and Ehrmann,
French Society; Bazin, What Is Film?

908. THE CHANSON: POETRY AND MUSIC IN
RENAISSANCE FRANCE
Brown U; Fr, Music; Providence, RI 02912.
Laura G. Durand, Fr Studies; David
Josephson, Music Dept.
1-17; 2-2 hrs. 40 min x 15; 3-b; 4-spr /4//5;
5-1; 6-perhaps every other yr; 7-a; 8-1
course unit; 9-a; 10-specified levels of
preparation in Fr and music; more rigorous
for concentrators in either field; 11-in
addition to poetry and music (scores),
poetic theory, background readings in Fr
lit, performance, projects; 12-a,b,d,f; 13-
scores, records; 14-various.

909. PRE-HITLERIAN ART AND LITERATURE
California Lutheran C; Ger; Thousand
Oaks, CA 91360.
Robert M. Stanford
1-10; 2-4x14; 3-b; 4-73; 5-1; 6-c; 7-a; 8-4s;
9-a; 10-none; 11-major trends from 1900;
12-a,c,f, field trips; 13-a,b,e; 14-ng.

910. THE FRENCH ART SONG FROM
SYMBOLISM TO SURREALISM
U of California; Music, Fr & Ital; Santa
Barbara, CA 93106.
1-new; 2-8x30; 3-b; 4-spr 75; 5-1; 6-
undecided; 7-a; 8-4q; 9-a; 10-open to music
or Fr majors or with consent; 11-interdisc
study in a text-music relationship from
Faure to Poulenc; from Baudelaire to
Eluard; lectures in Eng, readings in Fr; 12-
a,d,f; 13-d; 14-Miller, The Ring of Words;
Noske, French Song from Berlioz to
Duparc.

911. POETS AND PAINTERS IN THE
TWENTIETH CENTURY
U of California; Fr & Ital; Santa Barbara,
CA 93106.
1-15; 2-8x10; 3-b; 4-73; 5-2; 6-b; 7-a,b; 8-
4q; 9-a; 10-reading knowledge, art
background; 11-confrontations between
verbal and visual images, especially as seen
in collaborations; 12-a,f, guest lectures,
readings in Fr; 13-b; 14-various.

912. LITERATURE AND OPERA
Canisius C; MLs; Buffalo, NY 14208.
Raymond L. Girard
1-40+; 2-3x15; 3-b; 4-72; 5-3; 6-b; 7-a,b; 8-
3s; 9-a; 10-none; 11-hist of opera; 12-
a,b,e,f; 13-records; 14-primary texts.

913. STUDIES IN TRANSLATION THEORY:
LITERATURE AND PAINTING
Carnegie-Mellon U; MLs & Lits, Art;
Pittsburgh, PA 15213.
Jean Paris
Study of how painting and lit "translate"
each other; interest to students in
aesthetics, art history, modern langs, and
comp lit; almost all lectures illustrated by
numerous slide projections.

914. HUMANITIES
U of Colorado; Integrated Studies; Boulder,
CO 80302.
Hazel Barnes
1-150; 2-7x15; 3-a; 4-long established
courses; 5-ng; 6-a; 7-a; 8-6s; 9-a; 10-none;
11-analytical and comparative study of
selected works in various arts, from Aegean
to contemporary multi-level program; 12-
a,b,f; 13-a,b,d; 14-ng.

915. PERSPECTIVES ON FRENCH FILMS
Curry C; Lang & Lit; Milton, MA 02186.
Frances M. Kohak
Taught in cooperation with the hist area;
one discussion section is conducted in Fr.
Further info ng.

916. CHEKHOV, STANISLAWSKY AND THE
RUSSIAN REALIST TRADITION
U of Delaware; Theater, Langs & Lit;
Newark, DE 19711.
Brian Hanson, Theater; Eugenia Slavov,
Lang & Lit
1-16; 2-8x7; 3-b; 4-74; 5-1; 6-occasionally;
7-a; 8-4s; 9-a; 10-none; 11-detailed study of
several plays culminating in staging of The
Three Sisters; 12-a,b,d,f; 13-a,e; 14-
primary texts.

917. 17th CENTURY FRENCH DRAMA AND
STAGECRAFT
U of Delaware; Theatre, Langs & Lit;
Newark, DE 19711.
Spire Pitou, Lit & Lang
1-8; 2-6x14; 3-b,c; 4-74; 5-1; 6-once; 7-a; 8-
6s; 9-a; 10-none; 11-reading of classical
drama, studying of staging, acting
techniques, presentation of play; 12-
a,b,c,d,f; 13-a,b,c,d; 14-primary texts.

918. THE DON JUAN THEME
Eastern Washington SC; FL; Cheney, WA
99004.
Cornelius J. Groenen
1-25; 2-5x10; 3-b; 4-74; 5-1; 6-b; 7-a; 8-5q;
9-a; 10-none; 11-Don Juan theme in lit, art,
music; 12-a,b,f; 13-d; 14-primary texts.

919. ROMANTICISM IN THE ARTS AND
LITERATURE
Elmhurst C; Ger, Art; Elmhurst, IL 60126.
1-10; 2-3x14; 3-b; 4-71; 5-1; 6 once; 7-a; 8-

4s; 9-a; 10-courses in lit or arts; 11-study of painting, music, lit of romantic period in England and on the Continent; 12-a,c,f; 13-b,d, concerts, museums; 14-ng.

920. THE EXPRESSIONIST ERA IN GERMANY 1910-1920
Haverford C; Ger; Haverford, PA 19041.
John R. Cary
1-12; 2-3x4; 3-b,c; 4-71; 5-3; 6-b; 7-a; 8-3s; 9-a; 10-sophomore standing; 11-movement which flourished 1910-22 as major source of modern Western esthetic; 12-a,b,c,f; 13-a,b,d; 14-primary texts.

921. ARTISTIC AND CULTURAL FRANCE
Indiana U; Fr & Ital, Fine Arts; Bloomington, IN 47401.
Michael Berkvan, Fr & Ital
1-65; 2-3x14; 3-b; 4-73/74; 5-1; 6-uncertain; 7-a; 8-3s; 9-a; 10-none; 11-jr interdisc course, recommended for Fr majors, doesn't count as part of major; from Celtic & Roman periods through eve of WW I; in 2 sems; 12-a,f; 13-b; 14-primary texts.

922. ASIAN FILM AND LITERATURE
Indiana U; Comp Lit Program; Bloomington, IN 47401.
1-22; 2-2½x16 plus a film once a wk; 3-b; 4-spr 75; 5-1; 6-b; 7-a; 8-3s; 9-a; 10-none; 11-ng; 12-a,b,f; 13-a; 14-primary texts.

923. ASIAN LITERATURE AND THE OTHER ARTS
Indiana U; Comp Lit Prog; Bloomington, IN 47401.
1-18; 2-3½x8; 3-b,c; 4-spr 74/75; 5-1; 6-b; 7-a; 8-2s; 9-a; 10-none; 11-analysis of arts of past 200 years; 12-a,b,f; 13-a,b; 14-primary texts.

924. COMEDY IN FILM AND LITERATURE
Indiana U; Comp Lit Program; Bloomington, IN 47401.
1-96; 2-2½x16 plus 1 film per wk; 3-ng; 4-74/75; 5-1; 6-b; 7-a; 8-3s; 9-a; 10-consent of instructor or intro course; 11-evolution, styles & techniques to the present; 12-a,b,c,f; 13-a,b,c; 14-primary texts.

925. FILM ADAPTATIONS OF LITERATURE
Indiana U; Comp Lit Program; Bloomington, IN 47401.
1-25; 2-2½ x 16 plus one film per wk; 3-ng; 4-fall 74; 5-1; 6-b; 7-a; 8-3s; 9-a; 10-intro to film course or consent; 11-analysis of the processes, problems involved in turning a lit work into screenplay and then into film; close study of lit and film techniques and short exercises in adaptation; 12-a,b,c,f; 13-a,b,c; 14-primary texts.

926. LITERATURE AND POPULAR CULTURE
Indiana U; Comp Lit Program; Bloomington, IN 47401.
1-71; 2-1½x16; 3-a; 4-fall 74/75; 5-1; 6-b; 7-a; 8-2s; 9-a; 10-none; 11-course for general student, dealing with popular forms of lit, interacting with lit and the popular arts; each time offered it will focus on a special topic, e.g., lyrics & popular songs, the detective novel, sci fiction; 12-a,b,f; 13-d, records, scores; 14-primary texts.

927. MODERN LITERATURE AND THE OTHER ARTS (FIRST SEMESTER)
Indiana U; Comp Lit Program; Bloomington, IN 47401.
1-215; 2-1½ x16; 3-a; 4-fall 55; 5-51; 6-a; 7-a; 8-2s; 9-a; 10-none; 11-Analysis of arts covering past 200 years; 12-b,c,f; 13-b,d,e; 14-primary texts.

928. MODERN LITERATURE AND THE OTHER ARTS (SECOND SEMESTER)
Indiana U; Comp Lit Program; Bloomington, IN 47401.
1-22; 2-1½x16; 3-a; 4-fall 72/73; 5-6; 6-a; 7-a; 8-2s; 9-a; 10-preliminary course; 11-analysis of arts covering past 200 yrs; 12-a,b,f; 13-b,d; 14-primary texts.

929. THE AVANT-GARDE - ROMANTICISM & THE ARTS
Loma Linda U; ML; Riverside, CA 92505.
M. Hilts
1-12; 2-4x11; 3-b,c; 4-72/73; 5-2; 6-b; 7-a; 8-4q; 9-a; 10-none; 11-interdept approach; 12-a,b,c,f; 13-a,b,d; 14-primary texts.

930. MOLIERE
Loyola U; ML, Theater; Chicago, IL 60626.
John Trahey, Theater Dept.
1-30; 2-3x15; 3-b; 4-fall 73; 5-1; 6-perhaps every other yr; 7-a; 8-3s; 9-a; 10-none; 11-class discussion & presentation of plays; scenes in Fr & Eng performed in costume in evening program for univ; 12-a,b,d,f; 13-a, theater props; 14-various.

931. FILMS AND PEOPLE: ENJOYING FOREIGN FILMS
Meramec CC; MFLs, Eng; Kirkwood, MO 63122.
Jennie Davis
1-29; 2-3x15; 3-b; 4-75; 5-1; 6-b; 7-a; 8-3s; 9-a, part-time; 10-none; 11-acquaints student with outstanding for films from France, Germany, Spain, and Italy and with the cults of these countries; 12-a,b,f; 13-a,e; 14-ng.

932. CLASSICAL LITERATURE AND THE FILM
U of Michigan; Cl Studies; Ann Arbor, MI 48104.
H. D. Cameron
1-new course; 2-3x16; 3-b; 4-wtr 75; 5-0; 6-undecided; 7-a; 8-3q; 9-a; 10-none; 11-explores continuity of creative imagination as reflected in cl lit & cinema; 12-a; 13-a,b; 14-primary texts.

933. GERMAN EXPRESSIONISM
Montclair SC; German; Upper Montclair, NJ 07043.
John Moore
1-20; 2-3x16 plus field trips; 3-b; 4-74; 5-1; 6-b; 7-a; 8-3s; 9-a; 10-none; 11-period from late Wilhelm days to Hitler examined in variety of aspects; 12-a,b,c,d,f; 13-a,b; 14-primary texts.

934. CONTEMPORARY MEXICO THROUGH ITS ART

Monterey Inst of Foreign Studies; Langs & Civs; Monterey, CA 93940.
Burt H. Seidenberg
General survey of Mex myths, legends, popular lit, music, dances, costumes, & arts & crafts; no prerequisite; 2 credits; smr 74; taught in Eng; further info ng.

935.   MEXICAN DANCES
Monterey Inst of Foreign Studies; Langs & Civs; Monterey, CA 93940.
Burt H. Seidenberg
Instruction on typical dances from different regions of Mexico; no prerequisite; taught in Sp; 1 credit; smr 74; further info ng.

936.   MEXICAN SONGS
Monterey Inst of Foreign Studies; Langs & Civs; Monterey, CA 93940.
Burt H. Seidenberg
Study of Mex folk & current popular music of different parts of Mexico; includes class singing; no prerequisite; 1 credit; taught in Sp smr 74; further info ng.

937.   EXPRESSIONISM IN GERMAN ART AND LITERATURE
Regis C; Ger, Art; Weston, MA 02193.
Althea C. Wohlkopf
1-7; 2-3x14; 3-b,c; 4-72/73; 5-2; 6-every 2nd yr; 7-a; 8-4s; 9-a; 10-none; 11-exploration of expression in art & lit, early 20th cen; 12-a,b,f; 13-a,b, museum visits; 14-primary texts.

938.   LITERATURE AND MUSIC: ROMANTIC THEMES IN GERMAN LITERATURE AND MUSIC
Regis C; Ger; Weston, MA 02193.
Mary P. Hamilton, Sr. Margaret William McCarthy
1-17; 2-3x14; 3-b; 4-71/72; 5-1; 6-alt yrs; 7-a; 8-4s; 9-a, cont ed; 10-none; 11-examination of the relationship between the two art forms considered through a study of selected musical & lit works in which romantic thought is manifested; 12-a,b,c,e,f; 13-d, records, concerts, recitals; 14-primary texts; Prawer, The Penguin Book of Lieder.

939.   ART, MUSIC, AND LITERATURE SINCE THE RENAISSANCE
Rutgers U; Fr, Music & Art; New Brunswick, NJ 08903.
J. Undank
1-55; 2-3x30; 3-b; 4-48; 5-annually; 6-a; 7-a; 8-ng; 9-a; 10-course in art, music or lit; 11-study of basic similarities & differences among arts; 12-a,f; 13-b, musical recordings & lit texts; 14-primary texts.

940.   SPECIAL THEMES IN SPANISH: LITERATURE AND PAINTING IN SPAIN
St. Louis U; MLs; St. Louis, MO 63103.
Paul Garcia
1-new; 2-3x18; 3-b; 4-spr 75; 5-0; 6-on demand; 7-a; 8-3s; 9-a; 10-none; 11-ng; 12-a,b,c,f; 13-a,e,f,g; 14-Fleming, Art and Ideas; instructor's materials.

941.   DADA AND SURREALISM
Southwestern U; Interdisc; Georgetown, TX 78626.
Regine Reynolds
1-15; 2-3x13; 3-b; 4-74; 5-0; 6-irregularly; 7-a; 8-3s; 9-a, school personnel; 10-none; 11-lit, poetry, visual arts, music, psychology, dance, hist, govt, drama; 12-a,b,c,d,f; 13-a,e, dance, piano recitals, records; 13-ng.

See also 805, 947, 973, 976, 977, 985, 986, 996, 997, 1001, 1003, 1006, 1010, 1011, 1012, 1014, 1017, 1018, 1021, 1023, 1387.

The Social Sciences

CANADIAN

942.   CANADIAN-AMERICAN INTERNATIONAL RELATIONS SEMINAR
U of Maine; FLs, Hist; Farmington, ME 04938.
Douglas Becker
1-new; 2-2½-3x15; 3-b,c; 4-spr 75; 5-1; 6-as now constituted only once; 7-b; 8-3s or pass/fail; 9-a,b, general public invited to each lecture; 10-none; 11-ng; 12-a,b,c,d,f; 13-a,b,d,e,f; 14-ng.

CHICANO

943.   CHICANO!
Hastings C; Sp, Soci; Hastings, NE 68901.
Douglas K. Benson, Robert Stockton
1-12; 2-50x4; 3-b; 4-Jan interim 73; 5-1; 6-occasionally; 7-ng; 8-4s; 9-a; 10-reading ability in Sp; 11-study of Mex-Amer population of Colorado, Nebraska, New Mexico & Texas: soci problems, ed progress, discrimination, lit, field trips to these areas to talk to educators, community leaders, students; 12-a,b,c,d,f; 13-a,b,c,d,e,f, filmstrips, food; 14-various.

CLASSICAL GREEK

See 978.

FRENCH

944.   LITTERATURE, HISTOIRE ET SOCIETE DE MONTAIGNE
Bryn Mawr C; Fr, Hist; Bryn Mawr, PA 19010.

Mme. Roland, Michel Guggenheim
1-7; 2-3x13; 3-b; 4-73/74; 5-1; 6-every 3 yrs; 7-a; 8-4s; 9-a; 10-adv prof; 11-study of Fr society from the Religious Wars to the Revolution as reflected in letters, memoirs, plays, essays; emphasis on the hist background of 2 cens of Fr lit; 12-a,b,c,d,g; 13-e,g, books; 14-various.

945. SOCIAL, POLITICAL AND RELIGIOUS BACKGROUNDS OF THE EARLY 19th CENTURY IN FRANCE
U of Maine; FLs; Orono, ME 04473.
Josef Roggenbauer
1-16; 2-3x15; 3-b; 4-68; 5-3; 6-alt yrs; 7-a; 8-3s; 9-a; 10-none; 11-ng; 12-a,b,f; 13-a; 14-ng.

946. FRENCH IN INTERNATIONAL AFFAIRS
C of New Rochelle; Fr; New Rochelle, NY 10801.
Marie-Helene Nessager
1-new; 2-3x12; 3-b; 4-75/76; 5-0; 6-a; 7-a,b; 8-3s; 9-a,b; 10-3 yrs of Fr; 11-ng; 12-b,c,f,g; 13-e,f; 14-ng.

947. LITERATURE AND THE ARTS ON THE EVE OF THE FRENCH REVOLUTION
SUCNY; FL; Potsdam, NY 13676.
A. R. Plante
1-40; 2-3x15; 3-b,c; 4-72/73; 5-2; 6-b; 7-b; 8-3; 9-a,b; 10-none; 11-study of causes of Fr Revolution through the arts & lit; comparison with 20th cen; 12-ng; 13-a,b; 14-various.

948. FROM POINCARE TO GISCARD D'ESTAING
Webster C; MLs, Hist & Poli Sci; Saint Louis, MO 63119.
Jacques C. Chicoineau
1-15; 2-3x16; 3-b; 4-spr 75; 5-1; 6-every 2 yrs; 7-a; 8-3s; 9-a; 10-none; 11-poli, soci, cult, religious evolution of Fr people-1919-1974; 12-a,b,f; 13-a,b,d; 14-Shirer, The Collapse of the Third Republic; Servan-Schreiber, The Spirit of May.

See also 907, 985, 986, 997, 1003.

GERMAN

949. GERMAN LITERATURE AND SOCIETY OF THE TWENTIETH CENTURY
Roosevelt U; Langs, Hist; Chicago, IL 60605.
Leon Stein, Hist; Helena Szepe, Langs
1-12; 2-3x15; 3-b; 4-spr 75; 5-1; 6-undecided; 7-a; 8-3s; 9-a; 10-lit course, courses in soci scis or consent; 11-ng; 12-a,b; 13-ng; 14-Friedrich, Before the Deluge; Gay, Weimar Culture; Phillips, The Tragedy of Nazi Germany; Mosse, Nazi Culture.

950. CULTURAL, SOCIAL, & ECONOMIC TRENDS IN 16TH CENTURY GERMANY
U of Virginia; Ger; Charlottesville, VA 22903.
Thomas W. Best
1-c2; 2-3x15; 3-b; 4-new; 5-0; 6-unknown; 7-a; 8-3s; 9-ng; 10-reading knowledge; 11-survey of lit, artistic, and econ developments in Reformation Germany; 12-a,b,f,g; 13-ng; 14-primary texts; Holborn, History of Germany, Vol. I.

951. WEIMAR GERMANY
Wake Forest U; Ger, Hist; Winston-Salem, NC 27109.
R.S. Fraser
1-new; 2-3x11; 3-b; 4-spr 76; 5-0; 6-ng; 7-a; 8-3s; 9-a; 10-ng; 11-hist, poli, lit, econ developments in Germany of the 1920's. Readings from fiction and belles-lettres of the period; 12-a,b,c,f; 13-a,b; 14-ng.

See also 125, 1387.

LATIN AMERICAN

952. MEXICO: THE SEARCH FOR IDENTITY
Agnes Scott C; Sp; Decatur, GA 30030.
Constance Shaw
1-new; 2-3x10; 3-b,c; 4-75; 5-0; 6-b; 7-a; 8-3q; 9-ng; 10-none; 11-lit, art, anthro, soci, poli sci; 12-a,b,c,d,f; 13-a,b; 14-ng.

953. LA GENTE MEXICANO-AMERICANA EN LOS ESTADOS UNIDOS
Boise SU; FLs, Hist; Boise, ID 83725.
R. Bonachea, Hist
1-new; 2-3x3; 3-b; 4-fall 75; 5-0; 6-b; 7-a; 8-3q; 9-a; 10-prof in Sp; 11-biling/bicult course dealing with hist of Mex-Amers, development of Mex-Amer population in U.S., soci & poli movements; 12-ng; 13-ng; 14-ng.

954. THE FAMILY IN LATIN AMERICA
Brandeis U; Latin Amer Studies, Anthro, Hist; Waltham, MA 02154.
Luis Yglesias (LAS)
1-ng; 2-ng; 3-b; 4-ng; 5-2; 6-ng; 7-a; 8-4s; 9-a; 10-ng; 11-Latin Amer Studies, anthro, hist as components in LAS program; 12-f; 13-ng; 14-ng.

955. HISTORY AND LITERATURE OF LATIN AMERICA
Graceland C; Hist; Lamoni, IA 50140.
Larry Hunt
1-8; 2-3x16; 3-b; 4-74; 5-1; 6-student demand; 7-a; 8-3; 9-a; 10-hist course & basic lit course; 11-general survey of hist & lit of Latin Amer in Colonial period; novels & hist of important revolutions in 19th & 20th cens; 12-a,b,f; 13-hist text, Latin Amer novels; 14-various.

956. SOCIAL AND POLITICAL INSTITUTIONS OF LATIN AMERICA
Indiana SU; FL; Evansville, IN 47712.
Lomberto Diaz
1-12; 2-3 hrs per wk per sem; 3-b; 4-72; 5-4; 6-b; 7-b; 8-3s; 9-a,b; 10-ng; 11-study of poli & soci structures, dictatorships; 12-a,b,c,f; 13-d,e; 14-Needler, Political System of Latin America; Lambert, Latin America, Social Structures & Political Institutions.

957. HISTORY AND SOCIOLOGY (Program)
Monterey Inst of Foreign Studies; Langs & Civs; Monterey, CA 93940.
Leon Shoob

Offers 5 courses (2 in Eng) on variety of soci & cult problems of Mexico and of her hist; included is course on problems of acculturation of Sp-speaking minorities; 1 course includes field trips; each course 2 credits; smr 74.

958. HISTORY OF LATIN AMERICA
Monterey Inst of Foreign Studies; Langs & Civs; Monterey, CA 93940.
Ovid C. Fuente
Overall view of Latin Amer hist; no prerequisite; 2 credits; taught in Sp; smr 74; further info ng.

959. THE MEXICAN REVOLUTION
U of Utah; Eng, Langs; Salt Lake City, UT 84112.
James T. Svendsen, Langs
1-20; 2-10-15x6; 3-b,c; 4-73/74; 5-ng; 6-pilot program which they hope to offer every other yr; 7-a; 8-15q; 9-a; 10-jr or sr standing; 11-six weeks on campus study of causes and results of Mex revolution, revolutionary activity in rest of Latin Amer and the Chicano movement in U.S. Four weeks spent traveling in Mexico, classes in Sp available and integrated into program; 12-a,b,c,f; 13-a,d,f; 14-various.

See also 1291, 1566.

LINGUISTICS

960. HISTORY OF THE SPANISH LANGUAGE IN THE SOUTHWEST
U of Colorado; Denver, CO 80202.
1-16; 2-3x16; 3-b; 4-72; 5-3; 6-b; 7-b; 8-3s; 9-a; 10-4th sem Sp; 11-Sp of the Southwest is compared to that spoken in other areas of the world. Basic ling terminology introduced & applied; 12-a,b,c,d,g; 13-d; 14-Lehman, Historical Linguisticism.

961. WORKSHOP IN SOUTHWEST SPANISH
U of Colorado; Sp & Mex Amer Studies; Denver, CO 80202.
1-new; 2-2x16; 3-b; 4-spr 75; 5-1; 6-b; 7-b; 8-2s; 9-ng; 10-adv prof; 11-research-oriented and designed to conduct an in-depth analysis of the Sp of the Southwest through field study; basic principles of field research; 12-a,b,c,d,g; 13-d, field research; 14-Samarin, Field Linguistics.

962. LANGUAGE AND CULTURE
Graceland C; Lang & Lit; Lamoni, IA 50140.
W.J. Slayton
1-7; 2-3xsem; 3-b, guest instructors; 4-fall 73; 5-3; 6-a; 7-a; 8-3s; 9-a; 10-jr standing; 11-examines the various ways a given lang mirrors its cult by means of readings, discussions, guest lecturers, special projects; 12-a,b,c,f; 13-b,d,f; 14-various supplementary readings.

963. LANGUAGE AND CULTURE
U of New Mexico; Lings; Albuquerque, NM 87131.
John Oller
1-30; 2-3x16; 3-b; 4-65; 5-6; 6-b; 7-a; 8-3s; 9-a,b; 10-intro to ling; 11-study of relationship between lang & speech & other elements of cult. Course in anthropological ling; frequently focuses on ed problems & communication across cults; 12-a,b,f; 13-ng; 14-Burling, Man's Many Voices; Blount, Language, Culture, and Society; Schaff, Language and Cognition.

964. SEMINAR IN SOCIOLINGUISTICS
U of New Mexico; Ling; Albuquerque, NM 87131.
John Oller
1-7; 2-3x16; 3-b; 4-fall 74; 5-1; 6-b; 7-a; 8-3; 9-a,b; 10-ling course; 11-grad seminar. Concentrates as a group on lang planning processes (lang standardization, development of orthographies, the role of academies, lang in sci & tech) 12-f; 13-ng; 14-ng.

965. SURVEY OF MULTILINGUAL EDUCATION
U of New Mexico; Ling; Albuquerque, NM 87131.
John Oller
1-new; 2-3x16; 3-b; 4-spr 75; 5-0; 6-b; 7-a; 8-a; 9-a,b; 10-ling course; 11-survey of multiling ed around world. Principles & practices; 12-f; 13-ng; 14-ng.

966. GENERAL LINGUISTICS
SUCNY; FLs & Lit, Anthro; Plattsburgh, NY 12901.
Craig Sample
Further info not available. Part of an inter-disc major in behavioral scis.

MEDIEVAL

967. MEDIEVAL STUDIES
Birmingham-Southern C; Cl & Art Hist; Birmingham, AL 35204.
S.J. Pezzillo
1-56; 2-3x15; 3-b; 4-74; 5-1; 6-irregularly; 7-a; 8-4s; 9-a; 10-none; 11-ng; 12-a,b,c,d,f; 13-b,d; 14-various.

968. MEDIEVAL STUDIES
Brandeis U; Hist, Eng, Rom Langs, Ger & Sl Langs; Waltham, MA 02154.
Angeliki E. Laiou
One course in Medieval Civ, sr seminar in Medieval studies, for lang, minimum of 3 courses relevant to this field of study; interdisc approach to the Medieval period; further info ng.

969. MEDIEVAL STUDIES
U of Georgia; Rom Langs; Athens, GA 30602.
James W. Alexander
Program involving Art, Comp Lit, Drama and Theatre, Eng, Ger and Sl Langs, Hist, Cls, Music, Philo, and Rom Langs Departs.

970. MEDIEVAL STUDIES
Indiana Central C; FLs; Indianapolis, IN 46227.
Marga Meir
1-15; 2-4x14; 3-b,c; 4-72; 5-2; 6-every 4th sem; 7-a; 8-4s; 9-a; 10-FL majors & minors: Fr, Ger or Sp, course also available to non-lang majors; 11-life, thought, cult seen in lit, art, music, & religion of France, Spain &

223

Germany from 9th-16th cens; 12-a,b,c,d,f; 13-b; 14-various.

971. MEDIEVAL CIVILIZATION
Pennsylvania SU; Liberal Arts; University Park, PA 16802.
Alan E. Knight
1-19; 2-4½x10; 3-b; 4-73; 5-2; 6-b; 7-a; 8-3s; 9-a; 10-none; 11-intro to art, hist, lit, thought of Middle Ages; 12-a,b,f; 13-a,b,d; 14-various.

972. MEDIEVAL STUDIES
Tulane U; New Orleans, LA 70118.
Robert Cook, Newcomb College, Eng
1-new; 2-ng; 3-b; 4-fall 75; 5-0;:6-a; 7-a; 8-ng; 9-a; 10-none; 11-interdisc studies involving 14 depts in medieval lit, soci studies, art, at least 1 course in medieval lang required; 12-a,b,f,g; 13-ng; 14-ng.

See also 1007.

RUSSIAN

See 1281, 1283.

MULTI-LANGUAGE

See 842.

MISCELLANEOUS

973. INTERDISCIPLINARY COURSES AFFILI-ATED WITH COMPARATIVE LITERATURE

U of Iowa; Comp Lit; Iowa City, IA 52242.

Alan F. Nagel
1-15-20; 2-3x15; 3-b; 4-73 first new inter-disc course; 5-one or more courses yrly; 6-several courses, at least one a yr; 7-a; 8-3-4s; 9-a; 10-soph standing; some courses require more thorough preparation in lit study and/or ling background; 11-Lit & Psychology; Lit & Society; Revolution in 20th Cen Writing; 12-b,f; 13-ng; 14-varies.

974. INTERNATIONAL AFFAIRS PROGRAM
U of Maine; FLs & Cl; Orono, ME 04473.
Josef Roggenbauer
1-19; 2-ng; 3-b; 4-66; 5-every sem since then; 6-a; 7-a,b; 8-this is a major program; 9-a; 10-ng; 11-as a major in FL, Poli Sci, Hist, or Econ: 24 hrs beyond the dept's intro courses & at least 9 hrs in each of the other depts; 12-a,b,c,d,f,g; 13-all; 14-ng.

975. THE WORLD OF THE RENAISSANCE
William Woods C; MLs; Fulton, MO 65251.
Adele Gorjanc
1-32; 2-3x16; 3-b,c; 4-73; 5-1; 6-every 2nd yr; 7-a; 8-3s; 9-a; 10-soph standing; 11-interdisc study of Renaissance cult, emphasis on art, hist, philo, sci; 12-a,b,c,d,f; 13-a,b,d, trips to museum; 14-various.

See also 976, 990, 996, 1002, 1006, 1008, 1009, 1010, 1011, 1012, 1016, 1017, 1018, 1020, 1021, 1023.

Themes and Concepts

976. THE CITY AS A CREATIVE CENTER: PARIS, BERLIN, NEW YORK
Carleton C; ML; Northfield, MN 55057.
Ulf Zimmermann, Carl Weiner
1-12; 2-4+ for 20+; 3-b,c; 4-74/75; 5-1; 6-b; 7-a; 8-6q; 9-a; 10-sr standing; 11-phenomenon of the city, its cult in the last cen and the interrelationships between the metropolis and the arts with a view to what makes the cities thrive in these terms; 12-a,b,c,d,f; 13-a,b,d,e,f; 14-ng.

977. TWO THEATERS OF THE ABSURD
Carleton C; Cl, Philo, Drama; Northfield, MN 55057.
David H. Porter
1-15-25; 2-4x10; 3-b; 4-74/75; 5-1; 6-b; 7-a; 8-6q; 9-a, one or two interested members of the Northfield or Twin Cities communities; 10-some study of theatre or drama; 11-study of cl & modern; 12-b,c,d,f; 13-a,e,f; 14-various.

978. GREEK HISTORY & PHILOSOPHY
Colorado C; Cl, Hist, Philo; Colorado Springs, CO 80903.
Owen Cramer, Cl; John Riker, Philo
1-26; 2-12x7; 3-b; 4-70/71; 5-4; 6-b; 7-a; 8-

7q; 9-a; 10-none; 11-work in Greek hist & philo through reading primary sources of cl Greek lit & philo; modern secondary sources; 12-a,b,f; 13-b; 14-various.

979. WAR, VIOLENCE & THE HUMANITIES
Colorado C; Cl, Philo, Hist; Colorado Springs, CO 80903.
Owen Cramer (Cl), William Hochman (Hist), J. Glenn Gray (Philo)
1-45; 2-12-15x3½; 3-b; 4-74/75; 5-1; 6-uncertain: may be offered once a yr; 7-a; 8-3½; 9-a; 10-none; 11-examination of ability of humanistic disciplines to describe & understand the phenomena of war & violence. Philo, hist, & lit insights into way war has been regarded in the West from Homer to present; 12-a,b,f; 13-a; 14-various.

980. HUMAN COMMUNICATION: SIGN AND SYMBOL
U of Detroit; Langs & Ling; Detroit, MI 48221.
L.W. Wedberg
1-12; 2-3x15; 3-b; 4-fall 74; 5-1; 6-b; 7-a; 8-3s; 9-a; 10-none, for freshmen only; 11-intro to sci study of lang, its relationship to cult, society & the individual, figurative

lang or the absence of it (the aesthetics of silence); 12-a,b,f; 13-e,f, handouts; 14-various plus Rich, Interracial Communication; Lindesmith & Strauss, Social Psychology; Roth, Our Gang.

981. CONTINENTAL TRENDS IN NOVELS FROM 1850 TO THE PRESENT
Immaculata C; Eng, MFLs, Philo; Immaculata, PA 19345.
Sr. Marie Eugenie, Eng
1-20-25; 2-3x sem; 3-b,c; 4-55; 5-ng; 6-alt yrs; 7-a; 8-3s; 9-a; 10-none; 11-lit & philo analysis of the novels of Dostoevski, Manzoni, Silone, Mann, Hesse, Kafka, Cela, Camus, Malraux; 12-b,c; 13-a,b; 14-various.

982. MODERN BRITISH AND CONTINENTAL DRAMA
Immaculata C; Eng, MFLs, Philo; Immaculata, PA 19345.
Sr. Marie Eugenie, Eng
1-20-25; 2-3x sem; 3-b,c; 4-approx 55; 5-ng; 6-alt yrs; 7-a; 8-3s; 9-a; 10-none; 11-existential nature of man as seen in study of continental novels from 1850-present; 12-b,c; 13-a,b; 14-various.

983. IDEAS IN LITERATURE
Indiana U; Comp Lit; Bloomington, IN 47401.
1-7; 2-2½x16; 3-a; 4-fall 68/69; 5-5; 6-b; 7-a; 8-3s; 9-a; 10-6 hrs of lit; 11-study of major philo themes which recur in Western lit; 12-a,b,c,f; 13-ng; 14-various.

984. SCIENCE AND THE NATURE OF MAN
U of Iowa; Chemical Engineering, Ger; Iowa City, IA 52242.
Dean Dewey Stuit, C of Liberal Arts
1-12; 2-3x17; 3-b; 4-late forties; 5-once a yr since 48; 6-b; 7-a; 8-2-4s; 9-a; 10-completion of core courses by upper classmen and grad students; 11-discussion course based on the philo & sci concept of man in the West contained in philo & sci texts beginning with St. Augustine through the present; 12-b,f; 13-e, texts; 14-various.

985. BIOGRAPHY OF A CITY: PARIS
U of Kansas; Fr & Ital, History of Art, Hist; Lawrence, KS 66045.
John D. Erickson
1-150; 2-3x15; 3-b; 4-spr 74; 5-1; 6-only offered once; 7-b; 8-3s; 9-a,b; 10-none; 11-course deals with Paris from the different perspectives of hist, art, & lit, major concern is to recreate the atmosphere of a great center of modernism from the mid-nineteenth cen to the present; 12-a,f; 13-a,b,d; 14-Green, From Versailles to Vichy; Ardagh, The New French Revolution; Hunter, Modern French Painting; primary texts.

986. 1913
U of Kansas; Fr & Ital, Art Hist; Lawrence, KS 66045.
J. Theodore Johnson.
1-new; 2-3x15; 3-b; 4-spr 75; 5-1; 6-unknown; 7-a; 8-3s; 9-a; 10-jr standing; 11-

course will focus on burst of artistic creativity in Europe & Amer early in 20th cen, its height in 1913, its interruption by World War I; main emphasis on the visual arts (film, photography, painting, sculpture, architecture) & lit; guest lectures in hist, philo, Ger, Eng & Amer lit & drama; 12-a,f; 13-a,b,e,f; 14-Gide, Lafcadio's Adventures; Proust, Swann's Way; Shattuck, ed., Selected Writings of Appollinaire; Haftmann, Painting in the 20th Century.

987. THE IMAGE OF THE HITLER ERA IN GERMAN NOVELS
Lawrence U; Freshman Core Program; Appleton, WI 54911.
John F. McMahon
1-22; 2-3x10; 3-Ger Dept; 4-73/74; 5-1; 6-a; 7-a; 8-3 1/3; 9-a; 10-none; 11-study of 4 post-WW II Ger novels concerned with the Nazi era; 12-a,b,c,f; 13-ng; 14-primary sources.

988. LITERATURE & THEOLOGY: VIOLENCE & THE SACRED
Loyola U; ML, Theology; Chicago, IL 60626.
John Miles, Dept of Theology, U of Montana, Missoula, MT
1-26; 2-3x15; 3-b; 4-spr 74; 5-1; 6-ng; 7-a; 8-3s; 9-a; 10-none; 11-relationship of lit form & content to violence in community and religion; discussion centered on Joseph Campbell's Hero with a Thousand Faces and Rene Girard's La Violence et le Sacre; 12-a,b,f; 13-a,b; 14-various.

989. SCIENTISTS' DILEMMA
Mankato SC; FL; Mankato, MN 56001.
Jean Strachan
1-16; 2-3x11; 3-b; 4-wtr 75; 5-1; 6-depending on demand; 7-b; 8-3q; 9-a; 10-none; 11-reading in trans of Ger plays in which a scientist is the central figure; 12-a,b,c; 13-ng; 14-various.

990. NATURE OF MAN & WESTERN SOCIETY
Merrimack Valley Branch of University of New Hampshire; Nat Scis, Soci Scis, Hums; Manchester, NH 03101.
William A. Cook, Chrm Liberal Studies
1-62; 2-3x15; 3-a; 4-73/74; 5-1; 6-a; cancelled this yr for revision; 7-a; 8-4s; 9-a,b; 10-none; 11-integrates materials from nat scis, soci scis & hums to explore nature of man & society, beginning with study of man as a primate & his primitive society through Christianity & Medieval civ; 12-a,b,c,d,f; 13-a,b,f; 14-various.

991. THE GOSPEL OF JOHN
U of Michigan; Cl Studies & Near Eastern Studies; Ann Arbor, MI 48104.
John A. Bailey
1-3; 2-3x16; 3-b; 4-wtr 70; 5-1; 6-occasionally; 7-a; 8-3s; 9-a; 10-knowledge of cl Greek; instructor's permission; 11-reading of the Gospel of John in the original with investigations of the hist and religious milieu; 12-b,g; 13-ng; 14-ng.

992. THE GOSPEL OF MATTHEW

U of Michigan; Cl Studies & Near East Studies; Ann Arbor, MI 48104.
John A. Bailey
1-6; 2-3x16; 3-b; 4-66; 5-2; 6-occasionally; 7-a; 8-3s; 9-a; 10-knowledge of cl Greek, instructor's permission; 11-reading in Greek the Gospel of Matthew and parallel material; exegesis of selected passages covering the philological, hist, and theological problems; 12-b,g; 13-ng; 14-ng.

993. LETTERS OF PAUL IN GREEK
U of Michigan; Cl Studies & Near Eastern Studies; Ann Arbor, MI 48104.
John A. Bailey
1-2; 2-3x16; 3-b; 4-wtr 69; 5-2; 6-occasionally; 7-a; 8-3s; 9-a; 10-knowledge of cl Greek; instructor's permission; 11-interpretation of selected texts from the Epistles of Paul, read in Greek, with attention to philological, hist, and theological problems; 12-b,g; 13-ng; 14-ng.

994. LITERATURE & PHENOMENOLOGY
U of Minnesota; Comp Lit, Ger; Minneapolis, MN 55455.
L. Duroche
1-10; 2-5x10; 3-b; 4-73/74; 5-1; 6-once every 2 yrs; 7-a; 8-4q; 9-a; 10-Fr or Ger, grad student or upper div lang or lit student; 11-study of specific lit texts from a variety of lits & langs by exploring a phenomenological perspective based on Merleau-Ponty's work; 12-b,f; 13-novels, plays, poetry; 14-ng.

995. PHILOSOPHICAL PROBLEMS IN TWENTIETH CENTURY LITERATURE
Molloy C; Philo, Sp; Rockville Center, NY 11570.
Rose Teresa Amor
1-19; 2-3x15; 3-b; 4-67; 5-4; 6-student request; 7-a; 8-3s; 9-a, part-time students; 10-none; 11-philo problems in 20th cen lit as seen in Fr, Sp, Eng & Amer lit, team-taught by members of the depts involved; 12-a,b,c; 13-e, reference; 14-various.

996. GREAT WOMEN OF THE 18th CENTURY
C of Mount St Vincent; Hist, Fine Arts, MFL; Bronx, NY 10471.
Arthur Murphy
1-15; 2-3x15; 3-b; 4-75; 5-1; 6-b; 7-a; 8-3s; 9-a; 10-none; 11-study of Catherine the Great, Maria Theresa, Mme de Pompadour, Marie Antoinette, Mme Vigie Lebrun, Mme du Chatelet, Mme de Deffand & their influence in 18th cen politics, lit, art; 12-a,f; 13-b, museum visits; 14-none.

997. SYMBOLISM OF THE FIN DE SIECLE
SUCNY; FLs, Hist, Philo, Soci, Art, Music, Dance; Potsdam, NY 13676.
A.R. Plante
1-40; 2-3x15; 3-b,c; 4-72/73; 5-2; 6-b; 7-b; 8-3s; 9-a,b; 10-none; 11-exploration of Fr cult of the fin de siecle through a study of hist, philo, soci, art, music, dance; 12-a,b,c,f; 13-a,b, a play, a concert; 14-Cobban, A History of Modern France; Bergson, Essay on Comedy; plus various others.

998. CLASSICAL TRADITION
C of Notre Dame; Cl; Baltimore, MD 21210.
Therese Marie Dougherty
1-29; 2-4x13; 3-b,c; 4-73/74; 5-2; 6-b; 7-a; 8-4s; 9-a; 10-none; 11-selections from Greek & Latin lit in trans dealing with values & comparison with writings from other periods; 12-a,b,c,f; 13-a,b,d; 14-primary texts.

999. THE HUMAN CONDITION & ALIENATION
C of Notre Dame; MLs; Baltimore, MD 21210.
Regina Soria
1-15; 2-3x14; 3-b,c; 4-67; 5-10; 6-a,b; 7-a; 8-4; 9-a, adults, part-time; 10-upper class or permission of coordinator; 11-topics vary, faculty drawn from approx 7 different depts; 12-b,c,d,f; 13-a,b,c,d,e,f, plus many different materials and artifacts, according to topic; 14-various.

1000. COURT OF CHARLEMAGNE
Ohio SU; Cl, Medieval & Rennaissance Studies; Columbus, OH 43210.
Joseph Lynch
1-75; 2-5x10; 3-b; 4-70; 5-5; 6-b; 7-a; 8-5q; 9-a; 10-none; 11-interdisc course on lit, art, music, hist, liturgy of Carolingian Age; 12-a,b,f; 13-b; 14-various.

1001. NINETEENTH CENTURY ROMANTICISM
Philadelphia C of Bible; Hums; Philadelphia, PA 19103.
Mae Stewart
1-25; 2-3x15; 3-b; 4-74/75; 5-1; 6-uncertain; 7-b; 8-3s; 9-a, some grad students; 10-jr status, 3 hrs of lit, 3 hrs of philo; 11-seminar course designed to examine the philosophical relationship of 19th cen lit, philo, painting & music; 12-a,b,c,f; 13-b,d,e, live music; 14-various.

1002. THE IDEA OF A UNIVERSITY
U of Pittsburgh; Fr & Ital; Pittsburgh, PA 15260.
Douglas Radcliff-Umstead, Director of Center for Medieval & Renaissance Studies; Arcadi Nebolsire, Comp Lit Program
1-12; 2-3x15; 3-b; 4-fall 72; 5-3; 6-b; 7-a; 8-4s; 9-a; 10-none; 11-hist & theory of univ ed from Middle Ages to present, emphasis on determining the goals of univs as they relate to society at large; 12-a,c,e,f; 13-ng; 14-various.

1003. PARIS 1300
Pomona C; MFL; Claremont, CA 91711.
Phyllis Johnson
1-25; 2-3x15; 3-b; 4-71; 5-1; 6-once; 7-a; 8-4s; 9-a; 10-none; 11-interdisc study of medieval music, art, lit, sci, hist, philo, theology; 12-a,b,f; 13-ng; 14-ng.

1004. PHILOSOPHY & LITERATURE
Purdue U; Eng, Philo; West Lafayette, IN 47907.
Robert Magliola, Coordinator, Program in Philo & Eng
1-12; 2-3x15; 3-b; 4-71; 5-7; 6-b (with

occasional hiatus of 1 yr); 7-a; 8-3s; 9-a; 10-for the Program: M.A. in Eng or philo; for this particular course 6 hrs in philo or lit or 3 hrs in each or permission of instructors; 11-intensive examination of the structure of lit, the bearing of lit style on philo idea, & the application of philo categories to lit criticism; 12-a,b,c,f; some texts read in for lang; 13-textbooks; 14-various.

1005. EXISTENTIALISM AND EXISTENTIAL THEMES IN MODERN GERMAN LITERATURE
Regis C; Ger; Weston, MA 02193.
Joan Murray
1-12; 2-3x15; 3-b; 4-73/74; 5-1; 6-alt yrs; 7-a; 8-4s; 9-a; 10-none; 11-study of existential thought in Nietzsche, Kierkegaard, Sartre, Heidegger, Husserl and its influence on Ger writers including Rilke, Musil, Kafka, Doeblin, Aichinger; 12-a,b,c,f; 13-ng; 14-various.

1006. MAN'S SEARCH FOR MEANING
Roanoke C; Philo & Religion, MLs, Fine Arts; Salem, VA 24153.
Patricia Dragon
1-89; 2-15x3 (Jan interterm course); 3-b,c; 4-Jan 74; 5-2; 6-every Jan interterm; 7-a; 8-4q; 9-a; 10-none; 11-man's search for meaning through various means: philo, religion, art, lit, soci interaction; 12-a,b,d,f; 13-a,b,d,e,f, reproductions of paintings; 14-various.

1007. MEDIEVAL MAN
Roanoke C; FLs; Salem, VA 24153.
Patricia M. Gathercole
1-70; 2-3x16; 3-b; 4-70; 5-4; 6-varies; 7-b; 8-1 unit; 9-a, evening; 10-none; 11-life and thought with some consideration of relevance to contemporary society; 12-a,b,f; 13-a,b; 14-primary texts; readings in hist and philo.

1008. RENAISSANCE MAN
Roanoke C; FLs; Salem, VA 24153.
Patricia Gathercole
1-new; 2-3 per wk for 4 months; 3-b,c; 4-to be offered; 5-0; 6-b; 7-b; 8-1 unit; 9-a; 10-none; two interdisc courses are required for graduation; 11-study of the life & thought of Renaissance man as reflected in Italian beginnings, Transalpine diffusion, and impact upon Europe; 12-a,b,f; 13-a,b, records; 14-various.

1009. THE SPIRIT OF LIBERATION
Roanoke C; FLs; Salem, VA 24153.
Patricia Gathercole
1-160; 2-3x4; 3-b,c; 4-72; 5-3; 6-every interterm; 7-day session during interterm; 8-1 unit; 9-a; 10-none, 2 interdisc courses required for graduation; 11-inquiry into some of the manifestations of the liberating forces at work in lit, politics, religion, & soci institutions & movements, from the late 18th cen to present; 12-a,b,f; 13-a,b, records; 14-various.

1010. INTELLECTUAL CURRENTS OF THE 18TH CENTURY
Roosevelt U; Langs, Eng; Chicago, IL 60605.
Otto Wirth, Dept of Langs
1-18; 2-2½x16; 3-b; 4-46/47; 5-19; 6-b; 7-a; 8-ng; 9-a; 10-1 course & consent; 11-seminar for outstanding students in the hums. Deals with the main ideas & intellectual currents of 18th cen, as manifested in art, lit, sci, philo, & poli of the period; 12-a,b,c,f; 13-b, records; 14-various.

1011. INTELLECTUAL CURRENTS OF THE 19TH CENTURY
Roosevelt U; Langs, Eng; Chicago, IL 60605.
Otto Wirth, Dept of Langs
1-2; 2-2½x15; 3-b; 4-46/47; 5-19; 6-b; 7-a; 8-3s; 9-a; 10-1 course & consent; 11-primarily a seminar for outstanding students in the hums; deals with the main ideas & intellectual currents of the 19th cen as manifested in the art, lit, sci, poli, philo of the period; 12-a,b,c,f; 13-a,b, records; 14-various.

1012. HUMANITIES SEMINAR ON VALUES
Rosemont C; Hums, Langs & Lits; Rosemont, PA 19010.
Margaret Healy
Seminar held spr 75; involving disciplines of: Theology, Philo, Hist, Lit, Arts; study of theoretical & illustrative readings, demonstrating how each discipline studies value systems.

1013. MYTHOLOGY AND LITERATURE
St. Vincent C & Seton Hill C; Cl, Ger, Fr, Sp; Latrobe, PA 15650.
Chrysostom Schlimm, St. Vincent C
1-new; 2-3x15; 3-c; 4-to be offered fall 75; 5-0; 6-b; 7-a; 8-3s; 9-a; 10-none; 11-study of recurrent mythical themes of Greek & Latin lit (Cl Dept) contrasted with myths which appear in Wagner & Romantic German lit (German Dept), Modern Fr lit (Fr Dept) & Mayan legend & lit of Guatemala (Sp Dept); 12-a,f; 13-b,d; 14-ng.

1014. TOWARD AN UNDERSTANDING OF MODERNISM
Stanford U; Comp Lit; Stanford, CA 94305.
Herbert Lindenberger
1-20; 2-3x10; 3-b; 4-70; 5-3; 6-one qtr every 2 yrs; 7-a; 8-5q; 9-a; 10-none; 11-provides intellectual background of modern lit through readings in writers such as Nietzsche, Kierkegaard, Freud. Analogies to modern lit are drawn from fields such as art hist, philo, music; 12-a,b,f; 13-ng; 14-Ellman & Feidelson, The Modern Tradition; plus various philosophical works.

1015. LATIN AMERICAN PHILOSOPHY
U of Texas; MLs; El Paso, TX 79968.
Diana S. Natalicio
1-30; 2-3x15; 3-b; 4-70; 5-3; 6-every 2 yrs; 7-a, smr; 8-3s; 9-a; 10-6 hrs jr level Sp; 11-selected works of Latin Amer thinkers (Rodo, Vasconcelos, Sarmiento, Faz Ferreira, Octavio Paz et al) are read & discussed both as contributions to lit & as

milestones in the formation of modern Latin Amer thought. Team-taught by MLs & Philo Depts; 12-a,b,c,f,g; 13-ng; 14-Ariel, La Raza Cosmica; Fermentario, Perfil del Hombre y la Cultura en Mexico; El Problema de Mexico y la Ideología nacional, Filosofía de la Persona.

1016. MODERN POLITICAL NOVEL
U of Texas; Lit, Govt; Odessa, TX 79762.
Owen Weddle, Lit; Kevin-John McIntyre, Govt
1-25; 2-3x15; 3-b; 4-spr 74; 5-1; 6-perhaps alt yrs; 7-b; 8-3s; 9-a, part-time students; 10-lower div courses in Eng & poli sci; 11-20th cen political novel as a subgenre and as a 'vehicle for normative poli thought'; 12-a,b,f; team-taught by prof of lit and prof of govt; 12-ng; 14-various.

1017. THEORIES OF CREATIVITY
U of Texas; Art; Odessa, TX 79760.
William A. King
1-27; 2-3x17; 3-b; 4-74; 5-1; 6-b; 7-a; 8-3s; 9-a; 10-jr standing; 11-3 presentations each from: engineering, lit, art, music, film, philo, psychology, theater, management, and creative writing. An examination of what creativity means in each of these disciplines. Students choose 20 of the 30 lectures to attend, each student designing his own course; 12-a,b,e,f; 13-a,b,c,d; 14-Gheslin, The Creative Process; Bloomberg, Creativity.

1018. FROM ROMANTICISM TO REVOLUTION
U of Utah; Eng, Langs; Salt Lake City, UT 84112.
James T. Svendsen, Langs
1-20; 2-4x10; 3-b,c; 4-73/74; 5-ng; 6-was pilot program but hope to offer it every other yr; 7-a; 8-5-8q; 9-a, faculty; 10-jr or sr standing; 11-investigates the transformation of Romantic ideals into revolutionary thought & action in Germany

of late 18th & early 19th cen intensive study of lit, theater, fine arts, & music, cult hist, philo & poli writings; 12-a,b,f; 13-a,b, dramatic performances & readings; 14-various.

1019. THE INTELLECTUAL TRADITION OF THE WEST
U of Utah; Langs; Salt Lake City, UT 84112.
Robert E. Helbling
1-758 in 20-22 sections; 2-4 or 5x30 (sequence course extending over 3 qtrs); 3-b; 4-55; 5-every yr; 6-a; 7-a,b; 8-5q; 9-a,c; 10-none; 11-traces the intellectual hist of the West; 12-a,b,f; 13-a,c, general lectures on closed circuit TV; 14-various.

1020. MYTH AND HISTORY
Wellesley C; Hist, Greek & Latin; Wellesley, MA 02181.
Mary R. Lefkowitz
1-14-; 2-2hrs 20minx13; 3-b,c; 4-74; 5-1; 6-b; 7-a; 8-4s; 9-a; 10-none; 11-analysis of eyewitness accounts, retrospective critical narrative & moralistic biography with a view to their having been rendered through subjective filter; readings in trans of Greek & Roman historical lit; 12-b,f; 13-ng; 14-ng.

1021. LANDSCAPES OF THE MIND'S INTERIOR
Wesleyan U; Fr, Religion; Middletown, CT 06457.
Richard Stamelman, Rom Langs
1-17; 2-4x13; 3-b; 4-spr 75; 5-1; 6-probably will not be repeated; 7-a; 8-2s; 9-a; 10-none, course limited to freshmen, some sophs; 11-probing of the mind's working through analysis of mystical texts, surrealist lit & art, mystical experience, poetic experience, psychotic experience; 12-b,c,d,f; 13-a,b; 14-various.

See also 918, 919, 920, 924, 929, 933, 937, 938, 941, 945, 1023, 1387, 1576, 1678A.

Miscellaneous

1022. INTERDISCIPLINARY HONORS
Chestnut Hill C; Honors; Philadelphia, PA 19118.
Irma Mercedes
1-10/15; 2-2x30; 3-b; 4-68; 5-c8; 6-a; 7-a; 8-3s; 9-a; 10-acceptance in Honors Program; 11-course topics vary; 12-b,f; 13-ng; 14-various.

1023. HUMANITIES PROGRAM
Parkland C; Communications; Champaign, IL 61820.
Eva Frayne
1-159; 2-4x11; 3-b; 4-71; 5-each term since

then 2 of the three courses have been offered; 6-a; 7-a,b; 8-4q; 9-a,b; 10-none; 11-man & creation-his relationship to the arts, religion, nature; 12-a,b,c,f; 13-a,b,d,e; 14-primary texts.

1024. MAJOR IN SPANISH (INTERDISCIPLINARY PROGRAM)
Southern Missionary C; ML; Collegedale, TN 37315.
Robert R. Morrison
1-new; 2-ng; 3-b; 4-74/75; 5-1; 6-a; 7-a; 8-30; 9-ng; 10-varies; 11-a 4 yr program built upon pre-existing courses, with exception

228

of "Masterpieces in Trans," team-taught; 12-a,b,c,e,f,g; 13-a,b,d,e,f; 14-ng.

1025. GERMAN LECTURES IN THE BIOLOGICAL SCIENCES
U of Wisconsin; Ger, Zoology; Madison, WI 53706.
1-24 in Ger, 20 in Zoology (credit registrations), 50-150 auditors; 2-2x14; 3-b; 4-fall '75; 5-1; 6-by demand and/or availability of lecturers; 7-b; 8-1s (cr/nc basis); 9-a,b, community; 10-for students at undergrad or grad level; inter prof helpful but not required; 11-lectures on a variety of topics related to professors' research specialties but directed toward a general audience; Eng glossaries and summaries and other aids provided; 12-a,b,g; 13-a,b,c; 14-Eng summaries prepared by lecturers; vocabs (Ger & scientific) prepared by depts; notes and grammar help prepared by Ger Dept; quiz materials.

See also 514, 1387, 1662.

INTERDISCIPLINARY (DEPARTMENTAL)

Culture and Civilization

NATIONAL

Armenia

1026. ARMENIAN LANGUAGE AND CULTURE
St. Joseph's C; MLs; Philadelphia, PA 19131.
James E. Iannucci
1-25; 2-3x14; 3-a; 4-75; 5-1; 6-a; 7-b; 8-3s; 9-ng; 10-none; 11-intro to Armenian lang & cult; 12-ng; 13-a,b; 14-ng.

Brazil

See 1486.

China

1027. CHINESE CULTURE AND CIVILIZATION
City C of San Francisco; FLs; San Francisco, CA 94112.
Jacquelyn W. Green
Additional info not available.

Cuba

1028. CULTURAL HERITAGE OF CUBA
Central Connecticut SC; MLs; New Britain, CT 06050.
Orlando Gomez-Gil
1-19; 2-3x15; 3-a; 4-74; 5-1; 6-on demand; 7-a; 8-3s; 9-a; 10-adv prof; 11-hist, geography, econ, cult, national character; 12-a, b, c, g; 13-b; records; 14-Fornet, El cuento cubano contemporanco; Lazo, Historia de la literatura cubana; Morales, Historia de Cuba; instructor-prepared materials.

France

1029. FRENCH CIVILIZATION
Boston U; MLs; Boston, MA 02215.
Susan Cate
1-8; 2-3x14; 3-a; 4-69/70; 5-4; 6-b; 7-a; 8-4s; 9-a; 10-adv prof; 11-cult, soci, poli, econ factors in hist development of France; 12-a,b,g; 13-ng; 14-Thoraval, Les Grandes Etapes de la Civilisation Francaise.

1030. FRENCH CIVILIZATION AND CONVERSATION
Bridgewater SC; MFL: Bridgewater, MA 02324.
Jacqueline Enos
1-13; 2-3x15; 3-a; 4-ng; 5-ng; 6-b; 7-a,b; 8-3s; 9-a; 10-adv prof; 11-cult and hist development; 12-b,c,g; 13-b,e,f; 14-Thoraval, Les Grandes Etapes de la Civilisation Francaise.

1031. FRENCH CIVILIZATION
Bucknell U; ML; Lewisburg, PA 17837.
Allan W. Grundstrom

229

1-20; 2-3x14; 3-a; 4-73; 5-3; 6-a; 7-a; 8-1 unit; 9-a; 10-inter prof; 11-life in contemporary France, structure of the family, structure of society, institutions; 12-a,b,g; 13-e,f; 14-Wylie, Les Francais; Christien & Lefebvre, Comprendre la France; L'Express.

1032. FRENCH MAJOR
U of California; Fr; Berkeley, CA 94720.
Leo Bersani
1-ng; 2-ng; 3-a; 4-75/76; 5-0; 6-a; 7-a; 8-49; 9-a; 10-ng; 11-present major (option A) has strong concentration in lit; Option B would include lit in a broader study of Fr civ in its hist, soci & artistic dimensions; 12-a,b,g; 13-a,f; 14-ng.

1033. FRENCH CIVILIZATION (series of four courses)
U of California; Fr & Ital; Riverside, CA 92502.
Robert Griffin
1-c25; 2-3x10; 3-a; 4-72/74; 5-1; 6-2 courses per year; 7-a; 8-ng; 9-a; 10-none; 11-interdisc approach to the Fr from the Gauls to present: society, cult, econ, arts; 12-a,b,f; 13-b,d; 14-varies with course.

1034. FRENCH CULTURE AND CIVILIZATION
City C of San Francisco; FLs; San Francisco, CA 94112.
Jacquelyn W. Green
Additional info not available.

1035. CONTEMPORARY FRENCH CULTURE
Davidson C; Fr; Davidson, NC 28036.
E.F. Jacobus, Jr.
1-10; 2-1 yr; 3-a; 4-73/74; 5-2; 6-jr yr; 7-ng; 8-1 course; 9-JYA participants in France; 10-course in Fr civ; 11-development of understanding of Fr character, cult, and soci structure, emphasis on univ life; 12-b,c,d,g; videotape making; 13-c,e,f; 14-various reference books.

1036. FRENCH CULTURE AND LIFE
Georgia Southern C; FLs; Statesboro, GA 30458.
Zoltan J. Farkas
1-30; 2-5x10; 3-a; 4-74; 5-1; 6-2 qtrs per yr; 7-a; 8-5q; 9-a; 10-none; 11-contemporary lit, arts, politics, cult, life, hist; 12-a,b,c,f; 13-a,b,d,e; 14-France: Comparative Culture and Government.

1037. FRANCE TODAY
Hood C; Lang; Frederick, MD 21701.
1-4; 2-3xsem; 3-a; 4-72; 5-2; 6-alt yrs; 7-a; 8-3s; 9-a; 10-inter prof; 11-the country today; hist, soci, econ, geographic factors shaping it and its people; 12-a,b,c,g; 13-a,b,e,f; 14-ng.

1038. THE FRENCH WORLD TODAY
Hope C; FLs; Holland, MI 49423.

Hubert Weller
1-23; 2-3x16; 3-a; 4-73; 5-3; 6-b; 7-b; 8-3s; 9-a; 10-none; 11-distinctive characteristics of Fr civ with emphasis on contemporary issues; 12-a,b,c,f; 13-b,e,f; 14-de Gramont, The French, Portrait of a People; Hoffman et al, In Search of France.

1039. FRENCH CULTURE THROUGH LITERATURE IN TRANSLATION
Marygrove C; FLs; Detroit, MI 48221.
E. DuBruck
1-18; 2-3x15; 3-a; 4-72; 5-4; 6-b; 7-a; 8-3s; 9-a, part-time; 10-for lang credit, inter prof; none for general credit; 11-France and the Fr; 12-a,b,f; 13-a,b,c; 14-primary texts, new every yr so that students can take course several times.

1040. FRENCH CIVILIZATION
U of Missouri; Rom Langs; Columbia, MO 65201.
K.B. Whitworth
1-86; 2-3x16; 3-a; 4-c65; 5-ng; 6-a; 7-a; 8-3s; 9-a; 10-none; 11-lit, artistic, poli, and soci hist of France; 12-a,b,f; 13-a,b; 14-varies.

1041. FRANCE TODAY
Molloy C; Fr; Rockville Centre, NY 11570.
Patricia Morris
1-38; 2-3x15; 3-a; 4-72; 5-5; 6-a; 7-a,b; 8-3s; 9-a,b; 10-none; 11-national and local govt, family life, ed system, cult and philo of life, role of the woman; relations with other countries, cult importance on world scene; 12-a,b,c,d,f; 13-a,b,e,f; 14-no formal text; materials and bulletins from France.

1042. FRENCH CULTURE
Monroe County CC; Hums; Monroe, MI 48161.
Paul E. Ross
1-5; 2-7½x6; 3-a; 4-72; 5-2; 6-interim; 7-a; 8-3s; 9-a; 10-none; 11-aspects of Fr cult not ordinarily covered in a formal classroom setting; 12-a,b,e,f; 13-a,b,e,f, guest speakers; 14- library texts.

1043. LIFE IN FRANCE: YESTERDAY AND TODAY
Montgomery County CC; MLs; Blue Bell, PA 19422.
Charlotte Anderson
1-47; 2-3x15; 3-a; 4-72; 5-6; 6-a; 7-a; 8-3s; 9-ng; 10-none; 11-events, personages, ideas that have contributed to the formation of present-day France; Fr cult abroad, its contribution to the modern world, its spread on other continents; 12-a,b,c,f; 13-a,b,c,e,f; 14-Buerard, France; primary texts.

1044. CONTEMPORARY FRENCH SOCIETY AND CULTURE
SUNY at Albany; Fr; Albany, NY 12222.

Georges V. Santoni
1-20; 2-3x15; 3-c; 4-73; 5-2; 6-b; 7-a; 8-3s (not acceptable for credit in Fr major); 9-a; 10-none; 11-concepts of time, space, human nature; family structures; ed system; family and ed (consequences in the behavior of adults); the urban soci classes; the rural soci classes; politics; econ; symbolic expressions and aesthetic creations; intellectual movements; Amer images of France and vice versa; 12-a,b,d,f; 13-a,b; 14-Nourissier, The French; Ardagh, The New French Revolution; Hoffman, In Search of France and Decline or Renewal?; Morin, The Red and the White; Wylie, Village in the Vaucluse

1045. FRENCH CIVILIZATION (IN ENGLISH OR IN FRENCH)
U of North Carolina; FL; Charlotte, NC 28213.
Newell R. Bush
1-10 (Eng), 17 (Fr); 2-3x14; 3-c; 4-71/72 (Fr), 72/73 (Eng); 5-3 (Fr), 2(Eng); 6-b (Fr), alt yrs (Eng); 7-a; 8-3s; 9-a; 10-inter prof (Fr), none (Eng); 11-taught as "sister courses," one in Fr and the other in Eng. A study of the Fr people, past and present, special attention to cross-cult contrasts in attitudes and values. Population problems, econ, religion, urbanization and housing, poli institutions, and child rearing psychology, as well as hist, sci, etc; 12-b,c,d,f,g; 13-a,b,e,f guest lectures; 14-Wylie, A Village in the Vaucluse; Les Francais; Ardagh, The New French Revolution; Hansen, France in the Modern World.

1046. FRENCH CIVILIZATION AND CULTURE
U of Notre Dame; Mod & Cl Lang; Notre Dame, IN 46556.
Bernard Doering
1-12; 2-3x14; 3-a; 4-68; 5-3; 6-alt yrs; 7-a; 8-3s; 9-a; 10-good reading prof in Fr; 11-identity of Fr in space and time; hist of ideas, soci insts, plastic arts, music; emphasis on 20th cen and contemporary problems; 12-a,b,c,g; 13-a,b,e,f, records; 14-Hardre, La France et Sa Civilisation; Ardagh, The New French Revolution.

1047. FRENCH CULTURE
Southeastern CC; FLs; Whiteville, NC 28472.
Samuel D. Sink
1-16; 2-2x11; 3-a; 4-73/74; 5-6; 6-a; 7-a,b; 8-2q; 9-a; 10-none; 11-geography, politics, and local customs; brief overview of lit and hist, current events; 12-a,b,c,f; 13-a,b,c,d,e,f; 14-none.

1048. FRENCH 400
U of Southern California; Fr & Ital; Los Angeles, CA 90007.
George W. Solovieff
1-18; 2-3x15; 3-a; 4-74; 5-1; 6-every third

sem; 7-a; 8-4s; 9-a; 10-none; 11-Fr cult since 1900; emphasis on major intellectual, sociopolitical & artistic trends, including cinema & TV; 12-a,b,d,f; 13-e,f; 14-no adequate textbook available in English; France, Documentation francaise, Paris, 1973.

1049. PROFESSIONAL MAJOR (FRENCH)
U of Southern California; Fr & Ital; Los Angeles CA 90007.
Max L. Berkley, Jr.
Change in emphasis from more traditional major in Fr lang & lit focus on general Fr cult of 20th cen & on complete mastery of the lang. Included in program are colloquia: French Studies (selected topics from lit of the Fr-speaking community, with emphasis on cult, philo, & soci issues).

1050. FRENCH LANGUAGE AND CIVILIZATION
Trinity U; FLs; San Antonio, TX 78284.
Olivia Sordo
1-6; 2-3½ per day for 14 days; 3-a; 4-smr 74; 5-2; 6-each smr mini-term); 7-a; 8-3s; 9-a; 10-inter prof; 11-conv & compostition, grammar review, cult, hist, poli, soci problems, music, art; 12-a,b,c,d,g; 13-a,b,c,e,f, guest speakers, records; 14-none.

1051. FRENCH CIVILIZATION
Upper Iowa U; Langs; Fayette, IA 52142.
F.A. Dupuis
1-9; 2-3x13; 3-a; 4-ng; 5-ng; 6-b; 7-a; 8-3s; 9-a; 10-World Civilization; 11-ng; 12-a,f; 13-e,f; 14-Knapton, France: An Interpretive History.

1052. CONTEMPORARY FRANCE
U of Washington; Rom Langs & Lits; Seattle, WA 98195.
Howard Nostrand
Currently 1 course is being offered: Contemporary France (1955-75): the soci & cult background; a prior course being planned for 76 to be called: The Making of Contemporary France: History; further info ng.

1053. FRANCE TODAY: CULTURE AND LANGUAGE
William Paterson C; FLs; Wayne, NJ 07470.
Catherine A. Barry
1-new; 2-3x17; 3-a; 4-ng; 5-0; 6-b; 7-a; 8-3s; 9-a; 10-none; 11-intro to France, its people and activities; contemporary cult; 12-a,b,c,f,g; 13-a,b,d,e,f; 14-Hachette, Le Francais Accelere.

1054. OTHER CULTURES THROUGH HUMANISTIC STUDIES (FRENCH)
U. of Wisconsin; Lang and Lit; Green Bay, WI 54302.
Louise R. Witherell
Broad background in many areas of cult, interdisc. Periodicals, newspapers, and

231

recent Fr-made documentary films will supplement the texts. Prepares for possible Jan trip. 3 credits. Work may be done in Fr or Eng.

See also 89, 716, 1230, 1348, 1370, 1379, 1551.

Germany

1055. GERMAN CIVILIZATION
Boston U; MLs; Boston, MA 02215.
Susan Cate
1-6; 2-3x14; 3-a; 4-74/75; 5-1; 6-b; 7-a; 8-4s; 9-a; 10-adv prof; 11-cult, poli, soci, and econ factors in hist development; 12-a,b,c,d,g; 13-a,b,e,f; 14-ng.

1056. THE MODERN GERMAN MIND
City C; Ger & Sl; New York, NY 10031.
Michael Rywkin
1-c10; 2-3xsem; 3-a; 4-early 70s; 5-ng; 6-b; 7-a; 8-3s; 9-a; 10-none; 11-intellectual and cult tradition through readings in Eng; 12-f; 13-ng; 14-primary texts.

1057. SPECIAL STUDIES IN GERMAN LITERATURE AND CULTURE
City C; Ger & Sl; New York, NY 10031.
Michael Rywkin
1-c10; 2-3xsem; 3-a; 4-early 70s; 5-ng; 6-b; 7-a; 8-4s; 9-a; 10-none; 11-rotating series of topics of special interest; 12-f; 13-ng; 14-primary texts.

1058. SEMINAR IN GERMAN CIVILIZATION
Duke U; Ger; Durham, NC 27706.
Frank L. Borchardt
1-19; 2-3x14; 3-a; 4-spr75; 5-1; 6-b; 7-ng; 8-3s; 9-a; 10-none but "German Life and Thought" recommended; 11-Expressionism: painting, graphics, architecture, film, poetry, drama, short prose, long prose--in that order; 12-b,c,f; 13-ng; 14-lengthy reading list of works in Eng and lit in trans.

1059. GERMAN CULTURE
Georgia Southern C; FLs; Statesboro, GA 30458.
H.J. Weatherford
1-40; 2-5x10; 3-a; 4-74; 5-1; 6-2q per yr; 7-a; 8-5q; 9-a; 10-none; 11- brief outline of hist, surveys of lit, music, art, philo, and modern life; 12-a,b,f, guest lectures; 13-a,b,e; 14-Germany: Comparative Culture and Government; Inside the Third Reich; novels.

1060. THE GERMANIC WORLD TODAY
Hope C; FL & Lit; Holland, MI 49423.
Gerhard Megow
1-17; 2-3x15; 3-a; 4-73; 5-3; 6-a; 7-b; 8-3s; 9-a; 10-none; 11-characteristics of Ger civ, emphasis on contemporary issues; 12-a,b,c,f; 13-a,f; 14-Dahrendorf, Society and Democracy in Germany; Smith, Germany beyond the Wall.

1061. GERMAN CULTURE AND CIVILIZATION
Luther C; ML; Decorah, IA 52101.
Barbara Bahe
1-new; 2-3x7½; 3-a; 4-75; 5-ng; 6-alt yrs; 7-a; 8-2; 9-a; 10-none; 11- Germany's contribution to Western civ as reflected in hist figures and events; may be combined with 'German Literature in Translation' for full-sem course; 12-a,b,c,f; 13-a,b,e; 14-McClelland & Scher, Postwar German Culture.

1062. GERMAN CULTURE THROUGH LITERATURE IN TRANSLATION
Marygrove C; FLs; Detroit, MI 48221.
E. DuBruck
1-18; 2-3x15; 3-a; 4-72; 5-4; 6-b; 7-a; 8-3s; 9-a, part-time; 10-inter prof for lang credit, none for general credit; 11-Germany and the Germans; 12-a,b,f; 14-a,b,c; 14-primary texts, new every yr so that students can take the course several times.

1063. GERMANY IN THE 20th CENTURY: WEIMAR AND NAZI CULTURE
U of Massachusetts; Ger; Boston, MA 02125.
Peter Ott
1-58; 2-3x13/14; 3-a; 4-71; 5-4; 6-b; 7-a; 8-4s; 9-a, part-time students; 10-none; 11-ng; 12-a,b,f; 13-a,b,d; 14-primary texts; Gay, Weimar Culture; Mosse, Nazi Culture; Remak, The Nazi Years; instructor-prepared materials.

1064. INTRODUCTION TO GERMANIC CIVILIZATION
Napa C; Hums; Napa, CA 94558.
Geza Kadar
1-30; 2-7x13; 3-a; 4-73/74; 5-6; 6-a; 7-a,b; 8-5q; 9-a, adults; 10-basic hums course; 11-independent study course; geography, hist and govt; contribution to U.S., art, music, theater, films, ed system, econ, scientists and inventors, lit, soci life, current affairs, travel experiences, special projects; 12-a,b,c,e,f; 13-a,b,c,d,e,f; 14-Reinhardt, Germany: 2000 Years; supplementary texts.

1065. GERMAN CULTURAL HISTORY
U of Notre Dame; MLs; Notre Dame, IN 46556.
Randolph Klawiter
1-5; 2-3x15; 3-a; 4-65; 5-3; 6-every 3 ys; 7-a; 8-3s; 9-a; 10-inter prof; 11-ng; 12-a,b,c,f,g; 13-b, records; 14-Kelling, Deutsche kulturgeschichte; Orthbrandt, Bildbuch deutscher Geschichte; Blume, German Literature: Texts and Contexts; Reinhardt, Germany: 2000 Years; Lindemann, History of German Art.

1066. GERMANY THROUGH THE AGES
Texas Lutheran C; FL; Seguin, TX 78155.
R.C. Lang

232

1-15; 2-4xsem; 3-a; 4-74; 5-1; 6-alt yrs; 7-a;
8-3s; 9-a; 10-instructor permission; 11-Ger
cult from its beginnings to the present;
emphasis on personalities who have made
lasting contributions to Europe and the
world; 12-b,f,g; 13-ng; 14-Kelling,
Deutsche Geschichte und Kultur: Bilder aus
2000 Jahren; Barraclough, The Origins of
Modern Germany.

See also 786, 1552.

Greece

1067. CLASSICAL CIVILIZATION: THE WORLD
OF THE ANCIENT GREEKS
U of Michigan; Cl Studies; Ann Arbor, MI
48104.
H.D. Cameron
1-45; 2-4x15; 3-b; 4-fall 73; 5-2; 6-b; 7-a; 8-
4s; 9-a; 10-none; freshmen, sophs, others by
permission; 11-lecture topics concern hist,
lit, philo, religion, law, archaeology, art
hist, tech, sci, mythology, econ, poli &
private life of the Greeks; 12-a,b,f; 13-b;
14-ancient primary sources in trans;
modern works.

Italy

1068. ITALIAN CIVILIZATION
Boston U; MLs; Boston, MA 02215.
Susan Cate
1-12; 2-3x14; 3-a; 4-73; 5-2; 6-b; 7-a; 8-4s;
9-a; 10-ng; 11-cult, poli, soci, and econ
factors in hist development; 12-f; 13-ng;
14-ng.

1069. ITALIAN CULTURE AND INSTITUTIONS
U of California; Ital; Los Angeles, CA
90024.
Giovanni Cecchetti
A 3-course sequence: History of the Italian
Language; Social Institutions of Italy;
History and Characteristics of
Contemporary Italy. Conducted mainly in
Ital. Prerequisite: inter prof.

1070. CLASSICAL CIVILIZATION: THE WORLD
OF THE ANCIENT ROMANS
U of Michigan; Cl Studies; Ann Arbor, MI
48104.
H.D. Cameron
1-24; 2-4x16; 3-b; 4-wtr 74; 5-1; 6-b; 7-a; 8-
4s; 9-a; 10-none; freshmen, sophs, others by
permission; 11-lectures focus on lit, hist,
philo, religion, law, archaeology, art, tech,
sci, mythology, econ, poli & private life of
the Romans; 12-a,b,f; 13-b; 14-ancient
primary sources in trans & modern works.

1071. ITALIAN CIVILIZATION
U of Missouri; Rom Langs; Columbia, MO
65201.
Wallace Craft

1-24; 2-3x16; 3-a; 4-c70; 5-ng; 6-a; 7-a; 8-
3s; 9-a; 10-none; 11-lit, artistic, poli, and
soci hist of Italy; 12-a,b,f; 13-a,b; 14-
varies.

See also 738.

Mexico

1072. AZTEC CIVILIZATION
Brandeis U; Flexible Curriculum; Waltham,
MA 02154.
Mr. Whittaker, Marguerite Robinson
1-38; 2-2½x15; 3-a; 4-72; 5-5; 6-a; 7-b; 8-4s;
9-a; 10-none; 11-2sem course; art,
architecture, the city, soci and poli
organization, ed, lit, morality, legend,
human sacrifice, poetry, philo, religion,
law, festivals, calendar, sci, medicine, war,
hist; 12-a,b,f; 13-b; 14-Soustelle, Daily Life
of the Aztecs; Leon-Protilla, Aztec
Thought and Culture; Leon-Protilla, Broken
Spears; trans Aztec accounts.

1073. A CULTURAL HISTORY OF MEXICO
U of Dallas; Sp; Irving, TX 75060.
Hazel Cazorla
A new course to be offered one sem per yr
starting 75. Given in Eng. Further info not
available.

1074. MEXICO, LAND OF CONTRASTS
Mississippi U for Women; FLs; Columbus,
MS 39701.
Philip Angeles
1-21; 2-3xsem; 3-a; 4-ng; 5-1; 6-a; 7-a; 8-
3s; 9-a; 10-none; 11-the land, the people,
mores, dances, songs, traditions; 12-a,b,f;
13-a,b,e; 14-none.

1075. INTRODUCTION TO MEXICO
Trinity U; Latin Amer Studies; San Antonio,
TX 78284.
Richard Woods
1-8; 2-3x15; 3-a; 4-fall 70; 5-5; 6-b; 7-a; 8-
3s; 9-a; 10-none; 11-interdisc presentation
covering Pre-Columbian, Colonial, and
Independence periods to the present; hist,
the soci scis, religion, fine arts, and lit; 12-
a,b,c,f; 13-a,b,ef; 14-Quirk, Mexico; Wolf,
Sons of the Shaking Earth; Gamio, The Life
Story of the Mexican Immigrant; Millon,
Zapata, The Ideology of a Peasant
Revolutionary; Fuentes, The Death of
Artemio Cruz; Lewis, Five Families.

North America

1076. INDIAN STUDIES PROGRAM
Black Hills SC; Communications; Spearfish,
SD 57783.
Arthur F. Prosper
This program, instituted very recently,
features courses in the Lakota (Sioux
Indian) language & oral lit, tradition & hist;

courses offered are Lakota Conversation I & II; Lakota Grammar; Lakota Oral Lit; Advanced Composition in Lakota; Lakota Public Speaking.

Puerto Rico

1077. LANGUAGE AND CULTURE OF PUERTO RICO
Central Connecticut SC; MLs; New Britain, CT 06050.
Arnaldo Sierra
1-22; 2-3x15; 3-a; 4-70; 5-6; 6-a; 7-a,b; 8-3s; 9-a, part-time, grad students; 10-none; 11-lang, music, lit, art, folklore; 12-a,b,c,d,f; 13-a,b; 14-Padilla, Up from Puerto Rico; Wagenheim, Puerto Rico: A Profile; Vivas, The History of Puerto Rico; Cordasco, The Puerto Rican Experience; Maldonado Denis, Puerto Rico: A Socio-Historic Interpretation.

1078. PUERTO RICAN CULTURE
Central Connecticut SC; MLs; New Britain, CT 06050.
Arnaldo Sierra
1-10; 2-3x15; 3-a; 4-71; 5-3; 6-on demand; 7-a; 8-3s; 9-a, grad students; 10-adv prof; 11-cult development through the study of selected authors in econ and poli context; 12-a,b,c,d,g; 13-a,b; 14-Vivas, Historia de Puerto Rico; Arce de Vazquez, Lecturas Puertorriquenas; Babin, Panorama de la cultura puertorriquena; Teatro Puertorriqueno.

1079. PUERTO RICAN CIVILIZATION AND LITERATURE
Cuyahoga CC; FLs; Cleveland, OH 44115.
Lenore V. Buford, Diana Dawson
1-26; 2-4x10; 3-a; 4-74; 5-1; 6-2q per yr; 7-a,b; 8-4q; 9-a, part-time; 10-inter prof; 11-ng; 12-a,b,c,e,g; 13-a,d; 14-extensive reading list.

1080. PUERTO RICAN CULTURE
Gettysburg C; Rom Langs; Gettysburg, PA 17325.
John C. Miller
1-10; 2-20x4; 3-a; 4-74; 5-2; 6-b; 7-a; 8-4s; 9-a; 10-none; 11-interdisc study of the hist, sociology, and lit on the island and the mainland; one-week residence in New York City; 12-a,b,c,f; 13-a,b,e,f; 14-various.

1081. CONTEMPORARY PUERTO RICO
SUNY; For Studies Center, Hispanic Program; Oswego, NY 13126.
Jose Perez, Wilfredo Figueroa, John P. Demidowicz
1-15; 2-3xsem; 3-a; 4-71; 5-3; 6-b; 7-a; 8-3s; 9-a; 10-none; 11-current poli problems; Puerto Rico in relation with the U.S. and the Puerto Rican population on the mainland; 12-a,b,c,d,f; 13-a,b,e,f; 14-Anderson, Party Politics in Puerto Rico; Goodsell,

Administration of a Revolution; Rand, The Puerto Ricans.

1082. HISTORY OF PUERTO RICO
SUNY; For Studies Center, Hispanic Program; Oswego, NY 13126.
Jose Perez, Wilfredo Figueroa, John P. Demidowicz
1-12; 2-3xsem; 3-a; 4-72; 5-3; 6-every 3 sems; 7-a; 8-3s; 9-a; 10-instructor permission; 11-analytical survey of cult and hist heritage; 12-a,b,c,d,f; 13-a,b,e,f; 14-ng.

1083. URBAN DEVELOPMENT OF PUERTO RICO
SUNY; For Studies Center, Hispanic Program; Oswego, NY 13126.
Jose Perez, Wilfredo Figueroa, John P. Demidowicz
1-20; 2-6x2 sems; 3-a; 4-72; 5-1; 6-alt yrs; 7-a; 8-6s; 9-a; 10-none; 11-hist, soci, econ, and cult development of Puerto Rico and on the mainland; 12-a,b,c,d,f, guest lectures; 13-a,b,e,f; 14-Sexton, Spanish Harlem; Ross, A Historical Study of Puerto Rico's Program in Economic Development.

See also 1408.

Russia

1084. RUSSIAN CIVILIZATION
Boston U; MLs; Boston, MA 02215.
Susan Cate
1-new; 2-ng; 3-ng; 4-ng; 5-ng; 6-ng; 7-ng; 8-4s; 9-ng; 10-adv prof; 11-art and cult from Middle Ages to present; painting, sculpture, architecture, music, dance, film; 12-g; 13-ng; 14-ng.

1085. RUSSIAN CULTURE
Bucknell U; MLs; Lewisburg, PA 17837.
Robert E. Beard
1-6; 2-3x13; 3-a; 4-69; 5-3; 6-alt yrs; 7-a; 8-1 unit; 9-a; 10-adv prof; 11-hist of art and music especially in their relationship to lit; 12-a,b,g; 13-a,b,d; 14-Beard, The Cultural History of Russia: Readings in the Art and Music; Rice, A Concise History of Russian Art.

1086. RUSSIAN CIVILIZATION AND CULTURE
Canisius C; MLs; Buffalo, NY 14208.
Michael Burtniak
1-22; 2-3x15; 3-a; 4-spr 75; 5-1; 6-unknown; 7-a; 8-3s; 9-a; 10-none; 11-art, architecture, music, religion in hist and geographical contexts; 12-a,b,c,f; 13-b,d,maps, transparencies; 14-ng.

1087. CONTEMPORARY SOVIET SOCIETY
City C; Ger & Sl; New York, NY 10031.
Michael Rywkin
1-c10; 2-3xsem; 3-a; 4-early 70s; 5-ng; 6-b; 7-a; 8-4s; 9-a; 10-none; 11-development of

Soviet society from 1917 to present; 12-f; 13-AV aids; 14-ng.

1088. RUSSIAN CIVILIZATION
Emmanuel C; Russ; Boston, MA 02115.
Pranas A. Sveikauskas, Luba Dyky
1-6; 2-3x13; 3-a; 4-70; 5-3; 6-alt yrs; 7-a; 8-4s; 9-a, part-time; 10-inter prof; 11-hist, lit, art, architecture, music; 12-a,b,c,f,g; 13-e,f, Radio Liberty bulletins; 14-Wasys & Krypton, Russian Area Reader; Davydoff & Pauliat, Civilisation et Litterature Russes; Tschebotariova-Bill, The Russian People.

1089. SOVIET MAN AND HIS WORLD
Middlebury C; Russ; Middlebury, VT 05753.
Robert L. Baker
1-new; 2-3x13; 3-a; 4-74/75; 5-1; 6-b; 7-a; 8-1 unit; 9-a; 10-inter prof; 11-Russ and Soviet cult and civ; 12-a,b,c,f,g; 13-a,b,d,e,f; 14-undetermined.

1090. RUSSIAN CIVILIZATION
SUNY; Sl Langs; Albany, NY 12222.
Natalia Kisseleff
1-35; 2-3x15; 3-a; 4-fall 72; 5-3; 6-b; 7-a; 8-3s; 9-a, special students; 10-none; 11-cult and soci survey in hist context; 12-a,c,f; 13-a,b,d, records; 14-none required.

See also 1361, 1650, 1651.

Spain

1091. SPANISH CULTURE THROUGH MEDIA
East Stroudsburg SC; FLs; East Stroudsburg, PA 18301.
Barbara Oberlander
1-14; 2-3x8; 3-a; 4-74; 5-1; 6-b; 7-a; 8-2s; 9-a; 10-none; 11-units on bullfights, Santiago de Compostela and Galicia, Andalucia, Madrid; 12-a,b,f; 13-a,b, realia, records; 14-Michener, Iberia.

1092. SPANISH CIVILIZATION
Lawrence U; Sp; Appleton, WI 54911.
R.W. Winslow
1-20; 2-3½x10; 3-a; 4-61; 5-6; 6-alt yrs; 7-a; 8-5q; 9-a; 10-inter prof; 11-Sp hist; Sp soci today; 12-a,b,c,g; 13-b,f; 14-varies.

1093. SPANISH CULTURE THROUGH LITERA-TURE IN TRANSLATION
Marygrove C; FLs; Detroit, MI 48221.
E. DuBruck
1-18; 2-3x15; 3-a; 4-72; 5-4; 6-b; 7-a; 8-3s; 9-a, part-time; 10-inter prof for lang credit, none for general credit; 11-Spain and the Sp; 12-a,b,f; 13-a,b,c; 14-primary texts, new every yr so that students can take the course several times.

1094. SPAIN TODAY
Molloy C; Sp; Rockville Centre, NY 11570.
Libe Aranguren

1-8; 2-3x15; 3-a; 4-72; 5-5; 6-b; 7-a, 8-3s; 9-a, part-time; 10-inter prof for Sp section, none for Eng section; 11-cult, hist, soci viewpoints showing evolution from histor-ical past; 12-a,b,c,d,f,g; 13-a,b,e,f; 14-Poyatos, Espana por dentro; Michener, Iberia.

1095. SPANISH CULTURE
Southeastern CC; FLs; Whiteville, NC 28472.
Samuel D. Sink
1-12; 2-2x11; 3-a sequence of 3 courses; 4-73/74; 5-3; 6-a; 7-a; 8-2q; 9-a; 10-none; 11-geography, econ, politics, and local customs; brief overview of lit and hist, current events; 12-a,b,c,f; 13-a,b,c,d,e,f; 14-none.

1096. SPANISH CIVILIZATION
Trinity U; FL; San Antonio, TX 78284.
Margaret Stovall
1-16; 2-3x15; 3-a; 4-spr 72; 5-2; 6-alt yrs; 7-a; 8-3s also given for grad credit; 9-a; 10-inter prof; 11-soci, poli and cult hist of Spain; 12-a,b,c,g; 13-a,b,e,f, records, filmstrips, handouts; 14-Mallo & Castellano, Espana: Sintesis de su civilizacion.

1097. THE SPANISH WORLD TODAY: CULTURE AND LANGUAGE
William Paterson C; FLs; Wayne, NJ 07470.
Catherine A. Barry
1-16; 2-3x17; 3-a; 4-74; 5-1; 6-b; 7-a; 8-3s; 9-a; 10-none; 11-Sp pronunciation; contem-porary cult--rasa cosmica, immigration, commerce, communication, religion, poli-tics, universities, theater, music, art, sports; 12-a,b,c,d,f,g; 13-a,b,d,e,f, field trips; 14-Rubia Garcia, Lengua y cultura.

See also 1123.

Yugoslavia

1098. SEMINAR ON YUGOSLAVIA
Muskingum C; ML; New Concord, OH 43762.
Mirco M. Mitrovich
1-8; 2-5/7x4; 3-a; 4-74/75 interim; 5-3; 6-on demand; 7-a; 8-b (pass/fail); 9-a; 10-none; 11-interdisc program, emphasizing modern lit, poli, soci, and econ aspects of the country. For those interested in the lang, a special section was arranged (5 students); 12-a,b,c,d,f (and g for special section); 13-b,d,e,f; 14-Barac, A History of Yugoslavian Literature; primary texts.

SUPRANATIONAL

African

See 1130A-1130D

235

1099. MIDDLE EAST/NORTH AFRICAN PRO-GRAM
U of Southern California; School of Intl Relations; Los Angeles, CA 90007.
W.A. Beling
1-11; 2-6x12; 3-a; 4-61; 5-consistently; 6-a; 7-b; 8-4q; 9-a, outside community; 10-none; 11- modern standard Arabic; 12-a,b,c,e,f,g; 13-d,f; 14-Monterey Defense Lang Inst, Modern Standard Basic Arabic.

Central American

1100. INDIAN CIVILIZATIONS OF MESOAMERICA
Amherst C; Rom Langs; Amherst, MA 01002.
Ernest A. Johnson
1-8; 2-3x13; 3-c; 4-72; 5-3; 6-every yr; 7-a; 8-4s; 9-a; 10-speaking, reading, writing knowledge of Sp; 11-lit, art, music, myth & hist of precolonial Central Amer. Emphasis on the Olmecs, Zapotecs, Mixtecs, Aztecs, Mayas; their significance in the 20th cen as seen in the works of Azuela, Lopez y Fuentes, Vasconcelos, Asturias, and the Mexican muralists; 12-a,b,c,d,g; 13-a,b,e; 14-Portilla, De Teotihuacan a los Aztecas.

Chicano

1101. CHICANO LITERATURE
Bethany Nazatene C; ML; Bethany, OK 73008.
Dolores Wood
1-new; 2-3x15; 3-a; 4-spr 75; 5-1; 6-alt yrs; 7-a; 8-3s; 9-a; 10-ng; 11-ng; 12-a,b,c,d,f,g; 13-ng; 14-ng.

1102. CHICANO LITERATURE
U of Iowa; Sp and Port; Iowa City, IA 52242.
Oscar Fernandez
1-14; 2-5x8 (smr), 2x18 (sem); 3-a; 4-72/73; 5-4; 6-a; 7-b; 8-2/3s; 9-a/ 10-none; 11-lit in hist, soci, econ context; 12-a,b,c,d,e,f,g; 13-a,b,e,f; 14-extensive reading list available.

1103. INTRODUCCION A ESTUDIOS CHICANOS
New Mexico SU; FLs; University Park, NM 88003.
Sergio D. Elizondo
1-55; 2-3x16; 3-a; 4-fall 72; 5-4; 6-a 7-a; 8-3s; 9-a; 10-inter prof; 11-life of the Mex Amer, seen primarily through the hums and soci scis, including lang, hist, ed, politics, and the family; 12-a,b,g; 13-b; 14-Von Hagen, The Aztec; McWilliams, North from Mexico; Pitt, The Decline of the Californios; Acuna, Occupied America; Parkes, A History of Mexico.

Classical

1104. THE CLASSICAL TRADITION
Ohio SU; Cl; Columbus, OH 43210.
D.M. Wratz
1-18; 2-3x10; 3-a; 4-73; 5-2; 6-b; 7-b; 8-3q; 9-in-service Eng teachers; 10-graduate standing; 11-varies; 12-a,b,f; 13-b; 14-primary texts.

1105. CLASSICAL CIVILIZATION
U of St. Thomas; Cl; Houston, TX 77006.
J.W. Embser
Greek and Roman hist and cult; poli, constitutional, archaeological, and intellectual development stressed. Further info ng.

European

1106. EUROPEAN CULTURE AND CIVILIZATION
Eastern Oregon SC; FL; La Grande, OR 97850.
Johannes M. Spronk
1-15; 2-3x10; 3-a; 4-74; 5-1; 6-every other yr; 7-a; 8-3q; 9-a; 10-none; 11-course intended to bring together into one class students of Fr, Ger & Sp, & other students with general interest in European civ. Three professors (Fr, Ger, Sp) examine events & movements that have shaped the cult & civ of Fr, Sp & Ger-speaking countries until the beginning of the 17th cen; next term continues this study & tries to determine how these elements have shaped the contemporary cult and civ of Europe; 12-a,b,f; 13-b,d, records, maps; 14-text assigned in either Eng, Fr, Sp or Ger, depending on a student's particular preparation (e.g., Bruchant, La France au Cours des Ages; Kelling Deutsche Kulturgeschichte; Ugarte, Panorama de la Civilizacion Espanola.

1107. CONTRIBUTIONS OF EUROPEAN LINGUISTIC GROUPS TO THE AMERICAN HERITAGE
U of Maine; FLs; Orono, ME 04473.
Josef Roggenbauer
1-16; 2-3x15; 3-a; 4-73; 5-ng; 6-b; 7-a; 8-3s; 9-a; 10-reading knowledge of one FL recommended; 11-cult contributions of European lang groups to the development of Amer; roots of Amer traditions, place names, words; ways groups or individuals adapted to the new environment; 12-a,b,f; 13-a,b; 14-ng.

1108. CULTURAL GEOGRAPHY OF CONTINENTAL EUROPE
U of Maine; FLs; Orono, ME 04473.
Josef Roggenbauer
1-new; 2-3x15; 3-a; 4-spr 75; 5-1; 6-b; 7-a; 8-3s; 9-a; 10-none; 11-geography of those countries in Europe where Fr, Ger, Sp, Ital, or Russ is spoken; 12-a,b,c,f; 13-a,b; 14-ng.

1109. FRENCH-SPEAKING CULTURES AND LITERATURES OUTSIDE EUROPE
U of Alaska; MLs; Anchorage, AK 99503.
Monique J. Pourny
1-14; 2-3x14; 3-a; 4-72; 5-6; 6-cycle of 5 with one offered every sem; 7-b; 8-3s; 9-a, part-time; 10-inter prof for Fr section, none for Eng section; 11-Fr Canada, North Africa, Black Africa, Carribean, Indochina, Louisiana; 12-a,b,c,f,g; 13-a,b,d,e,f; 14-primary texts.

1110. FRENCH OUTSIDE FRANCE
Hood C; MLs; Frederick, MD 21701.
1-new; 2-3x14; 3-a; 4-75/76; 5-0; 6-alt yrs; 7-a; 8-3s; 9-a; 10-inter prof; 11-concept of Francophony; readings from several areas of the world; concept of negritude; 12-a,b,c,d,g; 13-b; 14-ng.

See ms. p. 110)

1110A. AFRICAN LITERATURE IN FRENCH
Howard U; Rom Langs; Washington, DC 20059.
Maurice Lubin
1-12; 2-3x18; 3-a; 4-70; 5-10; 6-a; 7-a; 8-3s,b; 9-a; 10-inter prof; 11-intensive reading of texts dealing with African lit and cult, with emphasis on speaking and writing, along with vocab expansion; 12-a,b,c,d,f; 13-ng; 14-ng.

1110B. AFRICAN LITERATURE OF FRENCH EXPRESSION
Howard U; Rom Langs; Washington, DC 20059.
Maurice Lubin
1-3; 2-2 per wk; 3-b; 4-64; 5-every sem; 6-a; 7-a; 8-3s; 9-a; 10-prof in Fr; 11-ng; 12-a,b,c,g; 13-texts, photocopied; 14-ng.

1110C. HAITIAN LITERATURE
Howard U; Rom Langs; Washington, DC 20059.
Jacques C. Antoine
1-ng; 2-ng; 3-a; 4-68; 5-ng; 6-a; 7-ng; 8-3s; 9-a; 10-ng; 11-familiarization with Haitian writers from Haiti's independence to the present; various stages of Haitian lit evolution in their hist and cult contexts as well as the lit characteristics of the works of the various generations of writers, particularly in the field of poetry; 12-g; 13-ng; 14-ng.

1111. FRANCO-AMERICAN SEMINAR SERIES
U of Maine; FLs; Farmington, ME 04938.
Raymond J. Lagueux
1-20; 2-2½/3x15; 3-c; 4-spr 74; 5-1; 6-unknown; 7-b; 8-3s; 9-a,b,general public; 10-none; 11-series of presentations by specialists; aspects of Franco-American life in Maine; 12-a,b,c,f; 13-a,b,d,e,f; 14-Rumilly, Les Franco-Americains.

1112. FRANCO-AMERICAN CIVILIZATION
U of Maine; FLs; Orono, ME 04473.

Josef Roggenbauer
1-18; 2-3x15; 3-c; 4-72; 5-3; 6-b smr; 7-a,b; 8-3s; 9-a,b; 10-none; 11-Fr heritage in North Amer; 12-a,b,c,d,f,g; 13-a,b,d; 14-Eccle, France in America; Rioux, French-Canadian Society.

1113. FRENCH-SPEAKING AREAS OUTSIDE FRANCE
U of Massachusetts; Fr and Ital; Amherst, MA 01002.
Thomas Cassirer, Marjorie Fitzpatrick, J.P. Berwald, J. Bragger
1-14; 2-3x13; 3-a; 4-73; 5-3; 6-a; 7-a; 8-3s; 9-a; 10-none; 11-civ of Fr-speaking areas outside France: Switzerland, Belgium, Canada, the Antilles, and Africa south of the Sahara; 12-a,b,c,f, team-taught by 4 faculty; 13-ng; 14-handouts, background bibliographies. Students put together a bibliography on the area of their individual project.

1114. THE FRANCOPHONE WORLD
U of Rhode Island; Langs; Kingston, RI 02881.
Kenneth H. Rogers
1-5; 2-3x15; 3-a; 4-spr 75; 5-1; 6-one-time course; 7-b; 8-3s; 9-a,h; 10-B,A. in Fr; 11-survey of Fr in North Amer, Belgium, Switzerland, Orient, Carribean, Africa, etc; socioling as well as phonological and syntactic; 12-a,b,c,g; 13-e,f,maps; 14-various.

See also 1630, 1668.

German

1115. HISTORY AND CULTURE OF THE GERMANS FROM RUSSIA
Dickinson SC; Lang & Lit; Dickinson, ND 58601.
LeRoy A. Oberlander
1-10; 2-2x11; 3-a; 4-72; 5-3; 6-b; 7-a,b; 8-2q; 9-a, community; 10-none; 11-why and how the Germans moved to Russia in the 18th and 19th cens and why in the latter 19th cen many left Russia and came to Amer; traces the hist and customs of the Germans from Russia; 12-a,b,f; 13-b,e; 14-various.

1116. LIFE IN GERMANY: TODAY AND YESTERDAY
Montgomery County CC; For Studies; Blue Bell, PA 19422.
Charlotte Anderson
1-54; 2-3x30; 3-a; 4-72; 5-6; 6-a; 7-a,b; 8-3s per sem; 9-a,b; 10-none; 11-modern-day Germany and the poli, soci, and cult forces which shaped it; impact on other cults; perspectives on life in Austria and Switzerland; discussion of Ger ethnic groups in Amer; 12-a,b,f; 13-a,b,c,d, field trip; 14-Schalk, The Germans; primary texts.

1117. DEUTSCHE KULTURLANDSCHAFTEN
Pennsylvania SU; Ger; University Park, PA
16802.
Vickie Ziegler
1-new; 2-4½x10; 3-a; 4-wtr 75; 5-0; 6-alt
yrs; 7-a; 8-3s; 9-a; 10-inter prof; 11-cult
diversity in Austria, Germany and
Switzerland; hist and customs of other Ger-
speaking areas; 12-a,c,g; 13-a,d,e,f; 14-
various materials.

1118. PENNSYLVANIA GERMAN LANGUAGE
AND CULTURE
Pennsylvania SU; Ger; University Park, PA
16802.
Willard Martin
1-10; 2-4½x10; 3-c; 4-74/75; 5-1; 6-b; 7-a;
8-3s; 9-a; 10-none; 11-background,
customs, lang, lit, religion, folklore, folk
art, music, and ed of the Pennsylvania
Germans; 12-a,c,f; 13-b, guest lectures,
field trip; 14-Rosenberger, The
Pennsylvania German, 1891-1965;
instructor-prepared materials.

1119. GERMANY EAST AND WEST
Rice U; Ger; Houston, TX 77001.
Margret Eifler
1-17; 2-3x15; 3-a; 4-75; 5-1; 6-b; 7-a; 8-3s;
9-a; 10-none in Eng sections, adv prof in
Ger sections; 11-poli, econ, and soci trends
and issues of East and West Germany on a
comparative basis; examination of lit works
as reflections of sociopolitical situation;
12-a,b,f,g; 13-f; 14-Grosser, Germany in
Our Time; novels; documentary materials.

1120. GERMANIA USA
Winona SC; FLs; Winona, MN 55987.
Jordan V. Hodgson
1-new; 2-4x10; 3-a; 4-spr 75; 5-1; 6-every 2
or 3 yrs; 7-a; 8-4q; 9-a,b, extension; 10-
none; 11-ling, sociological, cult, econ, and
poli impact of Ger-speaking groups and
individuals in USA; 12-a,b,f; 13-a,b,d,e,f;
14-O'Connor, The German-Americans; An
Informal History; Gilbert, The German
Language in America.

See also 1290, 1339, 1642, 1643, 1669.

Hispanic

1121. SPANISH CULTURE AWARENESS
U of Albuquerque; Langs; Albuquerque, NM
87140.
Jorge Alarcon
1-15; 2-3x16; 3-c; 4-73; 5-3; 6-b; 7-a; 8-3s;
9-a,b, part-time; 10-ability to understand
Sp; 11-Hispanic cult with emphasis on Amer
Southwest; 12-a,b,c,g; 13-a,b,d,e,f,
records, field trips; 14-Ortega, We Are
Chicanos; Castro, Iberoamerica; Shular,
Literatura Chicana.

1122. THE LITERATURE AND CULTURE OF
THE SPANISH-SPEAKING IN THE U.S.
Allentown C of St. Francis De Sales; FL;
Center Valley, PA 18034.
Gerard R. Clarke
1-10; 2-3x15; 3-a; 4-spr 75; 5-1; 6-cyclical;
7-a; 8-3s; 9-a; 10-none; 11-designed to
explore through the novel, poetry, drama, &
the essay the various aspects-lit & cult-of
biling & bicult of Puerto-Ricans, Cuban
exiles, Mex-Amers, & Chicanos in the US;
12-a,b,c,d,f,g; 13-a,b,f; 14-Alford, The
Proud Peoples; Babin, Puerto-Rican Spirit;
Gonzales, Yo soy Joaquin; Gonzales, Los
Primos.

1123. SPANISH CIVILIZATION
Boston U; MLs; Boston, MA 02215.
Susan Cate
1-18; 2-3x14; 3-a; 4-73; 5-2; 6-b; 7-a; 8-4s;
9-a; 10-adv prof; 11-Spain as bridge
between the Christian and Arab worlds, in
the discovery and conquest of Amer, as a
leading power in the 16th and 17th cens;
contributions to the Western tradition in
art, music, thought, religion, letters; Sp
heritage in USA; 12-a,b,g; 13-ng; 14-Crow,
Spain, the Root and the Flower.

1124. HISPANIC AND HISPANIC AMERICAN
STUDIES
Bryn Mawr C; Sp; Bryn Mawr, PA 19010.
Willard King
Program provides two interdisc courses for
majors from other depts. Further info ng.

1125. HISPANIC INFLUENCE IN THE
AMERICAN SOUTHWEST
U of Dallas; Sp; Irving, TX 75060.
Alexandra Wilhelmsen
1-new; 2-ng; 3-a; 4-75; 5-ng; 6-ng; 7-ng; 8-
3s; 9-ng; 10-B.A. in Sp; 11-hist, cult, and lit
traces left by Spain and Mexico in the U.S.
Southwest; 12-a,b; 13-b; 14-various.

1126. SPANISH AND LATIN AMERICAN
CULTURE
Georgia Southern C; FLs; Statesboro, GA
30458.
Nancy C. Barrett
1-36; 2-5x10; 3-a; 4-74; 5-2; 6-a; 7-a,b; 8-
5q; 9-a, cont ed; 10-none; 11-govt, art, cult,
music, lit in trans; traditions, customs,
modes of expression that reveal the
character and style of these cults; 12-
a,b,c,e,f; 13-a,b,e,f; 14-Miller et al, From
Spain and the Americas; Ellis, Latin
America, Its People and Institutions;
Hilton, Spain: Comparative Culture and
Government.

1127. BICULTURAL STUDIES
Georgian Court C; Mod & Cl Langs;
Lakewood, NJ 08701.
Mary Catharine Sullivan
1-20; 2-3x15; 3-a; 4-spr 75; 5-1; 6-ng; 7-b;

8-ng; 9-a; 10-none; 11-principal cult developments in Hispanic Amer (emphasis on Mexico, Cuba, Puerto Rico); problems encountered by persons emigrating to U.S.; 12-a,b,c,f,g; 13-a,b,e,f; 14-Pendle, A History of Latin America; Franco, The Modern Culture of Latin America: Society and the Artist; Arciniegas, Latinoamerica: El continente de siete colores.

1128. CHICANOS, PUERTO RICANS, AND OTHER SPANISH SPEAKING AMERICANS
Hood C; ML: Frederick, MD 21701.
(See ms. p. 110) Chairperson
1-13; 2-3xsem; 4-fall 74; 5-1; 6-alt yrs; 7-a; 8-3s; 9-a; 10-Sp inter prof; 11-hist and cult background, econ, soci, and ling problems of Hispanic groups in U.S.; 12-a,b,c,d,g; 13-a,b,e; 14-Literatura Chicana, Prentice Hall; Voces del Bario.

1129. LATIN AMERICA TODAY
Hood C; Lang; Frederick, MD 21701.
Chairperson
1-5; 2-3xsem; 3-a; 4-72; 5-2; 6-alt yrs; 7-a; 8-3s; 9-a; 10-inter prof; 11-hist, soci, econ, geographic factors shaping contemporary Latin Amer and its people; 12-a,b,c,g; 13-a,b,e,f; 14-various.

1130. THE HISPANIC WORLD TODAY
Hope C; FLs and Lits; Holland, MI 49423.
Antonia Iglesias Searles
1-36; 2-3x15; 3-a; 4-73/74; 5-3; 6-a; 7-a,b; 8-3s; 9-a; 10-none; 11-distinctive characteristics of Hispanic civ with emphasis on their relevance to contemporary issues; 12-a,b,c,f; 13-a,b,e,f; 14-Franco, The Modern Culture of Latin America; Michener, Iberia; Payne, Franco's Spain; etc.

1130A. AFRO-HISPANIC POETRY OF THE 20th CENTURY
Howard U; Rom Langs; Washington, DC 20059.
Miriam D. Willis
1-8; 2-3x18; 3-a; 4-72; 5-2; 6-a; 7-a; 8-3s; 9-a; 10-good background in Sp; 11-study and interpretation of Caribbean and Sp-Amer poetry which emphasizes Black themes (undergrad); interpretation and analysis of Caribbean and South Amer poetry which expresses the Black or African experience (grad seminar); 12-a,b,c,e,g (grad students do extensive research); 13-d,e, original mss and rare books; 14-La poesia negroide; various books by Guillen, El ritmo negro del Peru; books of the teachers in the Moorland Spingarn Coll, and Library of Congress sources.

1130B. AFRO-HISPANIC PROSE OF THE 20th CENTURY
Howard U; Rom Langs; Washington, DC 20059.

Stanley Cyrus
1-6; 2-3x18; 3-a; 4-72; 5-3; 6-every third sem; 7-a; 8-3s; 9-a; 10-good background in Sp; 11-a study of Sp-Amer writers who express Black themes, with emphasis on Black novelists of selected countries (undergrad); study and investigation of Black novelists and their works in eight Sp-Amer countries (grad seminar); 12-a,b,c,g; 13-e,f; 14-primary.

1130C. BLACK THEMES IN HISPANIC LITERATURE
Howard U; Rom Langs; Washington, DC 20059.
Martha Cobb
1-15; 2-3x17; 3-a; 4-71; 5-4; 6-b; 7-a; 8-3s; 9-a; 10-for grad, adv undergrad, majors and minors in Sp; 11-study and analysis of lit themes by or about Black people in Hispanic poetry and prose from medieval Spain through nineteenth/twentieth cen Sp Amer; 12-a,b,c,g; 13-ng; 14-primary.

1130D. INTRODUCTION TO AFRO-HISPANIC LITERATURE
Howard U; Rom Langs, Washington, DC 20059.
Martha Cobb
1-10; 2-3x16; 3-a; 4-71; 5-9; 6-a; 7-a; 8-3s; 9-a; 10-interprof; 11-open to non-majors and minors for completion of FL requirement; central emphasis is the reading and discussion of selected works by and about Black men and women in the Hispanic cult; 12-b,d, reading discussion, taught in Sp when possible; final class skits from readings, music, etc.; 13-b,d; 14-Cyrus, El cuento negrista sudamericano; Noble, Literatura Afro-Hispanoamericana.

1131. CONTEMPORARY PROBLEMS OF THE SPANISH WORLD
Indiana SU; Hums; Evansville, IN 47712.
Lomberto Diaz
1-8; 2-4xsem; 3-a; 4-73; 5-2; 6-b; 7-a; 8-4s; 9-a, cont ed; 10-inter prof; 11-ideas of contemporary Sp-speaking writers through their most important work in soci scis, especially that relating to underdeveloped countries; 12-a,b,g; 13-f; 14-ng.

1132. LATIN AMERICAN CIVILIZATION
Lawrence U; Sp; Appleton, WI 54911.
H. Martines
1-22; 2-3½x10; 3-a; 4-69; 5-3; 6-alt ys; 7-a; 8-5q; 9-a; 10-inter prof; 11-racial, soci and poli developments to the present; 12-a,b,f; 13-f; 14-varies.

1133. HISPANIC CIVILIZATION
U of Missouri; Rom Langs; Columbia, MO 65201.
Albert Brent
1-74; 2-3x16; 3-a; 4-c65; 5-ng; 6-a; 7-a; 8-3s; 9-a; 10-none; 11-lit, artistic, poli, and

soci hist; 12-a,b,f; 13-a,b; 14-varies.

1134. LATIN AMERICA TODAY
Molloy C; Sp; Rockville Centre, NY 11570.
Libe Aranguren
1-11; 2-3xsem; 3-a; 4-73; 5-6; 6-b; 7-a; 8-
3s; 9-a, part-time; 10-inter prof for Sp
section, none for Eng section; 11-critical
study of cult, hist, soci, econ aspects of
20th cen Latin Amer showing development
and change from earlier civs 12-a,b,c,d,f,g;
13-a,b,e,f; 14-Phillips & Marquez, Visiones
de Latinoamerica; Plakemore, The Modern
World: Latin America.

1135. THE CULTURE OF LATIN AMERICA
U of Nebraska; FLs; Omaha, NE 68101.
Woodrow L. Most
1-15; 2-3x15; 3-a; 4-73; 5-1; 6-alt ys; 7-a; 8-
3s; 9-a; 10-soph standing; 11-cult of Latin
Amer, its origins, development, and the
present scene; art, lit, architecture,
politics, econ; 12-a,b,c,f; 13- a,b,d,e,f; 14-
Arciniegas, Latin America, A Cultural
History; Franco, The Modern Culture of
Latin America: Society and the Artist.

1136. HISPANOAMERICA Y ESPANA EN EL
MUNDO DE HOY
New York U; FLs; New York, NY 10003.
Santiago Luppoli
1-15; 2-2x15; 3-a; 4-72; 5-2; 6-alt yrs; 7-b;
8-3s; 9-ng; 10-fluency in Sp; 11-role of
Latin Amer and Spain in our contemporary
world; soci, poli, ed, econ and cult developments; 12-a,b,g; 13-e,f; 14-ng.

1137. HISPANIC CULTURE IN THE UNITED
STATES
SUCNY; FLs & Lits; Brockport, NY 14420.
Ethnicity and the Hispanic experience in
the U.S. Theme of cult in contact through a
comp and contrastive study of Cuban, Mex
Amer and Puerto Rican groups in this
country, from the perspectives of their
hist, soci institutions, and future as ethnic
units. In Eng; no prerequisites.

1138. LATIN AMERICAN STUDIES: LA RAZA
Pontifical C Josephinum; Latin Amer
Studies; Worthington, OH 43085.
Fina Querol-Kroenberg
1-12; 2-3x16; 3-a; 4-60s; 5-3; 6-every 3 yrs;
7-a; 8-3s; 9-a; 10-inter prof; 11-hist and
present condition of the Mex Amer heritage
of Mexico, pioneer heritage of the
Southwest, conflict of culs, awakening of
the Mex Amer; 12-a,b,c,d,f,g; 13-a,b,e; 14-
various.

1139. LATIN AMERICAN CULTURE
Southeastern CC; FLs; Whiteville, NC
28472.
Samuel D. Sink
1-ng; 2-2x11; 3-a; 4-ng; 5-ng; 6-a; 7-a; 8-2q;
9-a; 10-none; 11-sequence of 3 courses;
geography, econ, politics, and local cus-

toms; brief overview of lit and hist; current
events; 12-a,b,c,f; 13-a,b,c,d,e,f; 14-none.

1140. LATIN AMERICAN CIVILIZATION
Trinity U; Latin Amer Studies; San Antonio,
TX 78284.
Richard Woods
1-29; 2-3x15; 3-a; 4-spr 71; 5-2; 6-alt yrs; 7-
a; 8-3s, also given for grad credit; 9-a; 10-
inter prof. 11-topical approach, man and
landscape, races, revolution, and reform
and expression through art; 12-a,b,c,g; 13-
a,b,e,f, records, filmstrips, handouts; 14-
Castro, Iberoamerica: su hustoria y su cultura.

1141. OTHER CULTURES THROUGH HUMAN-
ISTIC STUDIES (SPANISH)
U of Wisconsin; Lang and Lit; Green Bay, WI
54302.
(See ms. Raquel Kersten
#1054) May be taken for Sp credit. Humanist
approach to cult. A basic goal is to
encounter people of other cults as they see
us and themselves, rather than through
stereotyped ways. Latin Amer cult as
reflected in lit, arts, and other means of
communication.

See also 89, 342, 368, 494, 505, 703, 761, 1243,
1404, 1417, 1497, 1568, 1670.

Italian

1142. ITALIAN AMERICANS: LITERATURE
AND SOCIETY
SUCNY; FL; Buffalo, NY 14222.
1-35; 2-3x15; 3-b,c; 4-spr 72; 5-7; 6-a; 7-a;
8-3s; 9-a, teachers, cont ed, grad students;
10-none; 11-lit, hist, soci; 12-a,b,c,f; 13-a,
outside speakers; 14-varies.

Polish

1143. POLES IN AMERICA
Central Connecticut SC; Hums; New
Britain, CT 06050.
S.A. Blejwas
1-new; 2-3x15; 3-a; 4-75; 5-1; 6-b; 7-b; 8-
3s; 9-a,b, part-time; 10-none; 11-origins of
Polish immigration; problems of assimila-
tion and adjustment; development of religious, soci, and econ organizations; impact
of post WW II immigration; problems of the
contemporary community; 12-a,b,f; 13-ng;
14-Polzin, Polish Americans, Whence and
Whither?; Renkiewicz, The Poles in America; Novak, The Rise of the Unmeltable Eth-
nics.

Scandinavian

1144. INTRODUCTION TO SCANDINAVIAN
CULTURE
U of Washington; Scand; Seattle, WA

240

98195.
Birgitta Steene
1-62; 2-2x9; 3-a; 4-c50; 5-c100; 6-a; 7-a; 8-2q; 9-a; 10-none; 11-broad survey of Scand experience from Viking age to present; emphasis on cult, poli, and religious development; 12-a,f; 13-ng; 14-Connery, The Scandinavians.

1145. THE SCANDINAVIAN HERITAGE IN THE MIDWEST
U of Wisconsin; Scand Studies; Madison, WI 53706.
Harold S. Naess
1-45; 2-3x3; 3-a; 4-73; 5-2; 6-intersession; 7-a; 8-2s; 9-a; 10-jr standing or permission; 11-topics covered include: 19th-cen Norway, migration and settlement, daily life in the new country, the Scand church in Amer, the Amer-Scand press, lit, higher ed, and hist research; 12-a,d, field trips; 13-ng; 14-Haugen, The Norwegians in America; A Student's Guide to Localized History; Blegen, Norwegian Migration to America, Vol. 2; Rolvaag, Giants in the Earth.

Slavic

1146. SLAVIC CULTURES AND CIVILIZATIONS
City C; Ger & Sl; New York, NY 10031.
Michael Rywkin
1-c10; 2-3xsem; 3-a; 4-early 70s; 5-ng; 6-b; 7-a; 8-4s; 9-a; 10-none; 11-development of the various Sl cults and institutions from the Middle Ages to 1917; intellectual developments, customs, traditions, arts; 12-f; 13-AV aids; 14-ng.

See also 1115.

Yiddish

1147. YIDDISH LITERATURE: FROM SHTETL TO SUBURBIA
Tufts U; Ger; Medford, MA 02155.
Sol Gittleman
1-181; 2-3x14; 3-a; 4-71; 5-4; 6-b; 7-a; 8-1 unit; 9-a; 10-none; 11-soci, hist, lit survey of East European Jewry, from the beginnings of the Diaspora to the movement to the US; 12-a,b; 13-a,f; 14-Zborowski & Herzog, Life Is with People: The Culture of the Shtetl; Hapgood, The Spirit of the Ghetto: Studies of the Jewish Quarter of New York; primary texts.

Miscellaneous

1148. WORLD CULTURE
Briar Cliff C; MLs & Cults; Sioux City, IA 51104.
Roman de la Campa, Attorney-at-Law (2219 Allan St., Sioux City, IA 51103)
1-18, 2-3½x10; 3-a; 4-73/74; 5-2; 6-b; 7-a; 8-3s; 9-a; 10-none; 11-characteristics of modern cults as a background for traveling; arts, foods, music, and way of life; 12-a,b,c,d,f; 13-a,b,c,e,f; 14-Vilar, Spain: A Brief History.

1149. EAST-WEST CULTURE
City C of San Francisco; FLs; San Francisco, CA 94112.
Jacquelyn W. Green
Interdisc course.   Additional info not available.

1149A. BLACK LITERATURE IN THE AMERICAS
Howard U; Rom Langs; Washington, DC 20059.
Martha Cobb
1-14; 2-3x16; 3-a; 4-75; 5-1; 6-every 3 sem; 7-a; 8-3s; 9-a; 10-for majors and minors in Sp, Fr, and Eng, and for grad students in these fields; 11-point of departure for the comparative study of Hughes, Guillen, and Roumain, as well as other authors selected for research and reading; 12-a,b,c,f (readings in lang of students' major field); 13-ng; 14-primary; Johnson, The Devil, the Gargoyle and the Buffoon--the Negro as Metaphor in Western Literature; Shapiro, Negritude: Black Poetry from Africa and the Caribbean.

1150. ANCIENT INDIA AND IRAN
U of Maryland; Ger & Sl; College Park, MD 20742.
Jere Fleck
1-ng; 2-3xsem; 3-ng; 4-spr 74; 5-ng; 6-ng; 7-a; 8-3s; 9-ng; 10-none; 11-intro to cult; 12-ng; 13-ng; 14-primary texts in trans.

1151. CULTURAL INTRODUCTION TO LANGUAGES
Murray State U; FLs; Murray, KY 42071.
John W. Ferguson
1-17; 2-3x14; 3-b; 4-74; 5-2; 6-a; 7-a; 8-3s; 9-a; 10-none; 11-one professor each from Fr, Sp, Ger, Russ will contribute to the course; the land; origins of lang; deep cult of lang; similarities, differences between langs; sample dialogues in the 4 langs; lang & sci; lit as the flower of lang; the arts reflected in lang; natural lang & artificial lang; 12-a,b,c,f; 13-a,b; 14-none.

See also 782, 1665, 1666.

CLASSICS

1152. ART AND MYTH IN THE BRONZE AGE: CRETE AND MYCENAE
St. Louis U; Cl Lang; St. Louis, MO 63103.
Marcus A. Haworth, Carolyn Valone
1-29; 2-3x13; 3-b; 4-fall 73; 5-2; 6-b; 7-a; 8-3s; 9-a; 10-designed to show students how knowledge of a prehistoric era can be derived from archaeology, anthropology, oral epic tradition, and philology; 12-a,b,f; 13-a,b; 14-Matz, The Art of Crete and Early Greece; primary texts.

1153. CLASSICAL PERSONALITIES ON FILM
Seton Hall U; Cl; South Orange, NJ 07079.
Robert Antczak
1-130; 2-3x15; 3-a; 4-71; 5-8; 6-a; 7-b; 8-3s; 9-a; 10-none; 11-study of the lit of Greece and Rome concerning great personalities and relationship to modern portrayals of them on film 12-a,b,g; 13-a,f; 14-personal notes.

1154. INTRODUCTION TO CLASSICAL HUMANITIES
Syracuse U; Cl; Syracuse, NY 13210.
Louis Roberts
1-35; 2-3x17; 3-b; 4-72; 5-4; 6-a; 7-a; 8-3s; 9-a; 10-none; 11-intensive intro to the major influential genres of lit, art, archaeology; heroic tradition and tragic spirit of epic and drama; 12-a,b,f; 13-a,b,d; 14-primary texts, mostly classical--plus Cervantes, Shakespeare, Nietzsche; Dodds, The Greeks and the Irrational; Clagett; Greek Science in Antiquity.

FRENCH

1155. APOLLONAIRE AND MODERN MOVEMENTS IN ART AND LITERATURE
Amherst C; Rom Langs; Amherst, MA 01002.
Jeffrey J. Carre
1-8; 2-3x13; 3-a; 4-71; 5-2; 6-alt yrs; 7-a; 8-4s; 9-a; 10-intro course in Fr lit; 11-study of Apollinaire as poet, theoretician, spokesman and moving force of new art in France during first 2 decades of 20th cen; inquiry into relationships of art and lit with particular attention to Cubism and Futurism; 12-a,b,c,g; 13-b; 14-primary texts.

1156. FRENCH FILM: SOCIAL CONTENT
Amherst C; Rom Langs; Amherst, MA 01002.
Jeffrey Carre
Further info not available.

1157. FRENCH TYPES: LITERATURE AND MUSIC
Bowling Green SU; Rom Langs; Bowling Green, OH 43403.
Clifford J. Gallant
1-new; 2-4x10; 3-a; 4-spr 75; 5-1; 6-on demand; 7-a; 8-4q; 9-a; 10-grad standing; 11-interdependence of lit and music in France; 12-a,b,g; 13-c; 14-primary texts.

1158. FRENCH PLAY PRODUCTION
Clark U; FL & Lits; Worcester, MA 01610.
Michael Spingler
1-ng; 2-ng; 3-a,b; 4-73; 5-ng; 6-a; 7-a; 8-4s; 9-a; 10-2 yrs college Fr; 11-course will concentrate on the playwright, studying him in terms of all the problems peculiar to the staging of his plays, sets, props, costumes, acting styles, gesture & blocking-with research into the dramaturgy, themes, soci context & style of the author's period; 12-b,c,d,e,g; 13-a,c, props, viewing of plays studied; 14-primary texts.

1159. THEATRE WORKSHOP
U of Colorado; Fr; Boulder, CO 80302.
Andree Kail
1-9; 2-6x10; 3-a; 4-spr 72; 5-2; 6-alt yrs; 7-a,b; 8-3s; 9-a; 10-perm; 11-course offered non-credit since 1954; 12-d,g; 13-ng; 14-primary texts.

1160. FAMOUS OPERAS AND THEIR FRENCH LITERARY SOURCES
Gettysburg C; Rom Langs; Gettysburg, PA 17325.
Amie Tannenbaum
1-new; 2-20x4; 3-a; 4-75; 5-1; 6-irregularly; 7-a; 8-4s; 9-a; 10-reading knowledge of Fr; 11-stories which have been the basis for operas will be read in original and compared with libretti; 12-a,b,g; 13-a,d, records; 14-primary texts.

1160A. FRENCH THEATER AND WORKSHOP
Howard U; Rom Langs; Washington, DC 20059.
1-6; 2-3 per wk; 3-a; 4-72; 5-3; 6-a; 7-a; 8-3s; 9-a; 10-inter prof; 11-Fr plays are read, cast, and presented to school and community when possible; students are taught all the technical lang needed for every aspect of theatrical performance as they learn to actually perform on stage; comedy, tragedy, and phantasy are offered; learning to speak Fr through the medium of acting; 12-g; 13-ng; 14-primary.

1161. TRANSLATION OF FRENCH OPERA LIBRETTI
U of Illinois; Fr; Urbana, IL 61801.
1-new; 2-3x16; 3-a; 4-75/76; 5-0; 6-ng; 7-ng; 8-3s; 9-a; 10-elem prof; 11-ng; 12-

a,b,f,g; 13-ng; 14-ng.

1162. NARRATIVE IN PAINTING AND LITERATURE
Johns Hopkins U; Rom Langs; Baltimore, MD 21218.
Louis Marin
1-15; 2-2x14; 3-a; 4-74; 5-1; 6-ng; 7-a; 8-3s; 9-a; 10-grad standing, outstanding srs; 11-distinction between discours and recit, basic assumptions of this distinction, test of the hypothesis in painting and lit, semiotic requirements of the hist discourse in painting and lit; 12-a,b,c,g; 13-b; 14-extensive reading list.

1163. PEINTURE ET LITTERATURE
Johns Hopkins U; Rom Langs; Baltimore, MD 21218.
Jean Paris
1-35; 2-2x14; 3-a; 4-73; 5-1; 6-irregularly; 7-a; 8-3s; 9-a; 10-inter prof; 11-ng; 12-a,c,g; 13-b; 14-ng.

1164. RELATIONSHIP OF FRENCH LANGUAGE AND LITERATURE TO MUSIC
U of Kansas; Fr & Ital; Lawrence, KS 66045.
Robert Anderson
1-ng; 2-2x15; 3-a; 4-spr 73; 5-2; 6-b; 7-a; 8-2s; 9-a; 10-jr standing; 11-lit background of Fr vocal music with emphasis on interpretation and performance of musical texts in Fr; drills in phonetics, speech patterns, phrasing; readings in lit hist; 12-a,c, sung, f; 13-records; 14-Cruikshank, Background of French Literature, 19th Century; Bernac, Interpretation of French Vocal Music.

1165. TOPICS IN FRENCH FILM
Middle Tennessee SU; FLs; Murfreesboro, TN 37130.
T. Coy Porter
1-new; 2-3x15; 3-a; 4-75/76; 5-0; 6-b; 7-b; 8-3s; 9-a,b; 10-inter prof; 11-history of Fr film; 'nouvelle vague' filmmakers and their impact; impact of cinema on the contemporary novel; in-depth study of one or two films; novel as film; novelists as filmmakers; 12-e,g; 13-a; 14-ng.

1166. MUSIC IN FRENCH CIVILIZATION
Montclair SC; Fr; Upper Montclair, NJ 07043.
Helene Klibbe
1-15; 2-3x16; 3-a; 4-72; 5-5; 6-a; 7-a; 8-3s; 9-a; 10-stylistics and composition; 11-relates each period in Fr music hist to artistic and cult environment; 12-a,b,f,g; 13-b; 14-Barraud, La France et la Musique occidentale; instructor-prepared materials.

1167. TWENTIETH CENTURY ART MOVEMENTS
Moore College of Art; Hums; Philadelphia,

PA 19103.
Thelma Richman
1-10; 2-3x13; 3-a; 4-ng; 5-ng; 6-a; 7-a; 8-3s; 9-a,b; 10-inter prof Fr; 11-advanced readings in Fr in art hist and art criticism with emphasis on 20th-cen material; 12-a,b,c,g; 13-a,b,e,f; 14-instructor-prepared materials.

1168. PARIS 1920
C of Mt. St. Vincent; Eng, MFL; Bronx, NY 10471.
Kathleen Knowles
1-12; 2-3x15; 3-b; 4-74; 5-2; 6-b; 7-ng; 8-3s; 9-a,b; 10-none; 11-examines the lit and artistic creativity in Paris in the 20's that was to nourish surrealism, imagism, and stream of consciousness; 12-f; 13-a,b,f; 14-primary texts.

1169. DADA AND ALL THAT: LITERARY MOVEMENTS IN TWENTIETH CENTURY FRANCE
Pfeiffer C; Lang & Lit; Misenheimer, NC 28109.
Elizabeth Ann Shaffer
1-30; 2-1x5; 3-a; 4-73/74; 5-1; 6-every 3 yrs; 7-a; 8-2½ units (125 required for grad); 9-a; 10-none; 11-lectures on surrealism, humanistic existentialism, Fr anti-lit movement of today; recreation of a Dada art show; 12-a,b,d, skit, f; 13-b, "art gallery"; 14-primary texts.

1170. HISTORY OF THE FRENCH CINEMA
Rutgers U; Fr; Camden, NJ 08102.
English Showalter, Jr.
1-new; 2-4x14; 3-a; 4-75/76; 5-0; 6-b; 7-a; 8-4s; 9-a; 10-none; 11-films will be shown and discussed from a non-tech point of view; reading will include screenplays, statements of filmmakers, hist of film; 12-a,b,f; 13-a; 14-not yet decided.

1171. CONTEMPORARY FRENCH LITERATURE
Upper Iowa U; Langs; Fayette, IA 52142.
F.A. Dupuis
1-12; 2-3x13; 3-a; 4-ng; 5-ng; 6-a, smr; 7-a; 8-3s; 9-a; 10-inter prof; 11-works of contemporary Fr authors plus theater, cinema, etc.; 12-a,f; 13-e,f; 14- primary texts.

See also 1311.

GERMAN

1172. EPIC AND OPERA (GERMAN)
Boise SU; FL; Boise, ID 83725.
H. Schoonover
1-10; 2-3x3; 3-a; 4-Jan 75; 5-1; 6-alt yrs; 7-ng; 8-3; 9-a; 10-none; 11-compares medieval world with romantic world; compares the use of ancient legends and motifs in epic and dramatic form and in lit

and musical form; 12-ng; 13-ng; 14-ng.

1173. MUSIC IN GERMAN LITERATURE AND THOUGHT
Clark U; FLs and Lits; Worcester, MA 01610.
Hartmut M. Kaiser
1-35; 2-2½x14; 3-a; 4-72; 5-2; 6-every 2nd or 3rd yr; 7-a; 8-1 unit; 9-a; 10-none; 11-thematic approach; studying successful attempts to employ musical devices and structures in lit and philo works; Wackenroder, Kleist, Schopenhauer, E.T.A. Hoffmann, Goethe, Grillparzer, Heine, Moerike, Wagner, Nietzsche, Hesse, Thomas Mann; 12-a,b,f; 13-d; 14-primary texts.

1174. LITERATURE AND MUSIC: TOWARDS A DEFINITION OF CULTURE
U of Colorado; Ger Langs and Lits; Boulder, CO 80302.
W.V. Blomster
1-26; 2-9x4 plus required attendance at numerous concerts, special lectures, films, discussions, etc; 3-a; 4-73; 5-2; 6-every smr; 7-smr; 8-6s; 9-a; 10-none; 11-course is conducted in Aspen against the background of the Aspen Music Festival. Study of common and formal aesthetic qualities in the music and lit of a given period; 12-a,b,f; 13-concerts, etc; 14-Nietzsche, The Birth of Tragedy; Hoffman, Don Juan; Mann, Doctor Faustus; Hesse, The Glass Bead Game; Broder, Norton, eds, Great Operas by Mozart.

1175. THE GERMAN FILM FROM 1920 TO 1933
Elmhurst C; Ger; Elmhurst, IL 60126.
Dr. Caltvedt
1-new; 2-9x4; 3-a; 4-Jan 75; 5-1; 6-ng; 7-a; 8-4s; 9-a; 10-none; 11-hist background of period; examples of Expressionism and New Objectivity in lit and art; 12-b,f; 13-a,b; 14-Kracauer, From Caligari to Hitler.

1176. GERMAN LITERATURE AND FILM
U of Illinois; Ger Langs & Lits; Urbana, IL 61801.
James M. McGlathery
Further info ng.

1177. GERMAN FILM
Indiana-Purdue U; Ger; Indianapolis, IN 46202.
John D. Barlow
1-9; 2-3x15; 3-a; 4-72; 5-2; 6-alt ys; 7-b; 8-3s; 9-a; 10-jr standing; 11-selected novels and films produced in Central Europe relating to Ger life and cult from 1918 to 1933; 12-f; 13-a; 14-Eisner, The Haunted Screen; primary texts.

1178. NIETZSCHE AND THE GERMAN ARTS
U of Massachusetts; Ger; Boston, MA 02125.
Lynn Dhority

1-30; 2-3x14; 3-a; 4-71/72; 5-1; 6-ng; 7-a; 8-4s; 9-a; 10-instructor permission; 11-ng; 12-a,b,f; 13-ng; 14-primary texts; Kaufmann, Nietzsche; Hollingdale, Nietzsche.

1179. THE GERMAN LIED
Montclair SC; Ger & Russ; Upper Montclair, NJ 07043.
John V. Moore
1-50; 2-3x15; 3-a; 4-72; 5-2; 6-alt yrs; 7-a; 8-3s; 9-a; 10-none; 11-lit analysis of poetry (parallel Eng trans for non-readers of Ger), musical analysis of setting, analysis of the Lied as a combination of the two; attempt to develop an aesthetic of the Lied and investigate validity of it as genre; 12-a,b,c,d,e,f; 13-d, piano, records; 14-mimeographed materials.

1180. GERMAN LITERATURE AND FILM IN THE TWENTIES
Ohio SU; Ger: Columbus, OH 43210.
David Miles
1-30; 2-3x10; 3-a; 4-74; 5-2; 6-b; 7-b; 8-3q; 9-a; 10-none; 11-cult of Weimar Republic from Expressionism to Third Reich; 12-a,f; 13-a,b; 14-primary texts; Delmer, Weimar Germany.

1181. THE GERMAN OPERA
C of St. Thomas; FL; St. Paul, MN 55105.
Paul A. Schons
1-10; 2-4x14; 3-a; 4-72; 5-2; 6-alt yrs; 7-a; 8-4s; 9-a; 10-inter prof; 11-analysis of the drama and music; hist and cult relationships and interaction; 12-a,b,c,g; 13-a,b,d; 14-primary texts.

1182. EXPRESSIONISM AS REVOLUTION
Transylvania U; MFLs; Lexington, KY 40508.
Gerhard F. Probst
1-32; 2-4x10; 3-a; 4-fall 72; 5-4; 6-b, plus smr; 7-a; 8-4q; 9-a; 10-none; 11-art and lit of Ger expressionism, emphasis on revolutionary and messianic aspects; 12-a,b,c,d,f,g; 13-a,b,d,e, records; 14-primary texts.

1183. THE GERMAN CINEMA: THE HISTORY AND DEVELOPMENT OF FILM AS AN ART FORM
Washington U; Ger Langs & Lits; St. Louis, MO 63130.
Peter U. Hohendahl
1-20; 2-3½x14; 3-a; 4-fall 72; 5-3; 6-b; 7-a; 8-3s; 9-a; 10-none; 11-important thematic and psychological qualities of Ger film; emphasis on early expressionistic films and pre WW II propaganda films; selected dramas, novels, screenplays read; similarities & differences of film and lit as art forms; 12-a,b,c,f; 13-a,b,e; 14-Eisner, The Haunted Screen; Kracauer, From Caligari to Hitler.

1184. MAJOR FOREIGN DRAMA: THE GERMAN STAGE AS POLITICAL FORUM
U of Wisconsin; Lang and Lit; Green Bay, WI 54302.
Heinz W. Geppert
Modern Ger playrights, their representative works and theories, styles of acting, scenic elements in the context of the soci, poli and cult aspects of the time. Lectures, presentations of scenes, discussions. 3 credits.

1185. ORAL INTERPRETATION OF GERMAN POETRY
U of Wisconsin; Humanism & Cultural Change; C of Creative Communications; Green Bay, WI 54302.
Heinz Geppert
1-10; 2-10x4; 3-a; 4-71/72; 5-2; 6-depending on student interest; 7-a,b; 8-3s; 9-a; 10-2 yrs Ger; 11-reading & discussion of Ger poetry; oral interpretation of individual poems; workshop culminates in presentation of public project; 12-a,b,c,d,e,g; 13-b,d, recording of poetry readings; 14-Foltin & Heinen, Paths to German Poetry.

1186. RADIO PLAY WORKSHOP
U of Wisconsin; Humanism & Cultural Change; C of Creative Communications; Green Bay, WI 54302.
Heinz Geppert
1-16; 2-3x10; 3-b; 4-69; 5-5; 6-depending on interest; 7-a,b; 8-3s; 9-a; 10-varies according to level of students; 11-Ger workshop: reading & discussion of radio plays; study of radio plays as art-form in hist context; students prepare & present a play for an audience; 12-a,b,d,e,g; 13-b,c,d; 14-varies.

See also 1292.

HISPANIC

1187. CONTEMPORARY CULTURE: ART AND ENTERTAINMENT IN THE SPANISH SPEAKING WORLD
Boston U; MLs; Boston, MA 02215.
Susan Cate
1-ng; 2-3x14; 3-a; 4-72/73; 5-1; 6-c; 7-a; 8-4s; 9-a; 10-inter prof; 11-fictional prose, visual arts, popular music studied as reflections of different soci problems & mentalities; emphasis on reading, aural comprehension, speaking; for non-majors wishing to continue lang study; 12-g; 13-ng; 14-ng.

1188. SPANISH ART HISTORY
U of Dallas; Sp; Irving, TX 75060.
Alexandra Wilhelmsen
1-12; 2-ng; 3-a; 4-71; 5-4; 6-b; 7-a; 8-3; 9-a; 10-general background in European hist; 11-architecture, sculpture, painting from prehistoric times to the present; emphasis on Baroque; 12-ng; 13-b; 14-Bozal, Historia del arte espanol en Espana.

1189. COMMUNICATION ARTS
Florida International U; MLs; Miami, FL 33144.
James O. Crosby
1-16; 2-5x11; 3-a; 4-73; 5-2; 6-every 2nd yr; 7-a; 8-5q; 9-a; 10-4 sems of college Sp; 11-discussion of poems chosen by students, dramatic readings with colored spot lights & musical accompaniment; 12-b,g; 13-see 11; 14-Antologia de la poesia hispanoamericana contemporanea; Siete poetas contemporaneos.

1190. THEATRE IN SPANISH
South Dakota SU; FLs; Brookings, SD 57006.
Beatriz Sanz
1-ng; 2-3x15; 3-a; 4-spr 74; 5-1; 6-on demand; 7-a; 8-3s; 9-a; 10-inter prof; 11-equal emphasis given to theoretical and practical aspects of theater; read and analyze plays; act, stage, cast, Brechtian theories; trans, discuss techniques in staging; 12-a,b,g; 13-ng; 14-ng.

1191. SPANISH THEATRE (WITH INTERNSHIP IN THEATRE)
Staten Island CC; MLs; Staten Island, NY 10301.
M.P. Holt
1-14; 2-3x15; 3-c; 4-72/73; 5-2; 6-b; 7-a; 8-3-6s; 9-a, students from other campuses; 10-course taught bilingually; for Sp credit 4 sem Sp, for Hum credit students may read works in Eng; 11-representative plays from Golden Age to present treated as total theater; production values as well as ideas are investigated. Qualified students may receive additional credits through participation in an internship program with an Off-off Broadway Sp theater company; 12-a,b,c,d,e,f; 13-a,b; 14-primary texts, depending on productions scheduled by Sp theater groups during a particular sem.

1192. SPANISH PLAY PRODUCTION
U of Texas; Sp and Port; Austin, TX 78712.
Phyllis Harmon
1-22; 2-3x14; 3-b; 4-59/60; 5-ng; 6-b; 7-a; 8-3s; 9-a; 10-inter prof; 11-intensive analysis of several plays, with emphasis on problems involving staging; public performance of at least one play at end of sem; 12-a,b,d,g; 13-ng; 14-none.

1193. TOPICS: MEXICAN-AMERICAN LITERATURE
Texas A & I U; Ethnic Studies; Corpus Christi, TX 78411.
Leonardo Carrillo
A consideration of the lit developments among Mex-Amers, particularly of the Southwestern U.S. Influences, purposes and

innovative themes are studied in essays, short stories and poetry. Taught in Eng. 3 hrs credit.

See also 1408, 1464, 1565.

ITALIAN

1194. ITALIAN ART AND CULTURE
Adelphi U; Langs; Garden City, NY 11530.
Romano Giachetti
1-21; 2-3x14; 3-a; 4-70; 5-5; 6-b; 7-a; 8-3s; 9-a; 10-none; 11-survey of the hist of Ital art in its relationship with other aspects of cult, hist, lit, music, etc.; 12-a,b,d,f; 13-b, records; 14-Chastel, Italian Art.

1195. THE ITALIAN FILM SINCE 1945
Adelphi U; Langs; Garden City, NY 11530.
Romano Giachetti
1-27; 2-3x14; 3-a; 4-70; 5-5; 6-b; 7-a; 8-3s; 9-a; 10-none; 11-critical presentation from post WW II period to present; 12-a,b,d,f; 13-a; 14-instructor-supplied materials.

1196. ITALIAN FILM AND LITERATURE
U of California; Ital; Berkeley, CA 94720.
Gavriel Moses
1-105; 2-4x10; 3-a; 4-fall 74; 5-1; 6-b; 7-a; 8-4q; 9-a; 10-none; 11-considers two central periods of Ital cinema--the early silent film and neorealism; novels from both periods read and discussed; 12-f; 13-a; 14-primary texts; Leprohon, The Italian Cinema.

1197. LITERARY AND SOCIO-POLITICAL TRENDS IN ITALIAN CINEMA
U of California; Ital; Los Angeles, CA 90024.
Giovanni Cecchetti
A 2-course sequence designed for students with majors other than Ital (given in Eng). The influence of Ital lit and socio-political thought on development and evolution of Ital cinema after WW II; and on the development, thematic emphasis, and aesthetic treatments of specific Ital directors and/or Ital cinematic genres.

1198. ITALIAN CINEMA (ALTERNATES WITH FRENCH, GERMAN, SPANISH CINEMA COURSES)
(See ms. #1191) Staten Island CC; MLs; Staten Island, NY 10301.
M.P. Holt
1-30; 2-4x15; 3-b (Dept of Performing and Creative Arts); 4-fall 74; 5-Fr course offered before; 6-alternates with the other courses; 7-a,b; 8-3s; 9-a,b; 10-none; 11-presentation & discussion of important Ital films with emphasis on their cult background; comparisons with the lit, music, & other art forms of the contemporary period; 12-a,b,f; 13-a; 14-various background readings.

1199. ITALIAN REALISM AND NEO-REALISM
Temple U; Ital; Philadelphia, PA 19122.
Raymond J. Cornier
1-new; 2-3x14; 3-a; 4-75; 5-0; 6-3 yrs; 7-a; 8-4s; 9-a; 10-inter prof; 11-study of verismo with emphasis on Sicilian writers from Verga to Sciascia and manifestation of this movement in the post-war neo-realismo of Ital cinema; 12-a,b,c,g; 13-a; 14-primary texts.

See also 1285.

RUSSIAN

1200. DRAMATIC ARTS IN RUSSIA
Boston U; MLs; Boston, MA 02215.
Susan Cate
1-ng; 2-3x14; 3-a; 4-69/70; 5-3; 6-b; 7-a; 8-4s; 9-a; 10-intro to Russ lit; 11-intro to Russ drama in 19th and 20th cens, emphasis on thematic concerns and character development; attention also paid to aspects of performance of the plays in traditional and modern experimental theaters; 12-ng; 13-ng; 14-ng.

1201. RUSSIAN AND SOVIET FILM (ENGLISH TRANSLATION)
Boston U; MLs; Boston, MA 02215.
Susan Cate
1-15; 2-3x14; 3-a; 4-74/75; 5-1; 6-b; 7-a; 8-4; 9-a; 10-none; 11-development and hist of Russ and Soviet film; screenings of films from the classical era and the 'New Cinema;' reading and discussion of theoretical works on film; 12-a,b,f; 13-a; 14-Leyda, A History of Russian Film; Lindgren, The Art of the Film.

1202. LITERATURE AND THE SOVIET FILM
Indiana U; Sl Langs and Lits; Bloomington, IN 47401.
Rodney B. Sangster
1-22; 2-3x15; 3-a; 4-spr 73; 5-2; 6-b; 7-a; 8-3s; 9-a; 10-none; 11-characteristics of Soviet films; theory and practice of filmmaking in the Soviet Union; the Soviet cinema in the context of its relationship to European cinema art; 12-a,b,f; 13-a; 14-Gianetti, Understanding Movies; Arms, Film and Reality.

SCANDINAVIAN

1203. THE SCANDINAVIAN CINEMA: THE DEVELOPMENT OF FILM AS AN ART FORM
Washington U; Ger Langs & Lits; St. Louis, MO 63130.
Peter U. Hohendahl
1-150; 2-3x14; 3-a; 4-spr 72; 5-3; 6-b; 7-a; 8-3s; 9-a; 10-none; 11-lyrical, thematic, and psychological qualities important to evolution of film forms in commercial Scand cinema; 12-a,b,c,f; 13-a,b,e; 14-

Cowe, Sweden 2; Wood, Ingmar Bergman; Milne, The Cinema of Carl Dreyer; Simon, Ingmar Bergman Directs; Durgnat, Films and Feelings; Donner, The Films of Ingmar Bergman.

1204. KIERKEGAARD TO BERGMAN
U of Washington; Scand; Seattle, WA 98195.
Birgitta Steene
1-26; 2-2x10; 3-a; 4-spr 74; 5-1; 6-irregularly; 7-b; 8-0; 9-a,b; 10-none; 11-spiritual and intellectual tradition of Scand through lit; Bergman's works in light of this tradition; 12-a,b,f; 13-a; 14-primary texts.

1205. SCANDINAVIAN FILM AND LITERATURE
U of Washington; Scand; Seattle, WA 98195.
Birgitta Steene
1-new; 2-4x11; 3-a; 4-ng; 5-0; 6-b; 7-ng; 8-3q; 9-a; 10-grad standing; 11-study of film adaptations by Sjostrom and Stiller of the works of Lagerlof; consideration of film adaptations by Dreyer; analysis of relationship between Strindbergian dreamplay tecnique and Bergman's films; 12-ng; 13-ng; 14-primary texts; Cowe, Sweden 2.

MISCELLANEOUS

1206. WORLD CINEMA
U of California; Fr & Ital; Santa Barbara, CA 93106.
1-150; 2-4x30; 3-a; 4-71; 5-9; 6-a; 7-a; 8-12q; 9-a; 10-drama courses recommended; 11-survey of intl tradition in cinema; 3q sequence: 1) contribution of major intl film traditions to universal art of film; 2) major Amer genres and study of the Amer hero; 3) Ital cinema since WW II; 12-a,f; 13-a; 14-Mast, Short History of the Movies.

1207. THE CLASSIC BAROQUE VISION
U of Dallas; FL; Irving, TX 75060.
Hazel Cazorla, Mrs. Bartscht, Dr. Dupree
1-10; 2-ng; 3-a; 4-74; 5-1; 6-b; 7-a; 8-3; 9-a; 10-ng; 11-ng; 12-a,b,f; 13-b; 14-various.

1208. THE ARTS TODAY: FROM 1950 TO PRESENT

Indiana U; Comp Lit; Bloomington, IN 47401.
1-new; 2-1½x16; 3-a; 4-75/76; 5-0; 6-b; 7-a; 8-3s; 9-a; 10-2 sems of "Modern Lit and the Other Arts"; 11-ng; 12-a,b; 13-b,d; 14-ng.

1209. COLLOQUIUM IN LITERATURE AND THE OTHER ARTS
Indiana U; Comp Lit; Bloomington, IN 47401.
1-8; 2-1 3/4x16; 3-a; 4-spr 74; 5-1; 6-every 3rd sem; 7-a; 8-4s; 9-a; 10-none; 11-problems of methodology based on concrete examples; analysis of secondary texts; two-sem sequence; 12-a,b,c,d,f; 13-b,e; 14-extensive reading list.

1210. CONTEMPORARY   THEATRE   AND CINEMA
Seattle U; FLs; Seattle, WA 98122.
Additional info ng.

1211. THE 20's THROUGH THE MEDIA
U of South Carolina; Ger; Columbia, SC 29208.
Margit Resch
1-50; 2-3-4x15; 3-a,b; 4-73; 5-twice; 6-every 2 years; 7-a; 8-3s; 9-a; 10-none; 11-broad look at 1920's based on lit, film, including guest lecturers from various cult fields; 12-a,b,d,e,f; 13-a,c; 14-primary texts.

1212. LITERATURE AND FILM
U of Wisconsin; Comp Lit; Milwaukee, WI 53201.
Davy Carozza
1-18; 2-3x15; 3-b; 4-Jan 72; 5-3; 6-ng; 7-a; 8-2/4s; 9-a; 10-soph standing; 11-examination of various aspects of inter-relationship between cinema and fiction; 12-a,b,f,g; 13-a,c,f; 14-varies each yr.

1213. LITERATURE AND THE OTHER ARTS
U of Wisconsin; Comp Lit; Milwaukee, WI 53201.
Davy Carozza
1-14; 2-3x15; 3-a; 4-Jan 72; 5-1; 6-ng; 7-a; 8-3s; 9-a; 10-grad standing; 11-relation-ships of lit with architecture, music, painting, photography, sculpture, etc; 12-a,c; 13-ng; 14-varies.

See also 1269, 1309, 1330.

AFRICAN

1214. AFRICAN LITERATURE AND CULTURAL NATIONALISM
Gettysburg C; Rom Langs; Gettysburg, PA 17325.
Fredric Michelmo
1-19; 2-20x4; 3-a; 4-74; 5-2; 6-b; 7-a; 8-4s; 9-a; 10-none; 11-affirmation of African cult values as a rebuttal to the European colonizers' civilizing mission; lit works of the last 40 yrs from Black Africa and the Caribbean; 12-a,b,f; 13-a,e,f; 14-primary texts; Wallerstein, Africa: The Politics of Independence; Cook & Henderson, The Militant Black Writer in Africa and the U.S.

BRAZILIAN

1215. BRAZILIAN LITERATURE OF SOCIAL CONFLICT
Temple U; Port; Philadelphia, PA 19122.
John B. Means
1-12; 2-3x15; 3-a; 4-72; 5-2; 6-alt yrs; 7-a; 8-4s; 9-a; 10-none; 11-analysis of poli, econ, socio conflict in Brazilian society and its reflection in Brazilian lit from the colonial period to the present; 12-a,b,c,f; 13-e; 14-primary texts.

CLASSICS

1216. AN INTRODUCTION TO ROMAN LAW
U of Michigan; Cl Studies; Ann Arbor, MI 48104.
Frank Copley
1-10; 2-3x16; 3-b; 4-wtr 71; 5-1; 6-occasionally; 7-a; 8-3s; 9-a; 10-none; 11-30 lectures & discussion sessions with occasional Socratic dialogue; 12-a,f; 13-ng; 14-ng.

See also 1152.

FRENCH

1217. READING THE FRENCH PRESS
Adelphi U; Langs & Intl Studies; Garden City, NY 11530.
M.R. Myron
1-10; 2-3x16; 3-a; 4-74; 5-1; 6-b; 7-a; 8-3s; 9-a; 10-permission of instructor; 11-competence in reading newspapers, magazines, periodicals; increasing comprehension of idiomatic phraseology and journalistic style; 12-b,c,g; 13-e,f; 14-Paris Match, France Amerique, Le Figaro.

1218. FRENCH PRESS, RADIO AND TV

Boston U; MLs; Boston, MA 02215.
Anne Slack
1-11; 2-3x17; 3-a; 4-73; 5-2; 6-ng; 7-a; 8-4s; 9-a; 10-consent; 11-study of current events, issues, and developments through the use of recent interviews with leading Fr personalities and through the use of some leading newspapers and magazines; 12-a,b,d,g; 13-d,e,f, lectures by Fr journalists in Boston; 14-course based on current mass media.

1219. MAN AND SOCIETY: PSYCHOLOGY AND SOCIAL COMMENTARY IN THE CLASSICAL PERIOD (FRENCH)
Boston U; MLs; Boston, MA 02215.
Susan Cate
1-new; 2-3x14; 3-a; 4-new; 5-1; 6-c; 7-a; 8-4; 9-ng; 10-inter prof; 11-17th cen thinkers who speculate on the human psyche and on motivation in personal and public life; 12-a,g; 13-ng; 14-ng.

1220. LA VILLE DE PARIS AUX XVIIe ET XVIIIe SIECLES
Bryn Mawr C; Fr; Bryn Mawr, PA 19010.
Catherine Lafarge
1-15; 2-3x13; 3-a; 4-74/75; 5-1; 6-every 3 yrs; 7-a; 8-4s; 9-a; 10-excellent command of Fr; 11-a study of Paris in representative texts (letters, memoirs, plays, novels), with emphasis on historical & aesthetic developments of the city as they appear in writings and paintings of these two periods; 12-a,b,c,d,f; 13-b,e,f; 14-ng.

1221. PARIS
U of California; Fr and Ital; Riverside, CA 92502.
Robert Griffin
1-25; 2-3x10; 3-a; 4-72/73; 5-2; 6-c, every other yr; 7-b; 8-ng; 9-a; 10-none; 11-soci and cult hist of Paris, with emphasis on the 19th and 20th cens and on the city's role as lit and artistic center; 12-a,b,f; 13-a,b,d; 14-Holmes, ed, Daily Living in the Twelfth Century; Ranum, Paris in the Age of Absolutism; primary texts.

1222. THE FRENCH WOMAN
Davis and Elkins C; FLs; Elkins, WV 26241.
David Seaman
1-6; 2-2x11; 3-a; 4-74; 5-1; 6-irregularly; 7-a; 8-2/4s; 9-a; 10-none; 11-readings in lit, hist, psychology, sociology, and contemporary media about women in France; 12-b,c,f; 13-a,e; 14-primary texts.

1223. FRANCE AND THE THIRD WORLD
Fisk U; MFLs; Nashville, TN 37203.
David W.H. Pellow
1-10; 2-3x15; 3-a; 4-spr 73; 5-1; 6-c; 7-a; 8-

3s; 9-a; 10-none; 11-hist and contemporary study of Fr colonialism in the Amers, Africa, Asia, the Pacific; geographical, poli, and econ aspects; 12-a,b,c,f; 13-b,e,f; realia, maps, photos; 14-Memmi, Colonizer and Colonized; Fanon, Towards the African Revolution.

1224. THE FRENCH PRESS
Hood C; ML; Frederick, MD 21701.
1-5; 2-3xsem; 3-a; 4-fall 74; 5-1; 6-b; 7-a; 8-3s; 9-a; 10-inter prof or permission; 11-reading and discussion of periodicals and newspapers; articles in various fields of cult, econ, poli, and sci interest; 12-a,b,c,d,g; 13-e,f; 14-ng.
(See ms. p. 110)

1225. WOMEN IN FRANCE
Hood C; ML; Frederick, MD 21701.
1-7; 2-3xsem; 3-a; 4-spr 75; 5-1; 6-alt yrs; 7-a; 8-3s; 9-a; 10-inter prof or permission; 11-roles and images of women in Fr society and lit; 12-a,b,c,d,g; 13-e,f; 14-ng.
(See ms. p. 110)

1226. A LA RECHERCHE DE LA FRANCE
Lawrence U; Fr; Appleton, WI 54911.
Bruce Cronmiller
1-15; 2-3x10; 3-a; 4-72; 5-2; 6-alt yrs; 7-a; 8-1 unit; 9-a; 10-inter prof; 11-3 parts: study of some of the basic elements and structures of contemporary Fr society which most puzzle Amers; study of a group of students of college age; study of several of Simenon's Maigret novels, emphasizing the author's preoccupation with the relationship between lieu and milieu; 12-b,g; 13-ng; 14-Ortali, Entre Nous; Wylie & Begue, Les Francais; books by Simenon.

1227. ETUDES DE CIVILISATION FRANCAISE
Lawrence U; Fr; Appleton, WI 54911.
Bruce Cronmiller
1-20; 2-3x10; 3-a; 4-69; 5-4; 6-b; 7-a; 8-1s; 9-a; 10-inter prof; 11-student uprisings and general strike of May 1968 are the focal point of this study of Fr society and institutions; 12-b,f; 13-e; 14-workbook/anthology edited by instructor.

1228. LA PRESSE FRANCAISE
U of Maryland; MLs; Baltimore, MD 21228.
Claud DuVerlie
1-15; 2-8x4; 3-a; 4-73; 5-2; 6-Jan session; 7-ng; 8-2s; 9-a,b; 10-inter prof; 11-further conv abilities, to give a comprehensive view of Fr journalism, to learn about the important questions facing France and Europe today, to look at America from a European perspective, and to perceive differences in the interpretation of intl events; 12-a,b,c,d,g; 13-e,f; 14-none.

1229. POLITICS AND MODERN FRENCH LITERATURE
New York U; Fr & Ital; New York, NY 10003.
Tom Bishop

1-c5; 2-2½x14; 3-a; 4-72/73; 5-1; 6-alt yrs; 7-a; 8-4s; 9-a; 10-adv prof; 11-examination of the opposing political forces of the Left and Right as expressed in novels, plays, poems representing differing viewpoints; 12-a,b,f,g; 13-ng; 14-primary texts.

1230. CONTEMPORARY FRANCE
U of Washington; Rom Langs & Lit; Seattle, WA 98195.
Howard Nostrand
1-10 ng; 11-study of women, the family, political situation, concept of Fr cult, nationalism vs. internationalism, industrialism and its transition to post-industrialism, class & race relations, ed, mass media, the arts with emphasis on lit and the visual arts, the lang and its evolution; 12-14-ng.

1231. DU MYTHE A LA RECETTE: ASPECTS SOCIO-CULTURELS DE LA FRANCE A TABLE
U of Wisconsin; Fr & Ital; Madison, WI 53706.
Yvonne Ozzello
1-ng; 2-10x3, plus 5 optional 3-hr workshops in Fr House kitchen; 3-a; 4-ng; 5-ng; 6-intersession (May-June); 7-a; 8-2s, plus 1s for optional workshops; 9-a; 10-perm prof; 11-exploration of the myths, cliches, and taboos governing attitudes of the Fr toward food and meals; in the workshops, students plan, prepare, and consume authentically researched illustrative meals; 12-b,d,g, field trips, individual research; 13-a,b,f; 14-Mathiot, La cuisine pour tous; Hall, The Silent Language; instructor-prepared materials.

See also 106, 1168, 1290A, 1296, 1348, 1436.

GERMAN

1232. CULTURE AND POLITICS OF THE THIRD REICH
Albion C; MLs; Albion, MI 49224.
Henry Rottenbiller
1-27; 2-4x17; 3-a; 4-72; 5-2; 6-b; 7-a; 8-1s; 9-a; 10-European hist; 11-multiperspective study of an authoritarian state; 12-a,b,c,f; 13-a,b,f; 14-ng.

1233. CONTEMPORARY GERMAN PRESS
Boston U; MLs; Boston, MA 02215.
Susan Cate
1-ng; 2-3x14; 3-a; 4-73/74; 5-ng; 6-ng; 7-a; 8-4s; 9-ng; 10-inter prof; 11-reading and discussion of current newspapers and periodicals; 12-a,b,c,f,g; 13-e,f; 14-ng.

1234. JUNGIAN PSYCHOLOGY AND GERMAN LITERATURE
California SC; FL; Rohnert Park, CA 94928.
Sterling Bennett

1-7; 2-3x14; 3-a; 4-fall 74; 5-1; 6-unspecified; 7-b; 8-3s; 9-a; 10-speaking knowledge, preferably srs; 11-readings from Jung's autobiography and works plus selections from Ger lit; analysis of myth and fairy tales in terms of Jungian psychology and in comparison with archetypes; 12-a,b,c,g; 13-ng; 14-primary texts.

1235. THE WORLD OF GUNTER GRASS
Carleton C; MLs; Northfield, MN 55057.
Ulf Zimmermann
1-25; 2-4x5; 3-a; 4-73/74; 5-1; 6-alt yrs; 7-a; 8-6q; 9-a; 10-none; 11-exploration of modern Ger hist and politics through the work of Gunter Grass and contemporary studies; 12-a,b,c,f; 13-e,f; 14-primary texts; Dahrendorf, Society and Democracy in Germany.

1236. THE TWO GERMANIES
Federal City C; FL: Washington, DC 20001.
1-7; 2-3x10; 3-a; 4-72/73; 5-3; 6-b; 7-a,b; 8-3q; 9-a, part-time; 10-none; 11-rise of the two Ger states after WW II; present contrasts & similarities, likely developments; 12-a,b,c,f; 13-misc; 14-ng.

1237. SOCIETY IN THE GERMAN NOVEL IN TRANSLATION
U of Illinois; Ger Langs & Lits; Urbana, IL 61801.
James McGlathery
Further info ng.

1238. JUNG AND HESSE
U of Massachusetts; Ger; Boston, MA 02125.
Lynn Dhority
1-ng; 2-3x13-14; 3-a; 4-73; 5-ng; 6-b; 7-a; 8-3s; 9-a, part-time students; 10-none; 11-ng; 12-a,b,d,f; 13-a; 14-primary texts.

1239. THE GERMANS UNDER HITLER: THE 30'S
U of South Carolina; Ger; Columbia, SC 29208.
Margit Resch
1-30; 2-3/4x15; 3-a; 4-74; 5-1; 6-alt yrs; 7-a; 8-3s; 9-a; 10-none; 11-Germany in the 1930's to the end of WW II based on lit and film; guest lecturers from hist, philo, art, music, intl studies; 12-a,b,d,e,f; 13-a,b,c; 14-Mosse, Nazi Culture; Remak, The Nazi Years: A Documentary History.

1240. GERMAN EXPRESSIONISM: THE ROAD TO HITLER
Tufts U; Ger; Medford, MA 02155.
Sol Gittleman
1-240; 2-3x14; 3-a; 4-69; 5-7; 6-b; 7-a; 8-1; 9-a; 10-none; 11-Ger Expressionism in its European context; its relationship to Nazism; painting and film are discussed; 12-a,b,f; 13-a,b; 14-Viereck, Metapolitics: The Roots of the Nazi Mind; Mosse, The Crisis of German Ideology; Willet, Ex-

pressionism; Sokel, The Writer in Extremis; Stern, The Politics of Cultural Despair; Kracauer, From Caligari to Hitler: History of the German Film.

1241. CURRENT ISSUES IN THE GERMAN PRESS
Winona SC: FLs; Winona, MN 55987.
Jordan V. Hodgson
1-9; 2-4x10; 3-a; 4-74; 5-1; 6-every 2 or 3 yrs; 7-a; 8-4q; 9-a,b, extension; 10-none; 11-topics of current interest--poli sci, econ, soci, bus, ed, and other areas; 12-a,b,f; 13-e,f, newsletters; 14-none.

See also 1063, 1177, 1180, 1182, 1184, 1315, 1552, 1639, 1642.

HISPANIC

1242. THE SPANISH LANGUAGE PRESS
Adelphi U; Lang & Intl Studies; Garden City, NY 11530.
Nicholas Garbo
1-22; 2-3x15; 3-a; 4-74; 5-1; 6-b; 7-a; 8-3s; 9-a; 10-adv prof; 11-development of reading, comprehension skills utilizing contemporary journals, periodicals, & related media; analysis of the journalistic terms & idiomatic expressions, of current issues, & of varied functions of journalism in Hispanic world; 12-b,c,g; 13-e,f; 14-Alegria, La Prensa; Garcia-Pons, Manuel de Estilo.

1243. MEXICAN-AMERICAN LITERATURE
Arizona SU; FLs; Tempe, AZ 85281.
Douglas C. Sheppard
1-38; 2-ng; 3-a; 4-fall 73; 5-2; 6-b; 7-a; 8-3s; 9-a; 10-inter prof; 11-lit in Sp and Eng by Mex Amers emphasizing sociocult as well as literary values; 12-b,g; 13-a,b,c,d,e,f; 14-ng.

1244. HISTORY OF MEXICO
U of Dallas; FL; Irving, TX 75060.
Alexandra Wilhelmsen
1-12; 2-ng; 3-a; 4-71; 5-4; 6-b; 7-a; 8-ng; 9-inservice teachers; 10-ng; 11-Mex hist from Pre-Columbian days to the Revolution of 1910; usually taken in conjunction with Mex art hist and week-long study trip to Mexico; 12-g; 13-b; 14-Cuevas, Historia de la nacion Mexicana.

1245. WOMEN IN THE HISPANIC WORLD
Hood C; ML; Frederick, MD 21701.
1-new; 2-3xsem; 3-a; 4-76; 5-0; 6-alt yrs; 7-a; 8-3s; 9-a; 10-inter prof, permission; 11-roles and images of women in Hispanic society and lit; 12-a,b,c,d,g; 13-e,f; 14-ng.

1246. READINGS AND DISCUSSION ON CONTEMPORARY PROBLEMS OF THE SPANISH WORLD
Indiana S U; Hums; Evansville, IN 47712.

Lomberto Diaz
1-8; 2-4xsem; 3-a; 4-73; 5-2; 6-b; 7-a; 8-4s;
9-a, cont ed; 10-elem prof; 11-preliminary
study of ideas of contemporary Sp-speaking
writers through their most important work
in soci scis, especially those related to the
underdeveloped countries; 12-a,b,g; 13-f;
14-ng.

1247. LANGUAGE AND SOCIETY IN THE
HISPANIC WORLD
Indiana U; Sp & Port; Bloomington, IN
47401.
Mark G. Goldin
1-16; 2-3x15; 3-a; 4-75; 5-1; 6-unknown; 7-
a; 8-3s; 9-a; 10-ability to read Sp; 11-ng;
12-a,b,f; 13-d,e; 14-ng.

1248. HISPANIC MINORITIES IN THE U.S.
Keene SC; FLs; Keene, NH 03431.
Donald Flemming
1-14; 2-3x15; 3-a; 4-74; 5-1; 6-one time
only; 7-a; 8-3s; 9-a; 10-none; 11-study of
Chicanos, Puerto Ricans, and Cubans
residing in the U.S.; 12-a,b,f; 13-e,f; 14-
Aztlan: An Anthology of Mexican American
Literature; The Chicanos: Mexican
American Voices; Thomas, Down These
Mean Streets; Growing Up Puerto Rican.

1249. NARRATIVA Y POLITICA EN LATINO-
AMERICA
U of Maryland; Sp & Port; College Park, MD
20742.
Henry Mendeloff
1-14; 2-3x15; 3-a; 4-fall74; 5-1; 6-alt yrs; 7-
a; 8-3s; 9-a; 10-grad standing; 11-lit
artifact as consumer goods; poli analysis of
several novels; participation of the writer
in the poli system; poli influence exerted by
his works; 12-a,b,g; 13-c,f; 14-various.

1250. LATIN-AMERICAN LITERATURE IN A
SOCIAL CONTEXT
Stanford U; Sp & Port; Stanford, CA 94305.
Jean Franco
1-ng; 2-7x13; 3-a; 4-73/74; 5-2; 6-a; 7-a; 8-
4q; 9-a; 10-reading knowledge; 11-different
content each time offered; explore the
meeting of the Hispanic, African, and
indigenous races in the Amer through
imaginative lit; focus on the colonizer and
his attempts to bring the indigenous peoples
within his ideological order; 12-a,b,c,g; 13-
b; 14-Arguedas, Los rios profundos; various.

1251. LANGUAGE AND THE MEXICAN-
AMERICAN
Texas A & I U; Ethnic Studies; Corpus
Christi, TX 78411.
Leonardo Carrillo
A philosophical and sociological
examination to demonstrate the
significance of lang in Mex Amer
communities especially those in South
Texas. Taught in Eng. 3 hrs credit.

1252. MEXICAN-AMERICAN LANGUAGE
Texas A & I U; Ethnic Studies; Corpus
Christi, TX 78411.
Leonardo Carrillo
1-16 (1st sem), 10 (2nd sem); 2-4x16; 3-a; 4-
74/75; 5-2 (1st sem), 1 (2nd sem); 6-a; 7-a,b;
8-3s; 9-a, public servants; 10-none; 11-the
Sp spoken by South Texans as a vital form of
communication; humanistic approach
designed to broaden understanding of
Texas' unique cult; 2-course sequence; 12-
e,g; 13-b,d; 14-none.

1253. LATIN AMERICAN STUDIES
Ursinus C; Rom Langs; Collegeville, PA
19426.
A.L. Reiner
1-7; 2-ng; 3-a; 4-74/75; 5-1; 6-b; 7-a; 8-3s;
9-a; 10-ng; 11-hist, poli, and socioecon
background of Latin Amer as brought out in
studies of its major writers; 12-a,f; 13-e,f;
14-ng.

1254. THE SPANISH CIVIL WAR
Vassar C; Hispanic Studies; Poughkeepsie,
NY 12601.
German Bleiberg
1-35; 2-2x13; 3-a; 4-69; 5-3; 6-alt yrs; 7-b;
8-3s; 9-a; 10-jr or sr standing; 11-hist and
myth of the Sp Civil War; lit and poli
impact, artistic influence, intl
implications, etc.; 12-a,b,c,f; 13-ng; 14-
works of Hugh Thomas and Gabriel Jackson.

See also 159, 1083, 1102, 1290A, 1310, 1404, 1417,
1526.

ITALIAN

See 1142, 1286, 1312.

JAPANESE

1255. JAPANESE LITERATURE IN ITS
CULTURAL CONTEXT
Merrimack C; MLs; North Andover, MA
01845.
Lawrence J. Gillooly
1-8; 2-3x14; 3-a; 5-70; 5-4; 6-sufficient demand; 7-a; 8-3s; 9-a; 10-none; 11-
geography, hist, soci, religion, and art;
readings in classical and mod lit; 12-a,b,d,f,
museum visits; 13-a,b; 14-primary texts;
Tsunoda et al, Sources of Japanese
Tradition.

LINGUISTICS

See 1359.

RUSSIAN

1256. CONTEMPORARY SOVIET PRESS

Boston U; MLs; Boston, MA 02215.
Susan Cate
1-3; 2-3x14; 3-a; 4-71/72; 5-4; 6-b; 7-a; 8-4s; 9-a; 10-consent of instructor; 11-special problems related to reading and interpreting current Soviet journalistic lit; emphasis on reading daily editions, but individual assignments geared to student interests; 12-a,b,c,d,g; 13-f; 14-ng.

1257. READING PRAVDA

● Bucknell U; MLs; Lewisburg, PA 17837.
Robert E. Beard
(See ms. #1085)
1-1; 2-varies x 4; 3-a; 4-70; 5-4; 6-Jan program; 7-ng; 8-b (special cr for completion); 9-a; 10-reading knowledge; 11-reading selected articles in Pravda for underlying poli assumptions, stylometric poli analysis, etc; 12-ng; 13-f; 14-none.

1258. SOVIET SOCIETY

● Bucknell U; MLs; Lewisburg, PA 17837.
Robert E. Beard
(See ms. #1085)
1-5; 2-3x13; 3-a; 4-68; 5-4; 6-alt yrs; 7-a; 8-1 unit; 9-a; 10-reading and speaking knowledge; 11-reading Soviet overview textbook on Soviet society and comparing it with Western sources; fundamentals of Soviet soci order, their underlying assumptions; 12-a,b,g; 13-a,b,d,f; 14-Sofinskii et al, Sovetskii sojuz; Inkeles, Social Change in Soviet Russia.

1259. THE LITERATURE OF SOCIAL CONSCIOUSNESS IN RUSSIA
Case Western Reserve U; Sl & EE Langs; Cleveland, OH 44106.
Thomas J. Watts
1-14; 2-3 per sem; 3-a; 4-73; 5-2; 6-alt yrs; 7-a; 8-3s; 9-a,b; 10-none; 11-survey of lit works from 18th cen to present in which the author displays concern for some oppressed group; approach is hist, soci, lit, poli; 12-a,b,f; 13-b, records; 14-primary texts.

1260. RUSSIAN LANGUAGE, LITERATURE, AND HISTORY
Fairleigh Dickinson U; Russ Area Study; Rutherford, NJ 07070.
E.C. Brody
1-15; 2-3x17; 3-a; 4-70/71; 5-4; 6-b; 7-a; 8-3s; 9-a; 10-be in Russ Area Study Program; 11-elem Russ; survey of 19th cen Russ lit; survey of Russ hist from 9th to 17th cen; 12-a,b,e,f; 13-d,e,f; 14-Smith & Afansy, Introduction to Russian; Proffer, From Karamzin to Bunin; Kochan, The Making of Modern Russia.

See also 143, 152, 155, 156, 1281.

SCANDINAVIAN

1261. THE VIKINGS
Pennsylvania SU; Ger; University Park, PA 16802.

E.A. Ebbinghaus
1-15; 2-4½x10; 3-a; 4-69/70; 5-3; 6-alt yrs; 7-a; 8-3s; 9-a; 10-none; 11-life and cult of the Vikings from their appearance in hist to the 12th cen; readings, discussion, significance of Viking cult in European medieval times; 12-a,b,f; 13-ng; 14-Arbman, The Vikings.

1262. HISTORY OF SCANDINAVIA
U of Washington; Scand; Seattle WA 98195.
Further info ng.

MISCELLANEOUS

1263. ETHNOPOETICS
Brandeis U; Rom & Comp Lit; Waltham, MA 02154.
Luis Yglesias
1-ng; 2-3x12; 3-a; 4-73/74; 5-1; 6-alt yrs; 7-a; 8-ng; 9-a; 10-none; 11-nature and function of poetry among native peoples, theory of origins, structural analysis, relation to written lits of past and present; 12-a,b,c,f; 13-d,e; 14-Trask, The Unwritten Song, Vols. I & II; Boura, Primitive Song.

1264. IDEOLOGICAL BACKGROUND OF TOTALITARIANISM
Federal City C; FLs; Washington, DC 20001.
Additional info ng.

1265. LANGUAGE AND CULTURE

● Loyola U; MLs; Chicago, IL 60626.
Lawrence Biondi
1-19; 2-3x16; 3-a; 4-74; 5-2; 6-a; 7-a; 8-3s; 9-a; 10-none; 11-course is cross listed in catalogue under Urban Ethnic Studies. It investigates the multiple cult & soci factors affecting use of lang in its many varieties of speech performance. Some field work in another cult setting is required; 12-a,b,c,d,f; 13-a,b; 14-Powdermaker, Stranger and Friend; Tiger, Men in Groups; Tiger & Fox, The Imperial Animal; Fromkin & Rodman, Introduction to Language.

1266. LIFE STYLES IN EUROPE PAST AND PRESENT: YOUTH REVOLT
Madison C; FLs; Harrisonburg, VA 22801.
Rinehart Kyler
1-new; 2-1x16; 3-a; 4-spr 75; 5-1; 6-ng; 7-a; 8-1s; 9-a,b,c; 10-none; 11-various periods in European cult in terms of the individual's life experiences, frustrations, feelings and attitudes as reflected in relevant lit docs; topic changes each year; 12-a,b,c,f; 13-ng; 14-primary texts.

1267. ON LANGUAGES AND LINGUISTICS
Muskingum C; ML; New Concord OH 43762.
Mirco M. Mitrovich
1-10; 2-3x10; 3-b; 4-73/74; 5-3; 6-b, on

252

demand; 7-a; 8-3s; 9-a; 10-none; 11-hist of lang; origin, changes & characteristics; in cooperation with Cl Dept; 12-a,b,d,e; 13-d,e,f; 14-various.

1268. LANGUAGE AND SOCIETY
U of New Mexico; Ling; Albuquerque, NM 87131.
John Oller
1-new; 2-3x16; 3-a; 4-spr 75; 5-1; 6-b; 7-a; 8-3s; 9-a,b; 10-Ling 292; 11-examination of the nature of ling variation and its relationship to soci interaction and soci stratification; 12-f; 13-ng; 14-Fishman, Advances in the Sociology of Language; Gumperz & Hymes, Directions in Sociolinguistics; Wolfram & Fasold, The Study of Social Dialects in American English; Labov, Sociolinguistic Patterns.

1269. AGE OF ROMANTICISM: ART, HISTORY, AND LITERATURE OF EARLY 19th CENTURY
New York U; Fr & Ital; New York, NY 10003.
Charles Affron
1-c45; 2-2½x14; 3-b; 4-73/74; 5-1; 6-alt yrs; 7-a; 8-4s; 9-a; 10-none; 11-poli, soci, and cult development of Western society as it faced the impact of industrialization; artistic and lit reflections of these developments; 12-a,b,f; 13-ng; 14-ng.

1270. LITERATURE AND ANTHROPOLOGY
Queens C; Comp Lit; Flushing, NY 11367.
Vincent Crapanzano
1-30; 2-3x14; 3-a; 4-73/74; 5-2; 6-a; 7-a; 8-3s; 9-a; 10-soph standing; 11-how man conceives of his personal hist has varied considerably from cult to cult & from age to age; at times he attempted to formulate his 'autobiography' using the genres and conventions at his disposal; Western and non-Western autobiographies read and discussed; nature of writing autobiography and writing exercises; 12-a,b,f; 13-ng; 14-primary texts; varies.

1271. GEOLINGUISTICS
U of Rhode Island; Langs; Kingston, RI 02881.
Kenneth H. Rogers
1-19; 2-3x5; 3-a; 4-74; 5-2; 6-c; 7-a; 8-1s; 9-a; 10-none; 11-survey of phenomena of lang distribution: biling, ling nationalism, contact problems; 12-a,b,f; 13-e,f, maps; 14-various.

1272. LITERATURE AND REVOLUTION
Skidmore C; MLs & Lits; Saratoga Springs, NY 12866.
Sonja Karsen, Rudolf Sturm
1-ng; 2-3x12; 3-a; 4-74/75; 5-1; 6-every 3rd yr; 7-a; 8-3s; 9-a; 10-none; 11-two-sem course; investigation of important non-Eng, 20th cen writings with a soci or poli bias; 12-a,b,c,f; 13-a,b; 14-primary texts.

1273. GREAT BOOKS: POLITICS AND LITERATURE
U of Wisconsin; Lang & Lit; Green Bay, WI 54302.
1-new; 2-ng; 3-ng; 4-spr 75; 5-1; 6-ng; 7-ng; 8-3; 9-ng; 10-ng; 11-explores the theme of poli action in selected ancient, medieval, and modern works emphasizing the relationship of the individual to the various govts portrayed in lit; 12-ng; 13-ng; 14-ng.

1274. THE ARTIST IN THE POLITICAL ARENA
U of Wisconsin; FL; La Crosse, WI 54601.
Shirley Toek
1 25; 2 3x16; 3-a; 4-73; 5-1; 6-ng; 7-a; 8-3s; 9-a; 10-none; 11-ng; 12-a,b,c,f; 13-ng; 14-primary texts.

1275. LITERATURE AND POLITICS
U of Wisconsin; Comp Lit; Milwaukee, WI 53201.
Davy Carozza
1-48; 2-3x15; 3-a; 4-Jan 72; 5-4; 6-ng; 7-a; 8-2/4s; 9-a; 10-none; 11-analysis of pressures exerted by politics from the creation of lit and by lit upon the world of politics; 12-a,b,f,g; 13-ng; 14-varies.

1276. LITERATURE AND SOCIETY
U of Wisconsin; Comp Lit; Milwaukee, WI 53201.
Davy Carozza
1-166; 2-3x15; 3-a; 4-Jan 72; 5-5; 6-a; 7-a; 8-2/4s; 9-a; 10-none; 11-famous utopias, women and lit, the pop arts and their lit concomitants, great cities in lit, etc.; may be repeated since topic changes; 12-a,b,c,f,g; 13-ng; 14-varies.

See also 1211, 1280, 1287, 1289.

1277. ITALIAN FOLKLORE
Albertus Magnus C; Ital; New Haven, CT 06511.
Juliana D'Amato
1-6; 2-3x10; 3-c; 4-fall 74; 5-1; 6-depends on student requests; 7-a, hope to offer it evenings also; 8-option (3s or no cr); 9-a, in future, will be open to general public, possible in Eng trans; 10-inter prof; 11-folklore, traditions, customs of Italy, investigated by region; 12-a,b,c,d,e,g; 13-a,b,d,e,f, realia; material is gathered by the students through personal interviews with the Ital-born people of New Haven and nearby towns; 14-Toschi, Invito al Folklore italiano; Il Folklore.

1278. PHILOSOPHY IN FRENCH LITERATURE
Allegheny C; MLs; Meadville, PA 16335.
Blair Hanson
1-11; 2-3 70 min hrs x 9½; 3-a; 4-72/73; 5-3; 6-b; 7-a; 8-3½s; 9-a; 10-none; 11-introduces student to several Fr and non-Fr philosophers to show relationship between them & the writings of some Fr litterateurs; 12-a,b,f; 13-ng; 14-students are encouraged to read the books in Fr if they can; primary texts.

1279. MEDIEVAL RUSSIAN SPIRITUALITY
Boston U; MLs; Boston, MA 02215.
Susan Cate
1-ng; 2-3x14; 3-a; 4-70/71; 5-2; 6-b; 7-a; 8-4s; 9-a; 10-intro to Russ lit; 11-survey of Russ lit during the medieval period considered in relation to its Orthodox religious context; intensive reading in Old Russ docs; 12-a,g; 13-ng; 14-ng.

1280. POLITICS AS REALITY AND UTOPIA IN 20th CENTURY LITERATURE
Brandeis U; Rom & Comp Lit; Waltham, MA 02154.
Peter Varkonyi
1-ng; 2-3x10; 3-a; 4-73/74; 5-ng; 6-ng; 7-a; 8-4s; 9-a; 10-knowledge of one FL; 11-examination of the discrepancy between utopian aspirations & poli & soci realities in modern European texts; 12-f; 13-ng; 14-primary texts.

1281. MARX AND RUSSIAN MARXISM
Bryn Mawr C; Philo & Russ Studies; Bryn Mawr, PA 19010.
George L. Kline
1-6; 2-2½x13; 3-a; 4-74/75; 5-1; 6-every second yr on average; 7-a; 8-3s; 9-a; 10-2 philo courses plus first half of this 2 sem course, called Russian Philosophy; 11-intensive study of selected works of Marx, Engels, Plekhanov, Lenin & a critical survey of contemporary Soviet Marxism-Leninism; 12-a,b,c,f; 13-books; 14-ng.

1282. PRACTICE AND THEORY OF MYTH
Bryn Mawr C; Greek; Bryn Mawr, PA 19010.
Mabel L. Lang
1-21; 2-3x13; 3-a; 4-72/73; 5-3; 6-b; 7-a; 8-4s; 9-a; 10-none; 11-Greek & other myths are examined from two points of view: as a testing ground for various approaches to the study & interpretation of myths, both ancient & modern; as raw material for lit exploitation & development; 12-a,b,f; 13-none; 14-various.

1283. RUSSIAN PHILOSOPHY
Bryn Mawr C; Philo & Russ Studies; Bryn Mawr, PA 19010.
George L. Kline
1-6; 2-2½x13; 3-a; 4-67/68; 5-5; 6-every second yr on average; 7-a; 8-3s; 9-a; 10-2 philo courses; 11-critical study of major trends in Russ thought from the 18th cen to present, special attention to ethics, soci philo, philo of hist; first half of 2-sem course of which the second half is called Marx and Russian Marxism; 12-a,b,c,f; 13-books; 14-Edie, Scanlan, Zeldin, & Kline, Russian Philosophy; plus various.

1284. FOLK TRADITION IN ITALIAN LITERATURE
U of California; Ital; Los Angeles, CA 90024.
Giovanni Cecchetti
Cross-referenced in catalog as a folklore course. Further info ng.

1285. FROM BOCCACCIO TO BASILE
U of California; Ital; Los Angeles, CA 90024.
Giovanni Cecchetti
Cross-referenced in catalog as folklore. A study of the origins & development of the Ital novella in its themes, structure, hist context, & European ramifications. Intended for majors in Folklore & Mythology & for students in other depts who wish to become acquainted with either the premises or the growth of similar lit genres. Given in Eng.

1286. TRADITION AND INNOVATION IN ITALIAN CULTURE
U of California; Ital; Los Angeles, CA 90024.
Giovanni Cecchetti
Italy's basic soci structures and cult institutions are delineated through their hist development and then as they are manifest

in the stresses to which the industrial state currently is subject. An upper-div course requiring 16 qtr units Ital for admission. Conducted mainly in Ital.

1287. FICTIONS OF SELF AND THE LANGUAGE OF HISTORY
Cornell U; Rom Studies; Ithaca, NY 14853.
Philip Lewis
1-new; 2-3x14; 3-a; 4-fall 74; 5-1; 6-ng; 7-a; 8-4s; 9-a; 10-ng; 11-critical questions about rhetoric of the self & hist; memory, autobiography, geography of the self and hist, trans, work, utopia, revolution, modernity; 12-a,b,f, taught by four staff members; 13-ng; 14-primary texts.

1287A. GERMANIC MYTHOLOGY
Rutgers U; Ger; Douglass C; New Brunswick, NJ 08903.
Marlene Ciklamini
1-new; 2-3x15; 3-a; 4-spr 75; 5-1; 6-b; 7-a; 8-3s; 9-a,b; 10-none; 11-religious practices & myths of the migration period & Viking age; 12-a,b,c,f; 13-b,e; 14-primary texts; hist and ecclesiastical sources.

1288. SPANISH FOLKLORE
East Stroudsburg SC; FLs; East Stroudsburg, PA 18301.
Aurora Gonzalez
1-19; 2-3x7½; 3-a; 4-74/75; 5-1; 6-b; 7-a; 8-2s; 9-a; 10-none; 11-insight into the characteristic cult ways of Sp-speaking people as expressed in music, tales, dances; peninsular and Latin Amer facets analyzed; 12-a,b,d,f; 13-a,b,d, instruments, realia; 14-ng.

1289. IDEOLOGICAL BACKGROUND OF TOTALITARIANISM
Federal City C; FL; Washington DC 20001.
1-new; 2-3x10; 3-ng; 4-ng; 5-0; 6-ng; 7-a; 8-3q; 9-ng; 10-course in Ger civ; 11-authoritarian & racist currents in men and movements from Romanticism to present; influence of non-Germans; 12-a,b,d,f,g; 13-ng; 14-ng.

1290. IMPACT OF GERMAN THOUGHT AND LETTERS IN AMERICA
Federal City C; FL; Washington DC 20001.
1-new; 2-3x10; 3-ng; 4-ng; 5-0; 6-ng; 7-ng; 8-3q; 9-ng; 10-soph standing; 11-using a comp & selective approach, seeks to show the influence of Ger writers on their Amer counterparts; 12-a,b,c,d,f; 13-ng; 14-ng.

1290A. WOMEN: THEIR SOCIAL IMAGE IN FRENCH AND HISPANIC LITERATURE
Howard U; Rom Langs; Wahington, DC 20059.
Paula G. Lewis, Moraima Donahue
1-20 expected; 2-2x15; 3-a; 4-75; 5-1; 6-either 1 sem per yr or alt yrs; 7-a; 8-3s; 9-a; 10-lang prof, and background in lit and/or civ; students of Eng, hist, soci, poli sci, and psychology can take course with all requirements completed in Eng; 11-the image will be seen as expressing cult stereotypes; in many cases ironic creations of authors or part of prejudiced vision; class discussions in Eng; texts in original or trans; 12-b,f; 13-a,d,e; 14-primary.

1291. SPANISH AMERICAN LITERATURE OF PROTEST
Indiana SU; FL; Terre Haute, IN 47809.
Lomberto Diaz
1-new; 2-3 per wk x sem; 3-a; 4-ng; 5 ng; 6-b; 7-b; 8-3s; 9-a,b; 10-ng; 11-study of contemporary Sp-Amer protest lit pertaining to revolutionary, soci, poli, & religious goals; 12-a,b,c,f; 13-e,f; 14-ng.

1292. LITERATURE AND MYTH IN GERMAN ROMANTICISM
Johns Hopkins U; Ger; Baltimore, MD 21218.
William McClain
1-30; 2-2x13; 3-a; 4-72/73; 5-2; 6-every third year; 7-a; 8-ng; 9-a; 10-inter prof; 11-ideas of Ger romantic writers on the mythopoetic nature of poetic creativity and on representative romantic works which exemplify these ideas; 12-a,b,c,f; 13-b, records; 14-primary texts.

1293. GERMANIC MYTHOLOGY AND FOLKLORE
U of Maryland; Ger & Sl; College Park, MD 20742.
Jere Fleck
1-23; 2-3x15; 3-a; 4-72/73; 5-f; 6-b; 7-a,b; 8-3s; 9-a, part-time students, faculty; 10-none; 11-hist, cult, lit, law; 12-a,f; 13-projects; 14-various.

1294. GERMANIC MYTHOLOGY
U of Massachusetts; Ger; Boston, MA 02125.
Peter Ott
1-65; 2-3x13-14; 3-a; 4-72; 5-3; 6-b; 7-a; 8-4s; 9-a, part-time students; 10-none; 11-ng; 12-a,b,f; 13-b,d; 14-primary texts; instructor-prepared materials.

1295. PROTEST AND REVOLT IN GERMAN LITERATURE
U of Massachusetts; Ger; Boston, MA 02125.
Alfred Hoelzel
1-35; 2-3x14; 3-a; 4-73; 5-1; 6-alt yrs; 7-a; 8-4s; 9-a; 10-none; 11-selective analysis of works since Goethe dealing with themes of protest against established authority ranging from insurrection to revolution; 12-a,b,c,f,g; 13-ng; 14-primary texts.

1296. THE MOVEMENTS OF IDEAS AND LITERATURE DURING THE SECOND EMPIRE
CUNY, Grad Center; Fr; New York, NY 10036.

Henri Peyre
1-ng; 2-2x14; 3-a; 4-72; 5-ng; 6-irregularly; 7-a; 8-4s; 9-a; 10-Ph.D. students; 11-historians & poli thinkers & their relationship to novelists, essayists, & poets; 12-a,c; 13-ng; 14-primary texts.

1297. NATIONAL SCHIZOPHRENIA AND THE MODERN JAPANESE NOVELIST
Oberlin C; Hist; Oberlin, OH 44074.
Ronald J. DiCenzo
1-13; 2-3x13; 3-a; 4-74/75; 5-1; 6-alt yrs; 7-a; 8-3; 9-a; 10-none; 11-colloquium; novels of leading modern writers discussed in terms of the modernization vs tradition problem; 12-b,f; 13-ng; 14-primary texts.

1298. FOLKLORE OF HISPANIC CULTURES
Occidental C; Langs & Ling; Los Angeles, CA 90041.
Eva M. Nieto
1-ng; 2-1x10; 3-ng; 4-ng; 5-1; 6-b; 7-a; 8-1/3q; 9-a; 10-none; 11-aspects of music, art, myth that comprise the folklores of Spain & Sp Amer; 12-a,e,g; 13-records, dance groups, musicians; 14-ng.

1299. THE REBEL IN GERMAN LITERATURE
Occidental C; Langs & Ling; Los Angeles, CA 90041.
Erich Frey
1-9; 2-4x10; 3-a; 4-75; 5-1; 6-alt yrs; 7-a; 8-4s; 9-a; 10-inter prof; 11-examination of works which deal with man's struggle to maintain his individuality; 12-a,b,g; 13-ng; 14-primary texts.

1300. WOMEN IN FRENCH LITERATURE
Occidental C; Langs & Ling; Los Angeles, CA 90041.
Annabelle M. Rea
1-16; 2-4x10; 3-a; 4-wtr 74; 5-2; 6-irregularly; 7-a; 8-1 unit; 9-a; 10-none if given in Eng; inter prof if given in Fr; 11-hist background of women in France from Middle Ages to present; readings, discussion; 12-a,b,c, d,e,f,g; 13-a,e; 14-primary texts.

1301. EXISTENTIALISM IN LITERATURE
U of Pittsburgh; Fr & Ital; Pittsburgh, PA 15260.
F.C. St. Aubyn
1-25; 2-3x15; 3-a; 4-74; 5-1; 6-unknown; 7-a; 8-3s; 9-a; 10-none; 11-readings and discussion; 12-a,b,f, written reports; 13-ng; 14-primary texts.

1302. TEOLOGIA DE LA LIBERACION
Pontifical C Josephinum; Latin Amer Studies; Worthington, OH 43085.
Fina Querol-Kroenberg
1-7; 2-3x16; 3-a; 4-73; 5-1; 6-alt yrs; 7-a; 8-3s; 9-a; 10-inter prof; 11-study of the soci implications, with respect to the Chicano, of the theological development springing from the Latin Amer situation; 12-a,b,c,f,g; 13-e; 14-Gutierrez, Teologia de la Liberacion; Documentos de Medellin.

1303. WORLD LITERATURE
Ripon C; Ger; Ripon, WI 54971.
James F. Hyde, Jr.
1-4; 2-3x16; 3-b; 4-62; 5-7; 6-alt yrs; 7-a; 8-3s; 9-a; 10-freshman Eng; 11-selected works from Western European lit organized about a theme which differs each time course is offered, e.g., the nature of physical reality; 12-b; 13-ng; 14-primary texts.

1304. ALIENATION IN EUROPEAN LITERATURE
Rosary Hill C; MFLs; Buffalo, NY 14226.
G.R. Shchurowsky
1-18; 2-3x13 or 14; 3-a,b; 4-72/73; 5-2; 6-every 2nd or 3rd sem; 7-a,b; 8-3s; 9-a; 10-none; 11-study of alienation on poli, soci, religious levels in Russ, Ger, Sp & Fr lit; 12-a,b,c,f; 13-a,b; 14-various.

1305. FROM HERO TO ANTI-HERO: STUDIES IN EUROPEAN LITERATURE
Rosary Hill C; MFLs; Buffalo, NY 14226.
G. R. Shchurowsky
1-13; 2-3-4x13-14; 3-a; 4-73; 5-1; 6-irregularly; 7-a; 8-3s; 9-a, community; 10-none; 11-study of the development of the 'hero' to 20th-cen 'antihero'; various genres; 12-a,b,c,f; 13-a,b, three faculty members involved; 14-trans of Fr, Ger, Russ, & Sp texts.

1306. NIHILISM IN PHILOSOPHY AND GERMAN LITERATURE OF THE 20th CENTURY
Rosemont C; Langs & Lits; Rosemont, PA 19010.
Erlis Glass
Tentative course for the future; further info ng.

1308. THE MEXICAN ESSAY AND THE CHICANO SEARCH FOR IDENTITY
St. Mary's C; MLs; St. Mary's College, CA 94575.
O. DeSales Perez
1-12; 2-3x15; 3-a; 4-72; 5-2; 6-alt yrs; 7-a; 8-3s; 9-a; 10-ability to read Sp; 11-principal essayists and their search for identity; the correlation, irrelation, misrelation to Mex-Amer thought; 12-a,b,f,g; 13-ng; 14-Ramos, Perfil del hombre y la cultura en Mexico; Paz, Laberinto de la soledad; Fuentes, Tiempo Mexicano; selected essays.

1309. GOTHICISM IN LITERATURE AND ART
Stanford U; Comp Lit & Eng; Stanford, CA 94305.
John Bender
1-10; 2-4x10; 3-a; 4-73/74; 5-1; 6-occasionally; 7-a; 8-5q; 9-a: 10-none; 11-the Gothic

256

and Gothicism prior to 18th cen; the 18th cen; Gothicism and Gothic revival of 19th cen; 12-b,c,d,f; 13-b; 14-primary texts.

1310. THEMES IN HISPANIC CREATIVITY AND THOUGHT
Staten Island CC; MLs; Staten Island, NY 10301.
M.P. Holt
1-new; 2-1x15; 3-a; 4-fall 75; 5-0; 6-a; 7-a,b; 8-1s; 9-a,b; 10-none if offered in Eng, inter prof for lang credit; 11-varied mini-courses on writers, events, regions, problems of Sp-speaking world; 12-a,b,c,d,f,g; 13-a,b,c,e,f; 14-varies.

1311. TOPICS IN FRENCH LITERATURE AND THOUGHT
Staten Island CC; MLs; Staten Island NY 10301.
M.P. Holt
Writers, creative artists, themes. Further info not available.

1312. TOPICS IN ITALIAN LITERATURE AND THOUGHT
Staten Island CC; MLs; Staten Island, NY 10301.
M.P. Holt
Writers, creative artists, themes. Given 2 times per week for 2s credits. In Eng or bilingually; no prerequisite for Eng section, inter prof for bilingual section.

1313. RELIGION IN MEXICAN CULTURE
Trinity U; FLs; San Antonio, TX 78284.
Francisco Garcia
1-12; 2-3x15; 3-b; 4-ng; 5-ng; 6-b; 7-a; 8-3s; 9-a; 10-inter prof; 11-pre-Columbian religions, impact of Sp Catholicism, religious aspects of Mex cult; 12-a,b,g; 13-a,b; 14-primary source materials.

1314. RUSSIAN FOLKLORE
U of Virginia; Sl; Charlottesville, VA 22903.
Natalie K. Moyle
1-25; 2-2½x14; 3-a; 4-75; 5-1; 6-1 sem every other yr; 7-a; 8-3s; 9-a; 10-none; 11-intro survey of Russ folklore; 12-various.

1315. FASCISM AND GERMAN LITERATURE
Washington U; Ger Langs & Lits; St. Louis, MO 63130.
P.U. Hohendahl
1-25; 2-3x14; 3-a; 4-spr 72; 5-2; 6-irregularly; 7-a; 8-3s; 9-a; 10-none; 11-study of the soci hist conditions for the rise of European fascism, particularly in Germany; readings & discussion of a variety of authors; 12-a,b,c,f; 13-e,f; 14-material translated and Xeroxed.

1316. THE HERO IN SCANDINAVIAN TRADITION
U of Washington; Scand; Seattle, WA 98195.
Further info ng.

1317. KIERKEGAARD
U of Washington; Scand; Seattle, WA 98195.
Further info ng.

1318. SCANDINAVIAN FOLKLORE: BELIEFS AND LITERATURE
U of Washington; Scand; Seattle WA 98195.
2 sem course, 3 cr each. Futher info ng.

1319. THE SCANDINAVIAN FOLKTALE
U of Washington; Scand; Seattle WA 98195.
Further info ng.

1320. SCANDINAVIAN MYTHOLOGY
U of Washington; Scand; Seattle WA 98195.
Further info ng.

1321. SWEDENBORG AND MYSTICISM
U of Washington; Scand; Seattle WA 98195.
Further info ng.

1322. THE VIKINGS
U of Washington; Scand; Seattle WA 98195.
Further info ng.

1323. CLASSICAL MYTHOLOGY
Wellesley C; Greek & Latin; Wellesley, MA 02181.
Mary R. Lefkowitz
1-83; 2-140 min x 13; 3-a; 4-62; 5-13; 6-b; 7-a; 8-4s; 9-a & cont ed; 10-ng; 11-reading of myths in primary sources in Greek and Latin lit; supplementary readings in religious hist, ritual, anthro; 12-a,d,f; 13-primary texts.

1324. CHRISTIAN PERSPECTIVES ON FRENCH LITERATURE
Wheaton C; FLs; Wheaton, IL 60187.
John Miles
1-12; 2-4x11; 3-a; 4-73/74; 5-1; 6-alt yrs; 7-a; 8-4q; 9-a,b; 10-reading ability in Fr; 11-critical study from a Christian viewpoint of selected texts & authors from the 16th to the 20th cen; 12-a,b,c,f; 13-ng; 14-primary texts.

1325. BUDDHIST EPISTOMOLOGY
U of Wisconsin; South Asian Studies; Madison, WI 53706.
Geshe Sopa
1-6; 2-3x16; 3-a; 4-69/70; 5-2; 6-every 4 yrs; 7-a; 8-3s; 9-grad standing; 10-2 yrs Tibetan and/or Sanskrit; 1 yr Buddhist philo; 11-examination of Buddhist theories of knowledge; focus on the system of Dignaga and Dharmakirti; 12-a,b,c; 13-ng; 14-Pramanavarttika of Dharmakirti; Tibetan Sanskrit commentaries.

1326. BUDDHIST LOGIC
U of Wisconsin; South Asian Studies; Madison, WI 53706.
Geshe Sopa
1-6; 2-3x16; 3-a; 4-69/70; 5-2; 6-every four

yrs; 7-a; 8-3s; 9-grad standing; 10-2 yrs Tibetan and/or Sanskrit; 1 yr Buddhist philo; 11-Buddhist theories dealing with inference, judgment, syllogism, formal fallacies; Dignaga and Dharmakirti; 12-a,b,c; 13-ng; 14-Pramanavarttika of Dharmakirti; Tibetan and Sanskrit commentaries.

1327. INDIAN PHILOSOPHY
U of Wisconsin; South Asian Studies; Madison, WI 53706.
Geshe Sopa
1-13; 2-3x32; 3-a; 4-73/74; 5-2; 6-alt yrs; 7-a; 8-6s; 9-a; 10-2 yrs Tibetan and/or Sanskrit; 1 yr Buddhist philo; 11-variable contents, e.g., systems of Buddhist philo, Madhyamika system; 12-a,b,d; 13-ng; 14-Dbus ma la 'jug pa.

1328. LITERATURE AND RELIGION
U of Wisconsin; Comp Lit; Milwaukee, WI 53201.
Davy Carozza
1-23; 2-3x15; 3-a; 4-Jan 72; 5-2; 6-ng; 7-a; 8-2-4s; 9-a; 10-none; 11-topic varies from sem to sem; study of the interrelationship of lit & religion across an hist spectrum; 12-a,b,f,g; 13-b,e; 14-varies with topic.

1329. TWENTIETH-CENTURY HUMANITIES
U of Wisconsin; Comp Lit; Milwaukee, WI 53201.
Davy Carozza
1-23; 2-3x15; 3-a; 4-May 74; 5-1; 6-ng; 7-a; 8-3s; 9-a; 10-none; 11-reason & unreason in 20th cen art & thought; 12-a,b,f,g; 13-a,b,d; 14-varies.

1330. UTOPIAN LITERATURE: SCIENCE FICTION
U of Wisconsin; Comp Lit; Milwaukee, WI 53201.
Davy Carozza
1-32; 2-3x15; 3-a; 4-ng; 5-1; 6-ng; 7-a, 8-3s; 9-a; 10-jr standing; 11-ng; 12-a,b,f,g; 13-ng; 14-varies.

1331. NEW TESTAMENT
C of Wooster; Fr; Wooster, OH 44691.
D. Wilkin
1-15; 2-4x10; 3-a; 4-66; 5-6; 6-b; 7-a; 8-1 unit; 9-a; 10-adv prof; 11-descriptive, critical, interpretive study of the New Testament; 12-a,b,c,g; 13-ng; 14-Bible.

1332. OLD TESTAMENT
C of Wooster; Fr; Wooster, OH 44691.
D. Wilkin
1-15; 2-4x10; 3-a; 4-66; 5-6; 6-b; 7-a; 8-1 unit; 9-a; 10-adv prof; 11-descriptive, critical interpretive study of the Old Testament; 12-a,b,c,g; 13-ng; 14-Bible.

1333. INTRODUCTION TO INDO-EUROPEAN LANGUAGES AND FOLKLORE
York C; Langs; York, PA 17405.
Heinz L. Hosch
1-37; 2-3x43; 3-a; 4-73/74; 5-3; 6-a; 7-a; 8-3s; 9-a; 10-none; 11-elem study of origin, development, relationships of the major Indo-European langs; comparative study of their fairy tales, legends, fables, mythology; 12-a,b,f; 13-ng; 14-Pei, The Story of Language; instructor-prepared materials.

See also 1056, 1152, 1178, 1182, 1204, 1266, 1653, 1654, 1660, 1661.

Miscellaneous

1334. LIFE AND THOUGHT IN MODERN FRANCE
California SU; FLs & Lits; Northridge, CA 91324.
Maja Reid
1-ng; 2-3x15; 3-a; 4-fall 72; 5-ng; 6-unknown; 7-a; 8-3s; 9-a; 10-none; 11-study of the ideas and events which have influenced the development of modern Fr intellectual and soci life; emphasis placed on intellectual currents reflected in essays and memoirs; 12-a,b,f; 13-a,d,f; 14-primary texts.

1335. LIFE AND THOUGHT IN MODERN GERMANY
California SU; FLs & Lits; Northridge, CA 91324.
Maja Reid
1-30; 2-3x15; 3-a; 4-72; 5-ng; 6-every 3 or 4 sems; 7-a; 8-3s; 9-a; 10-none; 11-study of the intellectual, cult, and soci trends in 20th cen Germany as reflected in Ger lit; 12-a,b,f; 13-a,d,e; 14-primary texts.

1336. LIFE AND THOUGHT IN MODERN SPAIN

California SU; FLs & Lits; Northridge, CA 91324.
Maja Reid
1-ng; 2-3x15; 3-a; 4-fall 70; 5-ng; 6-unknown; 7-a; 8-3s; 9-a; 10-none; 11-ideas and events which have influenced the development of modern Sp intellectual and soci life; emphasis placed on intellectual currents; 12-a,b,f; 13-a,d,e; 14-Jackson, The Spanish Republic and the Civil War.

1337. STUDIES IN FRENCH LITERATURE
Case Western Reserve U; MLs; Cleveland, OH 44106.
Steven Ungar
1-new; 2-3x13; 3-a; 4-75/76; 5-0; 6-irregularly; 7-a; 8-3s; 9-a; 10-grad standing; 11-two-sem sequence; contemporary lit and psychoanalysis, philo, and music; 12-a,b,c,f,g; 13-ng; 14-not yet decided.

1338. COMPARATIVE STUDIES IN LITERATURE
U of Chicago; Sl Langs & Lits; Chicago, IL 60637.
Edward Wasiolek
For Ph. D. in Comp Lit, students are required to take a national lit oral & a special field exam in some hist period which requires 2 lits & langs; students permitted option of linking study of lit with another discipline of the students' choosing; further info ng.

1339. MODERN TOPICS
U of Cincinnati; Ger Langs and Lits; Cincinnati, OH 45221.
Helga Slessarev
1-8; 2-3x30; 3-a; 4-70; 5-every yr; 6-a; 7-a; 8-3q; 9-a; 10-inter prof; 11-reading course with discussions and papers dealing with materials other than lit; concerned with Ger art, poli, econ, lifestyle, sci, etc. and improvement of lang skills; 12-a,b,c,f,g; 13-b,e,f; travel brochures, official propaganda; 14-Sevin & Sevin, Zur Diskussion; Sparks & Vail, German in Review; Smith & Duncan, Konfrontation: Themen aus der deutschen Presse; dictionary, supplemented by outside materials.

1340. AB/AM PROGRAM IN COMPARATIVE LITERATURE
Clark U; FLs & Lits; Worcester, MA 01610.
Walter Schatzberg
Program offered since 73/74; students required to take six courses in FL beyond inter level & to acquire reading knowledge of a 2nd FL; students are encouraged to pursue lit studies into non-lit fields. Further info ng.

1341. HISPANIC AUTHORS / INTERNATIONAL LITERARY RELATIONS
U of Colorado; FL and Lit; Colorado Springs, CO 80907.
D.R. McKay
1-15/15/15; 2-2½x5; 3-b; 4-70/71; 5-10; 6-a; 7-b; 8-1s; 9-a,b; 10-inter prof; 11-three independent five-week mini-courses offered each sem; content varies every yr; Hemingway in Spain: A biling approach (interdisc with Eng); Feminist writers of Latin Amer; Masterworks of Spanish pornography; 12-a,b,c,g; 13-a,b,e; 14-ng.

1342. MARTIN LUTHER
U of Illinois; Ger Langs & Lits; Urbana, IL 61801.
James M. McGlathery
Further info ng.

1343. HUMANITIES SEMINAR (VARIABLE TOPICS)
Marygrove C; FLs; Detroit, MI 48221.
E. DuBruck
1-20; 2-2x15; 3-a; 4-72; 5-4; 6-b; 7-a; 8-4s; 9-a, part-time; 10-inter prof for lang cr, none for general coll cr; 11-varies by topic; 12-a,b,c,f; 13-a,b,c; 14-varies, also available in Eng trans.

1344. GREEK AND ROMAN SPORTS AND RECREATION
U of Michigan; Cl Studies; Ann Arbor, MI 48104.
Waldo E. Sweet
1-44; 2-4/5x15; 3-a; 4-fall 73; 5-2; 6-b; 7-a; 8-4s; 9-a; 10-none; 11-athletics and recreation in the cult life of the Greco-Roman world, based on ancient sources trans into Eng, visual aids from archaeological evidence, and modern scholarship; 12-a,b; 13-b, pictures; 14-instructor-prepared materials.

1345. LITERATURE AND THE OTHER DISCIPLINES
U of Wisconsin; Comp Lit; Milwaukee, WI 53201.
Davy Carozza
1-ng; 2-3x15; 3-a; 4-Jan 72; 5-ng; 6-ng; 7-a; 8-3s; 9-a; 10-grad standing; 11-relations of lit studies to various academic disciplines; topics vary; 12-a,c,f,g; 13-ng; 14-varies.

See also 203, 1348.

Approach

MEDIATED

Classics

1346. CLASSICAL BACKGROUND OF SCIENTIFIC TERMINOLOGY
Ohio S U; Cl; Columbus, OH 43210.
Mark Morford
1-500; 2-3x10; 3-a; 4-51; 5-every qtr for 23 yrs; 6-a; 7-a; 8-3q; 9-a; 10-none; 11-tech and sci terms from Greek and Latin; word formation and elements, analysis; 12-taught entirely by CAI; 13-ng; 14-Tebben, Medical and Technical Terminology.

1347. BEGINNING LATIN
Stockton SC; Lit/Lang; Pomona, NJ 08240.
Fred Mench
1-10; 2-5x24; 3-a; 4-73/74; 5-1; 6-alt yrs; 7-a; 8-8s; 9-a; 10-none; 11-inductive approach, computer assisted drills, taped drills, 2 sem sequence; 12-b,e,f,g; 13-b,d, filmstrips; 14-Oerberg, Lingua Latina.

French

1348. COMMUNICATION WITH THE FRENCH
Harvard U; Rom Langs & Lits; Cambridge, MA 02138.
Laurence Wylie
1-15; 2-4x13; 3-b; 4-75; 5-1; 6-experimental; 7-a; 8-4s; 9-a; 10-some knowledge of Fr; 11-study & practice of face-to-face interaction; analyzes film clips of communicative situations--verbal expression, spatial relationships, touch, body posture & movement, formal & unconscious gesture, facial expression, eye behavior; relates each situation to its cult & psych context, students learn to reproduce each situation using videotape; 12-a,b,d,e,f; 13-a,c; 14-no specific text.

1349. COMPUTER ASSISTED ELEMENTARY FRENCH
U of Illinois; Fr; Urbana, IL 61801.
N. Gillespie
1-13; 2-4x16; 3-a; 4-68; 5-7; 6-a; 7-a; 8-4s; 9-a; 10-none; 11-2- sem sequence; 12-a,b,e,f; 13-ng; 14-ng.

1350. COMPUTER ASSISTED INTERMEDIATE FRENCH
U of Illinois; Fr; Urbana, IL 61801.
N. Gillespie
1-4; 2-4x16; 3-a; 4-69; 5-6; 6-a; 7-a; 8-4s; 9-a; 10-elem prof; 11-2- sem sequence; includes modern Fr lit & civ; 12-a,b,e,f; 13-ng; 14-ng.

1351. MEDIATED FRENCH
U of Wisconsin Center System; Fr; Baraboo, WI 53913.
Madeleine Wright
1-62; 2-self-paced; 3-a,b; 4-fall 74; 5-1; 6-a; 7-a,b; 8-4s; 9-a,b; 10-none; 11-videotapes, grammar, pronunciation, explanations, exercises, tapes, unit exams; 12-a,e,f,g; 13-c,d; 14-syllabus is text.

See also 89, 103, 1377, 1430, 1432, 1434, 1438.

German

1352. PROGRAMMED GERMAN READING FOR THE PH.D. READING EXAM
U of Delaware; Langs & Ling; Newark, DE 19711.
William McNabb
1-10; 2-1x14; 3-a; 4-60; 5-23; 6-a; 7-a; 8-1s; 9-a; 10-none; 11-programmed instruction in lang lab; 12-e; 13-c; 14-German A. & B. (Behavioral Research Laboratory Programmed Text).

1353. COMPUTER-ASSISTED GERMAN
U of Illinois; Ger Langs & Lits; Urbana, IL 61801.
James M. McGlathery
Elem lang courses being developed; further info ng.

1354. MULTI-MEDIA GERMAN
Loyola C; FLs & Lits; Baltimore, MD 21210.
Randall P. Donaldson
1-8; 2-12x4; 3-a; 4-Jan 74; 5-1; 6-interterm; 7-a; 8-1 unit; 9-a; 10-inter prof; 11-numerous media presentations designed as a point of departure for discussion; 12-b,c,g; 13-a,b,d; 14-Hammond, Fortbildung in der deutschen Sprache.

1355. BEGINNING GERMAN
SUCNY; Foreign Studies Center-Ger Program; Oswego, NY 13126.
Guenther J. Gerlitzki
1-12; 2-10x5; 3-a; 4-70; 5-8; 6-when needed; 7-a,b; 8-3s; 9-a,b, auditors; 10-none; 11-forms & structures; comprehension, speaking, reading, writing; understanding of the people, their country

& cult; TV course; 12-e,g; 13-a,b,c,d,e,f, records; 14-Schneider, Guten Tag; Gerlitzki, Beginning German I.

1356. COMPUTER ASSISTED INSTRUCTION IN GERMAN GRAMMAR
Ohio SU; Ger; Columbus, OH 43210.
Charles W. Hoffman
Deutscher Computer Unterricht & Tutorial Computer developed over period of 3 yrs; started 74; goal of these two programs to provide individualized, highly controlled instruction in Ger grammar for first-yr course. Each program designed to be additional, supplementary ed tool.

1357. GERMAN PROGRAMMED INSTRUCTION
U of Washington; Ger Langs & Lits; Seattle, WA 98195.
George C. Buck
1-50; 2-5x30; 3-a; 4-64; 5-40; 6-a; 7-a,b; 8-0; 9-a,b, grad, hs students, community; 10-none; 11-ng; 12-e,g; 13-d; 14-Ellert & Ellert, Britannica Program.

See also 574, 575, 591, 693, 1388, 1608.

Italian

1358. COMPUTERIZED ITALIAN
U of Minnesota; Fr & Ital; Minneapolis, MN 55455.
Marilyn Schneider
1-new; 2-individualized pacing; 3-a; 4-fall 75; 5-0; 6-a; 7-a; 8-15s; 9-available to any category of student; 10-none; 11-the basic material of a first-year Ital lang course as transcribed to a computer; 12-e,f; 13-c, computer lang tapes; 14-none, just computer material.

Linguistics

1359. LANGUAGE AND SOCIETY
U of Texas; Ling; Austin, TX 78712.
Winfred P. Lehman
1-28; 2-3x15; 3-a; 4-73; 5-4; 6-a; 7-a; 8-3s; 9-a; 10-none; 11-essential part of course is series of computerized ling materials prepared by Solveig Pflueger & Lalita Katre in conjunction with CBE staff. They are designed to permit the student to arrange a self-paced course; 12-a,b,f; 13-a,d; 14-Wolfran & Fasold, Study of Social Dialects in American English; Danes et al., The Speech Chain.

Norwegian

See 1452.

Polish

See 1453.

Russian

1360. ELEMENTARY & INTERMEDIATE RUSSIAN
Gallaudet C; Russ; Washington, DC 20002.
Charles H. Yeager
1-7 (elem), 4 (inter); 2-1x15; 3-a; 4-73/74; 5-2; 6-b; 7-a; 8-3s; 9-a; 10-none; 11-computer-based course; 4-sem sequence; 12-f; 13-computer, teletype; 14-handouts; material based on Silman & Harkins, Introductory Russian Grammar.

1361. RUSSIAN CIVILIZATION AND CULTURE
Purdue U; FLs & Lits; West Lafayette, IN 47907.
William Buffington
1-12; 2-3xng; 3-a; 4-fall 73; 5-3; 6-a; 7-a,b; 8-3s; 9-a, general public; 10-none; 11-45 ½ hr lectures recorded on videotape & broadcast over local cable system, course created especially for T.V. & for the broad spectrum of the viewing audience; univ students receive cr by taking the final exam; 12-a, f; 13-all; 14-none.

1362. COMPUTER-AIDED ELEMENTARY RUSSIAN
Rutgers U; Sl Langs & Lits; New Brunswick, NJ 08903.
William W. Derbyshire
1-50; 2-5x15; 3-a; 4-74/75; 5-1; 6-b; 7-a; 8-4s; 9-a,b; 10-none; 11-review sessions & supplementary drills for course conducted at computer terminal; 12-a,g; 13-computer; 14-Rudy et al, Russian: A Complete Elementary Guide.

See also 1454, 1455.

Spanish

1363. SPANISH
Tarrant County JC; FLs; Hurst, TX 76053.
Jane Harper
1-323 in several classes; 2-3x16; 3-a; 4-spr 74; 5-2; 6-a; 7-a,b; 8-4s; 9-a, auditors; 10-none; 11-fundamentals of Sp, emphasis on audiolingual presentation; 12-a,b,c,e,g; 13-a,b,c,d,e,f, small group sessions, peer tutors; 14-EMC Corp., Zarabanda.

See also 89, 323, 406, 636, 1462, 1463, 1464.

Multi-language

1364. MULTI-MEDIA LANGUAGE COURSES
American U; Lang & Foreign Studies; Washington, D.C. 20016.
Gisela Huberman, Vadim Medish
Further info ng.

See also 1471, 1476, 1477.

Miscellaneous

See 1019.

INTENSIVE/IMMERSION

Chinese

1365. INTENSIVE BEGINNING CHINESE
Connecticut C; Chi; New London, CT
06320.
Charles J. Chu
1-ng; 2-10x13; 3-a; 4-65; 5-c20; 6-a; 7-a; 8-
8s; 9-a; 10-ng; 11-ng; 12-b,e,g; 13-d,e,f; 14-
Speak Mandarin; Read Chinese.

1366. FALCON (CHINESE)
Cornell U; MLs & Ling; Ithaca, NY 14850.
John McCoy
1-12; 2-30 per wk all yr; 3-a; 4-72; 5-in 3rd
yr; 6-a; 7-a; 8-16s; 9-a; 10-consent; 11-
allows student to devote full, uninterrupted
attention to learning Chi over relatively
short period of time; brings him to a level of
competence that is at least the equivalent
of several yrs of part-time study, often
more; all drill sessions conducted by native
speakers; 12-all; 13-all; 14-De Francis,
Biginning Chinese Reader; Huang, Twenty
Lectures on Chinese Culture; Yale Series,
Read Chinese, Bk. III; Mills, Intermediate
Reader In Chinese; Peking, Han Yo Du Ben.

English as a Second Language

1367. ENGLISH AS A SECOND LANGUAGE
Monterey Inst of Foreign Studies; ESL;
Monterey, CA 93940.
Sandra Schachter
Program designed for foreign students; lang
& cult of U.S.; students follow Eng
curriculum of 4 hrs of classroom work, 1 hr
of lang lab per day, 5 days per wk for 1 sem;
to   ensure   fluency,   most   students
encouraged to study Eng for full academic
yr.

French

1368. INTENSIVE FRENCH
Bowling Green SU; Rom Langs; Bowling
Green, OH 43403.
Clifford J. Gallant
1-22; 2-20x10; 3-a; 4-wtr 75; 5-1; 6-on
demand, preferably initiating a series in Fr;
7-a; 8-16q; 9-a; 10-none; 11-elem & inter
Fr;   12-a,b,c,d,e,g;   13-a,b,c,d,   cult
activities; 14-Hansen & Wilkins, Le
Francaise Vivant and workbook; Easy
French Reader.

1369. INTENSIVE FRENCH
Earlham C; Langs; Richmond, IN 47374.
Guy Mentha
1-18; 2-15x10; 3-a; 4-72; 5-3; 6-b; 7-a; 8-3q;

9-a; 10-none; 11-3 hrs per day of
conversation, grammar, vocab, tapes, visit
to France; 12-g; 13-a,b,c,d,e; 14-Benamou,
Mise en Train.

1370. LA FRANCE ENTRE GUERRES
Evergreen SC; FLs; Olympia, WA 98505.
Susan Fiksdal
1-30; 2-35x6; 3-b,c; 4-smr 75; 5-1; 6-every
smr; 7-a,b; 8-16q; 9-a,b; 10-beg no
requirement; inter 1-2 yrs coll lang;
advanced 3-4 yrs coll lang; 11-total
immersion, incl lang dorms, grammar,
conversation, lit, art hist, soci hist; evening
workshops in folk dancing, folk singing,
cuisine, and talks by native speakers,
emphasis on the Dadaists and Surrealists;
12-a,b,c,d,e,g; 13-a,b,d,e,f; 14-Ostyn & Le
Texier, Fluent Spoken French; Valette,
France: A Cultural Review; plus others not
yet chosen.

1371. TOTAL IMMERSION IN FRENCH
Lowell U (South Campus); Langs; Lowell,
MA 01854.
Joseph Garreau, Robert Bousquet
1-to be offered; 2-15x16; 3-a; 4-75/76; 5-0;
6-b; 7-a; 8-15s; 9-a; 10-inter prof; 11-
conversation, lit advanced-5 contact hrs;
composition, advanced-4 contact hrs;
phonetics and diction-3 contact hrs "Sound
and Light"-5 contact hrs advanced
grammar & syntax-5 contact hrs; 12-
a,b,c,d,e,g; 13-a,b,c,d,e, filmstrips, radio;
14-not yet determined.

1372. EN FRANCAIS, S'IL VOUS PLAIT
U of Maryland; MLs; Baltimore, MD 21228.
Claud DuVerlie
1-34; 2-16x4 (25 would be closer to reality
since many activities were not officially
scheduled); 3-c (natives); 4-72; 5-2; 6-Jan
session; 7-a; 8-4s; 9-a, community; 10-elem
prof; 11-immersion experience; open
classroom framework to make possible cult
activities, group and individual projects at
all levels of ability and in any area of
personal   interest;   12-b,c,d,e,g;   13-
a,b,c,d,e,f, field trips; 14-taught in Lang
Media Center, with c300 books divided into
levels of Fr, a place for reference tools,
newspapers.

1373. EXPERIMENTAL FRENCH
Miami U; Fr & Ital; Oxford, OH 45056.
L.F. Luce
1-25; 2-4x11; 3-a; 4-fall 74; 5-1; 6-a; (it is a
3-qtr sequence); 7-a; 8-4q; 9-a; 10-students
must be ready to accept heavy workload
first 3 wks of course; 11-core of
grammatical structure is given the first 3
wks; next 3 wks concentration on oral work;
last 3 wks reading writing; 12-a,b,c,d,e,g;
13-ng; 14-chosen by instructors.

1374. FLASH FRENCH
U of New Mexico; Mod & Cl Langs;

262

Albuquerque, NM 87131.
Truett Book
1-13; 2-15x1 sem; 3-a; 4-72; 5-5; 6-a,b,
formerly every sem, now 1st sem only; 7-a;
8-15s; 9-a; 10-ng; 11-five sems of Fr done in
1 sem; student normally takes no other
courses; 12-a,b,c,d,e,g; 13-a,b,d; 14-
Swanson & Book, Elements of French;
Kretsch, Images et Reflets Litteraires;
Valette, France: A Cultural Review
Grammar; Ellis, Prose Classique; Mondelli,
French Conversational Review Grammar;
Butor, L'Art de Michel Butor; Hammond,
Creative French; Myron, Perspectives.

1375. BEGINNING FRENCH
San Diego Mesa C; FLs; San Diego, CA
92111.
J. Michael Moore
1-25; 2-8x16; 3-a; 4-70; 5-1; 6-a; 7-a; 8-8s;
9-a; 10-none; 11-total immersion, taught
entirely in FL; 12-a,b,c,d,e,g; 13-
a,b,c,d,e,f, field trips, food sampling,
singing; 14-ng.

1376. INTERMEDIATE FRENCH
San Diego Mesa C; FLs; San Diego, CA
92111.
J. Michael Moore
1-25; 2-8x16; 3-a; 4-70; 5-1; 6-a; 7-a; 8-8s;
9-a; 10-elem prof; 11-total immersion,
taught entirely in the FL; 12-a,b,c,d,e,g;
13-a,b,c,d,e,f, field trips, food sampling,
singing; 14-ng.

1377. ELEMENTARY FRENCH I & II
Tarrant County JC; MFL; Fort Worth, TX
76119.
E. Guzman
1-20; 2-25½x4; 3-a; 4-smr 74; 5-1; 6-each
smr; 7-a; 8-8s; 9-a; 10-none; intensive, self-
paced, continuous progress approach; 12-
individualized packages; 13-multi-media;
14-ng.

1378. INTENSIVE FRENCH
Washington SU; FLs & Lits; Pullman, WA
99163.
Joseph Labat
1-38; 2-40x8; 3-a; 4-74; 5-1; 6-smr only; 7-
a; 8-10s; 9-a; 10-none; 11-provides active
knowledge of the four lang skills; 12-
a,b,c,d,e,g; 13-a,b,e,f, songs; 14-Mauger,
Le Francais Accelere; Lenard & Lester, L
'Art de la Conversation; Sartre, Les Jeux
Sont Fait; Valette, France.

1379. INTENSIVE FRENCH
West Georgia C; FLs; Carrollton, GA
30117.
Warner Blumenthal
1-33; 2-20x10; 3-a; 4-71; 5-5; 6-b; 7-a; 8-
15q; 9-a; 10-none; 11-intro to cult and lang
with emphasis on the inseparability of both;
readings in arts and scis; 12-a,e,f,g; 13-b,d,e;
14-Hansen et al, Le Francais Vie (text and
workbook).

1380. PRACTICAL FRENCH
U of Wisconsin; FL; Platteville, WI 53818.
John G.W. Robertson
1-13; 2-1x16; 3-a,c; 4-69; 5-5; 6-a; 7-this is
dormitory lang "wing," students speak FL in
dorm; 8-1s; 9-a; 10-speaking knowledge of
lang; 11-varies from slides to actual course
content of other courses, guest speakers,
FL club activities, inventories of rooms and
clothing, personal belongings, speaking FL
while in the FL dorm wing area; 12-
a,b,c,d,e,g; 13-a,b,c,d,e,f; 14-ng.

See also 191, 193, 526, 1159, 1158.

German

1381. ELEMENTARY READING COURSE
Columbia U; Ger; New York, NY 10027.
Inge D. Halpert
1-67; 2-2x14; 3-a; 4-50; 5-every yr; 6-a; 7-
a,b; 8-0; 9-a,b; 10-jr, sr, grad; 11-rapid
survey of grammar and extensive reading
program; for those with one yr to study the
lang; 12-g; 13-e,f; 14-Fehling & Paulsen,
Elementary German; Goedsche & Glaettli,
Sutter, Carl Schurz, Beethoven.

1382. INTERMEDIATE INTENSIVE READING
COURSE
Columbia U; Ger; New York, NY 10027.
Inge D. Halpert
1-53; 2-2x14; 3-a; 4-50; 5-every yr; 6-a; 7-
a,b; 8-0; 9-a,b; 10-jr, sr, grad; 11-non-
fictional readings from a variety of fields
other than the natural and pure scis, vocab
building and stress on syntax; 12-g; 13-e,f;
14-Bergethon, Grammar for Reading
German, Form B; Heller et al, German
Essays and Expository Prose.

1383. INTENSIVE GERMAN COURSE
U of Connecticut; Ger & Sl Langs; Storrs,
CT 06268.
Herbert Lederer, Stephen J. Kaplowitt
1-12; 2-20x14; 3-a; 4-73; 5-3; 6-b; 7-a; 8-
16s; 9-a,b; 10-none; 11-covers work
normally done during 2 yrs in 1 sem;
students enrolled do not register for any
other course; 12-b,e,g; 13-a,b,d; 14-Feld et
al, Anfang und Fortschritt; workbook for
this text; Goedsche & Glaetti, Sutter,
Thomas Mann, Beethoven; Loram & Phelps,
Querschnitt; Durrenmatt, Die Physiker;
Goedsche & Spann, German Oral Practice.

1384. TOTAL IMMERSION GERMAN CAMP
Hendrix C; ML; Conway, AR 72032.
Hal Allen
1-35; 2-up to 24 hrs per day for 9 days; 3-a;
4-fall 72; 5-3; 6-before 1st term of school;
7-total immersion; 8-3 1/3s; 9-students,
faculty, others of coll age; 10-none; 11-
total functioning in Ger; 12-a,b,c,d,e,g; 13-
a,b,d,e,f, total environment; 14-ng.

1385. BEGINNING GERMAN

263

San Diego Mesa C; FLs; San Diego, CA 92111.
J. Michael Moore
1-25; 2-8x16; 3-a; 4-70; 5-1 per sem; 6-a; 7-a; 8-8s; 9-a; 10-none; 11-total immersion, taught entirely in FL contact with native speakers; 12-a,b,c,d,e,g; 13-a,b,c,d,e,f, field trips, singing; 14-ng.

1386. INTERMEDIATE GERMAN
San Diego Mesa C; FLs; San Diego, CA 92111.
J. Michael Moore
1-25; 2-8x16; 3-a; 4-70; 5-1 each sem; 6-a; 7-a; 8-8s; 9-a; 10-elem prof; 11-total immersion, taught entirely in FL; 12-a,b,c,d,e,g; 13-a,b,c,d,e,f, field trips, food sampling, singing; 14-ng.

1387. GERMAN SEMESTER
U of Southern California; Ger; Los Angeles, CA 90007.
Rudolf Hirschmann
1-32; 2-16x15; 3-b,c; 4-73; 5-1; 6-once in 2 yrs; 7-a; 8-16s; 9-a; 10-3 or 4 sem of Ger; 11-Ger lang (standard Ger, colloquial Ger, phonetics); Ger lit; soci studies (hist of Germany, Austria & Switzerland from 1880 to present; between East & West; contemporary soci and poli structures of the Ger-speaking countries); art & music; sci, philo, & psych; 12-a,b,c,g; 13-all, guest lecturers from Europe; 14-ng.

1388. INTENSIVE GERMAN
Washington SU; FLs & Lits; Pullman, WA 99163.
Gertrud Mazur
1-48; 2-40x8; 3-a; 4-71; 5-4; 6-smrs; 7-a; 8-10s; 9-a; 10-none; 11-modified total immersion approach; 12-a,b,c,d,e,g; 13-a,b,e,f, realia; 14-Schultz et al, Deutsche Sprachlehre fuer Amerikaner; Zobel, Deutsche Schwaenke; Hagboldt, Allerlei; Weiss & Anderson, Begegnung mit Deutschland; Guten Tag films.

1389. INTENSIVE GERMAN
West Georgia C; FLs; Carrollton, GA 30117.
Warner Blumenthal, Mr. Sapp
1-20; 2-20x10; 3-a; 4-71; 5-3; 6-b; 7-a; 8-15q; 9-a; 10-none; 11-emphasis on the oral/aural method; 3 qtrs covered in one; complete immersion; 12-a,e,f,g; 13-a,b,d,e, native speakers; 14-Schutz et al, Auf deutsch, bitte!

See also 214, 568, 569, 1184, 1185, 1186.

Greek

1390. THE GREEK WORKSHOP
U of California; Cl; Berkeley, CA 94720.
Thomas G. Rosenmeyer
1-24; 2-30x10; 3-a; 4-72; 5-3; 6-each smr;

7-a; 8-15q; 9-a, grad students; 10-none; 11-intro to cl Greek, structure, idiom, and hist of the lang, reading of ancient texts; 12-a,f; 13-handouts prepared by director; 14-Plato, Ion; Euripides, Alcestis; additional poetry and prose.

Hebrew

1391. HEBREW
Brandeis U; Near Eastern & Judaic Studies; Waltham, MA 02154.
Nahum Sarna
1-32; 2-6x13; 3-a; 4-ng; 5-74/75; 6-annually; 7-a; 8-ng; 9-a; 10-none; 11-grammar, vocab, oral & written work; 12-a,b,e,g; 13-c,d,e; 14-modern Hebrew lit, Jewish philo, and modern press.

Italian

1392. INTENSIVE ITALIAN: FOR ROMANCE LANGUAGE MAJORS AND MINORS
U of Minnesota; Fr & Ital; Minneapolis, MN 55455.
Marilyn Schneider
1-11; 2-4x10; 3-a; 4-72; 5-3; 6-b; 7-a; 8-5q; 9-a; 10-2 yrs Rom lang study; 11-grammar covered through comparative study of Fr, Sp, and Ital grammar; oral and reading practice; 12-b,c,d,e,f,g; 13-e; 14-Cioffari, Italian Review Grammar & Composition; Heatwole, A Comparative Practical Grammar of French, Spanish & Italian.

1393. BEGINNING ITALIAN
San Diego Mesa C; FLs; San Diego, CA 92111.
J. Michael Moore
1-25; 2-8x16; 3-a; 4-70; 5-1 each sem; 6-a; 7-a; 8-8s; 9-a; 10-none; 11-total immersion, taught entirely in FL; 12-a,b,c,d,e,g; 13-a,b,c,d,e,f, field trips, food sampling, singing; 14-ng.

See also 599.

Japanese

1394. FALCON (JAPANESE)
Cornell U; MLs & Ling; Ithaca, NY 14850.
Eleanor H. Jorden (Japanese)
1-14; 2-30 per wk all yr; 3-a; 4-72; 5-in 3rd yr; 6-a; 7-a; 8-16s; 9-a; 10-consent; 11-allows student to devote full uninterrupted attention to learning Jap over relatively short period of time; brings him to a level of competence that is at least the equivalent of several yrs of part-time study, often more; all drill sessions conducted by native speakers; 12-all; 13-all; 14-Jorden, Reading Japanese; Chaplin & Martin, A Manual of Japanese Writing.

1395. INTENSIVE JAPANESE
U of Washington; Asian Langs; Seattle, WA 98195.

264

Tamako Niwa
1-15; 2-30x10; 3-a; 4-62; 5-13 plus smr qtrs; 6-entire sequence is offered yearly; 7-a; 8-15q; 9-a,b,c; 10-none; 11-1st qtr: basic Jap taught through the oral-aural method; covers fundamental grammer, Hiragana and about 100 characters are introduced; 2nd qtr: reading emphasized, oral conversation; 3rd qrtr: reading, tapes, and lectures in Jap; 12-a,b,e,g; 13-b,d,f; 14-Niwa, First Course in Japanese; Hibbett & Itasaka, Modern Japanese, A Basic Reader.

See also 1560, 1561.

Latin

1396. THE LATIN WORKSHOP
U of California; Cl; Berkeley, CA 94720.
Thomas G. Rosenmeyer
1-37; 2-30x10; 3-a; 4-67; 5-8; 6-each smr; 7-a; 8-15q; 9-primarily grad students; 10-none; 11-designed to enable M.A. and Ph.D. candidates in other fields to pass dept requirements & to read and interpret Latin; grammar, reading, techniques in lit/criticism, intro to quantitative rhythm & scansion; 12-a,f; 13-handouts prepared by director; 14-Moreland, Latin: An Intensive Course; Vergil, Aeneid IV; Horace, Odes; Catullus, Poems; Cicero, Somnium Scipionis.

Latvian

1397. SUMMER LATVIAN LANGUAGE PROGRAM (5 COURSES)
Western Michigan U; Ling; Kalamazoo, MI 49001.
Robert A. Palmatier
1-110; 2-8x7½; 3-c; 4-smr 70; 5-5 smrs; 6-smr; 7-a; 8-4s; 9-a,b, guest students; 10-none for basic (505); 505 for inter (506); 506 for adv (507); 507 for both reading and writing; 11-structure of lang, phonetics, vocab, reading, conv, writing; 12-a,b,c,d,e,f,g; 13-b,d,e,f; 14-materials designed by teaching faculty.

Portuguese

1398. ACCELERATED FIRST-YEAR PORTU-GUESE
U of Texas; Sp & Port; Austin, TX 78712.
Phyllis Harmon
1-13; 2-6x14; 3-a; 4-61/62; 5-19; 6-a; 7-a; 8-6s; 9-a; 10-consent; 11-covers first yr of the lang; designed primarily for lang majors or other students of high academic standing or exceptional lang ability; 12-a,f,g; 13-d; 14-Ellison et al, Modern Portuguese.

See also 748.

Russian

1399. THE RUSSIAN PRACTICUM

Columbia U; Sl Langs; New York, NY 10027.
Robert L. Belknap
1-15; 2-40x8; 3-c; 4-72; 5-3; 6-every smr; 7-a; 8-8s; 9-a; 10-3rd yr Russ or equiv; 11-reading, conv, comp & syntax, comp & correspondence, lang of Soviet soci sci; lang of Russian prose & poetry; objective of courses to give scholars and other professions the lang they need to deal actively with their Soviet counterparts; 12-a,b,c,d,g; 13-a,b,e,f; 14-varies.

1400. RUSSIAN CERTIFICATE PROGRAM
Indiana U; Sl; Bloomington, IN 47401.
Pamela Hawks
1-16; 2-25x10; 3-c; 4-smr 72; 5-3; 6-every smr; 7-a; 8-10s; 9-a, high school teachers; 10-3 yrs coll Russ; placement exam; 11-concentrated instruction in grammar and structural analysis, phonetics, oral comprehension and fluency, vocab through reading and lang control through comp, housing in Russ Lang House; 12-a,b,c,g; 13-a,e,f; 14-ng.

See also 150, 151, 1563.

Spanish

1401. SPANISH HOUSE
Beaver C; FLs; Glenside, PA 19038.
Gerardo Rodriguez
1-5; 2-30x4; 3-a; 4-73; 5-1; 6-every 2 yrs; 7-dorm arrangement; 8-b; 9-a; 10-some knowledge of Sp; 11-ng; 12-a,c,d,g; 13-a,b,e,f, records, games; 14-none.

1402. INTENSIVE SPANISH
Cabrillo C; Sp; Aptos, CA 95003.
Joanne Allen
1-35; 2-16x16; 3-a; 4-72; 5-5; 6-a; 7-a; 8-16s; 9-a; 10-none; 11-equivalent of first 4 sems in one sem; native speakers as conv session leaders; conv session 8 hrs week; 12-b,d,e,f,g; 13-b,c,e,f,g; 14- Anderson, Basic Spanish; Da Silva, On With Spanish; Matute, Doce Historias de la Artanila; Pimsleur, Sol y Sombra; Da Silva, Voces de Manana; various mimeo materials.

1403. INTENSIVE SPANISH
Earlham C; Langs; Richmond, IN 47374.
Guy Mentha
1-18; 2-15x10; 3-a; 4-72; 5-4; 6-b; 7-a; 8-3q; 9-a; 10-none; 11-3hrs per day of conv, grammar, vocab, tapes, working with Sp-speaking student instructors; visit to Sp-speaking country; 12-g; 13-a,b,c,d,e; 14-Segreda & Harris, Listening, Speaking, Reading, Writing.

1404. ESPANA Y AMERICA DEL SUR ENTRE LAS GUERRAS
Evergreen SC; FLs; Olympia, WA 98505.

Susan Fiksdal
1-30; 2-35x6; 3-b,c; 4-smr 75; 5-1; 6-smr; 7-a,b; 8-16q; 9-a,b; 10-beg none, inter 1-2 yrs college lang, advanced: 3-4 yrs college lang; 11-total immersion, including lang dorms, grammar, conv, lit, art hist, soci hist; evening workshops in folk dancing, folk singing, cuisine, and talks by native speakers, emphasis on Sp Civil War & its effects in Latin Am; 12-a,b,c,d,e,g; 13-a,b,c,d,e,f; 14-Osborne, Voces y Vistas; plus books not yet chosen.

1405. SPANISH LIVE-IN
Lenoir Rhyne C; MLs; Hickory, NC 28601.
Robert Eckard
1-9; 2-total immersion for 4 weeks; 3-c (as resource people & informants); 4-75; 5-none; 6-once every 3-5 yrs as interim offering probable; 7-a,b; 8-4; 9-a; 10-completion of 1st yr Sp; 11-conv, singing, written and oral presentation, vocab; 12-a,b,c,d,g; 13-a,b,c,d,e,f, games, radio, 14-no text.

1406. INTENSIVE ELEMENTARY SPANISH
Lone Mountain C; Sp; San Francisco, CA 94118.
M.P. Valdes
1-10; 2-12x15; 3-a; 4-69/70; 5-6; 6-b; 7-a; 8-8s; 9-a, part-time; 10-none; 11-pronunciation, vocab, grammar, hist of Spain and Latin Amer; emphasis on oral skill; 12-b,c,d,e,g; 13-b,c,d; 14-Turk & Espinosa, Foundation Course in Spanish; Sedwick, Conversation in Spanish: Points of Departure.

1407. TOTAL IMMERSION IN SPANISH
Lowell U; Langs; Lowell, MA 01854.
Joseph Garreau, Robert Bousquet
1-to be offered; 2-15x16; 3-a; 4-75/76; 5-0; 6-b; 7-a; 8-15s; 9-a; 10-inter prof; 11-conv, adv Sp 5 contact hrs; comp, adv Sp-4 contact hrs; phonetics & diction-3 contact hrs; lit of 20th cen 3 contact hrs; "Sound & Light"-5 contact hrs; adv grammar & syntax-5 contact hrs; 12-a,b,c,d,e,g; 13-a,b,c,d,e,f, filmstrips, radio; 14-ng.

1408. IMMERSION IN PUERTO RICAN CULTURE
Manchester CC; FLs; Manchester, CT 06040.
Toby Tamarkin
1-23; 2-12x1; 3-c; 4-72; 5-3; 6-b; 7-spr break; 8-2; 9-a,b,c; 10-none; 11-preparation of series of minidramas depicting cross-cult conflicts as noted by students, recorded in their daily diaries, and discussed by them in small group sessions each day; 12-f,g; 13-first-hand info and items through pre-planned activities; 14-no texts; written handouts about the hist of Puerto Rico and some of the cult concepts to be studied.

1409. TOTAL IMMERSION PROGRAM IN SPANISH
Northern Arizona U; ML; Flagstaff, AZ 86001.
Orazio Giusti
1-14; 2-40x1 sem; 3-a; 4-spr 74; 5-1; 6-b; 7-a; 8-19s; 9-a; 10-none; 11-ng; 12-a,b,c,e,g; 13-a,b,e,f, evening cult activities; 14-MLA, Modern Spanish; Da Silva, On With Spanish; Duran & Duran, Vivir Hoy.

1410. SUMMER IMMERSION COURSE IN SPANISH
Rockland CC; FLs & Lits; Suffern, NY 10901.
Norman D. Arbaiza
1-14; 2-27½x9; 3-a; 4-smr 74; 5-1; 6-every smr; 7-a; 8-12 (for entire course, but students may register for 1st or 2nd half); 9-a,b, adults; 10-none; 11-full-day program with a lunch break during which the students speak Sp; 12-a,b,c,d,e; 13-a,d,e, field trips; 14-ng.

1411. BEGINNING SPANISH
San Diego Mesa C; FLs; San Diego, CA 92111.
J. Michael Moore
1-25; 2-8x16; 3-a; 4-70; 5-1 each sem; 6-a; 7-a; 8-8s; 9-a; 10-none; 11-total immersion, taught entirely in FL; contact with native speakers; assignments to Sp speaking families for reports; 12-a,b,c,d,e,g; 13-a,b,c,d,e,f, field trips, food sampling, singing; 14-ng.

1412. INTERMEDIATE SPANISH
San Diego Mesa C; FLs; San Diego, CA 92111.
J. Michael Moore
1-25; 2-8x16; 3-a; 4-70; 5-1 each sem; 6-a; 7-a; 8-8s; 9-a; 10-elem prof; 11-total immersion, taught entirely in the FL; 12-a,b,c,d,e,g; 13-a,b,c,d,e,f, field trips; 14-ng.

1413. ELEMENTARY SPANISH I & II
Tarrant County JC; MFL; Fort Worth, TX 76119.
Ernesto Guzman
1-28; 2-25½x4; 3-a; 4-smr 74; 5-1; 6-smr or mini semester; 7-a; 8-8s; 9-a; 10-none; 11-intensive, self-paced, continuous progress approach; 12-g; 13-multi-media; 14-Spanish ILS package, Basic Spanish I & II.

1414. INTENSIVE SPANISH
U of Texas; FL and Ling; Arlington, TX 76019.
Norman A. Whitlock
1-22; 2-20x15; 3-a; 4-71; 5-5; 6-b; 7-a; 8-14s; 9-a; 10-none; 11-intensive study of 4 sems of lang; 12-a,b,e,f,g; 13-a,b,c,d,e,f; 14-Settgast and Anderson, Basic Spanish; Sol y Sombra; Visiones de Latinoamerica.

1415. ACCELERATED BEGINNERS' SPANISH

U of Texas; Sp & Port; Austin, TX 78712.
Phyllis Harmon
1-36; 2-6x14; 3-a; 4-61/62; 5-17; 6-a; 7-a; 8-6s; 9-a; 10-consent of the coordinator of lower-div Sp; 11-covers the first yr of the lang. Primarily designed for lang majors or other students of high academic standing and/or exceptional lang ability; 12-a,f,g; 13-d; 14-Wolfe, Curso Basico de Espanol; Pimsleur, Sol y Sombra.

1416. ACCELERATED SECOND-YEAR SPAN-ISH
U of Texas; Sp & Port; Austin, TX 78712.
Phyllis Harmon
1-38; 2-6x14; 3-a; 4-48/49; 5-17; 6-a; 7-a; 8-6s; 9-a; 10-Sp 604 with a grade of B or 407 with a grade of A; consent of coordinator required; 11-covers second yr of the lang; primarily for lang majors or students of high academic standing or exceptional lang ability; 12-a,g; 13-d; 14-Phillips & Marquez, Visiones de Latinoamerica; Casona, La Dama del Alba; Wolfe, Curso Intermedio de Espanol.

1417. MEXICAN-AMERICAN LANGUAGE (INTENSIVE)
Texas A & I U; Ethnic Studies; Corpus Christi, TX 78411.
Leonardo Carrillo
1-new; 2-ng; 3-a; 4-ng; 5-new; 6-b; 7-ng; 8-6s; 9-a, public servants; 10-none; 11-equivalent of 2 sems in one; Sp spoken by South Texans as a vital form of communication; humanistic approach designed to broaden understanding of Texas' unique cult; 12-e,g; 13-b,d; 14-none.

1418. INTENSIVE SPANISH
West Georgia C; FLs; Carrollton, GA 30117.
Kenneth Bunting
1-ng; 2-20x9; 3-a; 4-71; 5-4; 6-c; 7-a; 8-15q; 9-a; 10-none; 11-total immersion program; approx equal time given to conv, structure, lab and cult activities; 12-a,b,e,f,g; 13-a,b,d, books on music and fine arts; 14-Kasten and Neale-Silva, A Lo Vivo; readers vary.

1419. AN INTENSIVE PROGRAM IN CONVERSATIONAL SPANISH
William Paterson C; FL; Wayne, NJ 07470.
Catherine A. Barry
1-13; 2-4 per wk per one yr; 3-a; 4-74; 5-1; 6-every yr; 7-b; 8-3s; 9-a,b; 10-none; 11-intro to lang in U.S. today, pronunciation, conv, vocab related to community use, Hispanic Amer cult; 12-a,b,c,e,g; 13-c,d,f; 14-Turk & Espinosa, Foundation Course in Spanish; Del Rio & Hespelt, Lecturas Hispanicas.

See also 88, 258, 263, 313, 396, 631, 675, 1080, 1465, 1191, 1192.

Multi-Language

1420. TOTAL IMMERSION PROGRAMS: IN GERMAN, FRENCH, RUSSIAN
U of Maine; FLs; Orono, ME 04473.
Josef Roggenbauer
1-25; 2-24x3; 3-a; 4-smr 74; 5-1; 6-smr; 7-ng; 8-3q; 9-a; 10-inter or equivalent; 11-curriculum mainly cult, although some formal work will be conducted. Pledge to use FL exclusively for duration of course must be signed by each participant; 12-b,c,d,g; 13-a,b,c,d,e,f, songs, skits, games, plays; ng.

1421. INTENSIVE LANGUAGE PROGRAMS
Middlebury C; Sunderland Language Center; Middlebury VT 05753.
Roger M. Peel
Smr courses for grad credit: Fr, Ger, Ital, Russ, Sp. Courses for undergraduate credit in Chi, Greek, Ger, Ital, Jap, Russ, Sp.

1422. SUMMER WORKSHOPS IN MODERN LANGUAGES
Purdue U; FL & Lit; West Lafayette, IN 47907.
Joe Wipf
1-79; 2-18x3; 3-a; 4-smr 74; 5-1; 6-every smr; 7-smr intensive sessions, 3 hrs 15 min each; 8-3s; 9-temp & perm grad student under grads; 10-minor in FL; 11-workshops offered in either Fr, Sp, or Ger; in addition there are 2 workshops in afternoon, one dealing with latest AV equipment & material & their utilization in teaching langs; other workshop will deal with problems of lang in attracting students, lunch hour lang tables giving student opportunity to practice; 12-a,b,c,d,e,f,g; 13-a,b,c,d,e,f, filmstrips, journals; 14-no required text, newspapers, periodicals, journals, hand-outs, audio recordings.

1423. RIDER COLLEGE SUMMER INSTITUTE
Rider C; FL & Lit; Trenton, NJ 08602.
H. Reske
1-30; 2-20x5; 3-c; 4-smr 74; 5-1; 6-smr only; 7-a; 8-6q; 9-a,b; 10-acceptable academic record; 11-aural-oral work, grammar, syntax, vocab, written work offerings in Fr, Ger, Ital, Russ, Sp on elem & inter levels; 12-d,e,g; 13-d,e,f; 14-ng.

See also 711.

INDIVIDUALIZED

Arabic

1424. SELF-INSTRUCTED ARABIC
Warren Wilson C; MLs; Swannanoa, NC 28778.

William Rowell
1-5; 2-2x16; 3-a; (student native speaker as tutor), c (certified instructor of Arabic for testing); 4-73; 5-a; 6-a; 7-b; 8-3s; 9-a; outsiders; 10-none; 11-elem Arabic, written forms & spoken lang; 12-tutoring & drilling; 13-a,b,e; 14-Aɒɒud, Elementary Standard Arabic.

Chinese

1425. SELF-INSTRUCTION COURSES IN CHINESE
Colby C; MFLs; Waterville, ME 04901.
Henry Holland
1-1; 2-3x24; 3-c; 4-70; 5-9; 6-a; 7-a; 8-3s; 9-a; 10-ling ability & permission of dept; 11-independent study of lang, involving weekly tutorial sessions with a native speaker of lang. Final course evaluation made by resident or by visiting faculty member; 12-e; 13-d, native informant; 14-De Francis, Beginning Chinese; Character Text for Beginning Chinese.

1426. SELF-INSTRUCTED CHINESE
Warren Wilson C; MLs; Swannanoa, NC 28778.
William Rowell
1-1; 2-2x16; 3-a (student native speaker as tutor) c (certified instructor of Chinese for testing); 4-73; 5-a; 6-a; 7-b; 8-3s; 9-a; outsiders; 10-none; 11-elem Chi, written forms & spoken lang; 12-tutoring & drilling; 13-a,b,e; 14-DeFrancis, Beginning Chinese.

Classics

See 170, 174.

English as a Second Language

See 712, 776.

French

1427. FOREIGN LANGUAGE ALTERNATIVE PROGRAMS: ELEMENTARY FRENCH
Bellevue CC; FL; Bellevue, WA 98007.
Edward Matkowick
1-22; 2-5x11; 3-a; 4-fall 73; 5-2; 6-b; 7-a,b; 8-5 to 15q; 9-a,b; 10-none for beginning of course; 11-student placed in course according to level; individual pace. Students may choose to engage in extra practice in one or more of the 4 basic lang skills for extra credit; 12-b,e,f,g; 13-d; 14-Lenard, Parole et Pensee.

1428. FOREIGN LANGUAGE ALTERNATIVE PROGRAMS: INTERMEDIATE FRENCH
Bellevue CC; FL; Bellevue, WA 98007.
Edward Matkowick
1-18; 2-5x11; 3-a; 4-73/74; 5-2; 6-a, on demand; 7-a; 8-5q; 9-a,b; 10-elem prof; 11-consists of 3 tracks: lit and/or vocational; cult; conv; allows student choice of

emphasis on one of the four lang skills; 12-b,c,e,g; 13-a,b,d,e, programmed materials; 14-Brown, Langue et Litterature; Valette, France; Pimsleur, C'est la vie; Sullivan, Programmed French Phonetics; Nachtmann, Exercises in French Phonetics; AMSCO Workbook Series.

1429. INDIVIDUALIZED - READING COURSE FOR GRADUATE STUDENTS
U of California; Fr & Ital; Santa Barbara, CA 93106.
1-15; 2-7x10; 3-a; 4-wtr 75; 5-1; 6-every other qtr; 7-a; 8-ng; 9-grad students; 10-consent of instructor; 11-basic intro to grammar & work on individual projects within the field of interest; 12-b,e,f,g; 13-a,e,f, articles, journals; 14-none.

1430. MODERN FRENCH A & B
Florissant Valley CC; FL; St. Louis, MO 63135.
Eleanor McCluskey
1-40; 2-5x16; 3-a; 4-72; 5-6; 6-a (2 sem sequence); 7-a; 8-4s; 9-a,b, part-time; 10-none; 11-programmed course, independent study method at student's own pace, unit tests; 12-e; 13-d; 14-Burroughs, Modern French A & B.

1431. MULTI-LEVEL FRENCH PROGRAM
Forest Park CC; Fr; St. Louis, MO 63110.
Rosemary H. Thomas
1-50; 2-4x16; 3-a; 4-72; 5-7; 6-a; 7-a,b; 8-3,4, or 5s; 9-a, and any others; 10-none; 11-open-classroom, open-enrollment in Fr lang, civ &/or conv. Course work is offered in modules, based on small groups & team teaching. Students work with modules suitable to their skills, interest, & purpose; 12-b,d,f,g; 13-b,d,e, programmed materials, games, locally prepared cult units; 14-Morton & Thomas, Basic Programmed French Course; Rendez-vous en France; Les Francais comme ils sont, Laboratoire de Lecture (SRA Associates).

1432. SUPERVISED SELF-INSTRUCTION IN FRENCH
Hampshire C; Foreign Studies; Amherst, MA 01002.
James M. Watkins
1-35; 2-private appts only, 15-45+ weeks, depending upon individual; 3-a; 4-72; 5-continuously; 6-student may begin at any time; 7-a; 8-Hampshire C associated with 4 other schools, thus cr varies with each school; 9-a, staff employees; 10-none; 11-primarily for students who plan to work or study in Fr-speaking country; stepped program in which student must demonstrate prof in 1 level before proceeding to next; 12-f,g; 13-d, private interview & programmed text, computer; 14-ng.

1433. FRENCH INDIVIDUALIZED
Kellogg CC; Lit, Lang & Journalism; Battle

Creek, MI 49016.
Carole Edmonds
1-57; 2-4 or 5x16; 3-ng; 4-65; 5-11; 6-a; 7-a;
8-4s; 9-a; 10-none; 11-4 sem sequence using
semi-individualized modules; 12-b,c,d,e,g;
13-all, records; 14-Parole et Pensee; Ren-
dezvous en France.

1434. WEDNESDAY FRENCH
Kirkwood CC;.FLs; Cedar Rapids, IA 52406.
Florence Masters
1-14; 2-3½x12; 3-a; 4-73/74; 5-ng; 6-a,
variable entry; 7-a; 8-3 or 4q; 9-a, part-
time; 10-none, except to take in sequence;
11-elem (1st yr college), inter (2nd yr
college), civ (3rd yr college), traditional
skills development, using multi-media; 12-
e,f,g, individualized self instructional; 13-
a,b,d, packets, books, cassettes; 14-
Ecouter et Parler; C'Est la Vie; C'Est de la
Prose; Chez les Francais.

1435. ELEMENTARY FRENCH (INDIVID-
UALIZED)
Raymond Walters C; FL; Cincinnati, OH
45236.
J. Baughin, Dorothy Wartenberg
1-12; 2-5x10; 3-a; 4-73/74; 5-1; 6-a; 7-a; 8-
5q; 9-a,b, adults from community; 10-none;
11-self-paced; students encouraged to attend classes but required to attend only one
conv session per wk; written and oral tests
on the four lang skills; tests may be
repeated as often as necessary until 80%
accuracy is achieved; 12-a,b,d,e,g; 13-
b,d,e,f, packets; 14-Harris & Leveque,
Basic Conversational French.

436. FRENCH HISTORIANS & BIOGRAPHERS
C of St. Thomas; FL; St. Paul, MN 55105.
Herbert M. Willging
1-individual study; 2-½x15; 3-a; 4-48; 5-6;
6-every yr or two to individuals; 7-a; 8-4s;
9-a; 10-inter prof; 11-either 15 one-hr
tapes with written reports or about six
texts; 12-c,e,g; 13-d; 14-various.

437. FRENCH
Tarrant County JC; FLs; Hurst, TX 76053.
Jane Harper
1-80 (in 3 courses); 2-3x16; 3-a; 4-70; 5-9;
6-a; 7-a,b; 8-4s; 9-a,b, any student; 10-
there are 3 courses in sequence, for first in
sequence no prerequisite; 11-fundamentals
of Fr with emphasis on audio-lingual skills,
option of individually-paced program.
Total testing bank for evaluation of listening, speaking, reading, writing skills; 12-
a,b,c,d,e,g, individualized instruction, self
pacing, test banks; 13-a,b,c,d, peer tutor;
14-Brown, Listening, Speaking, Reading,
Writing French; Harper & Gunter, An
Individualized Approach.

438. MODULAR FRENCH
U of Wisconsin-Center System; Fr; Wau-

kesha, WI 53186.
Sara Toenes
1-ng; 2-self paced; 3-a; 4-73; 5-3; 6-a; 7-
a,b; 8-4s; 9-ng; 10-none; 11-audiotapes,
texts; self paced, students listen to tapes,
confer with instructor, record their own
tapes & submit written exercises & exams
(oral & written); 12-e,f,g; 13-d; 14-Brown,
French.

See also 486, 776, 1377.

German

1439. FOREIGN LANGUAGE ALTERNATIVE
PROGRAMS (ELEMENTARY GERMAN)
Bellevue CC; FL; Bellevue, WA 98007.
Franz Pfister
1-35; 2-5x11; 3-a; 4-fall 73; 5-2; 6-a; 7-a,b;
8-5-15q; 9-a,b; 10-none; 11-individualized
first-yr FL program; self-paced with no min
or max work required in a given time period. Students may engage in extra practice
in one or more of the 4 basic lang skills for
extra credit; 12-b,e,f,g; 13-d; 14-Pfister,
Deutsch durch Deutsch.

1440. INDIVIDUALIZED GERMAN
California SC; FLs; Rohnert Park, CA
94928.
Philip H. Beard, Sterling Bennett
1-c45; 2-varies x15; 3-a; 4-73/74 (1st yr); 5-
4 (1st yr), 2 (2nd yr); 6-a; 7-a; 8-1/5s (1st yr)
74/75 (2nd yr); 1/3s (2nd); 9-a; 10-none for
1st; 11-4 sem self-paced instruction ir
grammar & conv; 12-b,e,g, individual sessions with instructor; 13-d, parlor games,
phone books, catalogs; 14-Rogers & Watkins, German through Conversational Patterns; DuVal & DuVal, Wiederholung und
Fortsetzung.

1441. ELEMENTARY GERMAN (INDIVID-
UALIZED INSTRUCTION)
Emory U; Ger; Atlanta, GA 30322.
Maximilian A.E. Aue
1-19; 2-4x11; 3-a; 4-74; 5-1; 6-a; 7-a; 8-
variable; 9-a, auditors, including faculty in
other depts; 10-none; 11-individualized
instruction. Students are provided with
detailed instructions, and each can proceed
at his/her best pace. Instead of a variable
grade for a fixed number of hours of credit,
the student is guaranteed an A or a B, but
the number of credits depends on how fast
he/she works; 12-a,b,c,d,e,f; 13-d; 14-
Lohnes & Strothmann, German, A Structural Approach.

1442. GERMAN, INDIVIDUALIZED
Kellogg CC; Lit, Lang & Journalism; Battle
Creek MI 49016.
1-20; 2-5x16; 3-a; 4-65; 5-11; 6-a; 7-a; 8-4s;
9-a, part-time; 10-none; 11-4-sem sequence using individualized-modularized
system; 12-b,c,d,e,g; 13-a,b,d,e,f, sound on
slide programs; 14-Werba, Basic Conversa-

tional German; Haas, Die Deutschen und die Oesterreicher; Guten Tag film series.

1443. GOAL-DIRECTED LANGUAGE ACQUISI-TION PROGRAM
U of Maryland; Ger & Sl; College Park, MD 20742.
Gunter Pfister
1-450; 2-4x16; 3-a; 4-fall 72; 5-5; 6-a; 7-a,b; 8-3s; 9-a,b; 10-none for the beginning; 11-4 sem sequence, goal-directed program; students & teachers make a contract for a specific goal-90% mastery of the course content; student and teacher work together, often individually, to reach this goal. Team taught. In addition to lang skills, the program promotes cult awareness, both of Ger and of Amer cult; 12-"incentive quizzes" (a student who scores 90% on all of them receives an A in the course and is exempted from the final exam); 13-ng; 14-various.

1444. APPLIED GERMAN
Middle Tennessee SU; FLs; Murfreesboro, TN 37130.
T. Coy Porter
1-new; 2-3x15; 3-a; 4-75; 5-0; 6-b; 7-a; 8-3s; 9-a; 10-3 sem of Ger; 11-special terminology, letters, specialized syntax related to the student's major; 12-individualized; 13-Ger soci texts, psych, etc; 14-various.

1445. SUPERVISED SELF-INSTRUCTION
Pennsylvania SU; Ger; University Park, PA 16802.
Keith O. Anderson
1-20; 2-1x10; 3-a; 4-69/70; 5-16; 6-a; 7-a; 8-3s; 9-a; 10-B av or better and some experience with another FL; 11-material same as in elem and inter Ger, but student does not attend class; works with the textbook & in the lang lab & consults dept native informant once a wk; 12-b,c,e,g; 13-d; 14-Lehmann et al, German Language and Culture (Elem); Moeller et al, Blickpunkt Deutschland (Inter).

See also 776, 1356.

Greek

1446. INTRODUCTION TO GREEK
Northeastern JC; Hums; Sterling, CO 80751.
Jerry Spoon
3-credit individual study course; further info ng.

Hindi

1447. SELF-INSTRUCTED HINDI
Warren Wilson C; MLs; Swannanoa, NC 28778.
William Rowell

1-3; 2-2x16; 3-a (student native speaker as tutor), c (certified instructor of Hindi for testing); 4-73; 5-a; 6-a; 7-b; 8-3s; 9-a, outsiders; 10-none; 11-elem Hindi, written & spoken lang; 12-tutoring & drilling; 13-a,b,e; 14-Landour Lang School (Mussoorie, India), Introductory Hindi.

Italian

1448. SELF-INSTRUCTED ITALIAN
Warren Wilson C; MLs; Swannanoa, NC 28778.
William Rowell
1-6; 2-2x16; 3-a (student native speaker as tutor), c (certified instructor of Ital for testing); 4-73; 5-a; 6-a; 7-b; 8-3s; 9-a, outsiders; 10-none; 11-elem Ital, written & spoken lang; 12-tutoring & drilling; 13-a,b,e; 14-Cioffari, Beginning Italian Grammar.

See also 776, 1358.

Japanese

1449. INDIVIDUAL STUDIES IN JAPANESE
Foothill C; Lang Arts; Los Altos, CA 94022.
Nayan McNeill, M. Hiramatsu
1-17; 2-4x11; 3-a; 4-74; 5-3; 6-a; 7-a; 8-4q; 9-a; 10-none; 11-grammar, calligraphy, reading, writing; 12-a,b,e,f,g; 13-b,d; 14-ng.

1450. SELF-INSTRUCTION IN JAPANESE LANGUAGE
Graceland C; Lang & Lit; Lamoni, IA 50140.
Arthur Gardner
1-8; 2-2x15; 3-b; 4-fall 71; 5-4; 6-a; 7-a; 8-3 or 4 q; 9-a; 10-none; 11-Jap Lang 1: Basic grammar, vocab of about 1000 modern colloquial words, primary emphasis on speaking & hearing, some writing learning kana & kanji (200 characters). Inter Jap seeks to develop prof in major sentence patterns. Written lang work with command of hiragana, katakana, 500 kanji; 12-g; 13-c,d; 14-Jorden, Beginning Japanese.

1451. SELF-INSTRUCTED JAPANESE
Warren Wilson C; MLs; Swannanoa, NC 28778.
William Rowell
1-1; 2-2x16; 3-a (student native speaker as tutor), c (certified instructor of Jap for testing); 4-73; 5-a; 6-a; 7-b; 8-3s; 9-a; outsiders; 10-none; 11-elem Jap, written forms & spoken lang; 12-tutoring & drilling; 13-a,b,e; 14-Jorden, Beginning Japanese.

See also 776.

Latvian

See 1397.

Linguistics

See 1359.

Norwegian

1452. SELF - INSTRUCTIONAL LANGUAGE PROGRAM: NORWEGIAN
Wheaton C; FLs; Wheaton, IL 60187.
Gary C. Rundquist
1-12; 2-3x11; 2-b,c; 4-spr 74; 5-2; 6-a; 7-a,b; 8-4q; 9-a,b; 10-successful score on MLAT & valid reason for wanting to learn Norwegian; 11-a self-instructional course in beginning Norwegian using text, lab, tapes, native informants. No formal class work. Testing by visiting examiners from Norwegian Depts of neighboring schools; 12-e,g; 13-d, native informants used as tutors 3 hrs per wk; 14-Haugen, Spoken Norwegian.

Polish

1453. SPOKEN POLISH
California SC; MLs; California, PA 15419.
Bruce Weston
1-25; 2-6x15; 3-a; 4-74; 5-1; 6-every other yr; 7-b; 8-3s, no credit given for community; 9-a, citizens from community; 10-none; 11-self-instructional materials, cassettes & players, class sessions with instructor not qualified in Polish but knows Slavic ling & teaching methods; 12-f,g; 13-d, pattern drills & explanations; 14-Schenker, Beginning Polish Vol. I.

Russian

1454. THE RUSSIAN ROOM: AN INDIVID-UALIZED APPROACH TO TEACHING COLLEGE RUSSIAN
U of California; Russ; Davis, CA 95616.
1-64; 2-determined by student; 3-a; 4-72; 5-ng; 6-ng; 7-ng; 8-ng; 9-ng; 10-none; 11-contract-graded instructional system, cursive & printed alphabets, phonetics, Russ room open 50 hrs per wk so that students may use all of the AV facilities & avail themselves of an instructor who is always on duty; grammar, course of study made available in stepped unit so that student can contract for an A grade and continue studying same unit until mastery is achieved; 12-b,c,e,g; 13-a,c,d,e,f; 14-Clark, Russian for Americans.

1455. ELEMENTARY, SELF-PACED, CON-TRACT-GRADED RUSSIAN
SUNY; Sl; Albany, NY 12222.
Rodney L. Patterson
1-ng; 2-determined by students; 3-a; 4-74; 5-1; 6-a; 7-a,b; 8-5s; 9-a; 10-none; 11-a systematic study of 15 chapters of Russ grammar (equivalent to the lock-step norm

of 1st sem Russ, next 12 chapters equivalent to lock-step norm of 2nd sem); 12-a,b,e,f,g; 13-a,b,c,d; 14-Stilman & Harkins, Introductory Russian Grammar; Baker, Mastering Russian Pronunciation and the Writing System.

1456. RUSSIAN TUTORIAL
Pennsylvania SU; Sl; University Park, PA 16802.
L.T. Kapitanoff
1-21; 2-½x10 plus individualized work; 3-a; 4-69; 5-10; 6-fall & wtr terms; 7-a; 8-3q; 9-a; 10-1 previous Russ class; 11-tutorial course; instructor meets each student ½ hr per week. Student completes 30pp of Russ material in particular field of interest. Grad students may use a grade of B or better as sub for lang exam; intensive training in trans techniques & grammar; 12-f; 13-e,f, books in Russian on tech topics; 14-no text.

See also 776.

Spanish

1457. INDIVIDUALIZED INSTRUCTION IN EL-EMENTARY SPANISH
U of California; Sp & Port; Berkeley, CA 94720.
J.R. Craddock
1-32; 2-6x10; 3-a; 4-fall 74; 5-1; 6-a; 7-a; 8-2-5q; 9-a; 10-3 level course; no prerequisites for entry into 1st level; 11-beginning Sp; 12-a,b,c,e,f,g; 13-books; 14-Turk & Espinosa, Foundation Course in Spanish; Teacher's & Student's Manuals for the individualized instruction program.

1458. INDIVIDUALIZED FIRST-YEAR SPANISH
U of Colorado; Sp & Port; Boulder, CO 80302.
Charles W. Stansfield
Course allows for self-pacing & individually chosen activities. In order that students not fall behind, strict time limitations for the completion of each unit have been set. Students may move ahead even to the point of not attending class (these students participate in FL house activities, etc.) Programmed materials are used.

1459. INTRODUCTORY SPANISH (SELF-PACED)
Florissant Valley CC; FL; St. Louis, MO 63135.
Eleanor McCluskey
1-45; 2-5x16; 3-a; 4-72; 5-7 or 8; 6-a (2 sem sequence); 7-a; 8-4s; 9-a,b, part-time; 10-none; 11-programmed course, independent study method at student's own pace; 12-e; 13-d; 14-Sullivan, Introductory Spanish.

1460. INDIVIDUALIZED PERFORMANCE IN SPANISH

271

Independence CJC; FL; Independence. KS 67301.
Leo Carvalho
1-42; 2-2x15; 3-a; 4-73; 5-8; 6-a, any time anyone wants to learn Sp; 7-a,b; 8-1-5s, and given for no credit; 9-a,b, adults or anyone who wants to learn Sp; 10-none; 11-individualized performance oriented practical approach to Sp; 12-f,g; 13-d; 14-ng.

1461. SPANISH, INDIVIDUALIZED
Kellogg CC; Lit, Lang, & Journalism; Battle Creek, MI 49016.
Carole Edmonds
1-57; 2-4 or 5x16; 3-ng; 4-65; 5-11; 6-a; 7-a; 8-4s; 9-a; 10-none; 11-4 sem sequence using semi-individualized modules; 12-b,c,d,e,g; 13-all, records; 14-various.

1462. SELF-INSTRUCTIONAL SPANISH
U of Kentucky; Sp & Ital; Lexington, KY 40506.
H.B. Saunders
1-5; 2-60 (self-paced); 3-a; 4-fall 73; 5-continuously; 6-the student begins when he wishes; 7-students study on own; 8-b; 9-students in other colleges, professors; 10-none; 11-spoken Sp through imitation & responses to taped material; minimum grammatical concepts; 12-e (contact with "tutor"); 13-d; 14-Temac, Spanish A.

1463. WEDNESDAY SPANISH
Kirkwood CC; FLs; Cedar Rapids, IA 52406.
Florence Masters
1-24; 2-3½x12; 3-a; 4-73/74; 5-ng; 6-a, variable entry; 7-a; 8-3 or 4q; 9-a, part-time; 10-none, except to take in sequence; 11-elem (1st yr college), inter (2nd yr college), civ (3rd yr college); traditional skills development through multimedia; 12-e,f,g, individualized self-instructional; 13-a,b,d, packets, books, cassettes; 14-Entender y Hablar; Sol y Sombra; Mexico.

1464. HISPANIC CIVILIZATION AS REFLECTED IN THE ARTS
Manhattanville C; FLs; Purchase, NY 10577.
Marta de la Portilla
1-12; 2-2 hrs each wk of sem; 3-b,c; 4-spr 74; 5-2; 6-b; 7-self instructed; 8-3s; 9-a, outside students; 10-adv prof; 11-study of Hispanic civ through use of slides & tapes; 12-e,g; 13-b,d; 14-specially prepared materials.

1465. SPANISH: ELEMENTARY, INTENSIVE, SELF INSTRUCTION
U of Massachusetts; Sp & Port; Amherst, MA 01002.
Fresia Bradford, Nina Galvin
1-5; 2-3 half hrs x 18; 3-a; 4-73/74; 5-2; 6-6; 8-6s; 9-a; 10-high motivation; 11-weekly contact with instructor; grammar consultation; drill sessions; testing. 12-c,e,g; 13-d, workbook; 14-Wolfe, Curso basico de espanol; workbook & tapes for Curso basico

de espanol.

1466. SPANISH
Tarrant County JC; MFL; Hurst, TX 76053.
Jane Harper
1-ng; 2-3x15; 3-c; 4-74/75; 5-1; 6-b; 7-a,b; 8-1s; 9-a,b; 10-mastery of listening, speaking, reading, writing skills in Sp equivalent to two sems study in college to be demonstrated by placement exam, proficiency in steno & typing in Eng & completion of course in Eng comp; 11-instruction in form of Sp bus letter, typing in Sp trans of Eng bus letters into Sp; 12-f,g, packaged individualized; 13-4; 14-various.

1467. SELF-PACED FIRST YEAR SPANISH
Washington SU; FLs & Lits; Pullman, WA 99163.
Angelo Cantera
1-ng; 2-4x15; 3-a; 4-72; 5-5; 6-a; 7-a; 8-4s; 9-a; 10-none; 11-elem Sp, self-paced; 12-a,b,e,f,g; 13-flashcards; 14-Lamadrid, Bull, Briscoe, Communicating in Spanish.

See also 404, 776, 1363, 1413, 1573, 1587.

Swahili

1468. SELF - INSTRUCTION COURSES IN SWAHILI
Colby C; MFLs; Waterville, ME 04901.
Henry Holland
1-2; 2-3x24; 3-c; 4-70; 5-9; 6-a; 7-a; 8-3s; 9-a; 10-ling ability & permission of dept; 11-ind study of a critical lang, involving weekly tutorial sessions with a native speaker of the lang; final course evaluation made by resident or by visiting faculty member; 12-e; 13-d, native informant; 14-Zawawi, Kiswahili Kwa Kitendo.

1469. SELF-INSTRUCTED SWAHILI
Warren Wilson C; MLs; Swannanoa, NC 28778.
William Rowell
1-3; 2-2x16; 3-a (student native speaker as tutor), c (certified instructor of Swahili for testing); 4-73; 5-a; 6-a; 7-b; 8-3s; 9-a; outsiders; 10-none; 11-elem Swahili, written forms & spoken lang; 12-tutoring & drills; 13-a,b,e; 14-Zawawi, Kiswahili Kwakitendo.

Swedish

See 766.

Multi-Language

1470. CRITICAL LANGUAGES
Allegheny C; MLs; Meadville, PA 16335.
Louis Wagner
1-varies with lang; 2-individual study + 3 drill sessions per wk per sem; 3-c + student tutors on campus; 4-69/70 (1 or 2 langs per yr); 5-whenever there are one or more students interested in a given lang; 6-upon demand by interested students and upon availability of student tutors; 7-a; 8-3 1/3s;

9-a; 10-interest & ability to study on their own; 12-e,g; 13-d, drill session with tutors; 14-Foreign Service Tapes & various programs used by the big univs.

1471. SELF-INSTRUCTIONAL PROGRAM IN UNCOMMONLY TAUGHT LANGUAGES
Bates C; FLs; Lewiston, ME 04240.
Alfred J. Wright, Michael O'Dea
1-27; 2-1x13; 3-c; 4-71/72; 5-8; 6-a; 7-a; 8-ng; 9-a,b; 10-ng; 11-learning of the spoken lang through tapes & native consultants with supervision by member of the FL dept, staff, & final testing by a visiting examiner of recognized qualifications; offered in 74/75: Brazilian, Port, Jap, Modern Greek; 12-d,g; 13-d; 14-Foreign Service Institute, Greek Basic Course; MLA-Knopf, Modern Portuguese; Beginning Japanese.

1472. GERMAN, FRENCH, SPANISH-INDIVIDUALIZED
Central Wyoming C; FLs; Riverton, WY 82501.
Earl McDaniel
1-new; 2-2-3x8; 3-a,c; 4-fall 75; 5-0; 6-a; 7-a,b; 8-variable 9-a, special interest; 10-none for beginning students; 11-same as that for langs offered in standard approach; 12-e; 13-a,b,d,f; 14- German Through Conversational Patterns; Blaisdell, L'Echelle; Spanish text, ng.

1473. INDEPENDENT STUDY
Federal City C; FLs; Washington, DC 20001.
Both jr and sr ind study courses are offered by FL dept each for period of 1 qtr. Further info ng.

1474. SELF-PACED CONVERSATIONAL LANGUAGES
Greenville Tech Ed Center; MLs; Greenville, SC 29606.
Margaret Rice
1-30; 2-5x11; 3-a; 4-73; 5-6-yr-round course; students may enroll any time; 7-Sats; 8-b; 9-b; 10-none; 11-students work on their own in lab on Fr, Sp, Ital, Ger, or ESL. Practice sessions in small groups with a native speaker are arranged; 12-e; 13-d, workbook; 14-Brown, French; Communicating in Spanish; Lo Dica in Italiano; Auf deutsch, bitte!; Modern American English.

1475. CRITICAL LANGUAGES PROGRAM
McPherson C; FLs; McPherson, KS 67460.
Ian Van Asselt
1-1; 2-1x12; 3-c; 4-68; 5-5; 6-on demand; 7-on demand; 8-2-4s; 9-a; 10-desire to work ind and take exams produced or given by outside persons; 11-beginning lang study; 12-ind work; 13-d; 14-ng.

1476. SELF-INSTRUCTION IN ARABIC, HEBREW, CHINESE
SUCNY; FL; Geneseo, NY 14454.
G.P. Orwen
1-3-5 in each lang; 2-2x15; 3-in cooperation with a native speaker on campus; 4-Chi 67; Arabic, Hebrew 72; 5-each sem; 6-a; 7-a; 8-3s; 9-a; 10-lang aptitude test, high motiva-

tion; 11-standard texts & tapes; 12-c,g; 13-ng; 14-ng.

1477. SPECIAL LANGUAGE PROGRAM
Ohio Wesleyan U; Rom Langs; Delaware, OH 43015.
Hugh A. Harter, Donald Lenfast
1-15-20; 2-4x10; 3-student tutors & outside examiners; 4-69/70; 5-every qtr; 6-a; 7-a,b; 8-4q; 9-a; 10-none; 11-students listen to tapes & meet with native speakers to prepare for exam by professors from other univs. Langs offered are: Chi, Jap, Hebrew, Arabic, Modern Greek, & Port; 12-e,g, tutorial sessions; 13-d; 14-Tewksberry, Speak Chinese; Chang, Read Chinese; Jorden, Beginning Japanese; Hayon, Modern Hebrew; Center for Applied Linguistics, Damascus Arabic; Foreign Service Institute, Greek Course; Ellison, Modern Portuguese.

1478. INDIVIDUALIZED PROGRAMS
Providence C; MLs; Providence, RI 02918.
Students may study MLs individually; further info ng.

1478A. SELF-PACED LANGUAGE LEARNING: SPANISH, GERMAN, FRENCH
U of South Carolina; FLs; Columbia, SC 29208.
Bruce Fryer, Francis Dannerbeck, Carl Johnson

1479. FRENCH, GERMAN OR SPANISH
Tarrant County JC; FLs; Hurst, TX 76053.
Jane Harper
1-72; 2-variable, average 1-2 hrsx16; 3-a; 4-73/74; 5-3; 6-a; 7-a,h; 8-1s; 9-any student meeting prerequisite; 10-elem prof; 11-variable, self-paced, includes lab work, short stories; 12-b,d,e; 13-b,c,d,e,f, FL typewriters, records, tutoring; 14-ng.

1480. LANGUAGE PRACTICUM
Tarrant County JC; MFL; Fort Worth TX 76119.
Ernesto Guzman
1-15; 2-2x15; 3-a; 4-73/74; 5-3; 6-a; 7-a; 8-1s; 9-a; 10-2 sem of lang; 11-individualized package offered for: Fr, Ger, Sp, Russ; course varies from sem to sem; genres, poetry, short story, bus & tech writing, conv, individual projects, lit dramatization; 12-g; 13-individualized instruction, multimedia approach; 14-ng.

1481. CRITICAL LANGUAGES
U of Toledo; FLs; Toledo, OH 43606.
John W. Pullyn, Jr.
1-2; 2-5x2; 3-c; 4-fall 74; 5-1; 6-a; 7-arranged; 8-5q; 9-a; 10-none (later: appropriate score on MLAT); 11-various langs at elem & inter levels-currently: Chi & Russ; to be added fall 75 Jap, Hebrew, Port, Swahili, Yoruba, Modern Greek; 12-e,g; 13-d, native informants; 14-as recommended by NASILP.

1482. DIRECTED INSTRUCTION IN MODERN FOREIGN LANGUAGES
Western Washington SU; FLs; Bellingham,

WA 98225.
W. Robinson
1-8; 2-2x11; 3-b; 4-73; 5-2; 6-b; 7-a; 8-3q;
9-a; 10-inter level experience in college in
a FL course; 11-fundamentals of the lang;
pronunciation, grammar, aural comprehension, reading, speaking. Only those non-
traditional langs for which established
curricular materials are available will be
offered (73/74 Persian; 74/75 Ital); 12-
d,e,g; 13-d; 14-ng.

1483. SELF-INSTRUCTIONAL MALAY, JAPA-
NESE, SWEDISH, ESPERANTO
Wilmington C; MLs; Wilmington, OH 45117.

Sheri Scott
1-1-5 per lang; 2-2x10; 3-c, tester from
outside institutions, student tutors; 4-wtr
74; 5-3; 6-a; 7-up to participating
tutors/students; 8-3; 9-a, local people,
foreign students, full time faculty; 10-
none; 11-emphasis on spoken lang; 12-g; 13-
d,e,f, pictures, mini store (real props); 14-
Jorden, Beginning Japanese; Kursus Bahasa
Kebangsaan, Svenska For Er; Auld, A First
Course in Esperanto; Incontro con
l'Italiano.

See also 1017, 1577A.

Native Speakers

FRENCH

1484. FRENCH FOR FRANCO-AMERICANS
U of Massachusetts; Fr & Ital; Amherst, MA
01002.
Micheline Dufau
1-6; 2-3x14; 3-a; 4-spr 74; 5-2; 6-a; 7-a; 8-
3s; 9-a; 10-near-native prof; 11-review of
grammar focusing on phonology, morphology, syntax; readings of Fr-Canadian
authors; 12-a,b,c,f,g; 13-ng; 14-Porte
Ouverte, La Guerre, Yes Sir!

1485. FRENCH FOR THE FRENCH
Occidental C; Langs & Ling; Los Angeles,
CA 90041.
Edric Cane
1-new; 2-4x10; 3-a; 4-spr 75; 5-1; 6-alt yrs;
7-a; 8-4s; 9-a; 10-adv prof; 11-reading &
discussion of non-lit books; present ideas in
a variety of ways; debates, speeches,
written summaries; 12-b,c,d,e,g; 13-e,f;
14-various.

PORTUGUESE

1486. PORTUGUESE LANGUAGE AND LUSO-
BRAZILIAN CIVILIZATION FOR SPANISH
SPEAKERS
U of Texas; Sp & Port; Austin, TX 78712.
Phyllis Harmon
1-new; 2-3x14; 3-a; 4-spr 75; 5-1; 6-
unknown; 7-a; 8-3s; 9-a; 10-native or near-
native prof; 11-intro to grammar & pho-
netics; readings in cult & civ; 12-a,g; 13-ng;
14-Bastide, Brasil: Terra de Contrastes;
Diegues, Etnias e Culturas do Brasil; Prado
Jr., Formacao do Brasil Contemporaneo;
Freyre, Interpretacao do Brasil; Ramos,
Las Poblaciones del Brasil; de Hollanda,
Raizes do Brasil; Prado, Retrato do Brasil.

SPANISH

1487. ELEMENTARY SPANISH (BILINGUAL)
Adams SC; FLs; Alamosa, CO 81101.
Luis Trujillo
1-30; 2-5x10; 3-a; 4-72; 5-3; 6-a; 7-a; 8-5q;
9-a; 10-ng; 11-principles of pronunciation,
essentials of grammar, written comp, reading materials; emphasis on grammar &
formal writing; 12-a,b,c,e,f,g; 13-d; 14-ng.

1488. SPANISH FOR NATIVE SPEAKERS
Adelphi U; Langs & Intl Studies; Garden
City, NY 11530.
Nicholas Carbo
1-24; 2-3x16; 3-a; 4-75; 5-1; 6-b; 7-a; 8-3s;
9-a; 10-instructor's permission; 11-formal
grammatical & cult foundation; 12-b,c,d,g;
13-d; 14-Barker, Espanol para el Bilingue;
Lewald, Latinoamerica: Sus Culturas y
Sociedades.

1489. SPANISH FOR HISPANOPARLANTES
U of Albuquerque; Langs; Albuquerque, NM
87140.
John Archibeque
1-new; 2-3x16; 3-a,b; 4-75; 5-1; 6-a; 7-a; 8-
3s; 9-a, part-time students; 10-native
speaker; 11-basic grammar, correction of
slang, increase in vocab, readings, conv; 12-
a,b,c,f,g; 13-ng; 14-Spanish for the Bilingual Class.

1490. SPANISH FOR NATIVE SPEAKERS
Angelo SU; ML; San Angelo, TX 76901.
1-ng; 2-3x18; 3-a; 4-67; 5-ng; 6-a; 7-a; 8-3s;
9-a; 10-speaking ability; 11-ng; 12-a,c,g;
13-e,f; 14-varies.

1491. ELEMENTARY SPANISH, INTERMEDIATE
SPANISH
Arizona SU; FLs; Tempe, AZ 85281.
Douglas C. Sheppard
1-79; 2-ng; 3-a; 4-71/72; 5-4; 6-b; 7-a; 8-4s;
9-a; 10-native speaker; 11-emphasis on the
needs of the biling student through comp,
lit, conv, review of grammar fundamentals;
4-sem sequence; 12-b,g; 13-a,b,c,d,e,f; 14-
Armitage & Meiden, Beginning Spanish.

1492. BILINGUAL PROGRAM
U of Arizona; Sp; Tucson, AZ 85721.
Edward G. Brown
1-basic lang program in existence 1 sem; 2-
sem program for Sp bilings with option of 5
courses emphasizing either oral, reading,

writing, grammar skills or a comprehensive course which covers all lang skills. Further info ng.

1493. SPANISH FOR NATIVE SPEAKERS
U of Arizona; Rom Langs; Tucson, AZ 85721.
Charles Olstad
1-40; 2-4x14; 3-a; 4-67/68; 5-13; 6-b; 7-a; 8-4s; 9-a; 10-native speaker; 11-reading, writing, speaking, understanding, vocab building, standardization; 12-a,b,c,d,e,g; 13-a,b,d,e,f; 14-ng;

1494. SPANISH FOR NATIVE SPEAKERS
Bee County C; Lang & Lit; Beeville, TX 78102.
Norman G. Damerau
1-41; 2-2½x15; 3-a; 4-ng; 5-ng; 6-a; 7-a,b; 8-ng; 9-a, local citizens; 10-ng; 11-two-course sequence; analysis, study of problems in reading, writing, speaking; exercises to minimize dialectal deficiencies; 12-a,b; 13-b, transparencies; 14-Barker, El Espanol para el bilingue.

1495. SPANISH FOR THE NATIVE SPEAKER
Boise SU; FL; Boise, ID 83725.
Rudi Pena
1-10; 2-4x18; 3-a,c; 4-Jan 74; 5-2; 6-b; 7-b; 8-3s; 9-a,b; 10-some native familiarity; 11-vocab building, speaking, control of the written lang, grammar, readings from Mex & Mex Amer sources; 12-ng; 13-ng; 14-ng.

1496. SPANISH FOR NATIVE SPEAKERS
Bowling Green SU; Rom Langs; Bowling Green, OH 43403.
Richard Hebein
1-20; 2-4x10; 3-a; 4-72/73; 5-2; 6-on demand; 7-a; 8-4q; 9-a,c; 10-elem prof; 11-ng; 12-a,b,e,g; 13-ng; 14-Barker, Espanol para el bilingue.

1497. SPANISH FOR SPANISH SPEAKING
Butte C; Sp; Oroville, CA 95965.
Richard A. Clark
1-6; 2-1x12; 3-a; 4-73; 5-8; 6-a; 7-a; 8-1q; 9-a; 10-native speaker; 11-reading, writing skills; cult of Mexico & Western hemisphere; 12-a,b,g; 13-a, clippings; 14-Nassi, Workbook in Spanish, Three Years.

1498. ADVANCED SPANISH FOR BILINGUAL STUDENTS
U of California; Sp & Port; Berkeley, CA 94720.
L.A. Murillo
1-17; 2-4x10; 3-a; 4-74; 5-2; 6-b; 7-a; 8-4q; 9-a; 10-inter prof; 11-unified study of phonetics, grammar, lexicon, comp; 12-a,b,e,g; 13-d,e; 14-Seco, Gramatica esencial del espanol.

1499. SPANISH FOR SPANISH-SPEAKING STUDENTS
U of California; Sp & Port; Riverside, CA 92502.
Philip O. Gericke
1-6; 2-4x40; 3-a; 4-70; 5-4; 6-4 qtr sequence; 7-a; 8-4q; 9-a; 10-native background; 11-intensive lang study; reading &

discussion of selected texts; 12-a,b,g; 13-b,d,f; 14-Leal, Mexico; Soto, Repaso de gramatica; Eoff & Ramirez, Composicion-conversation; Rogers, Escritores contemporaneos de Mexico; Usigli, El gesticulador.

1500. SPANISH GRAMMAR FOR NATIVE SPEAKERS
Central Connecticut SC; ML; New Britain, CT 06050.
Arnaldo Sierra
1-12; 2-3x15; 3-a; 4-71; 5-4; 6-b; 7-a; 8-3s; 9-a; 10-ng; 11-remedial course in grammar, diction, spelling; 12-a,b; 13-ng; 14-Hesse, Spanish Conversational Review Grammar; Baker, Espanol para los hispanos; Diaz Alfaro, Terrazo; Arce de Vazquez, Lecturas Puertorriquenas.

1501. SPANISH FOR NATIVE SPEAKERS
City C; Rom Langs; New York, NY 10031.
Gabriela Mora
1-23; 2-4x14; 3-a; 4-fall 73; 5-3; 6-a; 7-a; 8-4s; 9-a; 10-spoken prof; 11-1 yr course; fundamentals of grammar, diction; 12-a,b,g; 13-ng; 14-Crow & Crow, Panorama de las Americas; Anorga, Espanol: Elementos gramaticales y ortografia.

1502. SPANISH FOR SPANISH-SPEAKING
Cypress C; Eng & FL; Cypress, CA 90630.
1-25; 2-3x2 sem; 3-a; 4-ng; 5-ng; 6-a; 7-ng; 8-3s; 9-ng; 10-spoken ability; 11-speaking, writing; standard usage; 12-ng; 13-ng; 14-Barker, Espanol para el bilingue.

1503. SPANISH FOR SPANISH SPEAKERS
Eastern Connecticut SC; ML; Willimantic, CT 06226.
Pedro Rivas
1-15; 2-3x15; 3-a; 4-70; 5-2; 6-alt yrs; 7-a; 8-3s; 9-a; 10-ng; 11-ng; 12-a,b,c,g; 13-ng; 14-ng.

1504. SPANISH FOR NATIVE SPEAKERS
Eastern Oregon SC; FL; La Grande, OR 97850.
Jose A. Troncoso
1-7; 2-3x31; 3-a; 4-71; 5-4; 6-3 qtr sequence; 7-a; 8-3; 9-a; 10-native speaker, some reading & writing ability; 11-basic grammar & orthography, techniques in trans, vocab building, identifying & remedying native errors, bus correspondence, advanced oral expression & composition; 12-a,b,c,g; 13-ng; 14-Da Silva & Lovett, A Concept Approach to Spanish; Cuyas, English-Spanish, Spanish-English Dictionary; reader; instructor prepared materials.

1505. SPANISH SYNTAX AND COMPOSITION
Florida International U; MLs; Miami, FL 33144.
Frances M. Aid, Florence Yudin
1-15; 2-5x11; 3-a; 4-72; 5-3; 6-b; 7-a; 8-5q; 9-a, part-time students; 10-native speaker; 11-orthography; syntax; structures; paragraph, expository, descriptive writing; 12-a,b,g; 13-f; 14-Revilla, Gramatica espanola moderna; Martin Vivaldi, Curso de redaccion; Arena, Linguistics and Composi-

tion: A Method for Structural Finger-printing.

1506. REVIEW SPANISH
Hardin-Simmons U; FL; Abilene, TX 79601.
Don R. Whitmore
1-30; 2-3x16; 3-a; 4-fall 73; 5-3; 6-a; 7-a; 8-3s; 9-a; 10-native speaker; 11-study of the fundamental grammatical structures, development of reading & writing skills; 12-a,e,f,g; 13-e,f; 14-Dalbor, Beginning College Spanish; del Prado & Calvo, Primeras lecturas.

1507. SPANISH FOR NATIVE SPEAKERS
Hobart and William Smith C; ML; Geneva, NY 14456.
Judith Merrill
1-5; 2-3x10; 3-a; 4-73/74; 5-1; 6-b; 7-a; 8-3s; 9-a; 10-near-native ability; 11-improvement of written Sp; stress on orthography & syntax; 12-b,c,f,g; 13-e,f; 14-various grammars; short stories.

1508. SPANISH FOR NATIVE SPEAKERS
Hostos CC; MLs; Bronx, NY 10451.
Manuel Ramos
1-36; 2-3x15; 3-a; 4-73/74; 5-ng; 6-a; 7-a,b; 8-3s; 9-a; 10-native prof; 11-2 sem sequence; 12-a,b,g; 13-d; 14-instructor-developed materials.

1509. SPANISH FOR NEAR-NATIVE SPEAKERS
U of Illinois; Sp, Ital & Port; Urbana, IL 61801.
Anthony M. Pasquariello
1-15; 2-3x15; 3-a; 4-72; 5-5; 6-a; 7-a; 8-3s; 9-a; 10-spoken prof; 11-materials for biling speakers; 12-a,b,g; 13-d; 14-Barker, Espanol para el bilingue.

1510. SPANISH FOR BILINGUALS
Imperial Valley C; FL; Imperial, CA 92251.
Alicia Ortega
1-ng; 2-4x18; 3-a; 4-ng; 5-ng; 6-a,b; 7-a,g; 8-3 or 4s; 9-a, part-time students; 10-ng; 11-4 sem sequence; reading, writing, vocab building, cult, trans, grammar, oral skills; 12-a,b,c,d,g; 13-a,e; 14-Bourne et al, El espanol: La teoria y la practica; Espinosa et al, Cultura, conversacion y repaso.

1511. SPANISH FOR SPANISH SPEAKERS
Indiana U Northwest; MLs; Gary, IN 46408.
Nicolas Kanellos
1-ng; 2-5x15; 3-a; 4-spr 71; 5-5; 6-a; 7-a; 8-4s; 9-a; 10-native speaker; 11-ng; 12-b,c,d,e,g; 13-a,d,f, records; 14-Gil, Espanol contemporaneo; Rivera, And the Earth Did Not Part; Marques, La Carreta.

1512. SPECIAL PROBLEMS OF SPANISH FOR NATIVE SPEAKERS
Kean C; FL; Union, NJ 07083.
Charles Wendell
1-24; 2-3x15; 3-a; 4-74; 5-1; 6-b; 7-a; 8-3s; 9-a; 10-native speaker; 11-ng; 12-a,c,e,g; 13-d; 14-ng.

1513. SPANISH FOR NATIVE SPEAKERS
Kingsborough CC; FL; Brooklyn, NY 11235.

Julio Hernandez-Miyares
1-30; 2-3x15; 3-a; 4-73; 5-4; 6-a; 7-a; 8-3s; 9-a; 10-native speaker; 11-ng; 12-a,b,c,e,g; 13-a,b; 14-Del Rios & Garcia Lorca, Lengua Viva y Gramatica.

1514. SPANISH FOR NATIVE SPEAKERS
Lehman C; Rom Lang; Bronx, NY 10468.
Emita B. Hill
1-ng; 2-ng; 3-a; 4-71; 5-ng; 6-a; 7-a; 8-3s; 9-a; 10-ng; 11-ng; 12-b,g; 13-ng; 14-ng.

1515. SPANISH FOR NEAR-NATIVE SPEAKERS
Loop C; FL; Chicago, IL 60601.
Judith Moses, Eileen Lucietto
1-10; 2-3¼x16; 3-a; 4-fall 73; 5-3; 6-b; 7-a,b; 8-4s; 9-a, part-time students; 10-interview; 11-review of formal structure & sound system; emphasis on oral expression; 12-b,d,f,g; 13-b,e,f; 14-Nassi & Bernstein, Workbook in Spanish; Two Years; Shular et al, Literatura Chicana: Texto y Contexto.

1516. SPANISH FOR BILINGUALS
Manhattanville C; Sp; Purchase, NY 10577.
Marta de la Portilla
1-12; 2-per wk x 1 sem; 3-b,c; 4-69; 5-6; 6-b; 7-b; 8-3s; 9-a,c; 10-native speaker; 11-grammatical structure; readings; expository writing; vocab building; 12-b,c,g; 13-d,e,f; 14-instructor-prepared materials.

1517. SPANISH GRAMMAR AND LITERARY READINGS FOR BILINGUALS
Manhattanville C; Sp; Purchase, NY 10577.
Marta de la Portilla
1-12; 2-2 hrs per wk each sem; 3-b,c; 4-69; 5-6; 6-b; 7-b; 8-3s; 9-a, outside students; 10-native speakers; 11-2 sem course; grammatical structure of Sp adapted to the students' needs & readings in different fields; 2nd sem: modern expository writing & vocab enrichment; 12-b,c; 13-d,e,f; 14-specially prepared materials.

1518. SPANISH TO NATIVE SPEAKERS
U of Massahcusetts; Sp & Port; Amherst, MA 01002.
Jose L. Monserrate
1-39; 2-3x15; 3-a; 4-72/73; 5-4; 6-a; 7-a; 8-3s; 9-a; 10-none; 11-grammar, reading, comp; open only to native speakers of Sp; 12-a,b,d,g; 13-b,e,f; 14-Gramatica Castellana.

1519. SPANISH FOR NATIVE SPEAKERS
Medgar Evers C; Hums; Brooklyn, NY 11225.
Gladys A. Seda-Rodriguez
1-21; 2-3x28; 3-a; 4-72; 5-3; 6-a; 7-a; 8-6s; 9-a; 10-spoken prof; 11-2-sem sequence; pronunciation, spelling, grammar, comp, reading, vocab building; 12-g; 13-ng; 14-del Rio, El espanol es nuestra lengua; Anorga, Gramatica bilingue; Bague, Seleccion de lecturas y practicas de redaccion; instructor-prepared materials.

1520. SPANISH FOR NATIVE SPEAKERS
Mesa CC; FL; Mesa, AZ 85201.
Elias Y. Esquer
1-28; 2-4x16; 3-a; 4-74/75; 5-1; 6-a; 7-a; 8-

4s; 9-a; 10-oral comprehension & communication; 11-reading, writing; correction of
slang; discussion of the Chicano experience
in Amer; 12-b,c,g; 13-a,f; 14-Da Silva,
Beginning Spanish: A Concept Approach.

1521. SPANISH FOR CHICANOS
U of Michigan; FL; Flint, MI 48503.
F.C. Richardson
1-25; 2-5x14½; 3-a; 4-72; 5-8; 6-a; 7-a; 8-4s;
9-a; 10-interview; 11-development of confidence & facility in speaking & reading Sp
for whose with some oral comprehension;
12-b,e,g; 13-a,d; 14-Da Silva, Beginning
Spanish: A Concept Approach.

1522. SPANISH FOR NATIVES
Montclair SC; Sp & Ital; Upper Montclair,
NJ 07043.
Norman H. Fulton
1-ng; 2-3x15; 3-ng; 4-ng; 5-ng; 6-a; 7-ng; 8-
3s; 9-a,b, part-time; 10-ng; 11-two-course
sequence; 12-a,b,c,d,f,g; 13-d,e,f; 14-ng.

1523. CREATIVE WRITING FOR NEW MEXICO
SPANISH-SPEAKING STUDENTS
U of New Mexico; Mod & Cl Langs;
Albuquerque, NM 87131.
S.R. Ulibarri
1-22; 2-3x1 sem; 3-a; 4-ng; 5-ng; 6-usually
every other yr (on demand); 7-a; 8-3s; 9-a;
10-ng; 11-writing of original short stories &
poems; emphasis on use of New Mexican Sp;
12-ng; 13-ng; 14-Ulibarri, Tierra Amarilla.

1524. ESPANOL AVANZADO PARA ESTUDI-
ANTES DE HABLA ESPANOLA
U of New Mexico; Mod & Cl Langs;
Albuquerque, NM 87131.
Leon Marquez
1-62; 2-3x2sems; 3-a; 4-ng; 5-ng; 6-a; 7-a;
8-3s; 9-a; 10-Espanol elemental para es-
tudiantes de habla espanola; 11-standard Sp
(inter level-for New Mex Sp-speaking students; 12-a,b,c,g; 13-ng; 13-Barker, Espanol para el bilingue; Rogers, Escritores
contemporaneos de Mexico; Shular et al,
Literatura Chicana: Texto y Contexto.

1525. ESPANOL ELEMENTAL PARA ESTUDI-
ANTES DE HABLA ESPANOLA
U of New Mexico; Mod & Cl Langs;
Albuquerque, NM 87131.
Leon Marquez
1-152; 2-3xsem; 3-a; 4-ng; 5-ng; 6-a; 7-a; 8-
3s; 9-a; 10-ng; 11-intro to standard Sp for
New Mex Sp-speaking students; 12-
a,b,c,e,g; 13-ng; 14-Barker, Espanol para el
Bilingue; Canton, Nosotros somos dios;
Ulibarri, Tierra Amarilla; Shular et al,
Literatura Chicana: Texto y Contexto.

1526. SOUTHWEST SPANISH
U of New Mexico; Mod & Cl Langs;
Albuquerque, NM 87131.
Ruben Cobos
1-61; 2-3xsem; 3-a; 4-ng; 5-ng; 6-every
other yr; 7-a; 8-3s; 9-a; 10-adv comp &
conv; 11-study of Sp of US Southwest, esp
New Mexico; comparisons with standard Sp;
12-a,b,c,d,g; 13-ng; 14-none.

1527. SPANISH FOR NATIVE SPEAKERS
SUNY; Sp, Ital & Port; Buffalo, NY 14214.
Jorge Guitart
1-25; 2-3x15; 3-a; 4-74/75; 5-1; 6-a; 7-a; 8-
4s; 9-a; 10-none; 11-standard Sp for oral &
written communication; 12-a,b,e,g; 13-ng;
14-various.

1528. SPANISH COMPOSITION FOR STUDENTS
WITH   SPANISH-SPEAKING   BACK-
GROUND
SUNY; Hispanic Langs; Stony Brook, NY
11794.
Giorgio Perissinotto
1-10; 2-3x16; 3-b; 4-71; 5-ng; 6-a; 7-a; 8-3s;
9-a; 10-none; 11-improvement of oral &
written skills of native speakers; 12-
b,c,d,g; 13-e; 14-Alegria, La Prensa.

1529. SPANISH   FOR   SPANISH-SPEAKING
AMERICANS
U of Oregon; Rom Langs; Eugene, OR
97403.
David Curland
1-20; 2-4 hrs per wk x full yr; 3-a; 4-70; 5-4;
6-yr course; 7-a; 8-4q; 9-a; 10-native
speaker; 11-develops ability to read, write,
speak standard Sp; 12-b; 13-a,e; 14-Aarom,
Cartas de Luis; Perera, Ortografia; Y no se
lo trago la tierra.

1530. ELEMENTARY SPANISH FOR THE SPAN-
ISH SPEAKING
Pasadena City C; FLs; Pasadena, CA 91106.
Marina Cobb
1-18; 2-5x18; 3-c; 4-fall 74; 5-3; 6-a; 7-b; 8-
4s; 9-a; 10-understanding & speaking ability; 11-practice in pronunciation, reading,
writing, speaking; intro to Hispanic cult;
12-a,d,e,g; 13-a,b,d; 14-Barker, Espanol
para el Bilingue; Nassi, Workbook in Spanish, Three Years; Mexican textbooks of
various grade levels.

1531. BILINGUAL PROGRAM
Rockland CC (and St. Thomas Acquinas C);
FLs & Lits; Suffern, NY 10901.
Director of Admissions
2-yr program designed for Sp-speaking
students to take college courses in their
own lang & for Eng-speaking students to
improve their command of Sp.   Classes
started at the Haverstraw, N.Y. campus in
Sept 75. Further info ng.

1532. SPANISH   FOR   SPANISH-SPEAKING
STUDENTS
Sacramento City C; Sp; Sacramento, CA
95822.
Jose Gonzalez
1-20; 2-5x18; 3-a; 4-72; 5-4; 6-a; 7-a; 8-4s;
9-a; 10-understand & speak Sp; 11-speak-
ing, reading & writing elem Sp; vocab
building; structure; cult; 12-a,b,c,d,e,g; 13-
a,b,f; 14-Amsco, Workbooks I, II; Cuentos
de hoy; handouts for poetry and short
stories.

1533. PRINCIPIOS DE COMUNICACION ORAL
St. Mary's U; MLs; San Antonio, TX 78228.
O.H. Rechtschaffen; H. Rodriguez Fleming

277

1-23; 2-3x16; 3-b; 4-fall 73; 5-1; 6-b; 7-a; 8-3s; 9-a; 10-spoken prof; 11-dialogues, group discussion, oratory, formal & informal discourse, famous Sp & Latin Amer speeches; 12-c,e,g; 13-c, public speakers; 14-Reina Reguera, La Escuela del Orador.

1534. SPANISH FOR NATIVE SPEAKERS
Santa Rosa JC; FLs; Santa Rosa, CA 95401.
Ruth Parle Craig, Jesus de la Ossa
1-20; 2-2x17; 3-a; 4-late 60's; 5-18; 6-a; 7-a; 8-2s; 9-a,b; 10-literate native speaker; 11-reinforce reading & writing skills; 12-b,c,d,g; 13-ng; 14-ng.

1535. INTERMEDIATE SPANISH
Southwest Texas SU; MLs; San Marcos, TX 78666.
Robert A. Galvan
1-49; 2-3x15; 3-a; 4-fall 64; 5-25; 6-a; smr; 7-a; 8-3s; 9-a; 10-native speakers with some formal training in Sp; 11-ng; 12-a,b,c,d,e,g; 13-a,d,e,f, interviews; 14-Crispin & Crispin, Progress in Spanish; McKay, Misterio y Pavor, 13 Cuentos.

1536. SPANISH FOR SPANISH SPEAKERS
U of Texas; MLs; El Paso, TX 79968.
Diana S. Natalicio
1-263; 2-3,4½x15; 3-a; 4-74/75; 5-1; 6-a; 7-a,b; 8-3 or 4s; 9-a, part-time students; 10-4-course sequence; 1st course no prerequisite; subsequent courses, previous course in sequence; 11-ng; 12-a,b,c,d,e,g; 13-a,b,c,d,e,f; 14-Vivir Hoy; Perspectivas; Tesoro Hispanico; Literatura del Siglo XX; Marcario.

1537. FIRST-YEAR, THIRD-YEAR, FOURTH-YEAR SPANISH FOR CHICANOS
U of Utah; Langs; Salt Lake City, UT 84112.
Robert Helbling
1-20/25; 2-4 or 5x30 (fourth-year, 4-5x10); 3-a; 4-71/72; 5-12; 6-a; 7-a; 8-5q; 9-a; 10-written or oral placement exam; 11-grammar, reading, comp; 12-a,b,c,e,f,g; 13-b,f; 14-various.

1538. SPANISH FOR THE SPANISH SPEAKING
Ventura C; Lang Arts; Ventura, CA 93003.
Rene Rodriguez
1-32; 2-6x18; 3-a; 4-71; 5-1; 6-a; 7-a; 8-4s; 9-a; 10-aural-oral prof; 11-improving oral-aural skills, writing skills, principles of grammar, comparison of 'barrio' Sp to standard Sp; 12-a,b,e; 13-a,d; 14-Leal, Mexico: Civilizaciones y culturas; del Rio, Lengua Viva y Gramatica; Williams, New College Spanish and English Dictionary.

1539. SPANISH GRAMMAR AND COMPOSITION
Westchester CC; MLs; Valhalla, NY 10595.
Jacqueline Rosay
1-15; 2-3x16; 3-a; 4-fall 74; 5-1; 6-a; 7-a; 8-3s; 9-a; 10-native speaker; 11-two courses, one-year sequence; 12-g; 13-a,b,d,e,f; 14-Baker, Espanol para los Hispanos; Carralde, Mejore su vocabulario.

1540. INTERMEDIATE SPANISH FOR THE SPANISH SPEAKING
Western Michigan U; Mod & Cl Langs; Kalamazoo, MI 49001.
Roger L. Cole
1-9; 2-4x15½; 3-a; 4-fall 74; 5-1; 6-b; 7-ng; 8-4s; 9-ng; 10-native speaker; 11-ng; 12-g; 13-ng; 14-ng.

1541. CONTEMPORARY SPANISH FOR NATIVE SPEAKERS
William Paterson C; FL; Wayne, NJ 07470.
Catherine A. Barry
1-13; 2-3x17; 3-a; 4-74; 5-1; 6-b; 7-a; 8-3s; 9-a; 10-Sp advisor's permission; 11-correction of oral Sp, grammar, syntax, comp; 12-a,b,c,g; 13-e,f; 14-Alonso & Urina, Gramatica castellana; Crow & Dudley, El cuento.

1542. SPANISH FOR SPANISH SPEAKERS
U of Wisconsin; Sp & Port; Milwaukee, WI 53201.
Marguerite C. Suarez-Murias
Proposed course for fall 75; further info ng.

1543. SPANISH FOR THE SPANISH SPEAKING STUDENT
Yuba C; La Raza Studies; Maryville, CA 95901.
Corine Andrews, Salvador Soto
1-15; 2-4x18; 3-b; 4-71; 5-ng; 6-a; 7-a; 8-4s; 9-a; 10-Sp fluency; 11-reading, spelling, comp, grammar; offered at 3 levels of prof; 12-a,b,g; 13-e,f; 14-Pimsleur, Sol y Sombra; Perea, Ortografia; Perea, Acentuacion y Puntuacion; Anorga, Elementos Gramaticales.

TRAVEL AND/OR STUDY ABROAD

Chinese

1544. CHINESE LANGUAGE PROGRAM IN TAIWAN
Miami U; Ger, Russ & East Asian Langs; Oxford, OH 45056.
Chiang-tsu Chow
1-15; 2-20x8; 3-a; 4-71; 5-4; 6-every smr; 7-a; 8-12q; 9-a, students from other univs; 10-none for first yr Chi, 1 yr of Chi for second yr; 11-courses offered are the same as on Oxford campus; 12-a,e,f,g; 13-none; 14-Fenn, Speak Mandarin, Student Workbook; Wang, Read Chinese, Bks. I and II; Wang, Chinese Dialogues; Huang, 20 Lectures on Chinese Culture.

French

1545. FRENCH STUDY TOUR
Cabrillo CC; Fr; Aptos, CA 95003.
Bette Silverblatt
1-ng; 2-15x3; 3-a; 4-wtr 74/75; 5-1; 6-b, Jan intersession; 7-a; 8-3s; 9-a,b; 10-none; 11-travel-practical experience; 12-f; 13-none; 14-none.

1546. FRENCH-CANADIAN LIVE-IN
Mary C; Fr; Bismark, ND 58501.
Helen Kilzer
1-9; 2-all dayx3½; 3-c; 4-75; 5-1; 6-Jan Interim; 7-all day; 8-b; 9-a; 10-min one sem Fr; 11-live with Fr-Canadian families, share in family activities, spend ½ days in Fr school K-9 assisting in classes, partici-pating on a paraprofessional basis when possible (kindergarten); 12e,g; 13-experi-ence, daily log; 14-none.

1547. INTERMEDIATE FRENCH - QUEBEC
Nasson C; Hums; Springfield, ME 04083.
Gilles E. Auger
1-18; 2-4x16; 3-a; 4-74/75; 5-1; 6-a; 7-a; 8-4s; 9-a; 10-elem Fr; 11-ng; 12a,b,c,d,f,g, field trip to Quebec; 13-a,b,f, travel brochures; 14-Bessette, Histoire de la Litterature Canadienne -Francaise.

1548. LIVING YOUR SECOND LANGUAGE: A JOURNEY TO QUEBEC
Peabody C; MLs; Nashville, TN 37203.
T.G. Herder
1-18; 2-126x2; 3-c; 4-74; 5-1; 6-upon suffi-cient demand; 7- interim/smr; 8-1-3s; 9-a,b,c; 10-elem prof; 11-14-ng.

1549. CONVERSATIONAL FRENCH AND SKIING
Queens C; FLs; Charlotte, NC 28207.
E. Cobb
1-ng; 2-45x3; 3-a; 4-Jan 75; 5-1; 6-perhaps every 3 yrs; 7-a; 8-3; 9-a; 10-1 sem Fr; 11-3 hrs daily conv lessons; skiing in Fr Alps

afternoon; 12-b,c,g; 13-e,f; 14-ng.

1550. PARIS-FRENCH ORIENTATION
Ripon C; Rom Langs & Lits; Ripon, WI 54971.
Virginia Avery, Registrar, AYA, Inc., 221 E. 50 St., New York, NY 10022.
1-c60; 2-15x4/6; 3-c; 4-64; 5-ng; 6-a; 7-a; 8-b; 9-a; 10-none; 11-preparation in lang & civ for students in all fields so that they can pass entrance placement exams at univ. Ripon C gives 2 credit hrs for passing; 12-a,b,c,d,e,g; 13-e,f; 14-teachers prepare own materials.

1551. LES ACTUALITES FRANCAISES
U of Southern California; Fr & Ital; Los Angeles, CA 90007.
Michelle Buchanan
1-18; 2-4x15; 3-a; 4-74; 5-1; 6-every two yrs; 7-a; 8-4s; 9-a; 10 reading knowledge of Fr; 11-readings in Fr periodicals, viewing Fr films & art exhibits; 12-a,b,c,d,f; 13-a,b,e,f; 14-none.

See also 305, 479, 792, 793, 1035, 1054, 1369.

German

1552. SPRING SESSION IN GERMANY
Central Michigan U; FLs; Mt. Pleasant, MI 48858.
Charlotte Evans
1-9; 2-24x3; 3-a; 4-71; 5-3; 6-every other spr; 7-ng; 8-3s; 9-a; 10-for hum credit, for Ger credit: 2 yrs Ger; 11-based in Munich; approach is cult, interdisc & informal; three courses offered: Ger Cult in the Post-War Era (no lang requirement), Ger Cult in the Post-War Era (Ger required), Independent Study in Ger Cult; 12-a,b,c,d,f,g; 13-e,f, guide books; 14-none.

1553. INTRODUCTION TO SPOKEN GERMAN
DePauw U; Ger & Russ; Greencastle, IN 46135.
C. Van Zwoll
1-30; 2-2x14; 3-a; 4-73; 5-3; 6-a; 7-a; 8-2s; 9-a; 10-none; 11-oral & aural Ger; admis-sion to a DePauw Univ sem in Europe program immediately following the course; 12-e,g; 13-a; 14-Experiment in Inter-national Living, Living German.

1554. THE AUSTRIAN EXPERIENCE
Emory U; Ger; Atlanta, GA 30322.
James V. McMahon
1-3; 2-10x6; 3-c; 4-73; 5-2; 6-spr & smr; 7-a; 8-10q; 9-a; 10-1 yr college Ger; 11-taught in Vienna. Covers development of Austrian cult in context of European cult. Hist approach; 12-a,b,d, field trips; 13-ng; 14-some readings in Austrian lit.

1555. INTERMEDIATE GERMAN
Hudson Valley CC; MLs; Troy, NY 12180.
Ausma Mursch

1-5; 2-ng; 3-b,c; 4-74/75; 5-1; 6-ng; 7-ng; 8-3s; 9-a; 10-Ger III; 11-extension of first sem of inter level, at Goethe Inst in Germany; 12-a,b,c,g; 13-a,b,e,f; 14-ng.

1556. INTENSIVE GERMAN IN LUXEMBOURG (I)
Miami U; Ger, Russ & East Asian Langs; Oxford, OH 45056.
Gisela E. Bahr
1-9; 2-24x6; 3-c; 4-72/73; 5-2; 6-every smr; 7-a; 8-15; 9-a,c; 10-none; 11-elem Ger at the Miami U European Center; 12-a,b,c,f,g; 13-b,e, Silent Way; 14-Fremdsprache I & II.

1557. INTENSIVE GERMAN IN LUXEMBOURG (II)
Miami U; Ger, Russ & East Asian Langs; Oxford, OH 45056.
1-5; 2-18x6; 3-c; 4-73/74; 5-1; 6-every smr; 7-a; 8-12q; 9-a; 10-1 yr coll Ger; 11-at the Miami U European Center; 12-a,b,c,f,g; 13-b,f, Silent Way; 14-Deutschland Erzaehlt.

1558. INTERNATIONAL STUDY CENTER-BONN
Ripon C; Ger; Ripon, WI 54971.
James F. Hyde, Jr.
Now in its 6th year, the Ripon ISC is designed primarily to assist talented students, regardless of their majors, in attaining prof in the Ger lang & learning about Ger cult. As part of a Jr Yr program officially integrated into Bonn Univ, individually adjusted curricula are available. Prerequisites: at least jr standing; basic knowledge of Ger.

1559. GERMAN TRAVEL SEMINAR
U of Wisconsin; FLs; Eau Claire, WI 54701.
Vernon Gingerich, Adam Bors
1-15; 2-72x3; 3-a; 4-74; 5-2; 6-once a yr in May; 7-entire May interim, all day and all night; 8-3s; 9-a, and auditors from community; 10-must be a jr to receive coll credit; 11-travel through southern Germany & Austria; 12-a,b,d,f; 13-a,b,d, travel; 14-Pinson, Modern Germany; German govt, The Strange German Ways; Berlitz, German for Travelers; primary texts.

See also 30, 305, 800, 801, 1176.

Japanese

1560. SUMMER INTENSIVE JAPANESE AND FIVE MONTHS IN JAPAN
Colgate U; Cl, Sl & Oriental Langs; Hamilton, NY 13346.
Thomas E. Swann
Intensive lang experience & study of Jap cult. Students live with Jap families. Inaugurated in 72. A full yr of lang study & completion of a course on Jap society & culture required prior to departure. The smr intensive course meets these requirements.

1561. JUNIOR YEAR IN JAPAN
Divine Word C; Epworth, IA 52045.
Robert Riemer
In cooperation with Nanzan Univ, Nagoya, Japan, students take a full load of courses in Jap hist, cult, philo, art, lit, including two intensive sems of Jap. Program initiated 74/75 with 3 students.

Russian

1562. ADVANCED STUDIES IN RUSSIAN LANGUAGE AND CULTURE
Amherst C; Russ; Amherst, MA 01002.
Dan E. Davidson
1-19; 2-3x14; 3-a; 4-71/72; 5-3; 6-b; 7-a; 8-4s; 9-a, part-time area teachers, faculty spouses; special students; 10-inter prof; 11-topics and texts of a general cult significance; discussion of prominent figures & current events in the artistic & intellectual life of the USSR; culminates in a 3-4 week optional study tour of Moscow & Leningrad during Jan interterm; 12-a,b,c,g; 13-b,e,f; 14-ng.

1563. RUSSIAN STUDIES PROGRAM (OFF CAMPUS)
Colgate U; Cl, Sl, and Oriental Langs; Hamilton, NY 13346.
Virginia Bennett
Intensive study of inter Russ & cult; 11 wks, 3 at Colgate & 8 in Russia. Students meet in small groups 3 hrs daily for 5 wks with native instructors; keep a diary in Russ, make class presentations, participate in debates & dramas & attend Soviet guest lectures. For cult course, students have texts and observe & study in the field, submit a diary of impressions, & write on one aspect of Russ cult. Program approved for smr 75.

See also 808, 835, 1085.

Spanish

1564. SPANISH AMERICAN STUDIES PROGRAM
Columbus C; Langs; Columbus, GA 31907.
Philip D. Battle
1-28; 2-25x6½; 3-a; 4-smr 72; 5-3; 6-each smr; 7-2 wks on Columbus campus, 4½ wks in Bogota, Colombia; 8-15q; 9-a, or anyone who meets prerequisite and coll entrance requirements; 10-elem prof; 11-designed to attract non-Sp majors; cult the main emphasis, lang the vehicle; 12-a,b,c,g, living with family; 14-phrase books.

1565. MEXICAN ART HISTORY
U of Dallas; Sp; Irving, TX 75060.
Alexandra Wilhelmsen
1-12; 2-ng; 3-a; 4-71; 5-4; 6-b; 7-smr; 8-3; 9-grad students & teachers; 10-ng; 11-study of Mex architecture, sculpture, & painting from early Pre-Columbian times to 20th cen. Includes a one-wk study trip to Mexico; 12-a,b,g; 13-a,b; 14-Fernandez, Arte Mexicano-De Sus Origenes a Nuestros Dias.

1566. MEXICO: A MODERN REVOLUTION
Hastings C; Sp & Soci; Hastings, NE 68901.
Douglas K. Benson (Sp), Robert Stockton (Soci)

280

1-13; 2-allx4; 3-b (Soci); 4-Jan interim 75; 5-1; 6-as needed; 7-ng; 8-4s; 9-a; 10-for Sp credit, reading knowledge of Sp; 11-study the effects of the Mex "Social" Revolution of 1910 with respect to soci & cult change; trip gives first- hand experiences with Mex academic & govt representatives, exposure to land reform patterns & the artistic milieu generated by the Revolution; interaction with Mex students; 12-a,b,c,d,f; 13-a,b,c,d,f, student journal; 14-Cumberland, Mexico: The Struggle for Modernity; Lewis, Five Families; Azuela, The Underdogs; Fuentes, Where the Air Is Clear; Guzman, El Aguila y la Serpiente; Paz, The Labrynth of Solitude. Upper div students must do outside research.

1567. WINTERIM IN SPAIN
Houghton C; Sp; Houghton, NY 14744.
Robert L. Crosby
1-15; 2-ng; 3-c; 4-73; 5-2; 6-by demand; 7-three wks in Jan; 8-3s; 9-a; 10-1 yr coll Sp; 11-1st week based in Madrid followed by overland travel through La Mancha to Andalucia, region of Arabic influence; 3rd wk living in Sp homes.

1568. PRE-COLUMBIAN CULTURES
Lone Mountain C; Sp; San Francisco, CA 94118.
M.P. Valdes
1-3; 2-all dayx4; 3-a; 4-Jan 75; 5-1; 6-on demand; 7-ng; 8-4s; 9-a; 10-knowledge of Sp; 11-in-depth study of Maya, Aztec, & Inca cults; includes trip to Mexico, Yucatan, Guatemala, Ecuador, Peru; 12-a,b,c,d,g; 13-a,b,e,f; 14-von Hagen, Los Incas; Von Hagen, Los Mayas; Von Hagen, Los Aztecas; a specially designed reading list of books to be read before departure.

1569. STUDY OF MEXICAN CULTURE AND LANGUAGE
Marion C; Lang & Ling; Marion, IN 46952.
Owen Snyder
1-7; 2-100+x3; 3-b; 4-71; 5-5; 6-every Jan term; 7-ng; 8-3s; 9-a; 10-1 sem coll Sp for Sp credit, none for "cultural" credit; 11-travel, daily paper in Sp, reading about Mexico; 12-b,d,f,g; 13-e,f; 14-no text.

1570. TRAVEL STUDY IN FOREIGN LANGUAGE
U of Nebraska; FLs; Omaha, NE 68101.
Woodrow L. Most
1-10; 2-20x2-3; 3-b; 4-73; 5-2; 6-Christmas interim every other yr; 7-ng; 8-1-3s; 9-a, townspeople; 10-2nd sem standing; 11-latest trip: study & appreciation of Mexico, its institutions & people through primary & secondary sources; 12-a,b,d,f; 13-e,f; 14-Simpson, Many Mexicos; Castillo, The Discovery and Conquest of Mexico; Paz, Labrynth and Solitude: Life and Thought in Mexico.

1571. SUMMER GRADUATE PROGRAM IN MEXICO
Rice U; Cl, Sp & Port; Houston, TX 77001.
1-21; 2-6-9x6; 3-a; 4-73/74 in Argentina; 5-

3; 6-every smr; 7-a; 8-6-9; 9-a; 10-admission to grad program; 11-research & study; alternates between Spain & Latin Amer; 12-a,b,c,d,g; 13-all, plus ling field work & play attendance.

1572. MADRID-SPANISH ORIENTATION
Ripon C; Rom Langs & Lits; Ripon, WI 54971.
Virginia Avery, Registrar, AYA, Inc. (Academic Year Abroad), 221 E. 50 St., New York, NY 10022.
1-20; 2-15x4-6; 3-c; 4-64; 5-ng; 6-a (Sept 15-Nov 1 and Jan 5-25); 7-a; 8-b; 9-a; 10-none; 11-preparation in lang & civ for students in all fields so that they can pass entrance placement exams at Univ of Madrid. Ripon gives 2 credit hours for passing; 12-a,b,c,d,e,g; 13-e,f; 14-teachers prepare own materials.

1573. INTERMEDIATE SPANISH I (INDEPENDENT STUDY)
C of St. Thomas; FLs; St. Paul, MN 55105.
Shelly Ann Moorman
1-1; 2-ng; 3-a; 4-74/75; 5-1; 6-irregularly; 7-ng; 8-4s; 9-a; 10-elem prof; 11-reviews & emphasizes understanding another cult; involves living-learning experience in a foreign country. (1) reading & research about the country to be visited; (2) living with a family in a foreign country; (3) reports in Sp to advisor, daily log, final paper & oral summary.

1574. MINI-TERM IN MEXICO
Trinity U; FLs; San Antonio, TX 78284.
Kenneth Taggart
1-12; 2-2 wks; 3-a; 4-smr 74; 5-2; 6-each smr; 7-a; 8-3s; 9-a; 10-4 sems Sp; 11-varies, 74: Hispanic Theater, Civ, Cult; 75: Mexico, Rural & Urban; 12-a,b,c,d,g; 13-e,f, complete immersion in foreign cult; 14-74: Leal, Mexico--Civilizaciones y Culturas; 75: Rulfo, El llano en llamas; Paz, El laberinto de la soledad.

1575. SPANISH STUDIES ABROAD
U of Wisconsin; FLs; Eau Claire, WI 54701.
1-29; 2-6 wks; 3-c; 4-smr 65; 5-10; 6-smr; 7-a; 8-6s; 9-a; 10-elem prof; 11-ng; 12-a,b,c,f,g; 13-a,b,e,f, field trips; 14-ng.

1576. SPANISH-RELIGION QUARTER IN MEXICO
C of Wooster; Sp & Ital, Religion; Wooster, OH 44691.
Kent O. Brimhall, Glenn R. Bucher
1-45; 2-variesx10; 3-b,c; 4-wtr qtr 74/75; 5-1; 6-not sure; 7-a; 8-1 qtr course; 9-a; 10-none, provision made for required Sp study for registrants without Sp training; 11-Sp lang; Mex and Sp-Amer cult, art, anthro, religion; mini-courses at Cemanahuac Inst, Cuernavaca; 12-a,b,c,d,f,g; 13-personal contacts mostly; 14-ng.

1577. STUDY TRAVEL SEMINAR
C of Wooster; Sp; Wooster, OH 44691.
Kent Brimhall
First offered wtr qtr 74/75 with 45 stu-

dents. Constitutes a full qtr of study, with many courses available. In Cuernavaca, Mexico. No prerequisites.

See also 258, 269, 305, 867, 957, 959, 1141, 1244, 1403, 1411, 1412, 1566.

Multi-Language

1577A. INDEPENDENT STUDY AND TRAVEL
Howard U; Rom Langs; Washington, DC 20059.
Miriam D. Willis
1-3; 2-3x18; 3-a; 4-73; 5-every sem; 6-a; 7-a; 8-3s; 9-ng; 10-none; 11-to enable students to research ind topics under the guidance of an advisor or to gain the experience of living abroad with the objective of gaining insights into a foreign cult (undergrad); academic credit to students who initiate and complete an original research project abroad as part of their grad program; 12-c, examination of experiences abroad; 13-materials for oral presentation; 14-none.

See also 300, 842.

INTERNSHIP AND/OR FIELD WORK

French

See 303.

German

See 212, 303.

Portuguese

See 749.

Spanish

1578. SPANISH IN THE CITY
Albertus Magnus C; Sp; New Haven, CT 06511.
Sr. Fidelis Bell
1-ng; 2-3x32; 3-a; 4-73/74; 5-1; 6-every other yr; 7-b; 8-6s; 9-a,b; 10-elem & inter Sp; 11-functional conv: everyday problems & vocab; topics of current interest-urban or Hispanic; project working with Puerto Rican Association; 12-b,c,d,g; 13-e,f; 14-Duran, Vivir Hoy.

1579. INTERNSHIP
Emmanuel C; Sp; Boston, MA 02115.
Sr. Margaret Pauline Young
1-ng; 2-varies x 15; 3-c; 4-spr 75; 5-1; 6-b; 7-a; 8-4s; 9-a; 10-near native fluency; 11-students teach H.S. equivalency courses in Sp & help with ESL courses; or students assist Sp and/or Port speaking people at Logan Airport; 12-ng; 13-ng; 14-ng.

1580. COMMUNITY SPANISH
George Washington U; Rom Langs; Washington, DC 20052.
Shirley Barnett
1-8; 2-2 class hrs, 4 hrs of community work

per wk for 13 wks; 3-a; 4-72; 5-4; 6-a; 7-a; 8-3s; 9-a; 10-4 sems coll Sp; 11-improving oral & written fluency; 12-b,g; 13-ng; 14-no texts; class periods devoted to discussion of outside activities, correction of compositions.

1581. NON-TRADITIONAL/SPANISH INTERN-SHIP
Lake Forest/Field Museum of Natural History of Chicago; FL, Ed; Lake Forest, IL 60045.
George L. Speros
1-6; 2-20x7; 3-a, dept at museum; 4-wtr 73/74; 5-1; 6-b; 7-a; 8-8s; 9-a; 10-adv prof; no freshmen; 11-interns work with biling programs for children, trans museum material from Eng, & trans for museum instructors; 12-b,d,f,g; 13-g, material published by museum; 14-all material translated supplied by the Dept of Ed of the Museum; material substantially different each year.

1582. FIELDWORK IN THE SPANISH COMMUNITY
Lowell U; Sp (Langs); Lowell, MA 01854.
John Mendicoa
1-6; 2-6x16; 3-c; 4-73/74; 5-3; 6-a; 7-a; 8-3; 9-a; 10-4 sems of Sp; 11-students work in community under supervision of one agency & instructor; 12-ng; 13-ng; 14-ng.

1583. SPANISH FOR HUMAN RELATIONS
Marian C; Sp; Fond de Lac, WI 54935.
Sr. Marilyn Homiak
1-4; 2-ng; 3-b (Dept of Soci Behavioral Scis), c (field work); 4-ng; 5-2; 6-a; 7-a; 8-3s; 9-a; 10-ng; 11-ng; 12-e,g; 13-a,b,c; 14-Duran, Vivir Hoy.

1584. FIELD STUDY IN THE PUERTO RICAN COMMUNITY
U of Massachusetts; Sp & Port; Amherst, MA 01002.
Ana M. Galvin
1-6; 2-7x14; 3-c; 4-fall 73; 5-3; 6-a; 7-a; 8-3s; 9-a; 10-adv prof; permission; 11-class meetings; textbook plus knowledge of bibliography in field; outreach work in community; living with Puerto Rican family; attendance at related functions, meetings & lectures; research project; 12-a,b,c,g; 13-input from community; 14-Cordasco and Bucchioni, The Puerto Rican Community on the Mainland.

1585. TUTORING SPANISH-SPEAKING STUDENTS
U of Massachusetts; Sp & Port; Amherst, MA 01002.
Nina M. Scott
1-15; 2-3x14; 3-c; 4-fall 71; 5-10; 6-a; 7-a; 8-3s; 9-a; 10-2 yrs coll Sp; 11-the students are bused to Holyoke & work directly in the classrooms on elem levels, one-to-one secondary schools, under supervision of the classroom teacher; one paper on background reading, one paper upon completion of the tutorial, based on an experiential journal; 12-a,b,f; 13-f; 14-Wagenheim, Puerto Rico, A Profile; Fitzpatrick, Puerto

Rican Americans: The Meaning of Migration to the Mainland.

1586. LANGUAGE INTERNSHIP
Molloy C; Sp; Rockville Centre, NY 11570.
Sr. Mary William Posthauer
1-2; 2-5x15; 3-c; 4-72; 5-5; 6-a; 7-a; 8-3s; 9-a, part-time students; 10-fluency in Sp; 11-students work as translators in one of the local Nassau County social agencies 4 hrs wkly. There is a one-hr wkly seminar to develop trans skills & cult implications; 12-b,g; 13-f and forms pertaining to soci work; 14-none.

1587. EXPERIENTIAL LEARNING IN SPANISH: FIELD WORK
C of St. Catherine; Sp; St. Paul, MN 55105.
C.A. White
1-3; 2-either 40 hr work wk/4 wks or 6 hr work wk/14 wks; 3-a; 4-72/73; 5-5; 6-a; 7-time arranged according to project; 8-either 4s or 2s; 9-a; 10-inter level Sp; 11-practical application of Sp in working with community projects, biling ed, migrant workers; program initiated by student, approved by dept; 12-b; 13-varies; 14-varies, e.g. Snyder & Ochia, Voces del Barrio.

1588. EXPERIENTIAL LEARNING
C of St. Thomas; FLs; St. Paul, MN 55105.
Lyn Loudon
1-1; 2-ng; 3-a; 4-74/75; 5-1; 6-irregularly; 7-ng; 8-4s; 9-a; 10-adequate mastery of Sp; 11-teaching Sp to school children 6-10 yrs old in a parochial school under supervision of the principal and Ms. Loudon; 12-ng; 13-ng; 14-ng.

1589. SPANISH FIELD WORK SEMINAR
Simmons C; FLs & Lits; Boston, MA 02115.
Louise G. Cohen
1-9; 2-2 class hrs, 3 or more hrs in field for 13 wks; 3-a (class), c (field work); 4-71; 5-4; 6-b; 7-a; 8-4s; 9-a; 10-some speaking knowledge of Sp; 11-sustained, wkly contact with Boston's Sp-speaking community; discussion of Puerto Rican cult; 12-a,b,c,e,f,g; 13-a,b,d,e,f; 14-Thomas, Down These Mean Streets; Sexton, Spanish Harlem; Lewis, La Vida; Soto, Spiks; Vivas & Maldonado, A Vellon la Esperanzas Mela-

nia; Maldonado-Denis, Puerto Rico: A Socio-Historic Interpretation.

1590. INDEPENDENT STUDY-SPANISH
Westfield SC; FLs; Westfield, MA 01085.
Raymond Durand
1-3; 2-3-6x16; 3-c; 4-spr 75; 5-1; 6-b; 7-a; 8-3-6s; 9-a; 10-fluency; 11-interpreting for doctors & patients at Springfield Med Center. Wkly reports to advisors of problems; 12-b,e,g; 13-ng; 14-ng.

See also 258, 303, 961, 1191.

Miscellaneous

1591. COMMUNITY INVOLVEMENT PROJECT
California SC; FLs; Rohnert Park, CA 94928.
F. Gaona
1-5; 2-1-3x14; 3-c; 4-70; 5-9; 6-a; 7-a,b; 8-1-3s; 9-a; 10-none; 11-the student helps teachers with pupils who speak little or no Eng; 12-f,g; 13-none; 14-none.

1592. FIELD WORK IN FOREIGN LANGUAGES
U of Maine; FLs; Orono, ME 04473.
Josef Roggenbauer
A new course as of spr 75. 1-12 credits, only 6 of which may be counted toward the major. Activities considered for credit: radio & T.V. announcing or script writing in a FL; trans & interpreting; library work, e.g. cataloguing FL material; health service using an FL, e.g., reading to patients; soci work, including VISTA, Peace Corps; work abroad for a least one month.

1593. FIELD STUDY
Moravian C; FLs; Bethlehem, PA 18018.
Dorothy Tyler
Student may receive 13 course units per term (not to exceed 4 units of the 31 for the degree) for: full or part-time employment, volunteer work, internships or research assignments, or individual study. Dept has been involved in 3 programs: work in a hospital in Nicaragua; work in a Gymnasium in Germany; & Fr to Eng trans of articles in the electronic data processing industry abroad.

See also 1265.

DUTCH

1594. SPECIAL READINGS IN DUTCH
Berry C; FL; Mount Berry, GA 30149.
August J. de Berdt
1-1; 2-2x10; 3-a; 4-72; 5-3; 6-when needed;
7-a; 8-2/5q; 9-a; 10-adv Ger; 11-for students traveling to Europe; 12-b,c,e,g; 13-d,e; 14-Lagerway, Speak Dutch.

FRENCH

Texts used (#14):
a. Amado, En France Comme si Vous y Etiez
b. Kany & Dondo, Spoken French for Students and Travelers

1595. FRENCH FOR STUDENTS AND TRAVELERS
Claremont Men's C; MLs; Claremont, CA 91711.
Jean-Antoine Bour
1-9; 2-3x15; 3-a; 4-74/75; 5-1; 6-b; 7-a; 8-½s; 9-a; 10-none; 11-ng; 12-b,g; 13-b, realia; 14-Harris & Leveque, Basic Conversational French; instructor-prepared materials.

1596. FRENCH LIFE AND CONVERSATION FOR THE TRAVELER
Cleveland SCC; FLs; Cleveland, TN 37311.
Renate Hufft
1-32; 2-3x10; 3-a; 4-spr 74; 5-1; 6-b; 7-b; 8-3q; 9-a, part-time; 10-none; 11-customs, points of interest, travel hints; beginning conv Fr; hums elective; 12-b,c,d,g; 13-a,b,d,e,f; 14-b; instructor-prepared materials.

1597. FRENCH FOR TRAVEL
Columbia C; MLs; Columbia, MO 65201.
Hortense P. Davison
1-ng; 2-2x18; 3-a; 4-73; 5-3; 6-a; 7-b; 8-2s; 9-a; 10-none; 11-vocab and expressions useful to the traveller; 12-g; 13-d; 14-French in a Nutshell; instructor-prepared materials.

1598. FRENCH FOR TRAVELERS
U of Detroit; Langs & Ling; Detroit, MI 48221.
L.W. Wedberg
1-c12; 2-2x15; 3-a; 4-72; 5-ng; 6-a; 7-a; 8-2s; 9-a; 10-none; 11-essential functional vocab to get along in everyday situations; 12-d,g; 13-visuals; 14-Conversa-phone records and booklet.

1599. FRENCH FOR TRAVELERS
U of Georgia; Rom Langs; Athens, GA 30601.
J.P. Lee
1-9; 2-5x10; 3-a; 4-74; 5-1; 6-b; 7-a; 8-5q; 9-a; 10-inter prof; 11-vocab and oral prof for travel or living in Fr-speaking countries; 12-b,c,g; 13-a,b,e,f; 14-Bonnell & Sedwick, Conversation in French: Points of Departure; Limouzy & Bourgeacq, A Vous la Parole.

1600. FRENCH FOR TRAVELERS
U of Kansas; Fr & Ital; Lawrence, KS 66045.
Corinne Anderson
1-50; 2-2x15; 3-a; 4-spr 74; 5-2; 6-a; 7-a; 8-2s; 9-a; 10-none; 11-basic communication patterns, practical vocab, exercises in comp and con; 12-b,e,g; 13-a,b,d,e,f; 14-Berlitz, French for Travelers; EMC, Rendez-vous en France.

1601. FRENCH FOR TRAVELERS
Michigan SU; Rom Langs; East Lansing, MI 48824.
Leonard J. Rahilly
1-new; 2-3x10; 3-a; 4-74; 5-1; 6-b; 7-a; 8-3q; 9-a; 10-none; 11-basic outline of grammar, basic vocab for communication when traveling, info on travel abroad; 12-a,b,f; 13-b,g; 14-Madrigal, See It and Say It in French.

1602. FRENCH FOR TRAVELERS
SUCNY; Foreign Studies Center; Oswego, NY 13126.
Patrick Sullivan
1-new; 2-15x3; 3-a; 4-smr 75; 5-1; 6-on demand; 7-a; 8-3s; 9-unknown; 10-none; 11-intensive conv Fr for travel; basic vocab and phrases; 12-b,c,d,e,g; 13-a,b,c,d,e,f; 14-no formal text.

1603. FRENCH FOR TOURISTS
U of North Carolina; MLs; Wilmington, NC 28401.
Jackson G. Sparks
1-9; 2-3x15; 4-74; 5-1; 6-b, smr; 7-a; 8-3s; 9-a; 10-none; 11-transportation, hotel, restaurant, shopping, 12-b,f,g; 13-b,f, menus; 14-b.

1604. FRENCH AROUND THE WORLD
Roanoke C; FLs; Salem, VA 24153.
Patricia M. Gathercole
Non-credit conv course for travel. Further info ng.

1605. FRENCH FOR TRAVEL
Wayne SC; Hums; Wayne, NE 68787.
Rafael Sosa
1-15; 2-3x14; 3-a; 4-72; 5-3; 6-b; 7-a,b; 8-3s; 9-a; 10-ng; 11-vocab for travel abroad; 12-a,b,g; 13-a,b,f; 14-ng.

See also 195, 196, 478.

GERMAN

Texts used (#14):
a. Braun et al., Deutsch als Fremdsprache, I
b. Schneider, Guten Tag

1606. GERMAN FOR TRAVEL
Columbia C; MLs; Columbia, MO 65201.
Hortense P. Davison
1-ng; 2-2x18; 3-b; 4-73; 5-3; 6-a; 7-b; 8-2s; 9-a; 10-none; 11-vocab and expressions

useful to the traveller; 12-g; 13-d; 14-instructor-prepared materials.

1607. GERMAN FOR TRAVELERS
U of Detroit; Langs & Ling; Detroit, MI 48221.
L.W. Wedberg
1-c12; 2-2x15; 3-a; 4-72; 5-ng; 6-a; 7-a; 8-2s; 9-a; 10-none; 11-functional vocab for everyday situations encountered abroad; 12-d,g; 13-visuals, records; 14-Conversa-Phone records and booklet.

1608. GERMAN FOR TRAVELERS
East Stroudsburg SC; FL; East Stroudsburg, PA 18301.
Blossom S. Brooks
1-11; 2-3x7½; 3-a; 4-74; 5-4; 6-twice a sem; 7-a; 8-2s; 9-a, part-time; 10-none; 11-useful phrases in travel situations; 12-g; 13-a,b,d, transparancies; 14-Langenscheidt dictionary, b.

1609. GERMAN FOR TRAVELERS
Miami U; Ger, Russ & East Asian Langs; Oxford, OH 45056.
Gisela Bahr
1-c55; 2-3x10; 3-a; 4-spr 73; 5-3; 6-ng; 7 b; 8-3q; 9-a; 10-none; 11-basic knowledge of the spoken lang for everyday encounters; 12-a,b,f,g; 13-realia; 14-Miller, Auf Deutsch bitte, Stufe Eins, instructor prepared materials.

1610. GERMAN FOR TRAVEL AND STUDY ABROAD
St. Louis U; MLs; St. Louis, MO 63103.
Margarete Moon
1-new; 2-3x18; 3-a; 4-spr 75; 5-1; 6-b; 7-a; 8-3s; 9-a; 10-none; 11-ng; 12-a,b; 13-b,e,f; 14-Weiss & Anderson, Begegnung mit Deutschland; Those Strange German Ways; Mann, Unser Vaterland; Seydlitz fuer Gymnasion, Vol. 1.

1611. GERMAN FOR TRAVEL
Wayne SC; Hums; Wayne, NE 68787.
Rafael Sosa
1-15; 2-3x14; 3-a; 4-72; 5-3; 6-b; 7-a,b; 8-3s; 9-a; 10-ng; 11-vocab for travel abroad; 12-a,b,g; 13-a,b,f; 14-ng.

JAPANESE

See 383.

NORWEGIAN

1612. NORWEGIAN FOR TRAVELERS
Moorhead SC; Langs; Moorhead, MN 56560.
Kenneth Smemo
1-new; 2-4x12; 3-a; 4-74/75; 5-1; 6-sufficient demand; 7-a; 8-4q; 9-a; 10-none; 11-beginning course; listening, reading, speaking, writing; 12-b,e; 13-d, visuals; 14-Haugen, Spoken Norwegian.

RUSSIAN

1613. RUSSIAN FOR TRAVELERS
U of Detroit; Langs & Ling; Detroit, MI 48221.
L.W. Wedberg

1-new; 2-2x15; 3-a; 4-75; 5-0; 6-a; 7-a; 8-2s; 9-a; 10-none; 11-essential functional vocab for everyday situations encountered abroad; 12-d,g; 13-visuals, records; 14-Conversa-Phone records and booklet.

1614. INTRODUCTION TO RUSSIAN
Ohio SU; Sl Langs & Lits; Columbus, OH 43210.
Leon Twarog
For those planning a trip to the Soviet Union and needing enough Russ to read street signs, use a dictionary and phrasebook intelligently--or for those who are simply interested in learning something about how Russ works. Introduction to the Cyrillic alphabet, basic elements of grammar, some speaking and reading.

SPANISH

1615. SPANISH FOR TOURISTS
U of Alaska; MLs; Anchorage, AK 99503.
Diana Berkowitz
1-20; 2-3x14; 3-a; 4-73; 5-3; 6-a; 7-b; 8-3s; 9-a, part-time; 10-none; 11-intro to basic grammar, pronunciation, vocab; 12-b,f,g; 13-a,b; 14-none.

1616. SPANISH FOR TRAVEL
Columbia C; MLs; Columbia, MO 65201.
Hortense P. Davison
1-ng; 2-2x18; 3-a; 4-73; 5-3; 6-a; 7-b; 8-2s; 9-a; 10-none; 11-vocab and expressions useful to the traveler; 12-g; 13-d; 14-Spanish in a Nutshell; instructor-prepared materials.

1617. SPANISH FOR TRAVELERS
U of Detroit; Langs & Ling; Detroit, MI 48221.
L.W. Wedberg
1-c12; 2-2x15; 3-a; 4-72; 5-ng; 6-a; 7-a; 8-2s; 9-a; 10-none; 11-essential functional vocab for everyday situations encountered abroad; 12-d,g; 13-visuals, records; 14-Conversa-Phone records and booklet.

1618. SPANISH FOR TRAVELERS
U of Georgia; Rom Langs; Athens, GA 30601.
Ruth Hanson
1-20; 2-5x10; 3-a; 4-74; 5-1; 6-b; 7-a; 8-5q; 9-a; 10-inter prof; 11-vocab and oral prof for travel or living in Sp-speaking countries; 12-b,c,g; 13-a,b,e,f; 14-Kany, Spoken Spanish for Students and Travelers.

1619. SPANISH FOR TRAVELERS
Michigan SU; Rom Langs; East Lansing, MI 48823.
William DeSua
1-21; 2-3x10; 3-a; 4-spr 74; 5-1; 6-b; 7-a; 8-2q; 9-a; 10-none; 11-grammar, vocab, useful phrases; intro to Sp cult and life; 12-a,b,e; 13-b,e; 14-instructor-prepared materials.

1620. BASIC SPANISH CONVERSATION FOR TRAVELERS
Molloy C; Sp; Rockville Centre, NY 11570.
Libe Aranguren

1-8; 2-3x15; 3-a; 4-75; 5-1; 6-unknown; 7-a; 8-3s; 9-a, part-time; 10-none; 11-basic idioms to help the traveler; customs and cult differences; 12-c,d,e,g; 13-a,b,f, realia; 14-FSI Sp materials.

1621. **SPANISH AROUND THE WORLD**
Roanoke C; FLs; Salem, VA 24153.
Patricia M. Gathercole
Non-credit conv course for travel. Further info not available.

1622. **SPANISH FOR TRAVELERS**
Santa Ana C; FLs; Santa Ana, CA 92706.
Lyle P. Johnson
1-80; 2-2x18; 3-a; 4-73/74; 5-4; 6-a; 7-b; 8-2s; 9-a, part-time; 10-none; 11-conv approach; emphasis on basic vocab and terminology useful to travelers; 12-a,b,c,e,f; 13-a,b,d,e,f, guest speakers; 14-Spanish Made Simple; phrase books.

1623. **SPANISH FOR TRAVEL**
Wayne State C; Hums; Wayne, NE 68787.
Rafael Sosa
1-15; 2-3x14; 3-a; 4-72; 5-3; 6-b; 7-a,b; 8-3s; 9-a; 10-ng; 11-vocab for travel abroad; 12-a,b,g; 13-a,b,f; 14-ng.

See also 248, 267, 268, 498, 505, 658.

MULTI-LANGUAGE

See 1148.

In-Translation

CHINESE

1624. **CHINESE LITERATURE IN TRANSLATION**
Connecticut C; Chi; New London, CT 06320.
Charles J. Chu
This course includes topics such as: Survey in Chi Lit; Women in Chi Lit; Revolution in Chi Lit; further info ng.

CLASSICS

1625. **CLASSICAL DRAMA IN TRANSLATION**
Western Michigan U; Mod & Cl Langs; Kalamazoo, MI 49001.
Roger L. Cole
1-9; 2-3x15½; 3-a; 4-wtr 71; 5-2; 6-ng; 7-ng; 8-3s; 9-ng; 10-none; 11-reading and analysis of selected plays as dramas and as expression of the Greek view of life; some attention to Roman drama; 12-f; 13-ng; 14-ng.

See also 1020, 1150, 1151, 1153, 1154, 1211.

DANISH

1626. **MODERN DANISH LITERATURE IN TRANSLATION**
Pennsylvania SU; Ger: University Park, PA 16802.
E.A. Ebbinghaus
1-new; 2-4½x10; 3-a; 4-spr 75; 5-1; 6-alt yrs; 7-a; 8-3s; 9-a; 10-none; 11-main lit movements of 19th cen Denmark; current trends in context; major Danish authors of today; 12-a,b,c,f; 13-ng; 14-Jansen & Mitchell, Anthology of Danish Literature, Vol. 2.

FRENCH

1627. **EARLY FRENCH LITERATURE**
TRANSLATION
Arkansas Polytechnic C; Eng & FLs; Russellville, AR 72801.
Louise Mobley
1-new; 2-3x16; 3-a; 4-ng; 5-0; 6-every 2nd or 3rd yr; 7-a; 8-3s; 9-a; 10-jr standing; 11-survey of Fr lit to 19th cen; 12-a,b,c,e,f; 13-a,b,c,d; 14-not yet chosen.

1628. **19TH CENTURY FRENCH LITERATURE IN TRANSLATION**
Arkansas Polytechnic C; Eng & FLs; Russellville, AR 72801.
Louise Mobley
1-new; 2-3x16; 3-a; 4-spr 75; 5-1; 6-every 2nd or 3rd yr; 7-a; 8-3s; 9-a; 10-jr standing; 11-survey of 19th cen Fr lit; 12-a,b,c,e,f; 13-a,b,c,d; 14-primary texts.

1629. **20TH CENTURY FRENCH LITERATURE IN TRANSLATION**
Arkansas Polytechnic C; Eng & FLs; Russellville, AR 72801.
Louise Mobley
1-new; 2-3x16; 3-a; 4-ng; 5-0; 6-every 2nd or 3rd yr; 7-a; 8-3s; 9-ng; 10-jr standing; 11-survey of 20th cen Fr lit; 12-a,b,c,e,f; 13-a,b,c,d; 14-not yet chosen.

1630. **BLACK FRENCH LITERATURE IN TRANSLATION**
East Stroudsburg SC; FLs; East Stroudsburg, PA 18301.
Bernard S. Hawrylo
1-12; 2-3x8; 3-a; 4-fall 75; 5-1; 6-unknown; 7-a; 8-2s; 9-a; 10-none; 11-thought, action, problems of black Francophone writers and their peoples; hist and cult of the countries concerned; 12-a,b,f; 13-a; 14-primary texts.

1631. **THE DRAMA OF MODERN FRANCE IN ENGLISH TRANSLATION**
King's C; FL & Lit; Wilkes-Barre, PA 18711.

Margaret Corgan
1-2; 2-3x15; 3-a; 4-73/74; 5-3; 6-a; 7-a; 8-3s; 9-a; 10-none; 11-major trends and themes in modern Fr theater; 12-a,b,f; 13-a,b,c,d, records; 14-primary texts.

1632. FRENCH LITERARY (IN TRANSLATION)
Millersville SC; FLs; Millersville, PA 17551.
Byron Detwiler
1-15; 2-3x15; 3-a; 4-fall 74; 5-1; 6-b; 7-a; 8-3s; 9-a; 10-none; 11-present topic: plays from the Fr repertory from 17th cen to present; 12-a,b,f; 13-a,d; 14-primary texts.

1633. FRENCH LITERARY MASTERPIECES IN ENGLISH TRANSLATION
Rutgers U; Fr; Camden, NJ 08102.
English Showalter, Jr.
1-new; 2-4x14; 3-a; 5-75; 5-ng; 6-b; 7-a; 8-4s; 9-a; 10-none; 11-varies from yr to yr; interdisc; 12-a,b,f; 13-a,b,d, museum visits; 14-varies.

1634. FRENCH THEATRE IN TRANSLATION
South Dakota SU; FLs; Brookings, SD 57006.
Michael G. Paulson
1-ng; 2-3x15; 3-a; 4-spr 74; 5-1; 6-on demand; 7-a; 8-3s; 9-a; 10-ng; 11-origins and development of Fr theater; 12-b,f; 13-ng; 14-primary texts.

1635. FRENCH LITERATURE IN ENGLISH TRANSLATION
Western Michigan U; Mod & Cl Langs; Kalamazoo, MI 49001.
Roger L. Cole
1-8; 2-3x15½; 3-a; 4-wtr 72; 5-2; 6-ng; 7-ng; 8-3s; 9-ng; 10-none; 11-thematic and stylistic analysis of major writers from LaFayette to present; 12-f; 13-ng; 14-ng.

1636. 20th CENTURY FRENCH MASTERPIECES IN TRANSLATION
U of Wisconsin; Fr & Ital; Madison, WI 53706.
Dr. Rossi
Novel form, existentialist authors, drama, cinematographic novel. Offered smr 75. Further info not available.

1637. FRENCH MASTERPIECES IN TRANSLATION
U of Wisconsin; MLs; River Falls, WI 54022.
Erwin F. Ritter
Further info not available.

See also 1039, 1045, 1054, 1551.

GERMAN

1638. GERMAN LITERATURE IN TRANSLATION
U of Colorado; Ger Langs; Boulder, CO 80302.
W.V. Blomster
1-has varied 8 to 40; 2-2/3x16; 3-a; 4-69; 5-ng; 6-a; 7-a; 8-2/3s; 9-a; 10-upper div course; 11-varies; period, genre, specific authors, etc.; 12-f; 13-various; 14-various.

1639. SOCIETY IN THE GERMAN NOVEL IN TRANSLATION
U of Illinois; Ger Langs & Lits; Urbana, IL 61801.
James M. McGlathery
Further info ng.

1640. MODERN GERMAN DRAMA IN ENGLISH TRANSLATION
King's C; FL & Lit; Wilkes-Barre, PA 18711.
Joseph Krawczeniuk
1-6; 2-3x15; 3-a; 4-73/74; 5-3; 6-a; 7-a,b; 8-3s; 9-a; 10-none; 11-representative plays; 12-a,b,f; 13-a,b,d; 14-primary texts.

1641. GERMAN LITERATURE IN TRANSLATION
Luther C; ML; Decorah, IA 52101.
Barbara Bahe
1-new; 2-3x15; 3-a; 4-75; 5-ng; 6-alt yrs; 7-a; 8-2s; 9-a; 10-none; 11-lyric, drama, Novelle; 12-a,b,c,f; 13-a,b,e; 14-primary texts.

1642. IMAGES OF MEN AND WOMEN IN GERMAN LITERATURE
U of Massachusetts; Ger; Boston, MA 02125.
Joey Horsley
1-20; 2-3x13; 3-a; 4-72; 5-2; 6-unknown; 7-a; 8-4s; 9-a; 10-none; 11-images of women and men in Ger lit from 18th cen to the present; understanding the soci forces and hist contexts and cult attitudes; 12-a,b,f; 13-ng; 14-primary texts plus contemporary readings from women's movement.

1643. GERMAN INFLUENCES ON AMERICAN LITERATURE
SUCNY; FLs & Lits; Brockport, NY 14420.
Ger influences on Amer lit and theater from early times up to the 'German craze' of the mid-19th cen. Amer authors read. In Eng; no prerequisites.

1644. MAJOR WORKS OF GOETHE
SUCNY; FLs & Lits; Brockport, NY 14420.
In Eng; no prerequisites. Further info not available.

1645. THE GERMAN QUEST FOR HUMAN FREEDOM
SUCNY; FLs & Lits; Brockport, NY 14420.
The Ger search for serenity, truth, and human freedom as found in post WW II lit: novels, short stories, essays. In Eng; no prerequisites.

1646. CONTEMPORARY GERMAN DRAMA IN TRANSLATION
South Dakota SU; FLs; Brookings, SD 57006.
Erhard Gross
1-ng; 2-2x15; 3-a; 4-spr 74; 5-1; 6-on demand; 7-b; 8-2s; 9-ng; 10-ng; 11-effect of Ger authors on the Amer stage; post WW II Ger theater and reception in U.S.; 12-b,f; 13-ng; 14-primary texts.

1647. GERMAN LITERATURE IN ENGLISH TRANSLATION
Western Michigan U; Mod & Cl Langs; Kalamazoo, MI 49001.
Roger L. Cole

1-6; 2-3x15½; 3-a; 4-wtr 71; 5-3; 6-ng; 7-ng; 8-3s; 9-ng; 10-none; 11-comparative study of lit themes and techniques of major Ger writers from Hauptmann to present; 12-f; 13-ng; 14-ng.

1648. GERMAN MASTERPIECES IN TRANSLATION
U of Wisconsin; MLs; River Falls, WI 54022.
Erwin F. Ritter
Further info ng.

See also 1056, 1061, 1062, 1177, 1179, 1180, 1182, 1237.

ITALIAN

See 1196, 1312.

RUSSIAN

1649. RUSSIAN LITERATURE IN TRANSLATION
Millersville SC; FLs; Millersville, PA 17551.
Daniel E. Kogut
1-33; 2-3x32; 3-a; 4-71; 5-6; 6-a; 7-a; 8-3s; 9-a; 10-none; 11-1st sem: 19th cen lit; 2nd sem: Soviet lit; 12-a,b,f; 13-a,b,d, e; 14-primary texts.

1650. RUSSIAN LITERATURE IN ENGLISH TRANSLATION
Western Michigan U; Mod & Cl Langs; Kalamazoo, MI 49001.
Roger L. Cole
1-7; 2-3x15½; 3-a; 4-fall 72; 5-2; 6-ng; 7-ng; 8-3s; 9-ng; 10-none; 11-survey of the development of great Russ prose in hist and cult context; 12-f; 13-ng; 14-primary texts.

1651. TRENDS IN RUSSIAN CULTURE AND LITERATURE
U of Wisconsin; Sl; Madison, WI 53706.
James Bailey
1-35; 2-2x16; 3-a; 4-52; 5-10; 6-b; 7-a; 8-2s; 9-a; 10-jr standing; 11-development of Russ cult within the framework of Russ lit; 12-a,f; 13-none; 14-primary texts, various secondary texts.

See also 784, 1201.

SERBO-CROATIAN

See 1098.

SPANISH

1652. LATIN AMERICAN LITERATURE IN ENGLISH TRANSLATION
King's C; FL & Lit; Wilkes-Barre, PA 18711.
Daniel DiBlasi
1-27; 2-3x15; 3-a; 4-73/74; 5-3; 6-a; 7-a; 8-3s; 9-a; 10-none; 11-study of major writers and trends; 12-a,b,f; 13-a,b,c,d,records; 14-primary texts; Urena, Literary Currents in Hispanic America.

1653. SPANISH LITERATURE IN TRANSLATION
New Mexico Inst of Mining & Technology; Hums; Socorro, NM 87801.
Ruth L. Gross

1-10; 2-3x15; 3-a; 4-73; 5-2; 6-b; 7-a; 8-3s; 9-a; 10-adv prof for Sp credit; 11-development of Sp thought through outstanding works of lit, cl period through the present; for Sp credit, all reading and reports done in Sp; 12-a,b,c,f; 13-none; 14-bilingual materials, handouts, primary texts.

1654. SAINTS AND SINNERS OF GOLDEN AGE SPANISH LITERATURE
SUCNY; FLs & Lits; Brockport, NY 14420.
Study of selected works of the Sp Golden Age with emphasis upon hist, soci, philo, and psycho roles of lit types. In Eng; no prerequisites.

1655. SPANISH GOLDEN AGE: LITERATURE IN TRANSLATION
South Dakota SU; FLs; Brookings, SD 57006.
Michael G. Paulson
1-ng; 2-3x15; 3-a; 4-spr 74; 5-1; 6-on demand; 7-a; 8-3s; 9-a; 10-ng; 11-Cervantes, drama; 12-b,f; 13-ng; 14-primary texts.

1656. SPANISH-AMERICAN LITERATURE IN ENGLISH TRANSLATION
Western Michigan U; Mod & Cl Langs; Kalamazoo, MI 49001.
Roger L. Cole
1-6; 2-3x15½; 3-a; 4-wtr 72; 5-1; 6-ng; 7-ng; 8-3s; 9-ng; 10-none; 11-selected prose and poetry from late 19th cen to contemporary writers of Hispanoamer; 12-f; 13-ng; 14-ng.

1657. SPANISH MASTERPIECES IN TRANSLATION
U of Wisconsin; MLs; River Falls, WI 54022.
Erwin F. Ritter
Further info ng.

See also 417, 1024, 1093, 1141, 1193, 1291, 1310, 1566.

MULTILANGUAGE

1658. CONTINENTAL LITERATURE IN TRANSLATION: THEORY AND PRACTICE
King's C; FL & Lit; Wilkes-Barre, PA 18711.
Daniel DiBlasi
1-77; 2-3x15; 3-a; 4-72/73; 5-5; 6-a; 7-a; 8-3s; 9-a; 10-none; 11-developing understanding of value and meaning of lit as expressed in a number of national lits of continental Europe; students choose between Fr, Ger, and Sp; 12-f; 13-a,b,c,d; 14-primary texts.

1659. WORLD LITERATURE: UNDERSTANDING OTHER CULTURES THROUGH LITERATURE
Meramec CC; FL, Eng; Kirkwood, MO 63122.
Jennie Davis
1-22; 2-3x15; 3-b; 4-75; 5-1; 6-b; 7-a; 8-3s; 9-a; 10-none; 11-major 20th-cen writers; poetry, fiction, non-fiction, drama of Fr, Ger, Sp Latin Amer writers; focus on shared cult themes; relationships between the cults; impact of a particular cult on its lit; 12-a,b,c,f; 13-a,b; 14-primary texts.

1660. DEMONIC POSSESSION IN WESTERN LIT-

ERATURE: ECSTASY
SUCNY; FLs and Lits; Brockport, NY
14420.
Emphasis upon demonic possession and
related states: transcendence of the self in
mysticism, eroticism, sadism, drugs, romantic love, destructive rage, aesthetic
pleasure, artistic creativity. In Eng; no
prerequisites.

1661. EXISTENTIALISM TO THE ABSURD IN
CONTEMPORARY EUROPEAN LITERA-
TURE
SUCNY; FLs & Lits; Brockport, NY 14420.
Existentialism, the fantastic, the gro-

tesque, antiforms, the absurd in Sp, Fr, Ger,
and Russ lits. In Eng; no prerequisites.

1662. MINOR IN WORLD LITERATURE (PRO-
GRAM)
Western Michigan U; Mod & Cl Langs;
Kalamazoo, MI 49001.
William Combs
Interdept program administered jointly by
Eng and Mod and Cl Langs; lit read in Eng;
courses from a variety of depts; further
info not available.

See also 1343.

Miscellaneous

1663. GERMAN PRONUNCIATION
Adrian C; MLs; Adrian, MI 49221.
J.C. Hanson
1-7; 2-1x13; 3-a; 4-74; 5-1; 6-b; 7-b; 8-1s; 9-
a; 10-none; 11-performance oriented pronunciation course; 12-e,f; 13-d; 14-Waeng-
ler, German Pronunciation.

1664. GERMAN VOCABULARY
Adrian C; MLs; Adrian, MI 49221.
J.C. Hanson
1-19; 2-1x13; 3-a; 4-74; 5-1; 6-a; 7-b; 8-1s;
9-a; 10 none; 11 strengthening vocab, AV,
reading; 12-b,e; 13-b,d,e; 14-Pfeffer,
Grunddeutsch: Basic (Spoken) German
Word List: Grundstufe.

1665. SURVEY OF NON-WESTERN LAN-
GUAGES
Austin Peay SU; MLs; Clarksville, TN
37040.
Joseph V. Thomas
1-15; 2-3x10; 3-a; 4-74; 5-1; 6-b; 7-a; 8-3q;
9-a; 10-none; 11-Russ, Chi, Swahili: elem
lessons in pronunciation, sentence structure, word-study, writing systems; importance of these langs in world affairs, their
ling relationships, cult differences
reflected in them, important works written
in them; 12-a,b,e,f; 13-d, duplicated maps,
pictures, lists, etc.; 14-Say It in Russian;
Say It in Swahili; Modern Chinese-A Basic
Course.

1666. SURVEY OF WESTERN LANGUAGES
Austin Peay SU; MLs; Clarksville, TN
37040.
Joseph V. Thomas
1-18; 2-3x10; 3-a; 4-74; 5-1; 6-b; 7-a; 8-3q;
9-a; 10-none; 11-Fr, Ger, Sp, Ital: elem
pronunciation, sentence structure, word
study; discussion of importance of these
langs in world affairs, their ling relationships, their influence on Eng, the cult
differences reflected in them, sci & lit

works written in them; 12-a,b,e,f; 13-d,
maps, pictures, etc.; 14-Say It in French,
German, Spanish, Italian.

1667. INTRODUCTION TO THE ROMANCE
LANGUAGES
Boston U; MLs; Boston, MA 02215.
Anne Slack
1-ng; 2-4 or 5x14; 3-a; 4-71/72; 5-4; 6-b; 7-
a; 8-4s; 9-a; 10-for concentrators in one of
the romance langs or with consent; 11-
intensive course providing simultaneous
instruction in Fr, Ital, & Sp, designed for
concentrators to acquire rapid reading
facility in the other two langs. Presentation of basic structural patterns; emphasis
on grammatical relationships among the
langs, study of cognates; 12-a,b,d,f,g; 13-
ng; 14-Heatwole, A Comparative Practical
Grammar of French, Spanish and Italian; 2-
3 graded readers for each of the langs.

1668. TRANSLATION WORKSHOP: FRENCH
Carnegie-Mellon U; MLs & Lits; Pittsburgh,
PA 15213.
Juris Silenieks
Small, informally conducted seminar group
in which students from all disciplines are
invited to come together & study the
process of trans through practical exercises, discussions, critiques. Purpose of
course is not "professional" but more
broadly cult, even hedonistic: to study, as
an act of pleasure, structures of communication among peoples; to analyze & try to
understand hist & geographical values
underlying lang systems.

1669. TRANSLATION WORKSHOP: GERMAN
Carnegie-Mellon U; MLs & Lits; Pittsburgh,
PA 15213.
Juris Silenieks
Small, informally conducted seminar group
in which students from all disciplines are
invited to come together & study the
process of trans through practical exer-

cises, discussions, critiques. Purpose of course is not "professional" but more broadly cult, even hedonistic: to study, as an act of pleasure, structures of communication among peoples; to analyze & try to understand hist & geographical values underlying lang systems.

1670. TRANSLATION WORKSHOP: SPANISH
Carnegie-Mellon U; MLs & Lits; Pittsburgh, PA 15213.
Juris Silenicks
Small, informally conducted seminar group in which students from all disciplines are invited to come together & study the process of trans through practical exercises, discussions, critiques. Purpose of course is not "professional" but more broadly cult, even hedonistic: to study, as an act of pleasure, structures of communication among peoples; to analyze and try to understand hist & geographical values underlying lang systems.

1671. ENGLISH FOR INTERNATIONAL STUDENTS
U of Cincinnati; Eng; Cincinnati, OH 45221.
Margo Kempf
1-61; 2-2 to 10x10; 3-b; 4-69; 5-6; 6-a; 7-a; 8-2q; 9-a,b; 10-inter prof Eng; 11-diagnostic test determines primary areas of weakness; then student enrolls in one or more of the following: Tech Writing for Intl Students; Reading Skills and Vocab Development; Basic Grammar; Speech and Communication; Basic Writing Skills; 12-a,b,c,d,e,f; 13-ng; 14-Lawrence, Writing as a Thinking Process; Praninskas, Rapid Review of English Grammar; Grindall, Marelli, & Nadler, American Readings.

1672. CONVERSATIONAL SPANISH, FRENCH AND GERMAN
Citrus C; FLs; Azusa, CA 91702.
Lilian Gracial, Edith Howe, Roger Taylor
1-300 in all; 2-2x20; 3-a,c; 4-65; 5-every sem since 65; 6-a; 7-a,b; 8-2s; 9-a, eve students; 10-depends on level; 11-team teaching is the success of these classes, 2-3 teachers used in large classes; 12-a,b,c,d,e,g; 13-a,b,d; 14-Hablamos en Espanol; Moudelli, Conversational French; German through Conversation Patterns.

1673. FRENCH LANGUAGE HOUSE
U of Colorado; Fr; Boulder, CO 80302.
Susan Barela
1-40; 2-70 to 90x16; 3-a; 4-72/73; 5-5; 6-a; 7-a,b; 8-2s; 9-a; 10-inter prof; 11-coed living in Fr-speaking environment; 12-b,d,g; 13-a,b,e,f, talks by professors & students, composition of yearly book by the students in Fr; 14-none.

1674. ENGLISH AS A SECOND LANGUAGE
Dixie C; Hums; St. George, UT 84770.
O.G. Hammond
1-9; 2-10x10; 3-a; 4-74; 5-5; 6-a; 7-a; 8-3q; 9-a; 10-for foreign students with little or no knowledge of Eng; 11-basic lang skills; 12-

b,d,e,f; 13-d,e, first-hand experience in community; 14-none.

1675. TUTORING IN FOREIGN LANGUAGES
Federal City C; FLs; Washington, DC 20001.
1-3; 2-3x10; 3-a; 4-72/73; 5-3; 6-b; 7-a; 8-3q; 9-a; 10-jr level; 11-FL majors & others prof in lang may serve as tutor with the consent & sponsorship of dept; pass-fail. Up to 6 credits depending on number of hrs worked. 12-b,c,e,g; 13-d; 14-ng.

1676. PROBLEMS IN READING AND INTERPRETATION (ESL)
Florida International U; MLs; Miami, FL 33144.
Lilliam Hernandez
1-13; 2-5x11; 3-a; 4-74; 5-2; 6-ng; 7-a,b; 8-5q; 9-a; 10-none; 11-course aims to detect and correct errors in syntax, usage, reading & comprehension experienced by the non-native speaker of Eng; 12-b,d,f; 13-e,f; 14-Jacobus, Improving College Reading.

1677. CONVERSATIONAL ESL
Greenville Tech Ed Center; MLs; Greenville, SC 29606.
Margaret Rice
1-18; 2-4x11; 3-a; 4-74; 5-5; 6-a; 7-b; 8-b; 9-a,b; 10-none; 11-ng; 12-a,b,e,f,g; 13-d,e,f; 14-Dixson, Modern American English.

1678. READING SPANISH FOR UNDERGRADUATES
U of Kentucky; Sp & Ital; Lexington, KY 40506.
H.B. Saunders
1-175; 2-6x16; 3-a; 4-fall 72; 5-7; 6-a; 7-a; 8-3s; 9-a; 10-4 sem reading track in sequence; 11-reading material carefully graded, grammar prepared for the reading skill only; 12-f; 13-textbooks, handouts; 14-ng.

1678A. VALUES OF FOREIGN CULTURES
Mars Hill C; MFL; Mars Hill, NC 28754.
Gwyndola P. Fish
1-150; 2-4x15; 3-b; 4-74; 5-5; 6-a; 7-a,b; 8-4s; 9-a,b; 10-soph with background in Amer cult preferred but not required; 11-see ms; 12-a,b,c,d,f,g; 13-a,b,e,f, reserve books, resource persons; 14-ng.

1679. ELBERT COVELL COLLEGE (SUBJECT MATTER COURSES TAUGHT IN SPANISH)
U of the Pacific; Stockton, CA 95204.
Gaylon L. Caldwell
1-c200; 2-4x13½; 3-a; 4-fall 63; 5-10; 6-individual courses usually offered 1 sem a yr; 7-a; 8-4s; 9-a; 10-none (for most courses); 11-subject matter course taught in Sp; 12-a,b,c,d,e,g; 13-a; 14-ng.

1680. ENGLISH AS A SECOND LANGUAGE
C of St. Elizabeth; Eng; Convent Station, NJ 07961.
Elena Francis
1-6; 2-3x15; 3-a; 4-72/73; 5-c6; 6-a; 7-a; 8-3s; 9-a, auditors; 10-none; placement by diagnostic testing; 11-development of basic oral-aural, reading, writing skills; pro-

nunciation; fundamental speech patterns; drill in basic structures; use of authentic cult items; contrast of Eng with Sp; 12-b,c,d,e,f; 13-a,b,d,e,f; 14-Developing Fluency in English; English 900 Series; Lado English series; Encounters: A Basic Reader.

1681. THE NATURE OF LANGUAGE
Southeastern CC; FLs; Whiteville, NC 28472.
Samuel D. Sink
1-14; 2-3x11; 3-a; 4-fall 74; 5-1; 6-b; 7-a; 8-2q; 9-a; 10-none; 11-basic intro to semantics, body lang, comparison of langs, dialects, effects of lang; 12-b,c,d,e,f; 13-a,b,c,d,e, games; 14-none.

1682. PRACTICAL PHONETICS (MEXICAN-AMERICAN DIALECTOLOGY)
U of Texas; Sp & Port; Austin, TX 78712.
Phyllis Harmon
1-20; 2-3x14; 3-b; 4-72; 5-4; 6-b; 7-a; 8-3s; 9-a; 10-4 sems of coll Sp; 11-phonetics and phonemics through describing, characterizing, comparing, contrasting Mex-Amer dialects & other Sp dialects in relation to each other; analysis of sound systems in contemporary & hist perspective; 12-a,g; 13-ng; 14-Fernandez and Quilles, Curso de Fonetica y Fonologia Espanola.

See also 77, 476, 1025.

Part III: Index of Institutions